THE STATUS OF LAW IN
INTERNATIONAL SOCIETY

PUBLISHED FOR THE
CENTER OF INTERNATIONAL STUDIES,
PRINCETON UNIVERSITY

A list of other Center publications
appears at the back of the book.

THE STATUS OF LAW IN INTERNATIONAL SOCIETY

BY RICHARD A. FALK

PRINCETON UNIVERSITY PRESS
PRINCETON, NEW JERSEY
1970

On behalf

of the people of Vietnam (and elsewhere)

who have been victims of *Pax Americana*

> . . . *I saw, long before this war,*
> *wrath move in the music that troubles me.*
> Robert Duncan,
> *Bending the Bow*, p. iii

Introduction

THIS VOLUME complements *Legal Order in a Violent World*. Whereas the earlier volume was concerned with the relevance of international law to the regulation of international violence, this second volume widens the arc of substantive concern to encompass the range of subject matter susceptible to international regulation. However, *The Status of Law in International Society* does not undertake a comprehensive description of what is going on within the international legal order. The effort is rather to analyze the jurisprudential and sociopolitical foundations of modern international law. A special part of this effort is to identify what is distinctive about the system of international legal order that has emerged and continues to evolve in the period since the end of World War I, as compared to the classical or traditional system of international law that had developed in the period between the Peace of Westphalia (1648) and World War I.

My objective in these two volumes is to produce a coherent and self-consistent interpretation of the role of law in world affairs. Such an interpretation purports only to create a tool for continuing analysis. There is neither a claim nor an inclination to achieve any kind of interpretative finality. In fact, one of the contentions in the chapters comprising this book is that we need a process of dynamic thought *about* international legal order to be able to capture the processive reality *of the* international legal order.[1] In this spirit, the substance of international law is studied in segments rather than as a whole, with the objective of acquiring insight into the overall system of international law taking precedence over the objective of comprehending the specific subject matter under consideration.

Part of my own concern with developing appropriate tools of analysis for the study of international law is to enable an intellectually rigorous appraisal of the strengths and weaknesses of the international legal order as it now exists. To be intellectually rigorous is an ideal to be pursued rather than an attribute to be acquired. This pursuit is at once consistent with ongoing approaches to international legal studies (see Chapter XV) and quite at odds with several other prominent traditions of inquiry: First, the purely passive styles of inquiry associated with traditions of legal positivism that pride themselves on describing international law as "it is" and, thereby, refraining from prescribing international law as "it ought to be"; second, the normatively confusing styles of inquiry associated with traditions of natural law that posit the relevance of an

---

[1] For distinction see Myres S. McDougal, "Some Basic Theoretical Concepts About International Law: A Policy-Oriented Framework of Inquiry," *Journal of Conflict Resolution* 4 (1960), 337-54, at 337.

immutable moral order to the affairs of nations without, in general, either ascertaining the extent of its actual relevance to the behavior of states or without even determining why the particular moral order that they posit ought to be relevant; and third, the activist and energetic styles of inquiry associated with the advocacy of world government that posit what the international legal order ought to be without bothering themselves about how to transform it from what it is to what it ought to be. Admittedly, each of these three styles of inquiry has been characterized in such a salient fashion as to neglect the richness of conception and depth of awareness exhibited by its best practitioners, but the point remains valid that the orientations of these three styles of inquiry have helped establish an intellectual climate for international legal studies that my own work endeavors to avoid.

To be more specific, I believe that it is necessary to initiate inquiry by explicating as clearly as possible the contours of realistic expectation applicable to the world legal order. Such realistic expectations require, first of all, a sense of why and in what sense international law functions as law even though the structure of the international legal order does not in crucial respects resemble the structure of the domestic legal order. In particular, it is essential to understand the characteristics of legal order in a social setting—such as the international setting[2]—in which there is absent an established central government. The quality of realistic expectations, then, entails some sense of what decentralized substitutes exist for such normal incidents of domestic law as compulsory adjudication of disputes, disarmament, police protection, and legislation. As well, it is necessary to assess the specific conditions under which decentralized substitutes work. These substitutes arise mainly from the perceived common interests of national governments in an orderly and just world and from the reciprocal dependence of sovereign states on each other's willingness to sustain legal expectations on most occasions. As well, there exists a need to identify the situations in which decentralized forms of world legal order fail.

At the same time, it is important *not* to establish the domestic legal order as an *ideal* toward which the world legal order is actually evolving, nor should this necessarily be transformed into a *goal*. The actual and preferred future of the world legal order is itself a subject deserving systematic inquiry.[3] The failure to conduct this inquiry, including the

[2] For considerations of the distinctive character of international law see H.L.A. Hart, *The Concept of Law*, Oxford, Clarendon Press, 1961, pp. 208-31; C.A.W. Manning, *The Nature of International Society*, London, G. Bell, 1962, pp. 100-27.

[3] There are several projects under way that emphasize the future of world legal order. The World Order Models Project of the World Law Fund has assembled regional teams of scholars who are expected to posit models for world order systems that are more desirable than the existing system and within reach of attainability by the end of the twentieth century. At Princeton University there is a

failure to consider the preconditions of such a centralization of the world legal order, is one of the reasons why proposals to reform the legal order of international society so blandly and so consistently endorse some model of world government as the natural culmination of ideological dreams. Another reason for the endorsement, also relevant here, is that the domestic legal order appears to depend upon the functioning of a central government and this dependence is presupposed to be the crucial element of adequate legal order in every human setting.

The domestic analogy of legal order is misleading on quite another ground. It is not at all clear that government on an international scale is capable of dealing with the main challenges to world order that might motivate its creation. National societies—even those with well-established governments—have experienced costly civil wars. Given the lesser cohesion of international society, the early decades of a world government might well be marked by a series of civil wars of a magnitude and frequency more detrimental than the pattern of warfare that is characteristic of the existing international system for the management of military power. Surely from the perspective of creating a preferred future it is essential at this preliminary stage that inquiry is initiated with a question rather than with a solution. And the question that seems most useful initially to emphasize (but not exclusively) is: what are the costs and benefits of plausible alternative systems for the management of military power in international society.[4] Other questions, too, are essential ingredients of inquiry, often more essential than those related to military power, depending upon the socioeconomic position of the inquirer. What system for the use of economic resources appears most likely to facilitate the modernization and self-sufficiency of the poorer nations of the world? Or what system of organizing influence is most likely to rectify and avoid racial oppression and other forms of perceived injustice throughout the world? Western oriented observers tend to identify world order with the minimization of violence, especially nuclear violence, writing as they do in a context wherein concerns of justice and welfare appear either subordinate (if subject to eventual realization, then, if at all) or realizable through domestic capabilities. The priority schedule of a militant African leader intent on the downfall of apartheid in South Africa, or an Indian scholar confronted by developmental trends that disclose increasing food shortages on the Asian subcontinent is certain

---

parallel project devoted to the evolving character of the international legal order in the period of the near future. The World Law Fund project is concerned with the study of system change, whereas the Princeton project is devoted to evolutionary trends within the existing system. Both projects are examining the prospects for strengthening world legal order.

[4] Very suggestive speculation along these lines is contained in Oran R. Young, *The World System: Present Characteristic and Future Prospects*, Hudson Institute (HI-277D), August 29, 1963. See also Chap. XXI.

to be different from that of North American or European inquirers. These differences can be generalized by ascribing to the developed countries a security orientation toward world order, and ascribing a welfare orientation and social-change orientation to the leadership of many non-modernized countries. Obviously such a dichotomy disguises many complexities and diversities of thought, not least of which is the cross-cutting ideological range of positions that encompass both commitments to global revolution and to various sorts of status quo on the part of political elites within each country.

The normative mood that is reflected in this book commences in the spirit of inquiry. It proceeds, however, to the discernment of vulnerabilities and weakness in the existing international legal system and to the consideration of ways to improve the system—both modest ways of reform and drastic ways of revolution. Having postulated world order alternatives, emphasis is then placed on preconditions for change and on procedures of change within the international legal order. Part of the task of comprehending change—both directed and undirected change that influences the quality of world legal order—is to learn how to manage its phases and impacts more effectively. International lawyers are only beginning to consider the significance of a dynamic, future-oriented attitude toward the international legal order. Such an orientation presupposes that the future is susceptible to the methods of intellectual inquiry of a rigor comparable to those that previously have guided generations of jurists in their studies of the present and the past.

Underlying any adequate normative mood—that is, a concern with directed change—is a set of jurisprudential attitudes that are used to specify the character of the international legal order.[5] It is desirable to make these attitudes as explicit as possible so that they can be challenged either in form or in application. My own outlook has been very much shaped by the intellectual dialectic that exists between the work of Hans Kelsen and Myres S. McDougal, two great international lawyers of our era who have each developed and sustained a coherent interpretation of the international legal order.[6] From Kelsen one learns the importance of acknowledging a framework of values and beliefs about the facts of international life that, if possessed, guide inquiry almost inevitably toward certain types of conclusions. Without such an acknowledgment, the biasing framework will nevertheless be present, but it will be secretly embodied in the work and detract from both its veridical character and from its analytic merit. Kelsen demonstrates successfully that an inter-

---

[5] See Myres S. McDougal, Harold D. Lasswell, W. Michael Reisman, "Theories About International Law: Prologue to a Configurative Jurisprudence," 8 *Virginia Journal of International Law* 188-299 (1968).

[6] For a comparison of jurisprudential virtues and some effort to identify the limit of each approach see Chap. II.

national lawyer should avoid any kind of *spurious* objectivism that, in effect, purports to resolve the great moral and political problems of the day *as if* they were legal problems. Such overreaching of the limits of legal analysis can only lead to barren legalism (explaining nonlegal factors in legal terms) or to legal apologetics (using law in the service of political actors, especially national governments). Kelsen's own solution is to evolve a *genuine* objectivism by way of adopting such a narrow definition of international law that moral and political factors are excluded from the proper province of inquiry. I do not regard this as an adequate solution: It removes the legal element from its conditioning context of moral and political values. Such autonomy for international law tends to result in its irrelevance in the realms of thought and action.

Myres S. McDougal and his associates, in an extraordinary corpus of cooperative legal scholarship, have demonstrated intellectual strategies that certainly restore international law to a position of relevance. By explicating fully the manner in which the processes of international law unfold within the wider settings of moral values and political orientations, McDougal's group have shown the way in which the dimension of law influences the patterning of international behavior under all conditions of interaction, including adversary relationships. But McDougal's enterprise of reconciliation (between international law and international politics and between international law and international morality) seems to have been overconsummated, given a world of sovereign states each of which interprets behavior in an egoistic and, hence, distorting fashion. In the absence of central institutions of authority, it becomes difficult in any concrete instance of international controversy to differentiate between violations of law and compliance; in such event, law loses its capacity to furnish authoritative guidance to national officials who are most generally entrusted with the power of decision.

It seems desirable, therefore, to react against McDougal's approach to the extent of seeking to establish a clearer distinction between "law" and "policy" for international legal studies, preserving at the same time the relevance of international law to ongoing processes of international behavior.

The general issue of reconciliation raised by the distinct conceptions of international law relied on by Kelsen and McDougal can be stated as follows: How can the *relevance* of international law to the conduct of international relations be maintained without sacrificing its *autonomy* altogether? Or to put the issue more precisely—What is the most beneficial compromise between autonomy and relevance given the existing character of the international legal order? In my judgment Kelsen has gone too far to establish the autonomy of international law, whereas McDougal has gone too far to establish its relevance. This book is an attempt to develop a conception of the international legal order that effectuates a reconciliation between these intertwined considerations of autonomy and relevance.

The present sociohistorical situation creates a strong incentive to approximate the reconciliation to which we aspire. The need for autonomy is especially critical in relation to the management of military powers, given the wide-ranging types of international conflict and given the capacity of principal states for mutually self-destructive forms of confrontation. The need for relevance is especially critical in relation to the management of social change on the international level, both with regard to the modernization process and with regard to the fulfillment of certain justice demands bearing on questions of human rights. This new emphasis is responsive to the relatively recent participation of the strongly revisionist Afro-Asian and Moscow-Peking groups of states in the world legal order. In effect, the reconciliation of the concerns of autonomy and of relevance is a means to express the simultaneous need for *minimum stability* in the relations among principal sovereign states and for *minimum social change* in the relations between the advantaged and disadvantaged sectors of international society.

This description of the overall setting of international law needs to be completed by brief reference to several structural factors of great contemporary significance. First of all, the present possession of nuclear weapons by five states (and the awesome prospect of many more) creates for a nuclear power both the capacity to inflict great destruction on all other states and also introduces an unprecedented vulnerability to total and instantaneous destruction into the calculations of even the most powerful of sovereign states. Second, many of the sovereign units that enjoy the status of international states in the postcolonial period are unable to govern their own national societies with any degree of success, whether success is measured by reference to stabilizing domestic patterns or by the ability to satisfy minimum justice demands. And third, supranational arenas created by international institutions of regional and global scope are becoming an increasingly important element in international society, creating new patterns of authority, expectation, and loyalty that at once complement and compete with the sovereign state as the focal point of interaction in international life. These structural factors condition inquiry into the character of world legal order and give specific shape to the underlying jurisprudential search for a reconciliation between the divergent needs for autonomy and relevance. For my own purposes, then, these two volumes together might be thought of as prolegomena to a conception of international legal order. What remains to be done is to explicate as comprehensively and systematically as possible the conception itself. Easily a stone for Sisyphus.

Acknowledgments

MY APPROACH to international law has been increasingly influenced by a growing conviction that the present structure of international society cannot solve the problems of technetronic man. We have two or three decades, at the most, to bring a new system of world order into being, a system that is arranged to identify and implement human interests on a planetary scale. If the sovereign state remains the organizing center of political life in international affairs, then the outlook for human affairs is indeed bleak. We are living along the precipice of dire calamity. The danger is no longer alone a matter of fear for nuclear war, but the cumulative and interrelated dangers that stem from steeply rising curves of violence, population, and pollution in a world of shrinking space and dwindling resources. The chapters that comprise this volume foreshadow the emergency consciousness that now dominates my understanding of the scholarly and professional concerns of international lawyers.

My debts to other scholars are very great. Once again the work of Professor Myres S. McDougal lies at the intellectual center of everything that I have written. My continuing collaboration with Saul H. Mendlovitz and the World Law Fund has helped greatly to expand the horizons of my concerns beyond those traditional for professors of international law.

Most of the work on this book was done with the support of the Center of International Studies at Princeton University. At all times I have been encouraged by Klaus Knorr and Cyril E. Black who have served successively as Directors of the Center. Elsbeth Lewin again provided me with valuable assistance in countless ways and with endless patience. And once more Jean McDowall, as commander of the Center staff, always mobilized the secretarial resources needed to accomplish the job. As before, I thank Priscilla Bryan, especially, for the high quality of her work, mind, and disposition. June Traube and Mary Merrick also helped, and always with skill and good spirits.

Marjorie Putney has once more given me the benefit of her editorial skills. William McClung has continued to be interested and supportive, and has, thereby, enhanced the pleasure of my relationship with the Princeton University Press.

At the final stages, I was greatly assisted by Edith Levin of the Stanford Law School who rectified some errors that persisted through galleys and by Priscilla Jones of the Center for Advanced Study in the Behavioral Sciences, who with sprightly cunning tracked down some elusive citations.

Once more my wife, Florence, has given me the strength and love to carry on with this kind of work. She has, as well, been a participant at every stage, allowing me the full and tender benefit of her fine critical intelligence and unfailing sense of judgment.

Earlier versions of a number of chapters have been previously published. I wish to thank the publishers and journals for granting permission in connection with the following chapters: Chapter I in the *Virginia Law Review*; Chapter II in Karl W. Deutsch and Stanley Hoffmann, eds., *The Relevance of International Law* published by Schenkman and Co.; Chapter III in C. J. Friederich, ed., *Revolution* published by Atheneum; Chapter IV in Lawrence Scheinman and David Wilkinson, eds., *Studies in Crisis and International Law* published by Little, Brown; Chapters VI and XIII in the *American Journal of International Law* and Chapter X in the *Proceedings of the American Society of International Law*; Chapter VII previously appeared as a research memorandum of the Center of International Studies and as an article in *Rutgers Law Review*; Chapter VIII in R. J. Stanger, ed., *Essays on Espionage and International Law* published by the Ohio State University Press; Chapter XI in the *Virginia Journal of International Law*; Chapter XII in *International Organization*; Chapter XIV in the *Indiana Law Journal*; Chapter XV in Morton A. Kaplan, ed., *New Approaches in International Relations* published by St. Martin's Press and the *American Journal of International Law*; Chapter XVI in the *Columbia Journal of Transnational Law*; Chapter XVII in *World Politics*; Chapter XVIII in the *Journal of Conflict Resolution*; Chapter XXI in Richard B. Gray, ed., *International Security Systems* published by the P. E. Peacock Publishers; Chapter XXII in the *Stanford Journal of International Law*. An earlier version of Chapter XX was presented as a paper at the College of Fisheries of the University of Washington, and Chapter XXIII at a conference of Episcopal student leaders held at Princeton University.

Contents

PART ONE

AN ORIENTATION TOWARD THE

POLITICAL SETTING OF THE

INTERNATIONAL LEGAL ORDER

Introduction

THIS initial group of chapters attempts to specify an overall intellectual context. Part One, above all, seeks to depict the implications of acknowledging the *quasi-dependence* of international law upon the international political system of which it is a part. The notion of quasi-dependence is used despite its semantic inelegance, to express both the *subordination* of international law to the shape and character of the overall international environment and to identify areas of actual and potential *independence* wherein international law acts as a causative agent of its own. The task set for the international lawyer is to delimit as clearly as possible this sector of actual and potential independence, and to explain the conditions of its existence, as well as to describe the conditions and processes of its expansion or contraction.

The inquiry discussed in the previous paragraph has several main components each of which will be dealt with in later chapters:

1. A description of the international political system that conditions the operation of international law.

2. A consequent consideration of the special law tasks created by such factors as the expansion of international society by the emergence of additional states and by the activity of several types of international institutions, the shifts in the patterns of conflict arising from the technology of nuclear weapons and from the existence of many states vulnerable to interventionary penetrations of their domestic spheres of operation, as well as the crystallization of new justice demands with regard to the welfare of poorer states and with regard to the promotion of those human rights defied by racial discrimination.

3. An interpretation of the international legal order in light of its capability to deal with these sets of issues that bear on the quantity and quality of international stability by examining first, the nature of authority in international law, and second, the processes by which authority claims are translated, or not, into patterns of conforming behavior.

A part of this initial effort is to disclose the early stages of a law-creative global consciousness that characteristically expresses its claims to influence the growth of international law through the acts and operations of the political organs of the United Nations, especially the General Assembly. To assess the legal status of these claims presupposes a conception of the nature of law. These chapters espouse the view that the identifying characteristic of law is the existence of identifiable and assertive expectations of the relevant constituency that certain behavior is legally permissible and other behavior is not. The existence or not of these identifiable and assertive expectations about the limits of permissibility requires clarification as to what is meant and as to who is entitled in different international settings to draw authoritative inferences as to what are the relevant rights and duties of the parties to a controversy. In effect, then, the scope of law on a given subject is related to predictions as to how different kinds of decision-makers will treat different sorts of legal data that affect issues that fall within the scope of their authority. Since international behavior relating to intense conflict is governed almost exclusively by the decisions of adversary officials of the participant governments, it is obvious that the constructive roles of law, to the extent that these exist, are often to provide bases for *communication* rather than to impose guidelines of *restraint*. With regard to the more routine subject matter of international relations, however, the converging incentives of states to establish stable guidelines of restraint may produce substantive accommodations through state-to-state interaction, i.e. without any supranational or third-party intermediary.

The capacity of a more centrally based law-creating consciousness to influence international behavior depends on a number of factors, among which the following might be noted:

1. The quality and quantity of the consensus that underlies the purported embodiment of global consciousness, the percentage of states, the percentage of powerful states, and the presence or absence of the language of obligation and the expectation of enforcement in the final document;

2. The arena of interpretation, whether national or supranational, whether judicial, executive, or legislative, and whether calling for self-implementation or community action;

3. The subject matter involved—whether by tradition or necessity a matter of international concern or a matter of domestic jurisdiction, whether accommodation involves issues of convenience, prestige, power, or principle, and whether the purported globally based claim was premised on a requisite understanding of the other side's position;

4. The trust reposed in the fairness and objectivity of the proceedings giving rise to the globally based claim.

More descriptively, the chapters in Part One take up different segments of the problem of clarifying the conditioning context of contemporary international law. Chapter I catalogues the main kinds of challenges to the international jurist who would develop an adequate conception of the international legal order—challenges stemming from changes in the structure and character of the international political system. Chapter II examines, in particular, the legal consequences of characterizing as "revolutionary" the dominant patterns of contemporary international conflict. Chapter II, taking more or less for granted the altered structure of international relations (Chapter I) and the revolutionary quality of international conflict (Chapter III), proceeds to examine the appropriate ways to relate the international legal order to its wider political context. In Chapter II the opposing solutions to the law/context relationship developed by Hans Kelsen and Myres S. Mc-Dougal are subjected to critical scrutiny on the ground that they represent the two most prominent and promising jurisprudential strategies of our time, the weaknesses of each casting light on the strengths of the other.

I. Gaps and Biases in Contemporary Theories of International Law

THERE IS, in my judgment, always present a useful temptation to be highly selective in an essay that considers the adequacy of the body of international legal theory now being relied upon in the academic community of the United States. Such a temptation is especially strong at the present time when many procedures of inquiry are being developed by talented scholars. I have decided not to make a synoptic survey of the work now being done by those international lawyers whose work exhibits theoretical interests.[1] Such a decision does not imply that such a survey would not be worthwhile; it is merely an indication of limited intentions on my part.

This chapter will discuss some major gaps and shortcomings that have emerged in international legal theory at its present stage of development in the United States. I shall first examine several aspects of the relation of theory to practice in contemporary thought about international law. This examination will stress the distinction between practice and policy. It is one thing to argue that improved theoretical constructions promote a deeper understanding of international legal phenomena than did earlier approaches; it is quite another to contend that any contemporary theoretical approach is sufficiently perfected to provide government officials and others with an adequate basis for objective or scientific judgment.[2] I shall attempt to show that, because of problems peculiar to international law, international legal theorists simply have not developed criteria that provide adequate guidelines for evaluating particular decisions, although existing theory can be used to improve the rationality of the decision-making process. Since this inadequacy exists, it is especially unfortunate to note the current tendency to argue in legal support of official decisions based on national policies adopted for such essentially nonlegal reasons as national security or the containment of Communism by an appeal to the objective character of the legal analysis. This tendency undermines the necessary objectivity of scholarship and obscures the fact that an adequate theory of international law must take account of global as well as national interests.[3] The scholar who fails to separate legal theory from national

[1] Cf. Chap. IV; and see Richard C. Snyder, "Some Recent Trends in International Relations Theory and Research," in Austin Ranney, ed., *Essays on the Behavioral Study of Politics*, Urbana, University of Illinois Press, 1962, pp. 104-71.

[2] The more modest form of the latter argument is that international legal theory can improve the rationality of decision.

That is, if its methods are adopted, inquiry will gradually grow more disciplined. For an impressive attempt to modernize the theoretical basis of diplomacy see Richard W. Cottam, *Competitive Interference and 20th Century Diplomacy*, University of Pittsburgh Press, 1967, esp. pp. 1-33.

[3] The distinction between the systemic or international level of analysis and the

policy tends to ignore the systemic properties of international law in the nuclear age.

The current inflamed climate of political opinion in the United States threatens an increasing nationalization of scholarship. This danger will be considered in connection with the relevance of international legal theory to the decisions (as distinct from the decision-making process) of government officials. It is important to bear in mind the difference between using a theory of analysis to clarify and improve the governmental process of decision-making and using a theory to uphold or attack the outcome of the process. In fact, the core of my argument is a plea for emphasis on the former task and avoidance of the latter pretension.

Having considered the necessity for restraint and detachment on the part of international legal theorists, I shall consider certain gaps in our understanding of contemporary international law. These gaps arise in part from a failure to give an adequate account of the distinctive character of international law as a legal system. The central theoretical challenge arises from the persisting need to explain how law is even possible in a social system that lacks strong central institutions and that finds itself in no position to take formal action in order to punish serious violations of its fundamental ordering norms.

A final brief section is devoted to the place of theory in international legal studies today. One should appreciate the fact that the theorist swims against a strong operational current in the mainstream of legal research in the United States. Most international lawyers, whether inside or outside of universities, profess to be antitheoretical. Such a profession is often accompanied, or even justified, by a conviction that theory is a waste of time in legal studies. The serious work of legal research, the argument proceeds, is to organize and analyze the knowledge that has grown up as a consequence of attempts by lawyers, judges, government officials, and other scholars to solve specific legal problems. This hostile attitude toward theory, if ever defensible, certainly appears ill-suited to a proper understanding of law in a social environment that is changing as rapidly and as fundamentally as is the environment of international law. To refuse to reexamine the theoretical basis of inquiry into the international legal order is to be reconciled to an old theory rather than to be rid of theory altogether. The difference between the antitheorist and the theorist is that the former is the servant of implicit theory, whereas the theorist, if competent, is the master of an explicit

---

subsystemic or national level of analysis has been demonstrated with effective clarity by J. David Singer, "The Level-of-Analysis Problem in International Relations," in Klaus Knorr and Sidney Verba, eds., *The International System*, Princeton, Princeton University Press, 1961, pp. 77-92.

theory that he refines as an instrument suitable for whatever substantive study he proposes to undertake.

I. On the Need for Humility and Restraint by Contemporary Theorists of International Law in the United States

International legal theory has special problems of its own. The absence of a world government compels theorists to speculate on whether it is plausible to posit the existence of an international society and, if so, of what character. Thus, the social environment within which international law is expected to function cannot be taken for granted to nearly the extent that it might be in investigating the borderlands of the known, knowable, and unknowable in a domestic legal context. For the theorist to assume the social and political environment of international law is to risk other perils, the most frequent of which is implicit reliance upon a model of law transferred from domestic life. Since such a domestically derived model does not fit the international setting, the effect is likely to be a theory of international law that is excessively formal (Kelsen) or simplistically cynical (Morgenthau).

The first requisite of an adequate theory of international law is a concern with the distinctive attributes of law in an environment with the characteristics of the international system. Because Myres McDougal has made such a powerful demonstration of his awareness of this starting point for a theory about international law,[4] I regard McDougal as the most important international law theorist of our time. McDougal's position is not jeopardized even if one reaches the conclusion that his method for coping with the extralegal environment is so complicated as to be unworkable.[5] McDougal has demonstrated in great detail the manner in which international law functions, taking into account the special quality of law in a decentralized social system. Because of his insistence upon contexual analysis, McDougal makes the environment of world affairs relevant to any particular decision about the meaning of a legal rule. The necessity for this reference to context suggests that international legal theory is quite undeveloped, for as long as it is

---

[4] The work of McDougal is essentially a group endeavor and one in which the work of Harold D. Lasswell has figured particularly prominently. Cf. Chapter XI for further discussion of the New Haven Group Approach. Reference to Professor McDougal as an individual should be understood to connote a wider reference to his wider collaborative base of intellectual operation. See, e.g., McDougal and Associates, *Studies in World Public Order,* New Haven, Yale University Press, 1960, Chaps. 1, 2 and 12 [hereinafter cited as *Studies*]; Myres S. McDougal, "International Law, Power and Policy: A Contemporary Conception," 82 *Recueil des Cours* 133-258 (1953).

[5] Cf. Singer, note 3 *supra* at 79n5, where, in referring to a criticism often directed at Richard C. Snyder's decision-making models, the author said that "one might call attention to the relative ease with which many of Snyder's categories could be collapsed into more inclusive ones." The same criticism could be applied to McDougal's framework.

necessary to take so much into account in making each legal appraisal, it is evident that there is no agreement about the role and character of law in the social order. The more that can be taken for granted without upsetting the validity of an inquiry, the sharper the focus of knowledge and awareness tends to become. In fact, the primitiveness of a theory can be roughly gauged by the extent to which the environment can be held constant without affecting its application.

A recognition of the implications of this primitiveness seems crucial for developing an improved theory of international law. This issue of primitiveness goes to the heart of whether and to what extent a theoretical explanation provides normative guidance or, stated differently, expresses the relationship between theory and practice. What insight does a theory of international law presently yield with respect to a dispute about whether specific behavior is, was, or will be legal? The arguments[6] about the legality of the 1962 quarantine imposed by the United States to prevent the emplacement of Soviet missiles on Cuban territory are a forceful illustration of how hazardous it is to be confident about what is legal and what is illegal.[7]

Moreover, there are the more general difficulties of using a primitive theory as a basis for engineering applications.[8] It is one thing to state a

---

[6] Carl Q. Christol and Charles R. Davis, "Maritime Quarantine: The Naval Interdiction of Offensive Weapons and Associated Material to Cuba, 1962," 57 *American Journal of International Law* 525-45 (July 1963); "Editorial Comment," *id.* at 588-613; L. C. Meeker, "Defensive Quarantine and the Law," *id.* at 515-24; Quincy Wright, "The Cuban Quarantine," *id.* at 546-65. I do not wish to disparage these articles. They constitute a thoughtful and provocative series of commentaries upon the legal issues raised by the quarantine. However, except for Quincy Wright, who is rather legalistic in his approach, the authors do not seriously consider the arguments that are available against the legality of the United States claims. The authors instead appear to mobilize legal arguments in support of a national position in a period of crisis. This one-sided argumentation is an appropriate perspective for an American official or perhaps even for a citizen, but it is inappropriate for international lawyers concerned with appraising legality from a global perspective in such a way that the nation of a scholar's origin is a factor of diminishing importance. The one-sided nature of the various analyses was particularly striking in those authors who used the rhetoric of a world community perspective but limited themselves to the arguments favorable to

the United States' (regional) interpretation of law.

[7] The most that a theory of a subject can contribute is to enhance the rationality of the process. This contribution is obscured as soon as the theoretical approach purports to generate authoritative outcomes for specific problems. It is this obscurity that gives rise to part of my complaint. What is disturbing is that none of the American commentators on the legality of the quarantine conceded uncertainty about the outcome of a legal appraisal, although such uncertainty appears to be the only reasonable conclusion. See note 6 *supra*. Oddly enough, Abram Chayes, Legal Advisor, Department of State, came closest to making this point: " 'Was the Quarantine legal?' A question put in that form is bound to elicit overgeneralized and useless answers. The object of first-year law school education is to teach students not to ask such questions." Chayes, "Remarks," *Proceedings of the American Society of International Law, 1963*, pp. 10, 11.

[8] See generally Morton A. Kaplan, "Problems of Theory Building and Theory Confirmation in International Politics," in Klaus Knorr and Sidney Verba, eds., *The International System*, Princeton, Princeton University Press, 1961, pp. 6-24.

general conception of international law that takes account of many variables; it is quite another to shift from general levels of conceptual analysis to concrete levels of disputed behavior. It is not that theory is irrelevant to a legal appraisal of behavior, but rather that it is not dispositive at this stage. No theory, impartially and rigorously applied, will reveal whether or not the Cuban quarantine was legal; nor may a theory of international law be relied upon for unambiguous guidance to, or for passing judgment on, an official entrusted with responsibility for acting in accord with law. On the other hand, a theory can contribute to the rationality of the decision-making process by enumerating those variables most relevant to a particular decision. Here again, the work of the McDougal group is very valuable since it systematically enlarges the legal horizon of relevance by pointing to the kinds of considerations that a decision-maker can and should take into account. However, this accounting of relevant factors is done in a manner that is too imprecise and cumbersome to produce uniform application. Thus, equally ardent disciples of the method of legal analysis could come to divergent legal conclusions with regard to any particular legal controversy.

Of course, the difficulty of applying a theoretical approach to a concrete situation is not peculiar to international law. The split decisions of the Supreme Court of the United States suggest that uncertainty continues to torment the operation, as well as the theory, of law even in a relatively stable domestic society. But there is a crucial difference. In a domestic society, there is an official decision-maker regularly available to render an authoritative judgment as to what the law is at a given time and place. With rare exceptions, such an authoritative interpretation is not obtainable in the international system. Again the Cuban quarantine is a useful example. There was no possibility of acquiring a judgment as to whether the quarantine was legal from an official decision-maker acknowledged as authoritative by the world community.[9] Even if one contends that the International Court of Justice has the status to give such a judgment, there is no routine obligation imposed upon disputing nations to have recourse to it; nor is there a consensus in the community that it is proper to settle a legal dispute of this kind by third-party settlement procedures. Adversary interpretations of law are set forth by national officials serving as legal experts in the national bureaucracy. The expectation of the international community is that a political dispute about national rights will lead to a clash of national

---

[9] Reliance upon Georges Scelle's interesting theory *de dédoublement fonctionnel* is more a proposal for the reorientation of attitude than a promise of objective decision-making at the national level. Scelle argues that a government official serves simultaneously as a national official and an agent of world order. See Scelle, "Le Phénomène juridique du dédoublement fonctionnel," in W. Schätgel and H. F. Schlochauer, eds., *Rechtsfragen der Internationalen Organisation: Festschrift für Hans Wehberg*, Frankfurt, Klostermann, 1956, p. 324.

interpretations of the type which international law allows, just as we in a domestic community expect that a private dispute about rights and duties will lead opposing counsel to develop contradictory interpretations of the relevant legal rules. The domestic clash usually can be authoritatively and effectively resolved, and this prospect often induces a reasonable settlement without recourse to the formal legal system, but the international clash of legal arguments cannot regularly be eliminated by a formal decision.[10] In such a situation, if the legal theorist duplicates the approach taken by the foreign office law expert, then the scholar forgoes an opportunity to play a distinctive role in the international system. And, what is worse, the most cynical disenchantment with law as a regulative process in international relations is vindicated. In this respect, it is unfortunate that members of the Legal Adviser's Office entered scholarly arenas to advance their adversary interpretations of the Cuban quarantine and also that scholars abandoned a detached perspective to become "of counsel" to the United States. The result was the confusion of adversary and scholarly perspectives, as well as a sacrifice of the objectivity and balanced response that might otherwise have come from the legal interpretations given by scholars. One way to compensate for the weakness of central institutions in world affairs is to encourage scholarly specialists to act as imparital judges of the legality of national behavior, thereby giving some objective status to a consensus among scholars.[11]

Of course, a special difficulty arises in appraising the legality of international activity if the observer is also a participant. The citizen's role often takes precedence over the scholar's; in other words, the dictates of national patriotism seem to shape judgments about legality to an extent too great to be consistent with the canons of scholarly detachment. This psychological assessment itself counsels against the assertion of scholarly conclusions about what is legal in a controversial international law case that engages national interests. Respect for the impartiality of international law is not engendered if, in the dramatic cases, the legal outcome appears to be more a matter of the national orientation of the analyst than the product of a detached analysis of legal prin-

[10] Julius Stone has been particularly sensitive to the consequences of the absence of either clear rules or effective remedies in the course of interpreting the permissible use of force in contemporary international relations. See Julius Stone, *Aggression and World Order*, Berkeley, University of California Press, 1958; Julius Stone, *Quest for Survival—The Role of Law and Foreign Policy*, Cambridge, Harvard University Press, 1961.

[11] The idea of encouraging scholarly objectivity also discloses the possibility of abandoning the primary attachment of the political man to the state. As such, it would be a step in the direction of building loyalties to world order of the sort that have been advocated by such diverse scholars as C. Wilfred Jenks and Percy Corbett. See Percy E. Corbett, *Law and Society in the Relations of States*, New York, Harcourt, Brace, 1951, pp. 259-300; Clarence Wilfred Jenks, *The Common Law of Mankind*, New York, Praeger, 1958, pp. 1-61.

ciples. Such partisanship destroys the fragile claim that the standards of international law can provide a basis for common restraint. If international law is unable to establish rules of common restraint, then the normal domestic function of law is so altered in international affairs that we are presented with an unpleasant choice: either to withdraw the label "law" from "the talk about norms" or to redefine law for international affairs in a way so radical that it refers to the rhetoric used by nations to justify their own ways or to state their complaints about the ways of others.[12] Law then becomes primarily a mode of international communication instead of an international system designed to restrain behavior.[13] Stanley Hoffmann has protested against policy oriented analysis precisely because it produces this shift in the meaning of international law: "It is . . . essential for the social scientist to understand that law is not merely a policy among others in the hands of statesmen, and that it is a tool with very *special characteristics and roles*: the social scientist who forgets this and advises the Prince accordingly will debase the instrument and mislead the Prince."[14] This comment underscores the importance of avoiding added uncertainty as to the nature of international law arising as a by-product of a theoretical approach that unconvincingly purports to interpret and guide the practice of sovereign states in authoritative terms. Although, surprisingly enough, McDougal himself has often failed to distinguish between the roles of scholar, citizen, and social engineer in his analysis of controversial questions in international law,[15] he has stated clearly "the fundamentally different standpoint and functions of the scholarly inquirer and the authoritative decision-maker": "*The scholarly inquirer assumes an observational standpoint relatively apart from the processes of authoritative decision being observed, attempting to free himself in the highest degree possible from the limiting perspectives of internal participants,* and seeks effectively to perform certain interrelated intellectual tasks about such processes."[16]

---

[12] Certainly, the introduction of legal language into the conduct of diplomatic relations is one important indication of the reality of international law. On the proposition that international law is in fact law, see H.L.A. Hart, *The Concept of Law*, Oxford, Clarendon Press, 1961, pp. 208-31; C.A.W. Manning, *The Nature of International Society*, London, G. Bell, 1962, pp. 100-27.

[13] One principal function of international law is to facilitate the process of international communication, especially in periods of crisis. For the general relevance of law to social communication see Apter, "Political Religion in the New Nations," in Clifford Geertz, ed., *Old Societies and New States*, New York, The Free Press, 1963, pp. 57, 73-77, where the legal order for any social system is identified as "a reconciliation system."

[14] Stanley Hoffmann, "The Study of International Law and the Theory of International Relations," *Proceedings of the American Society of International Law, 1963*, pp. 26, 33.

[15] Professor Harold Sprout of Princeton University suggested to me this way of distinguishing among roles.

[16] Myres S. McDougal, "Some Basic Theoretical Concepts About International Law: A Policy-Oriented Framework of Inquiry," *Journal of Conflict Resolution* 4 (Sept. 1960), 337-54, 337. (Emphasis added.)

However, one theoretical issue—a residue of the legal realist movement—is whether such impartiality is ever possible. McDougal inclines toward the view, easily overstated, that the policy bases of legal rules provide standards of interpretation and introduce an inevitable uncertainty and value perspective into the application of rules to behavior.[17] This leads McDougal to castigate those " 'schools' of jurisprudence, perhaps even the most influential contemporary schools, [that] continue to present 'law' as an 'autonomous' science or art, cleanly severable from the community processes which condition it and it in turn affects."[18] The result of McDougal's neo-legal-realist critique is the contention that law cannot be rationally applied without taking account of its "value consequences."[19] Furthermore, once these value consequences have been taken into account, the primary task of the law is to use legal doctrine to maximize the values at stake. These values may include the satisfaction of national objectives. This task is simplified because legal rules co-exist in complementary pairs, permitting opposing arguments to develop in relation to each complementary norm. "Omnipresent complementarity" enables the decision-maker to choose from the set of complementary norms those particular norms that serve to maximize the values of the community that he happens to serve. McDougal and his associates have recommended the explicit adoption of the values of human dignity as an international value objective.[20] The question, "Whose version of human dignity?" is not squarely faced, with the consequence that legal rules have one content for one's own society and quite another for its rival.[21] This bivocalism risks converting international law into an instrument of propaganda whenever the international community is deeply divided on value issues. Legal norms are understood to support the realization of values rather than the restraint of behavior. Although an instrumental jurisprudence is a virtual necessity to support an action philosophy, such as Existentialism or Marxism, it also does help to build a system of world order that is broad enough to encompass rivals.

There appears to be a contradiction in McDougal's theoretical posi-

---

[17] For a perceptive critical analysis of this aspect of McDougal's appoach, see Stanley V. Anderson, "A Critique of Professor Myres S. McDougal's Doctrine of Interpretation by Major Purposes," 67 *American Journal of International Law* 378-83 (April 1963). However, McDougal does not intend to invite decision-makers to determine the law in accordance with their personal outlook. See McDougal, note 16 *supra* at 339; McDougal, "A Footnote," 57 *American Journal of International Law* 383-84 (April 1963).

[18] Myres S. McDougal, "The Ethics of Applying Systems of Authority: The Balanced Opposites of a Legal System," in Harold D. Lasswell and Harlan Cleveland, eds., *The Ethic of Power*, New York, Harper and Brothers, 1962, pp. 221, 228.
[19] *Id.* at 229.
[20] *Id.* at 231, passim. For a particularly effective statement, see McDougal, "Perspective for an International Law of Human Dignity," in *Studies*, p. 987.
[21] For further consideration, see Appendix C.

tion between the argument that nuclear peace depends upon the adoption by all nations of universal rules of minimum order and the requirement that what is legal must express, in each context, that which is most conducive to the promotion of a national version of human dignity. One can accord priority either to a common set of rules or to an adversary set of goals, but one can hardly assert their compatibility without denying that element of consistency that is at the root of all rational thought. Either the rules of self-defense mean one thing for all actors or they do not; if they do not, then the rules will be self-interpreted to fulfill national interests, as well as national values. No national community can pretend to be so virtuous that its international behavior is a reflection of its proclaimed values rather than of its interests and capabilities. We need evidence from history and practice to show that national governments determine foreign policy by a primary reference to postulated values as distinct from selfish interests.[22] This kind of demonstration must be forthcoming if we are ever to be convinced that values, however conceived and by whom, serve or should serve as the dominant guide of conduct in world affairs. However, there is no proof that values serve this function; rather, the evidence suggests that, especially in international affairs, values, as distinct from interests, play a very subordinate role in the formation of national policy.[23]

The argument against the approach of the McDougal group reaches two conclusions on these issues. First, the correlation of law and values is a subjective process that is incompatible with the maintenance of nuclear peace by an objective system of norms, i.e. by principles of minimum world public order. Second, national behavior, especially in foreign spheres of action, is more characteristically shaped by interests and capabilities than by values.

McDougal's analysis of the legal process in world affairs seems mistaken in certain serious respects. The significance of complementary norms is exaggerated. Granted, it is *logically possible* either to maintain that the 1962 quarantine was illegal because it violated the freedom of the high seas during peacetime or to allege that the interference was a proper exercise of the rights of self-defense, but is it *equally plausible* to maintain either argument? What kind of argument is it? Is this an argument about the meaning of clear rules, the differing values of rival national actors, or is it an argument about the content of community expectations about what constitutes permissible behavior in such a con-

[22] There are many interpretations of international relations that stress the distorting effect of national egoism. Among the most perceptive are Charles de Visscher, *Theory and Reality in Public International Law*, Princeton, Princeton University Press, 1957 (Corbett trans.), and

Reinhold Niebuhr, *The Structure of Nations and Empires*, New York, Scribner, 1959.

[23] It should be observed that an insistence upon common values discredits the attempts to increase public order by reliance upon common interests.

text? And if values are relevant, do we consider the values of the actors with respect to the subject matter in dispute or with respect to overall objectives? Are we interested in both tactical values and strategic values? McDougal does not fully answer these questions, with the result that an acceptance of McDougal's position virtually severs the link between language and meaning. For if complementary norms are equally plausible under most circumstances, then no predictable impact upon behavior derives from the adoption of a new prohibitive rule—unless by some mysterious and undisclosed process the rule can also be thought to amend community values. Most of the time a legal rule is capable of conveying its content without requiring any consideration of its relation to community values. Furthermore, there is a clear and uniform right or duty created, the content of which is commonly understood by actors with different, even antagonistic, values. That is, a universal legal order combining actors with incompatible values seems to be *theoretically*, although not necessarily *existentially*, possible.[24] Its existential possibility, or rather the range, quality, and degree of approximation, involves an assessment of the behavior and intentions of the dominant actors in world affairs at a given time in history with respect to a specified set of issues.[25] An assessment in real-world terms, as distinct from in utopian or dysutopian terms, depends on precise and specific observation of the relationships between behavior and normative claims to regulate behavior.

Although legal rules, especially broad principles of world order such as are embodied in the doctrine of self-defense, are not delineated precisely enough so that violative behavior can be identified with confidence, something quite definite is communicated by the basic conception. Legal rules usually have meanings that can be stretched to provide an adversary argument in order to support the policies of an actor, but not all arguments are equally convincing, partly because the meaning of legal rules is not indefinitely elastic. There are world community expectations about what is permissible and impermissible that draw upon even wider cultural expectations about the meaning of these rules.

To allege the pervasive complementarity of legal norms is to make a false allegation, as well as to blur the perception of quite another matter: namely, the idea that law can be manipulated to rationalize policy goals, even those of the most anarchic character. To illustrate, the Soviet Union invokes norms of sovereignty and nonintervention with regard to its management of Eastern Europe affairs, whereas at the same

---

[24] Compare McDougal and Lasswell, "The Identification and Appraisal of Diverse Systems of Public Order," in *Studies* 1, with Jenks, *op.cit. supra*, note 11, at Chap. 2.

[25] See Roscoe Pound, "Philosophical Theory and International Law," 1 *Bibliotheca Visseriana*, Leyden, E. F. Brill, 1923, pp. 71, 75-76, 89-90.

time it invokes norms of popular self-determination with regard to Asian and African affairs. This illustration of Soviet policy-oriented jurisprudence expresses in part, or can be so construed, a revolutionary commitment to spread Marxist-Leninist values of "human dignity." Certainly Marxist ideology develops a vision of human society that promises to realize the optimal dignity of its individual members. If we look at law from the perspective of an antagonist, we confront more vividly the dangers of a policy approach to the content of norms in a divided world. As Oliver Lissitzyn has clearly shown, legal process and doctrine simultaneously serve the causes of conflict and cooperation, of social integration and disintegration.[26] But recognizing the *capacity* to manipulate rules for policy objectives is not tantamount to saying that the content of legal rules depends upon the policy context. In fact, the growth of world legal order depends on the gradual growth of a willingness on the part of principal governments to refrain from exercising this manipulative capacity, at least in instances when legal argument relies upon an interpretation of a rule that exceeds reasonable margins of tolerance. The policy objective of such an approach is to build attitudes and habits that encourage international law to develop into a *system of world order* rather than into a *style of argument in international relations.*[27]

From this perspective, a next step in the development of a theory of international law is to increase understanding of the relation between ideas and action. This understanding involves recognizing the difficulty of making engineering applications of high-order legal abstractions. Such an understanding also suggests that the theorist refrain from participation in adversary arenas (and, ideally, that an adversary refrain from entering scholarly arenas), or at least that the nature of participation in legal debate be clearly labeled. A theory of international law such as has been developed by the McDougal group can certainly clarify the implications of policy choices and identify for the policy-maker the kinds of considerations that are appropriate to emphasize, but such a theoretical approach is not yet in a position to guide the choice of policy in concrete circumstances or even to provide an objective account of what is legal when the policies and values of the actors diverge and when complementary legal rules are invoked in support of competing adversaries.

II. *Some Tasks for the Ambitious Theorist*

It would be most unconstructive to castigate the activism of a theorist of international law without hazarding some ideas as to how he might

---

[26] Oliver J. Lissitzyn, "International Law in a Divided World," *International Conciliation*, 542 (March 1963), 1, 6.

[27] When one asks, "Does international law really exist?" attention should be given to the word "exist" rather than to the word "really."

more profitably employ himself. This section discusses some things that need to be known and are knowable by whosoever would develop an adequate theory of international law. Such an emphasis may help to clarify the nature, function, and limits of international law in contemporary international society.

1. GLOBAL INTERESTS AND NATIONAL INTERESTS: A SYSTEMIC ORIENTATION

It is indeed difficult to adapt thought about international law to the rapidly changing environment of international relations. The pace of extralegal change, as well as the character and scale of conflict between nations and ideologies, has led some scholars to conclude that the current international system is best considered to be a revolutionary one.[28] Such an interpretation prompts a special set of inquiries about how law functions in a revolutionary social system.

Attributing a revolutionary quality to world politics as a whole is itself an unfamiliar style of thought for international lawyers.[29] It implies a willingness to treat world politics as a political system with its own patterns and processes of interaction, as well as its own forms of order.[30] This conception of an autonomous international system as a suitable object of study contrasts with the traditional approach of lawyers and political scientists which is to study international law as a series of restraints imposed upon the nation-state as principal actor. A primary theoretical need of international law is to complement the tradition of actor perspectives (sovereign states) with a rigorous concern with systemic perspectives. That is, there is a need to examine the role and destiny of international law within a global system of world order. The primary goals of this global system are to advance the values and interests of the overall world community rather than to promote the more special and diverse interests and values of national actors who are components of that system.

The current scope of international activities requires an overall framework of legal order. The study of the quality of this framework warrants attention now as much as does the status of particular rules and

[28] See Chap. 3; Stanley Hoffmann, "International Systems and International Law," in Klaus Knorr and Sidney Verba, eds., *The International System*, Princeton, Princeton University Press, 1961, pp. 205-37.

[29] The first major attempt to introduce systemic thinking into the analysis and presentation of international law is in Morton A. Kaplan and Nicholas deB. Katzenbach, *The Political Foundations of International Law*, New York, Wiley,

1961. Harsh, but effective, criticism of this book may be found in Robert W. Tucker, "A Review," *Journal of Conflict Resolution*, 7 (March 1963), 69-75.

[30] See generally, Morton A. Kaplan, *System and Process in International Politics*, New York, Wiley, 1957; George Liska, *International Equilibrium*, Cambridge, Harvard University Press, 1957; Richard N. Rosecrance, *Action and Reaction in World Politics*, Boston, Little, Brown, 1963.

transactions. Such a contention implies that we are as interested in the general atmosphere of international relations as in an exposition of the legal expectations that cluster about particular subjects, such as force, space, and foreign investment. Students of the international legal order can be usefully encouraged at this period of time to develop conceptions of the contributions of law to a worldwide system of order.

2. SHIFTING BASES OF OBLIGATION IN INTERNATIONAL LAW: FROM AUTHORITY TO CONSENT TO CONSENSUS

There is an absence of clarity about the role and character of international law in the contemporary world. Part of this unclarity stems from radical changes in the environment and composition of international society. Frequently, the explanation of why the international world of 1939 is discontinuous with that of 1969 is based principally upon the emergence of new states, the development of nuclear technology, and the activity of international institutions.[31] The multiplication of actors and their heterogeneity, the new parameters of rational conflict among states, and the emergence and authority of regional and global institutions are among the factors that greatly complicate the milieu within which international law is expected to function.

The older international law that had been developed and studied since the Reformation was concerned with the regulation of independent states that for the most part shared a common cultural heritage and exhibited a common political outlook in their relations with one another. Despite this degree of sharing, it was difficult to restrain the foreign policies of these states within mutually acceptable limits. After the Reformation states refused to acknowledge any source of legal authority superior to their sovereign will. For this reason, the collapse of Medieval unity visibly manifest in the Church and the Holy Roman Empire and the later disrepute of the rationalistic continuation of the Medieval conception of world society embodied in the various formulations of natural law eliminated any prospect of establishing an authoritative spiritual center for the organization of mankind; only very recently, in the decades since World War I, have the principal governments struggled to reestablish a new institutional and spiritual unity. This newer center of potential authority and order was born of necessity and urgency, however, rather than of faith and solidarity. After the Medieval center disappeared, theorists of state sovereignty began to attribute external reality to the ideas of sovereignty, ideas that had been

---

[31] See, e.g. Rosecrance, *op.cit. supra*, note 30. But see George Liska, "Continuity and Change in International Systems," *World Politics*, XVI (Oct. 1963), 118-36, where the alleged lack of continuity of successive international societies is questioned in a significant review of Rosecrance's book.

originally developed to substantiate the internal claims of national governments against the refractory vestiges of the feudal system. Doctrinal formulations of natural law were unable to posit effective, or even meaningful, restraints upon the behavior of states after the Reformation, and, accordingly, were not taken seriously enough to provide international society with a reliable supranational source of restraint. Each national government tended to construe natural law principles to conform to its national interests; therefore, stable patterns of order were not achieved, and widespread cynicism was generated.[32] Perceptive international jurists since Vattel have supported the development of a voluntaristic system of legal restraint which rested upon the express or implied willingness of the sovereign to be bound. Eventually, subjective consent replaced objective authority as the central basis of international legal obligation. This system of pseudo-restraint dominated international legal theory until World War I. It was a realistic but modest conception of international law. Such a conception of legal obligation made it clear that governments of sovereign states would not permit any diminution of their discretion to advance their own vital interests in areas of power, security, and wealth. Thus, international law, as premised upon sovereign consent, even tolerated national policies dependent upon recourse to war. Just as natural law engendered cynicism for claiming to do too much, so legal positivism stimulated cynicism by being content with too little.[33] After all, of what use was a legal system that allowed actors unrestricted discretion to use violence against one another? How could restraints imposed on lesser acts of nations be taken seriously if recourse to war was to be unregulated? These questions became even more crucial after World War I, which had disclosed the costs of modern war in suffering, resources, and political dislocation.

The aftermath of World War I led to a movement, doomed *ab initio* by ambivalence, to curb the discretion of sovereign states without disturbing the power and reality of sovereignty. The League of Nations can be understood as a rudimentary attempt to reestablish a visible center of international society responsible for the maintenance of permanent

[32] But let us not forget that the universalistic world view of the naturalists not only made possible the development of thought on the subject of international law but also introduced a cosmopolitan bias that international law has never lost, at least as compared to thought and action dealing with other international subject matter. Sir Henry Maine has even suggested that "the grandest function of the Law of Nature was discharged in giving birth to modern International Law," Maine, *Ancient Law*, Boston, Beacon Press, 1963, p. 92.

[33] The reliance of positivism upon a narrow conception of the sources of international law is particularly damaging. The refusal to acknowledge the legal status of informal and horizontal norms is a persisting failure within the positivist tradition, introducing legalism (excessive concern with formal rules) and underrating normative elements in international life. Kaplan and Katzenbach, *op.cit. supra*, note 29, at 341-54, develop an excellent appreciation of this normative element to a degree that would be impossible for a positivist to achieve.

world peace. But the gesture was not accompanied by the transfers of power necessary to make the new potential center of legal authority effective, and League voting rules based on unanimity revealed an unwillingness to impose obligations upon any unconsenting sovereign state. Furthermore, the League failed to include several powerful international actors. The United States never joined; the Soviet Union did not belong until 1934; Germany joined late and quit early; and Italy left during the Ethopian War.

The period between the world wars also featured notable efforts to negotiate comprehensive disarmament agreements. That is, an attempt was made to eliminate the capability to wage war by means of the mutual consent of states.[34] In addition, prohibitions upon recourse to force except for purposes of self-defense were formally accepted by almost every state.[35] War was to be banished from the system of international relations by the processes of sovereign consent. World War II indicated dramatically that these prohibitions, if effective at all, were not sufficient to eliminate war. The magnitude of the conflict, the suffering, and the destruction again emphasized the need to establish an international society that possessed the institutional capabilities and legal authority to maintain world peace.

Compared to the League of Nations, the United Nations constitutes a more ambitious attempt to create a visible institutional center for international society competent, if not capable, to restrain recourse to violence by nations. The Charter anticipated some transfers of power to the organization; the voting rules as enacted in the Charter and as shaped by practice have come increasingly to allow consensus to replace consent as a basis for action; and near universality of membership has been achieved. Nevertheless, power remains concentrated in the dominant states and in alliances among these states; the nuclear states now possess fantastic potentialities for causing destruction; and most crisis decisions about the use of force in world affairs continue to be made at the national level.[36] The shift from consent to consensus has, therefore, not been made for fundamental ongoing decision processes involving force and war at the strategic level. However, for local or regional conflicts and for such crucial matters as self-determination, colonialism, and human rights, there is increasing evidence of the role of consensus both in formation of authoritative practice and in the development of rules

---

[34] A useful study of international relations, including the disarmament effort, in the period following World War I is Edward Hallett Carr, *International Relations Between the Two World Wars (1919-1939)*, London, Macmillan, 1948.

[35] For a concise survey of developments, including pertinent documentary material, see Louis B. Sohn, ed., *Cases and Materials on World Law*, Brooklyn, Foundation Press, 1950, pp. 781-806.

[36] At the same time, it is important not to underestimate the peacekeeping achievements of the United Nations in Korea, Suez, Lebanon, the Congo, and Yemen.

of behavior.[37] A major task for an adequate contemporary theory of international law is to assimilate the significance and contours of this shift of the basis of legal obligation from authority (reason), to consent, to consensus.[38] At each stage, however, the earlier basis for legal obligation persists and coexists to some extent with the newer bases; for example, reason continued to underlie the perception of law in its positivistic stage, despite the emphasis upon the sovereign will and the requirement of consent. Similarly, if today we attribute a certain law-forming potency to consensus and acknowledge the growing reality of a global will, such awarenesses do not imply a denial of the continuing role played by sovereign consent or do not even challenge the persisting dominance of the state mechanism in many areas, including perhaps the most vital areas of human concern.

In fact, the limitations upon the processes of consensus and the stalemate at the level of sovereign consent contribute to what I would identify as the tragic paradox of contemporary international law: *the necessity for effective management of violence in world affairs exists alongside the impossibility of achieving management by consensual means.* Settled habits of political consciousness continue to identify national security with strength, disarmament with weakness, and world government with the sacrifice of national independence and character. Ideological hostility, political rivalry, and cultural diversity generate distrust and conflict. These pressures of habit and conflict militate decisively against any attempt to transfer significant power to a new center of authority or to reduce drastically the power of national actors. The elimination of national force will probably have to be accompanied by the growth of an international legislative competence. Processes of social and political change cannot and should not be brought to a halt in a disarming world. Even in domestic society, threats and symbolic eruptions of violence are the motive force behind a successful social protest on a fundamental issue.[39] Contentions that social and political

[37] This progress can serve as the basis for promoting the growth of legal order in world affairs. See, e.g., Richard A. Falk and Saul H. Mendlovitz, "Towards a Warless World: One Legal Formula to Achieve Transition," 73 *Yale Law Journal* 399-424 (Jan. 1964).
[38] Attention should also be given to Professor Wolfgang G. Friedmann's most important suggestion that the whole basis of international legal obligation is being transformed by the growing role of international cooperation activities, "for which the traditional concept of sanction is largely meaningless" since the actual sanction which provides the necessary enforcement is based merely "upon the privilege of participation in joint endeavors serving the common interests of mankind." Friedmann, "National Sovereignty, International Cooperation, and the Reality of International Law," 10 *University of California Los Angeles Law Review* 739, 748-53 (May 1963); see Friedmann, "The Changing Dimensions of International Law," 62 *Columbia Law Review* 1147-65 (Nov. 1962).
[39] This point has been the subject of two recent articles: H. L. Nieburg, "The Threat of Violence and Social Change," *American Political Science Review*, 56 (Dec. 1962) 865-73; Nieburg, "Uses of Violence," *Journal of Conflict Resolution*, 7 (March 1963), 43-54.

change can be adequately assured by processes of persuasion appear to reflect a dubious interpretation of human experience; at best, such contentions represents slogans that have been uncritically built into democratic ideology. It would appear that this relationship between violence and change applies *a fortiori* to international society. Therefore, substantial disarmament implies a lot of government and/or a lot of chaos, as well as some competence by international society to redistribute wealth and to promote human rights throughout the world.[40] There seems to be no disposition on the part of national actors to take such radical steps by voluntary action. Unless transformed by trauma induced by war or such other catastrophe as famine and disease resulting from overpopulation, the effective central management of violence in world affairs appears impossible to achieve.

And yet an effective centralization of authority over principal instruments of international violence appears to be necessary. There is no historical evidence to suggest that a central international war can be permanently avoided among national rivals. In fact, present levels of hostility and tension, together with the increasing cost of defense and the continuing uncertainties of the arms race, make the situation, if prolonged, appear very unpromising. The world is at the mercy of the leadership of the nuclear superpowers. Our recent past, which includes Hitler and Stalin, suggests that leaders of great states, and their supportive bureaucracies, may be motivated by pathological drives to assume self-destructive political risks. Thus, even assuming the capacity of reason to restrain the kind of provocative national behavior that prompts escalation of violence across the threshold of nuclear violence, there is considerable evidence in support of a forecast of eventual doom unless the situation is changed. On such a basis, a necessity for the centralized management of force appears presently to exist.

3. LEGAL SOLUTIONS FOR THE TRANSITION PROBLEM

The tension between this necessity for drastic modification of the structure of international society and its impossibility poses a further challenge for those working to evolve an adequate theory of international law. This simplified depiction of the tragic situation of international society is not intended to vindicate an attitude of complacent or despondent disregard. The analysis reaches pessimistic results, but the need to avoid a tragic outcome persists. What appears now to be impossible may unexpectedly turn out to be possible. It is quite consistent to combine a discouraging realism and a qualified commitment to pursue

[40] See B.V.A. Röling, *International Law in an Expanded World*, Amsterdam, Djambatan, 1960; Johannes Messner, "International Social Justice," *World Justice*, 3 (March 1961-62), 293-309.

utopian objectives. One task for international legal theory is to focus attention upon the selection of means by which to solve "the transition problem"—the problem of centralizing conflict management in international institutions and of replacing national security arrangements with a global security system.[41] Such a transition, variously described as the movement from a war-prone or threat system of international relations to a peace system or warless world, is one appropriate focus of legal inquiry in the decades ahead.[42] Legal thinking has been slow to study processes of social transformation, especially at the international level. It is important to encourage emphasis on these processes of change in present studies. We need to learn more about how law can contribute to the process of institution building at the global level. It is to be noted that the stress is upon the process of changing the world, rather than upon a model of a changed world.[43] A futuristic model can serve as a reminder that transition effort is worthwhile and it can portray in realistic detail the character of alternative systems of international order.[44] Nevertheless, the main conceptual challenge at present is to work out analytic techniques that illuminate the character of the transition process and to formulate various strategies of transition. The projection of terminal models—blueprints of world order—are secondary, more easily accomplished, intellectual acts.

4. VIOLATIONS OF INTERNATIONAL LAW

Parallel to the challenge of transition are a variety of problems that pertain to the operation of international law within the existing system. It is important to use existing legal resources to improve the quality of order in the world today while simultaneously encouraging efforts to change it. Among the most serious deficiencies in international law is the frequent absence of an assured procedure for the identification of a violation. Theoretical inquiry can clarify the problem and provide some

[41] For useful and stimulating suggestions about conflict management and legal order, see Hardy C. Dillard, "Conflict and Change: The Role of Law," *Proceedings of the American Society of International Law, 1963*, p. 50.

[42] See Walter Mills and James Real, *The Abolition of War*, New York, Macmillan, 1963; *Preventing World War III*, Quincy Wright, William M. Evan, and Morton Deutsch, eds., New York, Simon and Schuster, 1962; Arthur Larsen, ed., *A Warless World*, New York, McGraw-Hill, 1963.

[43] But note the relevance of models, so often unappreciated, in thought about current social reality. For an important recent explanation of the role of models in human thought, see Karl W. Deutsch, *The Nerves of Government*, New York, The Free Press, 1963, pp. 3-50.

[44] In furnishing a model, Grenville Clark and Louis B. Sohn, *World Peace Through World Law*, Cambridge, Harvard University Press, 2d rev. edn. 1960, performs a valuable service. We badly need a Soviet Clark-Sohn proposal worked out in comparable detail. This would help to concretize debate. In addition, we need a variety of Western Clark-Sohn models to suggest the lack of agreement in the West over the character of a warless world. The economic stability of the Clark-Sohn solution is challenged in Neil W. Chamberlain, *The West in a World without War*, New York, McGraw-Hill, 1963.

[24]

insight into the solution. The status of controverted behavior a or illegal is quite problematical, in the first instance, because no institutions are able to make judgments that will be treated as auth tive by states.[45] The absence of third-party judgment is a familiar weakness of international law that results from the tendency of national governments to insist upon rights of self-interpretation to discern the scope of permissible behavior. How is a violation of law to be identified in a decentralized social system? National officials may help shape behavior so that it minimizes conflict with legal rules, but once behavior is undertaken, then national officials normally set forth a legal argument to support the challenged action rather than attempt to reach a balanced impartial judgment as to whether the action is or is not legal. Furthermore, the strength of psychological allegiance to one's national sovereign often seems to render nongovernmental specialists incapable of divorcing their role as citizen from their role as expert. The consequence of this confusion of roles is to deprive the international system of the means to determine more definitively whether or not certain behavior constitutes a violation of law. This inability to identify violations is especially prominent when the action is performed by a leading international actor who is able to block censure resolutions in the political organs of the United Nations. In such event, scholars in third states might be capable of providing the most objective account, but their relative obscurity and the special interests that might underlie their outlooks act to restrict the influence of their judgment.[46] It may be worthwhile to consider forming a global council of distinguished international lawyers who would attempt to reach collective determinations (with dissenting views expressed) about the legal status of international conduct of states alleged (by anyone of their membership) to be of doubtful legality. Existing theory about international legal order does not take into sufficient account the difficulty that now attends establishing a violation of international law.

This problem has deep as well as obvious consequences. One obvious consequence is to provoke the contention that, since there is no assured way to identify what a sovereign state is forbidden to do, everything is permissible. How can international law purport to be a system of re-

---

[45] This characteristic of international law is the subject of preliminary analysis in Richard A. Falk, "International Jurisdiction: Horizontal and Vertical Conceptions of Legal Order," 32 *Temple Law Quarterly* 295-320 (Spring 1959).

[46] But compare the argument of Roger Fisher that it is preferable to technicalize the perception of *any* potential violation of international law since it is desirable not to engage a nation's honor by calling attention to its illegal conduct. The thrust of his position seems to be that, in fact, an alleged past violation of international law is a dispute as to the meaning of that law and that "any meaningful difference is necessarily over the future—over what the government should be doing starting right now." Roger D. Fisher, "Enforcement of Disarmament: The Problem of the Response," *Proceedings of the American Society of International Law, 1962*, pp. 1, 10. Compare Richard J. Barnet, "Violations of Disarmament Agreement," *Disarmament and Arms Control* (Summer 1963), 33-48.

straint if it lacks a means to identify transgressions of its rules? This question, far from suggesting the irrelevance of international law, points toward the need to achieve a better understanding of its function and purpose. For, although rules of restraint are the core of the system, their influence is often realized by a combination of self-restraint and reconciliation. A state bureaucracy refrains, under routine circumstances, from violating rules (crystallized expectations about permissible behavior) and approaches them in a spirit of impartiality. Once it is alleged that legal restraints have been broken, the extent of adherence to applicable rules has a great bearing upon the response of the complaining party. Therefore, the degree and manner of violation may be more crucial than the alleged fact of violation.[47] The possibility that a violation of international law may be a matter of degree should be introduced explicitly into international legal theory. A conception of compliance and of violation that draws inspiration from the idea of a spectrum or a prism, rather than insists upon a rigid dichotomy between legal or illegal conduct,[48] would appear well adapted to a largely decentralized legal system such as exists in international society.

In this regard, attention should also be given to the postviolation functions of law. Here, too, a deterioration of international relations may be prevented if there is minimal departure from applicable legal rules in response to allegedly provocative or illegal conduct by other international actors. This problem of moderating responses and counterresponses has received preliminary statement and study in the arms control and disarmament area, but it has not yet been adequately treated in a general statement about the character of international law.[49]

There are further problems about violations of international law that need theoretical refinement. First, the problem of persistent noncompliance—if a particular rule is persistently violated by certain actors and if there is no way to assure future compliance, does the rule remain in force? In other words, is the validity of a rule conditioned upon mutuality of compliance by the major actors in the system? The nonintervention norms that are such an important part of the ideology of world order for the states of Latin America, Asia, and Africa are an

[47] It is in this spirit that the most constructive study of the 1962 Cuban missile crisis could be made. That dispute illustrated a strong governmental policy to depart as little as possible from established norms regulating freedom of the high seas and prohibiting states from threatening or using force to resolve international disputes.

[48] This suggestion has been made in a stimulating essay, Fred W. Riggs, "International Relations as a Prismatic System," in Klaus Knorr and Sidney Verba, eds., *The International System*, Princeton, Princeton University Press, 1961, pp. 144-81.

[49] See note 46 *supra*. See also, Institute for Defense Analyses, *Verification and Response in Disarmament Agreements*, Woods Hole, Massachusetts, 1962 (Summary Report and two annex volumes).

obvious area of concern here.[50] In a bipolar world, or even in more multipolar international settings, adherence to nonintervention rules by certain actors, unless reciprocated, tends to benefit the noncomplying aggressor and to be detrimental to the complying states. One way to think about this issue is to consider allowing states to "violate" a norm in order to secure its enforcement, that is, to revert to the example, to accept counterintervention as a justifiable means of neutralizing previous acts of intervention.[51] But if one is dealing not with an *instance*, but with a noncompliance *pattern* of behavior, as by an expanding and revolutionary political system such as world Communism,[52] then it may be possible to deter intervention on one side only by regarding the rule of law as no longer applicable as a claim against behavior. For example, it has been argued that it is necessary to authorize what amounts to anticipatory or precautionary intervention by the West to forestall subsequent Communist intervention.[53] According to this view, the pattern of violation cannot be prevented by a pattern of counterviolations, but only by a discretionary right to commit similar violations.[54] Under these conditions, it would seem preferable to treat the rule as void rather than to come forward with a series of strained interpretations of what is permissible under it.

A further concern that is not adequately distinguished from the above problem is the proper response to what might be described as systemic noncompliance by an international actor. That is, if a state or a group of states is regarded as pursuing a consistent policy at variance with basic rules of world order, a situation is created which is quite different from a challenge directed at a particular rule or principle. There is a contrast between states that challenge such things as the traditional legal restraints upon the breadth of territorial waters and a revolutionary actor that challenges the entire prevailing system.[55] International legal

---

50 See Chap. IV, "The International Law of Internal War: Problems and Prospects," in Richard A. Falk, *Legal Order in a Violent World*, Princeton, Princeton University Press, 1968.

51 See Peter Calvocoressi, *World Order and New States*, New York, Praeger, 1962, pp. 11-23. In the response stage, there is an equivalence that can be maintained between a violation and a sanction. That is, the operation of a violation that intends to neutralize a prior violation is like a sanction. This is closely related to the argument used by the great powers prior to World War I in order to vindicate their interventionary role in world politics.

52 See George A. Modelski, *The Communist International System*, December 1, 1960, Research Monograph No. 9, Center of International Studies, Princeton University.

53 Compare the suggestions to this effect in Manfred Halpern, *The Morality and Politics of Intervention*, New York, Council on Religion and International Affairs, 1963.

54 There is a need for further clarity in distinguishing between a violation and a counterviolation in international law, especially with respect to whether force is or is not used in a particular case.

55 See authorities cited in note 28 *supra*; cf. McDougal and Lasswell, note 24 *supra*. However, for an article containing a pre-World War II optimism about peaceful coexistence between totalitarian and democratic states, see Hans Wehberg, "Civil War and International Law," *The World Crisis*, London, Longmans, Green, 1938, pp. 160-99.

theory has not developed any explicit body of thinking about the response of law to a revolutionary challenge, as distinct from its response to a series of specific demands for legal reforms. The most serious kind of revolutionary challenge is posed whenever an actor has the capability and intention of using violence to satisfy its demands for a radical reordering of international society. The problem of revolution for the international legal system is more closely associated with the existence of a powerful aggressor than it is with the espousal of an ideology. Hitler's Germany was a revolutionary actor even though it lacked a revolutionary ideology of the sort professed by states adhering to the doctrines of Marxism-Leninism. The endorsement of a revolutionary ideology if accompanied by a sincere commitment to the elimination of violence from interstate relations can make it useful to consider such a state as a nonrevolutionary actor. Yugoslavia under Tito appears to fit this classification,[56] whereas Indonesia, until the countercoup of 1965, often behaved like a revolutionary actor, at least from a regional perspective. It may be useful to develop ideas about systemic noncompliance with regard to regional, as well as global, systems of minimum order. Such ideas would be able to take some account of the emerging importance of regional actors, interests, and systems of order.

A third distinct problem is presented when a state engages in conduct that has been neither expressly authorized nor forbidden. The claim of the United States and of the Organization of American States to establish a partial quarantine upon shipping carrying "offensive" military equipment to Cuba illustrates the difficulty.[57] How does one distinguish in international law between the violation of an old rule and the creation of a new one?[58] Certainly the 1962 quarantine would constitute a useful precedent for a future claimant. In fact, one assumes that a future case would take for granted the legality of the 1962 precedent, just as the Eichmann litigation presupposed the validity of the Nuremberg trials. The international legal system contains only clumsy formal devices for extending and revising the existing law—agreement and the slow accretion of custom. A controversial claim could never qualify as a new rule of law by these processes. As Myres McDougal consistently emphasizes, international law is developed by the unilateral claims of states that are respected or tolerated because they are regarded by the world community as reasonable in their particular context of assertion and because the

[56] See, e.g., *New York Times*, Oct. 23, 1963, p. 14, cols. 2-8 (excerpts from President Tito's speech to the General Assembly of the United Nations). The speech included a nonrevolutionary exposition of peaceful coexistence.

[57] The United States' unilateral claim of the right to orbit surveillance satellites over the Soviet Union, despite Soviet objections, is another illustration. See Chap. VIII.

[58] See generally Hersh Lauterpacht, *Recognition in International Law*, Cambridge, Eng., Cambridge University Press, 1947, pp. 426-30.

claiming state has the power to make them effective.[59] In addition, the status of a controversial claim is increasingly determined by whether it is ratified or repudiated by the organized community as represented in the political organs of the United Nations. Nevertheless, it remains important for international legal theory to clarify existing procedures for the creation and reform of its rules. There is no doubt that positivistic accounts, as largely embodied in Article 38 of the International Court of Justice, are not descriptive of the way international law has grown in the past and are far too restrictive for orderly growth in response to the pressures for change and innovation that are now arising in international life. Most broadly stated, there is a need to find an adequate account of the distinctive character of the international legislative process. How can there be legislative change without a legislature?

Fourth, there is a widespread misimpression that the weakness of international law is reflected by the frequency with which its fundamental rules are violated. Such an attitude inspires an invidious comparison between the success of domestic law and the failure of international law. However, there is a double confusion here. The success of domestic law does not rest on its capacity to solicit the respect of its subjects; the incidence of homicide and civil violence, and even of rebellion, is high. International law is a weak legal system not because it is often or easily flouted by powerful states, but because certain violations, however infrequent, are highly destructive and far-reaching in their implications. International law will not necessarily solve its problems, therefore, by coming to resemble a domestic legal order. Its requirements are different. For international law cannot generate a sense of security among people until the capability and inclination to resort to major war disappears. This is more a problem of disarmament and of individual and group psychology than it is of an improved legal order. For this reason, the suggestion that institutional solutions—better courts and a stronger United Nations—will be sufficient or even nearly sufficient to provide a stable and just international order is properly regarded with skepticism.

International law can only succeed if it does what no legal system has been able to do—secure perfect compliance with its fundamental norms.[60] Any violence at the strategic level of international relations

---

59 I believe that the most successful sustained illustration of McDougal's analysis of the role of the claiming process in the formation of international legal order is Myres S. McDougal and William T. Burke, *The Public Order of the Oceans: A Contemporary International Law of the Sea*, New Haven, Yale University Press, 1962.

60 It has been almost forty years since most nations obligated themselves to refrain from the use of force in international affairs except for self-defense (Briand-Kellogg Pact of Paris, Aug. 27, 1928, 46 Stat. 2343 [1929]). This is not much time for a firm social attitude to develop in a social order with as little sense of community as is found in international affairs. Nevertheless, the trend to make the prohibition effective is certainly visible, despite certain lapses, such as the Communist approval of just wars of na-

threatens nuclear war and the downfall of the system; this prospect, however slight, renders fragile the ordering claims of the international system. It is the vulnerability of international society to a single destructive violator that makes the system weak and inadequate. This vulnerability can be explained, but not by emphasizing the weaknesses of central institutions in world affairs or by positing a model of international society comparable to a developed domestic legal order as a relevant utopia. The urgent, but unattainable, desideratum in international society is the capability to assure that the destructive violation never takes place.

Fifth, there has been no interpretation of the way in which the duty to respect international law correlates with other national duties, such as the duty to frustrate international aggression, to promote human rights, or to safeguard national security. It is unrealistic and probably unjustifiable to regard as absolute the duty to respect enacted or governing law. There is a need to conceive of a doctrine of civil disobedience on an international level. Of course, such a doctrine needs to be understood as having systemwide application; that is, every state actor should be equally entitled to assert a limited right of disobedience. How does one circumscribe this right of disobedience? If the conditions vindicating disobedience are outlined in advance, then they become part of the law. If they are not specified ahead of time, then the system is only as binding as is the goodwill, habits, and self-interest of the powerful states. But is this not the inevitable contingency of any legal claim in every legal system?

To assert an absolute duty to comply is to overlook the validity, and even the reasonableness, of the pressures to violate. Domestic systems often come to regret the myth of absolute compliance, as it was expressed, for instance, in the German atmosphere of Lutheran subservience to secular authority and in the unquestioning acceptance by legal positivists of the claim that positive law always deserves to be accepted as law.[61] The continuing appeal of natural law arises, in part, because it invokes a revered tradition of appeal to a criterion of just action that is higher than the directives of positive law. From the viewpoint of political and moral realism, it is essential to provide within a legal theory for the discretionary right to disobey the law under exceptional circumstances.[62]

---

tional liberation, the aggressive expansionism of some new states, and India's use of force to settle its dispute with Portugal over the status of Goa.

[61] Samuel I. Shuman, *Legal Positivism: Its Scope and Limitations*, Detroit, Wayne State University Press, 1963, pp. 12-18, carefully makes the distinction between analytical jurisprudence (a way-of-doing

jurisprudence) and legal positivism (a theory about the relation between law and morals and about the nature of legal obligation).

[62] Recognition of such a right introduces a contingency reserve that makes explicit the nonabsoluteness of any man-made system of restraint, whether legal or otherwise. There remains, however, a duty

The existence of a right of disobedience also identifies the limits of law and warns naive optimists to realize that no legal order, however perfected, can offer complete protection against the dangers of a destructive violation. The exigencies of conflict and passion may always generate pressures that produce full-scale war, and no set of legal rules and institutions can do more than reduce the risk of this eventuality.

Any ideas about international disobedience should also be reconciled with domestic requirements of maintaining government according to law. In the United States we never tire of citing the celebrated dictum in *The Paquete Habana* that "International law is part of our law, and must be ascertained and administered by the courts of justice of appropriate jurisdiction, as often as questions of right depending upon it are duly presented for their determination."[63] Rules of international law that are incorporated into treaties have constitutional status as supreme law of the land.[64] How is this internal reception of international law to be reconciled with a qualified right of governmental disobedience in exceptional circumstances? In a government of laws, we do not authorize officials to depart from domestic law to promote certain urgent policies. Can we find a rationale for such a departure from international law? Are we prepared to acknowledge that international law is less binding upon government officials than is domestic law?

A plausible allegation of noncompliance, such as complaints about the use of U-2 planes to observe foreign territory or attacks upon the participation by the United States in the Bay of Pigs invasion of 1961, may arouse criticism of the government for choosing an "unlawful" course of action, but it will not prompt attack upon the government as "lawless." Violations of international law are tolerated by the national publics of democratic states in a way that violations of domestic law would not be—a domestic incident comparable to the U-2 incident of 1960 might probably have led the opposition to propose impeachment.[65] There is no formal basis in our national system for differentiating in terms of authoritativeness between these legal rules deriving from domestic and those from international sources. The discrimination against in-

---

to explain the violation to the community as "a reasonable act," given all the relevant circumstances, including an element of perceived necessity.

[63] 175 U.S. 677, 700 (1900); cf. *Interhandel Case—Pleadings, Oral Arguments, and Documents* (Switzerland v. United States of America), Hague, International Court of Justice, 1959, pp. 55-56, 497, 504.

[64] *U.S. Constitution, Article VI.* Thus, the highest organic law and the most authoritative interpreter of law in the United States' legal system assert that international law is binding upon national

behavior.

[65] In an autocratic society, the public becomes hardened to and even expects lawlessness in the internal behavior of government. But it is precisely this feature that contributes to our horror when we contemplate life in an autocratic society. If international society is in some sense a social whole, then lawlessness, if habitual, would seem to have the same undermining effect that we come to dislike so much when it is exhibited in domestic societies.

ternationally based rules accords with community expectations. The national community does not expect, perhaps it would not even permit, its government to confine national policy strictly within the constraints of international law during a period when important national objectives are threatened. In this sense, domestic support of international law compares unfavorably with that given to domestic law. This weak domestic reception of international law is a characteristic weakness of the international legal system that is perhaps accentuated in autocratic national states and it is a weakness that should be considered in working out an adequate descriptive theory of international law. A useful theory of international law would facilitate the identification and explanation of the weaknesses of legal process and structure when the totality is conceived as a global system of world order.

There is a final problem connected with the duty of a state to comply with international law. How does the internal political structure of a nation distribute the legal authority to determine what the applicable rules of international law are? From the viewpoint of international law the distribution of internal authority is a matter of domestic discretion. It is also clear, however, that a state is treated as a unified entity within the international system and is responsible as a unit for any internal failures to apply international law properly. The problem is especially relevant for a federal state in which certain subject matter is beyond the apparent control of the central government and yet has a bearing upon that government's duty to uphold its international obligations.[66] Another set of issues arises from the way in which powers are separated at the federal level—namely, the extent to which the executive, the judiciary, or the legislature is the final domestic arbiter of the requirements of international law.[67] The apparently interminable *Sabbatino* litigation, highlighting the relevance of the act-of-state doctrine, raises many of these issues.[68] A theory of international law requires, however, a general or systemic account that classifies and appraises the various national approaches to a legal problem.[69] One characteristic of an adequate theory is its ability to explain, predict, and appraise from a general orientation rather than merely to reflect a given national, cultural, or ideological perspective.[70]

[66] See, e.g., United States v. Pink, 315 U.S. 203, 239-42, 249-56 (1942) (concurring opinion of Frankfurter, J. and dissenting opinion of Stone, C.J.).

[67] See, e.g., Mortensen v. Peters, 8 Sess. Cas. (5th ser.) 93 (Scot. Ct. Justiciary 1906).

[68] For a discussion of the first round of cases in the *Sabbatino* litigation see Chapter XIII.

[69] Among the most notable approaches to this task is McDougal, "The Impact of International Law Upon National Law: A Policy-Oriented Perspective," in *Studies*, p. 157.

[70] F.S.C. Northrop deserves credit as the first scholar to emphasize the role of cultural diversity in world order. See Northrop, ed., *Ideological Differences and World Order*, New Haven, Yale University Press, 1949; Northrop, *The Meeting of East and West*, New York, Macmillan,

5. A DISTINCTION BETWEEN BUREAUCRATIC AND CRISIS DECISION-MAKING

The challenge of compliance is most formidable when national actors perceive the situation to be one of crisis. Much automatic compliance with obligations of international law occurs because a modern state is a large bureaucracy that operates by means of conformity to rules and regulations. Ideas about bureaucratic autonomy have been stimulated by the writings of Max Weber, but their application to international law has been only partial and implicit.[71] A theory of international law needs a conception of compliance that distinguishes between the crisis and bureaucratic decision-making processes and provides an account of the role of law in each context.

Bureaucratic decision-making, depending generally upon the efficiency and tradition of a particular bureaucracy, normally strives to depart as little as possible from rules that govern. Civil servants in government give advice and seek to avoid exposing themselves to subsequent criticism in the event that a violation is charged. Higher government officials have neither the time nor the disposition to determine whether or not compliance with routine legal obligations serves the interests of the state in each particular circumstance; accordingly, they make no assessment of the national advantages that might accrue from a violation of a particular rule. There is thus a routine of compliance and inertia that assures any system of law a partial effectiveness as soon as it becomes subject to the bureaucratic practices of modern states. International law benefits from this routine bureaucratic compliance, which is seldom recognized as a source of legal effectiveness. Bureaucratic pressures to comply are reinforced by the logic of reciprocity, habits of restraint, ideas of fairness and reasonableness, and an overall tradition of respect for law.

However, as we have observed, there are a variety of occasions, especially those involving national power and wealth, upon which policy is shaped with much less regard for the constraints of law.[72] Indonesia's expansionism, Africa's anticolonialism and antiracism, Egypt's anti-Zionism, Chinese revolutionary Marxism, and American cold war politics are some prominent illustrations of policy orientations in the 1950's and 1960's that are adhered to with such uncompromising intensity that the standards of law cannot purport to be an effective restraining in-

---

1946; Northrop, *The Taming of Nations,* New York, Macmillan, 1952. For trenchant criticisms of Northrop's method of analysis, see Marion J. Levy, Jr., "A Philosopher's Stone," *World Politics,* 5 (July 1953), 555-68.

[71] See, e.g., Rogert D. Fisher, "Bringing Law to Bear on Governments," 74 *Harvard Law Review* 1130-40 (April 1961); Roger D. Fisher, "Constructing Rules that Affect Governments," *Arms Control, Disarmament, and National Security* 56-57 (1961).

[72] See, e.g., Falk, *op.cit. supra,* note 50, pp. 39-79, 184-323.

fluence. However, it is easy to exaggerate the irrelevance of international law to crises and to political decision-making—decision-making by top government officials who are far less bound by an obligation of subservience to a bureaucratic structure of obligation. Governments often seek to attain their objectives with a minimum provocation of others, and observance of law or minimum violation of law tends to diminish such provocation.

A distinction between means and ends may clarify the point. In crises dominated by political decision-making, the end of national policy is chosen with rather little deference to the rules of international law, although the means selected to attain the end may very likely, especially if rationality is present, reflect an intention to adhere as closely as possible to applicable law.[73] *Law provides a technique for narrowing controversial claims, for communicating the precise nature of the demand, for paying maximum respect to community expectations about right action, and for encouraging a rival to respond with arguments rather than weapons.*

Obviously, the distinction between crisis and bureaucratic decision-making must be refined. Here, as elsewhere, it is necessary to develop a range of categories to handle a range of experience. There are many varieties of "crisis" and of "bureaucracy." We require variables that will allow us to classify the situation as precisely as possible. Among the relevant variables are those of subject matter, tradition, capability, intention, perception, equilibrium, domestic political system, and public opinion. There are many kinds of crises that are capable of being studied in clusters or patterns. In addition, bureaucratic decision-making is not monolithic, but varies with the political, emotional, and perceptual environment within which it occurs.[74] It is also necessary to develop criteria that will facilitate a less impressionistic determination of what leads an international situation to be treated as "a crisis" and of how to identify when a decision or part of it has been removed from bureaucratic procedures. This need for more adequate description is a problem of comparative, as well as international, politics. It is always essential to consider international law as a public law system that operates on a global level and that must be studied in conjunction with other legal systems operating within more circumscribed political boundaries.[75]

[73] See Falk, *Legal Order in a Violent World*, Princeton, Princeton University Press, 1968.

[74] A typical set of factors are outlined in Rosecrance, *op.cit.* supra, note 30, at 228.

[75] Hans Kelsen makes very clear the relation between the circumscribed national legal systems and an uncircumscribed national legal system. See Kelsen, *Principles of International Law*, New York, Rinehart, 1952, pp. 207-99.

6. International Actors: Problems of Classification and Relationship

It is important for a theory of international law to take account of new actors in world affairs and to relate their functions to one another. It is very difficult to discard the conceptual apparatus that was developed to explain the role of law in a world composed of relatively few national actors; the simplicity of this world was increased by the common heritage and outlook of the national governments then dominant in international affairs. That this relative homogeneity did not produce harmony may be quickly realized by a study of the history of European warfare. Nevertheless, the international world prior to the twentieth century was easier to represent accurately. Since 1900 there has been an increasing diversification among national participants; states with sharply diverging cultures, ideologies, objectives, backgrounds, and stages of socio-economic development and of political cohesion have joined the older Europe-centered state system. In addition, there has been a progressive increase in the types of actors as a result of the creation and growth of regional and international institutions of both a functional and political character. As well, increasing formal recognition has been given to subnational units such as the individual, the corporation, and the political party.[76] A network of legal relations among these various types of actors has been created. Some sense of the allocation of competence is needed. How, for instance, does a claim based on an appeal to regional security and asserted by a regional institution expand, if it does at all, the national rights of self-defense that are expressed by Article 51 of the United Nations Charter?[77] There is, as well, a need to conceive of interregional law alongside traditional forms of state-oriented international law. International legal theory must work out a systematic presentation of the distinct roles of different kinds of international actors, as well as of their various interrelations. It is not enough to acknowledge the social fact that a proliferation of actor-types and actor-roles has significance for the international legal order. We want to know how, when, and why it is significant. A theorist is needed who will put forward new organizing concepts to take account of these radical changes in the international environment.

A jurisdictional map that points out the spheres of legal competence possessed by the various kinds of actors in the international legal system

[76] See, e.g., Quincy Wright, "Toward a Universal Law for Mankind," 63 *Columbia Law Review*, 435, 444 (March 1963).

[77] Is a regional concept of "just war" emerging? The attitude of the Arab states toward Israel and that of the African states toward Angola and South Africa are certainly based upon the justice of recourse to force in order to achieve regional objectives.

needs to be supplemented by a more refined sense of what constitutional restraints are applicable to action at the regional and global level. The effort to attach punitive consequences to Castro's deviation from regional political affiliations and methods led the United States in 1962-63 at Punta del Este and elsewhere to encourage the Organization of American States to impose various forms of sanctions against Cuba; the Arab governments of the Middle East feel similarly about Israel, as do sub-Sahara African governments about Angola, Mozambique, Rhodesia, and the Republic of South Africa. There is obviously a need to clarify the relationship between regional security and national rights of independence and self-determination. Furthermore, a broad interpretation of the status of regional claims to act in self-defense and complaints about regional aggression would be useful to obtain. States that deviate from a strong regional consensus may also require some kind of remedial procedure to protect minimum security rights guaranteed to them by the United Nations Charter, a global instrument that must be assumed to take precedence over contradictory regional claims.

Every kind of governmental center in world affairs should be subject to constitutional restraints. We have been so preoccupied with the effort to encourage transfers of national authority to international institutions that there is a tendency to overlook the dangers of lawlessness on the part of the international institutions that have been evolving in recent decades. Disarmament thinking has advanced somewhat further in analyzing limitations upon the legal authority of supranational actions than has the general theory of international law.[78]

7. WHAT IS A RULE OF INTERNATIONAL LAW?

The increasing importance of actors other than nation-states in world affairs complicates the task of identifying a rule of international law. Some of these complications arise because the underlying facts of obligation can no longer be adequately described by traditional terminology. The word "international" is not accurate in a literal sense if used to designate relations between actors, at least one of whom is not a nation. This verbal inaccuracy can be overcome by substituting the term "world law" for "international law." However, there is some danger that the utopian connotations of the adjective "world" do more damage to the idea of law in international society than does the retention of the outmoded adjective "international."[79]

[78] See Arthur I. Waskow, ed., *Quis Custodiet? Controlling the Police in a Disarmed World*, Peace Research Institute, 1963.

[79] I have used on one occasion the phrase "world law" rather than "international law" to emphasize developments that will tend to displace the nation as primary actor in world affairs. See Falk, note 73. *supra.*

In any event, such semantic issues are not very significant if it can be assured they do not constrict inquiry by international lawyers to the law arising from inter-nation relations *strictu senso*.[80] The *operative* meaning of international law can be broadened to embrace the multiplicity of new actor relationships without sacrificing the comparative hardness of the inter state tradition. One way to resist a narrowing of scope is to emphasize a systemic focus upon world politics and to consider the multiple forms of legal order emerging on a system level.[81]

A more fundamental issue is whether or not tacit and informal norms will be accorded the status of law and studied alongside the norms generated by formal rule-making procedures.[82] The role of reciprocity, self-restraint, fairness, habit, and inertia in the formation of national policy and in the interaction of national policies is a critical part of the ordering capability of the world community. This potentiality for decentralized modes of legal order can be promoted by self-consciousness. In this respect international legal studies can aid the policy-forming process by making more explicit the benefits and gains that might be expected to derive in various specific settings from horizontal forms of legal order.

Edward T. McWhinney has written usefully about the role of horizontal norms in his discussion of the "rules of the game" that have emerged on an inter-bloc basis in the course of cold war diplomacy.[83] These norms provide predictable boundaries for conflict and competition among international rivals. Effective restraints on the behavior of sovereign states may be introduced into international behavior by tacit means in certain situations. Such restraints could never have been agreed upon by formal negotiations. It is important to understand the relations between formal and informal norms and to appreciate their joint contribution to the systemic endeavor to improve world order and manage conflict among nations. Part of this understanding can be achieved by the adoption of a conception of law that is broad enough to include horizontal as well as vertical forms of legal order.[84]

III. The Place of Theory in International Legal Studies in the United States

There is today in the United States an unusually lively interest in the development of a general theory of international law. I think this interest

[80] See Falk, *The Province of Law in International Relations* (paper presented at the 1963 Annual Meeting of the American Political Science Association).
[81] Compare the discussion at 18-19 *supra*.
[82] Such a study is attempted in Richard A. Falk, *Law, Morality, and War in the Contemporary World*, New York, Praeger, 1963, pp. 66-85.
[83] See Edward T. McWhinney, "Soviet and Western International Law and the Cold War in the Era of Bipolarity," 1 *Canadian Yearbook of International Law* 40, 63-81 (1963).
[84] See Falk, note 45 *supra*.

is largely a tribute to the impact of the work done by McDougal and his close associates on the role of law in world affairs. The monumental attempt of the New Haven Group to develop an adequate theoretical framework is such a major intellectual event that it stimulates and forms the center of an intellectual dialogue among friends and enemies of this policy-science approach to international legal studies. An emphasis on theoretical issues overcomes rather formidable obstacles arising out of research traditions that have guided the work of American scholars. These obstacles remain relevant to the future of American thought about law in world politics and are thus worth enumerating. First, the Anglo-American temperament tends to be uncongenial to general theoretical approaches, although Talcott Parsons, Harold Lasswell, David Easton, Morton Kaplan, and Myres McDougal are exceptions that prove that a distrust of theory is not endemic to the social sciences. The traditional avoidance of theoretical issues is most pronounced in legal thinking, which has tended to adopt a method of descriptive analytical research that corresponds with the legal process itself in common-law countries.

Second, the interest in public international law has been increasingly displaced by the attention given to private international law, comparative law, the law of international institutions, and the legal aspects of arms control and disarmament. Thus, the classical heritage of international law created by Grotius, Wolff, Vattel, Gentili, and Vittoria is almost irrelevant to the main lines of current research interest and vocational training in the United States.

Third, the ahistorical quality of legal study in the United States, placing almost exclusive emphasis upon analysis and analytical sophistication, overlooks and undervalues the importance of social and political changes in the international society; orthodox assumptions about the behavior of states are thus retained rather than reexamined. This intellectual orientation toward particulars is part of a wider pedagogical strategy adopted by law schools in the United States to avoid the supposed sterility of theoretical concerns, a sterility that is thought to have often influenced adversely Continental legal education.

Fourth, the research methods and interests of political science are shifting away from formal structures and toward the elucidation and discovery of political life processes. Polls, interviews, content analysis, multivariant attention to context, gaming, and simulator devices are attempts to present and study the behavior of the polity at a level that is currently thought to be more rewarding than is the study of laws or legal behavior. Attention to the formal structure of a legal order is now regarded by many influential political scientists as a particularly unrevealing way to study international affairs, as the formative international forces are mainly politically, economic, and psychological rather than legal. The presentation of international order itself is now conceived to involve the depiction of the means to sustain various types of political equilibria. This unfortunate deprecation of law stems partly from an arid form of legalism that has been frequently adopted, ironically, by nonlawyers who have grown concerned with law as an area of political science and partly from an excessive disillusionment among modern students of political life about the role of law and legitimacy in any political system.

Fifth, deductively formulated theory is not directly related to specific problems. Pragmatic philosophic traditions in the United States identify general theory with metaphysics and tend to dismiss metaphysical concerns as irrelevant to specific human concerns. There is a tendency among American intellectuals to regard abstract theory as irrelevant to our practical lives. The irrelevance of theory to practice is a familiar American theme: "That is a very interesting theory, but now let's be practical"; or "That may be true in theory, but things are different in practice."[85] Such hostility to theoretical levels of inquiry apparently intimidates many members of the academic community, especially at a time when resources for research seem more easily available for behaviorally oriented research. Academicians, as others, seek some commodity to offer in the market place, and the outcome of theory building is rarely a commodity in present demand. Decision-makers appear to value guidance from experts who know relevant patterns of practice better than they do; government officials often resent and have no time to consider the basic reorientations of policy that may follow from the adoption of a new theoretical outlook. More than money, prestige, and dignity are involved. The search for societal relevance is a part of the human condition, and if the temper of a society is unreceptive to general theory, then it is likely that the calculus of rewards and punishments will affect the course of university studies. The argument for theory building and theorizing is difficult to sustain either on utilitarian or pragmatic grounds. Nevertheless, the adequacy of human knowledge is almost totally dependent upon the adequacy of the basic theoretical conceptions that guide inquiry.

Sixth, there is a tendency among theorists of international law to refrain from formulating their conclusions in the form of testable propositions. This tendency assures that there will be no cumulative development, since the major elements of a theoretical conception are rarely capable of either confirmation or refutation by the accumulation of ex-

[85] There is a very acute discussion of the foolishness of drawing an invidious distinction between theory and practice in the opening paragraphs of an essay by Immanuel Kant. Kant, "Theory and Practice Concerning the Common Saying: This May be True in Theory but Does Not Apply to Practice," in Carl J. Friedrich, ed., *The Philosophy of Kant*, New York, Modern Library, 1949, pp. 412-29.

perience. A greater sense of methodological responsibility of theorists may lead in turn to a more concerted interest in empirical validation by experiment and observation. In other words, theoretical conceptions about international law should be linked with a set of concrete applications. The relationship between theory and experiment that has proved beneficial in the natural sciences offers a suggestive model for theory building in future international legal studies.

This suggestion to seek empirical confirmation does not imply an insistence upon quantification, although it does stress the link between abstract concepts and observed behavior. Legal science, as other social sciences, depends for progress at this stage of its development upon gradually replacing traditions of undisciplined speculation with increasingly rigorous methods of analysis and observation. Improved methodology, too, should be part of an endeavor to advance international legal theory beyond heuristics.

II. The Relevance of Political Context to the Nature and Functioning of International Law: An Intermediate View

I

DESPITE several centuries of distinguished thought we still lack an established science of international law. There even remains considerable doubt as to the character of international law and great controversy as to its achievements and shortcomings. Part of the fundamental difficulty stems from the absence of any agreement as to the extent to which legal phenomena can be suitably appreciated as an autonomous dimension in international life, the extent, in other words, to which it makes sense to conceive of the role of law in world affairs by reference to legal doctrine, procedures, and institutions and without attention to the conditioning impact of the international environment. Quincy Wright may have had this uncertainty in mind when he wrote that "The discipline of international law is in a state of crisis. As understood by traditionalists it appears to be obsolete, and as understood by modernists it appears to be premature."[1] The way out of the crisis is, as Professor Wright seems to imply, the search for some way to take account of the social and political contexts within which the law jobs are done and yet at the same time to maintain a separation between law and fact.

One testing ground for an intermediate approach concerns the depiction of the functions of international law in the world today. A satisfactory statement of functions would provide both a framework for specific inquiry and an occasion for arguing about just how much of the international context is enough and why any less would tend to make international legal studies legalistic and formal and why any more would bring undue indeterminacy to the relationship between what the law prescribes and what nations do.

Those international lawyers who ignore context altogether, or almost so, tend to conceive of international law as a restraint system, as a system of prohibitions established in accordance with law-creating procedures sanctioned by custom or formal agreement. Undoubtedly the most lucid and influential exposition of international law as a restraint system is to be found in the writing of Hans Kelsen, although the jurisprudence of the approach is clearly foreshadowed in the work of John Austin. Kelsen's model of international law seems to derive from the functioning of law—especially criminal law—in a well-ordered do-

[1] Quincy Wright, *The Study of International Relations*, New York, Appleton, 1955, p. 233.

mestic society. Thus Kelsen puts stress upon the coercive claims of the norms comprising international law and upon the sanctions available in the event of violations. Kelsen employs great ingenuity to analogize features of international society with the constituents of legal order in a domestic society. Among the many merits of Kelsen's approach is his pervasive and systematic awareness of international society as a relatively decentralized social system. It is a merit because given the acceptance of a model of law as hierarchical Kelsen goes on to provide a way to think and talk coherently and comprehensively about international law *as if* it were a hierarchical system, and hence a system that qualified in conventional terms as law. With great ingenuity Kelsen argues that various decentralized features of international society can be understood to operate as jural equivalents to their centralized analogues in domestic society. For instance, potentially justifiable uses of force by states are identified as sanctions of self-help thereby filling the institutional vacuum created by the absence of police institutions.

One characteristic of Kelsen's approach that often antagonizes American audiences is his tendency to accept normative claims at face value, regardless of the prospect for their implementation. Thus Kelsen writes that the organized international community possesses a monopoly over the legitimate use of force because the rules of international law say so. No attempt is made, or rather only a slight attempt is made,[2] to qualify the significance of these rules in light of political realities, especially in light of the retention in fact, despite the renunciation in law, of military prerogatives by nation-states, both in the sense of the capability to wage war and of the discretion to bring that capability to bear by processes of unilateral decision. To a certain extent it is unfair to subject Kelsen to this sort of criticism. He clearly discloses why such a political accounting is not part of his undertaking. It is Kelsen's view that the role of the international lawyer is to present the normative phenomena —the norms that qualify as law by the law-creating rules of the system —in an analytically coherent fashion, thereby depicting what the law "is." Such a presentation is "scientific" as it is guided by objective canons of scholarship and avoids the pitfalls of conjecture or wishful thinking. And as Leo Gross has so aptly pointed out, Kelsen's whole undertaking is skewed toward a demonstration of what an international

---

[2] E.g., Hans Kelsen, *Principles of International Law*, New York, Rinehart, 1952, pp. 412-17. Kelsen here maintains that validity of particular legal norms rests upon the effective application of the legal order as a whole: "For if we analyze our judgments concerning the validity of legal forms, we find that we presuppose the first constitution as a valid norm only under the condition that the legal order established on the basis of this constitution is, by and large, effective, that is to say, that it is actually applied and obeyed" (p. 412).

law of peace requires.[3] Kelsen posits an international legal order that is an autonomous reality, a reality that has the normative properties needed for an orderly and just world. In one respect Kelsen's presentation of international law, despite its claim of positivity, is an ideal legal order, that is, an order which if actualized in the behavior of states as well as in their formal acknowledgments promises an end to war and lawlessness.

Certainly, although somewhat unfairly, Kelsen's approach to international law is "obsolete." It is obsolete because it refuses to introduce into its analysis the relationship between doctrine and what Kenneth Carlston has called "the social structures of action." Kelsen restricts an international lawyer's job to the normative phenomena—to rules and rule-making—and the complex engineering process by which these rules get somewhat translated (some more, some less, some not at all), into patterns of behavior is not examined. But it is precisely the understanding of this engineering process that enlightens us as to the degree to which states engage in law-oriented behavior, and enables jurists to distinguish between areas of effective law and wishful thinking. We require a model of statecraft as well as a model of an international legal order, or more aptly, we need a synthetic mode that combines the actualities of statecraft with the claims posited on behalf of international law as a restraint system. And this need is so deeply felt that it leads many international lawyers to neglect, if not deplore, Kelsenianism.[4]

One might cite the work of Myres McDougal as the prime example of what Quincy Wright identifies as a modernist approach to international law. McDougal combines the outlook of legal realism with the systematic policy science of Harold Lasswell. The result is a complex reorientation of emphasis in the presentation of international law. McDougal conceives of international law as comprised by the "processes of authoritative decision transcending the boundaries of particular territorial com-

[3] Leo Gross, "States as Organs of International Law and the Problem of Auto-Interpretation," in George A. Lipsky, ed., *Law and Politics in the World Community*, Berkeley, University of California Press, 1953, p. 59: "Kelsen's epochal contribution to the study of international relations consists in the theoretical conception of international law as the law above states, as 'law in the same sense as national law,' and in the practical proposals for making this law a more effective instrument of social control than it has been in the unhappy past. . . . Indeed, in my view, Kelsen's theory of law furnished the ideal foundation for the peace movement, that is, for all efforts directed at the substitution of international order for international anarchy, and its instrument, imperialism." And see also p. 60 where Gross goes on to illustrate that whenever two views of legal obligation are "scientifically" possible, Kelsen invariably chooses the one that inclines international society toward a peace system.

[4] But see Helen Silving, "The Permanent Value of Kelsenianism" in Salo Engel and Rudolf Métall, eds., *Law, State and International Legal Order—Essays in Honor of Hans Kelsen*, Knoxville, University of Tennessee Press, 1964, for a balanced assessment.

munities."[5] The focus of inquiry is upon the law-choices available to the decision-maker called upon to appraise contested action. Part of McDougal's outlook is conditioned by "the openness" of the legal system, by the availability of plausible legal arguments to vindicate whatever course of action is preferred for nonlegal reasons. The consequence of this openness is to shift emphasis from rules or norms to policies and goals.

McDougal, as Kelsen, is deeply sensitive to the decentralized character of international society, although McDougal puts this awareness to startlingly different use. McDougal emphasizes the decision-maker located in the national system as the prime actor in international law and calls upon such an actor to balance national interests against world community interests to the extent that the two perspectives collide. The main task of the decision-maker is to assess the alternatives in light of various preferred policies, preferred in terms of the values of the relevant community and specified in light of the accumulated knowledge of the social sciences. Thus McDougal does not encourage the decision-maker to advance personal preferences, but rather to reflect the scientifically established preferences of his community. In theory at least this nationalistic bias is diluted by the admonition to regard the world community as part of the relevant community and to consider the fulfillment of the expectations of others about legal outcome to be a significant policy objective, as it encourages confidence in the regulative role of law. If these expectations are respected then the role of precedent is conserved, law remains subject to prediction, and the potentialities for manipulation of legal doctrine are reduced.

McDougal posits a rather abstract and universalistic set of values— geared to the promotion of individual human dignity, the avoidance of war and disruption, and the establishment of freedom and prosperity— as providing a framework for decision about the requirements of international law. However, these abstract criteria are given a rather specific content by accepting an interpretation of contemporary international conflict as perceived through the rather inflamed eyes of Robert Strausz-Hupé. The result at times is to transform international law into a cold-war ideology—almost the contradiction of Kelsen's image of an impartial restraint system.[6] The Western oriented decision-maker is almost automatically vindicated and his opposite number in the Communist world is just as automatically condemned—international law is made to do service by providing the rhetoric for an international morality play

[5] Myres S. McDougal, "Some Basic Theoretical Concepts about International Law: A Policy-Oriented Framework of Inquiry," *Journal of Conflict Resolution*, 4 (Sept. 1960), 337-54, 345.

[6] See criticism to this effect directed at McDougal's approach to a leading Soviet jurist, G. I. Tunkin, *Droit International Public—Problèmes Théoriques*, Paris, Pedone, 1965, pp. 184-90.

that always comes to a happy ending for "our side." In this sense, Mc-Dougal has surely rescued international law from the pretension of providing a restraint system, but perhaps overmuch by engaging so unabashedly in exercises of national self-justification while retaining the scholar's mantle.

This presentation of McDougal's modernist approach takes account only of its most objectionable feature, a feature that is a consequence of a passionate political input rather than inherently a part of the underlying policy-science approach.[7] If one factors out the political content then international law as conceived and studied by McDougal does provide a highly developed and sophisticated way of taking into account everything that might—in an ideal decision-making situation—be properly taken into account. It is still possible to contend that McDougal exaggerates the openness of the legal system, and by so doing undercuts the stabilizing role of law and vastly and quite unnecessarily complicates the decision-making task.[8] But even if the actual decision-maker is neither prepared nor concerned to take account of conditioning variables, goals, trends, and so forth—the wide horizon of awareness enlivens one sense of what it means to take seriously the social and political context, and thereby permits a genuine understanding of the relevance of law to action in the various contexts of international behavior.

However, it remains apt to consider Quincy Wright's perhaps too pithy dismissal of modernist approaches as "premature." The validity of such a dismissal obviously depends upon one's assessment of the present character of international law as a legal system and upon passing judgment as to the relative priority of the various law jobs. McDougal's view might be assessed as premature to the extent that it undermines the guidance functions of international law, especially if it reinforces the susceptibility of the system to self-serving manipulation, thereby giving credence to the cynical view that international law is little more than a repository of legal rationalizations. In recent years whenever the United States has had recourse to force—almost necessarily dubious from the perspective of those viewing law partly, at least, as a restraint system—the Legal Adviser to the Department of State has felt obliged to come forth with an explanation of why the conduct of the United States was compatible with international law.[9] The Legal Adviser is in

---

[7] For a fuller treatment of McDougal's approach see Appendix C and *Legal Order in a Violent World*, Princeton, Princeton University Press, 1968, pp. 80-96.
[8] Cf. Leo Gross, "Problems of International Adjudication and Compliance with International Law; Some Simple Solutions," 59 *American Journal of Inter-*

national Law 48-59, 53-54 (Jan. 1965).
[9] Leonard C. Meeker, "The Dominican Situation in the Perspective of International Law," *Department of State Bulletin*, LIII (July 12, 1965), 60-65; Abram Chayes, "Law and the Quarantine of Cuba," *Foreign Affairs*, XLI (April 1963), 550-57.

an adversary role in the sense that a judgment as to legality is generally made out of the clash of diplomatic argument. That is, even if international law is conceived to function as a restraint system it is necessary to consider whether one party has improperly violated a restraining rule. One deficiency of international society when viewed as an international legal order is that generally there is no decision-maker available to move the argument beyond the adversary stage to the stage of authoritative judgment.[10] This deficiency arises from decentralization, especially from the limited and nonauthoritative role of third-party appraisal of contested state behavior. Even when a political organ of the United Nations is called into an international dispute it acts almost always to restore order rather than to assess legal responsibility, and there is little disposition to entrust neutral or nonaligned states with any privileged role in the determination of the respective rights and duties of disputing states. Partly this refusal to pass legal judgments reflects views on efficacy, partly it reflects deference to sovereignty, and partly it expresses both the reality of conflict and the reality of conflicting attitudes toward the requirements of law. But the effect is to produce a rather damaging impression of legal indeterminacy.

The United Nations response to the fighting in 1965 between India and Pakistan was to seek a cease-fire and to ignore almost altogether the relative merit of the contradictory appeals to legal rights and duties, going so far as to refrain from even considering whether one side might be justified and the other side not (or less so). The significance of this reluctance on the part of global institutions to pass legal judgment, certainly not an absolute reluctance—for instance, Korea (1950), Hungary and Suez (1956)—but a pronounced tendency, accents the inability of the international legal order to resolve this indeterminacy as to the status of challenged conduct.[11]

Added to the indeterminacy of legal status is an inevitable tendency to assimilate into the structure of law itself any claim effectively asserted by a state to be a matter of legal right. The claim might be challenged at the time of its assertion, it might even go against the prevailing sense of what international law requires, but in retrospect it stands forth as a precedent available to vindicate a similar claim in the future.[12] The powerful state, within certain limits of plausibility, enjoys a legislative

---

[10] See Chap. I, pp. 9-17.

[11] It leads some commentators to affirm the legitimacy of states pursuing remedies of self-help in defiance of legal rules of restraint and of the will of international institutions. This is the drift of the argument developed by Julius Stone in *Aggression and World Order: A Critique of United Nations Theories of Aggression,* Berkeley, University of California Press, 1958.

[12] Cf. full development of the role of effectiveness in generating international legal norms in Jean Touscoz, *Le principe d'effectivité dans l'ordre international,* Paris, Librairie Général de Droit et de Jurisprudence, 1964.

capacity, which when once exercised might bring into being a standard of conduct that not even its generative power can repudiate. The history of nuclear testing on the high seas is perhaps an instructive example. The claims to conduct such tests were first asserted and defended as a matter of legal right by the United States. To the extent that the organized community passed legal judgment it condemned these tests, but it was so helpless to inhibit the behavior that its response to challenges of illegality can be reasonably viewed as acquiescence.[13] Now years later when interests have shifted, when the prime nuclear powers consider it to be undesirable to permit atmospheric testing and nuclear aspirants and newcomers assert their claim to test, the precedent of earlier testing creates a powerful legal vindication of more recent claims.

One of the inhibitions on power in world affairs is an elemental respect for some imperfect measure of symmetry—that is, the claims of right that one nation asserts must generally be available to other nations to assert. Of course, inequalities of power introduce some asymmetry as the powerful state can emphasize distinguishing features of the two contexts to establish why a claim adverse to its interests is "illegal" despite its own earlier reliance upon the legality of a similar sort of claim. In a sense the ability of the United States to make good a distinction between its overseas missiles—for instance, those in Turkey—and those of the Russians based on the element of surprise and deception illustrates the asymmetrical potentiality of a perceived superiority in relevant power.[14] But if the symmetry of antecedent and current claims is too evident, as it is with respect to French and Chinese nuclear testing, then it is very difficult to protest on legal grounds and opposition must rest upon a moral appeal or outright coercive interdiction, the first not likely to be persuasive and the second not often feasible under modern conditions.

The point of this excursion into the vulnerability of international law to *ex parte* manipulation is to give some sense of what is involved in affirming or repudiating a modernist approach of the sort advocated by McDougal. It becomes clear that a stress on openness accentuates the potentiality for plausible manipulation of legal rights and duties by powerful, anarchistic, or desperate states. At the same time such openness impairs the capacity of legal criteria to provide the organized international community with impartial yardsticks by which to measure its

[13] On the law-creating role of acquiescence see I. C. MacGibbon, "The Scope of Acquiescence in International Law," *1954 British Year Book of International Law*, pp. 143-86.

[14] For the American outlook see W. T. Mallison, "Limited Naval Blockade or Quarantine-Interdiction: National and Collective Defense Claims Valid Under International Law," 31 *George Washington Law Review* 335-98 (Dec. 1962); Robert Crane, "The Cuban Crisis: A Strategic Analysis of American and Soviet Policy," *Orbis*, VI (Winter 1963), 528-63.

response to crisis and conflict, and thereby to legitimize its own role in resolving international disputes and to make possible a clear decision achieved after minimum debate. The Kelsenian image of law as a restraint system generating relatively clear criteria to assess legality serves well, it would seem, certain of the most crucial needs of international life, especially those arising out of the use of force by one state against another.[15] In contrast, the McDougalian image is at once too complex and too vague to provide guidance either to national actors or to global institutions. One way of putting this shortcoming is to say that a theory of international law stressing the outlook of adversary decision-makers, however accurate a reflection of international policy-making with regard to law, must be subordinated to a theory of international law stressing the outlook of a supranational decision-maker, however hypothetical his existence in particular instances. Such an attitude seems especially persuasive with respect to force used by one nation across an international frontier against another nation, that is, in an area where there exists a general agreement in support of a rather absolutistic rule of prohibition, and where the dilution of the prohibition promises to increase the potential for anarchy and violence.[16] It is much less persuasive with respect to internal wars, a subject matter for which the legal rules are so indeterminate and permissive as to provide almost no guidance, even assuming some commitment to law-oriented behavior.[17] Given this state of affairs and the great strategic incentives to influence the outcomes in internal wars, it is hardly surprising that law plays almost no role at present in regulating third-party participation in civil strife and intervention, although the laws of war have been of some relevance to the conduct of the hostilities themselves.[18]

This sort of assessment follows from the double nature of international law—an intellectual discipline devoted to the study of order in world affairs and an operative code of conduct capable of exerting varying degrees of beneficial and detrimental influence on the quality of

[15] The rules prohibiting aggression across boundaries serve the needs of the system best if they are kept as absolute as possible, thereby facilitating the identification of violations, the guidance of decision-makers, and the definition of the requirements of minimum world public order. A more sophisticated approach to legality of force based upon a contextual analysis of various conditioning variables sacrifices this clarity and blurs the distinction between self-defense and aggression.

[16] An effective statement of the policy reasons to oppose the McDougalian approach in the area of international law is found in a paper and its discussion at the 1963 Annual Meeting of the American Society of International Law. Louis Henkin, "Force, Intervention, and Neutrality in Contemporary International Law," *Proceedings American Society of International Law, 1963*, pp. 147-173.

[17] The rules of international law are little more than procedural devices by which states communicate their attitude toward the factions contending in a civil war. There are no standards by which to determine when it is "illegal" to recognize the insurgent faction.

[18] For some attempt to discuss these complicated issues see Falk, *op.cit. supra*, note 7, pp. 99-155.

international life. It is my view that the shape of the discipline must not
be oblivious to the living needs of international society for certain requisites of order, fairness, and restraint. This is admittedly a daring and
dangerous view, quite at odds with certain prevalent notions of scientific detachment, as it premises an invidious comparison of various
theories of international law upon a system-oriented judgment as to
which theory is most likely to advance overall needs. Intellectually,
even morally, it would be quite as acceptable to adopt some sort of subsystemic evaluative perspective—either national, regional, or bloc—
and ask which theory best promotes this set of needs. In fact, this
avowedly is what McDougal professes to be doing by urging the use
of international law as a strategy to attain the goals of the democratic
public-order states and to frustrate the designs of their totalitarian
adversaries.[19]

In contrast to McDougal I would urge the development of a systemic
orientation for the study of international legal order. Such an orientation is part of the effort to develop a body of thought on the character
of global interests that is as well worked out as is reflection upon the
character of national interest. So long as nations possess predominant
power, that is, so long as is foreseeable, it is also desirable to develop
subsystemic orientations toward world order of a national, bloc, and
regional variety; these orientations help to sustain the awareness that the
growth of legal authority must be conjoined with the locus of political
power. Such an awareness is elementary wisdom for any social system,
but its implications are more pervasively evident in a system so decentralized as international society. This reasoning leads to the conclusion
that the global perspective sets up on an ideal form of order, a form,
however, that may in view of the perils and opportunities of interdependence in matters of military security and economic welfare be made
increasingly relevant to the definition of subsystemic interests, including
those at the national level. Such a reconciliation of levels-of-analysis
may be regarded as alternate strategy of world order to system-changing
proposals, perhaps best exemplified by the Clark-Sohn plan, that urge
the transformation of the existing international system of order into a
supranational system.[20]

[19] See esp. Myres S. McDougal and
Harold D. Lasswell, "The Identification
and Appraisal of Diverse Systems of Public Order," in McDougal and Associates,
Studies in World Order, New Haven, Yale
University Press, 1960, pp. 3-41; cf. Harold D. Lasswell, "Introduction: Universality versus Parochialism," in McDougal
and Florentino P. Feliciano, *Law and
Minimum World Public Order*, New
Haven, Yale University Press, 1961, pp.

xix-xxvi.
[20] On the level of analysis see J. David
Singer, "The Level-of-Analysis Problem in
International Politics," in Klaus Knorr and
Sidney Verba, eds., *The International
System*, Princeton, Princeton University
Press, 1961, pp. 77-92; on the compari-
son of international and supranational
models of world order, see Klaus Knorr,
"Supranational versus International Mod-
els for General and Complete Disarma-

II

In the hope of liberating the discipline of international law from a sense of its own futility and of elevating the primary comprehension of the actual and various potential international legal orders above the outlook of the national actor, and certainly above the outlook of a particular nation—one's own—there is occasion to do serious thinking on the system level.[21] One way to initiate this undertaking is to set forth the functions of international law, given the characteristic patterns of interaction in the present international system.

Here, too, there is a preliminary need to plead for a realistic bias, that is, a bias that avoids both unwarranted despair and wishful thinking, extremes of attitude so often responsible for distorting the perception of international law in the direction either of cynicism or of utopianism. One way to cut into this problem is to emphasize the limits of legal ordering as an independent variable in the existence of a social system. No form of law, however much it is supported by the social environment, has been able to eliminate altogether violations of its most fundamental rules of restraint. When one examines the domestic incidence of murder or rebellion in the best-ordered society, the record discloses a frequency of violation that would disappoint any legal perfectionist.

No system of law can satisfy its membership—or intimidate it— sufficiently to attain perfect, or anything approaching perfect, compliance. And beyond this evidence of the persistence of the phenomena of lawlessness we know enough about active irrational and psychopathological wellsprings of individual and collective action to humble further any very optimistic assertions of the actual or potential legal control of human behavior. Thus it is not realistic to anticipate the perfection of international order through the perfection of the legal system, nor through the successful emulation in international society of the kind of legal system that has emerged in the most successful domestic states. A failure to heed such realism is partly why movements dedicated to "world peace through world law" seem so characteristically naive. And it is through an overawareness of this naiveté that invites critical observers to denigrate the role of law altogether in world affairs. Although it is the case that no amount of legal order can assure perfect compliance with the restraints of law imposed upon actors, nevertheless given

---

ment," in Falk and Richard J. Barnet, eds., *Security in Disarmament*, Princeton, Princeton University Press, 1965, pp. 384-410; on the change of one system into another see Falk and Saul H. Mendlovitz, eds., *The Strategy of World Order*, New York, World Law Fund, 1966; on the character of the transformed international system see Grenville Clark and Louis B.

Sohn, *World Peace Through World Law*, Cambridge, Harvard University Press, 3rd rev. edn., 1966.

[21] An important illustration of this approach is Stanley Hoffmann, "International Systems and International Law," in Knorr and Verba, eds., *The International System*, Princeton, Princeton University Press, 1961, p. 237.

amounts of legal order may decisively influence the frequency and distinctiveness of the violations that do occur, as well as make other aspects of international life more or less beneficial. The inability of international law to guarantee an altogether peaceful world does not imply its inability to promote a more peaceful world, or to deal adequately with the many aspects of international life having nothing directly to do with war and peace.

Part of the difficulty of accepting international law as a beneficial, albeit imperfect, source of order in world affairs, arises from the fear of a destructive violation of international law culminating in a general nuclear war. Such an awesome prospect cripples the imagination and inclines observers to conclude that a system of order that cannot offer assurance against such an occurrence is virtually worthless. It is certainly the case that the role of international law in the nuclear age is crucially related to making the system less war-prone or in assisting the transition to a new international system, one where the scale of violence is regulated in such a way that both the incentive and capability to cross the nuclear threshold is dramatically reduced. But while taking account of this nuclear coordinate of world order, it remains possible and necessary to grasp the more moderate, but nonetheless considerable, contributions of international law to the present and prospective attainment of world order, welfare, and justice. It is possible to exaggerate the relevance of nuclear weaponry to world legal order. There were bad, awesomely bad, wars without nuclear weapons, there are very catastrophic conflicts going on today with conventional weapons—the prolonged fighting in Vietnam has brutalized the life of that society for an entire generation—and there are many urgent needs other than the maintenance of peace. For instance, many of the governing elites in the Afro-Asian states appear to rate economic improvement and the avoidance of neocolonial subjugation as more important policy goals than the avoidance of nuclear war. To consider that war prevention is all that we require from our system of international order is to adopt a provincial outlook, one appropriate, if at all, only for a prosperous nuclear power, perhaps only for a superpower.

The task of legal analysis is to find a middle ground, conjoining law to politics without collapsing the one into the other and attaining a realism that neither expects law to guarantee a peaceful world nor concludes that law is irrelevant to international peace. Part of the task is to appreciate the distinctiveness of international law—and so refrain from measuring its quality or quantity by matching it up to the experience and structure of domestic law. Another part of the task is to honor the complexity of international life and the resulting multifariousness of law tasks—and so avoid the various reductionist temptations, especially the inclination to reduce the enterprise of law in world affairs to the control of international violence through norms of restraint. As well, this complexity emphasizes the importance of making a series of specific inquiries into the mode and adequacy of law in a variety of substantive settings, encompassing among other matters those of diplomatic immunity, conservation of whales, treatment of prisoners in civil war, respect for alien property, delimitation of territorial boundaries, demilitarization of outer space, and promotion of human rights. And finally, the task as set forth here requires a subordination of the policies of particular nations to the needs of world legal order, although recognizing that the reconciliation of national and world perspectives is one of the prime factors in improving the global system, as well as in altering the historically sanctioned possession over military capability by powerful nations.

One step toward the development of an adequate conception of international law consists in describing its various modes of impinging upon state behavior. The images of legal process and legal order embodied in the writings of both Kelsen and McDougal unduly impoverish the phenomenological reality of international law.

RULES OF THE GAME

In a most primitive sense international law posits boundaries upon conflict. These boundaries function as limits upon the means available to states in contention with one another. Especially in a period when warfare is perceived as mutually destructive, at least if it takes place between the most powerful states, respect for these boundaries is supported by strong common interests. These boundary rules are characteristically not formalized in accordance with procedures for law-making in world affairs, but arise from tacit assent and mutual forbearance. Among the most essential boundary rules the following may be mentioned:

1. No concerted use of military force across international boundaries in pursuit of unspecified objectives;

2. No use of nuclear weapons to influence the outcome of an armed conflict internal to a single national society;

3. No overt military intervention in ongoing warfare taking place within a state belonging to a rival superpower's bloc or sphere of influence;

4. No extension of the scope of overt violence associated with an internal war to reach covert participation if such an extension requires overt acts of violence across an international frontier;

5. No insistence upon victory in a violent encounter involving the substantial participation of rival blocs;

6. No deployment of nuclear weapons in a state formerly associated with a rival's sphere of influence.

It is obvious that these boundary rules are imprecise and subject to revision, violation, and misinterpretation. Nevertheless, these rules function to illuminate thresholds which when crossed endanger the confinement of conflict within previously accepted and acceptable limits. International law functions to specify the constituents of minimum world order, and the articulation of these constituents makes more evident the extent to which the survival of all states depends upon the moderation of the most powerful ones. The acceptance of these rules of the game strengthens the awareness that rivalry and cooperation are properly correlated. Given the upper limits of nuclear warfare and given the persistence of irrational political behavior these rules of the game create some sensitivity to the fragile character of nuclear peace, and act to bolster the search for transition techniques able to foster a system change.

A group of scholars working quite independently of one another has pointed to the role of international law in establishing the basic assumptions about the acceptable limits as a particular stage of international relations.[22] These scholars have each sought to clarify the role of international law by depicting the overall quality of the international system of which it is a part. Coplin has recently, on this basis, called attention to the use of the treaty mechanism, especially as it operates to formalize a peace settlement following a major war, as a way of communicating to states the character of the international system at a particular time, as well as to call their attention to basic changes in its character.[23]

CRISIS MANAGEMENT

International law as a process for the assertion and counterassertion of claims of right tends to encourage the employment of limited means to reach limited ends. Such communication amid crisis discourages overresponse and lessens the prospects for unlimited emotional involvements associated with the protection of vital interests and the receipt of wounds to national honor.[24] A reconciliation, at least temporarily, can be

[22] In addition to Hoffmann's article cited in the previous note, see William D. Coplin, "International Law and Assumptions about the State System," *World Politics*, XVII (July 1956) 615-34; Morton A. Kaplan and Nicholas deB. Katzenbach, *The Political Foundations of International Law*, New York, Wiley, 1961; Falk and Saul H. Mendlovitz, "Towards a Warless World: One Legal Formula to Achieve Transition," 73 *Yale Law Journal* 399-924 (Jan. 1964).

[23] Coplin, *op.cit. supra* 619 24; cf. also Leo Gross, "The Peace of Westphalia, 1648-1948," 42 *American Journal of International Law* 20-24 (Jan. 1948).

[24] C.A.W. Manning has contended that international law is primarily a language game that sets the rules for diplomatic communication. A violation consists of refusing to play this game rather than insisting upon certain behavior. In this spirit Manning finds India's use of force against Goa to be especially disturbing

achieved by a minor concession or adjustment of technical rights or by an agreement to use pacific procedures to assess the validity of competing claims. In this mode of functioning, international law serves as an adjunct to diplomacy. If international bargaining is carried on in relation to a disputed norm or a disputed interpretation of an accepted norm, the process seems more consonant with an order-oriented approach to international relations. In a democratic society the support of the population, or influential portions of it, for a dangerous position in foreign policy, seems significantly affected by whether or not a plausible claim of legitimacy can be made in explanation of a controversial and aggressive foreign policy. To seek such support by maintaining a respect for relevant norms tends also to moderate the choice of means used to achieve foreign policy objectives in the course of an international crisis. In this sense I think it is reasonable to ascribe a relevant restraining role to international law with respect to the choice among options that was made by the United States decision-making group during the Cuban Missile Crisis of 1962.[25]

Stable Expectations for Routine Transactions

Large modern states operate as law-oriented bureaucracies. This assures the automatic application of international law in many areas of transnational activity. The legal advisers to governments and the domestic courts of a large state take for granted the applicability of international law. Most often a government is interested in satisfying the expectations of the parties in controversy about the requirements of law, and does not have any inclination to assert any governmental policy at variance with international law—even in the event of such a variance. A recent example arises from an action for wrongful death arising from an air crash on international flight. By terms of the outmoded Warsaw Convention recovery is restricted to the pitiable amount of $8,300. Such a maximum was designed in 1929 to protect the then infant air transportation industry but such a low limit of liability is now absurd. Yet when the controversy came recently before a domestic court in the United States it did not even occur to the litigants, much less the court, to claim that recovery could be awarded independent of obligations validly contracted under international law. The plaintiff rather restricted itself to contending that Belgium—the country of destination—had

because India did not try to vindicate its conduct by using "law talk." For a more complete statement of this position see Manning's book *The Nature of International Society*, London, Bell, 1962, esp. pp. 101-13. In Manning's view one might point out that contrived legal rationalizations may cause international law to fall into worse disrepute by reinforcing the impression that this so-called legal order is merely talk.

[25] Abram Chayes, "A Common Lawyer Looks at the Common Law," 78 *Harvard Law Review* 1396-1413, esp. 1410-12 (May 1965).

never ratified the Warsaw Convention and therefore the defendant air line (Sabena) could not enjoy the privileges of limited liability.[26] Although the litigation is not yet finally resolved, the District Court upheld the applicability of the Warsaw Convention, thereby denying the American claimants the right to unlimited recovery.[27] It seems to me that this case is a paradigm for the operation of international law in regard to all sorts of routine activity. There never is even any serious question raised about violating international law provided its rules can be shown to be validly applicable by the normal means of construction.[28]

Such a legal setting exonerates the pretensions of the idealistic dictum in the *Paquete Habana* case: "International law is part of our law, and must be ascertained and administered by the courts of appropriate jurisdiction, as often as questions of right depending upon it are duly presented for their determination."[29] The point is that international law is domesticated and given the full deference accorded internal law of the highest rank by any of the branches of government, at least so far as they act bureaucratically. But when the validity of a rule of law is deeply challenged within international society then its impartial application is much less likely to take place. The bureaucracy assumes a political posture in relation to the controverted norm that tends to vindicate the national outlook. Prime illustration of the pressures upon bureaucratic automaticity is presented by the celebrated series of legal happenings in the *Sabbatino* controversy, a series culminating in a self-serving and unconvincing statutory directive establishing the content of a rule of international law (i.e., the obligation of an expropriating government to compensate promptly foreign investors for the full value taken in readily convertible currency) that tends to reinforce the cynical image of international law serving to smokescreen the crude maximization of national values at the expense of rival values held by other nations.[30] The

---

[26] A recent decision has held that the application of the provisions of the Warsaw Convention restricting damage liability "are unconstitutional and therefore not enforceable because they violate the due process and equal protection clauses of the United States Constitution." *Burdell v. Canadian Pacific Airlines* (Ill. Cir. Ct., Nov. 7, 1968) as reported in 8 *International Legal Materials* (Jan. 1969) 83-108, at p. 107.

[27] *Kelley v. Société Anonyme Belge D'Exploitation* 242 F. Supp. 129 (E.D. N.Y.) Warsaw Convention for the Unification of Certain Rules Relating to International Flight in which both places of departure and destination are located within states that have ratified the Convention.

[28] The United States denounced the Warsaw Convention on November 15, 1965, to be effective on May 15, 1966. On May 14, 1966 the United States withdrew its denunciation of the Warsaw Convention after reaching an agreement on a tariff provision with the world's major international carriers. The essence of the agreement was an acceptance by the carriers of a $75,000 ceiling on damages that was payable on the basis of strict or absolute liability. For texts of the withdrawal of the denunciation and related documents see 32 *Journal of Air Law and Commerce* 243-48 (1966).

[29] *Paquete Havana*, 175 U.S. 677, 700 (1900).

[30] For an account of the Sabbatino controversy and the relevant texts of the decisions, see Richard A. Falk and others, *The Aftermath of Sabbatino*, edited by Lyman M. Tondel, Jr., Dobbs Ferry, N.Y., Oceana, 1965.

Sabbatino context illustrates the vulnerability of the bureaucratic sphere of decision-making to nationalistic and provincial invasion abetted by interest groups (investors), and points to the need to pierce the veil of legal language used to justify a decision so as to examine whether the *Paquete Habana* expectation is being realized or undercut. The mere incantation of the formula is not enough.[31]

COOPERATIVE REGIMES

All law facilitates cooperation as well as imposes restraints; law fulfills its role partly by helping to provide means by which actors can fulfill their objectives and realize their values. It is common knowledge that international law facilitates a variety of cooperative undertakings including the operations of postal, telecommunications, safety, health, and sanitation services. Institutions such as the International Bank facilitate economic development in the modernizing states and also reinforce certain patterns of protection with regard to foreign investment. As Wolfgang Friedmann has so creatively stressed, the possibility of denying states the advantages of participation in these cooperative undertakings creates some pressure to comply with legal obligations. There is, as Friedmann suggests, a considerable possibility of influencing national behavior through the existence of this sanction of nonparticipation.[32]

The scope of cooperative regimes varies considerably with the subject matter. There are some areas—for example, technical matters of health, communication, and information—for which specialized agencies of global dimension are the appropriate form of ordering unit. There are other activities—for instance, those associated with human rights or economic integration—where the outer limit of cooperation is a consequence of some shared attribute, perhaps ideological harmony or a similar state of economic development, but perhaps only spatial proximity. In any event, there appears to be a promising future for partial, in the sense of nonglobal, international organizations. These entities can be identified as regional actors, although the notion of regionalism may have heretofore overstressed geography as a factor favorable to legal integration. An adequate conception of contemporary international law needs to find a way to assimilate nonnational actors who are both the subjects and origin of new standards and procedures of legal order in world affairs.

[31] It is in this spirit that some authors misuse the *Paquete* dictum. E.g., John R. Stevenson, "The Sabbatino Case; Three Steps Forward and Two Steps Back," 57 *American Journal of International Law* 97-99 (Jan. 1963).

[32] Wolfgang G. Friedmann, *The Changing Structure of International Law*, New York, Columbia University Press, 1964.

CRITERIA FOR GUIDANCE

International law posits criteria by which national governments and other actors can act reasonably if so inclined. In fact, to take relevant rules of international law seriously is to commit an actor to a stabilizing role in world affairs, provided, of course, a minimum of mutuality exists. That is, if there is an important law-breaker in international affairs, then compliance is a way of encouraging unscrupulous behavior. Hitler's plan of aggression was undoubtedly abetted by the law-oriented responses of the liberal democracies to German foreign policy in the early 1930's. But the rules of international law do give nations a way to perpetuate an era of normalcy, and present, as well, supranational actors with impetus and guidance in mobilizing responses to challenged conduct.

Their criteria of guidance also fix expectations about what constitutes both reasonable and unreasonable behavior. A state that satisfies or disappoints expectations thus can lead its foreign policy in either the direction of provocation or of restraint.

Matters of guidance may be cut off from issues of policy in many areas of international life, thereby facilitating the expansion of agreement as to standards of law. It may be useful to think about the adoption of traffic regulations, especially such basic rules of the road as the choice between right-hand and left-hand driving. Quite obviously the choice of which rule prevails is far less important than that one or the other is clearly and authoritatively adopted. And so it is for a variety of international subject matter; for instance, in relation to the fixing of safety and liability standards in relation to the hazards of travel in the airspace or on the high seas. States antagonistic to one another or matters of political saliency may still welcome common standards of guidance wherever the realities of interdependence and interaction lead to the perception that uniform standards serve the self-interest of states more than does the preservation of freedom of action on the national level.

THIS discussion of the several functions of international law makes it possible to orient, but no more than this, the point of intellectual departure for an intermediate view of the linkage between the functioning of international law and its international political context. The principal conclusion is that the challenges set for law by the evolving needs of international life must be taken into account, but not at the expense of sacrificing the autonomy of the legal order. As a matter of policy it seems essential in a world divided by tension and conflict to keep alive some respect for law as a transcendent social order, that is, to maintain some respect for law as a normative order that posits the way states ought to act as well as explains in legal language the way states do act. Even in highly political settings it remains useful to invoke rules of law as criteria of judgment, if for no other reason than to mobilize domestic and international public opinion on some basis other than a mere appeal to expediency. To carry out this objective it is essential to rehabilitate a careful distinction between adversary and judgmental roles in the assessment of legal right and duties, as well as to resist the implication that a state's self-serving legal explanation of challenged conduct has a jural status equivalent to the conclusions of a community review by centralized international institutions.

At present there is some danger of legal nihilism in world politics, a danger prompted by the behavior of such law-oriented states as the United States making use of adversary presentation to reconcile its foreign policy with some of the most fundamental rules of restraint in international law. An opportunistic use of legal argument by a state so conservative and powerful as the United States sets a tone for international life that is bound to influence the overall prospects for strengthening the law habit throughout international society, and especially among the new international actors in Asia and Africa. The point here is that our conception of international legal order to be responsive to the needs of the day must emphasize the transcendence of law over fact, and distinguish sharply between the legal rationalizations of an adversary and the assessment of legality made by more impartial agencies of decision.

But it is not enough to assert the transcendence of law. It is also necessary to develop a rationale of transcendence that takes satisfactory account of relevant developments in international society. We largely maintain a conceptual apparatus for international law that was evolved to explain the legal governance of inter-nation relations at a period in history when nation-states were the only participants in international life of any legal consequence. The emergence of regional and global actors, as well as the diminished scope of a purely private sector of domestic life, has altered greatly the stuff of international life out of which the legal order must take its shape.

Quincy Wright added to his concern about the tendencies to be obsolete or premature the following set of imperatives for an adequate conception of international law: "A system of law must look to the past and the values of continuity, predictability, and stability, but it must also look to the future and the values of justice, progress, and peace demanded by the public opinion of the community. A valid legal discipline must reconcile vested interests with public policies and in a progressive society, whose visions of the future and interpretations of the past are continually changing, it must include means of continuous self-correction."[33] To what extent can the discipline of international law be modernized to take intelligent account of this range of considerations? It should be emphasized that modernization of the international legal order itself is needed. The crisis of international law, as truly as the crisis of the discipline—that is, its systematic study—requires life-solutions within the terms Wright sets forth.

[33] Quincy Wright, *op.cit. supra*, p. 233, n1.

III. Some Notes on the Consequences of Revolutionary Activity for the Quality of International Order

THE RELEVANCE of revolution to the organization of international society is not a new subject. It was a dominant concern during the decades following the French Revolution when the great powers of Europe sought to reconcile the independent character of sovereign states with the defense of the principle of dynastic legitimacy. The development of collective procedures of intervention to protect the European monarchies against republican revolution was the most significant outgrowth of the Congress of Vienna. In fact, the response of the nineteenth century to the French Revolution resembles in critical respects the response of the twentieth century to the Russian Revolution.

Thus it is certainly true that a successful national revolution in a major state, especially if it results in the triumph of an alien and crusading ideology, has long been perceived as relevant to the maintenance of order in international society. If a revolution includes an ideological challenge, then it threatens all governments that resemble the first victim of the revolutionary cause. An example has been set; the discontent that provoked the first revolution can be assumed to be present at different levels of latent intensity throughout international society, not just in the society that experienced the outbreak. Contradictory interventionary pressures arise both to hasten the spread of the revolution and to staunch the revolutionary flames. The prevalence of intervention based upon ideological cleavage is profoundly inconsistent with the basis of order in an international society composed of states supposedly sovereign and independent. So long as there are no predominant supranational institutions in existence, one serious consequence of an active revolutionary movement is to undermine the ideological basis of international society, that is, of a society of nation-states, and thereby to restrict the effectiveness of the normative element in international life.[1]

The background of relevant experience is, however, scant. There have been very few revolutionary movements in the history of international relations that have attained such a magnitude as to have relevance for the conduct and character of world politics. In fact, the only two clear cases are the French Revolution and the Russian Revolution. There is, however, a wider conception of revolution that embraces any political,

---

[1] On the comparative role of international law in revolutionary and nonrevolutionary systems, see Stanley Hoffmann's "International Systems and International Law," in Klaus Knorr and Sidney Verba, eds., *The International System*, Princeton, Princeton University Press, 1961, pp. 205-37.

social, and scientific facts that challenge and transform the prevailing bases of international order. This essay adopts this wider usage, thereby treating the history of international relations as a sequence of numerous revolutions.

By using this broader conception of revolution, attention can be given to nonpolitical facts that threaten international stability and are, at the same time, intimately connected with the phenomenon of political revolution on a national scale. The connection between these various kinds of facts must be studied to achieve an overall understanding of the revolutionary challenge to international order. In this respect, it is important to consider the impact of both nuclear weaponry and guerrilla warfare upon patterns of international conflict, the drive toward economic and social development in the new states, and the growth of supranationalism on a regional and global level. These radical modifications of the international environment are crucial aspects of the revolutionary situation in world politics today.

This chapter also assumes that it is useful to study international politics as if it were carried on within a single political system.[2] The international system tends toward revolutionary transformation whenever there is present a combination of forces (including a transnational revolutionary movement) that imperil the prevailing modes of organizing international life.[3] The most obvious focus for these forces today is to contrast the adequacy of the international order since 1914. For this purpose "adequacy" is understood as referring mainly to the capacity of the international system to advance human welfare at tolerable rates, to prevent large-scale violence, to provide security for social groupings, and to rectify the most flagrant abuses of human rights.

These preceding paragraphs sketch the orientation that controls the analysis that follows. The rest of the chapter attempts to depict the revolutionary situation that exists in contemporary world politics and to develop certain categories that encourage an analysis of revolution as an attribute of international politics, as well as of national politics. Without the development of such an intellectual perspective it will be-

---

[2] For the contrary argument that it is not yet proper to consider international politics as taking place within a single system, see Kenneth S. Carlston, *Law and Organization in World Society*, Urbana, University of Illinois Press, 1962, pp. 66-69.

[3] "The idea of the international system is based on an analogy with the domestic political system: both 'systems' are intellectual constructs—i.e., schemes of analysis—that focus on a number of key factors, based on certain postulates: that the chaos of political data can be ordered, that there are distinguishable patterns of relations among the participants, that it is possible to select the key variables in a non-arbitrary way, and that changes in one of them will have identifiable repercussions on the others. The notion of an international system is a more chancy one than that of a domestic political system, since the scholar's construct risks being more remote from political reality, especially from the reality experienced by the participants." Stanley Hoffmann, *Gulliver's Troubles or the Setting of American Foreign Policy*, New York, McGraw-Hill, 1968, p. 11.

come increasingly difficult to understand the unstable quality of international society.

I

The contemporary Western mind tends to visualize the actual and optimal constituents of international order in topical terms as a response to the overlapping dangers created by the combination of nuclear weapons and of expansionist politics. From such a perspective, the desiderata of international order become a system that reliably prevents the coercive expansion of aggressive states and that reduces the risks of nuclear war to tolerable levels. Profound disagreements surround the selection of the means available to accomplish this goal. There is, first of all, the need to reassess the alleged expansiveness of Communism, and there is the further need to assess whether or not to regard the United States as expansionist and as an aggressive disturber of world order. Do Communist leaders entertain the prospect of a Leninist-Marxist world as a matter of conviction or of rhetoric? It may be possible, in part, to ascribe the ideological rift between the Soviet Union and China to different interpretations of this issue, that is, to China's contention that Soviet policies are tantamount to a repudiation of revolutionary strategy. Can the Soviet Union, or, for that matter, China be so transformed from without and within as to become a state that is content to refrain from force in the pursuit of its foreign-policy objectives? Does the United States Government seek to dominate the political processes of Asia and Africa through the use of its military power? Questions of this sort underscore the complexity of our time. It has grown increasingly difficult, especially since the major escalations of United States involvement in the Vietnam War after 1965, to identify the major sources of danger to the stability of international society. A consensus no longer exists in the West and there is less and less acceptance of a dualistic conception of international conflict in which the United States is leading the defensive effort against a concerted aggressive effort by the combined centers of Communist power.

Another set of disagreements about revolutionary prospects surrounds the extent to which current patterns of international conflict are war prone and, in particular, whether they are nuclear-war prone. Can we rely permanently upon alliances and postures of deterrence to keep the nuclear peace? It is, of course, true that the deterrent systems developed in prenuclear periods have never been able to avert major war. Does, however, the unprecedented potential for nuclear destruction add enough intimidation to restrain nations over an extended period of sustained conflict and recurrent crisis? Those observers who are distrustful of such reliance make demands for a greatly altered system of international order. Often, those who are most sensitive to the risks of nuclear war are indifferent to the problems of securing societies against aggression, either regarding aggression (even if it occurs significantly) as an insignificant evil compared to nuclear war or considering aggression, at least in the sense of outright conquest, as something that is no longer very likely to occur to any significant extent. According priority to war prevention goals tends to produce enthusiastic advocacy of major disarmament schemes and to engender support for greatly strengthened international institutions.

The revolutionary position includes demands to change international order by downgrading the role of the state in world politics. It favors the progressive displacement of states as the primary actors by the growth of multinational federations and international organizations on a regional and subregional basis, and especially by the development of the United Nations.

There is, in contrast, a more prevalent conservative attitude toward international relations. The conservative position emphasizes the intransigent quality of international conflict and human nature, deemphasizes nuclear weapons as transformative agents, and voices skepticism about the possibility of interfering with the dominance of the nation-state in the international political process. This conservative view may or may not be receptive to minor adjustments in response to the proclaimed dangers created by an intense bipolar struggle in a nuclear age, but it either is opposed to accepting the risks that attend fundamental alterations of the existing system of international order or is convinced that environmental restraints make fundamental changes politically infeasible and therefore highly improbable. Reform—or, for instance, "stabilizing the deterrent"—is consistent with the conservative or non-revolutionary viewpoint.

The non-Communist revolutionary viewpoint is at once more skeptical and more hopeful about engineering a drastic change in the structure of international society. Such an outlook tends to believe that fundamental changes in the existing international system are essential for the maintenance of nuclear peace, and possibly also for the reallocation of wealth to the poorer countries. This outlook is generally more dubious about the virtues claimed for the existing system than are those who propose reform. Advocates of a new world order are often fearful that unless something is done soon about the management of military power a catastrophic war is quite likely to result. On the other hand, this revolutionary viewpoint is more hopeful about the capacity of human reason and will to respond to the present dangers by devising an utterly new arrangement for social organization on a world level. Nuclear weapons have rendered the old system of nations and military self-sufficiency and self-help so obsolete, it is contended, that traditional patterns of reliance for security upon the state system can and must be abandoned. The revolutionary viewpoint has not penetrated deeply into the behavioral patterns of nations, nor has it been acknowledged as valid by elite members of major states—although such events as Pope John XXIII's *Pacem in Terris* encyclical, President Kennedy's "Towards a Strategy for Peace" (June 1962) commencement address at American University, widespread antiwar activity throughout the world prompted by the Vietnam War, and the commitment of every state to the goals and ideals of general and complete disarmament have given some encouragement to the adherents of the revolutionary approach.[4]

I have, perhaps, overstated the contrast between reformist and revolutionary approaches to the improvement of the quality of international order.[5] There is a compatibility between these two viewpoints that may be even stronger than their opposition to one another. We may seek to improve the existing system and, at the same time, work toward the creation of a new system. Simultaneous commitment to reformist and revolutionary approaches does raise the question of how the transition from one system to another is to proceed. An understanding of this process of transition is perhaps the crucial question facing persons who are consciously at work to improve the quality of international order. It is itself susceptible to useful analysis in terms of revolutionary and non-revolutionary attitudes, depending, for example, on the extent to which one believes in the potentialities for evolutionary transition from one system to another as distinct from violent or traumatic transition. There are many people who think that only a nuclear war of considerable magnitude can create the opportunity to reconstitute the international order on a scale sufficiently far-reaching to be called a system change. Such a conclusion, I think, correctly emphasizes the strength of system inertia, even when a particular system of international order has been widely perceived to be risky and inadequate, in the sense of being functionally unresponsive to the objective circumstances of the nuclear age. A "revolution" in the context of such a transition might be regarded, then, as the aftermath of a nuclear war. A revolutionary analysis describing the conditions of transition is obviously distinct from a revolutionary strategy advocating the creation of these conditions.

A prediction about how the new international order can be brought

---

[4] There is some doubt about the wisdom, or even the reality, of a national commitment to seek drastic disarmament. See Arnold Wolfers and others, *The United States in a Disarmed World*, Baltimore, Johns Hopkins Press, 1966; *Report from Iron Mountain on the Possibility and De-* *sirability of Peace*, New York, Dial Press, 1967.

[5] This contrast is more fully developed elsewhere: Falk, *Legal Order in a Violent World*, Princeton, Princeton University Press, 1968, Chap. I.

about does not, especially among those who regard the new order as an urgent necessity, imply advocating the precipitation of nuclear war. The international Communist movement, on the other hand, illustrates coupling a revolutionary analysis with a revolutionary strategy. In fact, the weakness of the revolutionary movement in the non-Communist world arises, in part, from the absence of any very powerful explanation of how to accomplish a system change other than by making a reluctant reference to the prospect of a nuclear war. Communist doctrine and theory, however, anticipates an eventual imperium, brought about by a series of national triumphs; this process will also lead to the reconstitution of international order in a manner that befits a world lacking in substantial grounds for conflict. Thus, the variants of Communist revolutionary strategy to achieve world revolution (or system change) are contingent upon the successful outcome of a series of national revolutions (or unit changes). This dependence relationship may involve violent transition, but the violence is broken into subconventional and conventional warfare situations (national revolutions) that normally contain political violence within those limits traditionally regarded as tolerable. Such an idea of the transition process is more plausible than the evolutionary image and less catastrophic than the traumatic image; such an idea of transition gives Communism a way of reconciling its aims with the dangers of the nuclear age.

The Sino-Soviet dispute is relevant to an appreciation of these issues for several reasons. First, the intensity of this ideological conflict, especially when the variations in position of Yugoslavia, Rumania, and Albania are noted, raises considerable doubt as to whether a fully Communized world would be a solution, even in Moscow's or Peking's terms, of the transition problem. And, second, the disagreement between the Soviet Union and China is partly a matter of the extent to which the selection of transition strategy should be influenced by the dangers of nuclear war; more specifically, this disagreement centers upon whether there is a serious risk of escalating a revolutionary war into a nuclear war by rendering certain forms of support to radical insurgents. Maoists have argued that unless the risks of escalation are assumed, at least on a rhetorical level, the Communist solution of the transition problem will be permanently frustrated. The basic Soviet contention, on the other hand, is that spontaneous historical forces will bring about a Communist transition without any need for Communists states to sustain positions of ideological militancy in their relations to non-Communist states.

II

The basic distinction between revolutionary and stable international systems is predicated on the failure of international society to evolve new forms for the management of power that correspond to important changes in the structures of power. This distinction also depends upon the objectives of the major actors and the extent to which these objectives are promoted by unauthorized violence. If disputes between principal states typically center upon controversies about the application of existing norms, then the system tends to be stable, even though fierce wars may be fought to establish a frontier or to secure possession of a disputed province; the political identity and legitimacy of existing actors are accepted. Conversely, in a revolutionary system, the significant actors seek to eliminate certain other actors or to change their basic identities by violent means, if necessary. The stakes of conflict are so large that they induce antagonists to adopt any expedient means to protect their interests. Such an atmosphere generates lawlessness. The obligation to adhere to legal norms do not often influence crucial decisions by those actors who either are trying to overturn the existing systems or are compelled to fight in order to survive. If the revolutionary challenge is substantial, as it appeared to be after the French and Soviet Revolutions, it then generates counterrevolutionary pressures. In other words, *a revolutionary component in world affairs, if significant, tends to determine characteristic behavior of all major actors in the system.* The Afro-Asian states today direct a revolutionary challenge toward Portugal's control of Angola and Mozambique and toward the internal policies of the Republic of South Africa; if there were no other revolutionary currents in the international system, then those actors interested in stability could probably moderate the challenge and constrain the tendencies to depart from basic norms. However, this challenge, posed in an environment that includes the revolutionary presence of the Communist states, produces revolutionary patterns of conduct—for instance, the overtness of the sanctuary and the support given southern African liberation movements by such countries as Algeria and Tanzania. Even more revealing, perhaps, is the extent to which the opposition of the United States to Castro's Cuba has inclined toward a revolutionary form of normlessness. Oddly enough, the behavior of nonrevolutionary actors may serve as a better indicator of the revolutionary condition of the international system than does the behavior of revolutionary actors.

Does a revolutionary international system exhibit patterns of international order? Actors in any international system, no matter how revolutionary it is, accept certain limits upon the means available for the pursuit of their objectives. A description of international order in a revolutionary international system requires the discernment and delineation of those limits on action that remain applicable. The popular assumption that revolutionary systems are characterized by the absence of limits is a dangerous exaggeration, tending to undermine respect for norms that might otherwise remain operative; the normative dimension of a revolutionary system may prevent intense conflict from degenerating into anarchy.[6] Even before revolutionary and antirevolutionary actors were intimidated by the development of nuclear weapons, there was a general willingness on the part of principal governments to accept certain restraints upon conflict as being in the common interest. For example, expectations continue high that, in the event of military conflict, most laws of war will be upheld, including such important restraints as prohibitions against the use of lethal gases and bacteria. A revolutionary system weakens or alters, rather than destroys, international order through dramatic departures from crucial norms (e.g., prohibitions upon aggression) and as a result of explicit repudiations of some traditional norms (e.g., the legitimacy of colonial administration or the sanctity of foreign investment). But no revolutionary actor can participate for long in the international system without disclosing some degree of political socialization, including a fundamental willingness to adopt hallowed procedures and to abide by routine norms (e.g., diplomacy and diplomatic immunity). In this respect, it is worth noting the retreat of Soviet theory and practice from its original repudiation of the entire system of international law as an international manifestation of class dominance by the bourgeoisie. More recent Soviet jurisprudence accepts international law as a valid constituent of international order, while reserving for attack several specific norms contrary to Socialist values. The dependence of every international actor upon mutual contact and communication is the most basic form of interdependence. Such interdependence presupposes a minimally reliable system of international order, despite the fact that revolutionary and nonrevolutionary actors are engaged in a struggle for supremacy and containment, and adhere to contradictory values and proceed toward incompatible goals.

III

It may advance our understanding of international relations if we are able to detach ourselves from immediate anxieties. This sort of detachment will permit a more abstract conceptualization of the relationship between revolution and international order, and thus focus our attention upon the more essential characteristics of international relations. It is fashionable nowadays to characterize as "revolution" any kind of drastic change in circumstances that we wish to call attention to; it is a way of letting people know that the change is important or, at least, that we think it is. The following items of international concern have each been

---

[6] This is the principal argument of my book *Law, Morality, and War in the Contemporary World*, New York, Praeger, 1963.

called, on occasion, "revolutionary": nuclear weapons, decolonialization, the loss of Christian faith, the cycle of rising expectations in poor countries, the increasing role of non-Western states in world affairs, and improved transportation and communication facilities. Thus conceived, a revolution is not just a national political movement that makes use of violent and illegal means to bring about a radical new social structure; it is a whole series of developments in political, moral, scientific, and economic life that are perceived as very important. This usage involves some looseness of language, appropriating the glamor of the word revolution for nonpolitical happenings whose importance for international society is often difficult to identify. This loose usage does, nevertheless, provide a suggestive richness of connotation for the word revolution. From the viewpoint of international relations, there is a high degree of functional equivalence among unsettling events in economic, social, political, technological, and moral spheres of human activity that is acknowledged by the use of a single dramatic word like revolution.

International order is perhaps even vaguer as a term than is revolution, especially since a reference to "international order" frequently confuses descriptive and normative considerations. Are we identifying the kind of order that exists at a given time in international society or are we trying to specify the requisites of minimum and optimum order in various international environments? Is "order" a condition that invariably pertains to a social system, or are there social systems that lack some of the qualities implied by employing the word order? It seems useful to delineate order in broad terms but to insist that it be understood as a descriptive concept; it is thus possible for order to be evaluated as beneficial or detrimental, as stable or unstable, or as increasing or decreasing. We propose to define order in international relations primarily by reference to the extent and frequency of political violence and, therefore, to consider a given international order as consisting of the rules, procedures, and institutions available to regulate and reduce unauthorized political violence in international affairs. This definition is sufficiently broad to encompass the ordering claims of international law, international diplomacy, and international organization; in fact, the traditional separation of these interrelated aspects of international affairs inhibits the growth of an integrated awareness and understanding of the political factors that operate in international relations. The diplomat, the lawyer, and the official of an international organizations are working on different aspects of a single process, better understood by joining an awareness of their interrelationships.

There is one further difficulty: the word "international" has been used in a way that violates its literal meaning and its Latin origin. The world is not composed of a network of actors that are national, infra-national (individuals, corporations), transnational (political parties, trading associations), and supranational (regional and global international organizations). "International order" can no longer be usefully understood as referring only to the quality of order that exists in the relations among states. Although states retain preeminent power and discretion in the international system, it has become almost essential to acknowledge the subsidiary roles that are being played in international affairs by these several additional types of actors. In fact, it might now be semantically progressive to substitute the term "world order" for "international order"; however, I will retain the term "international order" to emphasize the need to improve techniques for the management of interstate violence and to facilitate historical comparisons with earlier periods of international relations so as to observe the successes and failures of earlier forms of international order—that is, to observe forms of order in which states were the only significant actors.

Some substantive problems arise from a focus on the characteristics and requisites of international order. This focus makes less obvious the link between domestic violence and the maintenance of international order in the existing international system. An increasingly evident characteristic of the existing system is the extent to which supranational control is claimed over domestic events that produce, or threaten to produce, violence that might in turn become an arena for an international confrontation. Responses to civil strife and warfare in the Congo between 1960 and 1964 disclosed several supranational efforts to regulate violence confined within the borders of a single state; the Vietnam War has disrupted international relations because it is, at once, a civil encounter between rival domestic factions and treated by principal governments as a test of ideological, economic, and military position and destiny.

The attitude assumed by international institutions and by dominant national actors toward such civil strife is a crucial ingredient of any attempt to describe and assess international order in the present era. The relative merits of passive and active sponsorship of "national liberation movements" is one of the central arguments between the Soviet Union and China. The Soviet Union evidently inclines more toward the stability that seems to result from a passive role, whereas the Chinese appear eager to maintain the revolutionary dynamism that is alleged to follow from an active role. A comparable internationalizing attitude produces the contention that the obligations of the United Nations Charter to promote human rights are essential ingredients of international order. A long history of humanitarian interventions, prompted by alleged or actual persecution of national or religious minorities, suggests that ideas of international order have for centuries included a concern with certain

[69]

conditions *within* a state. The link between peace and human rights is accented, at present, by the formation of a worldwide consensus supporting racial equality; this consensus increasingly insists upon implementation of its ideals, especially in the General Assembly of the United Nations where a militant Afro-Asian majority dominates the proceedings.

It may appear that these "domestic" events—civil wars and struggles to promote human rights—have little relevance to a study of the connections between revolution and international order. But the connection seems vital, if not always visible. Civil wars are often revolutionary in character for either of two reasons: because the insurgent is a revolutionary faction, or because the civil war is treated by principal governments as part of the world revolutionary process that it is eager to promote or to inhibit. If a civil war is defined as a national war of liberation, it is then almost certain to attract United States opposition and Communist-bloc support, at least to the extent of opposing or offsetting aid to the contending factions. The denial of human rights is often the prelude to revolutionary action; as such, supranational intervention to establish certain minimum conditions of human dignity can be evaluated as a way to forestall national revolution, as well as to provide a safeguard against the outbreak of international violence.

IV

An adequate sense of the relationship between revolutionary phenomena and international order is not easy to achieve. At least, seven kinds of problems need to be considered. First, attention to environmental changes that tend to revolutionize the character of international relations. Second, an analysis of characteristic behavior by different types of revolutionary and nonrevolutionary actors in various systems of international order. Third, the response patterns exhibited by various international systems to the appearance of a revolutionary state. Fourth, the international effects of civil wars in which one of the factions possesses a revolutionary outlook. Fifth, the outlooks of a revolutionary actor in terms of his claims and demands. Sixth, the regulation by the international system of the transmission of revolutionary energy from one nation to another; there is a need for historical case studies of the responses of the international system to ecumenical revolutionary movements. And seventh, the extent to which the quality of a given international order, including its capacity for change, depends upon the existence of revolutionary movements, actors, and events.

1. *"Revolutionary" Impacts on the International System.* Various kinds of political, social, economic, and technological events may undermine the stability of international relations. The dominant moral author-

ity of the Pope was a target of the Reformation; the *levée en masse* was an outgrowth of the French Revolution; the rules of naval warfare could not be adapted to deal with the advent of the submarine and airplane; the doctrine of neutrality could not be adapted to the requirements of "total war"; norms of nonintervention and self-determination are incompatible with the struggle for power in a revolutionary international system; the scope of sovereign discretion with respect to force is progressively curtailed in response to the increasing destructiveness of warfare; assumptions of immunity for sovereign activities are rejected in face of the growth of state-trading and of the decline of laissez-faire economics; norms of independence are qualified by facts of interdependence and by the gradual emergence of an international welfare system in the form of foreign aid and international capital financing; sovereignty as an indication of national autonomy is reinterpreted in the light of the assertion of effective claims against the state on behalf of a world community increasingly more organized on a regional and global level; the necessity of national consent as the basis of state obligation is being gradually superseded by the authority of community consensus. This list of examples tries to illustrate the dependence of international order upon all dimensions of human activity.

Most clearly visible, perhaps, is the effort to adapt the international system to those new realities created by the existence and diffusion of nuclear weaponry. No structural changes in international society, reflective of a new distribution of power, seem presently feasible. It is possible, however, to attribute a more cautious style of risk taking in world politics to the presence of nuclear weapons. States have also taken some specific steps to reinforce precautions against accidental and unauthorized military provocations. Perhaps the most important impact of nuclear weapons has been to reduce the incentive of the major states to rely on military force to expand their zone of influence.[7] There remains a well-entrenched disposition to maintain the existing international structure of power and authority premised upon the primacy of the state and of national defense systems. This disposition remains strong, despite the vulnerability of all states to substantial destruction in the event of a major nuclear exchange and despite the failure of deterrent and alliance systems in prenuclear periods to maintain peace indefinitely.

A second crucial change that is even less assimilated, is the emergence of assertive non-European states as independent actors in world affairs. In addition to the disturbance of the Western dominance, other problems

[7] The diminishing role for traditional use of military power is one principal conclusion of a recent book on the subject. Klaus Knorr, *On the Uses of Military Power in the Nuclear Age*, Princeton, Princeton University Press, 1966.

are beginning to arise as a consequence of glaring and growing economic disparities between rich and poor states.[8] A restored stability for international affairs will depend, it is submitted, upon the gradual development of a supranational welfare mechanism that accomplishes a major redistribution of the world's wealth. This development of a global welfare operation, ideally reinforced by disarmament and by the supranational control of expanding national populations, is essential if the accommodation of the new nations is to be more than temporary and expediential.[9]

Certainly, we are not living in a period of international anarchy. The United Nations, the development of regional and international specialized agencies, and the quasi-formalism of nuclear deterrence suggest some active mechanisms for the ordering of contemporary world politics. Nevertheless, the combination of nuclear weapons and a large number of inexperienced, militant nations create a revolutionary situation in international affairs that threatens the present system of order. The responses of those actors that dominate the system have so far been limited to gestures of accommodation, steps falling far short of what seems necessary to avert eventual catastrophe. There is a lag between the procedures available to maintain minimum order and changes in objective circumstances that threaten decay and disorder. This lag is an assurance that procedures to sustain international order will remain insufficient. An awareness of this insufficiency induces a climate of pessimism with regard to the future of mankind.

2. *Behavioral Patterns in a Revolutionary International System.* It is important to grasp the methods and objectives of the actors in the international system. This system is revolutionary because the potential methods of conflict are mutually destructive and because the existence and identity of important actors have been placed in jeopardy on ideological and humanitarian grounds. There is no universal consensus about the character of legitimate government. This absence of agreement is symbolized by the high incidence of nonrecognition and premature recognition; normative (as distinct from factual) approaches to the diplomatic recognition of foreign governments and newly emergent states are a by-product of strategic controversy in world affairs about the nature of political legitimacy. This doctrinal controversy in its intense phases—both in our century as in the decades following the French Rev-

---

[8] On this, see Gustavo Lagos, *International Stratification and Underdeveloped Countries*, Chapel Hill, University of North Carolina Press, 1963, pp. 3-34; and S. J. Patel, "The Economic Distance Between Nations: Its Origin, Measurement, and Outlook," *The Economic Journal* (March 1964), 119-31.

[9] For a study of the connection between disarmament and the reallocation of the world's wealth and income, see Neil W. Chamberlain, *The West in a World without War*, New York, McGraw-Hill, 1963.

olution—prompts patterns of covert coercion, including subversion and intervention. The Organization of American States decides in 1962 that Cuba is "incompatible" with the Inter-American hemispheric system because it possesses a Marxist-Leninist government. African states accord status and support to exile groups at work to organize revolutionary opposition to racist and colonialist regimes in Southern Africa. China, Yugoslavia, and the Soviet Union argue with each other about the tactics and forms of support for national wars of liberation. The United States Government arms and trains armies for reactionary governments throughout the world, as well as uses the CIA as an instrument of covert interference in the affairs of foreign states.

An international system with high costs associated with waging strategic conflict tends to exhibit widespread interventionary and counterinterventionary behavior. The consequence of such competition is to cause a deterioration of norms and procedures designed to safeguard the autonomy, independence, and equality of sovereign states. The Spanish Civil War illustrates a failure by the governments of the dominant nonrevolutionary actors to perceive the transformation of the system into a revolutionary one; these states scrupulously adhered to a nonintervention system while revolutionary actors (Germany, Italy, and the Soviet Union) were intervening to the full extent of their capability. Only after World War II when the conflict between the West and the Soviet Union was perceived as a revolutionary struggle for world dominance did the United States adopt a style of behavior appropriate for a revolutionary system.

The search for the means to restore stability to international relations as a result of the intertwined dangers of nuclear war and of a large number of inexperienced and dissatisfied states is quite inconsistent with the pursuit of a revolutionary or counterrevolutionary program in international society. National governments normally seek to balance their varying interests in system stability and system change; superstates generally strive, in addition, to achieve system dominance. These generalizations about the behavior of states is sufficiently broad to include the outlooks of revolutionary, modernizing, and status-quo nations.

3. *International Response Patterns.* A revolution that occurs in a significant state usually arouses a hostile response from other states that identify their social system with the prerevolutionary government. This process of identification is especially true if the revolutionary elite has an ecumenical outlook, considering itself to be the herald of a new form of government and social organization. Wars of liberation, often loosely called revolutions (for instance, the American Revolution or the post-World War II anticolonial wars of independence) need to be sharply

distinguished from those missionary revolutions that seek to bring a new social and political system to all mankind. A revolutionary nation in a previously stable system of international relations is often disturbing because it threatens the security of domestic governments that resemble the victim of the revolution.

A stable international system usually includes a consensus about the character and orientation of legitimate government. The experience of a successful revolution—the seizure of national power by illegal and violent means—has occurred in systems of international order throughout history and is compatible with the maintenance of international stability. Certain national revolutions are unsettling if they entail radical reorderings of domestic society; domestic models of radicalism encourage discontented groups elsewhere to imitate a successful revolution. In addition, the leadership of ideological revolutions may often seek to spread their movement to foreign nations both for reasons of mission and for reasons of national security. Such a context induces a variety of international response patterns, among which several will be enumerated below.

a. *The Formation of Antirevolutionary Coalitions.* Status-quo powers will often join together in alliances and coalitions to oppose the spread of the revolution. This kind of reaction happened after the French, Soviet, and Chinese revolutions; it is descriptive of recent international history, although in the mid-1960's there were signs of disaffection in the antirevolutionary coalition. The minimum objective of a conservative coalition is to resist the coercive expansion of the principal revolutionary states.

b. *Intervention.* Coalitions of revolutionary and antirevolutionary states often give rise to interventionary patterns and practices. The minimum goal of such a coalition is to prevent the balance of internal forces in foreign countries from reaching a revolutionary or a counter-revolutionary situation. For the conservative states the coalition may take the form of collective defense arrangements designed to prevent the expansion of revolutionary states. The Protocol at Troppau, adopted by the leading monarchies of Europe in 1820, illustrates an extreme commitment of this kind: "States which have undergone a change of government, due to revolution, the results of which threaten other states, *ipso facto* cease to be members of the European Alliance and remain excluded from it until their situation gives guarantees for legal order and stability. If, owing to such alterations, immediate danger threatens other states, the powers bind themselves, by peaceful means, or if need be by arms, to bring back the guilty state into the bosom of the Great Alliance," and in the Declaration of Pillnitz (1791) the Emperor of Austria and the King of Prussia pledged themselves to secure the restoration of the French monarchy by joint force, if necessary. The evolution of American foreign policy toward world Communism from the Truman Doctrine in 1947, through the alliance systems of the 1950's, to the escalated involvement in the Vietnam War is the major modern illustration of a counterrevolutionary response pattern that claims for itself the right to practice an interventionary diplomacy.

c. *Nonrecognition.* Prevailing rules and procedures of international order give governments the discretion to refuse formal diplomatic relationships with a revolutionary nation. Prolonged nonrecognition has been used by the United States in the twentieth century to express disapproval and to isolate and harass a revolutionary government. Nonrecognition may also be used as a bargaining lever to obtain concessions from the revolutionary government. Recognition is withheld in the hope that certain guarantees can be extracted in exchange for a willingness to accord the revolutionary government status and contact. The United States failed to recognize the Soviet government until 1933; and continues to refuse recognition to the People's Republic of China although the Peking government has been in secure control of mainland China since 1949. The antirevolutionary majority manipulated by United States diplomacy has also been able so far to deny China representation in and admission to the United Nations. The governments of conservative states tend to argue that a militant revolutionary state must demonstrate its acceptance of the constraints of the international system before it is entitled to access and a right of participation.

International order as a constitutive system includes practices and rules that enable antirevolutionary states to organize against the threat posed by the emergence of a powerful revolutionary state. Presumably, a recourse to force to implement an antirevolutionary alliance is illegal under the Charter of the United Nations and is impractical in view of the defensive strength of the existing revolutionary coalition. But, short of force, states are authorized to form defensive alliances and build regional security systems to resist the expansion of the revolution.

4. *The International Dimension of Civil War.*[10] In stable systems, a civil war is generally regarded as a domestic event; in a revolutionary system, a civil war is frequently a confrontation between factions each of which replicates the principal adversaries on the global level. This process of replication is especially true in the present international system as the danger of nuclear war discourages principal adversaries from risking direct military confrontation; overt participation in a civil war is the most intense form of unauthorized violence characteristic of the

---

[10] A more detailed study of the problems in this section is given in Chap. IV of *Legal Order in a Violent World*, Princeton, Princeton University Press, 1968.

current competitive behavior of major states. The dynamics of the United States involvement in the Vietnam War, its massiveness, its high costs, and its monumental failure, may yet produce a reversal, if not an abandonment, of counterrevolutionary militancy.

Traditional sovereignty-centered norms of international legal order built in the aftermath of the Peace of Westphalia strongly emphasize the irrelevance of civil strife to the rights and duties of other states. Notions of domestic jurisdiction and self-determination express this insulation developed to preclude any justification for intervention by outside powers. Domination by the great powers was often a by-product of an intervention allegedly carried out to maintain or restore order; the United States exercised, at least until 1933, such rights of hegemony in relation to Latin America, often alleging as its justification for intervention the need to protect resident Americans and their property. The United States' forcible intervention in the Dominican Republic in 1965 suggests a revival of such hegemonial diplomacy.

Classical international law allowed outside states to help the incumbent during the early stages of a civil war and obliged third states to refrain from aiding an insurgent faction. If, however, the challenge to domestic control was sustained over time and space, then a formal condition of belligerency could be proclaimed that obliged third states that recognized belligerency to maintain strict neutrality as between the factions. The antirevolutionary interest in the security of constituted government is subordinated by the doctrine of belligerent recognition to the interest of the international community in keeping the scale of violence small by creating duties of nonparticipation in a foreign civil war.

This regulatory approach is not likely to enjoy success in an international system experiencing a revolutionary struggle for dominance. It may even be difficult to insulate a civil war from outside intervention if the insurgent faction is revolutionary in the sense of possessing a radical social program and a missionary ideology. In such a civil war the stakes in the outcome, especially given contemporary assessments of the French Revolution and the Spanish Cvil War, may be seen as too great to generate adherence to norms of nonparticipation. Modern means of communications and modes of transportation facilitate contact between exile groups and domestic dissidents. This same modern technology is also available to the modern state and can be and is used to suppress discontented groups that lack foreign support. Under such a combination of circumstances, the structure of international order has no reliable ways to deal with civil wars in which the incumbent is being challenged by a revolutionary or counterrevolutionary faction. The absence of such an ordering capability represents a major source of instability and danger in the present system.

The existence of the United Nations suggests two possible modifications in the traditional normative treatment of civil war: first, the selective adoption of military measures to keep outside states from intervening on either side and, second, the selective encouragement of intervention by the United Nations to prevent national interventions and to shorten civil strife. The Congo Operation illustrated this use of the United Nations, but it also disclosed a Soviet hostility to such a supranational enterprise if it appears to align itself against revolutionary forces. To the extent that a global consensus can be discerned, organs of the United Nations should be encouraged to anticipate the outbreak of a civil war by intervening to secure basic human rights. Once the revolutionary challenge has been posed in a system that contains revolutionary actors, it may already be too late for constructive action by international institutions that contain both revolutionary and antirevolutionary states.

5. *The Revolutionary Actor.* The "true" revolutionary actor needs to be distinguished from other actors that assume control of a national government after a successful revolt. A revolutionary actor seeks to transform the world, especially by spreading the ideals of its revolution to other national societies. National governments are not the only kind of revolutionary actor in world politics; political parties of transnational revolutionary significance exist, as well as liberation groups and groupings of revolutionary states organized into some form of coalition.

An ecumenical revolution necessarily seeks to bring a new world order into being, although perhaps not immediately and perhaps not by reliance on the export of violence. There tends to be, as after the French Revolution, a violent and multifaceted interaction between the hostile reception given a revolution by conservative forces and the aggressive policies adopted by the revolutionary actor; each feeds on the other. Each side comes to regard its security as depending upon the elimination of the other side from the international system; this dialectic of perception and objective leads both to a foreign policy entailing intervention and aggression and to a domestic policy entailing repression of radical opposition.

The revolutionary actor justifies its recourse to violence by insisting upon the necessity to remove gross injustices throughout the world and by citing counterrevolutionary activity as a danger to its very survival. The revolutionary actor also tends to feel strong bonds of sympathy with those insurgent groups abroad who seek to eliminate injustices to those that stimulated the original revolutionary cause. The American Revolution fostered, at the time, a tradition of support in the United States for anticolonial revolts elsewhere. As soon as the first major anticolonial revolt was successful in the United States no colony was secure. A model for coercive decolonialization had been brought into existence. This model catalyzed the formation and activity of anticolonial groups everywhere.

It is difficult to generalize about those demands that the revolutionary actor makes upon the international system. The demands may depend, first of all, upon the reception that the system gives to the revolution and, second, upon the degree to which the leaders of the revolutionary and of the nonrevolutionary actors share a common interpretation of the relevant portions of history. In 1848 the moderation of both the revolutionary demands and the conservative response was, in part, a consequence of sharing the awful memories of the experiences in 1789 when violence took over.

The Soviet Revolution had, from its ideological birth and conception, emphasized a universal outlook. This revolution was thought of as an expression of a necessary historical process that would eventually be duplicated everywhere. The restraining claims of the international system—that is, the pattern of international order—were regarded as nothing more than as an externalization of the interests of the reigning social class in the status-quo societies. International law enjoyed no more legitimacy in Soviet perceptions than did any other part of the state apparatus designed to carry out bourgeois domination. Law was always a reflection of the pattern of class dominance, and therefore embodied neither common interests nor social justice. The original Soviet denial of the international legal order by a Marxist style of analysis was gradually supplanted by patterns of selective repudiation and pragmatic participation. The Soviet Union denies that there exists any obligation to compensate aliens for expropriated property or that a colonial title to territory establishes political legitimacy. At the same time, the Soviet Union participates actively, although, in common with other principal states, somewhat opportunistically in the United Nations Organization. Soviet goals in the United Nations are difficult to summarize clearly, although they include limiting the growth of the United Nations in the peace and security field and the pursuit of national interests in different international settings, as well as acting to prevent the outbreak of major war.

A revolutionary actor, almost by necessity, favors some unauthorized violence as a means to achieve revolutionary objectives. This reliance on violence may take the form of outright wars of aggression with imperial goals—such as Napoleon's or Hitler's—in which case it inclines the international system toward a major war. However, the strategy of revolutionary expansion may only call for adoption of subversive and infiltrative strategies—in which case, the international system is certain to experience intense conflict, but there is no comparable prospect of major war. The emergence of a revolutionary actor normally disrupts whatever international consensus previously existed as to the character of permissible political objectives. This disruption process tends to raise continuously the stakes of conflict to a point where antagonists are constantly tempted to take added risks to achieve success. This escalating dynamic inclines an international system eventually toward total war. Other factors in the setting may also have this dangerous effect: ardent nationalism; bureaucratic centralism in the great states; rapid and uneven improvements in military technology; and the construction of mass industrial societies capable of supporting long and costly wars.

There is always some possibility that a revolutionary actor will abandon or at least dilute its commitment to revolutionary objectives. This process of derevolutionizing often happens when the perceived self-interests of the revolutionary actor become associated with goals that can no longer be easily reconciled with a serious implementation of a revolutionary program; among these impinging goals is the quest for a higher domestic standard of living, concern with the maintenance of world peace, a protective attitude toward what has been already achieved by "the revolution," an awareness that ideological similarity may not be a necessary condition for international solidarity, and a gradual realization that the revolutionary theory no longer provides a prudent guide for action. Revolutionary actors normally tend to become less revolutionary as time passes. If the international system can absorb the initial challenge of a revolutionary actor, then it seems likely that the mere passage of time will domesticate the revolution. There is quite a difference in response between the proscription of heresy in Catholicism and the assimilation of heresy in Hinduism. In the history of international relations, the periods from 1789 to 1822 and from 1917 to the present chiefly illustrate the Catholic approach, whereas the reactions after 1776 and 1848 suggest the Hindu approach. Perhaps a Hindu-oriented counterrevolutionary strategy may yet preserve the tenuous viability of the international system during this period of revolutionary challenge and counterrevolutionary crusade.

6. *The Containment of Revolutionary Energy.* Following the failure of natural law after the Reformation to develop common standards and community judgments capable of regulating recourse to force by states, the subject matter of war was largely entrusted to the discretion of sovereign princes. These princes were restricted in their discretion only

to the extent that they were responsive to appeals directed at their conscience or were inhibited by prudence and equilibrating coalitions (deterrence). The normative superstructure in international society contained contradictory affirmations of a discretionary right to wage war and of duties to respect national independence, practice nonintervention, acknowledge the equality of states, and uphold the principles of territorial jurisdiction. The French Revolution, at least in Europe, generated conservative coalitions that resolved the contradiction by a mere insistence upon the legitimacy of coercive interventions designed to remove revolutionary elites from political power.

In the present international system, revolutionary actors are strong and sufficiently well established to deter counterrevolutionary interventions, except in countries geopolitically closely associated with the security of the United States. Some alliances, all organized by United States initiative, are pledged to resist revolutionary penetrations. In Latin America, both before and after Castro, the OAS has insisted that Communist activity is necessarily an outcome of extrahemispheric aggression, thereby creating a legal basis for preventive intervention. In 1954 the United States intervened covertly to help dislodge a government in Guatemala that was tending toward Communism; in Cuba, the identification of Castro as "revolutionary" came after his power was already secure; Cuba's transfer of allegiance to the Soviet bloc seems firm; current efforts are designed to prevent the spread of Castroism to other parts of Latin America, whereas, in the Dominican Republic the overt intervention by the United States in 1965 was evidently motivated by the desire to avoid the emergence of an additional revolutionary actor in the hemisphere.

Containment is the basic ideological impetus of a moderate antirevolutionary strategy. Less moderate antirevolutionary leaders favor preemptive interventions, especially within spheres of regional dominance, although the claim is still to prevent the expansion of the revolutionary zone of hegemony by coercive means. The spread of the revolution by hostile propaganda, the training of exiled subversives, and the guidance and financial support of indigenous revolutionary groups are the activities associated with revolutionary actors that are relied upon to vindicate coercive counterrevolutionary responses.

The existing system of international order has been generally effective in its efforts to discourage overt aggression across national boundaries; this system is unable, however, to deter or defend against either indirect aggression or counterrevolutionary intervention. In fact, internal wars fought to expand or to contain the expansion of revolutionary influence are *tolerated* by the present international system as a proper arena of conflict; until the Vietnam War was expanded beyond South

Vietnam, norms designed to keep these conflicts subnuclear and physically within the boundaries of a single state had been increasingly, if tacitly, recognized and accepted as binding upon the conduct of the principal sovereign states.

7. *Intervention by the Organized Community to Promote Revolutionary Change.* There is an increasing prospect that the United Nations will sponsor changes in domestic political systems under certain circumstances that would have a revolutionary impact. This sponsorship does not imply fostering of revolutionary nations, nor does it suggest the relevant capabilities, but it does suggest that domestic system changes are likely to become a legitimate goal of supranational actors. The policies of the United Nations during the Congo Operation are illustrative of both the role and its dangers; the subsequent financial and political difficulties of the Organization suggest that the action attempted by the United Nations on the basis of a partial and temporary consensus that existed among its members at the outset was too ambitious.

Social injustice resulting from classical colonialism or constitutional racism has led the United Nations toward increasingly coercive strategies in the hope of influencing the behavior of South Africa, Portugal, and Rhodesia. The Goa solution (military self-help), the Algerian precedent (prolonged civil war), and breakdowns of order in Vietnam and Laos give some support to those who advocate supranational coercion as the least destructive among several dangerous and flawed alternatives.

Interventions by international institutions would seek above all to assure that the domestic struggle didn't become part of the cold-war competition. In these missions, the United Nations might not always be able to muster a great power consensus unless a general interest in the prevention of large-scale violence took precedence over the revolutionary struggle for system dominance. In fact, the use of supranational institutions to achieve revolutionary changes would be most successful if their interference preceded domestic violence. A competence on the part of the United Nations to establish minimum human rights might enable a genuine consensus of states to favor a revolutionary intervention—that is, an intervention that transferred sovereignty to a new elite pledged to uphold human rights.

Such a pattern of coercion entails a revolutionary change in the allocation of authority between sovereign states and the organized world community. At the same time, this pattern might promote stability in the international system; as such, it deserves consideration in any assessment of the future role of the United Nations with respect to the maintenance of international order. Communist ideology associates a secure basis for world peace with support for national revolutions and with the completion of the world revolutionary process. Nonrevolutionary actors might also consider whether to exploit revolutionary opportunities by acting first and selflessly. The use of supranational institutions to bring about revolutionary changes, dangerous though such a pattern could become, is one way to help bring into being the kind of international order that satisfies the values and the interests of the status-quo states.

One thing is certain. A revolutionary civil war for supremacy in a strategic nation is not a domestic event. It will attract foreign participation. The maintenance of international peace hinges upon the capacity to keep internal wars of this variety within limits.

V

National revolutions are formally compatible with an interstate system of international order. In the contemporary world if a revolutionary movement possesses a Communist or perceived Communist orientation, its attempts to seize power are likely to heighten international tension and to provide an occasion for a violent test of strength between the principal rivals for world dominance.

There is not much prospect of a breakthrough in military technology of a magnitude sufficient to make recourse to general warfare a rational means of achieving political expansion at the strategic level. In this sense, the nuclear stalemate generates an image of a rigid, but tolerably safe, future. The existence of powerful military weapons in a nation leads adversary actors to threaten one another so as to achieve certain proximate goals of foreign policy. Threats have utility in international crises and may influence behavior. The credibility of threats depends on a willingness to carry them out. But to carry out a nuclear threat is to initiate a nuclear war, an act widely regarded to be destructive and self-destructive in almost any conceivable circumstances. There is a temptation to discount such a threat as a bluff. This setting for crisis behavior in international society makes the balance of terror unstable, especially whenever the stakes of conflict are high and whenever revolutionary actors try to dominate and transform international affairs in order to fulfill their ideological mission. If the revolutionary quality of international rivalry at the strategic level were replaced by an *entente cordiale* or by a Soviet-American condominium, then the possession of nuclear weapons might provide a rather stable peace. Through the retention of nuclear weapons, their nonuse could be reliably developed and secured to ensure that minimum cordiality persisted. At such a point, the prospects for serious disarmament might improve as a result of a new spirit of international confidence—just then, when it is much less needed, because in a nonrevolutionary international system the danger of all-out war seems greatly diminished.

This relationship between reducing the danger and raising the prospects for disarmament illustrates a familiar paradox in global politics: so long as international relations are conducted in a revolutionary system, there is a need for a system change with respect to war and the distribution of power and discretion, but the revolutionary nature of the conflict generates tensions and hostilities that are incompatible with any kind of drastic change.[11] Without the revolutionary attribute, a system change may become feasible but it is much less essential, perhaps even undesirable; with the revolutionary attribute, system change is necessary but almost impossible to bring about. In that sense, revolution, as attribute and as challenge, is a decisive obstacle to the achievement of a qualitative improvement in international order.

The prevention of war, however, is not the only consideration. In fact, the adaptation of the international system to the needs of the poorer states for modernization may turn out to be the most essential requirement for international stability, a requirement more fundamental than either of our obsessive concerns: the avoidance of nuclear war or the frustration of Communist objectives.

[11] This analysis is more fully developed in Falk and Saul H. Mendlovitz: "Toward a Warless World: On Legal Formula to Achieve Transition," 73 *The Yale Law Journal* 399-424 (Jan. 1964).

PART TWO

EXPANDING HORIZONS OF AUTHORITY
IN THE INTERNATIONAL LEGAL ORDER

Introduction

THE NATURE of legal authority in international society and the conditions of its effective exercise are among the most elusive subjects in the vast scholarship of international law. Authority is such a fundamental coordinate of legal analysis that its treatment will be decisively shaped by an author's jurisprudential orientation. The early period of international law developed under the influence of natural law approaches grafted on to the rich tradition of Roman Law, tended to identify legal authority in international society with the nature of reason and with the inherently reasonable, a source of guidance that was at once universal and timeless, to be given concrete expression by secular rulers themselves endowed with a sacred mantle of rulership (by way of "divine right"). The empty pretensions of such a doctrine became evident as soon as the diversity of interpretations (to which the supposedly immutable doctrines of natural law were subject) by rulers of varying motivation became manifest. As a historical matter the supposed objectivism of natural law usually gave way to manipulative subjectivism, each sovereign leader invoking natural law to rationalize a preferred course of national conduct. The thought of the naturalists was so vague and abstract and the interpretation of each sovereign so absolute that no very clear guidance function could be performed by international law so long as it filtered through the natural-law tradition of thought.

From Grotius onward, most significantly in the treatise of the Swiss international jurist Emmerich de Vattel, published in 1758, the ideas of legal positivism began to interpenetrate those of natural law. In particular, it was the consent of the sovereign ruler that began to be taken as the critical law-creative act that transformed rational conduct into obligatory duty. In effect, the formal expression of sovereign acquiescence became the one basis for construing conduct as obligatory or not. In this formative period of the growth of modern international law, the character and extent of legal authority was determined by the express or tacit agreement of national governments, although a great deal of what became accepted as "customary international law" arose from the processes of claim and counterclaim that took place whenever states with divergent interests in the definition of permissible behavior struggled toward a voluntary accommodation (not relying on force) and a coercive accommodation (relying on the threat or use of force). An effective resolution of a dispute, whatever the means of resolution, established a precedent that was available to other states in subsequent controversies raising either similar or analogous issues. The rules of international law relating to the use of oceans and with regard to the conferral of diplomatic immunity both arose in this fashion. The sole explanation of international legal authority was connected, however, with the consent of the sovereign, such consent being treated as the means whereby to reconcile the idea of national sovereignty with that of international obligation.

The positivistic line explanation continues to exert influence, as reflected for instance in Article 38 of the Statute of the International Court of Justice (see Chapter V), but given changes in the structure of international society, a positivistic theory of legal authority is neither descriptive of practice nor functionally related to the requirements for order and justice in international life. It is not descriptive because international institutions play an authority role which has been rapidly increasing since the creation of the League of Nations, although foreshadowed even earlier by the operation of international specialized agencies such as the International Postal Union. A positivist orientation is not functionally adequate because it fails to posit the need for a limited legislative competence to deal with certain kinds of national conduct that are perceived by the overall international community to endanger international peace and security. The domestic supremacy of the sovereign state has been increasingly challenged in the form of authoritative claims of wider political communities, although implementation of these claims is still unimpressive. The most dramatic challenges directed at national sovereignty by claims asserted on behalf of an allegedly overriding international authority structure have been in connection with the racial and colonial policies of South Africa and Portugal in southern Africa, together with the formal reaction of the international community to Rhodesia's Unilateral Declaration of Independence in November 1965. The jurisprudential highwater mark in the formulation of a system of legal authority centered in the world community as *a collectivity* rather than in its constituent states as *an aggregation* is the Dissenting Opinion of Judge Tanaka in *The South West Africa Cases* (see Chapter XII).

A further problem arises in connection with identifying the role and relevance of national institutions in the development and maintenance of international law. It has now become commonplace to criticize the false emphasis on supranational judicial tribunals, given the more regular and significant developmental role of domestic judicial tribunals. It remains important, however, to fit the role and practice of domestic courts into an embracing theory of authority in the international legal order.

Furthermore, there are serious unassimilated problems involving the allocation of authority among different actors that operate at different levels of world legal order. There is a problem of *diagonal allocation* of authority that stems from the overlapping claims of legal authority asserted by global, regional, and national institutions. There are also the more familiar problems of *lateral allocation* arising from the over-lapping claims of actors enjoying equivalent legal status, as when two states attempt to govern the same subject matter by inconsistent legal policies, and each contends that only its policies are entitled to supremacy; these problems of lateral allocation have been traditionally discussed in terms of an overjudicial focus upon "jurisdiction" (Chapter XI).

The chapters in Part Two attempt to discuss many of these questions. Chapter IV deals with the interaction of levels of legal authority that were operative in the dispute provoked by President Sukarno's espousal of "Confrontation" in reaction to the creation of the federated state of Malaysia in 1963; this is a suggestive context for inquiry because the dispute in question has been so widely (and misleadingly) perceived as proceeding within a legal vacuum. Rejecting the image of a legal vacuum, Chapter IV argues that the three years of Confrontation exhibit, although admittedly in inconclusive fashion, creative recourse to new centers of legal authority on a regional and global level. These appeals to central decision-makers were prompted by the impulse to get beyond adversary contentions as to governing authority that were advanced on the national level.

Chapter V reviews in the context of the South West Africa Cases the traditional views on authority in international law and argues for their expansion by way of incorporating the activity of the political organs of the United Nations into the law-creating sources enumerated in Article 38 of the ICJ Statute. Chapter V also briefly compares Judge Tanaka's acceptance of this line of the argument with its rejection by Judge Jessup and argues that the former view accords more fully with both existing patterns of the exercise of international authority as well as with desirable trends as to its expansion in the future. Chapter VI continues the inquiry of Chapter V by broadening the substantive ambit of concern to encompass the extent of legal authority that might be attributed to the activity of the General Assembly.

Chapter VII involves a somewhat more exotic question of legal authority, that of the United Nations in relation to nonmember states. Such an inquiry entails a consideration of the basis and extent of the authority of the United Nations to act on behalf of the global community, and the degree to which this organizational authority is undermined by withdrawals, exclusions, or nonmemberhips of states.

Chapters VIII and IX involve the role of national legal institutions in the overall authority pattern of the international legal order. Chapter VIII considers the extent to which the effective assertion of controversial claims to act by single states are creative of legal precedents that can be relied upon by others; this general question is considered in the concrete instance of the novel claims by the United States to use space satellites to observe the subjacent territory of an overflown objecting state unable to destroy the satellite. Chapter IX deals with a classical problem of jurisdiction in the context of the extraterritorial application of the United States antitrust laws in the face of objection by foreign governments. The conflict of regulatory claims suggests the entire set of difficulties that attend the identification of the limits of national legal authority in the international system. These difficulties arise from the absence of generally effective central institutions authorized to prescribe patterns of reconciliation in the event that adverse national and international claims do not result in mutually satisfactory patterns of allocation among respective authority claimants.

IV. Confrontation Diplomacy: Indonesia's Campaign to Crush Malaysia

I

IN A Security Council debate provoked by a Malaysian complaint of Indonesian armed aggression Mr. Sudjarwo, the Indonesian representative, made the following comment:

> When Indonesia proclaimed its independence from Dutch colonial rule in 1945, asserting its own sovereignty, was not Indonesia—according to that international law—legally tied to the Netherlands as a colony, possessing legal existence only under Dutch sovereignty? What would have happened if we had had to abide by the application of legal arguments under that international law? The Indonesian Revolution would have been strangled and smothered.[1]

This candid repudiation of traditional international law as it related to the Indonesian struggle for independence summarizes Indonesia's attitude toward respect for international law, especially to the extent that such respect might appear to hamper President Sukarno's militant championship of a new political order for Asia. This militancy was most dramatically expressed by the adoption of a Crush Malaysia campaign in the period from September 1963 when the Malaysian Federation came into existence and June 1966 when the anti-Sukarno turn of Indonesian domestic politics led to an abrupt normalization of relations with Malaysia.

From one important point of view Indonesia's policy of "Confrontation" toward Malaysia was a self-consciously blatant violation of fundamental rules of international law. President Sukarno's avowed objective was "to crush Malaysia" and the means used included military action overtly undertaken against a member of the United Nations. The Charter of the United Nations in Article 2(4) expresses the basic constraint of international law upon the use of force by one state against another: "All Members shall refrain in their international relations from the threat or use of force against the territorial integrity or political independence of any state." Article 51 permits limited uses of force for self-defense against an armed attack, but Indonesia never contended that it was acting in self-defense, nor was there any substantial evidence of prior Malaysian aggression against Indonesia.

On the basis of the above situation it hardly seems worthwhile to consider the role of international law in the relations between Indonesia and Malaysia during the period of Confrontation. It hardly seems worth-

[1] SCOR, 1144th Mtg., Sept. 9, 1964, para. 86.

while because Indonesia seems clearly guilty of violating international law and Malaysia seems entirely innocent. However, closer scrutiny discloses several reasons for rectifying this first impression. First of all, the basic policies upheld by international law with respect to the use of force can rarely be disposed of merely by considering the relationship between legal rules abstracted from the international environment and challenged national behavior. The legal basis for Indonesia's approach to Confrontation rests upon a certain conception of political equilibrium and regional autonomy in the postcolonial world that has received diverse and quite widespread backing in the period since World War II. It is not necessary to claim that Indonesia's espousal of Confrontation was a consequence of its reinterpretation of international law, but merely that it is possible to make arguments in favor of Indonesia's contentions that conform to certain ideas about the evolving nature of international legal order, ideas that antedate the Charter and that find resonances in the work of an international lawyer as renowned as Emmerich de Vattel and in the practice of a country as strongly opposed to Indonesia's Confrontation as was the United States.[2] Therefore, my first point is that it may be valuable, precisely because it is not fashionable, to consider the kind of basis that does exist in international law, even as it is most traditionally conceived, for the legally discredited and politically discarded espousal of Confrontation.

Indonesia's claims against Malaysia might also have found expression in an argument for a new international legal order. Sudjarwo in the statement quoted at the outset refrained from doing this, but it could have been done on Indonesia's behalf, and it might be useful to put Indonesia's case in as good a legal posture as possible, if only to disclose the ease with which a plausible legal argument can be developed to defend action that appears to be so clearly a violation of international law.

But more important than restating the legal issues provoked by the Indonesian use of force against Malaysia in terms wider than as a dispute about compliance with Charter rules, the Confrontation gives us an opportunity to examine the ways in which international law forms an integral aspect of the diplomatic process, even when its legal rules of restraints are ignored by one of the parties to a dispute. Indonesia's objections to the formation of Malaysia were expressed in legal terms and Malaysia's response depended heavily on being able to use its strong position in international law to rally political support to offset its military weakness.[3] More and more international lawyers are growing aware that

---

[2] Emmerich de Vattel, *The Law of Nations*, esp. Bk. II, Chap. 1 (Fenwick trans., 1758 edn., Carnegie Classics, 1916).

[3] George Modelski reports that as of 1962 Indonesia was spending $1,301,000,-000 on defense whereas Malaysia was spending only $42,000,000 (the Malaysian figure refers only to Malayan expenditures, but these represented the preponderant share). Modelski, "Indonesia and Her

international law may provide the participants to a dispute with an agreed instrument of communication.[4] The role of international law as an integral part of the process of international communication is especially prominent with regard to the formulation of claims and responses and with regard to the expression of third-party and community expectations as to the nature of a reasonable outcome of an international dispute.[5] Malaysian Confrontation will illustrate such an interaction. Each side invoked legal norms to communicate with its adversary and to mobilize effective political support for its position within international society.

Confrontation also provides an instructive example of the form that an international dispute takes in the contemporary world when the protagonists are both newly independent Asian states, the one adopting an essentially conservative orientation at home and abroad and the other pursuing revisionist policies that seek a partial reconstituting of the international legal order. Malaysia's security, and even her survival appeared to depend upon mobilizing support external to Asia, whereas Indonesia sought to discourage this external support by a combination of ideological, diplomatic, economic, and military means. Neither side was altogether successful, but it is clear that the political variables affecting the course of Confrontation were themselves partly a consequence of the extent to which Indonesia and Malaysia presented their legal cases in convincing terms. We learn from a study of Confrontation, then, something about the styles of communication used by adversaries seeking to legitimate their respective claims and implementing acts in various international arenas. These arenas include not only those for traditional diplomacy, but the newer regional and global ones, including the *ad hoc* arenas constituted by periodic meetings of the non-aligned states of Asia and Africa. One of the interesting facets of the Indonesian campaign for external support was its effort, partly successful, to isolate Malaysia in the third world, even to the extent of seeking its formal exclusion from the meetings of the Afro-Asian states.[6]

International law in the wider sense also provided the protagonists and third-party mediators with various alternatives to Confrontation as a basis for revising the relations between Malaysia and Indonesia. Hover-

Neighbors," Policy Memorandum No. 30, Center of International Studies, p. 4, October 29, 1964.

[4] E.g., William Coplin, *The Functions of International Law*, Chicago, Rand McNally, 1966, pp. 168-71.

[5] This approach is exhibited to excellent analytic advantage in Myres S. McDougal and William Burke, *The Public Order of the Oceans*, New Haven, Yale University Press, 1962.

[6] Indonesia was successful in excluding Malaysia from formal participation in the 1964 Meeting of the Heads of State of Non-Aligned Countries that took place in Cairo. Compare the parallel efforts of the Arab nations to exclude Israel. The United States has sought successfully, in similar vein, to exclude Castro's Cuba from participation in the inter-American system.

ing ambiguously in the background throughout the dispute was an aspiration to attain subregional and ethnic harmony by implementing the loosely formulated idea of a confederation, called Maphilindo—to join together in friendship and cooperation the national destinies of Malaysia, Indonesia, and the Philippines.[7] This contrapuntal diplomatic melody was given credible expression by recourse to legal conceptions and procedures that might resolve the underlying political conflicts provoked by Indonesia's reaction to the formation of Malaysia on a basis that would not make it appear that either side was acquiescing in the demands of the other or backing down. The forms and procedures of international law thus provided a way to transform the antagonisms of Confrontation into the harmonies of Maphilindo. And in fact the end of Confrontation, which principally resulted from drastic reorientation of Indonesian foreign policy after the bloody countercoup of 1965-66, was signaled and symbolized by the formalities associated with the reestablishment of diplomatic relations between the two countries, and by the Indonesian resumption of active membership in the United Nations.

In sum, then, a legal study of the Confrontation staged by Indonesia against Malaysia offers insight into the use of international law to communicate diplomatic positions and to mobilize or undermine support for these positions in various international arenas. We do not learn much about the static dimensions of international law that are constituted by a framework of rules and a set procedure for their impartial interpretation and application. Such rules and procedures were *invoked* against Indonesia, but to no significant effect, except perhaps to induce her withdrawal from the United Nations in January of 1965. One point is obviously that Confrontation was a conscious and unambiguous repudiation of the restraints of international law, but a deeper point, one that has eluded students and critics of the subject for centuries, is that the failure of international law as a restraint system is not equivalent to the failure of international law. The dynamics of Confrontation are so suggestive for the international lawyer precisely because the relevance of international law is so clear, despite the refusal of Indonesia to be restrained by its rules.

II

This relevance of international law to Confrontation becomes clearer by a selective narration of the main phases of the dispute between Indonesia and Malaysia. We must begin, first, with a consideration of the decision to create a single sovereign state out of the separate po-

[7] These subregional movements preceded and followed upon the Malaysian confrontation, taking the form of proposals for an Association of South East Asia (ASA), a loose confederation working together on common problems especially in the area of security.

litical entities of Malaya, Singapore, Sarawak, and Sabah. Indonesia's response to the creation of Malaysia in 1963 was to initiate the policy of Confrontation. The second phase, then, of the narrative is to describe the acts and events that together constitute the Confrontation. Third, and briefly, a description of the termination of Confrontation in 1966 as a result of the shift of the domestic balance of power in Indonesia to the army.

The Malaysian Federation. Malaya became independent of British colonial rule in 1957.[8] It appears that Britain did not contemplate the inclusion of its Borneo territories of Sabah and Sarawak in a single sovereign state until 1961, partly because these territories were very backward compared to Malaya and Singapore. The first public statement proposing Malaysia was made on May 27, 1961 by the Prime Minister of Malaya, Tengku Abdul Rahman, in a speech made in Singapore to the Foreign Correspondents Association: "Malaya today as a nation realizes that she cannot stand alone and in isolation. Sooner or later she should have an understanding with Britain and the people of the territories of Singapore, North Borneo, Brunei and Sarawak."[9] Underlying this impulse toward federation were two sets of factors, one ethnic and the other geopolitical. The large Chinese populations in these political units would almost certainly come to dominate their political destinies unless kept in a subordinate position by means of some artificial scheme designed to assure Malay domination disproportionate to numbers, talents, or resources. Malay racism, then, gave some of the impetus to the idea of creating Malaysia under the banner of Malay nationalism, quite a deception if one recognizes that there are more Chinese than Malays in Malaysia.[10] There were also geopolitical factors present. The acquisition of Chinese political control in Singapore and the Borneo territories would also lead, it was thought, to an eventual allegiance to the policies of mainland China. Therefore, the creation of Malaysia was designed, at once, to thwart the extension of Chinese Communist influence in Asia by means of internal takeovers and to provide a viable political unit of anti-Communist commitment to thwart

[8] For the Mayalan background of Malaysia see R. S. Milne, *Government and Politics in Malaysia*, New York, Houghton Mifflin, 1967, pp. 1-48 [hereinafter cited as Milne].

[9] Quoted in "Malaysia—in Brief," at 120 (Department of Information, Malaysia, 1963); this pamphlet contains the official Malaysian perspectives on development up through the creation of Malaysia.

[10] "On Malaysia Day, the Malays totalled 40 per cent of the Malaysia population, the Chinese 43 per cent, Indians and Pakistanis 9 per cent, and the indigenous tribes of Borneo and other races 8 per cent." Harry Miller, *A Short History of Malaysia*, New York, Praeger, 1966, p. 15; the Malays became the dominant group after the withdrawal of Singapore from the Federation in August, 1965. According to the 1961 census the total population of Malaysia (excluding 1.7 million living in Singapore) is about 8.3 million, of 1.7 million in Singapore 1.3 are ethnic Chinese.

the expansionist policies of China and Indonesia, Peking's then friend and ally.[11]

There are indications that as of 1961 the politically sensitive leadership of the Borneo territories would have preferred either to remain somewhat longer under British rule or to achieve independence as a Borneo federation rather than being absorbed as a subordinate unit of Malaysia.[12] In 1962 a conservative bi-national commission (Malaya and Britain) headed by Lord Cobbold concluded that the populations of the Borneo territories desired to join Malaysia provided certain safeguards were granted their particular interests and some federal monies were diverted to hasten their economic development.[13] There was a disagreement among the members of the Commission about when Malaysia should be established. The two British members favored a transition period of three to seven years before merger, but the two Malayan members of the Commission argued that Malaysia should be brought into being within twelve months; to delay longer would lead to racial conflict and "expose these territories and their peoples to dangerously disruptive influences both internally and from the outside."[14] The British government was persuaded to accept the Malayan view on timing and it was announced that Malaysia would come into being as of August 31, 1963.

George Kahin speculates that it was the urgency of proceeding with the merger of Malaya and Singapore that accounted for the British willingness to encourage the merger of the Borneo territories before they could be prepared for a greater measure of self-government.[15] Until the middle of 1961 Tengku Abdul Rahman opposed the merger of Malaya and Singapore, evidently fearing that adding Chinese-dominated Singapore to Malaya would upset the ethnic balance sufficiently (44 percent Chinese, 42 percent Malay) to vest political control in the Chinese. As well, the political power of Tengku depended on support it received from conservative Chinese groups in Malaya; this support might be withdrawn once the more radical socialist Chinese leaders of Singapore's political life were allowed to compete for power in a merged political unit. Singapore was run by the socialist Lee Kuan Kew, an advocate of union with Malaya to achieve economic advantages, whose leadership seemed endangered by the rise of a pro-Communist opposition.

[11] For a perceptive account of the motivation to establish the Malaysian Federation, especially on the part of the British, see George Modelski, "Indonesia and the Malaysia Issue," *The Year Book of World Affairs, 1964*. London, Stevens and Sons, pp. 128-49.

[12] For an analysis along these lines see George McT. Kahin, "Malaysia and Indonesia," xxxvii, *Pacific Affairs* (Fall 1964), 253-70, 254-56 [hereinafter cited as Kahin].

[13] An account of the operation of the Cobbold Commission is contained in Milne, pp. 64-68; for a view critical of the Cobbold Commission see Kahin, p. 256.

[14] Kahin, p. 256.

[15] *Id.* at pp. 256-57.

The negotiation of merger was a delicate matter, as it depended on a trade-off of political influence for economic gain, a trade-off that later led to racial strife and secession in 1965.[16] The 1963 formula gave Singapore considerable local control over education and labor affairs, but involved underrepresentation in Malaysian political affairs as measured on a per capita basis and as compared to the other subparts of Malaysia.[17]

The Indonesian response to projected Federation is difficult to reconstruct and appears to reflect the interplay of a series of domestic and foreign considerations. The first major public Indonesian reaction was a friendly one by Subandrio, then Foreign Minister, in the General Assembly of the United Nations, in November 1961:

> We [the Republic of Indonesia] are not only disclaiming the territories outside the former Netherlands East Indies, though they are of the same islands, but—more than that—when Malaya told us of her intentions to merge with the three British Crown Colonies of Sarawak, Brunei and British North Borneo as one Federation, we told them that we have no objections and that we wish them success with this merger so that everyone may live in peace and freedom. For the sake of clarification, I may tell this Assembly that three-quarters of the island of Borneo (Kalimantan) is Indonesian territory, while the remainder constitutes the three aforementioned British Crown Colonies.
>
> Naturally, ethnologically and geographically speaking, this British part is closer to Indonesia than, let us say, to Malaya. But we still told Malaya that we have no objections to such a merger based upon the will for freedom of the peoples concerned.[18]

Indonesia was at the time preoccupied with securing a successful termination of its long campaign to acquire control over West Irian and quite evidently did not want to jeopardize its imminent victory by fostering the impression that West Irian was merely the first of a series of demands in Southeast Asia.[19] Therefore Subandrio's reassurance vis-à-vis Malaysia must be understood in terms of the earlier instance of Confrontation—West Irian. West Irian, however, was safely in Indonesian

---

[16] Useful description, Milne, pp. 49-73 (see pp. 73-74 for further sources).

[17] For a positive assessment of the operation of Malaysia as a multiracial community see George Modelski, "Indonesia and Her Neighbors," Policy Memorandum No. 30, Center of International Studies, Princeton University, pp. 14-15, October 29, 1964.

[18] Quoted in "A Survey on the Controversial Problem of the Establishment of the Federation of Malaysia," Information Division, Embassy of Indonesia, Washington, D.C., p. 2 (no date given).

[19] The United Nations was expected to administer West Irian for a transitional period from October 1962 to January 1963 when Indonesian administration began four months ahead of schedule. For a critical view of Indonesia's campaign to obtain control over West Irian see Modelski, pp. 6-12, n17.

hands by January 1, 1963 (or more than nine months before Malaysia came into being) and the basic settlement favorable to Indonesia had been reached several months earlier. Therefore, from August 1962 on, Indonesian statesmen were free to respond to the prospect of Malaysia without impairing their efforts to obtain West Irian.[20]

Several factors seem to have inclined Indonesia toward Confrontation. First of all, there was the recollection of the role played by Malaya in promoting the 1958-60 uprisings against Sukarno. These uprisings were centered on the ethnically Malay island of Sumatra and were partly financed and guided by the United Kingdom and the United States.[21] It is hardly reasonable to suppose that the prospect of a strong Malaysia with a permanent British military presence in Southeast Asia was welcome news in Djakarta, especially given the mandate to use British military power based in Malay for purposes wider than Malaysian security. For instance, Article VI of the 1913 Defense Agreement between Malaysia and the United Kingdom affirms the British right to maintain its base facilities in Singapore and use them "as that Government may consider necessary for the purpose of assisting in the defense of Malaysia and for Commonwealth defense and for the preservation of peace in South-East Asia."[22] So the creation of Malaysia maintained in existence a situation in which Western powers hostile to the Sukarno leadership in Indonesia could continue to threaten, if not actually engage in, covert military activity, a threat that had already been carried out during the 1958-60 period at great cost to Indonesia.[23] The Indonesian reaction to this kind of Western presence must be compared with the reaction of the United States to the establishment of a Soviet military presence in Cuba after Castro's accession to power in 1960, a comparison not lost to Indonesian leaders.

A second important factor was the revolt in the Sultanate of Brunei in December 1962. Brunei was the one territory in North Borneo that refused to join Malaysia, partly because it was rich due to oil resources and partly because its Sultan would not accept a protocol position in-

20 The negotiations between Indonesia and Malaysia led to a settlement of the West Irian Question as of August 15, 1962. Ellsworth Bunker, acting as private citizen and representative of U Thant, tendered his good offices to the parties and his presence seems to have helped produce an agreement.

21 For a popular, yet impressive, account of foreign participation (including the CIA) in these Indonesian uprisings see William Stevenson, *Birds' Nests in Their Beards*, Boston, Houghton Mifflin, 1964.

22 For other relevant provisions in defense agreements affecting Malaysia see A. G. Mezerik, ed., "Malaysia-Indonesia Conflict," Appendix H, pp. 109-10, International Review Service, 1965 [hereinafter cited as Mezerik]. These provisions and other principal documents referred to in this chapter are to be found in Appendix A, pp. 613-32.

23 This fact was much stressed in the Indonesian official presentations of their reasons for opposing Malaysia as it was constituted. E.g. Mr. Sudjarwo's presentation in the Security Council of Indonesia's argument in response to a Malaysian complaint about aggression in September 1964, esp. SCOR, 1149th Mtg., Sept. 14, 1964, paras. 12-30.

ferior to the Tengku of Malaya. At the time of the revolt Brunei was a British Crown Colony that was operated on a semi-feudalistic basis. The revolt was evidently led by A. H. Azahari, then in exile in the Philippines. The objective of the revolt was to promote the cause of Borneo Federation as an independent sovereign state. British and Gurkha troops and Malayan police sent from Singapore were used to crush the revolt and the Malayan government accused Indonesia of playing a leading role in instigating its outbreak.[24] The Indonesia government denied any role in the Brunei uprising, although it praised its anticolonial character and called upon Malaya to cease its unfriendly attitude toward Indonesia. The Brunei uprising, however, resulted in raising the issue of self-determination for the Borneo territories. This issue led to ever more clear-cut opposition by Indonesia to the proposed Malaysian Federation. This opposition was partially seconded by the Philippines through the revival of a historic claim to the ownership of the Borneo territory of Sabah.[25]

On January 20, 1963 Subandrio made an official declaration: "We cannot but adhere to a policy of confrontation toward Malaya because at present they represent themselves as accomplices of neo-colonialist and neo-imperialist forces pursuing a policy hostile toward Indonesia." Throughout early 1963 hostile incidents occurred with increasing frequency, and accusations were made that Indonesia was aiding dissident groups in the Borneo territories to fight against federation with Malaya. Domestic influences in Indonesia intensified Confrontation. The Communist party was quick to grasp the Malaysian project as a popular anti-colonialist issue and was responsible for the earliest Indonesian opposition to the federation. The Indonesian army was eager to appear as nationalistic as the Communists on Malaysia and was sensitive to the security hazards that would be created by the long common, porous "jungle-infested" border between Malaysia and Indonesia in Borneo. The West Irian campaign was a vivid model of a successful use of confrontation diplomacy that combined ideological truculence with military intimidation to achieve an expansionist goal of foreign policy and, at the same time, develop the image of an Indonesia on the move as a leading member of the Afro-Asian world.[26]

These, then, were the elements of the international dispute that developed between Indonesia and Malaya about the proposed federation of Malaysia. This dispute can be expressed as a series of legal issues:

24 Cf. Milne, pp. 185-87.
25 Milne, pp. 187-88; cf. articles by Lorenzo Sumulong, Jovito R. Salonga, Arturo A. Alafraz, and Juan M. Arreglado in 2 *Philippine International Law Journal* 6-28, 78-104 (Jan.-June 1963). (There is also a useful documentary supplement on pp. 216-339.)

26 Cf. Modelski, pp. 6-12, n17; also Arnold Brackman, *Southeast Asia's Second Front—The Power Struggle in the Malay Archipelago*, New York, Praeger, 1966, pp. 91-114.

1. The applicability of the principle of self-determination to the Borneo territories;

2. The incompatibility of a colonial military presence in Malaysia with regional security and with regional autonomy;

3. The danger to Indonesian security arising from a permanent Western extraregional military presence in contiguous territory.

Such legal issues are not conventional ones in international law. But the relevance of regional consensus to the competing rights and duties of states has been an evolving theme of the efforts to secure order in both Latin America and Africa, and it is the status of such a regional consensus that underlies Indonesian claims if these claims are considered in a legal setting.[27] In the formulation of its claims to oppose the creation of Malaysia, Indonesia relied upon arguments that tended to discredit the legitimacy of Malaya's position. First, Indonesia tried to create the impression that Malaya was a tool of British influence and therefore lacking in the possession of real national independence. Such an argument amounted to both questioning Malaya's sovereign status and contending that the United Kingdom was exercising covert colonial rulership. In addition, Indonesia argued that there had been no fair test made of the will of the populations in the Borneo territories and that federation was in violation of the principle of self-determination.

Throughout the dispute the dominant theme of conflict was set off against a subordinate theme of cooperation based upon joint action. In the background of Indonesian diplomacy was a vague project to sponsor a loose confederation of Malaya, Indonesia, and the Philippines—an objective basis for which was the common interest in controlling the influence of the Chinese overseas populations in these countries and to create a security bulwark against expansion by China. The disposition toward cooperation culminated in the Manila Conference held in August 1963 that included a Maphilindo proposal, an aspect of which was a procedure for settling the dispute over the imminent creation of Malaysia.

The framework for a peaceful resolution of the dispute was set forth in the Manila Accord of July 31, 1963, the outcome of a meeting among the Foreign Ministers of the three countries. Paragraphs 10 and 11 of the Manila Accord outline the basic approach:

10. The Ministers reaffirmed their countries' adherence to the principle of self-determination, for the people of non-self-governing

---

[27] Comparable assertions of a regional consensus have been relied upon in other parts of the world as a legitimizing influence and as a basis for objection to extraregional intervention in regional affairs. This kind of objection underlay the African reaction to Operation Stanleyville in December 1964. For an account see Falk, *Legal Order in a Violent World*, Princeton, Princeton University Press, 1968, pp. 324-35.

territories. In this context, Indonesia and the Philippines stated they would welcome the formation of Malaysia provided the support of the people of the Borneo territories is ascertained by an independent and impartial authority, the Secretary-General of the United Nations or his representative.

11. Tho Federation of Malaya expressed appreciation for this attitude of Indonesia and the Philippines and undertook to consult the British Government and the Governments of the Borneo territories with a view to inviting the Secretary-General of the United Nations or his representative to take the necessary steps in order to ascertain the wishes of the people of those territories.[28]

In paragraph 12 of the Manila Accord, the Philippines reserved the right to pursue its territorial claims against North Borneo "in accordance with international law and the principle of the pacific settlement of disputes" and enumerated "negotiation, conciliation, arbitration, or judicial settlement as well as other peaceful means of the parties' own approach" as suitable, and proposed settlement "in conformity with the Charter of the United Nations and the Bandung Declaration."[29] The Manila Accord thus embodies an approach to the settlement of an international dispute dangerous to international peace that relies upon a series of universally accepted postulates of international law:

1. The suitability of the principle of self-determination to resolve a dispute about the federation of internationally distinct political units;

2. Recourse to the machinery of the United Nations to obtain an authoritative decision as to whether the principle of self-determination had been truly implemented;

3. Recourse to traditional methods of peaceful settlement to resolve a territorial dispute.

In effect, the Malaysian question had been narrowed by the Manila Accord to challenging the authoritativeness of the prior efforts, principally by the Cobbold Commission, to apply the principle of self-determination to the Borneo territories.[30] The Philippine claim to Sabah was dealt with by agreement to find some peaceful means to obtain an impartial judgment as to its merits, but without any specification of time or form that this judgment should take.

---

[28] Full text in Mezerik, Appendix E, pp. 100-02. Also see Appendix A this volume.
[29] Ibid.
[30] In Paragraph 11 of the Joint Statement at Manila the three parties agreed to resolve the problem of the postcolonial military presence of the colonial power in the following vague, but apparently conciliatory, fashion: "The three Heads of Government further agreed that foreign bases—temporary in nature—should not be allowed to be used directly or indirectly to subvert the national independence of any of the three countries. In accordance with the principle enunciated in the Bandung Declaration, the three countries will abstain from the use of arrangements of collective defence to serve the particular interests of any of the big powers." Mezerik, p. 104. Also see Appendix A this volume.

At a meeting of the three Heads of Government held immediately thereafter, the Accords approved by the Foreign Ministers were endorsed in the Manila Summit Statement and Declaration of August 3, 1963. The main operative section of the Manila Statement called for "a fresh approach" to the dispute over the establishment of Malaysia. The fresh approach consisted of an elaboration of Paragraphs 10 and 11 of the Manila Accord by adding a reference to the specification of self-determination "within the context of General Assembly Resolution 1541(XV), Principle IX." The Secretary-General of the United Nations was advised to examine the basis for the creation of Malaysia by "taking into consideration":

(I) The recent election in Sabah (North Borneo) and Sarawak but nevertheless further examining, verifying and satisfying himself as to whether
    (a) Malaysia was a major issue, if not the main issue;
    (b) Electoral registers were properly compiled;
    (c) Elections were free and there was no coercion; and
    (d) Votes were properly polled and properly counted; and
(II) The wishes of those who, being qualified to vote, would have exercised their right of self-determination in the recent elections had it not been for their detention for political activities, imprisonment for political offense or absence from Sabah (North Borneo) or Sarawak.[31]

In addition, in Paragraph 7 of the Statement the three governments stated that they "deem it desirable to send observers to witness the carrying out of the task to be undertaken by the working teams," presumably constituted by the representatives of the Secretary-General. In formal terms this mode of approach appeared to involve an optional recourse of global institutions to resolve an intraregional dispute in terms of an agreed frame of reference. As such, it illustrates a new kind of settlement procedure in which a multinational conference selects the chief executive of the United Nations to provide an authoritative determination of facts to resolve an international dispute.[32]

---

[31] The text of Principle IX of General Assembly Resolution 1541 (XV) is as follows:
    Integration should have come about in the following circumstances:
    a) The integrating territory should have attained an advanced stage of self-government with free political institutions, so that its peoples would have the capacity to make a responsible choice through informed and democratic processes;
    b) The integration should be the result of the freely expressed wishes of the territory's peoples acting with full knowledge of the change in their status, their wishes having been expressed through informed and democratic processes, impartially conducted and based on universal adult suffrage. The United Nations could, when it deems it necessary, supervise these processes.

[32] The obvious analogue is the role played by the Pope in the late Medieval period in Western international relations.

However, the Manila Statement and its accompanying Declaration also indicate some commitment to the underlying principles of regional autonomy and the importance of eliminating colonial powers from the life of Asian states. In Paragraph 9 it was affirmed "that initial steps should be taken toward the establishment of Maphilindo by holding frequent and regular consultations at all levels to be known as Mushawarah Maphilindo"; furthermore "it is agreed that each country shall set up a national secretariat for Maphilindo affairs and as a first step the respective national secretariats will consult together with a view to coordinating and cooperating with each other in the study on the setting up of the necessary machinery for Maphilindo." But more directly in Paragraph 10 "The three Heads of Government emphasized that the responsibility for the preservation of the national independence of the three countries and of the peace and security in their region lies primarily in the hands of the governments and peoples concerned, and that the three governments undertake to have close consultations (Mushawarah) among themselves on these matters." And, finally, in Paragraph 11 the leaders of the three countries "agreed that foreign bases—temporary in nature—should not be allowed to be used directly or indirectly to subvert the national independence of any of the three countries. In accordance with the principle enunciated in the Bandung Declaration the three countries will abstain from the use of arrangements of collective defense to serve the particular interests of any of the big powers." The language of the Declaration is permeated by "the spirit of Afro-Asian solidarity forged in the Bandung Conference of 1955."[33] Such a regionalization of the political affairs of these countries goes a long way toward eliminating any reasonable basis for regarding Malaysia as a neocolonialist project. One may question whether Prime Minister Rahman of Malaysia subscribed with any sincerity to such a radical Afro-Asian stance; it would not appear compatible with the basic orientation adopted by his country in making its gradual and conciliatory transition from colonial to independent status without any basic alteration of socioeconomic structure and without any repudiation of the British role in Malayan affairs. With regard to President Sukarno one may doubt whether he desired to settle so amicably an external dispute that was useful to deflect Communist opposition at home and to glorify his Afro-Asian leadership abroad; one may wonder whether Sukarno was willing to cast aside so graciously the mantle of West Irian in a historical period that he was fond of calling "the era of Confrontation."[34] Despite these questions the

[33] Mezerik, p. 104.
[34] Cf. President Sukarno's speech, "One cannot escape history," delivered at the closing ceremonies of the Manila Conference and reprinted in George Modelski, ed., *The New Emerging Forces—Documents on the Ideology of Indonesian Foreign Policy*, pp. 77-80, Documents and Data Paper No. 2, Institute of Advanced Studies, Australian National University, 1963, pp. 77-80.

Manila framework taken on it own terms appears to be a viable compromise that takes account of the basic interests of each of the participating states. As such, it illustrates the flexible use of the concepts and forms of international law to clarify an agreed framework of an ensuing peaceful settlement.[35]

The events subsequent to the Manila meeting are complex and their interpretation difficult. U Thant promptly accepted the request contained in the Manila Statement and appointed a nine-member UN mission to ascertain whether the peoples of Sabah and Sarawak sought federation. The mission was scheduled to arrive in the Borneo area on August 16, 1963 and complete its work in about four weeks. In the period after Manila, guerrilla activities were reported in the Borneo territories, there were clashes between guerrilla troops and Gurkha army units under British command, and there were fairly reliable contentions made that the guerrilla operations were based in and guided by Indonesia. Anti-Malaysia demonstrations greeted the UN Mission on its arrival in Sarawak and a vigorous dispute arose as to the size and nature of the observer teams from both the Philippines and Indonesia.[36] Sukarno repeated on a nationwide radio broadcast as late as August 28th that "We will bow our heads [and] obey" if the mission found that the peoples of Borneo wanted to join Malaysia.

Malaya's announcement on August 29 that Malaysia would be formed on September 16, 1963 was a decisive occurrence.[37] Such an announcement, coming while the UN mission was engaged in its work, seemed to take for granted an outcome favorable to Malaya and, thereby to presuppose the outcome of the issue left open by the Manila compromise. Indonesia immediately sent a protest calling the announcement "a reckless and premature decision" that is "a unilateral act contravening the letter and spirit of the Manila Summit agreements."[38] The Tengku's statement can only be regarded as a betrayal of the Manila approach to the creation of Malaysia and can only have been expected to lead Indonesia to revive its confrontation diplomacy.[39] It is indeed

[35] Cf. the assessment of Professor Kahin who accompanied Sukarno to and from the Manila Conference and was in close contact with the Indonesian Delegation at this time. Kahin, p. 269, esp. note 18.

[36] For an anti-Indonesian interpretation of these events see Brackman, note 26 *supra*, pp. 193-97.

[37] See the official Indonesian account of the extent to which the Manila settlement was undermined by Malaya's announcement, in "A Survey on the Controversial Problems of the Establishment of the Federation of Malaysia," Information Division, Embassy of Indonesia, Washington, D.C., p. 4 (no date given). The description of these events concludes as follows: "Thus the confidence of Indonesia and Philippines in the honesty and loyalty of Malaya as a party to the Manila agreement has been greatly damaged. Whoever might have provoked Malaya into such disloyal behaviour, the fact remains that the Philippines and Indonesia face the bitter and bare reality of an undermining of the Manila Agreement."

[38] Mezerik, p. 76.

[39] Cf. the statement of the Deputy Prime Minister of Malaysia, Tun Abdul Razak, made on January 13, 1964 to discover Malaysia's view of these controversial events. Text in Mezerik, p. 112.

strange that the timing of Malaysia's creation had not been taken up at Manila, as the original plan called for a date of August 31, obviously too soon for the United Nations to carry out its mission with any care. In his "Final Conclusions" U Thant stated that Malaya's announcement "led to misunderstanding, confusion, and even resentment among other parties to the Manila Agreement."[40] And in the *Aide-Mémoire* attached by the official observers of the Philippines to the UN Malaysia mission was a stronger condemnation: "The announcement made while the survey was going on that Malaysia would be launched on September 16, 1963, had the effect of rendering the mission of the United Nations Malaysia Team virtually meaningless."[41] At face value, the Manila solution was tantamount to acquiescence by both Indonesia and the Philippines to the inclusion of the Borneo territories in the projected union of Malaysia. For instance, George Kahin, who attended the conference at Manila and had known the Indonesia leaders since 1948, has written that "both leaders [Sukarno and Macapagal] expected the U.N. to find in favor of Malaysia—and had privately so advised U Thant."[42] Recourse to the Secretary-General was evidently devised to save face for all concerned.

The Secretary-General's Report issued on September 14, 1963 came as an anticlimax. It did, in fact, confirm the expectation that the great majority of the inhabitants of Sabah and Sarawak favored joining Malaysia. The *Aide-Mémoire* of the Philippine observers criticized the mission for its failure to carry out its mandate from the Manila conference. In a rather persuasive analysis, the Philippine observers complain that the UN mission, although fair and impartial to the extent of its inquiry, did not have the time or manpower available to truly apply the intentions at Manila to use "a fresh approach" by way of Principle IX of the annex to G.A. Resolution 1541(XV).[43] The comparable *Aide-Mémoire* of the Indonesian observers was more extreme in its condemnation of the findings of the UN report, arguing that it provided no basis for concluding that merger of the Borneo territories with Malaysia was an application of the principle of self-determination. One wonders why U Thant did not impose terms on the carrying out of the mission so that it would be less vulnerable to persuasive criticism, especially insisting that no plans for the creation of Malaysia be created until the UN report has been made public and that the UN team be allowed

---

40 United Nations Malaysia Mission Report, Kuala Lumpur (reproduced by the Department of Information, Malaysia, 1963, p. ii).

41 Text of the Aide-Mémoire is reprinted in "A Survey," note 37 *supra*, pp. 14-15; the quoted statement is contained in numbered para. 17 on p. 15. See Appendix A.

42 Kahin, p. 269.

43 Cf. Aide-Mémoire from the Observers of the Philippines to the U.N. Malaysia Mission in Sarawak and Sabah, reprinted in "A Survey," note 37 *supra*, pp. 14-16. For text see Appendix A, pp. 629-31.

the time and resources to investigate the situation in sufficient depth to attach confidence to its results. Perhaps the three states really asked only that the United Nations ratify a political solution reached at Manila, instead of, as the request asks, having benefit of an independent assessment. But given the inflamed background, the continuation of Indonesia supported rebel activities in the Borneo territories, and the precarious basis of Singapore's relation to Malaysia, it was unwise not to safeguard the authoritativeness of the UN role to a far greater extent. As it was, the United Nations carried out its role in such an unconvincing fashion that there was created a plausible, if not fully persuasive, basis for Indonesia's later hostility and temporary withdrawal from that organization.

Malaysia came into being on schedule on September 16, 1963. Both Indonesia and the Philippines withheld diplomatic recognition from the new entity, and Indonesia went further by breaking diplomatic relations with Kuala Lumpur and by staging mass demonstrations outside the British and Malayan embassies in Djakarta. Further incidents took place in Indonesia, especially directed against Britain's role in promoting and securing Malaysia, to signify the intensification of Confrontation to heights well above those attained during the months preceding Manila. On September 18 the British embassy in Djakarta was burned by an angry mob, eliciting a protest from the United States, and a mildly conciliatory statement of explanation from Indonesia. But the line was drawn, and within a few days Indonesia ended all trade relations with Malaysia, thereby eliminating the extensive trade with Singapore upon which Indonesia depended heavily for foreign exchange.

The months that followed September 1963 witnessed a continuation of the Confrontation with the Western powers indicating their support of Malaysia's independence and integrity. This support was symbolized by collective security gestures by the United Kingdom, Australia, and New Zealand and by the U.S. move of sending part of the Seventh Fleet into the Indian Ocean. The United States refused to continue economic aid to Indonesia in reaction to the stepped-up military dimension of Confrontation, mainly taking the form of guerrilla operations and terrorist raids across the Borneo frontiers. The Soviet Union and China endorsed Confrontation and the Soviet Union agreed to meet Indonesia's needs for military equipment.

In December 1963 the Maphilindo theme, somewhat surprisingly, suddenly recurs amid the cacophonies of Confrontation. President Diosdado Macapagal of the Philippines proposed another tripartite meeting to overcome the Malaysian problem and Sukarno actually proposed that a second survey be conducted by the United Nations, provided it include interviewing imprisoned leaders as a basis for Indonesian acceptance of Malaysia.[44] In effect, the architects of the Manila compromise appeared prepared to try the same formula for resolution and scheduled a bilateral meeting in Manila from January 7 to 11. Despite all the relevant events since June 1963, Presidents Sukarno and Macapagal declared themselves "loyal adherents to the Manila Agreements" and affirmed that their just concluded talks "were held in the spirit of Mushawarah as the fundamental method of Maphilindo."[45] Their Joint Statement went so far as to say that "the two Presidents considered it essential to strengthen Maphilindo as a living reality, in the firm belief that within its framework constructive and equitable solutions could be found for many of the serious problems of the region, including those arising from the formation of the 'Federation of Malaysia,' the promotion of regional security, and the development of regional economic cooperation." Calling for a return "to the spirit and principles of the Manila Agreements" the Joint Statement said that the two Presidents "cherish the hope that a tripartite Mushawarah could be convened to resolve existing differences among the three signatories." Sukarno in Paragraph 5 of the Joint Statement explains "the Indonesia policy of confrontation" as follows:

It is not a policy of aggression, much less of territorial expansion. Its main purpose is to oppose neocolonialist policy of an outside power which, by distorting the procedures laid down in the Manila Agreements for the ascertainment of the wishes of the peoples concerned regarding the establishments of "Malaysia," is bent on wrecking Maphilindo. This divide and rule policy, backed by predominant military force, can only be checked by a firm defensive policy of confrontation, lest the national independence and security of the countries of this region succumb to foreign domination.[46]

Sukarno's statement emphasizes the anti-British character of Confrontation, but the return to regional harmony appears to be conditioned on the unrelated validation of the popular will in Borneo with regard to joining Malaysia and, somewhat, on Malaysia's willingness to identify openly with Maphilindo as a central aspect for its future security. Throughout the period of Confrontation it is difficult to assess the extent to which Sukarno was seeking to eliminate the British colonial presence from Southeast Asia. It is also plausible to contend that Sukarno was merely using this British presence as a convenient pretext on which to build moral validity for a neocolonialist policy of Indonesian expansionism being pursued at Malaysia's expense.[47]

[44] Cf. Chronology of Dispute in Mezerik, p. 79.
[45] For full text of Joint Statement see Mezerik, pp. 110-12.
[46] Mezerik, p. 111.

[47] For a detailed interpretation along these lines see Brackman, note 26 supra, pp. 42-243; Kahin's interpretation is much more sympathetic with Indonesia's contentions.

Deputy Prime Minister of Malaysia Razak denied the implication of the Joint Statement that Malaysia had failed to live up to the Manila Agreements.[48] As to the Second Tripartite Summit proposed in the Joint Statement, he asked a series of rhetorical questions that amounted to preconditions:

1. Does this meeting mean that the two countries recognize Malaysia as an Independent Sovereign State?

2. Does it mean that Indonesia agrees to withdraw her policy of confrontation so that the meeting could be held in an atmosphere of peace and goodwill?

3. Does it mean that Indonesia is prepared to withdraw her troops massed along the borders of Sarawak and Sabah?

4. Does it mean that Indonesia agrees to withdraw her troops now engaged in operations deep in Malaysian territory of Sabah and Sarawak?

5. If so, would Indonesia agree to accept a neutral nation acceptable to Malaysia and Indonesia to act as a referee to ensure that all the terms of the truce are strictly and scrupulously carried out?

Mr. Razak concludes the statement of reply by saying that "If we could be assured of all those points nothing would make us happier than to attend such a conference anywhere and at any time."[49] These requests for assurances appear tantamount to a demand that Indonesia renounce Confrontation prior to the next summit and that the reality of this renunciation be validated by a neutral nation. Malaysia was, in effect, insisting that Indonesia's use of force in violation of the United Nations Charter cease prior to a negotiation of "the dispute"; such an insistence is consistent with a rule-oriented approach to international law, as Indonesia's basis for Confrontation, whatever it was, could not be vindicated as a form of self-defense. Some international lawyers have argued, however, that until the international legal order is in a position to assure states that their just claims will find assured methods of satisfaction, it is impossible to take the Charter prohibitions on the use of force literally.[50] If states retain discretion to use force to pursue just claims, then it is necessary to test whether Indonesia has had a reasonable basis for contending that its claim is just. An argument on behalf of Indonesia's claims might take the following form:

[48] Razak's statement is reprinted in Mezerik, pp. 112-13; he is replying to three charges contained in the Joint Statement issued by Indonesia and the Philippines:

1. Premature announcement of the date of Federation;

2. Refusal by Malaysia to deal with the Philippine claim to Sabah in the manner established by the Manila Agreements;

3. Decision by Malaysia to break diplomatic relations with the Philippines and Malaysia.

[49] Mezerik, p. 114.

[50] Julius Stone, *Aggression and World Order: A Critique of United Nations Theories of Aggression*, Berkeley, University of California Press, 1958.

1. Malaysia was created in violation of the Manila Agreements because (a) Malaya undermined the settlement by its premature announcement, and (b) the UN mission team did not conduct a survey that established the wishes of the inhabitants of Sabah and Sarawak;

2. The military presence of Great Britain in Malaysia posed a threat to the regional security of Southeast Asia,[51]

3. The proposals for Mushawarah Maphilindo amounted to efforts in good faith to find a prior peaceful settlement for the disputes between Indonesia and the Philippines and Malaysia.[52]

An adversary presentation of Confrontation could then be based on the rules and procedures of international law. It is also helpful to realize that the assertion of claims by Indonesia and the Philippines and counterclaims by Malaysia is part of the interaction process by which international disputes are resolved, community expectations as to a reasonable settlement are formed, and degrees of legitimacy and illegitimacy are attached to the opposing positions by the responses made by third-party states and by international institutions.[53]

A few days after the Manila meeting of Sukarno and Macapagal, President Lyndon B. Johnson asked Robert F. Kennedy, then Attorney General, to bring about an end of the Malaysian conflict. Presumably recalling the successful role played by the third-party intervention of the United States in the last stages of the West Irian dispute, the American hope was evidently to explore whether this second instance of Confrontation diplomacy could not also be ended through the good offices of the United States.[54] Kennedy's mission did meet with an immediate, if limited and temporary success—as on January 23, 1964 during Kennedy's visit to Djakarta, Sukarno announced Indonesian adherence to a cease-fire in Malaysia, although he did assert that the "Crush Malaysia" policy would continue, even if its tactics might change. Kennedy also affirmed the basic Indonesian insistence that Asian problems be solved by Asian countries, not by outsiders, and encouraged the reconvening of tripartite talks first at the ministerial and then at the summit level. In both respects the aftermath of Kennedy's January visit

[51] The United States has insisted upon the same line of argument in opposing the extension of Communist influence to the western hemisphere in the period since World War II, as well as in opposing the extension of Fascist and Nazi influence during World War II. For an account see Falk, "The United States and the Doctrine of Nonintervention in the Internal Affairs of Independent States," 5 *Harvard Law Journal* 163 (June 1959).

[52] Cf. e.g. Article 33(1) of the United Nations Charter: "The parties to any dispute, the continuance of which is likely to endanger the maintenance of international peace and security, shall, first of all, seek a solution by negotiation, enquiry, mediation, conciliation, arbitration, judicial settlement, resort to regional agencies or arrangements, or other peaceful means of their own choice."

[53] For an account of this process see the studies contained in Myres S. McDougal and Associates, *Studies in World Public Order*, New Haven, Yale University Press, 1960.

[54] See Brackman, note 26 *supra*, pp. 101-14, 214-17.

appeared to confirm the value of his visit: a cease-fire of sorts was proclaimed and maintained in the Borneo territories and tripartite meetings were arranged for Bangkok in early February. Asian diplomacy involving Cambodia and Thailand, as well as the three protagonists, sought to establish a political climate suitable for a second summit. Rahman demanded Indonesian withdrawal as well as a cease-fire, but Sukarno refused to withdraw Indonesian guerrillas from Malaysian territories unless British troops were simultaneously withdrawn.[55]

The Maphilindo theme was again accented in the Joint Communiqué of the Bangkok Ministerial Meeting issued on February 11, 1964. Once again the text of the document was couched in the phraseology of Mushawarah Maphilindo, and once again the Manila Agreements were made the baseline for a settlement of the underlying dispute.[56] The Communiqué confirmed the cease-fire originally proclaimed during the Kennedy mission with regard to fighting in Sabah and Sarawak. A new component added by the Bangkok meetings was bringing in Thailand as a mediating state, evidently in response to Malaysia's request for a neutral state, a request contained in its January 13 reply to the Joint Statement of Sukarno and Macapagal issued two days earlier in Manila.[57] The Bangkok Communiqué indicated in Paragraph 6 that the three states "agreed to invite the Secretary-General of the United Nations to designate Thailand to supervise the ceasefire." Inviting the Secretary-General to designate Thailand is a striking acknowledgment of the legitimizing role of the United Nations, an acknowledgment that is not common in multilateral negotiations and is not characteristic in great power approaches to peaceful settlement.[58] As Malaysia did not include this feature in its original suggestion of neutral supervision it would seem reasonable to attribute its appearance at Bangkok to Indonesian diplomacy.

The use of formal documents to establish expectations of the parties at the end of a multilateral meeting was a characteristic feature of the diplomacy that involved the dispute about Malaysia.[59] The Manila Agreements acquired an aura of legitimacy that was sustained despite their failure to deal with the provoking cause of Confrontation—the British presence. Such an ascriptive legitimacy illustrates the ways in

---

[55] See Mezerik, pp. 44-45.

[56] For text of the Bangkok communiqué see Mezerik, pp. 114-15.

[57] To select Thailand as the third-party intermediary bears witness to Indonesia's conciliatory attitude at this juncture. After all Thailand was of all Asian states the most pro-Western in orientation, a member of SEATO, and generally opposed to the foreign policy and domestic programs

associated with Indonesia.

[58] See Inis L. Claude, Jr., "Collective Legitimization as a Political Function of the United Nations," *International Organization*, xx (Summer 1966), 367-79.

[59] This basis for a negotiated settlement was not characteristic of the West Irian dispute in which Indonesia's claim was posited in the form of a unilateral demand to receive satisfaction.

which international norms—stable expectations about permissible out-comes—are established in the course of diplomatic interaction. Also despite the enlarging and overt intervention of Indonesian armed forces in Sabah and Sarawak over the period from September 1963 to Febru-ary 1964 a considerable ideological basis for peaceful settlement evolved. The tripartite meetings resulted in an affirmation of Mush-awarah Maphilindo, in both its aspects—the meeting together and the search for solidarity, in the midst of an armed struggle reinforced by shrill invective.

On the formal level Indonesia appeared to be quite reasonable in seeking an ordered solution to its dispute with Malaysia. In deeds, how-ever, there appeared to be little clear evidence of an Indonesian disposi-tion to end Confrontation, although it is not clear that Malaysia ever offered Indonesia anything in exchange, even of a face-saving variety. Malaysia insisted that a cease-fire could only be implemented by arrang-ing the withdrawal of Indonesian troops, regulars and irregulars, whereas Indonesia contended that a cease-fire did not imply withdrawal and that it was not willing to withdraw until an overall political solution was reached. In the interim Indonesia claimed the right to reequip its troops and to have them hold their positions within Malaysian territory.

President Macapagal, sensing the redeterioration of the situation, sought to mediate once again by a state visit to Sukarno in Djakarta. On February 28, 1964 a Joint Communiqué was issued by the two lead-ers that reaffirmed Indonesia's adherence to (a) the cease-fire and (b) "reiterated their faith in the wisdom of solving Asian problems by Asians themselves in an Asian fashion and trust that the constructive and brotherly Mushawarah is inherent in the Asian way of finding solu-tions to common problems." The Joint Communiqué also called for a "summit Mushawarah" that would seek "a peaceful settlement of the problems of the region, without pre-condition, at a place and date still to be determined."[60]

In the succeeding months two opposed developments took place. First, the guerrilla fighting in Sabah and Sarawak resumed, and the rhetoric of the "Crush Malaysia" campaign was intensified. Second, diplomatic efforts to implement the cease-fire by searching for a way to secure the withdrawal of Indonesian troops from Malaysian territory and by seek-ing agreement on the preconditions for a second tripartite summit were continued. Thailand played a role as intermediary in this effort, and in June 1964 a provisional agreement was reached on withdrawal checkpoints on both sides of the Indonesian border. Some withdrawals of Indonesian troops were actually verified by Thai observers.[61] On this basis, a summit was scheduled for June 20, 1964 in Tokyo, preceded

60 Cf. Mezerik, p. 45.   61 Mezerik, p. 46.

by two days of meetings at the ministerial level. Shortly beforehand, the Malaysian posture of Rahman and his party toward Indonesia had been confirmed by a major election victory.

The Tokyo meeting failed to bring the dispute to an end, quickly stumbling over the familiar negotiating obstacles. Rahman insisted that all Indonesian troops be withdrawn within four weeks, withdrawal being an absolute precondition for a discussion of other elements in "the dispute." President Macapagal proposed a four-member Afro-Asian Conciliation Commission to be constituted by the appointment of one member each by Indonesia, Malaysia, and the Philippines, the fourth member being chosen by the unanimous agreement of the other three. The Tokyo summit meeting endorsed the idea of the Afro-Asian Conciliation Commission in its Final Communiqué. The Commission was called upon "to study the existing problems between the three countries and to submit recommendations for their solution."[62] Sukarno gave strong assurances that he was favorable to this approach and that Indonesia would abide by any recommendations made by the Commission. Malaysia, too, in its draft communiqué which was rejected by Indonesia because of its insistence on prior withdrawal, "agreed . . . in principle" to the establishment of the Commission "for the purpose of normalizing relations" among the three countries.[63]

The Tokyo meeting appeared to harden the adverse positions of the disputants. Both sides sought to intensify their campaign to secure international support of an economic, ideological, and diplomatic variety. Malaysia turned increasingly toward the West, Indonesia toward the Communist powers. The Confrontation became gradually transformed into an Asian phase of the global struggle going on between the forces of Communism and anti-Communism. The United States especially, abandoned its earlier pretense of neutrality to take the side of Malaysia. Indonesia received during the early months of 1964 increasing military assistance from the Soviet Union in the form of modern equipment. The guerrilla war in Malaysian territory was gradually expanded in scale and scope, with overflight and terroristic incidents being reported on the Malayan peninsula, as well as in Sabah and Sarawak. Rahman visited the United States in late July to rally greater support for Malaysia. On August 17 Malaysia reported to the United Nations about armed incursions into Malayan territory by Indonesian irregulars. Subandrio denied such allegations as "mere fabrications." But on September 2 an Indonesian aircraft flying over Malaya was observed dropping a band of about thirty armed paratroopers, who were subsequently captured.

[62] For text of Tokyo communiqué see Mezerik, p. 115.

[63] For text of rejected Malaysian communiqué see Mezerik, pp. 116-17.

At this point Malaysia requested an urgent meeting of the Security Council to consider its allegations of Indonesian aggression. The ensuing Security Council debate in September was the high point of the efforts of each side to mobilize support for its position by arguing in favor of the legitimacy of its claims. Just prior to the Security Council debates severe rioting took place in Singapore resulting in thirteen deaths and in the arrest of 800.[64] This rioting was provoked by racial tensions in Singapore and seemed largely independent of the dispute with Indonesia, although it did show the world some of the fragility of the Malaysian Federation.

The Security Council Debate. The Security Council debate was directed at the Malaysian complaint about a specific act of Indonesian aggression, the paratroop landing in Malaya on September 1 and 2, 1964.[65] This "blatant and inexcusable aggression against a peaceful neighbor" was the basis for requesting this "urgent meeting" of the Security Council. Underlying the Malaysian complaint was its contention that the whole Indonesian policy of Confrontation was a disturbance of international peace, especially insofar as it included the sponsorship of guerrilla activities being carried on within Malaysian territory.

The various positions taken in the Security Council during the discussions of the Malaysian complaint witnessed a sharp clash between Western-oriented conceptions of world order and the most militant postcolonial Afro-Asian conceptions. The representatives of Indonesia and Malaysia made long statements in the Security Council that recapitulated the dispute since its inception in 1963. The non-Communist Members of the Security Council, including Bolivia, Brazil, Ivory Coast, and Morocco opposed Indonesia; only the Soviet Union and Czechoslovakia favored the Indonesian interpretation of the dispute. The United States and the United Kingdom were most vigorous in their verbal denunciations of Indonesia's position, not only with regard to the specific allegation of aggression that was before the Council, but more generally, in denouncing Indonesia's overall espousal of Confrontation. The consequence of the debate in the Security Council was to give the impression that Indonesia's position was rejected by the majority of the organized international community, including the nonaligned and Afro-Asian portions of it.

International law entered prominently into the discussion. Supporters of the Malaysian complaint rested their case on the rather clear-cut incompatibility between an unrepudiated recourse to force by Indonesia

[64] Mezerik, p. 91.
[65] Consideration by the Security Council was initiated by a complaint contained in a letter of September 3, 1964 from the Permanent Representative of Malaysia at the United Nations to the President of the Security Council. Document S/5930.

and the requirements of the Charter. Indonesia and its Communist supporters brushed aside the specific allegation of aggression and concentrated upon developing an argument on the merits of Indonesia's Confrontation policy. Indonesia's argument was essentially that Malaysia was a neocolonialist creation fabricated to perpetuate British influence in the area. Indonesia reinforced this argument by reference to its desire for a peaceful settlement, first in the form of its early friendship with Malaya in the pre-Malaysia period, then by its willingness to work toward a peaceful accommodation with Malaysia within the Manila framework, and finally, by its continuing adherence to Maphilindo as the way out, an adherence manifested most recently by Sukarno's declaration that Indonesia was prepared to accept any recommendations made by the Afro-Asian Conciliation Commission that had been proposed at the Tokyo summit meeting.

In the Security Council the decisive issue from the perspective of international law was whether Indonesia's line of argumentation had any relevance. There is no entirely satisfactory way to resolve this issue. It is possible to construe the 9-2 vote in favor of the Norwegian resolution as a repudiation of Indonesia's line of contention; more legalistically, it is possible to maintain that the Soviet Union's negative vote was a veto that prevented the Security Council from reaching any conclusion, as formally the Council took no action on Malaysia's complaint and the Norwegian resolution was not adopted.[66]

Alternatively, one might examine the argumentation itself and seek to determine the relative persuasiveness of the contending positions. Adlai Stevenson, the Representative of the United States in the Security Council at the time, referred to Indonesia's position as "a new and dangerous doctrine of international law outside the Charter of the United Nations." He referred to the large number of active international disputes and pointed out that "If other nations involved in these disputes were to take the law into their own hands, drop armed forces on the territory of their neighbors, the precarious peace of our inflammable world would soon go up in smoke."[67] Stevenson relied heavily on the clear incompatibility between the Charter obligation to settle disputes peacefully and Indonesia's use of force against Malaysia for purposes other than self-defense.

Sudjarwo replied on behalf of Indonesia that this condemnation of Indonesia's position "is rather strange when it comes from the representative of the United States," and asked whether Stevenson had "forgotten occurrences, to mention only recent events, such as the 'Bay

<hr>

66 The Resolution introduced by Norway is Document S/5973; text reproduced by Mezerik, pp. 117-18 and in Appendix A, p. 632.
67 SCOR, 1145th Mtg., para 24, p. 5.

of Pigs' and 'Tonkin' affair?" The Indonesian representative analogized recourse to force by the United States in its dispute with Cuba to the Indonesian claim to use force against Malaysia. Sudjarwo contended, furthermore, that it is not *the fact* that force is used that determines its legal status, but rather the acceptability of *the justification* for its use. In this instance such a justification, according to Sudjarwo, depended on a fair examination of the British colonial record, consisting of exploitation and dominance, and of the use of the territory of Malaysia to molest the independence of Indonesia. Indonesia argued that the United States had used its great influence in the past to keep complaints about American uses of force from being considered by the Security Council, but with respect to Indonesia the United States was adopting a sanctimonious attitude about the literal character of Charter commitments.

There is no question that the United States has claimed for itself considerable discretion to use force within the territory of foreign states in situations other than self-defense. The military intervention of the United States in the Dominican Republic in 1965 provides a particularly clear example. In replying to critics of this undertaking, the Legal Adviser to the Secretary of State, Leonard Meeker, chided those who argued that such action was illegal with taking a fundamentalist attitude toward international law, and urged a greater appreciation of the need to reconcile the constraints of law with the realities of international conflict.[68]

Assuming that the United States has used force outside the Charter limits, how does such use affect the status of Indonesia's position vis-à-vis Malaysia? Even if such a demonstration of American practice in analogous situations would establish the proposition that the United States was being hypocritical about its condemnation of Indonesia, or that it was claiming for itself a discretionary right to use force that it was unwilling to grant Indonesia, why should such a double standard deprive Malaysia of the protection of the Charter?

This last question seems to depict the underlying issue for international legal order. It points toward the "legislative" status of international practice inconsistent with rules incorporated in documents such as the United Nations Charter.[69] Not every violation of a rule is a legislative revision of it, but if the violations are frequent enough or if their commission is vindicated or even acquiesced in by a consensus of the

[68] Leonard Meeker, "The Dominican Situation in the Perspective of International Law," *U.S. State Department Bulletin*, LIII (July 12, 1965), 60-65.
[69] For explanation see Falk, "On the Quasi-Legislative Competence of the General Assembly," 60 *American Journal of International Law* 782-91 (Oct. 1966); in general, see Oscar Schachter, "The Relation of Law, Politics, and Action in the United Nations," 109 *Recueil des Cours* 169-256 (1963).

members of international society then a legislative claim seems to be established. In this respect the opposition of the Latin American and other non-Western Members of the Security Council to Indonesia's position is of some significance and should be contrasted with the response to the Portuguese complaint about India's use of force against Goa in 1961.[70] India's claim to use force rested upon the illegitimacy of maintaining colonial title to a territorial enclave, whereas Indonesia's claim rested upon the illegitimacy of a neocolonialist political unit that had the characteristics of a sovereign state, including membership in the United Nations.

Therefore, it would seem possible to conclude that although some of Indonesia's main opponents in the Security Council had less than clean hands on the matter of Charter compliance, nevertheless there was insufficient support for Indonesia's case to give it much legislative status as a precedent looking toward the expansion of the occasions upon which it is legally permissible to use force. It should be appreciated, however, that in addition to the patterns of American practice (and supporting justification), both the Communist and the Afro-Asian groupings claim the right to use force to support in the first instance "wars of national liberation"[71] and in the second instance, force against the states in southern Africa that are either colonialist or racist in character. Given these broad claims to establish exceptions to the Charter system of constraints, it is at least arguable that there is no effective international law applicable to uses of force by one state against another, especially if the force used is of an unconventional variety that does not involve "war" in the traditional sense. "Confrontation" is a species, at worst, of "indirect aggression," and it is arguable that this form of international violence, including military responses to it by third powers, presently eludes legal control.[72]

Undoubtedly Indonesia's failure to receive more support in the Security Council contributed to Sukarno's subsequent decision to withdraw from the United Nations. The debate produced only the relatively mild Norwegian resolution of censure. A resolution cannot be adopted officially if any permanent member of the Security Council casts a negative vote; as the Soviet Union did vote against the Norwegian resolution it was not officially adopted. The resolution, although using fairly in-

---

[70] For the Goa debate see SCOR, Mtgs. 987-88, December 18-19, 1961; an interpretation of these events is offered in Falk, "The New States and International Legal Order," Hague Academy of International Law, *Recueil des Cours*, 1-102 (1966).

[71] There is, of course, considerable ambiguity surrounding the idea of "support" and concerning the identification of what constitutes "a war of national liberation." What levels of support are forbidden by international law and what kinds of support provoke countervailing geopolitical pressures?

[72] For an argument to this effect see Falk, *op.cit. supra*, note 27, Chap. IV, pp. 109-55.

direct language, in effect endorsed the Malaysian position rather completely. It *"deplores* the incident" that gave rise to the Malaysian complaint and *"Calls upon* the parties to refrain from all threat or use of force and to respect the territorial integrity and political independence of each other, and thus to create a conducive atmosphere for the continuation of their talks." Only "thereupon" does it call for an implementation of the Tokyo arrangement to create an Afro-Asian Conciliation Commission entrusted with recommending a solution.

This Resolution supported by nine-elevenths of the Security Council closely resembles the Malaysian view on "pre-conditions"[73]—namely, (1) acknowledging the validity of Malaysia as a political entity endowed with the attributes of sovereignty and (2) termination of the military aspects of "Confrontation" prior to talks on a settlement, including apparently both cease-fire and withdrawal. After satisfying these preconditions the issues that constituted the dispute remained: (1) self-determination for the Borneo territories; (2) consideration of the Philippines' claim to Sabah; and (3) agreement on the nature, size, and duration of the British military presence in Malaysia. However, it is hard to imagine how Indonesia, or the Philippines, could exert much leverage, especially as the voting rules of the Commission proposed at Tokyo were never laid down, and its mandate was, at best, only to make recommendations.

From the perspective of international law the outcome of the debates in the Security Council were quite ambiguous. Certainly a consensus repudiated Indonesia and supported Malaysia, despite the absence of formal action. The Indonesian reaction to such a repudiation was to turn against the United Nations and to attack the Organization as a hostile environment for a new state eager to carry on the struggle against the forces of reaction and neocolonialism. A second reaction by Indonesia was to move closer in alignment with China and the Soviet Union. And a third reaction was once again to step up the pace of guerrilla activity both in the Borneo territories and on the Malayan mainland, as well as virtually to abandon the conciliation motif.

Withdrawal from the United Nations. Indonesia's disenchantment with the United Nations was a partial consequence of its diplomacy of Confrontation. This disenchantment began, it would appear, in September 1963 when the Secretary-General issued his Report confirming the wishes of the inhabitants of Sabah and Sarawak to join Malaysia. Sukarno subsequently suggested a second survey by the United Nations to resolve the self-determination issue. There was, then, an inclination by

---

[73] See e.g. Malaysian reply to the Philippine-Indonesian Joint Communiqué of Jan. 11, 1964; text reprinted in Mezerik, pp. 112-13.

Indonesia early in the dispute to treat the Secretary-General, acting on behalf of the United Nations, as an impartial and authoritative decision-maker capable of resolving the controversy. It hardly seems plausible that a nation would refer these issues to the United Nations unless there had been some disposition to act in accordance with its recommendations. And it is the case, as the reaction of the Philippines bears out, that the Secretary-General did not conduct the survey of Sabah and Sarawak in a manner that would allow confidence to attach to its results, especially in view of his rather weak reaction to Malaya's premature announcement of the date on which Malaysia was to be formed. Such an experience might cause Indonesia to feel that its original confidence in the United Nations had been unwarranted.

Indonesia also resented the rapid acceptance of Malaysia as a Member of the United Nations on September 17, 1963, an acceptance that took place at a time when Indonesia questioned the legitimacy of the Federation. Such an acceptance can easily be contrasted with the long-sustained exclusion of mainland China from the organization. A contrast of this sort, especially given Indonesia's sensitivity about its status in the world, confirmed the view that the United Nations was controlled by the reactionary forces in the world.

The more general conditioning factor was the Western control of the United Nations, especially the Security Council. This was expressed forcibly during the debate on Goa in 1961, but became more relevant for Indonesia during the September 1964 debates. If Sukarno believed that international society was the scene of a sharp struggle between OLDEFO (Old Emerging Forces) and NEFO (New Emerging Forces), then it was reasonable to believe that the United Nations was in the control of OLDEFO and a parallel structure was needed to establish greater legitimacy for the claims of NEFO.

The event immediately precipitating withdrawal was the selection of Malaysia on December 30, 1964 to be a member of the Security Council. This development provoked Sukarno to say in the course of a speech on the following day that if Malaysia was seated in the Security Council, then Indonesia would quit the organization. Malaysia was seated on January 1, 1965 and Indonesia formally withdrew a few days later.

Subandrio in his letter of withdrawal addressed to the Secretary-General refers to the Indonesian decision as "a revolutionary one," but one that "could well entail a beneficial effect for the speedy solution of the problem of 'Malaysia' itself."[74] Two sets of important questions were posed for the international legal order by Indonesia's withdrawal: (1) the relation of the United Nations to a nonmember and (2) the pos-

[74] Letter dated January 20, 1965 addressed to the Secretary-General, U.N. Document A/5857. Text in Mezerik, pp. 120-22.

sibility of a rival international organization purporting to be an independent and equivalent source of authority vis-à-vis the world community.[75]

Article 2(6) of the Charter claims control over nonmember states to the extent necessary to maintain international peace and security. There is, thus, a legal basis for a continuing role for the United Nations subsequent to withdrawal, especially in a context disturbing to international peace. As a practical matter, however, the authority of the United Nations seems to depend heavily at this stage upon a voluntary attitude of deference toward its views by states in dispute. Indonesia's withdrawal seemed to symbolize its refusal to accord the Organization any further deference; the United Nations has not attempted to exert much influence on the behavior of mainland China, its principal nonmember.

With China excluded and Indonesia withdrawn, there did exist a real danger that the position of the United Nations as a center of international legal authority would be undermined. China and Indonesia threatened to establish a rival organization, a threat that was not carried out because no other states were willing to abandon the United Nations as of early 1965. The other kind of danger to the position of the United Nations was to remind disenchanted Members, especially states like Portugal and South Africa, of their withdrawal option and its bargaining potential.[76] Such a timely withdrawal by these states, although stimulated by reasoning opposite to that provoking Indonesia's decision, might have undermined the authority of the United Nations to speak with the legal voice of the organized community of mankind. In this regard, it is relevant to recall that the failures of the League of Nations were accented by a series of withdrawals by disenchanted members.[77]

The point brought home by Indonesia's withdrawal is that whatever legitimacy is enjoyed by the United Nations derives largely from the voluntary participation in its activities by almost all states, including especially the enterprise of community conciliation that such participation implies. Universality or quasi-universality is the keystone of a voluntary association of sovereign states; the loss of this keystone may well endanger the entire structure of authority that it supports. In effect, Indonesia's withdrawal, although short-lived, did serve to reveal the fragile foundation of United Nations authority and should, perhaps, prompt a renewed effort to approximate more closely the ideals of universal membership.

[75] For a general discussion see Chapter VII.

[76] The authority of the United Nations rests, in part, on its global and quasi-universal character. States under pressure could threaten withdrawal and by this threat possibly inhibit the United Nations, as the implementations of the threat would almost certainly weaken the organization.

[77] For a brief account see Francis P. Walters, *A History of the League of Nations*, esp. Chaps. 27 and 33, London, Oxford University Press, 1952.

Furthermore, the option of withdrawal clarifies the limits of United Nations authority in normal circumstances, as it emphasizes the costs to the Organization of completely alienating a state that has any substantial political role in international society. These limits may not apply if the state in question is as isolated as Portugal and South Africa appear to be; Indonesia, it should be recalled, received overt support throughout Confrontation from the Communist powers and sympathy from several militant anti-Western new states (e.g., Cambodia).[78] Besides, such pro-Western states as Thailand and the Philippines were careful to refrain from taking sides. Indonesia, then, was not nearly so isolated in the international system as it appeared to be in the Security Council debates.

It is interesting to note that the local and small-scale violence between Indonesia and Malaysia provoked an authority crisis of the first magnitude in the world community.

Termination of Confrontation. The drift of Confrontation into a full-scale cold war conflict was abruptly halted by the drastic political changes that ensued in Indonesia after the abortive coup of September 1 to October 1, 1965.[79] After domestic political control shifted from Sukarno to General Suharto in the aftermath of the countercoup and wide-scale purge resulting in the death of anywhere from 300,000 to 1,200,000 Indonesians, there was a notable determination by the Indonesian government to detach itself from the Communist orbits of influence and seek friendly relations with the West—no better way to signal this shift could be found than to repudiate the militant approach of Sukarno on the Malaysian class of issues and to resume participation in the affairs of the United Nations. In the hectic weeks immediately following the coup there were ritualistic reaffirmations of the Confrontation policy, but once the domestic situation in Indonesia calmed down it was evident that the era of Confrontation diplomacy was at an end, temporarily at least.

On June 1, 1966, normalization was negotiated at Bangkok in a very simple bilateral document drawn up at a meeting on the ministerial level.[80] The Bangkok Accord, as the document is known, was officially ratified and brought into force by the two countries on August 11, 1966. The Bangkok Accord involves an element of reciprocal obligation. In Article 1 Malaysia "agrees to afford the people of Sabah and Sarawak who are directly involved, an opportunity to reaffirm, as soon as practicable, in a free and democratic manner through General Elections,

[78] Indonesia's influence was also illustrated by the partial success of its efforts to exclude Malaysia from formal or active informal participation in Afro-Asian affairs during the period of the dispute.

[79] For a preliminary assessment see Brackman, note 26 *supra*, pp. 284-99.

[80] For an analysis see Michael Leifer, "Indonesia and Malaysia: The Changing Face of Confrontation," *The World Today* (Sept. 1966), 395-405.

their previous decision about their status in Malaysia," Article 2 looks toward the exchange of diplomatic representatives and entails Indonesian acknowledgment of the legitimacy of Malaysia as a sovereign state. And Artiel 3 affirms that "hostile acts between the two countries shall cease forthwith."[81] The political implementation of the Bangkok Accord seems fully successful and there are indications of renewed interest in working out subregional cooperation of the Malay peoples on security and economic matters. It is worth noting that the settlement of the dispute did not involve an explicit renunciation of Indonesian demands, but rather contained a formula that accorded them nominal deference—namely, the agreement to ascertain the wishes of the inhabitants of Sabah and Sarawak.

Indonesia's return to the United Nations followed a parallel path. The appointment of Adam Malik as Foreign Minister in March 1966 appears to have been the decisive act. As late as May 1966, however, Sukarno reiterated his view that Indonesia should remain outside the United Nations unless certain changes were made in its structure. But Malik was increasingly definite about his intention to return to the United Nations and by August, Sukarno, too, supported the move to return, a move acted upon shortly thereafter.

Indonesia's return to the United Nations thereby ended the crisis of authority provoked by its withdrawal a year and a half earlier. Such a return to the established structures of international authority was avowedly part of the effort of the new Indonesian leadership to pursue a more conservative foreign policy, a foreign policy that would be compatible with the receipt of economic aid from the West. It was evident that Confrontation had been a costly diplomatic adventure for Indonesia. Not only were there the military costs associated with supporting the guerrilla effort within Malaysian territory, but foreign trade with Singapore, a major source of Indonesian foreign exchange, had been terminated and Western economic assistance ended. These economic sacrifices associated with Confrontation were abetted by Indonesia's failure to achieve significant economic growth and by an inflation of runaway proportions.

Conclusions. In several respects, international law was relevant to the course of the Malaysia-Indonesia dispute:

1. *Stable Expectations.* At each stage of the dispute the parties sought to formulate an agreed statement that contained the results of their efforts to reach a settlement. Departure from these agreed statements was later perceived as "violations" by the aggrieved party. The

[81] Cf. issues of *News and Views* for background and relevant texts, including the Bangkok Accord, during the period between May 1, 1966 and August 30, 1966, issues Nos. 136-95.

consequence of this pattern is to inject a law element into an encounter between states. Without this law element the encounter would more easily degenerate into unmitigated conflict resolvable only by the clash of wills and arms; with this law element there is a braking mechanism that allows the disputing parties a certain flexibility to accelerate, decelerate, or even halt the conflict.

This process can be illustrated by reference to the Manila Conference held in 1963. That Conference led to the Manila Accords which proposed a reassessment of the wishes of the inhabitants of the Borneo territories to be carried out under the auspices of the Secretary-General to assure that their inclusion in the Federation was consistent with the principle of self-determination. In an accompanying Statement the disputing states affirmed their commitment to regional solidarity and to an Asian solution for Asian problems. Of course, a series of subsequent events undermined the Manila solution, but nevertheless the framework for settlement established at Manila remained the basis for efforts at conciliation up to and including the termination of the dispute at Bangkok in 1966. In a quite different setting, the Geneva Accords of 1954 have been invoked by all parties to the conflict in South Vietnam as containing the guidelines upon which a restoration of peace could be based. The extent of departure from the Manila Accords by each side is a matter of interpretation, but the reference back to those guidelines created a legal structure to which adversary diplomacy might revert from time to time.

2. *Political Mobilization.* Recourse to legal arguments by the adversary states in various international arenas was designed to mobilize support and neutralize opposition. Malaysia's greatest success, of course, was to complain about being the victim of unprovoked and illegal uses of force by Indonesia; such an argument was appealing to the Western powers and it went a long way to neutralize opposition from the non-aligned states to the neocolonialist elements in the Malaysian context. The highwater mark of Malaysian diplomacy in this latter regard was its success in acquiring support from all nine non-Communist members of the Security Council, including the Ivory Coast and Morocco, during the debates of September 1964. Indonesia, in contrast, relied upon arguments about the illegitimacy of neocolonial regimes bolstered by a continuing military and economic role by the ex-colonial power to rally support for itself in the Communist world and to solicit sympathy throughout the Afro-Asian world. The highwater mark of Indonesian diplomacy in this latter regard was the exclusion of Malaysia from the 1964 Cairo Meeting of the Non-Aligned, although Malaysia possessed all of the qualifications needed to participate including the wish to do so.

In general, the rhetoric of international law was used as an instrument of diplomatic persuasion by the participants in the dispute to demonstrate either the unreasonableness of the other side or to demonstrate the underlying justice of one's own cause. The effect on behavior is difficult to measure, but it is not implausible to contend that the weakness of Indonesia's case against Malaysia in legal terms had an effect on the relative failure of Indonesia to be successful in political terms. In this regard, Indonesia's success in the West Irian Case was in part at least explicable by the fact that its Confrontation diplomacy, including threats and uses of military force in violation of the Charter, was based upon a legal case plausible enough to attract support from independent jurists.[82]

3. *Signaling Intentions.* International law provides actors with symbols by which they can communicate intentions, including demands for rectification. Indonesia and the Philippines withheld recognition from Malaysia to signal their intention to regard the Federation as an "illegitimate" entity. The United Kingdom signaled its intention to remain a military presence in Southeast Asia by undertaking broad security functions as specified in the 1957 Agreement with Malaya and as renewed and extended in 1963. Malaysia's insistence on "pre-conditions" to settlement—withdrawal of Indonesian troops—conveyed its intention to refuse negotiations until Indonesia ceased to rely upon military intimidation; the norm of aggression was invoked to clarify the basis of Malaysia's refusal "to settle" the dispute so long as Confrontation diplomacy continued in its unabated form.

4. *Supranationalism.* Throughout the period of Confrontation there were repeated efforts to refer the dispute to a supranational forum. The original effort to avert a crisis at Manila in 1963 was highly supranational in character, inviting third-party intervention by the Secretary-General on the self-determination issue and looking toward a political settlement by means of creating a Maphilindo framework. Later on at Bangkok, Thailand was called upon to verify the agreed withdrawal of Indonesian troops from the Borneo territory. The Tokyo summit meeting recommended the establishment of a four-power Asian Conciliation Commission. Malaysia had recourse to the Security Council to complain about Indonesia's armed intervention in Malaya. These main efforts to rely upon the supranational resources of international society to resolve a predominantly bilateral dispute are an interesting reflection of new trends in crisis diplomacy, although the actual settlement was achieved by traditional nation-to-nation diplomacy.

The essence of legal order is the impartial determination of conflicting claims that arise between parties to a dispute. International

---

[82] E.g., B.V.A. Röling, *Nieuw Guinea, als wereld probleem* (New Guinea World Problem), Assen, The Netherlands, Van Gorcum, 1958.

legal order is basically decentralized, the extent of impartiality injected into a settlement of a dispute being a reflection of whatever adjustment is reached through the interaction of claims and counterclaims. Unless the parties are reasonably protective of each other's interests—not common in adversary settings—the tendency is for any kind of serious dispute to be resolved by ultimate reference to the relative power that each actually or potentially can bring to bear. As such, conflict resolution works to the grave disadvantage of the weaker party; the outcome of "legal" interaction is not sharply separable from the outcome reached by the application of naked force. To the extent, however, that supranational decision-makers are introduced into the context of dispute, there is a greater tendency to determine the dispute by reference to considerations other than the relative power of the disputants. This equalizing impact is, in effect, a consequence of the third-party resolution of an international dispute. When conciliatory, Indonesia stressed the role of third-party settlement procedure, whereas when antagonistic, insisted upon sovereign prerogatives to proceed against Malaysia in whatever manner it deemed warranted.

5. *Regionalism.* Indonesia's insistence, one supported even by the adverse Norwegian resolution in the Security Council and by Robert Kennedy's efforts to mediate the dispute, was that the proper mode of settlement was by Asian countries in brotherly concert. This claim of regional autonomy has important implications for the structure of world order and is paralleled by analogous claims made by the Organization of African Unity in response to Operation Stanleyville and by the Organization of American States in response to several hemispheric disputes. Such support for the regionalization of international disputes suggests an effort to insulate Afro-Asian instabilities from great-power interventions. If some kind of strong tradition of regional autonomy were to emerge with the support of both great powers and the Afro-Asian states, an improvement in the quality of world order might result.

In terms of traditional conceptions of international law, the growth of a regional competence to influence what is permitted national conduct and what is prohibited is a very significant development. A regional basis for legitimizing and delegitimizing national action establishes a community-based international law to complement the traditional sovereignty based international law. Furthermore, the insistence on a primary regional jurisdiction to control the settlement of disputes between members of a region is a significant attempt in the Asian (or African) context to safeguard independence from the great powers in the post-colonial context. As law evolves out of the expectations of the community of its subjects, it is most interesting and significant to take full account of the stress upon the legitimacy of regional settlement procedures and the illegitimacy of recourse to extraregional actors throughout the period of Confrontation. Indonesia's emphasis on the "neocolonial" impact of Britain's military presence in Malaysia seemed to draw some strength from the appeal to the principle of regional autonomy.

THE Indonesia-Malaysia dispute, in short, is quite susceptible to analysis from the perspective of international law. In fact, it is a revealing instance of diplomatic and legal interaction that is distinctively Asian in character. International lawyers may tend to underestimate the interest of this dispute either because their perception of it was slanted against Indonesia by the Western presentation of the argument, or because the new regime in Djakarta so quickly abandoned the Indonesian position. A closer scrutiny suggests that Indonesia had a credible, if somewhat novel, legal argument to support its claims vis-à-vis Malaysia, and that the argument is an extreme example of the sort of revisionist outlook that is becoming more and more explicit in the attitudes and behavior of the Afro-Asian group of states.[83]

[83] Cf. Final Act of the United Nations Conference on Trade and Development, E/Conf. 46/L.28, June 16, 1964.

V. An Argument to Expand the Traditional Sources of International Law— with Special Reference to the Facts of the South West Africa Cases

1

THE SECOND paragraph of Article 2 of the Mandate for South West Africa provides: "The Mandatory shall promote to the utmost the material and moral well-being and the social progress of the inhabitants of the Territory subject to the present Mandate." The most interesting and significant issue of substance presented by the *South West Africa Cases* was whether the practice of apartheid by South Africa was compatible with the obligations of the Mandatory set forth in the provision quoted above. Of course, the majority opinion of the International Court of Justice disposed of the complaints submitted by Ethiopia and Liberia by determining that these states lacked the legal interest to enforce "the conduct provisions" of the Mandate and, consequently, never discussed the legal status of apartheid.[1] Several of the dissenting judges, however, refused the guidance of the President of the Court, Sir Percy Spender, and proceeded to examine this central legal issue.[2] The parties to the dispute, as well, devoted extensive attention in their oral and written pleadings to developing arguments supportive of their opposite legal conclusions as to the compatibility of apartheid with Article 2(2) of the Mandate.

This legal question is of considerable jurisprudential interest as it raises a very intricate question touching upon "the sources" of international law. At issue, most fundamentally, is the establishment of legal criteria by which to construe the significance of "well-being" within the context of the Mandate. Ethiopia and Liberia relied upon two principal theories to support their contentions that apartheid violated the Mandate:

> (1) The continuous and virtually unanimous condemnation of *apartheid* by the institutions of the organized international community established the conclusion that *apartheid* was incompatible with the well-being of the inhabitants of South West Africa, at least as

[1] See Chap. XII for full analysis along these lines of *South West Africa, Second Phase, Judgment, ICJ Reports 1966* (hereinafter cited by page reference).

[2] Most notably the opinions of Judges Jessup and Tanaka, pp. 242-440; but see also the opinions of Judges Mbanefo, Padillo Nervo, and Forster, pp. 441-505,

as well as the opinion favorable to South Africa's substantive contentions written by their judge *ad hoc*, J. T. van Wyk, pp. 65-215. See, esp. President Sir Percy Spender's Declaration, pp. 51-58 and Judge Jessup's response on the issue of the propriety of considering the merits, pp. 327-37.

well-being is understood at the international level; this conclusion, furthermore, provides a decisive criterion for interpreting "well-being" because underlying the idea of the Mandates System was, in the language of Article 22(1) of the Covenant of the League of Nations, "the principle that the well-being and development of such peoples form a sacred trust of civilization."

(2) The law-creating impact of the continuous and virtually unanimous condemnation of *apartheid* resulted in the formation of a rule of international law that was authoritative as to the nature of "well-being"; South Africa itself must be governed in conformity with international law and so, it would appear, that South Africa, in the role of Mandatory, had an indubitable legal duty to govern South West Africa in conformity with international law.

The first line of argument proceeding by way of canons of interpretation that incorporate evolving community standards of right conduct leads to a treatment of the apartheid issue as purely one of construction, no different in kind than countless legal controversies centering on a dispute as to the meaning of a critical phrase in the underlying legal text. This is the approach to the adjudication of constitutional issues bearing on race relations that has been adopted by and large by the American member of the ICJ, Philip C. Jessup, in the distinguished dissenting opinion that he filed in the *South West Africa Cases*.[3] In the setting of the litigation, the argument by way of standards of interpretation— binding on South Africa as Mandatory—needs to be balanced against the discretion vested in the Mandatory by the first paragraph of Article 2 of the Mandate, to wit: "The Mandatory shall have full power of administration and legislation over the territory subject to the present Mandate as an integral part of the Union of South Africa, and may apply the laws of the Union of South Africa to the territory, subject to such modification as circumstances may require." How does one offset this broad grant of discretion to South Africa against the contrary claims contained in the standards of well-being proclaimed by international institutions on the subject of racial discrimination?[4] South Africa clearly was conforming with Article 2(1) in the sense of extending to South West Africa the very same conception of "well-being" that prevailed in South Africa. Such conformity is made legally more impressive by the awareness of the League and its administering organ, The Permanent Mandates Commission, that South Africa and South West Africa were governed on the basis of strict segregation combined with economic, political, and social dominance assured to the white sector of the population.

[3] See esp. pp. 430-42.

[4] Cf. postulation of the issue in these terms in the dissenting opinion of Judge Tanaka, pp. 282-84.

The second legal argument by way of an emerging rule of international law is not subject to the weaknesses mentioned in the preceding paragraph, but it is jurisprudentially novel and its adoption entails significant policy shifts that bear on the overall structure of the international legal order, especially on the distribution of legal authority between sovereign states and the organized international community. In rejecting this approach Judge Jessup provides this explanation of his conclusion:

> . . . at times the argument of Applicants seemed to suggest that the so-called norm of non-discrimination had become a rule of international law through reiterated statements in resolutions of the General Assembly, of the International Labour Organisation, and of other international bodies. Such a contention would be open to a double attack: first, that since these international bodies lack a true legislative character, their resolutions alone cannot create law; and second, that if Applicants' case rested upon the thesis that apartheid should be declared illegal because it conflicted with a general rule of international law, it might be questioned whether such a claim would fairly fall within the ambit of paragraph 2 of Article 7 which refers disputes about the interpretation or application of the provisions of the Mandate. If the Court were to hold that the practice of apartheid is a violation of a general rule (norm) of international law, it might seem to be passing on the legality of acts performed within the Republic of South Africa itself, a matter, which, as already noted, would be outside the Court's jurisdiction. On the other hand, if the Court had considered the question of the existence of an international standard or criterion as an aid to interpretation of the Mandate, it would have been pursuing a course to which no objection could be raised.[5]

The remainder of this chapter is devoted to developing an argument in opposition to Judge Jessup's conclusion. This argument will be presented within the conservative compass of Article 38 of the Statute of the International Court of Justice.[6] Such a format is intended to establish the position that the ICJ could have supported the adoption of the in-

---

[5] See pp. 432-33, and p. 441: ". . . I have already explained that I do not accept Applicants' alternative plea which would test the apartheid policy against an assumed rule of international law (norm)."

[6] Cf. Frederick Pollack, "The Sources of International Law," 2 *Columbia Law Review* 511 (1902); Clive Parry, *The Sources and Evidences of International Law*, Manchester University Press, 1965;

Karol Wolfke, *Custom in Present International Law*, Warsaw, Wroclaw Scientific Society, 1964; William W. Bishop, "General Course of Public International Law, 1965," 2 *Recueil des Cours* 214-50 (1965); Max Sorensen, *Les sources du droit international*, Copenhagen, 1946; Obed Y. Asamoah, *The Legal Significance of Declarations of the General Assembly of the United Nations*, The Hague, Nijhoff, 1966.

ternational law argument by reference to its own past traditions concerning the creation of international law. Judge Tanaka's dissenting opinion, an historical document of great importance on these issues, develops the same line of argument as that developed here.[7] The justification for treating these questions here again is to call further attention to the argument for endowing the organized international community with a limited law-creating competence in the setting of the ICJ and to broaden the argument by reference to the overall requirements of a system of international law-making adequate to the world of today. My effort, however, is at the margins of Judge Tanaka's achievement and draws central inspiration from his own intellectual point of departure:

Of course, we cannot admit that individual resolutions, declarations, judgments, decisions, etc., have binding force upon the members of the organization. What is required for customary international law is the repetition of the same practice; accordingly, in this case resolutions, declarations, etc., on the same matter in the same, or diverse, organizations must take place repeatedly.

Parallel with such repetition, each resolution, declaration, etc., being considered as the manifestation of the collective will of individual participant States, the will of the international community can certainly be formulated more quickly and more accurately as compared with the traditional method of the normative process. This collective, cumulative and organic process of custom-generation can be characterized as the middle way between legislation by convention and the traditional process of custom making, and can be seen to have an important role from the viewpoint of the development of international law.[8]

There are, it remains to be noted, two levels of inquiry interactive here:

(1) The preconditions for law-creation under Article 38(1) of the ICJ Statute;[9]

[7] See esp. pp. 278-301.
[8] P. 292; cf. also p. 294: "the method of the generation of customary international law is in the stage of transformation from being an individualistic process to being a collectivistic process. This phenomenon can be said to be the adaptation of the traditional creative process of international law to the reality of the growth of the organized international community." Although Judge Tanaka's remarks, as quoted, are made with reference limited to the arguments for considering that a norm of customary international law has emerged (within the meaning of Article 38(1)(b) of the ICJ Statute),

it can be taken to reflect his insistence on establishing a law-creating process suitable for the transition from a sovereignty-centered international order to a community-centered international order. See, e.g. summary paras., pp. 298-301. My own wider views on this matter are developed in Chap. VI.
[9] Article 38(1) does not purport to exhaust the potentialities for law-creation in international affairs; taken in a literal fashion Article 38(1) lays down rules of law-creation that are binding upon the ICJ. It is a separate question whether this formulation of the law-creation process is binding as a matter of practice or neces-

(2) The conclusion that a rule of international law has emerged in such a form as to permit an appraisal of the compatibility of apartheid with the obligation of Article 2 of the Mandate to promote the well-being of the inhabitants of South West Africa.

II

Several considerations underlie the Article 38 argument. These considerations will be enumerated in this section to suggest a general approach to the processes of law-creation at work in international society.

1. The addition to international society of many newly independent states with varying cultural backgrounds, ideological perspectives, and moral orientations; this expansion of the number of participants suggests comparison with the international legal order as it evolved up to World War I when a relatively small number of Western European states, sharing a common culture, owing allegiance to Christian values, and exhibiting a single level of economic development, dominated international society. Today, international society is far more diverse and, complex; as a result, new procedures have necessarily been brought into being to crystallize the rules of behavior needed to sustain minimum world order. Furthermore, it is especially significant and quite remarkable that in the face of cultural, ideological, and economic diversity such a high degree of consensus has been achieved on the incompatibility of apartheid with contemporary international law. This consensus has transcended such major political chasms as "the cold war" and the so-called conflict between the developed and underdeveloped world.

2. Technological developments in the spread of information, the crystallization of world opinion, and in the arts of war and transportation have made the world increasingly "smaller" and more interdependent; there is an increasing awareness that events going on in one state cannot be isolated from the effort of international society to maintain a system of minimum order. There is more awareness of what is going on in South West Africa and a greater collective demand that something effective be done about it in deference to minimum expectations about the content of human decency. This process of demands tends to decrease the autonomy possessed by states vis-à-vis the demands of the organized world community. This reasoning implies the diminished autonomy of sovereign states, but it is a conclusion that applies to an even greater degree for a Mandate, a political regime where the origin and terms of reference made abundantly clear from the outset the concern of the international community with the protection of the welfare of the inhabitants. Judge Jessup pointed out in his Separate Opinion

sity in such other law-applying arenas as domestic courts or political organs of regional and global international institutions.

in the 1962 Judgment that "The Mandates System was one of at least four great manifestations in 1919-1920 of the recognition of the interest of all States in matters happening in any quarter of the globe."[10] Well, how is that world interest to be maintained, if the Mandatory denies the relevance of judicial supervision? Judge Jessup's assertion also makes plain that the Mandates System was itself conceived in the spirit of global interdependence, in the recognition that an affront to peace and human dignity anywhere was a danger and affront everywhere. More than a high-sounding pronouncement was contemplated. A legal regime was created with machinery to enable recourse to administrative and judicial remedies in the event that the Mandatory failed to discharge its responsibility.

Today the acknowledgment of interdependence is much more wide-spread and profound than in 1920. It is widely appreciated that unless South Africa can be peacefully persuaded to adapt its racial policies to minimum international standards and norms a severe danger of violence exists. It is one of the characteristics of the nuclear age that a civil war frequently attracts foreign interventions and counterinterventions, thereby increasing risks of escalation and endangering the overall maintenance of international peace. The appeal for relief by Ethiopia and Liberia to the ICJ illustrated the effort to use the ordering procedures of the world community so as to forestall recourse to violence. It is part of the effort to achieve pacific settlement in the face of dangers to world peace, these dangers having been identified in increasingly strident and formal terms by those organs of the world community entrusted with the task and function of upholding world peace. The Security Council has *decided* that this danger exists as a formal matter.

3. This connection between world peace and the minimum protection of human rights has been increasingly acknowledged in light of Hitler's persecution of the Jews and other minorities as part of the background of World War II. From Nuremberg onward there has been a series of international documents and formal acts acknowledging the link between internal coercion and abuse of human rights and the risks of external violence and war. International activities in the human rights field have stated this premise as underlying all of their activities, and it has been especially evident in connection with the effort by the organs of the United Nations to deal with South Africa's racial policies. The organized international community has increasingly maintained the need to assert an international claim to correct abuses, as it perceived those abuses, of human rights, and especially in the case of South Africa where the abuses are proclaimed to be part of authorized government policy.

[10] *South West Africa Cases, (Ethiopia v. South Africa, Liberia v. South Africa), Preliminary Objections, Judgment of Dec.* 21, 1962: ICJ Reports 1962, p. 319, at 429.

Such a situation underscores the strength of the claim on behalf of international society in South West Africa where the mandated status of the Territory makes especially germane the concern and values of the international community.

If a national government indicates a willingness to correct abuses by itself or to cooperate with the international community in their correction, then deference to the primacy of national authority seems appropriate. But when, as in the case of South Africa, the national government repudiates the concern of the international community, the rationale for deference is weakened. In the mandate context such deference almost disappears, given the basic duty of the Mandatory to promote the well-being of the inhabitants. This disappearance is almost total if the organized international community can arrive at a virtually unanimous conclusion that the condition complained about is not only abusive of the inhabitants, but a serious danger to international peace and security.

4. Within the area of human rights the most significant developments have involved the evolution of standards pertaining to matters of racial equality. This is the subject matter that has dominated the human rights activities of international institutions and it is abuses in this area that have been identified as the greatest affront to human dignity, as the most serious impediment to well-being, and as the most grave threat to international peace and security. A remarkable degree of agreement among states attaches to this conclusion despite all the diversity in the changed and expanded international society of today. Part of the current foundation of international peace is the establishment and implementation of international standards pertaining to racial discrimination.

5. Closely connected with human rights is the trend toward national self-determination visible since the end of World War II in international society; part of this trend is to respect the claims of peoples for self-government and the administration of their own territory; the colonial system has been virtually abolished and colonial titles to territory have lost whatever legitimacy they may once have possessed; the mandatory system was created in an international climate in which the colonial system was respected and notions of dependent peoples and the white man's burden prevalent, although declining in respectability. Colonial ideas have been decisively repudiated, and the whole claim of a mandatory to exercise paternalistic control is at odds with the decisive trends of recent international history. At the very least this trend supports an increasing level of accountability by the Mandatory and an obligation to defer to the international community on such a matter of fundamental human dignity as the avoidance of racial discrimination and segregation. On no issue is there more uniform agreement than that

the welfare of a people cannot be promoted if they are forced to live in a racially segregated society. It is not an issue within the orbit of legitimate controversy as the international community, at whose sufferance the Mandatory administers the Mandate, has decisively and repeatedly evidenced its unwillingness to have any sovereign state, and *a fortiori* a Mandate territory where the authority of international standards is much more obviously relevant, maintain as a matter of official policy, a racially segregated social unit.

Even outside the Mandate or in the absence of it there is evidence of the development of international procedures to protect dependent peoples from exploitation by whatever governing authority controls their destiny. Such an increase in international concern for dependent people cannot be ignored in the context of a Mandate where, from its beginning in 1920, a decision was made to prevent annexation and to deny the Mandatory the claim of sovereignty over the mandated territory. South Africa seems to insist upon unrestricted discretion with respect to the implementation of its obligation to promote the well-being of the inhabitants of South West Africa.

6. International society lacks a legislative organ. For this reason it has had to rely upon other procedures to change and evolve international standards and norms. This need has grown especially acute in light of the expansion of international society and the increasing role of international institutions. For this reason writers have increasingly urged that a legislative effect be given to the official acts of international institutions. Only thus can an important gap in international legal order be filled.

The absence of a legislature in international society also has an important bearing upon the outlook of international judicial organs. As Sir Gerald Fitzmaurice has so helpfully put this matter:

> Domestic courts can, if they wish, plead with some plausibility as a ground for not going beyond what is barely necessary for a decision that a national legislature exists which can, by legislative action, remedy any gaps or obscurities in the law. In the international field there is at present nothing comparable to a legislature, and the operation of the so-called law-making treaty is both uncertain and leaves many loose ends. The international community is therefore peculiarly dependent on its international tribunals for the development and clarification of the law, and for lending to it an authority more substantial and less precarious than can be drawn from the often uncertain and divergent practices of States, or even from the opinion of individual publicists, whatever their repute.[11]

[11] Sir Gerald Fitzmaurice, "Hersch Lauterpacht—The Scholar as Judge: I," 37 *British Yearbook of International Law* 1, 18-19 (1961).

7. Closely connected with the need in international society for some sort of legislative capacity, is the appreciation of the ordering role that is being played by the organs of the United Nations and by regional institutions in world affairs. International law developed its basic concepts and its basic doctrine at a time when sovereign states were the only significant actors. The whole framework of world order needs some modernization to take account of the law-creating capacities and roles of international institutions, so as to acknowledge that actors other than states may evolve authoritative international standards and international legal norms. At the basis of this discussion is the degree to which a single recalcitrant state or a tiny minority of states can block the emergence of authoritative legal rules in international society, and paralyze the growth of international law by their stubborn opposition to its change. Underneath this question is the extent to which the reality of sovereign consent is an essential ingredient in the formation of an international legal norm or international standard binding upon *all* states. The time has come for the ICJ to confirm the role of *international consensus* as a source of international law within the meaning of Article 38 of the Statute of the Court, consensus being used to refer to an overwhelming majority, a convergence of international opinion, a predominance, to something more than a simple majority but something less than unanimity or universality. Only with this rudimentary legislative capacity will it become possible to use the resources of law to implement the will of the international community against those who defy it. And if the resources of law are not available, then what? Only force is left to implement that will. This competence to use force is possible in the context of a threat or breach of international peace or an act of aggression without awaiting the consent of all states. Why should this false notion of universality be an impediment to legal order when something less than force is at stake?

The requirement that consent is a precondition to the formation of an international legal norm is more a matter of *abstract doctrine* than of *empirical juridical reality*. The greatest increase in the authority of the organized international community that exists if one compares the League of Nations with the United Nations is a consequence of relaxing the requirement of consent in the decision-making procedures of the Organization. In the Security Council only the consent of the Permanent Members is a precondition for the emergence of an obligation; as a consequence of recent developments in the peace-keeping area, the opposition of even the Permanent Members may be circumvented by recourse to the General Assembly through the Uniting for Peace Resolution. That is, effective and authoritative action by the Organization may take place in the absence of the consent of every state that is a member, and that this action may result in binding legal obligations upon members is part of the significance of the Advisory Opinion in the Case of Certain Expenses. A further implication of this approach is that Recommendations of the General Assembly form an integral part of the law-creating process now functioning in international society. Ethiopia and Liberia argued that the law-making capacities of the General Assembly were doubly relevant to its submission that the norm of nondiscrimination is an international legal norm: first, to provide an authoritative definition of the scope, character, and applicability to South Africa's policies of the international legal norms found in Articles 55(c) and 56 of the Charter, these provisions being read in the light of the overall affirmation in the Charter of the connection between human rights and the obligations of its members; and second, the explicit judgment of the membership that the standards evolved by the organs in the United Nations do, in fact, constitute an international legal norm; this evidence serves to satisfy the traditional requirement of *opinio juris* as underlying the law-creating process in international society.[12]

Further dramatic evidence of the law-creating competence of the United Nations is contained in the claim posited by Article 2, paragraph 6 of the Charter: "The Organization shall ensure that States which are not Members of the United Nations act in accordance with these Principles so far as may be necessary for the maintenance of international peace and security." This provision goes as far as it is possible to go in making clear the extent to which the international legal order has found it necessary to qualify the requirement of sovereign consent.[13] If the organized international community now affirms its intention to impose control over *even* nonmembers whose conduct endangers international peace and security and if one accepts the reiteration of the determination that the continuation of apartheid does so endanger international peace and security, then even a nonmember could under this line of reasoning be obliged to conform to international legal norms and international standards on the subject of racial discrimination; so much more so, a member, and so much more than this, a Mandatory. This hierarchy of internationally asserted claims shows that Ethiopia and Liberia were not asking anything very radical or extreme from the ICJ, but were merely seeking a minimum confirmation of the capacity of the organized international community to carry out its fundamental tasks.

It may be helpful to summarize the structure of the argument up to this point:

---

[12] See Rosalyn Higgins, *The Development of International Law Through the Political Organs of the United Nations*, London, Oxford University Press, 1963, pp. 1-10.

[13] For an analysis along these lines of the claim embodied in Article 2(6) of the United Nations Charter to control behavior of nonmember states see Chap. VII.

(a) The augmented legal authority and role of the organized international community, including especially its augmented role in connection with law-creating processes;

(b) The historical and doctrinal link between fundamental human rights and the maintenance of international peace and security in contemporary international society;

(c) The identification and proscription of racial discrimination as essential for the maintenance of international peace and security;

(d) The identification of apartheid as practiced in South West Africa as a prime example of racial discrimination endangering international peace and security;

(e) The special subordination of a Mandatory to evolving international legal norms and international standards bearing upon the well-being of inhabitants of a Mandate;

(f) The increasing role of an international consensus in the law-creating processes at the disposal of the organized international legal community;

(g) The participation of the International Court of Justice in the contemporary system of international order requires it to take account of points (a) to (f) in the course of, first, interpreting Article 2 of the Mandate, second, determining the *existence* of international legal norms and standards, third, interpreting Article 38(1) of the Statute of the Court, and fourth, deciding whether this legal norm of nondiscrimination governs the obligation of well-being in Article 2.

8. *Banco Nacional de Cuba v. Sabbatino*, 376 U.S. 398 (1964) is a recent decision by the United States Supreme Court dealing with whether Cuban expropriation decrees that fail to compensate the property owner in accordance with the requirements of international law shall be given legal effect in the United States to transfer the title of the expropriated property to the Cuban Government.[14] The main legal issue presented concerned whether the so-called act of state doctrine prevented an enquiry into the validity of the Cuban expropriation decrees under international law. What is relevant to the background of applicants' case is that the Supreme Court regarded the concept of consensus as relevant to the presence or absence, in this case the absence, of authoritative international legal norms. For the Court held by a majority of 8 to 1 that where a consensus no longer existed in support of the claimed norm of customary international law, then it was inappropriate for a judiciary to apply it; the majority opinion also implied that where the international standard contended for was supported by a consensus, then it would be

---

[14] For a more detailed consideration of the *Sabbatino* litigation see Chap. XIII. For more recent developments arising as a consequence of the statutory reversal of the judicial outcome see Samuel E. Bleicher, "The Sabbatino Amendment in Court: Bitter Fruit," 20 *Stanford Law Review* 858-69 (1968).

more appropriate to suspend the act of state doctrine and treat the standard as if it were a governing norm. The *Sabbatino* case is illustrative of an international trend to regard consensus as a relevant juridical concept, needed in contemporary international society where no legislature exists to create, modify, or eliminate international legal norms.

9. *The Shimoda Case.* The District Court of Tokyo delivered an opinion on December 7, 1963 dealing with the legality of atomic attacks by the United States on Hiroshima and Nagasaki in the closing days of World War II.[15] The case arose because five survivors of the atomic attacks brought a claim against the Japanese Government, alleging an improper waiver of their claims for recovery in the peace treaty concluded with the allied powers, the underlying claim being that the use of atomic bombs against inhabited cities was a violation of international law. It should be pointed out that the *Shimoda* decision was rendered by a lower Japanese court; this fact is discounted to a large degree, however, by the reliance of the court upon a line of analysis supported by the unanimous conclusions of three experts in international law— distinguished Japanese professors of international law that were appointed by the court to prepare and submit separate reports on the relevance of international law to the litigation.

What makes the *Shimoda* case so instructive in the context of construing Article 2 of the Mandate is that the Japanese court was confronted by a situation in which there were no rules of customary or conventional international law directly applicable to the use of atomic weapons. In coming to their decision that the attacks violated international law, the court relied upon various nonbinding legal documents to demonstrate the existence of the various norms and standards relevant to an adjudication. In particular, the court relied heavily upon the contents of the Draft Rules of Air Warfare to posit the relevant norms and standards pertaining to what constitutes a permissible aerial bombardment. It may be pertinent to quote the following observation of the Japanese court:

> The Draft Rules of Air Warfare cannot directly be called positive law, since they have not yet become effective as a treaty. However, international jurists regard the Draft Rules as authoritative with regard to air warfare. Some countries regard the substance of the Rules as a standard of action by armed forces, and the fundamental provisions of the Draft Rules are consistently in conformity with international laws and regulations, and customs at that time.[16]

[15] For an analysis of this litigation see Falk, *Legal Order in a Violent World,* Princeton, Princeton University Press, 1968, pp. 374-413; for convenient text of decision see Falk and Saul H. Mendlovitz, eds., *The Strategy of World Order,* New York, World Law Fund, 1966, I, 314-54.
[16] *Id.,* at 339-40.

The court also relied unapologetically upon the St. Petersburg Declaration of 1886, the Declarations concerning dum-dum bullets and projectiles launched from balloons of 1899, and upon the 1925 Geneva Protocol (to which neither Japan nor the United States adhered) prohibiting the use in war of asphyxiating, deleterious or other gases.

The *Shimoda* decision illustrates the reliance of a court of law upon norms and standards contained in instruments that are not legally binding according to traditional notions in order to achieve authoritative guidance as to the character and content of international law. This point deserves emphasis because South Africa attempted to discredit evidence of international legal norms and standards by arguing that the obligations contained in the documents relied upon by Ethiopia and Liberia were not legally relevant because they were in the form of resolutions, declarations, draft conventions, and so on.[17] Although nonbinding instruments are, by definition, unable to create or impose legal obligations, they might nevertheless provide decisive evidence of the content of legal obligations, especially in the context of the Mandate. This position is very persuasive, it would seem, when the instrument in question is itself a statement of what states regard to be the character of legal obligations; thus a consensus[18] of states solemnly declaring that South Africa's racial policies of group differentiation violate the international legal rules prohibiting racial discrimination seems entitled to great respect in assessing the compatibility of Respondent's policies with Article 2 of the Mandate. Is there some better method to construe the obligations of Article 2 than to defer to the judgment reached over and over again by the organized international community as to the legal character of respondent's policies?

10. *Piracy*. The international crime of piracy provides a helpful context within which to examine the contention that a legal norm of nondiscrimination and nonseparation exists. It is helpful because it is an activity with respect to which the international community *acted as a whole* to uphold *its common interests*, making use of norms and standards to confer an extraordinary power of jurisdiction upon nation-states, a power that allowed for the capture and prosecution of a pirate, regardless of his nationality. Part of what makes piracy relevant to an understanding of the legal character of the current reaction of the international

---

[17] Cf. esp. 5 *South West Africa Case—ICJ Pleadings* 157-174 (1966) in response to 4 *South West Africa Case—ICJ Pleadings* 476-519 (1966).

[18] Such a consensus is virtually unanimous if one eliminates South Africa as the accused state incapable of judging impartially the merits of the issue; the disqualification of the views of South Africa is an application of the familiar dictum *nemo judex in re sua*. See further Hersch Lauterpacht, *The Development of International Law by the International Court of Justice*, London, Stevens, 1958, pp. 158-61.

community to apartheid is to underscore the difference in approach between an organized and unorganized international community. Without international institutions the manner of dealing with a perceived common danger was to expand the normal competence of states, making each the agent of the whole, and to count upon decentralized actions of self-help to promote the common interest of the world in the suppression of piracy. During this period when the competence to capture and prosecute pirates became established as law there were states along the periphery of Africa that tolerated, even protected, piratical activities, states whose consent to the new jurisdictional norm could not very reasonably be presumed.

The connection between the international legal response to piracy, and to such other phenomena that shock the conscience and undermine the common interests of states as trading in slaves and narcotics, genocide, and apartheid is clearly foreshadowed in the reply of Romania to the League of Nations Committee of Experts for the Progressive Codification of International Law in 1926: "Absolute piracy (piracy *jure gentium*) is regarded today as an offense of a special character, because it is *punishable wherever encountered*. We already see in embryo the principle—which, in future social relations will become the practice—of penalizing throughout the world violations of law which are common to every country."[19] In proposing a general convention for the suppression of piracy, the reply quoted above suggests the use of standards contained in municipal legal systems as the basis for an international legal norm.

Charles Cheney Hyde, who is very protective of sovereign prerogatives, has an interesting passage in his treatise that almost exactly expresses the position of Ethiopia and Liberia in the South West Africa litigation:

> The offense of piracy derives its internationally illegal aspect from the will of the international society. That society, by common understanding reflected in the practice of States generally, yields to each of its members jurisdiction to penalize any individuals who, regardless of their nationality, commit certain acts within certain places.[20]

Hyde's reasoning can be applied to apartheid by arguing that "apartheid derives its internationally illegal aspect from the will of the international society." What Hyde does not tell us is how, if challenged, the

[19] League of Nations Document C/196/ M/70/1927, V, p. 202.
[20] Hyde, *International Law Chiefly as* *Interpreted and Applied by the United States*, 2nd rev. edn., 1945, I, 768.

will of international society *is to be established consistent* with the doctrine of international law.

The best that Hyde does in the context of piracy is to make a vague reference to the confirmation of the norm by the general practice of states:

> This common yielding of jurisdiction to punish, which the individual State could not itself otherwise lawfully exercise, with respect, for example, to the acts of aliens on foreign vessels on the high seas, has important implications. It signifies that what is so punishable must be regarded as internationally illegal, in the sense that it defies what the law of international society is deemed itself to forbid. Of this fact, the legislation of some States, embracing the United States, appears to take cognizance in providing for the punishment of one who commits the crime of piracy as defined by the law of nations.[21]

The increasing social integration and interdependence of international society together with the need to justify the legal claim before an institution of the organized international community, that is, the ICJ—result in the conclusion that the only entirely satisfactory ground for such a justification would be in terms of the law-creating processes of co-ordinate institutions of the organized international community. The problem of proof and the character of juridical explanation were different so long as international society was truly decentralized and unorganized. The state claiming jurisdiction over piratical activities could merely invoke "the will of international society" and proceed with a prosecution without being worried about the need to reconcile their unilateral claim with the positivistic notion that law to be binding on a state must, as Robert Ago states the issue, be laid down and accepted by the states through a formal, constitutive expression of consent.

Ago's thinking is relevant to this entire presentation, we might parenthetically observe, as he starts with the convincing demonstration of the impossibility of accounting for the existence of much operative law by those sources of law that are accredited by traditional international law. For this reason he introduces the entire idea of the spontaneous generation of legal norms to take account of law as a social fact rather than to worry about reconciling operative norms with the doctrines that have developed to explain the law-creating process in a manner that does no offense to the presupposition that a state is not bound by any obligations to which it has not assented.[22]

---

[21] *Id*, at 768-69.
[22] For a summary of Ago's thought see Roberto Ago, "Positive Law and International Law," 51 *American Journal of International Law* 691-733 (1957).

III

As A.J.P. Tammes has pointed out if "we glance at the enumeration of the sources of international law in Article 38, paragraph 1, of the Statute of the International Court of Justice, it will be seen that decisions of international organs are not among the categories listed separately. Though the enumeration in Article 38 has been criticized," Professor Tammes goes on to say, "it may be safely stated that it represents the most authoritative enumeration of the sources of international law."[23] And it certainly seems to be an authoritative enumeration for states engaged in litigation before the ICJ. Article 38 is not an exhaustive list of the sources comprising the totality of international law; it is rather a directive to the Court to decide disputes before it in light of these sources. Now, obviously, the difficulty for the case presented by Ethiopia and Liberia arises because the norm of nondiscrimination has been brought about principally as a consequence of the activity of international organs. Therefore, it is necessary to fit this activity within the sources explicitly acknowledged by Article 38 if the nonbinding standard that has evolved is to be confirmed by a judicial body at the international level as a legal norm. What must be demonstrated, then, to sustain the argument is that the formal acts are either *evidence* of the existence, or are themselves *constitutive*, of either "conventions," "custom," or "general principles" within the scope of Article 38.

It should be noted, to quote Tammes again, that "In its practice the Court does not seem to have found any difficulty in applying and interpreting resolutions of international organs."[24] On the basis of examining this practice of the Court Tammes concludes as follows:

> One is drawn to the conclusion that the Court, in applying resolutions of international organs, is basically applying the international conventions such as the Charter of the United Nations, *from which the decision-making power of such organs is derived. The Court, therefore, has no need of an explicit reference, in Article 38, paragraph 1, to decisions of international organs as a source of international law distinct from conventions.* (Emphasis added.)[25]

This conclusion suggests that Article 38(1)(a) draws within its compass the law-creating process going on in international organs, at least to the extent of the authoritative interpretation of the obligations of their own organic law, in the case of the political organs of the United Nations Charter. A potential issue of judicial review is present here

[23] A.J.P. Tammes, "Decisions of International Organs as a Source of International Law," 94 *Hague Academy Recueil des Cours* 261-64, 267-68 (1958—II).
[24] *Id.*, at 268.
[25] *Id.* at 269.

since South Africa regards as arbitrary the characterization by the world community of apartheid as violative of both international law and of Charter obligations, and it might be said that the ICJ should review the judgment reached by other organs of the organized international community. However, in view of the unanimity of the conclusion reached by competent organs, if one excludes the state whose policies and practices are being appraised and in view of the qualitative nature of the condemnation of apartheid, it does not seem appropriate for the ICJ to appraise independently the validity of the norm-creating process. There are no criteria that a court might properly use. How could a court decide, for instance, that the organized international community was somehow wrong and misinformed about the nature of genocide? There is a value judgment that has been passed, and would become reviewable only in light of some other value judgment, one that is not proper to ask the court to make—namely, is the organized international community correct to characterize apartheid or genocide as violative of international law because it finds these phenomena to be reprehensible? For, as Ethiopia and Liberia underscored by bringing this case on the basis of a *per se* theory, the rule of international law has arisen to proscribe apartheid regardless of extenuating or justifying circumstance; the character of the rule is such that it cannot be made to coexist with apartheid, even if apartheid consists of only those methods and measures conceded by South Africa.

Article 38 represents a compromise between the jurisprudential traditions of legal positivism and natural law. Among those that have most convincingly expressed the relevance of the natural law tradition to a construction of Article 38 is Judge Spiropoulos.[26] The relevance of natural law enables the ethical consciousness of mankind to be set off against the will of the sovereign state, and thereby endows the collective will of the organized international community with a law-creating competence that can overcome the defiance of a deviant sovereign state, especially in matters where basic considerations of well-being are at stake, and most especially, where the challenged government is carrying out the functions of Mandatory under an authorization that was received from international society.

It is important to interpret the provision of Article 38 in a flexible manner. Former Judge Basdevant said at the San Francisco Conference after World War II that it was generally agreed that despite certain inadequacies in the formulation of the sources in Article 38 the Court had operated well under it and time should not be spent in redrafting it.[27] In similar vein, Alf Ross has observed that "It is a fortunate thing, how-

[26] Jean Spiropoulos, *Théorie général du droit international*, Paris, Pichon 1930, pp. 97ff., pp. 91-114.
[27] UNICO, xiv, 1945, pp. 36-295.

[142]

ever, that the precepts of the sources [in Article 38] are so spacious that they will hardly prevent a natural development of practice."[28]

The whole idea of sources is somewhat constraining. The several arguments are made as if independent of one another so as to fit within the categories of Article 38(1). In actuality, the case for the emergence of an international legal norm is most strongly made by viewing the evidence under each of the four subdivisions in a cumulative fashion, each reinforcing the other, which when taken together make an overwhelming case for finding the norm in existence. In this regard, then, the evidence of the norm as an authoritative interpretation of the Charter or as indicative of general practice or as a general principle of law or as expressive of an international moral consciousness should be considered as aspects of a single argument affirming the reality of this international legal norm, and not as a series of alternative appeals. To quote Ross once again: "The judicial decision is the pulse of legal life, and it is here that the analysis of the legal sources comes into play. A source of law, then, means *the general factors (motive components) which guide the judge when fixing and making concrete the legal content in judicial decisions.*"[29]

Article 38(1) (a): "international conventions, whether general or particular, establishing rules expressly recognized by the contesting states."

1. The first major argument under Article 38(1) (a) is to regard the Mandate as an international convention that is itself given authoritative content by the practice and operations of the organized international community. South Africa as a member of the United Nations must be regarded as having consented formally to the procedures of the organization and, by its continuing membership, to have acquiesced in the formal determinations reached thereinunder. No determination in this regard has been more decisively and repeatedly made during the life of the United Nations than that apartheid and human well-being are totally incompatible. Such a determination, given the administering function of the organized international community, provides a decisive criterion by which to construe Article 2 of the Mandate. South Africa by its participation in the organization is estopped from denying the relevance of its virtually unanimous actions to a subject matter as clearly within its claimed competence as the status of dependent peoples and their rights.

It should be noticed that using the operations of the United Nations as authoritative guidance for the interpretation of the Mandate con-

---

[28] Alf Ross, *A Text-Book of International Law*, London, Longmans, Green, 1947, p. 93.
[29] *Id.* at 80. (Italics in original.)

forms with Judge Jessup's rationale. No contention is made that the norm of nondiscrimination is operative outside of the Mandate context and, therefore, strictly speaking there is no need to endow the consensus within the United Nations as law-creative. But what makes the action of the United Nations "authoritative"? To avoid the need to balance off the claims of the United Nations against the discretion of South Africa it is essential to aver that the formal acts within the United Nations generate rules of international law that operate as decisive criteria for construing the meaning of well-being in the Mandate.

2. The second major argument under Article 38(1) (a) of the statute is to regard the Charter of the United Nations as itself the source that generates the legal criteria governing the interpretation of Article 2 of the Mandate. The language of Articles 55(c) and 56 taken together with the relevant practice of the United Nations discloses the emergence of a legally binding antidiscrimination norm. The Charter is the organic law of the organized world community and its character as a binding international agreement bears upon the proper resolution of the dispute over the administration of South West Africa.

This argument admittedly arises only at the frontiers of a developing international legal order; there is no firm foundation for this legal conception in the past decisions of this Court. The acceptance of this argument would produce an expanded and expanding role for the ICJ in carrying out the will of the international community, not in any vague Rousseauesque sense of will, but the will of the international community as it is embodied in formal acts of the organs of the United Nations.

Although the weight of juridical evidence is not decisive to this phase of our argument, we, nevertheless, claim that this line of appeal is consistent with a trend toward legitimizing the law-creating processes of the organized international community, as evidenced both by the claims of the international institutions themselves and by the writings of those international lawyers who have been devoting themselves to adapting international law to the needs of international life. It would have been most beneficial if the ICJ had chosen to ratify this trend in the very limited context of Article 2 of the South West Africa Mandate. This context is so limited because the Mandates System emphasizes the special duty of the Mandatory to administer the territory on behalf of international society. This duty of the Mandatory eliminates any consideration of whether the deference owed by the international community to a sovereign state might alter an analogous claim directed at *apartheid* in South Africa itself. The basic drift of argument set forth here to the effect that international standards proscribing racial discrimination have by now become an international legal norm makes the rule binding irrespective of the Mandate. Except for establishing judicial jurisdiction and standing to complain, this legal rule is as enforceable against a state in its role as sovereign state as in its role as Mandatory.

The following Charter provisions are relevant. A fundamental purpose of the United Nations, as these are enumerated in Article 1, is "to achieve international cooperation in solving international problems of an economic, social, cultural, or humanitarian character, and in promoting and encouraging respect for human rights and for fundamental freedoms for all without distinction as to race, sex, language, or religion." Article 13(1)(b) authorizes the General Assembly to make studies and recommendations "assisting in the realization of human rights and fundamental freedoms for all without distinction as to race, sex, language, or religion." Article 55 states that "(w)ith a view to the creation of conditions of stability and well-being which are necessary for peaceful and friendly relations among nations" the United Nations shall promote universal respect for, and observance of, human rights and fundamental "freedoms for all without distinction as to race, sex, language, or religion." And in Article 56 "All Members pledge themselves to take joint and separate action in cooperation with the Organization for the achievement of the purposes set forth in Article 55."[30] The promotion of human rights is a fundamental element in the United Nations system. It is also evident that the idea of promoting human rights irrespective of race is deemed so basic that it is listed first in the enumeration of categories subject to discrimination (race, sex, language, religion). Furthermore, the practice of the organization makes clear that South Africa's racial policies are deemed in violation of this Charter commitment to eliminate racial discrimination. The pleadings of Ethiopia and Liberia in the South West Africa litigation abound with evidence to document the conclusion that virtually all states have committed themselves in formal votes to the conclusion that South Africa's racial policies violate international law in general and the obligations of the Charter in particular.

Are these Charter provisions capable of generating binding rules of international law? At the outset it is important to recognize that the Charter is a constitutional document that is to be construed in light of the changing needs of international society. In the words of Oscar Schachter:

> The Charter is surely not to be construed like a lease of land or an insurance policy; it is a constitutional instrument whose proud phrases were designed to meet changing circumstances for an un-

30 See also Charter Articles 62 and 68.

defined future. Any doubt as to the flexibility and adaptability of the Charter must surely have been resolved by recent developments.[31]

Lauterpacht also affirmed the Charter as a constitutional document.

> The Charter of the United Nations is a legal document; its language is the language of law, of international law. In affirming repeatedly the fundamental human rights of the individual it must of necessity be deemed to refer to legal rights—to legal rights recognized by international law and independent of the law of the State . . . there ought to be no doubt that the provisions of the Charter in the matter of fundamental human rights impose upon the Members of the United Nations the legal duty to respect them . . . it is clear that a Member of the United Nations who is guilty of a violation of these rights commits a breach of the Charter.[32]

Another passage from Lauterpacht is also illuminating: "The Provisions of the Charter . . . constitute legal rights and obligations . . . they signify the recognition, in an international treaty . . . of rights of the individual as such. They transfer the inalienable and natural rights of the individual from the venerable, but controversial orbit of the law of nature to the province of positive law, of international law."[33] In fact, Lauterpacht suggests that the entire international legal system depends upon mobilizing the organized international community for the protection of minimum or fundamental human rights:

> . . . an international legal system which aims at effectively safeguarding human freedom in all its aspects is no longer an abstraction . . . international law . . . henceforth acknowledges the sovereignty of man. . . . For fundamental human rights are rights superior to the law of the sovereign State . . . the recognition of inalienable human rights . . . signify the recognition of a higher fundamental law not only on the part of States but also, through international law, on the part of the organized international community itself. *That fundamental law . . . constitutes both the moral limit and the justification of the international legal order.*[34]

It is evident from these quotations that this learned author deems the individual human being as the fundamental repository of human rights, as they are acknowledged by the Charter and international law.

Some jurists have questioned the legal character of Charter provisions on the ground of vagueness or because they are stated in aspirational rhetoric or because their enforcement is blocked by the domestic juris-

[31] Oscar Schachter, Book Review, 60 *Yale Law Journal* 189-93, at 193 (1951).
[32] Hersch Lauterpacht, *International Law and Human Rights*, New York, Praeger, 1950, p. 34.
[33] *Id.* at 159.
[34] *Id.* at 70-71. (Italics added.)

diction clause of Article 2(7) (at least in the absence of enforcement action under Chapter VII of the Charter) or because the Charter did not establish any machinery for implementation or because the views of those drafting the Charter at San Francisco reflected an intention to avoid legal duties arising for states in regard to human rights. These objections deserve great weight if one adopts the perspective of 1945. These objections do not seem tenable, at least with respect to racial discrimination, in 1969. The Charter is a dynamic treaty instrument, an organic law, developing legal norms in response to the changing needs and values of the organized international community.

But it is worth noting that even at San Francisco, the Rapporteur of the Subcommittee concerned with Article 1(3), the provision specifying the promotion of human rights as a fundamental "Purpose of the Organization," reported as follows: "The subcommittee held that assuring or protecting such fundamental rights is primarily the concern of each state. If, however, such rights and freedoms were grievously violated so as to create conditions which threaten peace or so obstruct the application of provisions of the Charter, then they cease to be the sole concern of each state."[35]

It seems significant also, in view of the leadership exerted by the United States at the San Francisco Conference, to appreciate its support for a Charter that laid down a framework within which growth and adaptation could take place and its opposition to a Charter consisting of a detailed specification of legal rights and duties. Quincy Wright's summary here is useful:

> John Foster Dulles, speaking for the United States and the other sponsoring powers, said the "principle" of domestic jurisdiction "was subject to evolution" and might permit the organs of the United Nations gradually to assume wider authority than was originally envisaged as, he pointed out, had been true in the parallel case of the relations of the state and the federal government in the United States.[36]

What underlies this whole controversy, of course, is the relative allocation of legal authority between these organs and South Africa in its role as Mandatory.

But 1969 is not 1945. Law-creating processes have been at work in international life. Great attention has been given to South Africa's racial policies in this regard by a variety of international organs. These organs agree and by a predominant or overwhelming majority of their membership, a majority approaching unanimity, that South Africa's racial poli-

[35] Doc. 723, I/1/A/19, 6 UNICO 696, 705, June 1, 1945.
[36] Quincy Wright, "The Strengthening of International Law," 98 *Hague Academy* *Recueil des Cours* 1, at 200. (1959—III); Dulles quotation taken from UNCIO, VI, 508.

cies violate the Charter and are contrary to international law. Resolutions and formal acts interpreting the Charter were conceived even at San Francisco to have a central role in developing the law of the Charter. Each organ was expected to interpret those parts of the Charter concerned with their particular functions. Oscar Schachter has lent his authority to some views on Charter interpretation that seem very relevant for present purposes:

> The question of primary interest to the international lawyer has generally been the extent to which the interpretations reached by, or within, the political organs are to be regarded as legally authoritative when the organ has not been accorded the competence to make binding decisions. In considering this, one might start with the principle that an "authentic" interpretation of a treaty by the parties is legally binding on them to the same degree as the treaty itself.[37]

Schachter suggests, then, that interpretations can attain a binding legal effect even though they are made by organs without capacity to render binding decisions. This suggestion bears especially to the issue of whether the General Assembly can develop specific international legal norms through the process of Charter interpretation. Schachter writes as follows: "I believe it is generally accepted that this conclusion would hold for an interpretation of the Charter adopted by all the Members (or even 'by the overwhelming majority' except for some abstentions) in the General Assembly; *the interpretation would be characterized by international lawyers as having the same legal force and effect as the Charter itself.*"[38] (Emphasis added.)

If one excludes South Africa itself, this process of Charter interpretation has gone on to an extent that it is now possible to say that an "authentic" interpretation has been achieved. The result is that South Africa's racial policies are in violation of the Charter obligations. The many condemnations of apartheid have as one objective to characterize apartheid as a violation of an international legal norm, and *a fortiori* to regard apartheid as a flagrant violation of nonbinding international standards, that is, of rules of conduct that have not yet ripened into legal norms.

This allegation of Charter violation has been asserted in general terms, but also in relation to Article 56. In 1957 a Resolution of the General Assembly called upon South Africa to observe Article 56 and reminded that country that it was "as much committed as any other Member to the principles enshrined in the Charter."[39] Further refer-

---

[37] Oscar Schachter, "The Relation of Law, Politics and Action in the United Nations," 109 *Hague Academy Recueil* *des Cours* 186 (1963—I).
[38] *Ibid.*
[39] G.A. Res. 1178 (XII).

ence to South Africa's obligations to uphold the pledge of Article 56 was made in Resolutions in 1958 and 1959.[40] And in 1961 Resolution 1598 at the XVth Session of the General Assembly went even further by its explicit finding that South Africa had been in wilful breach of its obligations under Article 56 and by its reminder to the South African Government that Article 2(2) of the Charter requires that "all Members shall fulfill in good faith the obligations assumed by them in accordance with the present Charter," and called upon South Africa to bring its conduct into conformity with its obligations. This pattern of practice bears on the construction of Article 2(2) of the Mandate in the following two important respects: first, it suggests, as a minimum, that it is the virtually unanimous judgment of the organized world community that apartheid violates the Charter, and that, since the Charter is the basic treaty underlying world order, these policies consequently violate international law. Therefore, South Africa as Mandatory is administering the Mandate in a manner incompatible with the Charter and hence with general international law with respect to the subject matter of well-being. And second, South Africa is administering the Territory in a manner that violates a legal duty that has now been imposed upon states as a consequence of an authoritative interpretation of Article 56 as it relates to apartheid, and that, accordingly, Article 56 incorporates or embodies an international legal norm of nondiscrimination.

There is also the broader basis of condemnation arising from the fact that South Africa is administering the Territory by imposing a governing policy that the organized international community has progressively characterized as a threat to international peace and security, so grave a threat, in fact, that it has finally led to a call for sanctions at the Seventeenth Session of the Assembly.[41] One student of the political organs of the United Nations has this to say about what she refers to as "the complicated history of United Nations practice on apartheid":

> The position seems to be—contrary to the professed beliefs of certain Western states—that the Assembly had adhered remarkably closely to international law in the face of rapid political change outside the Union of South Africa, and a change only for the worse within South Africa. The matter has been very thoroughly examined by the Special Committee appointed by the Assembly; and only when in possession of the findings of the Committee did the Assembly pass resolutions condemning an individual member, South Africa. The more recent resolutions tend to show that where there is a finding of an imminent—though not actual—threat to the peace, and

[40] G.A. Res. 1248 (XIII) and G.A. Res. 1375 (XIV).   [41] G.A. Res. 1761 (XVIII).

human rights are involved, the Assembly will condone the taking of appropriate action by individual states to bring South Africa's policies into conformity with Articles 55 and 56, and hence remove the potential danger to peace.[42]

Now if the organized community will take such action against South Africa, should it not be able with the aid of its main judicial tribunal, to take corresponding corrective action with regard to the Territory of South West Africa?

It may be suggested that the ICJ could not accept this argument about a Charter violation unless it undertakes a full and independent review of the relevant Charter obligations. It seems reasonable to suppose that the Court would either agree or defer to the organized international community, so many of whose institutions and organs have already passed on these matters. This case is fundamentally different from the Certain Expenses case where a basic dispute existed as to the correctness of the Assembly's interpretation of its powers under the Charter. Here we have virtually unanimity, aside from the state adjudged, as to the incompatibility of the policies complained of and the Charter. In this circumstance, there seems neither need nor occasion for judicial review. The degree of consensus visible in the international community operates to establish an *authoritative characterization* of South Africa's policies for purposes of litigating its compliance with Article 2(2) of the Mandate.

It is true that Sir Percy Spender in the Certain Expenses case observed: "However the Charter is otherwise described the essential fact is that it is a multilateral treaty. It cannot be altered at the will of the majority of the Member States, no matter how often that will is expressed or asserted against a protesting minority and no matter how large be the majority of Member States which assert its will in this manner or how small the minority."[43] And in another portion of his opinion, Sir Percy wrote:

Apart from a practice which is of a peaceful, uniform and undisputed character accepted in fact by all current Members, a consideration of which is not germane to the present examination, I accordingly entertain considerable doubt whether practice of an organ of the United Nations has any probative value either as providing evidence of the intentions of the original Member States or otherwise a criterion of interpretation. As presently advised I think it has none.[44]

Such passages suggest the essential differences between traditional

---

[42] Higgins, *op.cit. supra*, note 12, at 122.
[43] Certain Expenses of the United Nations (Article 17, para. 2, of the Charter),
Advisory Opinion of July 20, 1962, *ICJ Reports 1962*, p. 151 at 196.
[44] *Id.*, at 195.

conceptions about the development of international law and the approach taken here. Spender assumes, it would appear, that the consent of each and every sovereign state is a precondition to the creation of international norms. It would seem consistent with even Spender's remarks, however, to consider the practice of the organs of the United Nations as evidence for the existence of international standards in the sense of guidance as to the character of the Mandatory's obligations in Article 2(2).

In this argument we consider Article 2 to be an international legal norm, forming part of the Mandate, and thereby encompassed by Article 38(1) (a), and to be itself *interpreted* by an *independent* legal norm arising outside of the law-creating sources enumerated in Article 38. The norm itself is not being applied by the ICJ except in its special role of providing *authoritative* guidance as to the content of obligations embraced by Article 2(2). The reason to introduce this argument is because Ethiopia and Liberia rested their case on a theory of *per se* violation, and the Court might find it more acceptable to restrict respondent's discretion on *such a basis*. As indicated, the will of the organized international community is alleged capable of generating a valid international legal norm if expressed by a consensus approaching unanimity. It is capable both as a *formal* and as a *material* source of law: *formal* in the sense of being a law-creating process capable of generating valid norms in the same sense as Article 38(1) (a) (b) (c) are capable, and *material* in the sense of being able to translate international standards into international legal norms on whatever subject it acts. There is a problem, but not one relevant to the South West Africa dispute, although perhaps relevant to the affirmation of an additional source of international law by this Court, connected with the priority of norms deriving from different sources in the event of a conflict between them, but this is a problem already present to some degree, at least between Article 38 (1) (b) and 38(1) (c) of the statute.

Reliance on this argument permits us to derive the relevant international legal norm from the Charter, a convention within the meaning of Article 38(1) (a) and one to which South Africa is a party. Therefore, South Africa has *consented* to the legal obligations imposed by the Charter and has by its membership and participation in the organization also acquiesced, if not consented, to its law-creating processes.

For this reason the international legal norm, if it in fact exists, does not depend on abridging the normal requirement of consent, although consent must be understood in relation to the competence of the organized international community rather than with respect to the specific substantive obligation imposed by the norm.

That acquiesence operates as the equivalent of consent in the law-creating processes of international law has been ably demonstrated by Ian MacGibbon.[45]

Ethiopia and Liberia were acting as agents of the organized international community in a situation in which South Africa has persistently acted to frustrate the claims of supranational control that were implicit and explicit from the time the Mandates System came into being in 1920. These states asked the Court to reaffirm the role of the organized international community in specifying the nature of the well-being of the inhabitants, at least to the extent that such well-being has been specified in cognizable international legal norms and standards.

The argument here is that the needs and practices of international life confirm the role of the organized international community in the law-creating process. In fact, the expectations of nations are disclosed by their use of legal language in formal acts condemning apartheid. And as Myres McDougal, Roberto Ago, and others have shown, *the expectations* of the world community with respect to the nature and character of law is itself generative of norms. All of our reasoning in Part II is also relevant to the demonstration here. Given the facts of global interdependence, the link between human rights and the maintenance of international peace, the need for a social response in the face of a persistent and serious challenge to basic values, the expansion of international society, the growing reliance upon consensus as a crucial concept in international law, the formal and social position of this Court as itself an institution of the organized international community, there exist compelling reasons for the ICJ to legitimate the law-creating processes used and relied upon by coordinate institutions in the organized international community.

Certainly, the numerous resolutions and other formal acts by international institutions that have asserted apartheid to be in violation of Charter obligations and general international law manifest the convictions of the overwhelming majority of states that a norm of nondiscrimination and nonseparation, or its equivalent, exists and is applicable. A further argument is that the presence of this conviction as a social fact is itself evidence for the existence of the specific norm, especially once it is conceded that organ has the potential competence to generate norms.

The extralegal basis of this law-creating process is certainly associated with the natural law tradition. It is interesting to examine a passage from Sir Hersch Lauterpacht's assessment of the role of natural law as a

---

[45] See series of articles by Ian MacGibbon, "Some Observations on the Part of Protest in International Law," 30 *British Yearbook of International Law* 293-319 (1953); "The Scope of Acquiescence in International Law," 31 *id.* 143-86 (1954); "Customary International Law and Acquiescence," 33 *id.* 115-45.

source of international law that is quoted with approval by Judge Sir Gerald Fitzmaurice:

> The fact is that while within the State it is not essential to give the idea of a higher law—of natural law—a function superior to that of providing the inarticulate ethical premise underlying judicial decisions . . . in international society the position is radically different. There—in a society deprived of normal legislative and judicial organs —the function of natural law, *whatever may be its form, must approximate more closely to that of a direct source of law*. In the absence of the overriding authority of the judicial and legislative organs of the State there must assert itself—*unless anarchy or stagnation are to ensue*—the persuasive but potent authority of reason and principle derived from the fact of the necessary coexistence of a plurality of States. This explains the pertinacity, in the international sphere, of the idea of natural law as a legal source.[46] (Italics added.)

It should be remarked that Lauterpacht is trying here to develop his view of the Grotian conception of international law. It seems desirable to confirm the dependence of international law upon natural law, and to add that the organized international community possesses a limited competence, at least, to set behavioral standards on matters of human dignity and welfare so as to *declare* the content of natural law. It breeds "anarchy" to allow each state to adopt its own conception of natural law; it breeds "stagnation" to eliminate natural law altogether from international law. As a consequence of the increased role of international institutions and the almost universal participation of states in their activities, it seems both realistic and practicable to give a consensus approaching unanimity a law-creating effect.

This, of course, is the burden of the argument throughout. The special feature here is to persuade the ICJ of a non-Article 38 source of law and, what's more, have it serve to generate a norm that acts as an authoritative basis for interpreting South Africa's obligations under Article 2(2).

Article 38(1)(b): "international custom, as evidence of a general practice accepted as law."

The first thing to observe is that the language of this subsection says nothing about consent being a prerequisite of the coming into being of a customary norm or that practice be universal or that states in their individual capacity accept the practice as law. In fact, the language of the provision accords with the view that a consensus or preponderant

---

[46] Gerald Fitzmaurice, "Some Problems Regarding the Formal Source of International Law," in *Symbolae Verzijl*, The Hague, Nijhoff, 1958, pp. 153-76, at 168; quoting from Hersch Lauterpacht, "The Grotian Tradition in International Law," 23 *British Yearbook of International Law* 1-53, at 22-23 (1946).

majority of states can generate a customary norm. Certainly in common parlance, a custom can arise, despite objection, during its period of emergence. So long as international society was highly decentralized it was necessary to rest all law-creating procedures on state practice, but with the growth of the organized international community it certainly seems increasingly plausible to allow the collective acts of the competent international institutions to serve as evidence of "general practice accepted as law."

Therefore, the resolutions of the General Assembly identifying apartheid as contrary to the Charter and to international law seem highly relevant to a judicial appraisal of South African racial policies. As Goodrich and Hambro note, "All the various organs of the United Nations will simultaneously be engaged in thus interpreting different provisions of the Charter and will build up a practice which will gradually assume the character of customary law."[47] If there is agreement among the various organs of the international community about the illegal character of the conduct in question, then the view of Goodrich and Hambro takes on even greater persuasive force and merit.

Rosalyn Higgins writes that the greatest achievement of the political organs of the United Nations with regard to developing international law is in relation to the creation of rules of customary international law: "Of all these sources, international custom is the most flexible, the most fluid, and as such, is exceedingly responsive to the changing needs of the international community. . . . Customary international law is therefore perhaps the most "political" form of international law, reflecting the consensus of the great majority."[48] Note, especially, that the criterion relied upon by Mrs. Higgins is "the great majority," not unanimity. It stands to reason that anything worth regulating by law will be opposed at the time by those who are to be the object of the regulation. If we give every state in the world a veto power over the process by which customary law emerges we severely handicap the capacity of international society to develop international law to meet developing needs.

As Mrs. Higgins acknowledges, this power to form international custom is not equivalent to endowing the General Assembly with anything so radical as legislative competence: "Resolutions of the Assembly are not *per se* binding: though those rules of general international law which they may embody are binding on member States, with or without the help of the resolution. But the body of resolutions as a whole, taken as indications of a general customary law, undoubtedly provide a rich source of evidence. These resolutions of the Assembly *which deliber-*

[47] Leland M. Goodrich and Edvard I. Hambro, *The Charter of the United Nations*, Boston, World Peace Foundation, 2nd rev. edn., 1949, p. 547.

[48] Higgins, *op.cit. supra*, note 12, at 1.

ately—rather than incidentally—provide declarations on international law are invariably based on other quasi-judicial forms of support"—that is, on the work of international commissions and agencies, such as the International Law Commission.[49] This is precisely the case with respondent's policies in South West Africa, which have been subject to quasi-judicial scrutiny over the last decade by organs of the United Nations as distinct as the International Labour Organization and the Special Committee on the Policies of Apartheid of the Government of the Republic of South Africa.[50]

It is against this jurisprudential background that Ethiopia and Liberia contended that apartheid violates a *norm* of customary international law within the language of Article 38(1) (b) of the statute. South Africa based its argument against the existence of the norm on the assumption that South Africa's persistent opposition to its emergence is of decisive relevance. South Africa relied upon the dictum in the *Fisheries Case* to the effect that "In any event the ten-mile rule would appear to be inapplicable as against Norway inasmuch as she has always opposed any attempt to apply it to the Norwegian coast."[51] On the same page of the rejoinder, South Africa also quotes for support from an article by Judge Sir Gerald Fitzmaurice that suggests that a state dissenting from a general norm being formed in the international community may enjoy an exemption from such a rule even if the norm is brought into being for international society as a whole.

South Africa's citation of Judge Fitzmaurice's apt summary of the traditional doctrine on the subject would appear supportive only if the subject of this litigation was apartheid as practiced in the Republic of South Africa. This self-incriminating argument by South Africa seems quite persuasive. Let us consider the language of Judge Fitzmaurice as it is quoted in South Africa's Rejoinder:

> ... if (i) at some time in the past ... other "dissenting" State had in fact, under international law as it then stood, enjoyed rights wider than those conferred by international law in its present form, and (ii) on the emergence of a new and more restrictive rule, had openly and consistently made known its dissent, *at the time when the new rule came, or was in process of coming, into otherwise general acceptance, then the dissenting State could claim exemption from the rule even though it was binding on the community generally it was binding on the community generally and had become a general rule of international law.*[52]

[49] *Id.* at 5. (Italics added.)

[50] E.g., see *Report, S/6073*, Dec. 7, 1964.

[51] Fisheries Case, Judgment of December 18, 1951: *ICJ Reports 1951*, p. 116 at 131.

[52] Gerald Fitzmaurice, "The Law and Procedure of the International Court of Justice, 1951-1954: General Principles and Sources of Law," 30 *British Yearbook of*

This passage correctly admits all that we contend, or Ethiopia and Liberia needed to prevail. For Judge Fitzmaurice seems to be saying that a general rule, an international legal norm in our sense, can come into being over the dissent of a protesting state, but that the protesting state enjoys an *exemption* from its application. Thus the law-creating process at work in international society is not paralyzed by the veto power derived from an overly abstract doctrine of national sovereignty. Article 2(2) is governed on a *per se* basis by existing international legal norms, especially as a consequence of the special character of the Mandate as an *international regime* and the special claims to exercise control on behalf of the well-being of the inhabitants that derives from Article 22, especially if paragraphs (1), (2) and (6) are read in conjunction. South Africa may enjoy an exemption from the norm, but a Mandatory would not appear entitled to the same exemption as might arguably be possessed by a sovereign state. A state *qua* Mandatory seems to have no serious basis for maintaining discretion to violate the norm once it is granted that the Mandate must, whatever else, be administered in accordance with international law.

If South Africa is prepared to accept Judge Fitzmaurice's statement as a summary of "the basic principles of International Law," then, it has accepted almost everything that has been contended for here about the nature of the law-creating processes at work in international society. How can an international legal standard grow into a binding norm, although a norm subject to an exemption, over the dissent of a state? By what process provided for in Article 38? Judge Fitzmaurice's conception presupposes the role of *consensus* as a law-creating fact, although not necessarily consensus in the form of acts by the organized international community. In fact, in the context of Judge Fitzmaurice's discussion, it seems that the relevant consensus for the norms to which his discussion pertained, was to be derived from an aggregation of acts performed by individual states.

South Africa thought so well of this line of reasoning that it has repeated it in its oral argument again referring to *Fisheries* and the article by Judge Fitzmaurice: "such a norm would not be binding on Respondent, inasmuch as the basic principles of international law involve that legal rules are not enforceable against States which, during the period of the coming into general acceptance of the rules in question, openly and consistently made known their dissent therefrom."[53] Mr. de Villiers speaking on behalf of South Africa repeated: "The principle, in other words, that if a new principle of international law comes about over a certain period of time, then it is not binding upon a State which

International Law 1-70, at 25 (1953). (Italics added.)

[53] Oral Argument, April 23, 1966, 65/20, pp. 48-49.

openly and consistently makes known its dissent from it." South Africa evidently wants the best of both worlds. The first world: the absence of consent operates as a veto in the law-creating process; the second world: the absence of consent *only* gives a protesting state an *exemption* from the norm. Now if it is a principle of international law to allow the protesting state an exemption, must not the argument based upon consent as veto fall away? But what is more relevant, if a single recalcitrant state cannot block the law-creating processes, what possible objection can South Africa have to the use of legal documents to which it has not consented, if their use is introduced to disclose the generality of practice or consensus with regard to an emerging norm, and what difference can it make whether these documents are themselves binding or not?

There is in the history of the Court and in the literature of customary international law some dicta that would appear to oppose the contention that an international legal norm or international standards exist and therefore, in response to South Africa's skepticism about the existence of the norm, we feel compelled to examine the nature of the traditional doctrine on the formation of customary international law, both as it has been formulated by this Court and by some prominent international jurists. Most of the difficulty arises, as we have had occasion to observe already, from various statements to the effect that sovereign states are only bound by rules to which they give their consent, either expressly or tacitly; therefore, custom rests on tacit consent, at least on acquiescence, the absence of protest and so on. For instance, we might take as a guideline for this discussion the view of the International Law Commission that "the emergence of a principle or rule of customary international law is generally thought to require presence of the following elements: concordant practice by a number of States with reference to a situation falling within the domain of international relations; continuation or repetition of the practice over some period of time; conception by the States engaged that the practice is not forbidden by prevailing international law; and general acquiescence in the practice by States other than those engaged."[54] Such a formulation is geared to the emergence of customary international law as a consequence of state practice rather than as a result of the formal standard and norm-setting procedures of the organized international community. As such, it overlooks the centralization of the law-creating process in international society as a result of the existence and expanding role of international institutions. It is principally in light of this expanding role and its peculiar relevance to the nondiscrimination norm that it becomes desirable to construe Article 38(1) (b) in a liberal fashion.

The whole status of customary international law can be viewed in the

[54] *Yearbook, International Law Commission,* I, 1950, 275, n9.

perspective set forth by C. Wilfred Jenks in his major work, *The Prospects of International Adjudication* (1964). In the opening paragraph of the chapter on customary international law as it relates to the work of the International Court of Justice, Jenks writes:

> In recent times a cataclysmic rate of political, economic and social change has produced widespread uncertainty concerning much which was previously thought to be well-established law. In these circumstances the nature and extent of the proof of custom required in international adjudication may have a decisive bearing on the extent to which such adjudication promotes effectively the rule of law in world affairs or is a further unsettling factor which constitutes a new source of uncertainty.[55]

Jenks is leading up to a contention that if the requirements for proving custom are imposed either too rigorously or too rigidly by the Court, the entire relevance of international law to the concerns of men and nations is drawn into question: "A number of International Court decisions raise in an acute form the question of the degree of universality and generality of practice of which proof must be afforded to establish the existence of a rule of customary international law; a thorough re-examination of the question of proof of custom is therefore a necessary element in any satisfactory appraisal of the prospects of international adjudication."[56] It is not feasible to attempt "a thorough re-examination." A consideration of two relevant cases, *Fisheries* and *Asylum*, is called for as each seems to contain language damaging to the position urged here.

The *Asylum Case* appears to be relevant in the sense that the subject matter in dispute involved the existence of a norm in the field of human rights, the unreviewable discretion of a state to grant asylum in its embassy to a political fugitive so as to protect him from his political enemies. In the majority opinion of the *Asylum Case* there is the following statement: "The Party which relies on a custom of this kind must prove that this custom is established in such a manner that it has become binding on the other Party. The Colombian Government must prove that the rule invoked by it is in accordance with a constant and uniform usage practiced by the States in question, and that this usage is the expression of a right appertaining to the State granting asylum and a duty incumbent on the territorial State."[57] Despite the rhetoric of "constant and uniform usage" the Court rejected the claim of customary norm on the ground that

---

[55] C. Wilfred Jenks, *The Prospects of International Adjudication*, London: Stevens, 1964, p. 225.
[56] *Ibid*.

[57] Colombian-Peruvian Asylum Case, Judgment of Nov. 20, 1950, *ICJ Reports 1950*, p. 266, at 276.

The facts brought to the knowledge of the Court disclose so much uncertainty and contradiction, so much fluctuation and discrepancy in the exercise of diplomatic asylum and in the official views expressed on various occasions, there has been so much inconsistency in the rapid succession of conventions on asylum, ratified by some States and rejected by others, and the practice has been so much influenced by considerations of political expediency in the various cases, that it is not possible to discern in all this any constant and uniform usage, accepted as law, with regard to the alleged rule of unilateral and definitive qualification of the offence.[58]

The important point to realize is that asylum involves an adjustment of *competing interests* of states, whereas the norm and standards of non-discrimination and nonseparation involve the promotion of *common interests* of states and of the organized international community taken as a whole, and what is more, common interests that rest upon a widely shared and deeply felt humanitarian conviction. In this respect apartheid corresponds to genocide, and the nature of the law-creating process in response to both is remarkably similar, one in which the collective will of the world community has been shocked into unanimity and in which the moral basis of law is most visible. It is precisely because there is an "offender" that there is a drive to create a norm, and if that offender is allowed to prevent the legal condemnation of his action by stating a protest, then international law is rendered impotent in the face of the gravest challenges to the values underlying the entire global order.

In the *Fisheries Case*, the Court affirmed that "then ten-mile rule would appear inapplicable as against Norway inasmuch as she has always opposed any attempt to apply it to the Norwegian coast." But the Court emphasized many other factors, including Norway's long historical claim, its peculiar economic dependence on fishing, the general toleration of other states, and the acquiescence by Great Britain, itself, over a long period of time.[59] Here again the alleged customary norm was a matter of adjusting *competing interests* of states differently situated, that is, shore states versus maritime states, rather than enforcing a world community standard against a dissenting state. The proof of custom appropriate to the evolution of a customary norm of international law of the latter type is a consensus as manifest in the formal acts of the competent organs of the organized international community. Such a law-creating procedure is a functional requirement of a world exhibiting even the rudimentary degree of centralization now present. This procedure is parallel to the evolution of custom by state practice, ascertained by the *interaction of states* rather than by their expressions through manifesta-

[58] *Id.*, at 277.   [59] See note 51.

tion of a *collective will*. The ICJ has in the past only been faced with claims alleging the existence of norms arising out of *interaction*; it is in this respect that Ethiopia and Liberia regarded the case as one of first impression where the background of precedents is less relevant than might, at first, appear from the generality of the language previously used in opinions of the Court.

Hans Kelsen, with characteristic acuity, shows that the requirement of consent in relation to customary international law is, at best, a juristic fiction designed to reconcile the doctrine of national sovereignty with the birth of binding international obligations. Kelsen writes:

> International customary law could be interpreted as created by a consent of the states only if it were possible to prove that the custom which evidences the existence of a norm of international law is constituted by the acts of all the states which are bound by the norms of customary international law, or that a norm of customary law is binding upon a state only if this state by its own acts participated in establishing the custom in question. Since general international law is customary law and since it is binding upon all states of the international community, it would—according to the theory of custom as tacit consent—be necessary to prove that all the states of the international community have consented to all the norms of general international law by their actual conduct, by participation in the establishment of the custom which evidences the law. Such a proof is not required and is in all instances excluded where general international law is applied to states which never had the opportunity to participate in the establishment of the law-creating custom.[60]

Kelsen gives several examples, among them the birth of a new state that never participated in the creation of the norms and yet is considered bound, independent of its consent, or its willingness to consent, from the beginning of its existence. The relevance of this juristic exercise is to suggest that "something other" than consent must be the true explanation of the validity of customary international law.

Lauterpacht also seems to suggest that notions of sovereign consent and universality, at least if taken literally, would impoverish, the dynamic possibilities for the growth of international law, as well as undercut much of the law in being. Lauterpacht asks and responds to a very revealing rhetorical question:

> If universal acceptance alone is the hall-mark of the existence of a rule of international law, how many rules of international law can

[60] Hans Kelsen, *The Principles of International Law*, Berkeley, University of California Press, 1952, pp. 311-12.

there be said to be in effective existence? Any such acceptance of the standard of universality as the test of the existence of a rule of international law may be open to the objection that it puts into question the existence of most rules and principles of international law. For this would appear to be the result of a judicial method which declines to treat a widely adopted practice as constituting accepted international law and which elevates the attitude of a small number of States to the authority of a practice entitled to equal—or greater—respect.[61]

The essence of South Africa's insistence is precisely that its protest should be allowed to block the formation of a legal norm even in a context where the world community has an interest so manifest as in a Mandate. Judge Lauterpacht also wrote that "In few matters do judicial discretion and freedom of judicial appreciation manifest themselves more conspicuously than in determining the existence of international custom."[62] Such a discretion might be exercised with appropriate appreciation of the relevance of the will of the organized international community on the issue of whether or not the norm contended for actually exists. Such an appreciation, if taken together with Lauterpacht's advocacy of "predominance" rather than "universality" as the measure of general practice and of acceptance by nations, would seem to make out an overwhelming case for acknowledging the existence of the norm of nondiscrimination and nonseparation as a matter of customary international law.

Article 38(1) (c): "the general principles of law recognized by civilized nations."

In the jurisprudence of the Court "the general principles of law" have been generally used to fill in gaps in international law by relying upon private law analogies based upon legal rules and institutions commonly found in municipal legal systems. As such, Article 38(1) (c) provides a way to enrich international law on the basis of comparative law research. There is no tradition, as with customary international law, of premising the existence of a general principle of law upon evidence of universality, or the absence of any protest, or upon a sense of obligation with respect to the specific duty contended for. As such, "general principles" is the source of law least closely tied to the ideas of legal obligation connected with theories of legal positivism. On the contrary, 38(1) (c) has been frequently identified as the way in which the perspectives of natural law can be most easily accommodated in a developing international system. But, in addition, in relation to 38(1) (c) it

[61] Lauterpacht, *op.cit. supra*, note 18, pp. 191-92. [62] *Id.* at 368.

would seem most appropriate for the Court to confirm the role of *consensus*, as manifest in the formal acts and proceedings of the organized international community, as a source or basis of international legal norms.

In this respect, there would be two ways in which Article 38(1) (c) might establish or, at least, strengthen the contention that a legal norm of nondiscrimination and nonseparation has come into being in international society. The first way would regard the widespread pervasity of laws against racial discrimination and segregation in the municipal systems of virtually every state as establishing on a comparative-law basis the essential precondition for the assertion of the norm of non-discrimination as "a general principle of law" within the meaning of Article 38(1) (c). The second way would regard the *international consensus*[63] as a general principle of law recognized by civilized nations. Such a view would approach the interpretation of the subdivisions of Article 38 in light of the needs of a developing international legal order. Article 38 would then possess a dynamic, open-textured content that would itself give full scope to the fact that the Statute of the Court as an integral part of the Charter of the United Nations is itself capable of and entitled to the same flexible principles of interpretation as we have said are applicable to the Charter, or for that matter to the Mandate instrument. The statute as an integral portion of the Charter underscores the point we wish to stress that this Court is itself conceived and constituted as an institutional component of the organized international community, thereby making appropriate its role in giving effect to the law-creating processes now going on in other parts of this organized international community.

All legal systems have relied upon the formative influence of social consensus in evolving law applicable to matters of basic social rights and duties. And certainly international law evolved much of its earlier content by the efforts of great international lawyers to set forth crystallizations of the *jus gentium* or *consensus gentium* during the several centuries preceding the formulation of sources in Article 38. Did the adoption of Article 38 imply an end to this social basis for the renewal and extension of international law? Restrictive approaches to the interpretation of Article 38(1) (c) reflect an excessive attachment to legal positivism, or what amounts to the same thing, an exaggerated solicitude to absolutist doctrines of national sovereignty, making all legal obligations rest upon evidences of universal national consent. Such perspectives deny the functional requirements of an effective international legal system given the needs and structure of international society as it currently

---

[63] The cumulative evidence of consensus on the human rights issue is now overwhelming. For sample documentation see Applicants' Reply Pleading, pp. 476-519.

functions, but ignore, as well, the close association of "general principles" with ideas of equity and natural justice that have existed from the
time of the drafting sessions of the 1920 Committee of Jurists, the group
responsible for drafting the original Statute of the Permanent Court of
International Justice. For instance, Baron Deschamps, a leading figure
on that Committee, referred to this source of international law as incorporating the "legal conscience of civilized nations," a phrase curiously resembling Judge Alvarez' constant reference to the "juridical
conscience of the peoples" as a source of international law. And Mr. de
Lapradelle, also a prominent member of the 1920 Committee of Jurists,
said that "the general principles" would enable the International Court
to "judge in accordance with law, justice, and equity."[64]

S. Rosenne on the basis of his appraisal of the relevant practice of
the Court comes to a similar conclusion:

> These instances show that the general principles of law recognized
> by civilized nations are not so much generalizations reached by ap-
> plication of comparative law . . . as particularizations of a common
> underlying sense of what is just in the circumstances. Having an
> independent existence, their validity as legal norms does not derive
> from the consent of the parties as such, provided they are norms
> which the Court considers civilized States ought to recognize.[65]

This stress on underlying ideas of justice posits, quite obviously, a conception of Article 38(1) (c) that seems entirely ample to demonstrate
its relevance to the acceptance of the consensus of the organized international community as a source of international legal norms.

It might be useful to consider how the international crime of piracy
came to be defined as a crime in the law of nations. Without attempting a
discussion of this issue, the answer seems to involve a generality of practice reinforced by a moral consensus and a common set of interests in
the control of piratical activity. In the Court's advisory opinion in the
case of Reservations to the Convention on the Prevention and Punishment of Genocide the following passage appears:

> The origins of the Convention show that it was the intention of the
> United Nations to condemn and punish genocide as "a crime under
> international law" involving the denial of the right of existence of
> entire human groups, a denial which shocks the conscience of man-
> kind and results in great losses to humanity, and which is contrary to
> the moral law and to the spirit and aims of the United Nations [Res.

---

[64] Quotations taken from Manley O.
Hudson, *The Permanent Court of Inter-
national Justice 1920-1942*, New York,
Macmillan, 1943, pp. 194-95.

[65] Shabtai Rosenne, *The International
Court of Justice*, Leyden, Nijhoff, 1957,
p. 423.

96(I) of G.A.]. The first consequence of this conception is that the principles underlying the Convention are principles which are recognized by civilized nations as binding on States, even without any conventional obligations. A second consequence is the universal character both of the condemnation of genocide and of the cooperation required in order to liberate mankind from such an odious scourge.[66]

This quotation bears significantly on the proper resolution of the main substantive question present in the South West Africa litigation. For if we substitute the word "apartheid" for the word "genocide" we notice a logical, sociological, and moral symmetry of rather remarkable proportion. Note that the ICJ was willing to rely upon a General Assembly Resolution to construe the character of the international legal norms presented for its consideration *and*, furthermore, found it *legally* relevant to discuss the impact of genocide upon the conscience of mankind, the moral law, and the underlying spirit and aims of the United Nations. It is especially interesting that the ICJ apparently regarded genocide as violative of international law even without the convention before it. On the basis of what evidence and as a result of what law-creating process could this conclusion be reached except on the basis of the manifest will of the organized international community?

It is, of course, true that when the Genocide Convention came before the ICJ no state was defending the practice of genocide as the South Africans today defend the practice of apartheid. But let us assume so as to test the earlier reasoning of the ICJ that the Genocide Convention had been brought into being while Hitler was still in operation and suppose that Germany was advancing a defense of its policies of oppressing Jews and others. Would Germany's protest really undermine the capacity of the organized world community and the ICJ to take legal account of the international consensus emerging in opposition to the practice of genocide? The international community would be just as shocked and violated. Would it not be absurd to say that no international legal obligations can emerge until the offending state is defunct? The result of taking universality as a literal precondition is to make the organized international community absolutely incapable *in law* of taking action against any existing practice or policy perceived as *evil* and shocking. Ethiopia and Liberia in the *South West Africa Cases* were testing this capacity to take legal action against a perceived social evil that has shocked the conscience of mankind, although the regulatory action asked for was of a modest sort in view of the fact that South Africa as Mandatory was

[66] *Reservations to the Convention on Genocide, Advisory Opinion, ICJ Reports* *1951*, p. 15, at 23.

already supposedly subordinated to the will of the international community, at least so far as its conduct in the Territory was concerned.

Even if the ICJ, or a majority of it, found itself unable to regard the international legal norm as a general principle of international law recognized by civilized nations within the meaning of Article 38(1) (c), nevertheless this source of law should provide canons of interpretation supportive of the meaning of well-being contended for by Ethiopia and Liberia. At the very least, then, "general principles" guide an interpretation by the Court of a document like the Mandate instrument. For it is by "general principles" that the Court has consistently introduced considerations of equity and justice into its analysis of legal argument, and especially in connection with construing treaties and other legal documents.[67] Judge Manley O. Hudson in his opinion in the *Water from the Meuse Case* argued that the authority of the Court to apply "general principles of law recognized by civilized nations" gives it "some freedom to consider principles of equity as part of the international law which it must apply."[68]

In connection with the interpretative act Judge Lauterpacht's separate opinion in the *South West Africa (Voting Procedure) Case* seems to be very instructive. Judge Lauterpacht there emphasized the principle of *nemo judex in re sua* in approaching an interpretation of the Mandate, a principle that, given the character of the underlying instrument, provides good legal grounds for resisting South Africa's insistence that Article 2(1) confers almost boundless discretion. As Judge Lauterpacht expressed it:

> In so far as the principle *nemo judex in re sua* is not only a general principle of law expressly sanctioned by the Court, but also a principle of good faith, it is particularly appropriate in relation to an instrument of a fiduciary character such as a mandate or a trust in which equitable considerations acting upon the conscience are of compelling application. This, too, is a general principle of law recognized by civilised States.[69]

Judge Lauterpacht further elaborated this approach in his separate opinion in the Admissibility of Hearings of Petitioners by the Committee on South West Africa in a manner that bears indirectly on an in-

[67] See, e.g., Judge Winiarski's dissenting comment in *Interpretation of Peace Treaties, Advisory Opinion: ICJ Reports 1950*, p. 65 at 95, that the court should have declined to give an opinion, as otherwise "fundamental principles of law and justice, would be disregarded."

[68] Water from the Meuse Case, P.C.I.J.,

Ser. A/B, No. 70, 1937, p. 4 at 76-77.

[69] *South West Africa—Voting Procedure on Question Relating to Reports and Petitioners Concerning the Territory of South West Africa, Advisory Opinion of June 7, 1955, ICJ Reports 1955*, p. 67 at 105.

terpretation of Article 21. Judge Lauterpacht argued that where one party seeks to block the fulfillment of the rights of the other, then this colors the interpretation of each specific obligation in the interests of restoring the original objectives of the legal regime:

> What, apart from the general principles of interpretation as set out above, is the authority for the proposition that the Court may replace one means of supervision for another, not previously authorized—nay, expressly disallowed? . . . this is not a case of contract or even an ordinary treaty analogous to a contract. As already pointed out, this is a case of the operation and application of multi-lateral instruments, as interpreted by the Court in its Opinion of 11th July 1950, creating an international status—an international regime—transcending a mere contractual relation. . . . The essence of such instruments is that their validity continues notwithstanding changes in the attitudes, or the status, or the very survival of individual parties or persons affected. . . . The unity and operation of the regime created by them cannot be allowed to fail because of a breakdown or gap which may arise in consequence of an act of party or otherwise.[70]

In effect, Judge Lauterpacht is calling upon the ICJ to be creative enough to supply what is needed by way of interpretation to keep the regime going with the same set of relationships as originally intended, which in the context of the Mandate requires some way of reasserting the interests of the organized world community in view of the Mandatory's own unwillingness to implement the well-being of inhabitants, as well-being is generally understood.

> Article 39(1) (d): "subject to the provisions of Article 59, judicial decisions and the teachings of the most highly qualified publicists of the various nations, as subsidiary means for the determination of rules of law."

The juristic background for the consensus theory of legal obligation has been developed fully and explicitly in the writings of C. Wilfred Jenks, especially in an essay entitled "The Will of the World Community as the Basis of Obligation in International Law."[71] Several brief passages of this essay indicate its relevance. After commenting on the multiplicity of explanations for the binding character of international law that have been given through the centuries Jenks writes:

---

[70] *Admissibility of Hearings of Petitioners by the Committee on South West Africa, ICJ Reports 1956,* p. 23 at 48; cf. also *Case of Certain Norwegian Loans, ICJ Reports 1957,* p. 9 at 49 (Judgment of July 6, 1957).

[71] C. Wilfred Jenks, *Law, Freedom and Welfare,* Dobbs Ferry, Oceana, 1963, pp. 83-100.

May it perhaps be that we have hitherto failed to secure a satisfactory measure of agreement on the basis of obligation in international law because the law is only now reaching a stage in its development at which we can rationalize from experience, and from potentialities which are opening up before us, an analysis of the basis of obligation which is historically, logically and above all teleologically satisfactory? May it not be that only in the will of the world community as the expression of the brotherhood of man can a satisfactory basis of obligation be found, and that only now is it becoming realistic to find in the will of the world community the basis of obligation in international law?[72]

Jenks goes on to say that the traditional explanations of the basis of international obligations have been distorted by transplanting the notion of national sovereignty from studies by political philosophers of the state as an isolated entity to the environment of international relations where the interaction of states is the basic nexus for legal regulation. The classical expositions of sovereignty, for instance Jean Bodin, were concerned exclusively with providing a theory to explain and justify the centralization of national power in a single government, thereby giving the nation-state a rationale to overcome the residues of feudalism in this postmedieval period when ideas of sovereignty first were formulated. But a theory designed to vindicate *domination* in domestic society is not easily made to serve the needs of *coordination* in international life.

Jenks tries to demonstrate that a reliance upon the will of the international community builds upon, rather than repudiates past thinking of international lawyers, it is a synthesis conceived in light of contemporary international needs: "The law crystallises spontaneously by recognized procedures in accordance with the needs of international life because such is the will of the world community. The individual conscience recognizes the binding force of the law accepted by the world community. It is the will of the world community which defines and maintains the law which there is a moral obligation to obey."[73]

Jenks then goes on to view the traditional sources of law in light of the overriding relevance of the will of the world community. This aspect of his thought anticipates the attempt here to demonstrate the possibilities for accommodating law-creating by the organized international community within the three main subsections of Article 38(1) of this Court's Statute. Jenks writes on this matter as follows:

The will of the community constitutes the basis of obligation; but the law of the community comes into being by all the processes of legal development and growth known to mature legal systems; it is

[72] *Id.* at 83. [73] *Id.* at 91.

the will of the community that principles and rules evolved in accordance with these processes of development and growth shall be regarded as binding. Treaty, custom, the general principles of law recognized by civilized nations, judicial precedent and the opinions of the most highly qualified publicists all fall naturally into place as methods by which, in accordance with the will of the community, the law is developed to meet the changing and growing needs of an evolving society. "An expanding society demands an expanding common law." . . . law is not a limited set of settled rules but a method of resolving problems by recourse to a body of living principles of which the settled rules are, at best, an imperfect expression. . . . The concept that the basis of obligation in international law is to be found in the will of the world community recognizes that constant adaptation to changing needs in accordance with acknowledged laws of growth is a fundamental element in all law; the consensual theory ignores this element and the natural rights theory and a number of the modern theories, while recognizing it in varying degrees, appears to give it insufficient weight.[74]

As early as 1910 Pearce Higgins, an international lawyer not at all inclined to the grandiose, took note of the fact that "the social forces of the world are more and more becoming organized, directed and regulated, and the pressure of the public opinion of the world cannot if it be steadily persevered in and directed be resisted in the long run."[75] Jenks emphasizes the role of international institutions as vehicles for the expression of the will of the world community and as an important part of the law-creating process at work in international life. Jenks quotes from Lord Mansfield to show that the content of the will of the international community is, in general, to be expressed by "recognized procedures for appraising 'justice, equity, convenience, and the reason of the thing' and determining the law of nations as it results 'from the usages established between civilized nations, from the laws of humanity, and from the requirements of the public conscience.' " Jenks comments "We cannot find it in anything less."[76] In arguing that the novelty of the concept "the will of the world community" should not prevent its acceptance Jenks recalls Judge Jessup's happy use of a Chinese proverb: "It is always well to have in the background of one's mind a multitude of definitions covering the subject at hand to prevent oneself from accepting the most obvious."[77]

Nicolas Politis, building on the work of Krabbe and Georges Scelle, developed his conception of international law on the premise of "la con-

[74] *Id.* at 91-92.
[75] A. Pearce Higgins, *The Binding Force of International Law*, Cambridge, Oxford University Press, 1910, pp. 11-12.
[76] Jenks, *op.cit. supra*, note 71, at 97.
[77] *Id.*, at 90.

science juridique des peuples," conceiving of law as necessarily reflecting the moral consciousness of the times.[78] The orientation of Politis is remarkably close to that adopted by Judge Alvarez, and has certain resemblances, as well, to the judicial perspectives of such Judges as Azevedo and Bustamante. But just as the law of civil liberties in the United States was built on the foundations laid by lonely dissenters, so the work of Judge Alvarez is relevant not as indicative of the past approach of the ICJ to these issues, but as revealing an unprecedented sensitivity to the social and moral basis upon which all legal systems, whether national or international, rest. In the *Corfu Channel Case* of 1948 Alvarez wrote a separate opinion in which he said "In consequence of the demands of the juridical consciousness of the peoples, there is a new tendency to introduce the notion of delinquency as a fundamental precept of international law." Among the three forms of international delinquency the one pertinent to this case consists of "acts contrary to the sentiments of humanity committed by a State on its own territory, even with the object of defending its security and its vital interests."[79] South Africa as Mandatory, of course, "is committing a severe form of delinquency" by its reliance upon apartheid. Judge Alvarez's formulation is helpful because it identified so explicitly what is the true motive force in connection with the evolution of legal norms condemning genocide or apartheid—the sentiments of humanity have crystallized and intend a legal effect. It is, in this connection that Judge Alvarez's observation that "the Court is the most authoritative organ for the expression of this juridical conscience"[80] acquires its full significance.

Judge Alvarez was also fully cognizant of the role of the organized international community in giving content to his new international law of social interdependence. As he put it in the *Fisheries Case*: "For the principles of law resulting from the juridical conscience of peoples to have any value, they must have a tangible manifestation, that is to say, they must be expressed by authorized bodies."[81] And to remove all doubt about his reference Judge Alvarez suggests that "resolutions of diplomatic assemblies, particularly those of the United Nations" are reflective of the content of juridical consciousness.

Rosalyn Higgins in a major study of the development of international law by the political organs of the United Nations writes as follows:

> The United Nations is a very appropriate body to look for indications of developments in international law, for international custom is to be deduced from the practice of states, which includes their in-

[78] Nicolas S. Politis, *Les Nouvelles Tendances du Droit International*, Paris, Hachette, 1927, pp. 46-91.
[79] Corfu Channel Case, Judgment of April 9, 1949, ICJ Reports 1949, 4, at 45.

[80] Admission of a State to the United Nations (Charter, Art. 4), Advisory Opinion of May 28, 1948, ICJ Reports 1948, p. 57 at 69.
[81] See note 51 at 148.

ternational dealings as manifested by their diplomatic action and public pronouncements. With the development of international organizations, the votes and views of states have come to have legal significance as evidence of customary law. Moreover, *the practice of states comprises their collective acts as well as the total of their individual acts. . . . Collective acts by states, repeated by and acquiesced in by sufficient numbers with sufficient frequency, eventually attain the status of law.*[82]

It is on this basis that Ethiopia and Liberia contended that their legal norm of nondiscrimination came into being. Mrs. Higgins also has some helpful things to say about the political character of these law-creating processes, emphasizing that the context of controversy does not impair the legal relevance of what results from it. Mrs. Higgins aptly writes that if "international law is to be effective" it "*must* concern itself with the controversial and political."[83] Mrs. Higgins also refers to the role of the political organs in generating evidence of the existence of norms and standards: "such organs have from time to time promulgated declarations of purportedly existing rules of law; such pronouncements are not only evidence of a customary law—they may also affect the direction of that law."[84]

In this regard it may also be helpful to recall Judge Lauterpacht's observation in the *South West Africa (Voting Procedure) Case* on the legal significance of General Assembly action: "Whatever may be the content of the recommendation and whatever may be the nature and circumstances of the majority by which it has been reached, it is nevertheless a legal act of the principal organ of the United Nations which Members of the United Nations are under a duty to treat with a degree of respect appropriate to a Resolution of the General Assembly."[85] This suggests the *relevance*, although not the *decisiveness*, of the *competence of nonbinding legal instruments to generate binding interpretations of binding instruments.* Oscar Schachter, the former Director of the Legal Division at the United Nations, also has expressed the view rather strongly that a consensus approaching virtual unanimity, disclosed in a resolution, would establish an interpretation of a Charter provision entitled to great legal weight:

> . . . one might start with the principle that an "authentic" interpretation of a treaty by the parties is legally binding on them to the same degree as the treaty itself. I believe it is *generally accepted that this conclusion would hold for an interpretation of the Charter adopted by*

---

[82] Higgins, *op.cit. supra*, note 12, at 2. (Italics added.)
[83] *Id.* at 3.
[84] *Id.* at 4.
[85] See note 69 (add at 120).

all the Members (or even "by the overwhelming majority" except for some abstentions) in the General Assembly; the interpretation would be characterized by international lawyers as having the same legal force and effect as the Charter itself.[86]

Professor Myres S. McDougal in the course of his writing develops two ideas both of which are relevant to this discussion: first, his ideas about legal authority, and second, his emphasis on the international legal protection of basic human rights as integral to the regulation of violence in international society.

McDougal identifies "law" with "community expectations," thereby providing a social criterion for the identification of *who* in the system can create *norms*, as well as clarifying the *legal effects* of those norms. McDougal, writing with Harold Lasswell, defines "legal process" and "authority" in the following fashion: "Within the decision-making process our chief interest is in the legal process by which we mean the making of authoritative and controlling decisions. Authority is the structure of expectation concerning who, with what qualifications and mode of selection, is competent to make which decisions by what criteria and what procedures."[87] This orientation toward international legal authority emphasizes the degree to which law is a *social* fact. For McDougal the character of legal obligations is influenced by the prevailing patterns of community expectation, both with regard to the *sources* of law and to the *norms* thereby generated. In terms of the contention in the argument made here, this orientation supports the claim that the General Assembly is competent to generate norms in the area of human rights if it acts on the basis of virtual unanimity; furthermore, the failure to uphold these community expectations with regard to the norm of nondiscrimination will undermine the respect for law and legal procedures. If the ICJ under present international conditions repudiates the norm of nondiscrimination after it has been so frequently posited as authoritative by the organized international community then it will create the impression that the international judicial process is aloof from the shared values and policies of mankind, and that to promote these values and policies effectively requires the pursuit of nonjudicial means. McDougal's conception of the link between community expectations and legal authority also lends support to the claim that the formal acts of international institutions can constitute a source of law within the scope of Article 38.

Professor McDougal also articulates the centrality of human rights in the evolution of an international legal system capable of dealing with contemporary needs. Writing with Gertrude Leighton, McDougal states:

[86] Schachter, *op.cit. supra*, note 37, at 186. (Italics added.)
[87] Myres S. McDougal and Associates, *Studies in World Public Order*, New Haven, Yale University Press, 1960, p. 13.

It is only from a perspective of centuries that the United Nations program for "human rights" can be accurately observed or rationally appraised. This program, too often thought to be at the periphery of the purposes of the United Nations, represents in fact the main core of rational objectives not only of the United Nations but of all democratic government. It represents the converging and integration on a global scale of many movements, movements hitherto restricted in a real diffusion, but centuries-old and rooted deep in universal human nature and civilized culture.[88]

And in subsequent passage, human rights are connected with world peace:

It is commonly agreed, as the Charter states, that the principal purpose for which the United Nations was established is the maintenance of "international peace and security." Throughout the Charter, however, runs the wise recognition, which pervaded all the great declarations of war aims and general consciousness of mankind, that peace and security, even in the limited sense of freedom from physical violence, cannot be obtained by arbitrary fiat and sheer balancing of power. A peace to endure must include the conditions of peace and a reduction of the severe frustrations that drive men to violence.[89]

In the South West Africa context such a passage well expresses the effort to persuade the ICJ to enforce the norm of nondiscrimination against South Africa, thereby acknowledging the contention that apartheid involves such a severe frustration of human rights that it endangers peace and security. The organs of the world community entrusted with the responsibility for the maintenance of international peace and security have declared, in fact and repeatedly so, as authoritatively as possible, that apartheid is a threat to international peace.

McDougal also shares Judge Lauterpacht's view that the human rights provisions of the Charter create legal duties and specific obligations, and considers that the task for the world community is "to translate obligations already assumed into concrete detail in the practice of states." McDougal writes that "the practice of the various organs of the United Nations under the Charter during the past four years is relevant as evidence of the common consensus of mankind that all peoples everywhere are interdependent as to human rights and security."[90] Certainly, in the twenty years since McDougal and Leighton wrote this article the course of practice in international organization, especially in the area of racial discrimination, has abundantly reinforced this observation, gen-

[88] *Id.* at 335-36.
[89] *Id.* at 337-38.
[90] *Id.* at 369-70.

erating a variety of claims to exercise *legal* control over deprivations of human rights that have been found endangering international peace and security.

Conclusion

The argument presented here relied on looks forward to an interpretation of Article 38(1) that is wide enough to permit the ICJ to classify as binding rules of international law certain norms of conduct evolved by the consensus machinery of the United Nations. The analysis of the subdivisions of Article 38(1) has emphasized the extent to which foreshadowings of such an interpretation are already to be found in the authoritative literature of international law, as well as in the jurisprudence of the ICJ itself. Although the recommended development is foreshadowed, its explicit assertion by the ICJ would be a signal step forward in the painfully tormented struggle to build a world legal order adequate to the needs of our time. The outcome of the *South West Africa Cases* discloses some of these torments, but it also provides an occasion to assess what might have been done, and hence what could be done in the future.

VI. On the Quasi-Legislative Competence of the General Assembly

I

THE PROCESSES of law-creation in international society have never been very clearly understood by international lawyers. It has been traditional to associate the creation of international law with "the sources of international law" contained in Article 38 of the Statute of the International Court of Justice. Such an approach distorts inquiry by conceiving of law-creation exclusively from the perspective of the rules applicable in this one centralized, judicial institution,[1] an institution that expresses the positivistic assumption that international legal obligations must always be shown to rest upon some tangible evidence of consent on the part of the state that is bound.[2] The expansion of international society to include the active participation of the Afro-Asian states and the slow and uneven trends toward regional global consciousness has produced a situation that calls for a more sociologically grounded reinterpretation of the basis of obligation in international law. One way to attempt this reinterpretation is to complicate the relationship between state sovereignty and the growth of international law by examining the argument that the General Assembly is endowed with, and actually exercises, a limited legislative competence.

The idea of attributing quasi-legislative force to resolutions of the General Assembly expresses a middle position between a formally difficult affirmation of true legislative status and a formalistic denial of the law-creating role and impact. To affirm the legislative competence of the General Assembly in qualified terms is thus expressive of a certain well-founded uneasiness about how to give an account of the jurisprudential basis for General Assembly competence to develop new law and repeal old law.[3] I propose to consider, first, the jurisprudential basis for at-

[1] Such a perspective overlooks the role of unilateral claims to act posited by nation-states and community prescriptions about action laid down by nonjudicial international institutions. For a critical reinterpretation of "the sources of international law" see Clive Parry, *The Sources and Evidences of International Law,* Manchester University Press, 1965. On the interaction between traditional sources and U.N. resolutions as a source of international law, see Leo Gross, "The United Nations and the Role of Law," *International Organization,* 19 (Summer 1965), 537, 555-58.

[2] But see Hersch Lauterpacht, *The Development of International Law by the International Court of Justice,* London: Stevens, 1958, pp. 155-223.

[3] The distinction between the *declaration, development, creation,* and *repudiation* of rules of international law is not clear-cut. The decentralized quality of international society emphasizes the importance of the self-determined status of legal rules by various national actors. These acts of self-determination may be mutually inconsistent to varying degrees and, in the absence of stronger central institutions, there is no assured way to obtain an authoritative interpretation of the relationship between an "existing" rule and a formulation of a rule in a resolution of the General Assembly.

tributing a limited legislative status to those resolutions of the Assembly that are supported by a consensus of the membership, and, second, some examples of areas wherein this exercise of quasi-legislative competence has made and might continue to make a contribution to world legal order.

In 1945 at San Francisco the Philippines Delegation made the following proposal to endow the General Assembly with legislative authority:

The General Assembly should be vested with the legislative authority to enact rules of international law which should become effective and binding upon the members of the Organization after such rules have been approved by a majority vote of the Security Council. Should the Security Council fail to act on any of such rules within a period of thirty (30) days after submission thereof to the Security Council, the same should become effective and binding as if approved by the Security Council.[4]

The Philippine proposal was decisively rejected by a vote of 26-1 at a drafting session of Commission II.[5] If Charter intent is decisive and strictly construed, it becomes impossible to attribute binding legal force to resolutions of the General Assembly or to consider that the Assembly is in any sense an active, potential, or partial legislative organ. This conclusion has been recently reaffirmed by scholarly observers.[6]

But this formally persuasive denial of legislative status is not nearly so relevant to patterns of practice and expectation as one might be inclined to suppose. Increasingly in other legal contexts the characterization of a norm as *formally binding* is not very significantly connected with its *functional operation* as law.[7] A few examples may clarify this assertion. In the Japanese case of *Shimoda and Others v. Japan* the Tokyo District Court was trying to assess the extent to which the atomic bombings of Hiroshima and Nagasaki violated international law.[8] In reasoning to a conclusion the court made virtually interchangeable use of rules contained in fully binding international treaties (Hague Rules of Land Warfare) and those contained in draft rules (Draft Rules of Air Warfare). In the Shimoda setting, then, draft rules had the same (or at least an indistinguishable) role as did treaty rules widely adhered to on

---

[4] 9 UNCIO Docs. 316 (1945).
[5] *Ibid.*, 70.
[6] J. S. de Yturriaga, "Non-Self-Governing Territories," *1964 Yearbook of World Affairs*, pp. 178-212, esp. 209-12. For general treatment of these issues see selections, citations, and comments in Falk and Saul H. Mendlovitz, eds., *The Strategy of World Order, Vol. 3: The United Nations*, New York, World Law Fund, 1966, pp. 37-122, 227-48.

[7] By "functional operation as law" is meant a perceptible relevance to expectations about the permissibility of behavior, including a reference to the use of legal rhetoric to protest a violation of these expectations.
[8] For a text of the Shimoda decision, see the *Japanese Annual of International Law*, 1964, pp. 212-52; for an interpretation see Falk, *Legal Order in a Violent World*, pp. 374-413.

the subject of poison gas. The elaborately pondered American decision to refrain from ratification of the Protocol Prohibiting in War the Use of Asphyxiating, Poisonous, or other Gases, and of Bacteriological Methods of Warfare (1925) did not exert any influence on the presupposition by the Japanese court of an American obligation to comply.[9]

Another example of this tendency to view nonbinding undertakings as binding is presented by the moratorium on nuclear testing established by the United States and the Soviet Union in the autumn of 1958. Although it was made clear that neither country had renounced its right to test, the resumption of Soviet testing in 1961 was treated in many respects as similar to a violation of a legal duty.[10]

The outcome of the financing controversy has been widely interpreted as undermining or, at least, as diminishing the authority of the International Court of Justice because its analysis of the controversy in the Expenses Case has been cast aside in the process of searching for a settlement. The neglect by the parties in the dispute of the "judgment" has not been considered much less significant because the Court handed down an advisory opinion, and not a decision in a contentious case.

These examples are drawn from the recent practice of legal institutions to call attention to the rather indefinite line that separates *binding* from *nonbinding* norms governing international behavior. Thus the formal limitations of status, often stressed by international lawyers, may not prevent resolutions of the General Assembly, or certain of them, from acquiring a normative status in international life.[11]

The nature of legal obligation in international relations underlies any inquiry into the status of General Assembly resolutions. This subject is complex and controversial. Some distinguished writers have started to emphasize the will of the international community as the fundamental law-creating energy.[12] Such an emphasis contrasts with the more traditionalist assumption that all obligations in international law can be traced directly (via explicit agreement) or indirectly (via state practice) to the consent of the sovereign state or to some system of natural rights and duties that is valid in all places for all time.[13] The Permanent Court of International Justice lent the weight of its authority to this consensual and contractual view of law-creation in the famous majority opinion in the *Lotus Case*:

[9] *Loc.cit.*, at 241-42.
[10] See, e.g. Arthur Dean's testimony before the Senate Foreign Relations Committee, *Hearings, Nuclear Test Ban*, Exec. M, 88th Cong., 1st Sess., pp. 824-25, Aug. 1963.
[11] See citations in note 4.

[12] C. W. Jenks, *Law, Freedom, and Welfare*, Dobbs Ferry, Oceana, 1963, pp. 83-100. For a more detailed discussion see Chapter V.
[13] See, *e.g.*, James L. Brierly, *The Basis of Obligation in International Law*, Oxford University Press, 1958, pp. 1-62.

International law governs relations between independent States. The rules of law binding upon States therefore emanate from their own free will as expressed in conventions or by usages generally accepted as expressing principles of law and established in order to regulate the relations between these co-existing independent communities or with a view to the achievement of common aims. Restrictions upon the independence of States cannot therefore be presumed.[14]

France, the Soviet Union, and South Africa continue to insist upon a sovereignty-centered conception of obligation in international relations, but there is discernible a trend from consent to consensus as the basis of international legal obligations.[15] This trend reflects an adjustment to the altered condition of international society, especially the growing perception of social and economic interdependence, the increased numbers of states participating in international affairs, the growth of international institutions as focal points for the implementation of the will of the international community, and the diminishing willingness to insulate internationally important activity from international legal control by unrestricted deference to the claims of domestic jurisdiction. In a world fraught with conflict and instability there is a widely felt need to find ways to adapt international legal order to the changing character of social and political demands and to develop techniques of peaceful change as an alternative to violence and warfare. This need is given dramatic urgency by the tendency of civil wars to serve as the main arena for international conflict. If international society is to function effectively, it requires a limited legislative authority, at minimum, to translate an overriding consensus among states into rules of order and norms of obligation despite the opposition of one or more sovereign states.[16]

The United States Supreme Court recently found occasion in the *Sabbatino* case to rely upon the notion of consensus in the course of assessing the reality of an international legal obligation.[17] In that controversial decision the Court held, *inter alia*, that traditional rules of international law imposing a duty upon an expropriating government to pay an alien investor "prompt, adequate, and effective compensation" were

---

[14] P.C.I.J., Ser. A, No. 10, p. 19 (1927).

[15] There is a very illuminating presentation of the perspective of "Socialist states" in Wojciech Morawiecki, "Institutional and Political Conditions of Participation of Socialist States in International Organizations: A Polish View," 22 *International Organization*, 494-507, esp. 494-96, 499-501. Professor Morawiecki has stated very candidly that socialist states have adopted a conservative attitude toward quasi-legislative claims because they are sensitive to their position as "a numerical minority" in the membership of international institutions (p. 496).

[16] This argument is central to the presentation in Falk and Saul H. Mendlovitz, "Towards a Warless World: One Legal Formula to Active Transition," 73 *Yale Law Journal* 399-424 (Jan. 1964).

[17] Banco Nacional de Cuba *v.* Sabbatino, 376 U.S. 398 (1964); cf. also Chapters XIII and XIV.

no longer supported by a consensus of sovereign states and, as a result, the validity of such rules was so doubtful as to make them inapplicable to the dispute.[18]

Rosalyn Higgins, in her important study, *The Development of International Law Through the Political Organs of the United Nations*, properly emphasizes the extent to which an assessment of the legal status of General Assembly resolutions is associated with the overall character of the law-creating process applicable to customary international law: "Resolutions of the Assembly are not *per se* binding: though those rules of general international law which they may embody are binding on member states, with or without the help of the resolutions. But the body of resolutions as a whole, taken as indications of a general customary law, undoubtedly provide a rich source of evidence."[19]

Mrs. Higgins also calls attention to the inherent discretion enabling the drafters of a resolution to *develop* new rules of law in the guise of *declaring* old rules. If declaratory language is used in the resolution, then the problem of acknowledging the formal absence of legislative competence is more or less solved and at the same time the legislative character of the claim is maintained.

In a social system without effective central institutions of government, it is almost always difficult, in the absence of formal agreement, to determine that a rule of law *exists*. Normativity is a matter of degree, expressive of expectations by national governments toward what is permissible and impermissible. Certainly norm-declaring resolutions are legal data that will be taken into account in legal argument among and within states. A main function of international law is to establish an agreed system for the communication of claims and counterclaims between international actors and thereby to structure argument in diplomatic settings. Diplomats in search of grounds for justification or of objection readily invoke resolutions of the Assembly. These efforts at persuasion do not seem to be influenced by whether resolutions are capable of generating binding legal rules or merely of embodying recommendations. The degree of authoritativeness that a *particular* resolution will acquire depends upon a number of contextual factors, including the expectations governing the extent of permissible behavior, the extent and quality of the consensus, and the degree to which effective power is mobilized to implement the claims posited in a resolution. The degree of authoritativeness that the *process* of law-creating by Assembly action

[18] It must be noted, however, that the validity of these traditional rules has been rehabilitated, at least within the confines of the United States, by legislative action. Foreign Assistance Act of 1964, § 301 (d) (4), 78 Stat. 1013, 22 U.S.C. § 2370 (e) (2) (1964), 59 *American Journal of International Law* 368 (April 1965); see also Michael H. Cardozo, "Congress vs. Sabbatino: Constitutional Considerations," 4 *Columbia Journal of Transnational Law* 297 (1966).

[19] P. 5, Oxford University Press, 1963.

comes to enjoy depends upon the extent to which this process is incorporated into the inchoate framework of an evolving system and the treatment accorded such action by the science of international law. The authoritativeness of this process of law-creation will certainly be enhanced by serious acknowledgment and empirical study on the part of international lawyers.

II

The jurisprudential basis for attributing legislative force to Assembly resolutions is quite distinct from determining the effective limits of Assembly competence to influence behavior through resolutions. To assess the variable role of quasi-legislative competence in Assembly action is a complicated task. To encourage assessment some lines of general inquiry are suggested in this section.

It is, first of all, essential to classify as accurately as possible the nature of the quasi-legislative claim; we need to be able to identify the claim that is being made and what must be done by whom to comply. In making this assessment, the language of the resolution should be carefully analyzed to see whether it formulates specific duties to be discharged by specific actors. It is also necessary to describe the rights and duties of states in the absence of the resolution. What, in other words, is added in the directive contained in the resolution? In the same respect it is necessary to obtain some insight into the varying objectives pursued by those who supported or opposed the resolution to get a better image of its anticipated impact. The objectives, for instance, of the United States, of the Soviet Union, and of the African states are very different from each other with regard to the implementation of resolutions "declaring" apartheid "illegal," and calling upon states to take appropriate sanctioning action.

It is also essential to clarify the conditions surrounding the vote on a resolution as they bear upon the accuracy of attributing legislative status to it. If the resolution becomes part of a political process that is moving toward implementation, then the legislative nature of the claim is more clear-cut, that is, there seems to be some explicit connection between the status of the claim as legislative and the prospects for *effective* implementation: the better the prospects, the more appropriate the label "legislative."

But a certain caution is needed here. One of the main contributions of the General Assembly in the area of war and peace is to help establish a climate of opinion that is favorable to the growth of world order. This contribution cannot be assessed by any measurable impact or by any evidence of specific intent. However, it does not seem extravagant to contend that Assembly resolutions on the subject of nuclear testing and nonproliferation dramatized a global concern that may, at least, have helped to keep the nuclear powers negotiating at Geneva, despite a periodic sense of discouragement about the prospects for agreement. Perhaps one could describe these assembly initiatives as creating a "weak" legislative norm that operates to influence marginal decisions about nuclear testing and proliferation.

An interesting, more ambitious, attempt to use the Assembly in the war/peace area is Resolution 1653 (XVI) that declares that the use of nuclear weapons would constitute "a direct violation of the Charter of the United Nations," "is contrary to the rules of international law and to the laws of humanity," and that "(a)ny State using nuclear and thermo-nuclear weapons" is "acting contrary to the laws of humanity" and is "committing a crime against mankind and civilization."[20] At a minimum, this resolution provides persuasive material to those seeking to establish the illegality of nuclear weapons. The negative votes of several powerful states and the abstention of several others suggest the absence of the sort of consensus that is found in the area of racial discrimination or decolonization, but the objective of Resolution 1653 (XVI) is to influence public opinion by positing a weak legislative claim. In the event that nuclear weapons would ever be used, the resolution is likely to be involved by those reacting in opposition. The resolution provides a legal term of reference. In the interim the resolution joins, admittedly to an imperceptible degree, with other tendencies that together create some legal basis for the argument that an obligation exists to use nuclear weapons, if at all, only as a reprisal against a state that uses them first (as is the generally accepted status of the use of poison gas). The legislative process at work here can be analogized in some respects to the growth of law in the common law tradition, and the impact of a particular resolution is impossible to anticipate, as its particular effects are so contingent upon unintended and unpredictable consequences.

If we inquire as to the substantive areas wherein quasi-legislative development might be most fruitfully undertaken by the General Assembly, then we confront an initial limiting factor—the radical split in the world community created by global rivalries among the nuclear superpowers.[21] Each principal nuclear state possesses enough political strength in international society to resist the claims of the other. That is, unless a consensus formulated in the claim to govern national action transcends the fissures of central patterns of global conflict and finds

---

[20] U.N. General Assembly Res. 1653 (xvi), Nov. 28, 1961.

[21] The continuing reality of intense conflict between the United States and the Soviet Union in the cold war is now subject to debate. The point remains, however, that a policy disagreement among the superpowers prevents the assertion by the organs of the United Nations of effective claims to control international behavior.

a basis for agreement among the principal states of the world, it is unable to satisfy fully the pre-conditions for legislative action in the United Nations setting. A belated understanding of this pre-condition may be the most positive legacy of the financial crisis, and the abortive attempt of the United States to impose a binding obligation on states through the exercise of authority by the General Assembly backed up by Article 19. If law is to be effective, its growth must be conjoined with the distribution of effective power, especially to the extent that a legislative claim is posited. International society remains too decentralized to suppose that a voting majority of two-thirds can by itself satisfy the pre-conditions for quasi-legislative action in the event that either the Soviet Union or the United States is in the dissenting minority. To this extent the veto in the Security Council is expressive of the quality of a political consensus needed to support a quasi-legislative claim. To overlook this necessity for a *political*, as well as a *parliamentary*, consensus is to undermine the authority of the Assembly by overextending it, and thereby engendering skepticism about its law-creating role. Although the ingredients of a politically relevant consensus cannot be laid down usefully in the form of mechanical requirements specifying the requisite quality and quantity of voting support, Resolution 1653 (XVI), for instance, may come to acquire a legislative role in restraining recourse to nuclear weapons, even if at the time of its formulation the United States was part of the dissenting minority. Also the need for a political consensus is less important when the objective of a resolution is to promote *in general* the evolution of legislative standards rather than to posit a *specific* legislative claim directed at prohibiting the action of a particular nation-state.

To recall earlier elements in the argument, the limits upon quasi-legislative competence of the Assembly are less a reflection of the absence of the *formal competence* to legislate than they are a consequence of certain *political constraints* that result from the general requirement of mobilizing effective community power in support of legislative claims. In international society this mobilization can normally take place only in the event of converging interests on the part of powerful states, although the convergence may express varying degrees of agreement as to the means and speed by which to carry forth the policy embodied in Assembly action. It is also relevant—and complicates any interpretation of the limits of Assembly action that relies too heavily on power as the chief constituent of political effectiveness—to take note of the role of African and Asian states in providing the formal majority and often the political impetus for the assertion of legislative claims by the Assembly. It is the Afro-Asian group of states, much more evidently even than the Socialist states, that presently seek revision in the international order as part of an overall demand for retribution in the post-colonial world. However, in situations in which an Afro-Asian consensus does not attract at least the nominal support of both superpowers, then the drive toward a legislative solution is often diverted through the adoption of a very abstract, operationally irrelevant resolution. An example is the celebrated Resolution on Permanent Sovereignty over Natural Resources, in which broad principles are formulated in such a way as to solicit an affirmative vote from all states, but no attempt is made to legislate a solution of a real dispute going on in international society.[22] In the context of Resolution 1803 (XVII) the real dispute concerned the duties of the expropriating states to compensate alien investors. The resolution refers to the duty to pay "appropriate compensation" as determined by international law, but it also refers the question of compensation to "national jurisdiction." Interpretations from every ideological angle are possible; conservative United States international lawyers tirelessly point out that even the new states and the Socialist states have now accepted the principle of compensation according to international law. Revisionist international lawyers argue that the resolution was drafted in terms of "appropriate compensation," thereby acknowledging that it was no longer necessary to pay "prompt, adequate, and effective compensation," but that it becomes possible to take account of such factors as the previous unjust enrichment of the investors in assessing the obligations of the expropriator. Furthermore, the reference to settlement via national jurisdiction is said to lend support to the argument that the issue of compensation is a matter exclusively within domestic jurisdiction, an interpretation favorable to the views of the new states. Resolution 1803 (XVII), then, provides a way of organizing legal arguments in the settling of a legislative dispute, but it does very little by way of determination. In this sense it is quite different from Resolution 1653 (XVI), which, however ineffective in directly altering the status of nuclear weapons, clearly claims to decide the dispute about the legality of nuclear weapons as instruments of warfare by taking a definite stand on the controverted issues.

The contentions of Resolution 1653 (XVI) are not supported by a number of significant states. In contrast, Resolution 1884 (XVIII), calling upon all nations not to station in outer space "any objects carrying nuclear weapons or any other kinds of weapons of mass destruction," received a unanimous endorsement, including the active backing of both the Soviet Union and the United States—the states whose policy most obviously was curtailed by adherence to the legislative claim. The resolution served to formalize tacit agreement without requiring

[22] U.N. General Assembly Res. 1803 (XVII), Dec. 14, 1962.

recourse to the cumbersome, and politically hazardous, treaty method; the obligation imposed on space powers have been referred to by government officials as one of the major steps taken in the area of arms control.[23] The binding quality of the obligation has been questioned, however, by at least one eminent authority.[24]

A vague consensus among principal states is supportive of a strong Afro-Asian commitment to terminate the practice of apartheid in South Africa. A series of resolutions has "declared" in increasingly specific terms that apartheid is incompatible with the obligations imposed by the Charter and threatens international peace and security. The crystallization of the anti-apartheid consensus in these terms constitutes part of the legislative background of the South West Africa Cases recently decided by the International Court of Justice.[25] Here quasi-legislative action by the General Assembly may contribute to a political process the immediate outcome of which is to provide a firm legal basis for an eventual imposition of serious sanctions against South Africa. Without the existence of a firm legal basis and of intense political pressure, the United States and the United Kingdom are unlikely to proceed beyond the stage of a verbal condemnation of apartheid. The Assembly may indirectly contribute to a process of norm-creation that improves, as well, the chances for norm-implementation.

An analysis of the possibilities for quasi-legislative action by the Assembly cannot hope to set forth general conclusions. It is necessary to examine the specifics of the context, especially to determine the relation between the sponsoring majority, the intended and possibly unintended objectives of the resolutions, and the distribution of power in international society. But inquiry cannot even be content with achieving sophistication about the relevance of power to legislative effectiveness. In certain settings, for instance the status of nuclear weapons, a consensus among the less powerful may create an international atmosphere that exerts an eventual, if indirect, influence on the more powerful. It does not, however, seem extravagant to claim that the Assembly is in a position to play a crucial role on a selective basis of adapting international law to a changing political environment; that is, the Assembly seems to be in a position to strengthen the rudimentary legislative process at work in international society. To confine analysis of the legislative role of resolutions of the General Assembly to traditional processes of law-creation (i.e., those premising the validity of the legal prescrip-

[23] Cf. e.g., Adrian S. Fisher, "Arms Control and Disarmament in International Law," 50 *Virginia Law Review* 1200-19 (Nov. 1964).
[24] J. C. Cooper, "The Manned Orbiting Laboratory: A Major Legal and Political Decision," 51 *American Bar Association Journal* 1137-40 (Dec. 1965).
[25] Judgment in South West Africa Cases, July 18, 1966, [1966] *ICJ Rep.*, p. 6. See Chapter XII.

tion upon the evidence of national consent) in international society is artificial. The continuous growth and development of international law through the centuries has been achieved as a result of "legislative" pressures exerted by such diverse phenomena as war and morality. Even traditional sources of international law contain a disguised nonconsensual element. The legislative content of customary international law is the most dramatic area wherein the myth of consent is frequently supplanted by the reality of an inferred consensus. Professors McDougal and Burke have amply demonstrated in *The Public Order of the Oceans* that the dominant mode of law-creation in the law of the sea has been one of legislative accretion.[26] In this crucial respect, the attribution of a limited legislative competence to the formal action of the General Assembly is nothing more than a special case of the more pervasive processes by which the formation and decay of legal standards have always taken place in international society. The more recent saliency of the General Assembly and its mode of operation by way of norm-positing resolutions merely transforms an implicit legislative energy by making it more explicit, and hence more efficient. To take account of this legislative energy and to relate it to other less visible legislative forms is a major creative task confronting international lawyers of our era.[27]

[26] Myres S. McDougal, and William T. Burke, *The Public Order of the Oceans*, New Haven, Yale University Press, 1962.
[27] For a general study see Obed Y. Asamoah, *The Legal Significance of the Declarations of the General Assembly of the United Nations*, The Hague, Nijhoff, 1966.

VII. The Authority of the United Nations to Control Nonmembers

I. Introduction

This chapter analyzes the authority of the United Nations to take action against nonmember states. The natural emphasis of such a study is, of course, Article 2, paragraph 6, of the United Nations Charter: "The Organization shall ensure that states which are not Members of the United Nations act in accordance with these Principles so far as may be necessary for the maintenance of international peace and security." Unfortunately, neither the practice of the Organization nor the commentary of jurists yields a very convincing account of the intended scope and juridical character of Article 2(6).

Underlying the specific inquiry is the general correlation between the effectiveness of the political organs of the United Nations organization and of the extent of its membership. The United Nations as an organization that is necessarily global in the scope of its concerns is very much dependent on the active participation of the principal national units in the world. The authoritativeness of the voice of the United Nations correlates closely with the degree to which its membership approaches universality. The strength of such a correlation is reinforced by two additional factors: first, nonmember status normally implies an attitude of active hostility toward the main currents of United Nations policy, unless some special circumstance exists, as may exist for states defeated in World War II; second, the United Nations as an actor possesses insufficient independent capabilities to implement its policies even as compared to rather minor states, and therefore is normally dependent upon voluntary patterns of compliance, patterns more difficult to establish in the absence of participation in the activities of the organization.

In addition to these general comments bearing on nonmembership, there are more specific considerations that arise in relation to a particular dispute. In private discussions during June 1968 about the role of the United Nations in settling the Vietnam War, for example, North Vietnamese leaders laid considerable stress upon the fact of nonmembership as an explanation of their country's opposition to any major role for the United Nations in a Vietnamese peace settlement. Furthermore, the utility of the political organs of the United Nations, especially in the area of peace and security, centers principally upon their capacity to provide a forum for communication between adversaries in periods of crisis and conflict. The effects of communication on stability and peace are difficult to establish with precision, but there is considerable evidence that adversary contact facilitates the identification and implementation of converging interests. To take an extreme instance, the participation of both Israel and the Arab countries in the United Nations during the Middle East War of June 1967 appears to have helped establish and sustain a cease-fire. Obviously, the *sine qua non* of communication is participation, and the conditions of effective participation appear to depend strongly on continuing membership and status in the organization. An *ad hoc* arrangement enabling participation on a specific matter does not normally overcome the obstacles of nonmembership.

These comments are a prelude to an inquiry into what the organization is legally empowered to do in the event of nonmembership; they are designed to emphasize the sociopolitical shortcomings of claiming control over nonmembers regardless of the legally vindicated scope of such authority. The subject attracted some attention in early 1965 when Indonesia withdrew from the United Nations expressly to free herself from some of the burdens of membership, especially as those burdens related to the Indonesian policies of "confrontation" with Malaysia.[1] The United Nations Secretariat merely took note of Indonesia's announced intention of withdrawal without taking formal steps to convert Indonesia from member to nonmember status. Thus, when political events in Indonesia in 1965-66 produced a new regime that espoused a very different foreign policy, it was very easy to restore Indonesia to its earlier status as an active participant in the United Nations. The organization merely noted that Indonesia, as of September 28, 1966, resumed full participation in the work of the United Nations.

Indonesia's purported withdrawal in January 1965 came at a particularly bad time for the United Nations. The United Nations was already suffering from a financial and voting crisis created by the refusal of three of the five permanent members of the Security Council—the Soviet Union, France, and the Republic of China—to pay their share of the assessments levied by the General Assembly to pay for the peace-keeping operations of the organization in the Suez and the Congo. As such, Indonesia's effort to disengage herself from the United Nations recalled the failures of the League of Nations to stem the tides of aggression that culminated in World War II. The three principal aggressors in World War II—Germany, Italy, and Japan—each withdrew from the League of Nations to protest efforts by that international organization to interfere with and condemn their acts of aggression in the prewar period. Other states, notably several in Latin America, withdrew subsequently because they felt dissatisfied with the League's response to aggression,

---

[1] For account and analysis see Egon Schwelb, "Withdrawal from the United Nations: The Indonesian Intermezzo." 61 *American Journal of International Law* 661-72 (1967). On the dispute between Indonesia and Malaysia see Chap. IV.

especially with its failure to establish effective sanctions against Italy after its attack upon Ethiopia. By 1939 only 46 of the 63 states that had belonged to the League at one time or another had retained their membership.

Indonesia's purported withdrawal was potentially significant because it could be associated with the exclusion of the People's Republic of China from the United Nations. The governments of these two states, representing some 800 million people, appeared to contemplate at one stage setting up a competing "world" organization based on the "newly emerging forces." Such a prospect, although it never took shape, illustrates the potentiality of a permanent alternative for states dissatisfied with the policies of the United Nations. The United Nations incurs grave risks of collapse, or at least drastic curtailment, whenever it takes a position adverse to the interests of any of its principal members. And without the will or capability to pursue strong policies in the event of aggression, the organization is unable to contribute very effectively to the maintenance of international peace. For these reasons it seems very important to seek ways to reinforce the claims and stature of the United Nations by working toward the ideal of universality of membership. The most effective means of doing this at the present time would be to admit the People's Republic of China to membership on some basis that does not continue to compromise the capacity and will of the United Nations to deal with aggression and threats to world peace. The outlook, at present, for such a development does not seem promising, but the situation remains so fluid that it is difficult to predict the future with any confidence. It is against this political background that the analysis of Article 2(6) proceeds.

Surprisingly little scholarly attention has been given to the issues raised by Article 2(6)—that is, to the basis for and extent of legal authority by an international organization over nonmembers.[2] It is surprising, in part, because the operations of the United Nations in Korea involved so conspicuously the use of force by the United Nations against a nonmember, China. In one respect this neglect is not surprising, as it reflects a growing sense that formal restraints upon the exercise of political authority and power are not very critical to an understanding of political behavior. The tendency of observers has been to emphasize, instead, the will of the requisite majority and the capability of the institution to carry out that will. This is unfortunate to the extent that it

[2] But see the very thorough article on the related problem of expulsion and forced withdrawal from international organizations by Louis B. Sohn: "Expulsion or Forced Withdrawal from an International Organization," 77 *Harvard Law Review* 1381-1425 (June 1964). Cf. also Joseph Gold, "The Fund and Non-Member States—Some Legal Effects," Pamphlet Series No. 7, Washington, International Monetary Fund, 1966.

underrates the importance of establishing a governing constitutional tradition of limited rights and duties for any political actor, including the United Nations. Without a system of legal restraints, it becomes necessary to rely for restraint solely upon the prudence of the majority or upon the restricted ability of an institution to carry out its own policies. So long as the United Nations is relatively weak this protection suffices for most purposes. But if one seeks an augmented United Nations and yet hopes to avoid the concoction of a new behemoth, it seems important that the organization achieve a responsible position when construing its own competence to act. One sign of such responsibility is to take seriously constitutional questions bearing on the legal authority to act.

Article 2(6) has not yet been taken seriously as a source of constitutional constraint. The validation of the claim to exercise authority over nonmembers is inconsistent with the traditional consensual basis of obligation in international affairs. The United Nations was created to keep world peace and this task can be carried out only if the activities of all states, not just members, can be regulated. The claim asserted by Article 2(6) satisfies a functional prerequisite of the United Nations as the organization was conceived from its beginnings. However, we must be careful not to liberate the United Nations from the normal restraints of general international law in the process of trying to uphold this claim over nonmembers in the event that it cannot find persuasive juridical support.

Article 2(6) achieves a delicate balance between assuring the means needed for the dynamic growth of international order and facilitating some trend toward constitutional opportunism. The role of Article 2(6) is linked to the wider problem of establishing respect for limited powers on the part of the membership of the United Nations. Several more topical reasons exist to help account for why it seems worthwhile to explore the basis for the legal claim embodied in Article 2(6). First, there exists an interest in the juridical basis of actions against nonmembers in the effort of the organization to secure compliance with the purposes of the Charter. Second, there exists the related issue of assessing the significance of withdrawal from the organization with regard to the overall obligations of a state. And third, there exists the knotty problem of assessing the seemingly analogous problem that arises when a regional organization claims competence to act against a nonmember (e.g., the Arab League against Israel). This chapter confines itself to Article 2(6), but it tries to do so in a way that casts some light upon these three related issues.

The material is divided into three main sections. First, some claims made by the organized international community to control the activities of nonmembers in the period preceding the formation of the United

Nations are examined. Second, Article 2(6) is analyzed, both in regard to its background at San Francisco, and to the various juridical problems posed by the main alternative ways to validate its existence. And third, the practice of Article 2(6) is reviewed to discover the manner in which the various organs of the United Nations conceive of their authority over nonmembers.

II. Prior Claims over Nonmembers

A. THE DEVELOPMENT OF THE IDEA

Josef Kunz has written that the claim made by Article 2(6) is "revolutionary."[3] It seems more reasonable, if one is to adopt this perspective, to regard Article 17 of the League Covenant as the radical measure and Article 2(6) as merely a continuation.[4] The claim of an international organization to control nonmembers for any purpose is generally considered to be a sharp departure from the traditional system of international law. This much is conceded here, although a careful appraisal of the process by which customary international law arises and develops discloses the fundamental fact that obligations in international law have never depended upon the prior expression of consent by all states bound. However, the traditional system premised on the theory of national sovereignty, though normally dominant, has had to contend with strong counterpressures toward the supranationalization of authority, especially on issues concerning the maintenance of peace. Writers have urged and states have acted at various times as though there existed a basis for extending international competence beyond the limits of national consent and participation. Such a contention does not deny the significance, as a juridical development, of Article 2(6). It merely seeks to offer some evidence of its antecedent growth. Article 2(6), when seen in this light, can be regarded as an emergent norm rather than as a claim to create a new norm.

The notion of supranational political authority, at least in the West, has deep religious roots. The Old Testament's messianic expectation included the belief that a Kingdom of God would be established to overcome decentralized secular authority. With the conversion of the Romans, the religious conception was introduced into an existing political organization and reinforced notions of a Pax Romana. This combination of religion and empire dominated Dante's vision of world order in *De monarchia*.[5] Dante relies strongly upon the need for the

---

[3] Josef L. Kunz, "Revolutionary Creation of Norms of International Law," 41 *American Journal of International Law* 119 (Jan. 1947).

[4] See *infra* § II-B, for a discussion of Article 17.

[5] Dante Alighieri, *De monarchia*, New York, Liberal Arts Press, 2nd rev. edn., Herbert W. Schneider, trans., 1957.

unification of authority to preserve peace. He bases his argument upon divine will, but he also reasons that the Roman Empire, as worldly authority, constitutes the only alternative to war and discord. If one substitutes the notion that a substantial majority of the world community used to validate the claim of Article 2(6) at San Francisco, for that of divine will, the resemblance is evident. According to Dante, then, it is legitimate at least to maintain world peace to give competence to a single central political authority.

These ideas were kept alive in the Church and especially in the natural law tradition, despite the growing dominance of post-Machiavellian formulations of the unfettered power of the political prince. Natural law, as it operated in the mind of Grotius, asserts the objective primacy of certain obligations with regard to war and peace. Limitations upon the state's discretion to resort to war abound in this literature, and underlie the central conception of *bellum justum*. The absence of supranational machinery to implement these limitations led jurists to a reluctant acceptance of the state as the final arbiter of its own "objective" obligations, and thus made the very existence of the obligations precarious.[6] However, it is relevant to observe that the natural law foundation of the traditional system of international law includes nonconsensual restrictions upon state competence with an impact far in excess of the claim posited by Article 2(6).

Among the most prominent early efforts to organize the maintenance of world peace was a European confederation conceived of as the Grand Design by Henry IV of France. It was to have a senate with the duty to inquire into and settle disputes, not only as to members *inter se,* but also in regard to matters involving the relations of Europe with the rest of the world. The historian Phillips probably exaggerated its intellectual influence on world order thinking when he observed: "It is on this Grand Design that all other projects of peace, directly or indirectly, consciously or unconsciously, are based."[7] The next proposal to arouse widespread interest was made by Abbé de St. Pierre in 1713, directly after the Treaty of Utrecht. As with almost every celebrated proposal for a reorganization of international society, this plan was a response to the conclusion of a costly war. Here also, a European confederation was to be established by all sovereigns, but the competence of its Congress was evidently to be sufficient to act against any state that threatened the peace, whether a member or not. The proposal of Abbé de St. Pierre was ignored at the time by those in power, who were more eager to pro-

[6] For a general study of the relevant development in the history of international legal thought, see Walter Schiffer, *The Legal Community of Mankind*, New York, Columbia University Press, 1954, pp. 15-96.

[7] Walter Allson Phillips, *The Confederation of Europe*, New York, Longmans, Green, 2d edn. 1920, p. 24.

mote national interest by the use of force than by consent to its control. However, his main ideas were revived as sharp instruments of international negotiation a century later. As Phillips says, "It is impossible to examine this project without being struck by the fact that there is scarcely one of its provisions which does not emerge, at least as a subject of debate among the Powers, during the years of European reconstruction after 1814."[8] The idea that if an international organization is to maintain peace it needs the competence to cope with whoever threatens the peace was always assumed by these proposals, although it must be conceded that this competence was not conferred by explicit provision.

The defeat of Napoleon at the end of a costly series of wars provoked the first serious modern effort to establish international order on the basis of the cooperative effort of nations. Historians differ in their evaluation of the success and character of the experiment initiated at the Congress of Vienna in 1815. However, for the narrow purposes of this chapter, it constitutes the first significant *political* recognition that the maintenance of peace requires control over events taking place every where within the relevant political community. Alexander I of Russia, motivated by a deep religious impulse and a strong sense of Christian providence, encouraged the great powers of Europe to exercise responsibility for upholding peace and order. The desire to guard against the repetition of revolutionary challenges caused the contemplated peace system to be overshadowed by practical political considerations. Metternich, especially, convinced the monarchs of Europe that order depended upon the suppression of liberal ideas that would otherwise lead to revolution. He had a vivid appreciation of the interdependence of political phenomena, recognizing that states could no longer be assured of even internal peace by a policy of isolation. This led to a doctrine of intervention that was sharply at variance with conceptions of deference to sovereign rights that had grown to be traditional since the Peace of Westphalia (1648). Hazen describes the claim made by the great powers in the following way:

> The doctrine was that, as modern Europe was based upon opposition to revolution, the powers had the right and were in duty bound to intervene to put down revolution not only in their own states respectively but in any state of Europe, against the will of the people of that state, in the interests of the established monarchial order. A change of government within a given state was not a domestic but an international affair.[9]

This system of preserving order was more or less formalized in a suc-

[8] *Id.* at 27.

[9] Charles Downer Hazen, *Europe Since 1815*, New York, Holt, 1910, p. 47.

cession of treaties elaborating the harmony of purpose expressed at the Congress of Vienna and later in the Quadruple Alliance. England, committed to self-determination and liberal government, was the only important state to remain rather aloof from this method of preserving peace and order. In 1820, to implement the Vienna method, revolutions were successfully suppressed in the Kingdom of Naples and in Piedmont by the intervention of Austrian and Russian troops. In both instances the deposed monarchs were given back their thrones. Similarly, in Spain restoration of the deposed Ferdinand VII was a consequence of the intervention of French troops in 1823. These events indicate the early triumph of Metternich's version of internationalism. The current of events in Europe, and the discord among the powers themselves, led to the breakdown of this nineteenth-century order based upon monarchical legitimacy. However, the experiment to cooperate to keep the peace, and to impose the scheme of cooperation upon nonconsenting members of the relevant international community, has the same generic structure as Article 2(6). In fact, the 1946 proposals in the Security Council to act against Franco's regime in Spain on the basis of Article 2(6) were a mere inversion of Metternich's diplomacy. The community organization is responsible for assuring the presence of "peaceful" governments in the community, even if this requires action against a state that is not a member. The Holly Alliance resisted anti-monarchial governments, and the United Nations has considered resisting military dictatorships of the right. It seems correct to accept the appraisal of Phillips, who regards the period of European cooperation between 1815 and 1823 as the most significant historical precedent favoring the creation of the League of Nations.[10]

In any event, the Holy Alliance and its sequels illustrate systems of international order in which competence to act against nonmembers is claimed. In these earlier experiments with collective security, the power to respond was not inhibited by traditional restraints of international law. In fact, the proceedings at Vienna, as much as at San Francisco, rested upon an assumption by the participants of an unchallenged legislative capacity sufficient to achieve the task of maintaining international peace and security. The only problem in each case was to devise an acceptable means.

Despite the superficial character of this historical survey, it is hoped that two points emerge. First, past proposals and actions seeking to maintain international peace have never regarded their competence as fixed by strictly contractual and consensual limits. Second, this competence was either so self-evident or so little perceived that the broad

10 See Phillips, *op.cit. supra*, note 7, at 11.

claim to control nonmembers was not clearly articulated until the League Covenant. Furthermore, there exists evidence to qualify the extravagant claims made on behalf of national sovereignty in the literature of natural law. It is also true that Judge Negulesco of the Permanent Court once argued in the course of a dissenting opinion that "decisions of the Great Powers, met together as the Concert of Europe, . . . have never been held to be legally binding upon States not represented in the Concert."[11]

It seems reasonable to conclude from a study of the background of the twentieth century that Article 17 of the Covenant and Article 2(6) of the Charter are inappropriately regarded as juridical innovations without antecedent in the history of international relations.

B. THE LEAGUE OF NATIONS AND NONMEMBER STATES

The relation of the League to nonmember states is sufficiently analogous to that contemplated by the Charter to warrant specific consideration. The objective of this section is to examine the claim made by the Covenant and to compare it with that made by the Charter in Article 2(6).

The Covenant in Article 17[12] dealt with the relationship between the League and a nonmember state. Article 17(1) provides that, in the event of a dispute between a member of the League and a nonmember state, the nonmember shall be invited to accept the obligations (but not the advantages or privileges) of the League upon such conditions as are "deemed just" by the League Council for purposes of the dispute. If this invitation is accepted, then the dispute mechanism of the Covenant set forth in Articles 12 to 16 shall apply, with any modifications "deemed necessary" by the Council. Article 17(2) authorizes the Council to "immediately institute an inquiry into the circumstances of the

---

[11] Jurisdiction of the European Commission of the Danube, P.C.I.J., Ser. B, No. 14, at 95 (1927).

[12] The text of Article 17 is as follows:

1. In the event of a dispute between a Member of the League and a State which is not a Member of the League, or between States not Members of the League, the State or States not Members of the League shall be invited to accept the obligations of membership in the League for the purpose of such dispute, upon such conditions as the Council may deem just. If such invitation is accepted, the provisions of Articles 12 to 16 inclusive shall be applied with such modifications as may be deemed necessary by the Council.

2. Upon such invitation being given, the Council shall immediately institute an inquiry into the circumstances of the dispute and recommend such action as may seem best and most effectual in the circumstances.

3. If a State so invited shall refuse to accept the obligation of membership in the League for the purposes of such dispute, and shall resort to war against a Member of the League, the provisions of Article 16 shall be applicable as against the State taking such action.

4. If both parties to the dispute when so invited refuse to accept the obligations of membership in the League for the purposes of such dispute, the Council may take such measures and make such recommendations as will prevent hostilities and will result in the settlement of the dispute.

dispute and recommend such action as may seem best and most effectual in the circumstances." Article 17(3) states that if the invitation of Article 17(1) is refused and if the nonmember resorts to war, then the provisions of Article 16 become applicable. Article 16 sets forth the response of the League to any "resort to war," and indicates the sanctions to be imposed and the collaborative effort by League members that is expected to take place. Article 17(4) applies to those situations in which "both parties to the dispute when so invited refuse to accept" in accordance with Article 17(1). In such event, the Council "may take such measures and make such recommendations as will prevent hostilities and will result in the settlement of the dispute."

It is hardly necessary to observe that the claim over nonmembers made in Article 17 of the Covenant is much more specific than the analogous claim of Article 2(6) of the Charter. The mechanism of the League is provisionally made available to nonmember states for the resolution of their disputes. However, the League is restrained from action unless the nonmember gives explicit consent by an acceptance of the invitation extended under Article 17, with the single exception of a resort to war by the nonmember. This means that the League cannot *compel* a nonmember to collaborate with it in the interests of maintaining international peace. It appears that Article 17(2) allows Council inquiry and recommendation to occur without nonmember consent between the time the invitation is extended and the date of its refusal. The meaning of Article 17(4) is very obscure. It evidently is meant to concern a dispute between two nonmember states, and it gives rather unrestricted competence to the Council in the event that both parties to the dispute refuse the invitation. Why the League should possess greater competence if both states refuse its invitation than if only one does is rather puzzling.

To summarize, Article 17 claims competence over nonmembers only when they are parties to an international dispute. Even then, such competence ends if the nonmember refuses the invitation of Article 17, unless the nonmember resorts to war or, strangely enough, unless the dispute is between nonmembers and both refuse the invitation. In the event of resort to war by a nonmember, Article 16 applies, giving the League the full competence it would possess against a member that had resorted to war.[13]

There was relatively little discussion of Article 17 in the course of drafting the Covenant,[14] and in a sense its history parallels that of

[13] Such an interpretation is in accord with that made by Sir John Fischer Williams. See his *Some Aspects of the Covenant of the League of Nations*, New York, Oxford University Press, 1934.

[14] David H. Miller, *The Drafting of the Covenant*, New York, Putnam, 1928, p. 264.

Article 2(6). It was regarded as an incidental supplement to the early expectations that all important states would be members of the League. In 1934, Sir John Fischer Williams called attention to the actual and potential importance of Article 17: "Up to the present, the Article has never been used, and possibly its chief importance is as a record of the high ideals entertained in Paris when the Covenant was founded as to the extent of its authority. This is not to say that the Article may not conceivably in new circumstances have considerable importance in the future."[15] In a formal sense, Article 2(6) could well receive a similar evaluation today, although United Nations practice does reveal a greater awareness of its contribution to the competence of the organization.[16]

Although Article 17 of the Covenant never was the basis of League action, it was at the center of the Eastern Carelia dispute, and the results in this case vividly reveal the attitude of the League toward nonmember obligations under the Covenant and generally express the prevailing conception that an international obligation must be founded upon consent.[17]

Eastern Carelia is a small land area on the Arctic Ocean situated between Finland (member) and Russia (then a nonmember).[18] Its population was predominantly inclined toward Finland by race, language, and emotion. Despite a long history of Russian domination, the population retained aspirations to obtain either independence or union with Finland. Between 1906 and 1919, the situation became worse, and bloodshed was frequent. Finland, at this time, agreed to support the efforts of the Eastern Carelians. In 1920 at Dorpat, peace negotiations between Russia and Finland took place. Articles 10 and 11 of the Treaty of Dorpat and certain Declaratory Annexes provided for the autonomy of Eastern Carelia and certain related matters. However, Russia displayed no intention to carry out these provisions, and after bloody border skirmishes between Finland and Russia, Finland appealed to the League. In 1922, the Latvian delegation offered to mediate the dispute in the interests of maintaining peace in the Baltic area. After some debate, the Council passed a resolution on January 14, 1922, urging one of the interested states in the area (Estonia, Latvia, Poland, Lithuania) to "lend its good offices . . . to assist in the solution of this question."[19] The following year, Estonia reported to the Council that Russia refused to submit the dispute to the League under the provisions of Article 17. Finally, at a later meeting, the Council decided by resolution to submit

15 Williams, op.cit. supra, note 13, at 169.

16 For United Nations practice, see text § III infra.

17 Eastern Carelia Case, P.C.I.J., Ser. B, No. 5 (1923).

18 The discussion of the political background of the Eastern Carelia dispute is based upon Thorsten Kalijarvi, "The Question of East Carelia," 18 American Journal of International Law, 93-97 (Jan. 1924).

19 Id. at 95 (quoted from League of Nations Off. J., 3 Ass. 107-08 [1922]).

the following question to the Permanent Court for an advisory opinion: "Do Articles 10 and 11 of the Treaty of Peace between Finland and Russia, signed at Dorpat on October 14th, 1920, and the annexed Declaration of the Russian Delegation regarding the autonomy of Eastern Carelia, constitute engagements of an international character which place Russia under an obligation to Finland as to the carrying out of the provisions contained therein?"[20]

The Registrar of the Court was instructed to notify the Soviet government of the request for an advisory opinion. The Court received various relevant documents and listened to the argument of the Finnish representative, Rafael Erich. The Soviet Minister of Foreign Affairs, Tchitcherin, sent a telegram to the Court stating the adamant position of his government, of which the most relevant portion is this:

> The Russian Government finds it impossible to take any part in the proceedings, without legal value either in substance or in form, which the Permanent Court intends to institute as regards the Carelian question. . . . [I]n a Note . . . [Tchitcherin] . . . protested categorically against action taken by the Finnish Government in placing the Eastern Carelian question before the League of Nations, a course which in the view of the Russian Government constituted an act of hostility . . . and an intervention in its domestic affairs. . . .[F]urthermore, whereas on June 18th, 1922, the Commissary of the People for Foreign Affairs declared that the Russian Government absolutely repudiated the claim of the so-called League of Nations to intervene in the question of the internal situation of Carelia and stated that any attempt on the part of any power to apply to Russia the article of the Covenant of the League relating to disputes between one of its Members and a non-participating State would be regarded by the Russian Government as an act of hostility to the Russian State: the Russian Government categorically refused to take any part in the examination of this question by the League of Nations or by the Permanent Court.[21]

Referring to this telegram, the Court examined the documentary evidence, including the relevant provisions of the Treaty and the accompanying Declaration. It concluded that the parties were "in acute controversy" as to the extent of the obligation accepted by Russia at Dorpat.[22] The Court then determined that it was being asked by the Council whether these instruments "constitute engagements of an international character which place Russia under an obligation to Finland."[23]

---

[20] Eastern Carelia Case, P.C.I.J., Ser. B, No. 5, at 6 (1923) (request for advisory opinion).

[21] Id. at 12-13.
[22] Id. at 22.
[23] Id. at 25.

Russia contended in the Tchitcherin telegram that the autonomy of Eastern Carelia was an internal matter and that references at Dorpat were made solely for the information of the Finnish delegation.

The Court proceeded to examine whether it possessed the competence to answer the question asked by the Council. As Russia was not a member of the League, the Court said "the case is one under Article 17 of the Covenant."[24] The Court, declining to regard itself as a competent body of inquiry, placed primary reliance on the absence of Russian consent. Referring to Article 17, it said: "This rule, moreover, only accepts and applied [sic] a principle which is a fundamental principle of international law, namely, the principle of the independence of States. It is well established in international law that no State can, without its consent, be compelled to submit its disputes with any other States either to mediation or to arbitration, or to any other kind of pacific settlement."[25] Such consent had been given by members in advance by their acceptance of the Covenant. But,

> As concerns States not Members of the League, the situation is quite different; they are not bound by the Covenant. The submission, therefore, of a dispute between them and a Member of the League for solution according to the methods provided for in the Covenant, could take place only by virtue of their consent. Such consent, however, has never been given by Russia. . . . The Court therefore finds it impossible to give its opinion on a dispute of this kind.[26]

This appears to be a complete endorsement of the Tchitcherin position.

The Court went on to supply "other cogent reasons" why it would be "inexpedient . . . to attempt to deal with the present question." The question at issue involved a matter "of fact" (the existence of a contractual obligation as a result of the Dorpat Declaration) that would place the Court "at a very great disadvantage in such an enquiry, owing to the fact that Russia refuses to take part in it." The Court then said that "there is no absolute rule that a request for an advisory opinion may not involve some enquiry as to facts, but under ordinary circumstances, it is certainly expedient that the facts upon which the opinion of the Court is desired should not be in controversy, and it should not be left to the Court itself to ascertain what they are." Finally, the Court said it was "aware of the fact that it is requested not to decide a dispute but to give an advisory opinion," but it referred to the question as "not one of abstract law," but one concerning "directly the main point of the dispute between Finland and Russia." Thus, "answering the question would be substantially equivalent to deciding the dispute between the parties."[27]

24 Id. at 27.
25 Ibid.
26 Id. at 27-28.
27 Quoted phrases are from id. at 28-29.

Four judges dissented, saying simply in a single sentence that they were unable to share the views of the majority of the Court as to the impossibility of giving an advisory opinion on the Eastern Carelian question. It seems incredible that such a majority opinion did not provoke a fully reasoned dissenting opinion. The sweeping language of the Court, quoted above, to the effect that a state cannot be internationally obligated except on the basis of its explicit consent was left in unresolved conflict with the apparent intentions of Article 17(2), (3), and (4). If Article 17 meant what the Court says it does, then it would appear that 17(1) exhausted its content, but such a conclusion seems difficult to justify in view of the detail of the other three provisions. However, the decision discloses how conservative the juristic temper was with respect to the creation of international obligations, and it thereby restored to prominence the requirement of sovereign consent in the context of international organizations. It also indicated a great willingness by the Court to restrict its own competence. Note that here consent was made a requirement not only for the imposition of obligations by the League upon a nonmember, but that it also restricted the advice that one organ (the Court) of the League might give to another (the Council) on a question that might influence League proposals to a nonmember in regard to a pending dispute. The Council took note of the advisory opinion in language that seems to reject its broader implications:

> [T]he opinion expressed by the Court in connection with the procedure described by Article 17 of the Covenant could not exclude the possibility of resort by the Council to any action, including a request for an advisory opinion from the court, in a matter to which a state non-Member of the League and unwilling to give information, is involved, if the circumstances should make such action necessary to enable the Council to fulfill its function under the Covenant of the League in the interests of peace.[28]

And, in fact, the Assembly of the League did instruct the Council to continue to collect information "with a view to seeking any satisfactory solution rendered possible by subsequent events."[29] Evidently, the nonjudicial organs of the League seemed unwilling to accept a restrictive role for an international organization with regard to nonmember disputes.

The decision of the World Court was accepted as a reliable interpretation of the meaning of Article 17.[30] A commentator on the Covenant,

---

[28] As quoted in Manley O. Hudson, "The Second Year of the Permanent Court of International Justice," 18 *American Journal of International Law*, 1, 10 (Jan. 1924).

[29] *League of Nations Off. J.*, Supp. No. 11, at p. 29 (1923).

[30] Quincy Wright considers that the advisory opinion of the Permanent Court of International Justice in the dispute about Mosul undermines the authority of its opinion in the Eastern Carelia Case.

Jean Ray, felt that the Eastern Carelian decision made it plain that the dispute-settlement mechanism of the League could be extended to nonmembers only after they had accepted an invitation to submit the dispute.[31] Article 17(2), to the extent that it suggests otherwise, is regarded as "une divergence regrettable."[32] Ray seemed to feel that the portions of Article 17 dealing with recourse to hostilities by a nonmember endow the League with competence without signification of consent by the nonmember. But this is treated as a power of the League, and it is not said to rest upon an obligation of nonmembers to conform to the Covenant. This is the only construction that reconciles the dictum in the *Eastern Carelia Case* that nonmembers "are not bound by the Covenant" with the language of Article 17. This also appears to be the view of Anzilotti.[33]

The Harvard Research Draft on the Law of Treaties went further in a Comment, regarding Article 17 as totally dependent for its operation upon an acceptance by the nonmember of the invitation by the League.[34] The three other provisions of Article 17 were said to presuppose a prior satisfaction of the consent requirement established by Article 17(1). This means that even if a nonmember has had recourse to war, the League remains helpless unless the nonmember has accepted its competence. In effect, a nonmember is immune from the sanctions of Article 16 until it requests their imposition! This is an absurd reading, it seems to me, of Article 17, but it indicates how reluctant the legal community was to conclude that an international obligation could be founded upon anything other than the consent of the obligated state. After setting forth its interpretation of Article 17, the Harvard Research Draft said that "this view was that which the permanent Court adopted in the *Eastern Carelia Case*."[35]

There are other indications of the importance of consent as a basis of international obligation during the period of the League. In the celebrated *Lotus Case*, the Court said: "International law governs the relations between independent States. The rules of law binding upon States therefore emanate from their own free will."[36] And the report of the Blockade Committee of the League in 1926 on the impact of Article 16 of the Covenant upon nonmember states concluded that:

See Wright, "The Mosul Dispute," 20 *American Journal of International Law*, 453-64 (July 1926).

[31] Jean Ray, *Commentaire du Pacte de la Société des Nations*, Paris, Sirey, 1930, p. 538.

[32] *Id.* at 540.

[33] See Dionisio Anzilotti, *Cours de Droit International*, Paris, Sirey, Gidel trans., 1929, p. 415.

[34] The discussion of Article 17 appears in "Harvard Research Draft Convention on the Law of Treaties," 29 *American Journal of International Law* (Supp.) 912-18 (Oct. 1935) [hereinafter cited as Harvard Research].

[35] *Ibid.*

[36] Case of the S.S. "Lotus," P.C.I.J., Ser. A, No. 10, at p. 18 (1927).

A third State is not under *any treaty* obligation to acquiesce in the measures contemplated by Article 16 of the Covenant, and, on the principle: *"pacta tertiis neque nocent neque prosunt,"* the coming into force of the Covenant could not *in strict law affect ipso facto any rights* which it possesses under general principles of international law. . . . It is true that Article 16 places the third State's nationals and territory on the same footing as those of a Member. . . . A treaty must, however, *be assumed* to be intended to be interpreted subject to the rights of third States under international law.[37]

The obvious difficulty of reconciling the objectives of the Covenant with strict conceptions of nonmember autonomy produced almost meaningless prose, as illustrated by the quoted passage. However, part of the tacit morality of the League in regard to nonmembers was to treat formulations of this kind as accurate statements of the law. Hence one can understand the general approval that greeted the *Eastern Carelia Case.*[38]

In conclusion, Article 17 played no significant role in League practice, although it seemed intended, as is Article 2(6) of the Charter, to give the League the important competence to deal with nonmembers to the extent necessary for the maintenance of peace. Compared with the Charter, the Covenant took far less account of the existence of nonmembers and made a smaller effort to make available to an aggrieved nonmember the advantages of the existence of the League. The Court and commentators seemed completely unable to respond to the claim made by Article 17. This reflected a dogmatic acceptance of consent as a prerequisite for every international obligation; at the same time, there was an unwillingness to reject Article 17 altogether. The consequence was an unconvincing construction of Article 17 that deprived the provision of its intended role. The idea of quasi-legislative competence on the part of the League, in lieu of nonmember consent, was not even examined. One is led to conclude that an emergent idea had arisen to challenge the traditional system of international law during the period when the League was planned, but that this idea did not have enough general acceptance to shape the practice of the League itself, which was confined rather strictly to the traditional conception of consent as the prerequisite to obligation.

III. The Juridical Status of Article 2(6)

It now seems feasible to analyze Article 2(6) itself. The analysis will be divided in the following fashion: First, we will consider the intentions

[37] *League of Nations Off. Docs.*, A 14, V, at p. 86 (1927). (Emphasis added.)
[38] See description of reaction as reported by Kalijarvi, note 18, *supra*, at 97, and Hudson, note 28, *supra*, at 7-10.

of the drafters of the Charter as expressed at Dumbarton Oaks and then at the San Francisco Conference; second, the treatment of nonmembers in provisions of the Charter other than Article 2(6); third, the possible meanings of Article 2(6); fourth, three factors useful for an appraisal of an application of Article 2(6); and fifth, some theoretical problems that attend construing Article 2(6), as well as the major approaches taken to their solution by prominent jurists.

A. DUMBARTON OAKS AND SAN FRANCISCO

At Dumbarton Oaks there was apparently "ready agreement" that the contemplated international organization would exercise competence over nonmembers whenever necessary to assure the maintenance of international peace, but not for other purposes.[39] Article 2(6) was the outcome of this consensus. No attention was given to what converts an issue into one involving international peace. It seems clear that the early planners of the United Nations did not devote themselves very seriously to a specification of the rights and duties of nonmembers in the event that a dispute on such a question arose. At the same time, there was a general feeling that the claims of the organization against nonmembers should be balanced by conferring upon nonmembers certain privileges of availing themselves of the new structure even if they were not formally affiliated with it.

A reading of the San Francisco debates makes it evident that the delegates were unanimously committed to the creation of an organization with authority to uphold international peace wherever it was threatened.[40] This authority is obviously not compatible with the full autonomy of nonmember states. For example, it is obvious that the inability of the United Nations to end warfare between participants one or more of which are nonmember states would contradict the obligation of the organization to maintain peace everywhere. As Kelsen has written, "the purpose of the United Nations . . . is not only to maintain peace within the Organization but within the whole international community, that is to say: to maintain world peace."[41]

Some states sought to overcome the contradiction between the autonomy of nonmembers and the global scope of the organization's responsibilities by proposing obligatory membership in the United Nations. The Rapporteur of Committee I/2 at the San Francisco Conference in 1945 describes this viewpoint:

Let us explain immediately the position taken in the debate by the

[39] Ruth B. Russell and J. E. Muther, *A History of the United Nations Charter*, Washington, D.C., The Brookings Institution, 1958, pp. 437-38.
[40] 6 *U.N. Conf. Int'l. Org. Docs.*, 348, 400-91, 722 (1945).
[41] Hans Kelsen, *The Law of the United Nations*, New York, Praeger, 1950, p. 106; see also *id.* at 369 [hereinafter cited as Kelsen].

Delegation of Uruguay and in a smaller degree by other delegations. Faithful to the principle of the universality of the Organization it arrives at the conclusion that all communities should be members of the Organization and that their participation is obligatory, that is to say that it will not be left to the choice of *any nation* whether to become a member of the Organization or to withdraw from it.[42]

However, the position that won out was "that universality in this sense was an ideal toward which it was proper to aim, but which was not practicable to realize at once."[43] Kelsen reasons, however, that the Charter seeks the status of general international law and that to the extent this status is validated by "general recognition," it will oblige all states, not just members. Article 2(6) is regarded as an expression of this far-reaching claim, leading Kelsen to observe that "the idea of compulsory membership has not entirely been rejected."[44]

Article 2(6) can thus be regarded as a compromise with the principle of universal membership. Even though states are not obliged to participate in the United Nations, no state is immune from the authority of the organization to carry out its duties merely because it is a nonmember. Edward Stettinius, Jr., Chairman of the United States delegation at San Francisco, confirms this interpretation of Article 2(6):

At San Francisco this principle of Article 2(6) was unanimously adopted. The predominant sentiment was that unless the Organization undertook this responsibility with respect to states not members of the Organization, the whole scheme of the Charter would be seriously jeopardized. In the background of the thought of many delegates was the action of Germany and Japan, ex-members of the League, who menaced the peace until finally they wrought havoc throughout the world.[45]

Earlier in the hearings Stettinius said that the ability to control nonmembers "is, of course, an essential condition for the preservation of the general peace of the world."[46]

At San Francisco, as earlier at Dumbarton Oaks, there was relatively little argument about either the content or the juridical validity of Article 2(6). Initially at Dumbarton Oaks, Article 2(6) was written as a second subprovision of Article 2(5).[47] However, Committee I at San

[42] *Report of Rapporteur [Membership] of Committee I/2 to Commission I on Chapter III, U.N. Conf. Int'l. Org.*, Sel. Docs., Doc. No. 1178, at 504-05 (1946).
[43] *Ibid.*
[44] Kelsen at 75-76.
[45] *Hearings Before the Senate Committee on Foreign Relations on the Charter of the United Nations*, 79th Cong., 1st Sess., 56 (1945).
[46] *Ibid.*
[47] Article 2(5): "All Members shall give the United Nations every assistance in any action it takes in accordance with the present Charter, and shall refrain from giving assistance to any State against which the United Nations is taking preventive or enforcement action."

Francisco made Article 2(6) distinct from Article 2(5) for the following reason: "The Committee by establishing that section as a distinct paragraph intended to establish it more clearly as a general principle of general application and not limited only to refraining from giving the assistance mentioned in the first section of the original text of paragraph 6 [i.e. what later became Article 2(5)]."[48] The fundamental character of the duty of the United Nations to control nonmembers is revealed by the placement of the provision in the chapter of the Charter setting forth its principles. Thus, as a principle, Article 2(6) constitutes one of "the methods and regulating norms according to which the Organization and its members shall endeavor to achieve their common ends."[49] It is built into the formal mechanism to be used by the organization in its approach to the maintenance of peace, and it is not carefully confined to any single aspect of this approach.

The delegates at San Francisco assumed explicitly that they possessed the authority to confer upon their proposed organization the duty to control the conduct of nonmembers: "The vote [on Article 2(6)] was taken on the understanding that the association of the United Nations, *representing the major expression of the international legal community, is entitled to act in a manner which will ensure the effective cooperation of non-member states with it, so far as that is necessary for the maintenance of international peace and security.*"[50] Thus there is no doubt that those responsible for the existence of Article 2(6) felt that they had not exceeded the permissible limits of their competence.

In summary, it appears that the delegates at San Francisco viewed a minimum control over the activities of nonmembers to be both *indispensable* and *legitimate* mechanisms for the maintenance of peace. Article 2(6) is the direct product of this thinking.

B. CHARTER STATUS OF NONMEMBERS[51]

The claim to control nonmembers made in Article 2(6) must be viewed within the larger framework of nonmember participation in the United Nations as it is envisaged by the Charter. This larger Charter framework supports the inference that the United Nations owes a responsibility to a community larger than its membership. For example, "any State," not just a member, is assured in Article 2(7) that the organization is not authorized to intervene in matters essentially within domestic jurisdiction. By virtue of Article 32, nonmember states are to be invited to participate in the Security Council discussion of disputes to

[48] 6 *U.N. Conf. Int'l. Org. Docs.,* 401 (1945) (same language also at 722).
[49] *Id.* at 388; see also *id.* at 699.
[50] *Id.* at 722. (Emphasis added.)
[51] See generally Shou Sheng Hsueh,

L'Organisation des Nations Unies et les états non membres, Arbilly, Presses de Savoie, 1953, pp. 67-159 [hereinafter cited as Hsueh].

which they are a party; and Article 25(2) permits a nonmember to bring any dispute to which it is a party to the attention of the Security Council or the General Assembly if it accepts in advance the obligations of the Charter regulating pacific settlement.[52] In Article 50, a nonmember state that is confronted by special problems as a result of preventive or enforcement measures taken by the Security Council against some other state is given "the right to consult the Security Council with a view toward a solution." And Article 93(2) allows nonmembers to become parties "to the Statute of International Court of Justice on conditions to be determined in each case by the General Assembly upon the recommendation of the Security Council."

This conception of the rights and duties of nonmembers is also illustrated by Article 4, which makes membership in the United Nations open to all states that satisfy the criteria for admission. In theory, states, under normal conditions, are not obliged to accept nonmember status. As a consequence of cold war pressures, admission has frequently been prevented or delayed for long periods. It is difficult to restrict the broad discretion of members to interpret the criteria of Article 4.[53] Political considerations have also been used to promote the admission of non-peace-loving states. Despite the delays and the notable exceptions of mainland China and Germany, it is fair to say that the promise of open membership in Article 4 has been largely kept.

The Charter purports, then, to give nonmembers rights and privileges, as well as duties. It explicitly protects them against excessive interference by the organization, and it offers nonmembers some opportunities for participation in matters of their direct concern. Article 2(6) is properly understood as an aspect of the organization's larger expectation to make itself globally effective as a dispute-resolving and peace-maintaining institution. As such, Article 2(6) is not, as it may appear to be in isolation, a mere claim by the organization to uphold its interests against infringement by those states who are not in it. The Charter works to specify a reciprocally beneficial relationship between the organization and nonmembers.

C. An Analysis of Possible Constructions of Article 2(6)

It is necessary to determine what is meant by the language of Article 2(6) or, more precisely, what are the various meanings that might plausibly be given to the provision. Traditional sources of insight offer only

---

[52] Nonmembers cannot vote, nor participate in a Security Council discussion of a "situation," nor appear before the General Assembly as a matter of right.
[53] The International Court of Justice has acknowledged this broad discretion in an advisory opinion. Conditions on Admission of a State to Membership in the United Nations, [1948] *ICJ Rep.*, 57.

very partial guidance. Expounders of the Charter are useful since they highlight the significance of varying lines of possible interpretation. However, their suggestions for the preferred interpretation obviously cannot and do not control either the governing doctrine or the practice of the organization. The discussion that follows assumes that Article 2(6) has not been authoritatively construed as yet. Issues of interpretation and application are difficult to consider from contexts of actual dispute as to meaning. This analytical survey can be regarded as a background for a consideration of the practice of organs of the United Nations.

The most restrictive possibility is that of limiting Article 2(6) to the preceding provision of Article 2(5), which reads as follows: "All members shall give the United Nations every assistance in any action it takes in accordance with the present Charter, and shall refrain from giving assistance to any State against which the United Nations is taking preventive or enforcement action." Even if this restrictive interpretation is accepted, it would still be necessary to determine which actions of the United Nations may be used to invoke Article 2(6). When is action by the United Nations "action" which is necessary to ensure the maintenance of international peace and security? Unless we can answer this question, it is impossible to formulate the relevant standards of limitation. Subject to this proviso, however, it is possible to assess the contention that Article 2(6) is properly read as restricted by Article 2(5). This can be done most economically by outlining the reasons for and against such reading. First, the reasons favorable to it:

1. It is all that is needed to maintain peace.

2. It constitutes the minimum interference with nonmember independence.

3. Since Article 2(6) was a second paragraph to Article 2(5) in the Dumbarton Oaks Proposals, it was conceived only as a means to make Article 2(5) available in the event that peace-keeping involved nonmembers.

The reasons against:

1. The documents of the San Francisco conference suggest that Article 2(6) was severed from Article 2(5) in order to make it a principle of greater generality than it would have been if left as a subdivision of 2(5).

2. Article 2(5) does not by itself obligate nonmembers sufficiently to ensure the maintenance of peace by the United Nations.[54]

3. Existing practice of the United Nations in regard to nonmembers

[54] Article 2(5) may imply that nonmembers are expected to cooperate with the organization in the event of a peace-keeping operation (e.g.) Korea), but the provision does not seem to cover the situation in which the nonmember is itself the object of action by the organization.

indicates no willingness to limit Article 2(6) to actions of the organization under Article 2(5).

4. If the drafters of the Charter sought to limit Article 2(6) to the obligations imposed by Article 2(5), then this could have easily been expressed. As it is, there is no reason to read the phrase "act in accordance with *these Principles*" as "act in accordance with Article 2(5)."

As Kelsen observes, even this restrictive reading of Article 2(6) has the consequence of jeopardizing the legitimacy of nonmember neutrality.[55]

The middle view is to regard Article 2(6) as incorporating the Principles of Article 2, paragraphs 3, 4, 5; Kelsen believes that this is the minimum content that can be reasonably given to Article 2(6). He describes this content as follows:

> [N]on-Member states are obliged by the Charter just as Members are, to settle their disputes by peaceful means, to refrain in their relation to other States from the threat or use of force, to give the United Nations every assistance in any action it takes in accordance with the Charter, and to refrain from giving assistance to any state against which the United Nations is taking preventive or enforcement action.[56]

This approach enables the organization to fulfill the stated objective of Article 2(6) and so act to ensure the maintenance of international peace, and yet it is conservative enough to take seriously the distinction between the general duties of members and nonmembers. A nonmember is not obliged to cooperate when the organization is concerned with something other than peace maintenance. It does allow the organization to take broad action against nonmembers without the consent of the obliged state. This interpretation is objectionable to those who regard the Charter as a treaty applicable only to those governments that have given their consent with appropriate formality.[57]

A more radical interpretation extends Article 2(6) to cover Article 2(2), which by its language is said to incorporate the entire structure of Charter obligation: "All Members, in order to ensure to all of them the rights and benefits resulting from membership, shall fulfill in good faith the obligations assumed by them in accordance with the present Charter." Sometimes this extensive view is said to relate Article 2(6) indirectly back to Article 1 and to the Preamble.[58] The main argument used to support this line of extensive interpretation is that any operation of the organization may turn out to be necessary to ensure the mainte-

---

[55] Kelsen at 108; see also Hsueh at 78-79.
[56] Kelsen at 107.
[57] See text discussion of whether the Charter is a treaty or something more than a treaty, *infra* § III-E.
[58] Hsueh at 79; see also André Salomon, *Le Préambule de la Charte*, Geneva, Paris, Editions de Trois Collines, 1946, p. 179.

nance of peace. Both the concepts "necessary" and "peace" are given broad definitions, and the social interdependence of the world community is stressed. There are several arguments against this position:

1. It tends to abolish the distinction between membership and non-membership in so far as obligations are concerned; this seems plainly inconsistent with other parts of the Charter, such as Articles 4 and 25, and with the assumed consequence of rejecting a proposal to make membership in the United Nations compulsory.

2. It makes the choice not to join the United Nations illusory, and it makes a nonmember potentially as fully subject to duties as is a member, without sharing with members the decision-making power of the organization.

3. It undermines any consensual basis that the Charter possesses by virtue of its character as an international agreement and *fully* disregards the right of nonmembers to be immune from an obligation to which they have not consented.

4. It goes beyond the plain language of Article 2(6) by presuming that all the obligations of membership are necessary to ensure the maintenance of international peace; if this was intended, why was the provision not more explicit about the extent of competence claimed over nonmembers?

One grammatical difficulty results from reading Article 2(6) into any other portion of Article 2. Article 2(6) refers to some unenumerated quantum of "these Principles" in Article 2. But "these Principles" all explicitly refer only to "all Members." How can a nonmember be made part of a Principle that is limited by its language to members? Probably this is just a fastidious illustration of the limitations of language, but it does made a precise statement of the relation between Article 2(6) and the rest of Article 2 necessarily awkward.

United Nations practice indicates a less technical approach to the meaning of Article 2(6). There is no attempt to specify its limits by reference to the extent to which it incorporates other Charter provisions. A more general criterion of peace maintenance appears operative in the debates. Article 2(6) is available to authorize United Nations actions whenever an affirmative answer can be given to the following question: does the conduct of the nonmember interfere with the efforts of the organization to maintain international peace and security? However, even the practice by organs of the United Nations in regard to Article 2(6) cannot be accepted as fully authoritative. It is subject to change in response to changes in the political climate prevailing within the organization.

In United Nations debates, only Article 2(7) dealing with domestic jurisdiction has been asserted as a limitation on the scope of 2(6). Article 2(7) applies also to members. Its restraint upon the organization refers to "any State." If Article 2(7) is treated as the sole operative limit on the scope of 2(6), then one is led to conclude that United Nations practice supports the extensive interpretation of 2(6) that tends to eliminate the difference between members and nonmembers at least when viewed from the perspective of the authority of the organization to prohibit state behavior.

A controversy that arises from the extensive interpretation of Article 2(6) is the degree of authority possessed by the United Nations to attempt to change the internal political structure of a state, whether it is a member or nonmember state. Under what circumstances does the maintenance of peace depend upon the character of internal government? From a legalist perspective, Article 2(7) and the acceptance of the principle of national self-determination would appear to inhibit such an extension of authority, but the legal solution appropriate to world order must draw on far more complicated considerations. Paramount among these considerations is the developing community expectation that authority is possessed to withdraw legitimacy from certain governmental regimes that administer a society in violation of deeply shared values. Major examples include colonialism and apartheid in the five countries of southern Africa. Community interpretations of the principle of national self-determination make it increasingly difficult to argue that the incumbent government is *necessarily* entitled to respect as the center of political legitimacy for a particular sovereign state.

The Spanish Question (where action was recommended against the Franco government, then a nonmember, and to a small extent carried out) illustrated the practical relevance of this inquiry. The present political split within the organization between the Communist and non-Communist conception of what makes an internal government dangerous to world peace indicates that it is difficult to gain enough agreement within the organization to permit the use of Article 2(6) to compel a (member or) nonmember state to change its internal form of government, unless at least there exists a consensus that transcends the dividing lines between principal member states.

D. SOME RELEVANT FACTORS

Three factors deserve emphasis in any attempt to understand the role of Article 2(6) in the Charter scheme: (1) the reason for nonmembership status; (2) the relationship of the nonmember to the facts in issue; and (3) the claim asserted by the United Nations against the nonmember. Practice of the United Nations remains too scant to permit a useful analytical survey of the organization's experience with Article

2(6) in the light of these variables. However, it is possible to list a set of considerations that should be taken into account when studying a particular case in which there is occasion to apply Article 2(6).

I. *The quality of nonmembership*[59]

1. A state that had never applied for membership and was:
   a. of recent origin;
   b. of long existence.
2. A state that had applied for membership and had been refused admission.
3. A state that claimed neutral status by:
   a. preference;
   b. treaty.[60]
4. A state that had once been a member and had:
   a. been expelled in accord with Article 6;
   b. voluntarily withdrawn from the organization.

II. *The relationship of the nonmember to the controverted issue*

1. The nonmember might be a party to a dispute or a situation with:
   a. a member;
   b. a nonmember;
   c. a member and a nonmember;
   d. a regional organization;
   e. the United Nations.
2. The nonmember might be the direct object of United Nations sanctions because:
   a. It threatens international peace by
      (i) its form of government;
      (ii) its international policy;
      (iii) resort to threat or use of force.
   b. It suppresses fundamental freedoms and human rights protected by
      (i) international agreement;
      (ii) the Charter.
   c. It gives aid and comfort to an "enemy" of the United Nations— aid that is

---

[59] No attempt is made to deal with the legal relationship between the United Nations and entities that are "less" than states. Presumably, such a nonstate could not claim "sovereign" status under international law, nor would its consent be required in the event that the organization proceeded to act against it. The issue has some relevance for understanding the controversy caused by India's use of force against Goa, although in such a situation the concern involves whether a state, as distinct from the United Nations, was less legally inhibited in its rights to use force when it was dealing with a political entity lacking international personality.

[60] E.g. Switzerland. But see Art. 103 of the Charter, and Lazare Kopelmanas, *L'Organisation des Nations Unies*, Paris, Sirey, 1947, pp. 185-86.

      (i) military;
      (ii) nonmilitary.
  d. It violates international law by
      (i) failure to abide by agreements;
      (ii) failure to conform to customary international law.

III. *The character of the claim made by the organization*

When the nonmember is made the subject of obligations under the Charter:

  1. It may take the form of:
    a. a decision;
    b. a recommendation.
  2. The nonmember may be requested or ordered:
    a. to cooperate with the Organization;
    b. to refrain from interfering with the Organization;
    c. to terminate a course of conduct.
  3. It may be directed at:
    a. international relations;
    b. internal affairs.
  4. It may seek:
    a. *active* discharge of an obligation (e.g., participation in blockade, contribution of military equipment, pacific settlement of dispute);
    b. *passive* discharge of an obligation (e.g., allowing troops of the United Nations to cross territory).
  5. It may involve:
    a. military pressure;
    b. economic pressure;
    c. diplomatic pressure;
    d. psychological or moral pressure.

E. THEORETICAL PROBLEMS OF AN INTERPRETATION OF ARTICLE 2(6)

There are three main problems: first, the general considerations relevant to Charter interpretation; second, the special considerations relevant to an interpretation of Article 2(6), particularly with regard to its relationship to the traditional conceptions of international obligations; third, the various interpretations of Article 2(6) that give different answers to the second question.

1. General Considerations of Charter Interpretation. The Charter defines the powers and functions of the various organs of the United Nations with considerable generality.[61] This observation applies with

---

[61] A useful introduction to the problems of Charter interpretation can be found in Pollux, "The Interpretation of the Charter," 23 *British Yearbook of International Law* 54-82 (1946).

even greater force to the "Purposes and Principles" of the United Nations as enumerated in Articles 1 and 2. This vagueness makes necessary the exercise of continuous responsibility to interpret the relevant provision of the Charter. There is no way to make definite the meaning of a provision so as to terminate this continuing interpretative responsibility. As Oscar Schachter has said: "The Charter is surely not to be construed like a lease of land or an insurance policy; it is a constitutional instrument whose broad phrases were designed to meet changing circumstances for an undefined future. Any doubt as to the flexibility and adaptability of the Charter must surely have been resolved by recent developments."[62] The Charter itself does not indicate either the procedure or the nature of its own interpretation. Often major international treaties do contain such a provision that does establish procedure for interpretation. For example, the Constitution of the International Labour Organisation provides by Article 432 that "any question relating to the interpretation" of the Constitution shall be referred to the Permanent Court of International Justice; Article 18 of the International Monetary Fund gives interpretative power to the Fund's Executive Director.[63] Article 96 of the Charter does authorize organs of the United Nations to request an advisory opinion from the International Court of Justice on "legal questions," a provision that clearly includes questions of Charter interpretation. A celebrated use of Article 96 occurred when the General Assembly in 1947 requested the Court to interpret the meaning of Article 4(1) with respect to conditions of membership in the organization. More recently the advisory opinion in the case of Certain Expenses of the United Nations illustrates the use of this approach to interpret the Charter.[64] However, there is no requirement that this procedure be used, and the expectation at the San Francisco Conference was that Charter interpretation would mainly proceed on an *ad hoc* basis by the organ concerned with the meaning of a particular provision. The most authoritative statement appears to be found in the often-quoted final report of Committee IV/2 at San Francisco:

> In the course of the operations from day to day of the various organs of the Organization, it is inevitable that each organ will interpret such parts of the Charter as are applicable to its particular functions. . . . [I]t is not necessary to include in the Charter a provision either authorizing or approving the normal operation of this principle. . . . In brief, the members or the organs of the Organization might

[62] Oscar Schachter, Book Review, 60 *Yale Law Journal* 189, 193 (Jan. 1951).
[63] For other examples and discussion, see Leland M. Goodrich and Edvard I. Hambro, *Charter of the United Nations:* Commentary and Documents, Boston, World Peace Foundation, 1949, p. 548, 2d rev. edn. [hereinafter cited as Goodrich and Hambro].
[64] [1962] *I.C.J. Rep.*, 151.

have recourse to various expedients. . . . [Submission to the ICJ by Members or organs, determination by an *ad hoc* committee of jurists established by either the General Assembly or the Security Council, are "expedients" expressly mentioned in the report] in order to obtain an appropriate interpretation. It would appear neither necessary nor desirable to list or to describe in the Charter the various possible expedients.

It is to be understood, of course, that if an interpretation made by any organ of the Organization or by a committee of jurists is not generally acceptable it will be without binding force. In such circumstances, or in cases where it is desired to establish an authoritative interpretation as a precedent for the future, it may be necessary to embody the interpretation in an amendment to the Charter. This may always be accomplished by recourse to the procedure provided for amendment.[65]

Kelsen explores, with characteristic rigor, the theoretical character of the process of interpretation. It is not, he says, a search for the "true" meaning of legal norms, but an attempt "to render binding one of the several meanings of a legal norm, all equally possible from a logical point of view." This suggests that the choice of interpretations as a law-making act is determined by political motives. It is not the logically "true" but the politically preferable meaning of the interpreted norm that becomes binding.[66] Thus, there is no one *correct* meaning, according to Kelsen, that could be given to Article 2(6), and the task of the commentator is merely to suggest the possible meanings, leaving it to the appropriate authority "to choose from among the various possible interpretations the one which they, for political reasons, consider to be preferable, and which they alone are entitled to select."[67] One still is left with the problem of identifying who, in a particular case, is the appropriate source of political guidance.

Kelsen urges that scientific commentary on Charter interpretation is necessarily neutral, although Kelsen as a writer with strong political preferences is not silent after Kelsen as "scientist" has spoken. As Professor Leo Gross has so accurately noted, Kelsen's work expressed "his deep-seated desire to guide the development of law toward a more centralized and therefore more effective legal order." For, as Gross goes on to say, "whenever scientifically two conceptions appear to him to be equally possible, he invariably declares his preference in favor of that likely to promote that objective."[68]

---

[65] 13. *U.N. Conf. Int'l. Org. Docs.*, 709-10 (1945).

[66] Kelsen, p. xv.

[67] *Id.* p. xvi.

[68] Leo Gross, "States as Organs of International Law and the Problem of Auto-

Myres McDougal also arrives at the conclusion that the language of the Charter permits several possible interpretations.[69] However, McDougal rejects the dichotomy stressed by Kelsen between "scientific" and "political" models of analysis. For McDougal the most important undertaking of the expert commentator is to provide scientifically persuasive arguments for the politically preferable interpretation. In contrast to Kelsen, McDougal considers the most important task of a commentator to be to make persuasive his judgment as to the preferred interpretation, persuasive as measured by approximating the shared expectation of the parties and of the wider international community; he urges that we construe the meaning of a particular provision of the Charter to promote the major "Purposes" of the organization. In a similar vein, the late Judge Lauterpacht has written: "*Res magis valeat quam pereat.* It is a major principle, in the light of which the intention of the parties must always be interpreted, even to the extent of disregarding the letter of the instrument and of reading into it something which, on the face of it, it does not contain."[70] In an article developing this position, McDougal and Gardner defend the interpretation of the voting requirement in Article 27(3) that was made by the Security Council when it took action against North Korea in 1950 during the absence of the Soviet Union from the Council. They argue that the requirement that decisions of the Security Council must include "the concurring votes of the permanent members" does not preclude decisions reached during the absence of one of the permanent members (Soviet Union.)[71] These authors contend that "it would be a sad paradox indeed if the one act which gave the United Nations its greatest hope for survival in fact could be called beyond its competence in law."[72]

This approach of "interpretation for survival" by McDougal-Gardner finds a forceful parallel expression in the work of Judge Alvarez, who argues that "the Court has a free hand to allow scope to the new spirit which is evolving in contact with the new conditions of international life," and adds that Charter interpretation should be based upon "the

---

interpretation," in George A. Lipsky, ed., *Law and Politics in the World Community*, Berkeley, University of California Press, 1953, pp. 59, 60.

[69] Cf. Myres S. McDougal and Richard N. Gardner, "The Veto and the Charter: An Interpretation for Survival," in McDougal and Associates, *Studies in World Public Order*, New Haven, Yale University Press, 1960, p. 718; for a more complete discussion of McDougal's views on interpretation see Chap. XI. See also Myres S. McDougal, Harold D. Lasswell, and James C. Miller, *The Interpretation of Agreements and World Public Order*, New

Haven, Yale University Press, 1967.

[70] Hersch Lauterpacht, *The Development of International Law*, 69-70 (1930), [quoted by McDougal and Gardner].

[71] For an opposing interpretation of Article 27(3) based upon a more traditional analysis, see Leo Gross, "Voting in the Security Council: Abstention from Voting and Absence From Meetings," 60 *Yale Law Journal* 209-57 (Feb. 1951). McDougal and Gardner wrote their article in reply to Gross.

[72] McDougal and Gardner, note 69 *supra*, at 720.

requirements of international life" rather than upon technical considerations.[73] Schachter observes that, in fact, the direction of interpretation taken by those using the Charter has been beneficial and that the choice among interpretative possibilities has been generally resolved to promote the aims of the organization: "[I]t might be said that in the present state of affairs, many of us are grateful that we have at least an imperfect instrument for world order and, more important, that this instrument is being construed not in terms of its deficiencies but in order to make effective its principles and purposes."[74]

2. *Considerations Bearing on the Interpretation of Article 2(6).* This survey of the general problem of interpretation serves to introduce the more specific problems presented by Article 2(6). Kelsen is correct that it is necessary to explore the various possible meanings that those in authority can attach to a Charter provision. But McDougal is also correct, I feel, in placing emphasis upon an analysis of the consequences in relation to the purposes of the organization that inhere in the choice of alternative interpretations. And, finally, the positions of Judge Alvarez and Schachter, together with the envisioned flexibility of method described in the report of Committee IV/2, indicate that the various organs of the United Nations have been aware of the need to allow the interpretation of the Charter to be based upon an appraisal of what is necessary for the achievement of its dominant objectives. If we recall that the reason for Article 2(6) is to enable the United Nations to keep the peace on a worldwide basis, it is evident that advocacy and practice in regard to its interpretation should always endeavor to take account of the means necessary to achieve this goal. There is also a continuing need to inventory communitywide expectations that have been created by Article 2(6) and other communications related to nonmember status.

Does international law authorize the Charter to impose obligations upon nonmembers?[75] This is the central theoretical question posed by Article 2(6). It is necessary to clarify what is at stake when one argues that international law does or does not authorize the claim of competence made by Article 2(6). It is also necessary to consider the sociopolitical condition of expectations bearing on this subject matter.

The negative argument: The United Nations Charter is a multilateral treaty. The obligatory character of a treaty is universally based upon the explicit consent of the states that are bound by it. This consent is

[73] See, e.g., the individual opinion by Judge Alvarez in the case of Conditions on Admission of a State to Membership in the United Nations, [1948] *ICJ Rep.,* 57, 67.
[74] Schachter, note 62 *supra,* at 193.
[75] It is assumed in this discussion that

Article 2(6) purports to obligate nonmembers as well as to confer competence upon the organization to act. Later on an attempt will be made to support this assumption and to point out why the writings of some commentators to the contrary are misleading.

expressed by some variety of formal acceptance of the obligations of the treaty. This acceptance ordinarily makes such a state a party to the treaty. The nonmembers of the United Nations have not manifested their consent to be bound by the United Nations Charter. The attempt to impose Charter obligations upon nonmembers is thus contrary to accepted principles of international law. Therefore, Article 2(6) is without legal effect insofar as it purports to impose such obligations.[76]

The affirmative argument: The United Nations Charter possesses a world constitutional aspect. It is at least a quasi-constitutional instrument creating a legal regime, and drawing upon other elements in building up an overall constitutive order for international society. As such, it possesses *legislative* power to bind all states. The validity of the obligations that it imposes is quite independent of the acceptance of these obligations by formal acts of sovereign consent. The indisputable minimum legislative authority possessed by the San Francisco Conference concerned the means necessary to ensure the maintenance of international peace. Article 2(6) seeks to do no more than to obligate nonmember states to the extent necessary "to maintain international peace and security." Hence it is a valid expression of the legislative competence possessed by the Conference.

There is also a slightly different major formulation of this affirmative argument. Those parts of the United Nations Charter that deal with the maintenance of international peace are merely declaratory or creative of general (or customary) international law. Norms of general international law are binding without consent or—what is the same thing— by conclusively presumed consent. The maintenance of peace on a collective basis by the United Nations is thus no more than a structural extension of the norms of general international law that allows states to engage in collective self-defense against other states that threaten to, or do in fact, breach the peace. Therefore, Article 2(6) is a norm of general international law, and the consent of those bound by it is irrelevant to its juridical validity. The Charter, then, so far as it is concerned with the maintenance of international peace, is neither a treaty nor a constitution; it is a codification and an expression of norms of general international law. This is especially true if Article 2(6) is given a narrow construction so as not to bring it into conflict with other norms of general international law, such as the right to maintain a neutral status. And even if Article 2(6) does impose legal obligations upon nonmembers, it has validly done this in view of the failure of nonmembers to object to the claim. By the reasoning of the International Court of Justice in the North Atlantic *Fisheries Case,* it seems proper to argue that the

[76] Alfred Verdross, "Forbidden Treaties in International Law," 31 *American Journal of International Law* 571, 573 (Oct. 1937).

acquiescence of nonmembers has allowed Article 2(6) to enter into the corpus of general international law.[77]

3. *Article 2(6) and the Charter as a Legal Instrument.* The preceding analysis avoids the ambiguities that make it difficult to reach any firm conclusion about the juridical status of Article 2(6). The most significant of these ambiguities concerns the legal character of the Charter. Is it a treaty, a constitution, or does it codify general international law? Or is it a hybrid instrument that combines aspects of each? In at least a superficial sense, it seems necessary to agree with Goodrich and Hambro that the Charter is a multilateral treaty.[78] The Preamble to the Charter opens and closes with the consensual language of agreement that does not sound like a constitution or an instrument of codification. The Preamble begins: "We the peoples of the United Nations," and ends: "Accordingly, our respective governments, through representatives assembled in the city of San Francisco, . . . do hereby establish an international organization." Article 110 of the Charter requires "ratification" by the "signatory States in accordance with their respective constitutional processes." The Charter "comes into force" only by the deposit of ratification by a majority of states, a majority that must include all of the permanent members of the Security Council. Article 108 attaches similar ratification requirements to the Charter amendment procedure. Thus it is evident that internal to the Charter itself there exists strong evidence that the states participating at San Francisco acted, at least in part, as if they were creating a treaty. Domestic procedures used for routine treaty ratification were used by states to signify their decision to become members of the United Nations.

There is, however, some internal evidence to contradict this inference that the Charter should be regarded as an example of an orthodox treaty. Although Articles 108 and 109(2) employ the ratification technique, they allow changes in the Charter to become effective despite the absence of consent on the part of up to one-third of the members. Only the permanent members of the Security Council have been given protection by Article 108 against having the original content of the Charter varied to their dislike. Traditional international law requires a renewal of consent if the original obligations of a treaty are altered. However, one could say that this customary norm has itself been superseded by Article 108, which expresses the consent by all members to allow changes in the Charter by a prescribed method.

The *voluntary* character of the association envisaged by the United Nations is also suggested by the failure of the Charter to prohibit withdrawal. Thus a member can withdraw from the organization in order to

[77] [1951] *ICJ Rep.*, 116.   [78] Goodrich and Hambro, pp. 20-21.

[216]

avoid new obligations to which it did not wish to give its consent. By this possibility, then, one could conclude that the traditional requirement of consent as a condition of obligation has been preserved within the Charter structure. However, here again, the force of this conclusion can be questioned by pointing to the rejection at San Francisco of an Ecuadorian proposal to make such a withdrawal a matter of right incorporated into Chapter XI of the Charter.[79] Instead Committee I/2 made a "Declaration on Withdrawal" that acknowledged the right of withdrawal under "exceptional circumstances" but declared it to be "the highest duty of the nations which will become Members" to remain in the United Nations so as "to continue their cooperation within the Organization."[80] This Declaration could, I suppose, be disregarded in technical discussions as an assertion of sentiment rather than as a qualification upon the essentially consensual character of Charter participation. One must be careful to distinguish the largely consensual basis of *participation* in the United Nations from the nonconsensual basis of its *obligations*. Article 2(6) is itself the most bald separation of these two matters. This distinction was recognized clearly in relation to the expulsion of a member from the organization authorized by Article 6: "It was wrong to say that expulsion, as opposed to suspension, would release a state from obligations imposed on member states. In point of fact, by virtue of the principle contained in the Charter, it would still be bound by various obligations devolving upon non-member states in so far as such obligations affected the maintenance of peace."[81] This quotation is important because it unambiguously claims authority to obligate nonmembers.

The international usage of "constitution" is derived by demonstrating how the document in question is more ambitious than a treaty. Hence a constitution can be said to exist when the subject matter of an international instrument purports to base international obligations on *something other than* explicit and formal consent. This "something other than" is best described as at least a quasi-legislative competence. It seems useful to regard what is constitutional in an international sense as roughly equivalent to what is legislative in a domestic sense. In addition to the suspension of the consent requirement, there is the corollary fact pointed out by Alf Ross: an international instrument is constitutional when "according to its content . . . it aims at creating organs for a collectivity and establishing corresponding powers."[82] Article 2(6) seems to suggest that the Charter "aims at" a "collectivity" comprising the total world community, including those states that do not consent to

[79] *U.N. Conf. Int'l. Org.,* Sel. Docs., 525-26 (1946).

[80] *Id.* at 525.

[81] *Id.* at 508.

[82] Alf Ross, *Constitution of the United Nations,* New York, Rinehart, 1951, p. 40.

its obligations by becoming members. This constitutional claim is limited to that competence which is necessary to maintain peace. Ross feels that the constitutional character of the Charter is also revealed by Article 103, which subordinates the rights of nonconsenting nonmembers, deriving from international agreements with members, to the obligations of the Charter.[83] This is an "illegal" provision unless the San Francisco Conference possessed legislative competence to speak *ex cathedra* in the Charter. Ross also supports his inference of the constitutional character of the Charter by reference to the amendment procedures of Article 108 and 109(2). It is also evident that the delegates at the San Francisco Conference were convinced of their own competence to legislate, at least on the issue of the maintenance of peace, for the entire world community. The Report telling of the unanimous vote in Committee I/2 in favor of Article 2(6) also said the provision was adopted "on the understanding that the association of the United Nations, representing as it does the major expression of the international legal community, is entitled to act in a manner that will ensure the effective cooperation of non-member states with it, so far as that is necessary for the maintenance of international peace and security."[84] Mr. Stettinius in his Report to the President attributes a constitutional character to the Charter.

It is quite true that some authors regard the Charter as "constitutional" in a way that is irrelevant to the validity of Article 2(6). For example, Kunz refers to "the constitutions of particular international communities, like the United Nations, based on particular, treaty-created, international law."[85] In this view, the Charter binds only the "collectivity" of the membership and its "constitutional" status does not include any legislative competence to bind nonmembers. By reference to domestic usage, Kunz defines a constitution to mean the legal framework within which legal institutions operate. Thus a constitutional instrument becomes just one form of treaty, and the requirement of consent must be satisfied prior to the creation of valid obligations.[86] If one considers an international constitutional instrument as a contrast to a treaty, the issue of whether it is possible to impose obligations upon states without their consent is directly raised.

The Charter clearly purports to create an organization with a limited competence to regulate the activities of nonmembers. Accepting this as

---

83 *Id.* at 33-35.
84 *U.N. Conf. Int'l. Org.*, Sel. Docs., 487 (1946).
85 Josef L. Kunz, "Revolutionary Creation of Norms of International Law," 41 *American Journal of International Law* 119, 121 (Jan. 1947).

86 Kelsen's view that a treaty may create binding obligations on nonconsenting states under certain circumstances will be discussed below. It resembles the analysis that finds a legislative effect arising from certain types of multilateral treaties.

so, is it reasonable to argue that the Charter asserts an *ultra vires* claim? Is this the case, and, if so, what is its significance? Ross offers two reasons to validate the constitutional aspect of the Charter. First, international legislative competence exists whenever there is the intention to exercise it together with the expressed approval of "the great majority of states"; such a condition was satisfied at San Francisco, and hence such legislative provisions as Article 2(6) or 103 are fully valid.[87] And, second, legislative validity can be acquired by making effective the claim to such competence; Ross feels the Universal Postal Union possesses the requisite legislative competence because it would be so inconvenient for a nonconsenting state to depart from its norms that neither is the competence challenged nor does resistance to legislative claims occur.[88] If we apply this reasoning to Article 2(6), which Ross does not expressly do, it is evident that there exists a considerable basis for concluding that the United Nations in the Korean question has established the validity of its claim to control nonmember states to the extent necessary to maintain international peace and security. A further means of validating Article 2(6) is to emphasize the absence of any formal means to invalidate it. All organs of the United Nations, including the International Court of Justice, appear bound to accept as valid the provisions of the Charter.[89] It is, of course, possible that a tribunal in a nonmember state might declare some provision of the Charter—say, Article 2(6)—to be illegal by invoking general norms of international law.[90]

What would be the consequences under international law of classifying the Charter as a treaty?[91] Article 18 of the Harvard Research Draft Convention for the Law of Treaties contained the following first paragraph: "(a) A treaty may not impose obligations upon a State which is not a party thereto."[92] The attached comment takes such an unequivocal and self-assured position that it almost disdains discussion: "Paragraph (a) of this article affirms a general principle admitted by all writers on international law. In view of the virtual unanimity among them as to the validity of this principle, no purpose would be subserved in quoting their opinions here."[93] Of course, in one sense, such assurance is an automatic consequence of defining a treaty to include the requirement of consent. The Harvard Research Draft regards "treaty" as a term referring to all multinational arrangements. This would make it neces-

---

[87] Ross, *op.cit supra*, note 82, at 32. Ross makes an elaborate attempt to demonstrate that the process by which general international law is created may generate a valid norm in the face of a nonconsenting minority.

[88] *Id.* at 38.

[89] 1 Lassa Francis Lawrence Oppenheim-Hersch Lauterpacht, *International Law*, New York, Longmans, Green, 8th edn., 1955, pp. 928-29.

[90] Some writers facilitate this conclusion by emphasizing that the Charter is "nothing but a treaty." See, e.g., Goodrich and Hambro, pp. 108-09; Kunz, note 85 *supra*, at 124.

[91] For a survey, see Hsueh at 72-74.

[92] Harvard Research 918.

[93] *Ibid.*

sary to conclude that consent is a requirement coexistent with validity. The Harvard Draft is, therefore, quite dogmatic about the inability of a state to be bound in any way by a treaty to which it is not a party.

Roxburgh traces the roots of this consensual conception back to Roman law.[94] The whole subsequent "black-letter" development is summarized in the maxim: *pacta tertiis nec nocere nec prodesse possunt.* The *Code Napoléon* carried forward the notion that a contract "can never impose an obligation on a stranger."[95] Roxburgh concludes that no municipal legal system allows third-party obligations, and that similarly "a treaty cannot impose any liabilities upon a state which is not a party to it."[96] At the Hague Conference of 1907, the Rapporteur at the plenary session stated this conclusion in especially strong language: "Treaties bind none but the contracting parties; this is the only common law."[97] The practice of states is said to confirm fully this rule that a state may never be obligated by a treaty to which it is not a party.[98] Judicial experience in various tribunals (national and international) further reinforces the acceptance of the rule.[99] The Permanent Court of International Justice adopted this reasoning to refuse the suggestion that Article 17 of the Covenant of the League of Nations could be construed to bind nonmember states.[100] The force of all this evidence seems to compel the conclusion, accepted by so many commentators on the Charter, that Article 2(6) does not create legal obligations for nonmembers.[101]

Kelsen is the lone prominent exception. He interprets the Charter as a treaty and yet suggests the *possibility* that nonmembers may be subject to a legal obligation to conform to the Charter to the extent required by Article 2(6).

> That the Charter is a treaty concluded by the Members is not essential to the obligation to obey the norms created by the treaty. . . .
>
> In Article 2, paragraph 6, the Charter shows the tendency to be the law not only of the United Nations but also of the whole international community, that is to say, to be general, not only particular, international law. The Covenant of the League of Nations had the same tend-

[94] Ronald F. Roxburgh, *International Conventions and Third States*, New York, Longmans, Green, 1917, pp. 1-10.
[95] *Id.* at 13.
[96] *Id.* at 19.
[97] Quoted, *id.* at 20.
[98] Harvard Research 918.
[99] E.g., Territorial Jurisdiction of the Int'l. Comm'n. of the River Oder, P.C.I.J., Ser. A, No. 23 (1929); Factory of Chorzow, P.C.I.J., Ser. A, No. 17 (1928); Pablo Nájera Case, [1928] Ann. Dig. 393 (No. 271); Upper Silesia Case, [1926] Ann. Dig. 349 (No. 264); Trampler v. High Court of Zurich, [1925] Ann. Dig.

351 (No. 265).
[100] Eastern Carelia Case, P.C.I.J., Ser. B, No. 5 (1923).
[101] See Norman DeM. Bentwich and Andrew Martin, *A Commentary on the Charter of the United Nations*, New York, Macmillan, 1950, p. 14; Goodrich and Hambro, pp. 108-10; Paul Guggenheim, *Lehrbuch des Völkerrechts*, Basil, Verlag für Recht und Gesellschaft, 1948, p. 92; Kunz, note 85 *supra*, at 119-26; cf. Kunz, "General International Organizations," 48 *American Journal of International Law* 456, 457 (July 1953).

ency especially in its Article 17 and 18, but to a much smaller extent. The League, however, had no opportunity to realise *this tendency which is in contradiction to one of the fundamental principles of existing international law, that an international treaty can impose duties and confer rights only upon the contracting parties, that is to say, that an international treaty which is not concluded by all the states of the world does create particular, not general, international law. From the point of view of existing international law, the attempt of the Charter to apply to states which are not contracting parties to it must be characterized as revolutionary.* Whether it will be considered as a violation of the old, or as the beginning of a new international law, remains to be seen.[102]

Kelsen's analysis reaches results equivalent to those reached by Ross. However, Ross discusses the problem of Article 2(6) in connection with his demonstration of the constitutional character of the Charter. Ross also feels that validity of the Charter's claim to exercise *legislative power* cannot be fully determined until there has been an authoritative pronouncement.[103] Neither writer makes known how we will be able to obtain such an authoritative pronouncement. A pronouncement from a tribunal or other organ outside of the United Nations would hardly appear to be authoritative. Kelsen does mention that an *ad hoc* tribunal established to resolve a dispute between a member and a nonmember might conclude that the nonmember was not bound by the Charter.[104]

Kunz goes further and suggests that the International Court of Justice has a duty to relieve a nonmember from obligations said to derive from the Charter. He states:

> Even the International Court of Justice, . . . although, under Article 3 of the Charter, it is a "principal organ" of the U.N., *may not only possibly, but will be bound, to decide that a non-member is not legally bound by the Charter. . . .* For this Court, under Article 38 of its Statute, is bound to apply general customary international law, under which these treaty norms are not legally binding, and can apply to international conventions only if they "establish rules expressly recognized by the contesting parties."[105]

If this is a correct, it would be possible to receive an authoritative pronouncement of the validity of Article 2(6). However, the practice of the Court and other organs of the United Nations seems to reject de-

102 Kelsen, pp. 90, 109-10. (Emphasis added.) This is also the position taken by Alfred Verdross, in "Le Nazioni Unite e i Terzi State," 2 *La Comunità Internazionale*, at 445 (Oct. 1947).
103 Ross, *op.cit. supra*, note 82, at 32.

104 Hans Kelsen, "Sanctions in International Law under the Charter of the United Nations," 31 *Iowa Law Review* 499-543 (May 1946).
105 Kunz, *supra*, note 85, at 126. (Emphasis added.) See also Hsueh, p. 78.

cisively Kunz's view.[106] Lauterpacht, who agrees with Kunz that Article 2(6) does not impose "legal obligations upon non-member States," appears to give a more accurate presentation of the probable response of the Court to a challenge directed at the *legality* of the Charter: "This [Article 2(6)] is a mandatory provision which, upon analysis, constitutes a claim to regulate the conduct of non-members to the extent required for the fulfillment of the object of that Article. *It can not be admitted that the International Court of Justice or any other organ of the United Nations established under the Charter would be at liberty to hold that action taken in pursuance of Article 2 is contrary to International Law.*"[107] Given this conclusion, it is rather unimportant to argue about whether or not nonmembers can be bound by the Charter. In other words, once you carry the argument for validity to the point where there is no possibility of pronouncement of invalidity, and this argument is persuasive, then it seems idle bickering to resist the Ross-Kelsen conclusion that the claim made by Article 2(6) is legitimate.

If, however, one does not regard the absence of judicial review as decisive and goes on to insist that as a treaty the Charter cannot obligate a nonmember, then it becomes necessary to examine directly Kelsen's contention that a "revolutionary norm" has been created to overcome the former norm forbidding third-party obligations. Kelsen points out that unless the creation of new norms conforms to the framework provided by general international law, it is necessary to have recourse to the principle of effectiveness as a basis of validation. The consequence of doing this is antithetical to the basic purpose of international law to restrain power. As Verdross puts it: "[T]he principle of effectiveness can create new law only within the framework of international law; for a *boundless* recognition of the principle of effectiveness would legalize *any* illegality and thus abolish international law itself."[108] Kelsen's suggestion for validating Article 2(6) does have these dangerous implications of merging "law" with "power." This whole issue, it should be recalled, arises when one insists on classifying the Charter as a treaty. On balance it would seem that analogizing the Charter to a treaty, thereby making applicable the general norms governing the extension of a treaty, is unnecessary and undesirable. The Charter is a unique international instrument that creates the norms of general international law that are needed to validate its claims of competence.

This conclusion can be supported with more positive evidence. The need to regulate *all* states to assure the maintenance of peace, the experience of the League of Nations, the nearly universal participation in the

---

[106] Kunz's view does find some support in the dissenting opinions filed in the Interpretation of Peace Treaties with Bulgaria, Hungary, and Rumania, [1950] I.C.J. Rep. 65, 89-113 (advisory opinion).

[107] Oppenheim-Lauterpacht, *op.cit. supra*, note 89, at 928-29. (Emphasis added.)
[108] Alfred Verdross, *Völkerrecht*, Berlin, Springer, 1937, p. 126 [quoted by Kunz, *supra*, note 85, at 126].

San Francisco conference and in the United Nations, the absence of formal and explicit protest to the claims of competence made by the Charter over nonmembers, and the instances of action taken against nonmembers support the existence of a norm of general international law authorizing the Charter to claim legislative competence on the issue of the maintenance of peace. There exists enough basis to validate as legal Article 2(6). In fact, other analyses seem artificial by comparison, especially if one examines the way members and nonmembers react to the Charter in practice; no serious challenge has yet been directed at the legality of Article 2(6) except in scholarly literature. A sentence near the end of the Harvard Research Draft is relevant to this general line of reasoning: "Multipartite treaties enunciating new rules of international law cannot create obligations binding upon third States, unless perhaps they have been ratified by the vast majority of States, including all the important ones."[109] The acceptance as valid of the "unless" clause is all that is needed to validate the claims of Article 2(6). The Charter has been ratified by all important states in the world except Germany and China. Their failure to ratify derives from "special circumstances" that preclude their present admission to the United Nations; there is no indication that either objects to Article 2(6).

A subsidiary technique of validation could be achieved by regarding the Charter as an "international settlement." Such a settlement seeks to establish a new order that is binding upon the entire world community. Roxburgh says that "a presumption of a conviction of legal necessity ought perhaps to be made [if] . . . third states, knowing that the settlement is to be part of the international order, abide by its terms, and in the course of time they come to believe that they are legally bound by it." He adds, however, that "this conviction of legal obligation . . . does not admit of convincing or direct proof."[110] Quincy Wright has suggested that universal obligation may result from such an international settlement, but that it derives from the acceptance and the acquiescence of *the third states rather than from the instrument of agreement.*[111] The Harvard Research Draft observes that it is unimportant to resolve the question whether third-party obligations derive from the treaty directly or from the treaty indirectly as a consequence of acceptance and acquiescence: "In fact, however, whether or not they [the instruments of settlement] were regarded as 'legally binding' by the States which were not

[109] Harvard Research 924.
[110] Roxburgh, *op.cit. supra*, note 94, at 81-82.
[111] Quincy Wright, "Conflicts Between International Law and Treaties," 11 *American Journal of International Law* 566-79 (July 1917); but consider the previously quoted remark of Judge Negulesco in his dissenting opinion in the case of Jurisdiction of the European Commission of the Danube, P.C.I.J., Ser. B, No. 14, at 95 (1927): "Decisions of the Great Powers met together at the Concert of Europe . . . have never been held to be legally binding upon States not represented in the Concert."

parties to them, such decisions have been enforced and have been acquiesced in. It would serve no purpose to argue the question here."[112]
Of course, this dismissal is not fully convincing as the difference between
the two bases of validity could become crucial if a third state were to
make its nonacquiescence an issue. Again, however, the reasoning that
supports the universality of an international settlement is *a fortiori* available to support the claim of the United Nations to have the competence
through Article 2(6) to maintain world peace. The notion of "settlement" is useful as a rationale. Customarily, it refers to some disposition
made in a single act rather than to a continuing process of acting. A clas-
sic illustration of an international settlement binding on third states is
the Aaland Islands Dispute.

One problem with all of these arguments about the validity of Article
2(6) derives from the need to justify international legislation in a non-
legislative vocabulary. Article 2(6) makes a limited legislative claim
based upon the expression of the will of the participants in the San Francisco conference. This difficulty is based upon widespread deference,
repeated rather hypocritically in Article 2(1) of the Charter, to traditional conceptions of the sovereign character of states. The essence of
this traditional notion of sovereignty is to make the state the ultimate
arbiter of its own obligations. Thus all obligations must be based upon
consent, or at least acquiescence. Ross, among others, has shown that
such consent has never existed, except in a formal sense, with respect to
general international law.[113] The significance of sovereignty is not in
issue so long as one can "presume" acquiescence. But as soon as the
claim is made explicit in a written instrument, as it is in Article 2(6),
then it becomes necessary either to regard the claim as illegal or to conclude that the traditional description of sovereignty is inaccurate. This
choice seems inescapable if one does not argue that requisite consent
can be presumed by the acquiescence of nonmember states, or, in any
event, that nonmembers are estopped from protesting. If we face the
choice, then we must determine whether the San Francisco conference
could legislate rules binding upon nonmembers. The United Nations in
action discloses a divergence between theory and practice with regard
to the relevance of national sovereignty. International legal theory has
not yet developed a way to discuss the qualifications upon sovereignty
that seem operative in practice.

[112] Harvard Research 923. (Discussion
suggests that bilateral treaties neutralizing
the Straits of Magellan and the Panama
Canal have subsequently received universal respect. *But see* Roxburgh, *op.cit. supra*, note 94, at 71, where it is said that
this respect is without legal foundation
until the distant day when the subject
matter of the treaty can be said to have
been incorporated into the corpus of general international law—a very mysterious
process.)
[113] Ross, *op.cit. supra*, note 82, at 33.

This issue has been discussed at such length because the most eminent writers on international law have been unable to give a convincing account of the juridical status of Article 2(6). They have felt compelled to claim a legal revolution or to insist that a constitution for the world exists. If these modes of validation are not used, then writers, albeit with increasingly diminished assurance, conclude that Article 2(6) has no legal effect. Most writers are led to some variant of this position, despite the unquestioned confidence with which the United Nations proceeds against nonmembers.

It is perhaps instructive to compare the relevant portion of the comment to Article 2(6) found in the two editions of Goodrich and Hambro. A decisive pronouncement was ventured in the first edition: "The Charter *does not of course create any legal obligation* for states not Members of the Organization. They are therefore not obligated in a legal sense to act according to the Principles of the Charter for any purpose whatsoever. The Charter system therefore provides for the imposition, by force if necessary, of the prescribed conduct without any legal basis in contractual agreement."[114] The second edition used far more cautious language: "It is doubtful whether an international instrument can impose legal obligations on states which are not parties to it. The traditional theory which is not unanimously held [citing Kelsen] is that treaties cannot obligate third parties."[115] The change of tone, one supposes, is a consequence of the intervening United Nations practice in which Article 2(6) had been used without doubt as to its validity. No explanation of the change is offered by the authors.

Lauterpacht indulges in rather inconsistent assertions about the status of Article 2(6):

> The rule that treaties cannot validly impose obligations upon States which are not parties to them follows clearly from the sovereignty of States and from the resulting principle that *International Law does not as yet recognise anything in the nature of a legislative process by which rules of law are imposed upon a dissenting minority of States.* However, in proportion as international society is transformed into an integrated community *a departure from the accepted principle becomes unavoidable,* in particular in the sphere of preservation of international peace and security. . . . Both the Covenant . . . and the Charter . . . must therefore be regarded as having set a limit, determined by the *general interest of the international community, to the rule that a treaty cannot impose obligations upon States which are not parties to it.*[116]

---

[114] Goodrich and Hambro, p. 71 (1st edn., 1946). (Emphasis added.)

[115] Goodrich and Hambro, pp. 108-09.

[116] 1 Oppenheim-Lauterpacht, *op.cit. su-*

The constraints of traditional theory seem to induce so astute an observer as the late Judge Lauterpacht was to obscure a contradiction. Stripped of its protective coating of technical language, Lauterpacht's statement seems to contain two incompatible assertions: (1) International law does not allow the exercise of legislative power to extend the obligations of treaties to third parties; and (2) The Charter is a treaty that validly uses legislative power to extend some of its obligations to third parties. Thus a single instance (No. 2) of the violation of the general rule (No. 1) is said to modify the general rule (see last phrase of excerpt). Either this is nonsense or the general rule never "existed." Lauterpacht's analysis further illustrates that when the Charter is viewed as a treaty, the effort to state a validation of Article 2(6) is likely to appear strained and unconvincing.

Some writers have tried to resolve the question by concluding that Article 2(6) generates only a moral obligation. For example, Scheuner says that the Charter is a treaty that can create only particular international law (i.e., among members whose relations are governed by legal obligations to conform to the Charter) and that Article 2(6) results in *"nur eine Moralische Verpflichtung."*[117] And Judge Jessup has written that "under traditional international law, such treaty provisions [as Article 2(6)] do not bind a third state, but a third state would be *politically alive* to the possible consequence of action in defiance of the United Nations."[118] To be "politically alive" is a more direct way of expressing the operative impact of Article 2(6) regardless of its legal character.

A final approach, taken especially by Charter commentators, is to suggest, on the basis of a literal reading of the language used, that Article 2(6) creates an obligation only for the organization.[119] That is, the organization is obliged to take action against nonmembers to the extent necessary to ensure the maintenance of peace and security, but Article 2(6) does not purport to oblige nonmembers to conform to the Charter. According to this view, the obligations of nonmembers are presumably governed exclusively by general international law. Hence action taken by the organization is legal only insofar as it finds a basis in norms

---

pra, note 89, at 928-29. (Emphasis added.) Cf. the formulation in the 7th edn. at 652: "Non-members are not bound by this provision [Article 2(6)] and they may choose to react accordingly."

[117] Ulrich Scheuner, "Die Vereinten Nationen und die Stellung der Nichtmitglieder," in 29 *Völkerrechtliche und Staatsrechtliche Abhandlungen* 371, 379 (1954).

[118] Philip C. Jessup, *A Modern Law of Nations*, New York, Macmillan, 1948, p. 168. (Emphasis added.) Judge Jessup does hypothesize a "community interest" as supportive of the legality of the potential claims posited by Article 2(6).

[119] Bentwich and Martin, *op.cit. supra*, note 101, at 14; Goodrich and Hambro, p. 108.

of general international law, such as those authorizing "self-help," "self-defense," and recourse to collective action. This would tend to confine Article 2(6) to situations in which the organization concluded that the nonmember was guilty of breaches of the peace. It would not authorize, for instance, the United Nations to compel the cooperation of a nonmember to resist the aggression of some other state. Such a contemplated usage, certainly within the compass of the narrowest meaning reasonably attributable to Article 2(6), would thus require the organization to act "illegally" (on the basis of force or, as Bentwich and Martin quaintly put it, "as the result of the realities of power"). Kunz disposes of this formalistic approach as "no solution and no juridical explanation."[120]

Vellas, in a short monograph construing Article 2(6) as part of a broader "'décadence' des situations juridiques contractuelles," explains this phenomenon as follows: "Provoquées par des forces sociologiques profondes dues à des lois d'interdépendance accrue et d'intensification des relations sociales intergroupales ou intragroupales, cette évolution tend, en droit international, à étendre de plus en plus la force obligatoire des règles de droit bien au delà du group des signataires du traité qui les exprime."[121] This insight is crucial for it acknowledges the power of sociological reality to influence the content of law. Article 2(6) reflects the needs of a peace system in an interdependent world.[122] Judge Jessup has suggested that if one could risk "the hypotheses of community interest" (in regard to maintenance of peace), there would be no further difficulty in overcoming the obstacles to validating the claim of Article 2(6) despite the contrary thrust of traditional international law.[123] This hypothesis has been used on one prominent occasion by the International Court of Justice. In its advisory opinion, Reparation for Injuries Suffered in the Service of the United Nations, the Court declared that the United Nations possessed international personality in relation to nonmembers as a consequence of the Charter: "On this point, the Court's opinion is that fifty States, representing the vast majority of the members of the international community, had the power, in conformity

---

[120] Kunz, note 85 supra at 124; 1 Oppenheim-Lauterpacht, op.cit. supra, note 89, at 928, regards this type of formal analysis as distinct from the substantive issue raised by Article 2(6), i.e. the legality of the impact of the organization upon nonmembers.

[121] P. Vellas, Contribution à l'étude des obligations à la charge de tiers en droit international public, Paris, Pedone, 1950, p. 5.

[122] For a consideration of the relevance of interdependence for the development of a global system of law, see the various writings of Myres S. McDougal and his collaborators; esp. McDougal and Florentineo P. Feliciano, Law and Minimum World Public Order, New Haven, Yale University Press, 1961. See also Wolfgang Friedmann, The Changing Structure of International Law, New York, Columbia University Press, 1964, pp. 233-74.

[123] Jessup, op.cit. supra, note 118, at 168.

with international law, to bring into being an entity possessing objective international personality, and not merely personality recognized by them alone, together with capacity to bring international claims."[124]

It seems reasonable to conclude that Article 2(6) is a valid legal claim of competence. It is motivated by the fact of interdependence; it concerns subject matter clearly within the domain of world community interest; and it makes its claim in an instrument approved by the vast majority of states. This formulation appears realistic, although it presupposes the existence of a limited international legislative process. This approach allows us to validate Article 2(6) within the structure of general international law. Hence, it does not involve us in the choice of advocating either a "revolutionary" norm or of talking about the Charter as a limited world constitution. And, what is more important, it does not burden us with the conceptual framework appropriate for the analysis of treaties. This is so unsuitable that it leads commentators either to conclude that Article 2(6) is somehow "illegal" or to make very unconvincing demonstrations of its "legality." Given the need for a global peace system and given the willingness of the vast majority of states to participate in it, the claim of Article 2(6) is an indispensable corollary, the validation of which most naturally proceeds from accepting the will of the community, once it has been authoritatively declared, as a source of law in world affairs.

IV. Article 2(6) and the United Nations Practice

Since the inception of the United Nations, several questions have been concerned with the power of the organization in relation to nonmembers. However, Article 2(6) has not been used in a single instance as the explicit basis of United Nations action. And only in the cases of the Spanish Question and the Observance of Human Rights and Fundamental Freedoms in Hungary and Bulgaria can there be said to have been significant debate as to the meaning of Article 2(6). All other references to Article 2(6) are aptly characterized by the *Repertory of Practice of United Nations Organs* as "incidental" ones that "throw little light on the application of the provision."[125] There seems to be small justification for a duplication of the adequate summary of the rather extensive and insignificant practice that one finds in the *Repertory* and its 1958 and 1964 Supplements.[126] Instead, I propose to con-

---

[124] Reparation for Injuries Suffered in the Service of the United Nations [1949], *ICJ Rep.*, 174, 185.

[125] 1 Repertory of Practice of United Nations Organs 1955, at 39 (U.N. Pub. Sales No. 1955. V.2).

[126] *Id.* at 12-54; see also Supp. No. 1, at 21-24 (1958); in Supp. No. 2, Vol.

1, at 117, the following declaration is found: "During the period under review Article 2(6) was not expressly invoked by any U.N. organ. Nevertheless, certain resolutions adopted by the General Assembly at its 11th and 12th sessions may be said to bear upon Article 2(6) inasmuch as recommendations were made

sider two cases in detail and to offer some general observations. The Spanish Question is discussed because it illustrates an interesting early invocation of Article 2(6) and reveals the attitudes of some members toward its meaning. The Observance of Human Rights and Fundamental Freedoms in Hungary and Bulgaria is discussed because it did generate some discussion as to the proper scope of Article 2(6) and it produced an advisory opinion of the International Court of Justice that rejected some of the restrictive implications of the *Eastern Carelia Case.*

In a letter to the Security Council in 1946, the Polish representative requested the inclusion of "The Spanish Question" on the agenda of the Security Council. Referring to General Assembly Resolution 32(I), the letter stated that "the activities of the Franco Government have . . . caused international friction and endangered international peace." It went on to say:

> In view of the foregoing, the situation in Spain must be considered not as an internal affair of that country but as a concern of all the United Nations. Article 2 of the Charter in paragraph 6 provides that the United Nations Organization shall ensure that States not Members of the United Nations act in accordance with the principles of the Organization so far as may be necessary for the maintenance of international peace and security. The situation in Spain makes the application of this provision imperative.[127]

The Security Council placed "The Spanish Question" on its agenda. The debates concerned the issue of whether the Franco government constituted a threat to international peace and security. Draft resolutions, invoking Articles 34, 29, or 41, were submitted to the Security Council. In this respect, one argument made was that Article 2(6) imposed an obligation upon the organization to act against a nonmember state that constituted such a threat. For example, Mr. Lange, the Polish representative, in his main presentation, which emphasized the close association between Franco and the Nazis, recited the language of Article 2(6) and added: "The Fascist regime in Spain does not act in accordance with the principles of the United Nations, nor has it ever given any evidence that it intends to do so. It endangers the maintenance of international peace and security. It is, therefore, the duty of our Organization to ensure that any nation, whether a Member or not, does not endanger international peace and security."[128] This line of argument was reinforced by Mr. Bonnet, the French delegate, who disposed of arguments against

therein to 'all States and authorities' and to 'all States' regarding questions of international peace and security." See Res. 1236 GA(xii) and 1010 GA(xi).

[127] *U.N. Security Council Off. Rec.,* 1st year, 1st Sess., Supp. No. 2, at 55 (1946).
[128] *U.N. Security Council Off. Rec.,* 1st year, 1st Sess. at 167 (1946).

United Nations action by reference to Article 2(6): "Far from prohibiting us from doing so, in my opinion the Charter makes it an obligation. In fact, in pursuance of Article 2, paragraph 6, of which the Polish representative reminded us . . . we are required to ensure that States which are not Members of the United Nations act in accordance with the principles of the Charter."[129]

The main opposition was based upon Article 2(7) together with a belief that the Franco regime did not, in fact, constitute a threat to international peace and security, regardless of how oppressive the internal impact of Franco happened to be. For example, Mr. van Kleffens of the Netherlands expressed this position quite clearly:

> If we were to interfere in Spanish affairs on the basis of such evidence as has been placed before us, I think we would establish a most regrettable and harmful precedent for all sorts of ill-founded intervention. We are discussing the matter fully, and that is certainly useful. . . . But I cannot see that there are valid grounds, in the light of the Charter, to go beyond discussion.
>
> So long as Franco does not really threaten international peace and security, whether Spain wants to keep that regime, or not, is a matter for Spain alone. It is, in my opinion, in the language of the Charter, a matter which is essentially within Spain's domestic jurisdiction.[130]

And this point of view was expressed in a more technical manner by Sir Alexander Cadogan:

> Previous speakers have called attention to paragraphs 6 of Article 2 of the Charter, but I must point out that that paragraph is immediately followed by a further statement, in paragraph 7, to the effect that nothing in this Charter authorizes the United Nations to intervene in matters which are essentially within the domestic jurisdiction of any State. The nature of the regime in any given country is indisputably a matter of domestic jurisdiction.[131]

The Security Council resolved the question by the creation of a subcommittee that was given the task to determine whether there was, in fact, a threat to international peace. In a report, the subcommittee said that the evidence presented to it did not justify the conclusion that a "threat to the peace" within the meaning of Article 39 existed. It did suggest, however, that if Spain did not respond to measures taken as "appropriate procedures or methods of adjustment" under Article 36(1), then it would be proper for the General Assembly to adopt a resolution recommending that each member of the United Nations sever diplomatic relations with Spain. After consideration and rejection of the report, the Security Council decided "to keep the situation in Spain under continuous observation" but to take no immediate action.[132]

Later in 1946 the Spanish Question was placed on the agenda of the General Assembly. The item was referred to the First Committee, where the debate paralleled what had been said earlier in the Security Council. Mr. Mora of Uruguay, after invoking Article 2(6) to justify action of the organization, said that "the first of these principles is a reaffirmation of faith in fundamental human rights and in the dignity and worth of the human person." Thus he urged that the General Assembly make recommendations as to the situation in Spain on the basis of Article 13(1) (b).[133] Mr. Alfaro of Panama advocated a broad standard of limitation upon Article 2(7) and construed the Charter as emphasizing "the principle of collective action" expressed in Articles 39, 41, 42, and 2(6). He even went so far as to say that "the word *intervention* should not be used, but rather the word *inter-dependence* should be applied to the relations between nations of the world."[134] In December 1946, upon the advice of the First Committee, the General Assembly adopted Resolution 39(I), which contains the following strong recommendations:

The General Assembly. . . .

Recommends that the Franco Government of Spain be debarred from membership in international agencies established by or brought into relationship with the United Nations. . . .

Recommends that if, within a reasonable time, there is not established a government which derives its authority from the consent of the governed, committed to respect freedom of speech, religion and assembly and to the prompt holding of an election in which the Spanish people, free from force and intimidation and regardless of party, may express their will, the Security Council shall consider the adequate measures to be taken in order to remedy the situation;

Recommends that all Members of the United Nations immediately recall from Madrid their Ambassadors and Ministers Plenipotentiary accredited there. . . .[135]

Gradually, the General Assembly relaxed its pressure on Spain.[136] In 1950, the General Assembly passed a resolution revoking the recommendations of Resolution 39(I) that called for withdrawal of diplomats

132 See 1 *Repertory of Practice of United Nations Organs* 1955, at 41 (U.N. Pub. Sales No. 1955. V.2).
133 *U.N. Gen. Ass. Off. Rec.*, 1st Sess., 2d Pt., 1st Comm., 233-34 (1946).
134 *Id.* at 240-41.

135 *U.N. Gen. Ass. Off. Rec.*, 1st Sess., 2d Pt., Res., 63-64 (1946).
136 For a summary of these developments, see Louis B. Sohn, *United Nations Law*, Brooklyn, N. Y., Foundation Press, 1956, pp. 557-61.

and that debarred Spain from international agencies.[137] And, finally, in 1955 Spain was admitted to the United Nations as part of a "package deal" on admission concluded by the United States and the Soviet Union.[138]

Several considerations relevant to Article 2(6) emerge. In the course of extended debates on the wisdom of seeking to apply pressure on Franco, there was *no* suggestion that the United Nations was incompetent to act solely because Spain was a nonmember that had not consented to the Charter. Both sides assumed that if the situation in Spain had been found to constitute a threat to the peace, within the meaning of the Charter, the United Nations would have had the power and duty to act. The argument centered on the question of whether the internal form of government of Spain was protected against interference by the inhibitions of Article 2(7). But this determination is unrelated to the status of Spain as member or nonmember, since in either case the organization is equally inhibited.

Sir Alexander Cadogan's argument that Article 2(6) is to be construed as limited by Article 2(7) is an apparent acceptance of Kelsen's view that the Charter recognizes no significant distinction between members and nonmembers. This is also the minimum effect of Mr. Alfaro's virtual rejection of Article 2(7)'s role of protecting a state against intervention; the consequence is to remove almost every inhibition upon competence. Both positions assume the competence of the United Nations once a nonmember threat to the peace is established. The difference of interpretation results from the kind of test used to determine a threat to the peace. Mr. Lange felt that a Fascist form of government was sufficient; Mr. Mora and Mr. Alfaro felt that suppression of fundamental human rights was enough. Those opposing action by the organization regarded it as necessary to establish the existence of something more aggressive than the objectionable character of the nonmember's internal form of government.

It is rather interesting that, despite the many critical changes in circumstances, Sir Alexander Cadogan took the same attitude toward intervention, based on a threat to peace arising from the form of government, that Castlereagh and Canning had taken in the congresses of Europe during the nineteenth century. Then the European monarchs regarded it as essential to the maintenance of peace to assure the survival of the monarchial form, whereas now it is often urged that the democratic form is essential.[139] This difference is important, since its resolution

---

[137] *U.N. Gen. Ass. Off. Rec.*, 5th Sess., Res., 16-17 (1950).

[138] *Id.* 10th Sess., Annexes, Agenda Item No. 21 (A/2973) (1955).

[139] This position can be traced back to Kant's celebrated pamphlet *Perpetual Peace*, initially published in 1795. A more recent exposition developing the Kantian point of view and applying it to the conditions of the world immediately follow-

vastly influences the self-delimitation of competence by the principal organs of the United Nations. If the existence of fundamental freedoms and democracy were to be regarded as "necessary for the maintenance of international peace and security" within the meaning of Article 2(6), then nonmember states would be subject to considerable potential interference from the United Nations. The dominant tendency has been to accept the British approach, thereby giving vitality to the inhibition of Article 2(7), although, as with many crucial questions of United Nations practice, there is no authoritative determination as yet, nor is there any clear and consistent pattern set by the will of the political majority.

One can further observe that in the Spanish Question there was a failure to delimit the positive content of Article 2(6) by reference to other provisions of Article 2. The only limit evident from its invocation was a negative one derived from Article 2(7). Such an attitude seems to presuppose a sufficiency of competence for Article 2(6) to permit whatever the organization considers necessary to discharge its principal duty to maintain peace. The only disagreement concerns the quantum of evidence needed to establish the United Nations action as *necessary*. But this is a matter of general competence, and it places no added restriction upon the organization because it is being asked to act against a nonmember.

However, the discussions on the admission of Israel reflected a somewhat different attitude toward the difference in status of members and nonmembers. Several delegations urged admission, including Israel itself, precisely because it would make the state subject to a greater burden of obligation to the United Nations.[140] For example, Mr. Reyes of Uruguay, referring to the power of the organization under Article 2(6), went on to say: "The admission of Israel into the United Nations was necessary in order to compel it subsequently to fulfill its obligations with regard to the Holy Places and to carry out decisions on the refugees and the frontiers of Israel."[141] But why? If the matters referred to did not constitute a threat to the peace, the United Nations would be barred by Article 2(7) even if Israel were a member. If there were a threat to the peace, then Article 2(6) would allow action even if Israel were a nonmember. This is correct unless Article 2(7) is to be construed differently when the state that is the object of action is a nonmember. There is no evidence for such differentiation in the language of Article 2(7), which extends its protection to "any state." Mr. El-Khouri of Syria per-

---

ing World War II can be found in Karl Loewenstein, *Political Reconstruction*, Toronto, Macmillan, 1946.
[140] *U.N. Gen. Ass. Off. Rec.*, 3d Sess., 2d Pt., 15 (1948).
[141] *Id. 3d Sess., Ad Hoc* Pol. Comm. 299 (A/818) (1949).

haps reaches closer to the relevance of admission to the extent of obligation by his stress upon psychological factors and upon the greater convenience of acting against a member: "Thus it is our duty [under Article 2(6)] to try to make States which are not Members of the United Nations act in accordance with the principles of the Charter. Would it not be easier to do this if those States were here with us as Members instead of being applicants whose requests for membership have been rejected? This is a matter which touches upon the dignity of the States."[142]

Finally, in regard to the Spanish Question it would appear, especially from the statements of Mr. Lange and Mr. Bonnet quoted above, that the authority of the organization to act against nonmembers was derived directly from the duty-imposing language of Article 2(6). There was no evidence of concern about, or interest in, the possible legal difficulties that might surround a discharge of this duty by the organization.

As a result of letters from the representatives of Bolivia and Australia, in 1949 there was placed on the agenda of the second part of the third session of the General Assembly an item entitled "Observance of Human Rights and Fundamental Freedoms in Hungary and Bulgaria," to which was later added the consideration of similar subject matter in regard to Rumania. The essence of the issue concerned the alleged violations of provisions in treaties of peace concluded at the end of World War II that obligated these states to show respect for human rights and fundamental freedoms and that also contained provisions to enable settlement of disputes over the fulfillment of these obligations. It was alleged that the persecution of the clergy in these countries, most spectacularly the trial and conviction of Cardinal Mindszenty of Hungary, was a flagrant violation and that a further violation arose from a refusal to cooperate in the use of the treaty procedure of settlement. In addition, it was alleged that these practices constituted a violation of Article 55 of the Charter, which involved a duty to promote "universal respect for, and observance of, human rights and fundamental freedoms." Competence was based on the broad grant of power to the General Assembly contained in Article 14. In the initial stages of debate, there was no mention that the states involved were nonmembers. The main issue was whether or not the alleged practices were, in the sense of Article 2(7), matters "essentially within the domestic jurisdiction" of the states involved. Extended discussion ensued and at successive Assembly sessions several resolutions were passed that "expressed deep concern" and "decided to retain the question on the agenda."[143] Through an interesting shift in

[142] *Id.* 5th Sess., Plenary 567 (A/1353) (1950).
[143] See 1 *Repertory of Practice of*

United Nations Organs 1955, at 83-88 (U.N. Pub. Sales No. 1955. V.2).

political circumstances from those present in the Spanish Question, the Communist bloc reminded the organization not only that this was an intrusion upon domestic jurisdiction, but also that the United Nations was making completely unwarranted claims to exert its influence upon nonmembers.

In fact, it was the Polish delegate who reminded the organization that the limits of its competence were specified by the traditional requirement of consent. Mr. Katz-Suchy of Poland proposed a most rigid circumscription of Article 2(6):

> Article 2(6) dealt with something entirely different from human rights. And strictly speaking, that clause did not entail any legal obligations for States which were not Members of the Organization. Since the Charter was a multilateral treaty, the non-obligation on the part of a State which was not a Member of the Organization derived not only from the legal principle that no State could be bound by a treaty concluded by other States—that was the time-honored principle of *res inter alia gesta*—but also from a comparison between Article 2, paragraph 6 and Article 17 of the Covenant . . . which contained a similar provision.[144]

This is indeed a strange *volte-face* for the state that took the initiative in the Spanish Question and that assured the organization of its ample competence under Article 2(6). Here Mr. Katz-Suchy relied upon a most conservative legalistic approach to the Charter by his insistence that it be interpreted like a treaty. Not even the Soviet delegate, Mr. Malik, insisted on this approach, preferring to emphasize that Article 2(7) made Charter provisions pertaining to human rights inoperative for members and *a fortiori* inoperative for nonmembers.[145] The political motivation for the remarks of Mr. Katz-Suchy is more boldly revealed by the following statement by Mr. Drohojowski in a Plenary Meeting of the Assembly addressed to the relevance of Article 2(6):

> As for Article 2, paragraph 6, which has been invoked by some representatives, was it possible, by even the greatest stretch of the imagination, to believe that the cases of Cardinal Mindszenty and the Bulgarian clergy could constitute a threat to the maintenance of international peace and security? That Article, however, might well be applied to such questions as Franco Spain, restrictions on trade union rights or the position of Indians in South Africa. In the case under consideration, however, reference to that Article could have been made only in bad faith.[146]

---

[144] *U.N. Gen. Ass. Off. Rec.*, 3d Sess., 2d Pt., Gen. Comm. 11 (A/820) (1948).

[145] *Id.* at 26ff.

[146] *Id.* Plenary at 15.

This position on the law is similar to that taken by the United States and by other non-South American advocates of United Nations action; disagreement centers upon the facts and their relevance to world peace. Mr. Cohen of the United States also maintained that the United Nations could not take action unless it was established that the alleged violations of human rights amounted to "a threat to the peace."[147] This appeared to be the overwhelming approach of the delegates to Article 2(6). The Article could be invoked only to maintain peace, and to establish this it was necessary to produce evidence that at least a threat to the peace existed. The radical differences in approach depended on the kind of evidence necessary to satisfy the test.

Some South American delegates felt that any violation was per se a threat to the peace within the meaning of the Charter and therefore provided the basis for action under Article 2(6) against nonmember states.[148] The Communist bloc argued the opposite position. Whenever the subject of controversy concerned human rights, it was alleged to be impossible to establish the existence of a threat to the peace such as to justify Article 2(6) action. As Mr. Drohojowski stated this position: "Article 2(6) is applicable *only* so far as peace and security are threatened. No one, not even its sponsors alleged that human rights violations threatened peace and security."[149] The more general view was to regard the subject of human rights as *potentially* within the purview of Article 2(6). It was, for example, frequently mentioned that Hitler's suppression of human rights was a major cause of World War II, but it was recognized that internal administration, including human rights, was ordinarily to be treated as a matter of domestic jurisdiction.

There was some expression by the Communist nations that issues of human rights were so clearly within domestic jurisdiction as to prevent even their placement on the agenda or their discussion. This can be discounted as an argument for the occasion, since these same nations, especially the Soviet Union, have consistently taken the opposite position with great fervor on all questions affecting human rights in the Republic of South Africa. The United States, although cautious about associating itself with the extreme South American position, explicitly urged that such matters were at least appropriate for inclusion on the agenda and ripe for discussion by the Assembly.

It is difficult to evaluate the significance of the debates that have been discussed. The attack on the use of Article 2(6) based on the analogy of the Charter to a treaty appeared to have been an *ad hoc* defensive tactic resorted to by the Communist members under pressure. It aroused little sympathy among non-Communist states. In the Spanish Question,

147 *Id. Ad hoc* Pol. Comm. at 89.
148 *Id.* Plenary at 24ff.
149 *Id. Ad hoc* Pol. Comm. at 62.

the Western states did not use a similar tactic in their attempt to restrain the organization. The practice of the United Nations with regard to non-member states does not question the authority to act under Article 2(6) when a threat to the peace has been established to the satisfaction of the relevant majority of the Membership.[150] Beyond this basic authority, existing practice does not give us guidance as to the scope of Article 2(6) or as to the differences between the extent of the Charter obligations of members and of nonmembers.

Mr. Katz-Suchy stated that the Charter made a lesser claim upon nonmembers than did the Covenant: "It had been possible to maintain that Article 17 of the Covenant was worded in such a way that it imposed on States not members of the League of Nations an obligation not to resort to war; on the other hand, Article 2, paragraph 6, of the Charter had obviously been worded in such a way that it did not impose any legal obligations on non-member States even with respect to international peace and security."[151] This interpretation of Article 2(6) separates the grant of authority to the organization from the obligation of nonmembers to respect the Charter. It requires one to assume that the Charter instructs the organization to impose its will upon states that are not bound in any way, other than by force, to respect it. It also assumes a renunciation by the Charter of the claim in the Covenant to receive compliance by nonmembers with the obligations of the League to the extent needed to maintain peace. This position seems to contradict the expectations of the San Francisco conference in regard to Article 2(6) as well as to disregard the general willingness of the organization to direct resolutions to "all States."

Whenever the maintenance of peace is involved, the United Nations has not hesitated to direct its resolutions to "every State" or to "all States." This was most dramatically illustrated during the Korean War, when resolutions called upon all states to take certain negative action against the People's Republic of China and North Korea. For example, Resolution 500(V) called upon "every State to apply an embargo on the shipment to areas under control" in these two countries of "arms, ammunition and implements of war," and recommended the application of "controls to give effect to the embargo; to prevent the circumvention of controls on shipments applied by other States; to co-operate with other States in carrying out the purposes of the embargo."[152]

This resolution was not only directed against a nonmember, but attempted to solicit nonmember cooperation for the imposition of the sanc-

150 *Id.* Plenary at 9, 242.
151 *Id.* Gen. Comm. at 11.
152 1 *Repertory of Practice of United Nations Organs* 1955, at 344 (U.N. Pub. Sales No. 1955.V.2); for other resolutions affecting nonmember states, see Res. 707 (VII) at 344; 290 (IV) at 351; 291 (IV) at 351; 503A (VI) at 350.

tions that were recommended. None of these resolutions (except in a single draft submission to establish a special committee "to elucidate the acts alleged to have been committed in Bulgaria and Hungary against human rights and the fundamental freedoms") explicitly relied upon Article 2(6); even in this latter instance the reference was deleted from the final form of the resolution.[153] There is some doubt as to the general legal force of Assembly recommendations, and it may be that, with regard to nonmembers, unless coercive implementation is undertaken, such resolutions are only exhortatory and thus cannot be considered relevant to the present inquiry into the obligation of the United Nations to "ensure" that nonmembers "act in accordance with these Principles." There has as yet been no test or real indication of the consequences of non-compliance by nonmembers with either the "Decisions" of the Security Council or with "Recommendations" of the Assembly. It seems evident that, if the nonmember is itself the state threatening or breaching the peace, the United Nations will respond exactly as it would against a member.

In 1949, the General Assembly requested from the International Court of Justice an advisory opinion in relation to the interpretation of the peace treaties with Bulgaria, Hungary, and Rumania.[154] The questions presented concerned the applicability and interpretation of the procedures provided by the treaties themselves for the resolution of disputes involving questions of the observance of human rights. The opinion is significant because it does seem to restrict the broader implications of the *Eastern Carelia Case*, especially as to the prerequisite of nonmember consent to action by an international organization and as to the capacity of the Court to render an advisory opinion in the absence of such consent. Here, as in the *Eastern Carelia Case*, the nonmembers had not given their consent to the proceedings of the Court. In this case, there was no mention of Article 2(6). The general inquiry was treated in a technical manner and the Court did not venture to consider the claims made by the United Nations to control nonmembers. On the central issue, the majority opinion said:

> The consent of States, parties to a dispute, is the basis of the Court's jurisdiction in contentious cases. The situation is different in regard to advisory proceedings. . . . The Court's reply is only of an advisory character: as such, it has no binding force. It follows that no State, whether a Member of the United Nations or not, can prevent the giving of an Advisory Opinion which the United Nations considers to

[153] *U.N. Gen. Ass. Off. Rec.*, 3d Sess., 2d Pt., *Ad hoc* Pol. Comm., Annex I, 111-12.

[154] Interpretation of Peace Treaties with Bulgaria, Hungary, and Rumania, [1950] *ICJ Rep.* 65 (advisory opinion).

be desirable in order to obtain enlightenment as to the course of action it should take.[155]

The *Eastern Carelia Case* was explicitly confined to the situation in which "that Court declined to give an Opinion . . . because it found that the question put to it was directly related to the main point of a dispute actually pending between two States, so that answering the question would be substantially equivalent to deciding the dispute between the parties, and that at the same time it raised a questions of fact which could not be elucidated without hearing both parties."[156] This formulation can be construed as reducing the scope of *Eastern Carelia* to a rather self-evident declaration of judicial self-restraint. It is self-evident because even the contentious jurisdiction of the Court is confined to *voluntary* or consensual submission. Thus the view expressed is designed only to avoid an adjudication of a dispute under the guise of an advisory opinion when the requisites for contentious jurisdiction cannot be satisfied. As the Court has said in a later case: "To adjudicate upon the international responsibility of Albania without her consent would run counter to a well-established principle of international law embodied in the Court's Statute, namely, that the Court can only exercise jurisdiction over a State with its consent."[157] The dissenters in the *Interpretation of Peace Treaties Case* insisted that the *Eastern Carelia Case* precedent was reason enough to refuse the request for an advisory opinion.[158] The argument rests upon the refusal of consent by the states, together with the dispute-affecting nature of the advice solicited by the Assembly Judge Krylov in his dissent places some emphasis also upon the fact that Bulgaria, Hungary, and Rumania are not members of the United Nations: Members in a sense "consented" to the rendition of advisory opinions because Article 93 makes them *"Ipso facto* parties to the Statute of the International Court of Justice."[159] This argument appears unnecessary, since even members are not *required* to have the Court adjudicate without their consent. Therefore, if the advisory opinion is an "adjudication," it requires the consent of all parties whether members or not.

The *Interpretation of Peace Treaties Case* seems intelligently restricted to its context—an insistence upon voluntary submission as a condition precedent, but only if the Court is asked for an adjudication. This appears to be all that *Eastern Carelia* can be now taken to mean, despite its use of broad language. To construe either opinion as bearing upon the right of an international organization to control nonmembers

155 *Id* at 71.
156 *Id*. at 72.
157 The Case of Monetary Gold Removed from Rome in 1943 (Preliminary Question), [1954] *ICJ Rep.* 32.

158 Interpretation of Peace Treaties with Bulgaria, Hungary, and Rumania, [1950] *ICJ Rep.* 65 (advisory opinion).
159 *Id*. at 109.

for purposes of maintaining world peace seems unwarranted. This is important since commentators, such as the authors of the Harvard Research Draft, regarded the *Eastern Carelia Case* as establishing that the Covenant was a treaty and hence not binding without the consent of the nonmember. It is possible that the Court would today hold this way, but it is certainly not an implication of the earlier case. There is, in fact, no relevant decisional material of the Court that would indicate its response, although the case on Reparations for Injuries Suffered in the Service of the United Nations suggests a strong willingness to find authorization in international law for whatever appears necessary for the intended optimum functioning of the organization.[160] One could argue that Article 2(6) would probably receive a judicial endorsement as a result of a probable extension of such an approach, should it be put to a test, but such a prediction is certainly highly conjectural.

In conclusion, despite instances of United Nations practice involving nonmembers, there is, as yet, no authoritative delimitation of the scope of Article 2(6). Its use seems tied to a minimum conception of "threat to the peace," a concept that is without definite content and whose definition on a given occasion reflects political considerations. However, when there is "a threat to the peace," the organization seems ready to ask for as much cooperation from nonmembers as from members. Even members have not yet been *required* to participate in peacekeeping operations against their will. Thus, differentiation is minimal.

If a nonmember is accused of a Charter violation, its main defense appears to be Article 2(7). Members also rely mainly upon this provision when seeking a shield against the organization. Thus, in practice, when peace maintenance is in issue, the United Nations, as Kelsen has suggested, seems to treat members and nonmembers alike, except with respect to the obligation to pay.

The validity of such treatment has been challenged only as a defensive tactic by a badly outnumbered Communist minority in the *Observance of Human Rights and Fundamental Freedoms Case*. Even then, it was put in legalistic form only by one delegate and elicited no response. Controversy seems more to concern the relative difficulty of demonstrating "a threat to the peace." Here again the difference between members and nonmembers is formal and perhaps significant as an *implicit* inducement to self-restraint.

Article 2(6) has not been discussed in any opinion of the International Court of Justice. On the one possible occasion, the *Interpretation of Peace Treaties Case*, there was a rather evident effort to avoid facing the more general aspects of the relationship between the United Na-

---

[160] Reparation for Injuries Suffered in the Service of the United Nations [1949], *ICJ Rep.*, 174.

tions and nonmember states. The decision reasserted the consensual basis of adjudicative jurisdiction, but affirmed its own competence to render a nonadjudicative advisory opinion despite the absence of consent by a nonmember disputant whose interests were at stake. But here again, the principle would appear to apply equally if the objecting party were a member.

Thus, my conclusion is that the practice of the United Nations has not yet revealed any clear lines of differentiation between the *obligations* of members and nonmembers. Where the requisite political majority can be mobilized, the organization does not disclose any reluctance to act against nonmembers, nor is there much evidence of concern with the juridical issues at stake. However, the juridical issues can be raised and, once raised, are difficult to resolve.

V. General Conclusion

The juridical character of Article 2(6) of the Charter raises fundamental questions that bear upon the creation of international obligations. The most important issue presented is whether a substantial majority of states in the world may "legislate" for an absent or even a dissenting minority. It would appear, at least on the issue of maintaining the peace, that such legislative competence must be acknowledged in view of the increasing gravity of the threat of war and the growing interdependence of the world community, as well as the virtually unchallenged exercise of such competence in the practice of the United Nations. It is difficult to validate this competence, as claimed in Article 2(6), by resort to the modes of analysis traditional in international law. It is especially artificial to approach the Charter as a treaty, since it produces either an untenable repudiation of competence (Kunz), or a strained affirmation (Kelsen). If one suggests that the Charter is a "constitution" (Ross), then some confusion with domestic usage results, and it becomes necessary to invent a new term to describe the possible replacement of the Charter by a *genuine* world constitution. The Charter, and perhaps the Covenant, should probably be treated as *sui generis*, generating distinct norms of interpretation and limits. In any event, formulation of sovereignty should be revised to take account of the *potentially* nonconsensual obligations of the Charter imposed by Article 2(6). The Charter itself should be reformulated to the extent that it now exhibits signs of adherence to the older approach, as in Article 2(1) and 25. And, finally, an adequate juridical analysis must take account of United Nations practice and its persistent tendency to ignore the distinction between members and nonmembers in establishing its competence to act whenever world peace is at issue.

VIII. Unilateral Claims to Use Outer Space and the Development of World Legal Order

CONTROVERSIAL unilateral claims to use outer space raise issues of utmost importance for the future of the world legal order. First, the regulation of space is a substantive matter of major concern. Second, the problems of space regulation illustrate the pervasive difficulty of restraining the international behavior of powerful states. Third, the development of international law very much reflects the quasi-legislative authority of principal sovereign states.

The loosely structured character of international society partly explains why novel claims of states to act internationally may be troublesome. There is no regularly available legislative or executive authority to adapt the regulative framework to new and unanticipated areas of human development. If powerful sovereign states assert new claims of consequence not just to themselves but to the entire international community, then international society seems particularly unequipped, formally or actually, to insist that the interests of the international community take precedence over national interests. The ideology and realism of the doctrine of national sovereignty make powerful states unamenable to restraint imposed, so to speak, from above. This absence of higher legal authority is descriptive of the situation in the space field. The principal states are developing a new technology that has, and will increasingly have, a global significance. These claimant states are acting in almost exclusive response to the dictates of their national will. Even in the event that a wider community exists it would lack the capability to express itself effectively. This unevenness is part of the background of excitement that surrounds the opening of the space age.

If we acknowledge the primacy of the sovereign actor in the space field, then it is necessary to examine the prospects for a sovereign willingness to substitute regulation for anarchy. Perhaps the tradition of legal positivism gives grounds for hope. By asserting that valid international obligations can arise only as a result of the consent of the sovereign to be bound, it may appear possible to entice the space powers to generate their own regulatory scheme by drawing up a comprehensive space code. For the space powers are not cut off from interests that prompt the community of states to seek a regime of restraint, which includes safeguarding supranational interests at stake. There is a mix of national interests that supplements the traditional drive to preserve a maximum area of sovereign discretion with an equally traditional drive to substitute mutual restraint for unregulated competition. This drive for order is certainly present, even if it is not yet dominant, in the space area. For it is widely appreciated that it would be desirable to avoid the extension of the arms race between the Soviet Union and the United States to activities in outer space. Such military competition would be expensive and dangerous. The weapons are difficult to develop and it is hard to monitor the progress of one's rival(s). Some evidence of restraint is present.

At the same time, certain uses of space with military significance have been already undertaken. There has been no effort to prohibit the passage of guided missiles through outer space. The fact of space passage has not been regarded as a significant differentiating variable in discussions about the legality of missiles or nuclear weapons. Then, too, the collection by space satellites of information with military significance has been undertaken, but not without initially arousing strong Soviet protest. These Soviet protests emphasized the argument that a state should not be able to use space to gather information that it was not able to obtain legally by other means. Decisions about military uses of space have been made by sovereign states largely as a consequence of procedures internal to national government, the substantive workings of which are not fully disclosed to the public. This insulation from appraisal is especially true for the Soviet Union, but it is also apparent that the government of the United States has not revealed fully the military uses that it now makes and proposes to make of outer space in the future.

To examine the nature of the problem, it may be helpful to consider the Samos-Midas observation satellite program to illustrate the military use of space. The justification for Samos-Midas as a particular policy cannot be appraised. An appraisal depends, in part at least, upon elaborate security arguments in favor of information-gathering. These arguments cannot be evaluated without access to highly classified materials, for instance, the availability of alternate information sources, the success of satellite missions, the relation of this information to such matters as protection against surprise attack, the overbuilding and underbuilding of a deterrent force, and the development of a credible first and second strike posture. The military argument also requires a reliance upon unavailable estimates about Soviet capabilities, vulnerabilities, and intentions vis-à-vis nuclear war. Thus it is not possible to come to a prudent substantive conclusion about the advisability of the Samos-Midas program. What is possible, however, is to discuss considerations that are relevant to the formation of national policy with respect to a military use of space that has generated protests on the part of another dominant space power. Inquiry will concern the development of procedures to assure the adoption of a reasonable course of action, appraising "reasonableness" from the dual perspective of national and global interests. A basic assumption of this chapter is that a powerful state in the contemporary world is well advised to act to improve world order as well as to promote its own sovereign advantage.

An adequate understanding of this kind of problem rests upon the character of law and order in world affairs today. Part of an improved approach involves the adoption of a clearer policy toward the apt mixture of national interest and world community interest on various issues. No abstract formula is available to instruct states on the extent of deference that it is proper to accord formal expressions of consensus by the majority of states. Each substantive area presents distinct considerations about the scope of sovereign discretion. This kind of balancing analysis, common for federal states required to reconcile the powers of the central government with those of its member states, is rather new for international affairs. It is also a very different process. Unlike the characteristic federal state, there remains no disposition to move preponderant power and authority to the political center of international society. The national units in the international system, especially the space users, retain predominant power and competence. Given these facts of political dispersal, what is the extent of and the basis for the effective curtailment of national power? The contingent character of national restraint is the appropriate starting point for every appraisal of the foundations of world legal order.

This contingent character is an especially attractive point of origin for thinking about the legal regulation, if any, of contested uses of outer space. No background of use exists to provide a tradition of restraint. These space claims are new claims to act in a realm of activity that did not previously exist. It is possible, although not very convincing, to analogize claims to use outer space to earlier claims to use air space or maritime regions. Such reference points provide, by analogy, certain traditions of restraint, but there are so many significant differences and the analogous standards are so vague that the points of contact that do exist can be virtually manipulated at whim by representatives of national governments.

Another way to raise the issue of legal restraint is to question the applicability of the postulate of legal positivism that sovereign consent, presumed or express, must underlie the formation of every valid international obligation. Perhaps the United Nations can restrain space claims that are detrimental to world community welfare. But international practice indicates that the General Assembly does not possess the kind of legislative competence that will be respected, especially when exercised to control vital activities undertaken by major states. For instance, appeals by the United Nations in the areas of nuclear testing and disarmament, although perhaps responsible for creating a world climate conducive to arms control and disarmament discussions, and even to occasional agreements, still suggest the rather modest extent of United Nations effectiveness. Certainly norms posited by the organization, but not perceived as serving the common interests of the space nations, are not likely to constrain conduct, unless they are formulated on such abstract levels as to leave procedures of self-interpretation unencumbered. There are no central institutions in international society that possess the strength to impose their will upon dissenting powerful states.

This absence of centralized effective authority is a critical fact of international life. If the organized community cannot impose restraint, then restraint, if it is to exist at all, must be self-generated. An obvious inference is that the parties to be restrained must come to an agreement, i.e. that in this case the space powers must enter into a compact of mutual restraint that satisfies their joint and separate interests. But, as disarmament negotiations suggest, to advocate this end is not to disclose a way to reach it. Lack of trust, asymmetrical strategic space objectives, an absence of domestic consensus, an unwillingness to give up sovereign prerogatives, and an uncertainty about what will be uncovered by subsequent space development are factors that contribute to a climate of opinion that remains hostile to a search for a code of space law and administration at this time. Perhaps limited agreements of importance can be reached as, for example, to prohibit the orbiting of weapons, or broad agreements of almost useless generality can be achieved. It is clear, however, that no general regime of space restraint can be presently negotiated by the parties, nor can it be effectively imposed by the organized community of states.

Do these discouraging conclusions about the prospects for legal order warrant an acceptance of anarchy plus national egoism in the use of space? This assessment would endorse traditionalist assumptions about the absence of a prospect for formal order. This chapter explores the possibilities of a more constructive response, partly in the form of a policy argument about how the United States should act and partly in a discussion of how law-making proceeds in a horizontal (a relatively unstructured) social system. The basic argument is that a nation should adopt what amounts to the golden rule as a guide to its action and should refrain from making the kind of claim that it would not want made against it. Adherence to the ground rules of reciprocity is posited as an aspect of minimum world order in the nuclear age. But suppose this attitude of self-restraint is not reciprocated? Suppose the space rivals of the United States pursue an egocentric policy that is restrained only by the vagaries of their dubious prudence and the exertions of their growing capability? Shall the United States be expected to restrain itself unilaterally in the competitive struggle for strategic superiority in a world of conflict and hostility? The security considerations raised by these questions cannot and should not be avoided altogether. For this reason it is necessary in a specific case to assess the costs of unilateral restraint. It may be difficult, accordingly, to reach substantive conclusions on such a question as whether the United States should proceed with establishing a space observation system in the face of Soviet protest.

The logic of mutuality has not been tested in the space area or, for that matter, in any other area of developing national power. For this reason it is important to make explicit the reasons why a state acts or refrains from acting in the face of protest from another state. Such an inquiry will also serve to make it clearer whether or not Soviet claiming patterns will evolve to incorporate mutuality of restraint in their patterns of international behavior.

We are concerned here with the legality of claims asserted with respect to a subject that exists within a virtual normative vacuum. Where there are no preexisting rules and no persuasive analogies, is a sovereign state permitted to do everything? The examination of the legal status of observation satellites provides some basis for giving a partial negative answer. It is partial because it asserts a procedure for making novel claims, but it lacks substantive rules that might be used to identify an impermissible claim. The main elements in the procedure are easily summarized. First, there is an obligation to disclose to the extent possible the justification for asserting a claim to act in the face of protest by one or more sovereign states or an international institution; an unprotested national claim is permissible, if its nature is disclosed, at this stage in international law. Second, the argument opposing the claim must be fairly considered, including any detrimental effects on the future of world order. And, third, the sentiments of the community, especially as formally expressed through the United Nations, should be taken into account. Of course, this procedure is not very directive in a specific case. A national claim to act that relies upon an undisclosed military justification cannot be fully assessed. The destabilizing effect of asserting a claim that is arbitrary on the basis of what can be disclosed is apparent and should be an inhibiting feature of its assertion for a responsible actor. Of course, what is, in effect, the advocacy of the golden rule is only a plea for adherence to the logic of reciprocity that is characteristic of a primitive species of legal order. But a rudimentary system of legal restraint is better than none at all. The present choice of principal national governments seems to be primarily between the improvement of the claiming procedures of space states and the acceptance of dangerous anarchy. It is true that some opportunities for formal agreement on specific issues moderate the sharpness of this choice. The constructive task awaiting those who are building a stronger system of world legal order, then, is to examine the extent to which the development of more responsible national procedures for asserting space claims over relevant protest adds to these opportunities to moderate activity by formal international agreement.

The apparent strategic importance of observational intelligence to the security drives of the superpowers makes this subject matter an intractable area for direct international negotiation. We have seen increasingly that neither the Soviet Union nor the United States is likely to forgo strategic military advantages, either shared or unshared advantages, to promote the cause of world order. The Soviet resumption of nuclear testing in 1961, the Soviet intervention in Hungary in 1956, the initiation of nuclear testing by the United States on the high seas, and United States participation in the armed invasion of Cuba in April 1961 are illustrative of the tendency of cold-war pressures to overcome considerations favoring restraint. Viewed in this light, prospects are indeed slim for depoliticalizing controversy about the status of observation from outer space.

We can summarize the extralegal conditioning of the observational satellite program, then, by reviewing the opposed military strategies and contradictory interpretations of motive on the part of the superpowers in the early 1960's. The Soviet Union appeared to consider reconnaissance from outer space as a threat to its survival since it pinpointed targets for a possible thermonuclear surprise attack and impaired a tradition (with Czarist credentials) of territorial secrecy about military affairs. The United States, in contrast, linked its security more closely to an adequate warning system and a superiority in weaponry to stabilize deterrence and discourage surprise attack.

How can such a conflict of priorities be resolved? Is it a discretionary right of the United States to orbit reconnaissance satellites over the Soviet Union? And, is it a discretionary right of the Soviet Union to shoot them down if it can? Is there no way, other than by violence, to vindicate or refute such a claim on the frontier of technological development in outer space? How do we attain limits for national conduct in an area where there is neither authoritative practice nor converging interests to support an agreement? We require a technique of evaluation that enlarges the horizon of relevance beyond the confines of military strategy.

How shall we characterize the activity of the observational satellite program? Is it "espionage"? Does it matter? Traditional definitions of espionage emphasize its *clandestine character*, and thus it can be argued that the "openness" of satellite intelligence activity puts it outside the scope of espionage.[1] This attitude might view the satellite program as a unilateral attempt to do what the Open Skies proposal sought on a bilateral basis. This interpretation would, however, be more persuasive if the United States had come forward with a proposal for the internationalization of the activity under United Nations control.[2] Observation from outer space would then become assimilated into the special needs for the maintenance of peace in a nuclear age.[3] This form of internationalized observation deserves special consideration and requires careful differentiation from the *potential* role of this activity in the form of egoistic and secret traditional espionage.

Such an interpretative problem underlies the Soviet claims that outer space is only available for nonmilitary uses (except in the event of war) and that the observational intelligence program is a military use—since it is financed and administered by the United States armed forces and thus related to the military effort. The precedent of claiming the right to use outer space for peacetime military purposes is a very dangerous one. Reciprocity and estoppel are relevant to the structure of world order in an area of behavior that lacks clear legal norms. For example, use of outer space by A warrants an equivalent[4] use by B and diminishes the prospect for an effective objection by A. Thus, A's use establishes a permissive norm. This basic pattern of international law-making should encourage sober reflection before unilateral claims are asserted at the frontiers of military technique. For instance, in looking back on the assertion of claims to engage in nuclear testing, we wonder whether the United States would not have helped its cause *on every level* by pressing for a test ban or a limitation in advance rather than by following a unilateral pattern of claim, subsequent estoppel, and eventual anxious dismay.

[1] Robert D. Crane's "Planning for Space Legal Policy" (a paper presented to the American Rocket Society, Oct. 1961) develops a similar position in explicating what he calls the "motivation for space policy"; for instance, he says "the basic thesis of this paper is that law is gaining increasing value as an instrument to deny control of outer space to others, and that the potential advantage of a law-oriented space policy should be integrated into military contingency planning." Contrast this approach with that taken in "Aerospace Force in the Sixties," symposium in 12 *Air University Quarterly Review* 1 (Winter and Spring 1960-61).

[2] E.g., consider definition given in the "Espionage" article in the *Encyclopedia of the Social Sciences*, v, 594 (1931); "Espionage is the practice of obtaining information about an actual or potential enemy clandestinely for possible use against the enemy."

[3] Philip W. Quigg, "Open Skies and Open Space," Legal Problems of Space Exploration, prepared for Senate Committee on Astronautical and Space Sciences, Doc. No. 26, 87th Cong., 1st Sess. (1961), *Legal Problems* 463; Raymond W. Young, "The Aerial Inspection Plan and Air Space Sovereignty," *id.* at 46.

[4] Equivalent use does not mean identical use; thus a military use of outer space by A that serves its strategic needs makes a proportionate use by B legitimate, given its peculiar strategic needs. Cf. a rather unilluminating effort to compare the Sputnik and U-2 overflights by Leon Lipson, "The Gagarin and Powers Flights," 17 *Bulletin of the Atomic Scientists* 274 (Sept. 1961).

There are various ways to approach a legal analysis of space surveillance. For instance, one might emphasize the fact that satellites gather and transmit their information without entering the target state.[5] The attribute of nonentry means that here is no interference with the administration of the national society. There is no need to recruit and identify spies; these objectionable aspects of orthodox espionage activities are absent from space observation. It is true, of course, that observation from outer space by unmanned satellites does not inject an information-gathering foreign agent into the life blood of the social order. It has been suggested that there is an analogy between the space observation program and the permissible photographic observation of shore objects from aircraft overflying the high seas.[6] However, this legitimation is qualified by the general duty to use the high seas in a manner that does not infringe upon the rights of the shore state and, further, by the evident right of the observed state to view such observation as "aggressive" or "military" and to take appropriate protective measures.[7] This description of "the law" informs us only about the rhetorical techniques used by participants in a decentralized legal order faced with a conflict between claim (U.S. observation) and objection (Soviet retaliation). As will be shown, the international legal order possesses techniques for a decentralized appraisal of legality that applies to the surveillance controversy. It has been generally conceded that a state can forbid others to photograph strategic objects and events taking place within its territory. All sovereign states, including the United States and the Soviet Union, strictly regulate and punish land-based activity that seeks to obtain the information that satellites are able to collect from outer space. The Chicago Convention on International Civil Aviation, as well as many instances of uncontested national legislation and the 1960 U-2 incident in the Soviet Union all convincingly extend this power of prohibition to unauthorized information-gathering that is conducted in territorial air space. It seems generally agreed that unauthorized information-gathering and photographing fall within the developing concept of "espionage." In fact, even our newspapers have dubbed observation satellites as "space spies," "spy in the sky," and the like. State practice and general usage both argue for the treatment of unauthorized aerial observation as "espionage" that is subject to regulation by the victim state.

It is plausible to stress the extraterritorial character of space surveillance. This shifts attention to the territorial limits of national sovereignty and the nonterritorial status of outer space. From the perspective of

---

[5] This formulation implicitly assumes that the Samos-Midas satellites operate in "outer space" and that outer space is outside of national territory.

[6] See John Cobb Cooper, "Letter to the Editor," *Spaceflight*, III, No. 2, 99 (1961). [7] *Id.* at 100.

the state that is the target of observation, however, it matters little where the observer locates himself. The functional quality of espionage from outer space is, at least from the viewpoint of the information gathered, no different from espionage in air space. Nicholas deB. Katzenbach may have overstated this point when he suggested that the height of the activity is of no relevance to a proper determination of its validity.[8] Certainly, the trend is toward the replacement of mechanical criteria by contextual judgments that rely upon a functional analysis as the basis for the proper delimitation of jurisdictional competence. Rather than relying upon the physical locus of constituent acts or upon some other isolated qualifying element present in the facts (for instance, the nationality of the actor), it is thought preferable to urge a comprehensive appraisal of the reasonableness of the particular claim by a reference to all affected interests.[9] A jurisdictional decision, then, would involve balancing competing interests of the claimant and the protesting states. This jurisdictional model of decision-making is primarily applicable to the practice of national courts, but it is also useful here, where executive officials of the United States are called upon to decide about the assertion of a controversial unilateral claim. The process of rational decision is structurally similar, regardless of where the decision-maker is located in the social process.[10]

It seems reasonable for a state to characterize surveillance from outer space as "espionage." Such a characterization puts such activity easily within the legislative reach of Soviet law. A government is legally entitled to apprehend and punish the perpetrators of espionage even if the defendants act only in foreign territory. The reach of United States economic regulation serves to illustrate this kind of extraterritorial claim in a setting where the prosecuting state has a less direct and acknowledged interest;[11] that is, the assertion of extraterritorial claims to protect national security enjoys greater recognition than do claims to defend the economy. If a state can regulate espionage taking place in another sovereign state, then it certainly can impose equivalent regulation upon

---

[8] Nicholas deB. Katzenbach, "Law and Lawyers in Space," *Bulletin of the Atomic Scientists*, 14 (1958) 221-22: "Whether it [a satellite] is higher or lower is irrelevant to the objections an observer state would posit or the claims the observer would make."

[9] Falk, "Jurisdiction, Immunities, and Act of State: Suggestions for a Modified Approach," in Falk and Robert J. Nordstrom, eds., *Essays on International Jurisdiction*, Ohio State University Press (1961); Donald T. Trautman, "The Role of Conflicts Thinking in Defining the International Reach of American Regulatory Legislation," 22 *Ohio State Law Journal* 586

(Summer 1961).

[10] See especially Myres S. McDougal, "International Law, Power and Policy: A Contemporary Conception," 82 *Hague Recueil* 137 (1953 I).

[11] For instance, the controversial extraterritorial antitrust decisions: United States v. Timken Roller Bearing Co., 341 U.S. 593 (1951); United States vs. Aluminum Co. of America, 148 F. 2d 416, 443 (2d Cir. 1946); see generally *U.S. Attorney General's National Committee to Study the Antitrust Law Report*, pp. 66-91 (1955). A more complete discussion of these problems is contained in Chapter IX.

similar activity in outer space. Giving the status of "espionage" to the activity makes the locus of conduct irrelevant to the regulative claim. It seems clear, then, that the Soviet Union has the regulative competence to characterize the observation program as "espionage" and to prescribe appropriate remedies.

One of the most characteristic features of the international legal order is the wide discretion possessed by the institutions of national government to characterize activity for the purposes of applying their legal policy. The Nottebohm Case illustrates the attempt of a supranational tribunal to impose limits upon this power. It is enormously significant as a challenge to a tradition of unfettered decentralization. The extension of Nottebohm thinking is reflected in the "genuine link" requirement for merchant shipping that has found its way into the Geneva Convention on the Law of the High Seas as a rebuff to "flags of convenience."[12] Without vertical institutional development, however, it remains to be seen whether the quality of the international order loses or gains by attempts to centralize and objectify the power to characterize. The simple criterion of national discretion is lost without yet being able to provide an alternative means to specify legal status. Does not Nottebohm represent, then, a premature attempt to verticalize international legal order? Despite Nottebohm, it remains correct to affirm the continuing capacity of nations to characterize an activity that is a threat to its military security.[13] The United States claim to establish extraterritorial Air Defense Identification Zones provides a confirmatory instance of this competence.

However, in the surveillance context, and this lends novelty to the situation, the United States actually supports its claim by reference to its own military security. That is, the United States contends that the surveillance of the Soviet Union by our satellites is an essential precaution against surprise attack. The claim, in effect, makes espionage from outer space a matter of self-defense. Thus, in a formal legal sense, two irreconcilable claims are present. In a centralized system, this kind of disagreement would induce judicial or legislative action to adjust the competing claims by procedures of compromise or choice. But what is to be done to achieve reconciliation in a relatively decentralized legal order?

[12] Geneva Convention on the High Seas, UN Doc. A/CONF. 13/L. 53 and corr. 1 (1958) Article 5(1): "Each State shall fix the conditions for the grant of its nationality to ships. . . . There must exist a genuine link between the State and the ship; in particular, the State must effectively exercise its jurisdiction and control in administrative, technical and social matters over ships flying its flag."

[13] This does, however, relieve the claimant state of the duty to use a rational process of self-delimitation when it proposes to extend its competence by unilateral action; reciprocity and estoppel operate to limit the unilaterality of the process. See generally Falk, "International Jurisdiction: Horizontal and Vertical Conceptions of Legal Order," 32 *Temple Law Quarterly* 295-320 (Spring 1959).

The probable course of national conduct in a decentralized legal order is the maximum assertion of opposed national claims at each stage of the controversy. In this spirit, the United States would orbit surveillance satellites, and the Soviet Union would try to destroy them. Another Soviet response, the one that has actually come about, would involve the assertion of parallel claims by developing satellites of its own. The Soviet Union and the United States, as the dominant space powers in the world, have a converging set of interests in relation to nonspace powers. These converging interests have actually led to the emergence of tacit patterns of mutual toleration in the space relations of the United States and the Soviet Union. However, the protection of world community interests and of nonspace or lesser space states, as well as the reconciliation of Soviet-American claims, would favor the use of a procedure designed to assess and explicate the reasonableness of each particular claim to use space, given competing interests. It is especially important to justify a claim to the target or any other objecting state. This need for explanation exists especially in relation to the United States original decision to orbit satellites and applies only to a lesser extent for the derivative or counterdecision by the Soviet Union to interfere with them. The state that disturbs the *status quo ante* in a decentralized legal order normally bears the principal burden for the ensuing instability. In partial qualification of this assertion, however, it is also true that the state whose claim or counterclaim crosses the threshold of violence always possesses a significant burden of justification; there is some merit in the suggestion that the international legal order remains permissive so long as force is not introduced into the claiming and counterclaiming process.

The position of the United States, as the principal opponent of the revolutionary nations, emphasizes its special national interest in strengthening the quality of the international legal order. It is not that the United States needs to sacrifice national security to promote world order but rather that the responsible officials of government should closely examine whether the sacrifice in world order is worth the short-term putative gain in security. The U-2 incident, the sponsorship of the Cuban invasion of April 1961, the Connally Reservation, the fight to keep Formosa on the Security Council, and the practice of interventionary diplomacy throughout the world disclose an overly narrow and coercive conception of national interests that impairs the quality of contemporary world order without even any adequate selfish justification. Likewise, there is no evidence that the decision to put the surveillance program into operation takes adequate account of its possible destabilizing effects on other activity in outer space. Thus far, outer space has been used compatibly by the principal space rivals for peaceful purposes. It seems hazardous to risk transfer of the continuing uses of outer space into patterns of struggle for global supremacy. It is difficult, without access to intelligence appraisals, to suggest the probable net gain or loss derived from space observation. Nevertheless, it remains possible to urge a basis of national decision that considers and explicates the consequences for world legal order, as well as the gains for military intelligence.

Espionage possesses the peculiar quality of being tolerated while it is, at the same time, treated as illegal.[14] This odd status, comparable to prostitution in many European countries, encourages a practice whereby states engage in espionage but do not come forward to defend an agent who is caught by enforcement techniques. Consider, for example, the Soviet forbearance from comment during the long trial of Colonel Abel together with the recent Soviet willingness to exchange Powers and Prior for Abel. The silence of the state sending the agent usually leads sanctions to be imposed *only* upon the detected agent, and not directed against his country. The employing state is not drawn formally into the espionage trial, nor is there any effort to insist upon the legal responsibility of the state that commissioned the espionage.

The space observation program, unless it can be kept secret or unless its occurrence becomes sufficiently mutual and unthreatening, raises the same problems that proved troublesome in the U-2 incident. Space surveillance would seem to constitute "espionage" under *explicit* government auspices. Part of its legal quality would depend upon American motivation, especially the extent to which this information contributes to defensive rather than aggressive policies of national defense. In other words, the test for the relative illegality of espionage rests to some degree upon a judgment of the end being sought. However, in view of the potential usefulness of the satellites for aggressive purposes, this test would appear to impose a burden of demonstration upon the United States. The program certainly arose as an attempt to undermine the security regulations of an adversary sovereign state during a period of peace and, as such, would seem to infringe the national independence of the target state. A strong argument could be made to support reference of such a space claim to an impartial decision-maker. The United Nations Security Council would appear to provide an appropriate forum

---

[14] For the qualified assertion that "espionage of itself does not appear to constitute a violation of international law," see Note, "Legal Aspects of Reconnaissance in Airspace and Outer Space," 61 *Columbia Law Review* 1074-1102 (June 1961), (see esp. p. 1074n1). Authoritative doctrine seems to be available to support such a conclusion, as well as considerable persuasive policy available to oppose it. An adequate analysis of the issue of "legality" would have to distinguish between information-gathering and the various kinds of subversion. Espionage is increasingly a part of the pattern of coercion roughly identified as "indirect aggression." The attempt to make the issue of legality rest upon the fact of war or peace seems to oversimplify the issue. For a discussion of espionage in the context of political violence, see Richard R. Baxter, "So-Called 'Unprivileged Belligerency': Spies, Guerrillas, and Saboteurs," 28 *British Yearbook of International Law* 323-45 (1951).

for discussion and appraisal. Characteristically, as we have said, the government sponsoring "espionage" is not explicitly connected with its agents, and the enforcement state proceeds against the agent as an ordinary criminal defendant. But the satellite program presents a novel pattern of espionage activity that renders obsolete many of the enforcement concepts that were developed in the course of dealing with traditional espionage.

Presumably, the satellites, as governmental property devoted to public use, would be entitled to sovereign immunity by application of normal principles. However, the use of satellites to break the laws of target states would, at least after warning, allow coercive action to be taken in self-protection. Furthermore, the conferral of immunity is primarily only a judicial inhibition. In any event, it is unlikely that the disposition of the controversy will stress to any degree the sovereign ownership of the satellites.

It is also necessary to consider the legal status of any Soviet claim to engage in extraterritorial enforcement. If we grant that outer space is "outside" national territory, it is still quite tenable to reason through analogy to practice in contiguous zones on the high seas that a state may make extraterritorial claims to regulate to the extent these claims are reasonably necessary for its national security. There would be no need to claim sovereignty up to the heavens in order to show that Soviet enforcement of its espionage laws in outer space was legally well-founded. The USSR could quite reasonably assert a particularized claim to control espionage, even if the objectionable acts were all performed in outer space. In jurisdictional rhetoric, it can be said that a jurisdictional claim to assert control over a particular activity in outer space does not rest upon the prior establishment of national sovereignty over outer space. Neither the physical locus of conduct nor sovereignty is an indispensable basis for valid jurisdictional claims. On the contrary, it is important to encourage the formulation of particularized claims, defended by their reasonable link to national interest, in preference to wholesale extensions of sovereignty that will validate, among other things, the particular claim.

The experience with territorial waters is instructive. Several Latin American states have asserted claims of national sovereignty over wide belts (200 to 300 miles) of territorial waters. These claims were primarily prompted by a desire to exclude foreign trawling fleets from coastal fisheries. It would have served this coastal interest and kept a maximum area for free, unimpeded use of the oceans, had the governments of these states put their claim in the kind of specific language used to justify national control *beyond* territorial waters.[15] The particular claim, justified by reference to national interests, commends itself to the needs of world order far more than does the crude exclusivity of the notion of sovereignty. Wherever it is functionally advantageous to share use, then it is best to work out a solution along specific lines. The dichotomy between freedom (of high seas, of outer space) and sovereignty is an inept way to allocate legal competence in an area where most uses are inclusive but a few are exclusive.[16] World order advances by accommodating both sets of national interests: that is, by encouraging an awareness that national interests more often profit by forgoing exclusivity than by insisting upon it. The growth of supranationalism in Europe, the Antarctic Treaty, and the success of the specialized agencies of the United Nations bear witness to an emerging realization that sovereignty does not provide suitable criteria for the allocation of authority and of resources with respect to a subject matter that is of genuine interest to more than one nation. Such an auspicious development depends also upon the willingness of sovereign states to refrain from using a voting majority in a community forum to provide some legitimation for hostile operations against a member of the community. Here again, we are in a position to sense the potential harm that may be done by engaging in space observation over Soviet objection. In the struggle to minimize exclusive claims in outer space, it is dangerous to jeopardize the perceived safety of other nations. For this causes both the minimum basis for trust to disappear and the functional compatibility of interests to vanish from perception.

This discussion raises a general theoretical issue relevant to the future course of international legal development. The facts of progressive interdependence of the main subject matter of national life, something that is frequently acknowledged in recent literature, produces a need for sharper allocational concepts in the international legal system. At a time when states were relatively independent in the pursuit of their interests, it was generally desirable to stress the simplicity of the ideas of sovereign exclusivity and inclusive freedom. Interdependence requires more flexible categories of legal competence in international law so as to support the satisfaction of as many genuine national interests as possible. The encouragement of ad hoc justification for particular claims

15 See Morton A. Kaplan and Nicholas deB. Katzenbach, *The Political Foundations of International Law*, New York, Wiley, 1961, pp. 147-54; see also, Myres S. McDougal and William T. Burke, "Crisis in the Law of the Sea: Community Perspectives versus National Egoism," in McDougal and Associates, *Studies in World Public Order*, New Haven, Yale University Press, 1960, pp. 844-911. Cf. also Chapter XX.

16 The distinction between exclusive and inclusive is borrowed from McDougal and Burke.

is responsive to this need. Narrow patterns of justification help to assure that both the process of claim and of subsequent resistance will emphasize specific functional considerations rather than merely invoke abstract categories of legal status. A requirement of functional specificity seems to be the best way for an interdependent but decentralized legal order to solicit constructive participation by national actors in the highly sensitive and complex processes of law-creation. This participation is very important, since the slow growth of supranational legal order depends heavily on the prior development of trust and constructive participation on the national level. And trust is only likely to emerge from the perception of a nonarbitrary attempt to take account of the needs of the relevant community and of all its members.

This proposed orientation of space claims is related to the attempts of some commentators to solve the problems of outer space by relying upon an analogy to the status of the air space, the high seas, or the polar regions.[17] The historical process of claim underneath these crude doctrinal categories provides considerably more specific guidance, especially with regard to the administration of the high seas, than would be apparent from the broad doctrinal generalizations. Professor Lipson has made this point in an effective way:

> In maritime law and practice there is not merely a zone of territorial waters, a single contiguous zone, and the free high seas; there is a whole cluster of zones, overlapping and intersecting, established at different times for different purposes by different states (unilaterally, bilaterally, and multilaterally) with different degrees of formality, enforced by different methods, and accepted in different degrees by varying numbers of other states.

Lipson puts the general view in concrete perspective when he writes that:

> No unitary rule could or should be devised to cover this motley patchwork; there is no reason why one rule of law must apply to the regulation, control, prohibition, or mutual tolerance of such diverse activities as navigation, fishing, conservation of fisheries, and cable-laying; naval maneuvers and antisubmarine patrol; the use and conservation of resources on the sea bed; enforcement of customs regulation; and protection of neutrality. *It is this very diversity of legal order, stemming from the diversity of activities and conditions, that*

---

[17] Note, "National Sovereignty of Outer Space," 74 *Harvard Law Review* 1154, 1159-67 (April 1961); Leon Lipson and Nicholas deB. Katzenbach, *Report to the National Aeronautics and Space Administration on the Law of Outer Space*, Chi- cago, American Bar Foundation, 1961, pp. 77-83; Philip C. Jessup and Howard J. Taubenfeld, *Controls for Outer Space and the Antarctic Analogy*, New York, Columbia University Press, 1959, pp. 160-90.

*will provide a fruitful analogy for what must be a gradual develop-
ment of the law of outer space.*[18]

This sophisticated approach to the use of analogy, stressing concrete
legal problems rather than overarching doctrinal abstractions, provide
the true basis for rational law planning in outer space. The facts of
interdependence, highlighted by the problem of distinguishing between
military and peaceful uses, make it essential that nations assert their
claims with a clear sense of community welfare in mind. Allocations on
the high seas could allow specific unilateral assertions based on a narrow
view of national interest without often risking, until very recently, im-
pingement on community welfare. Rational allocation of authority to
act in outer space, however, already requires a broader view of national
interest that incorporates the genuine concerns of other nations, if it is
to foster the growth of a legal regime based upon maximum use and
minimum friction. It is with this emphasis that we find an appraisal of
the legal status of the Samos-Midas program to be such a good example
of the problems of building legal order into the evolving framework of
space activity.

Does it matter that the observation satellites are unmanned? Such an
inquiry is independent from, although related to, the earlier discussion
of jurisdiction. It looks upon the issue from the special perspective of
national sovereignty and its distinctive ordering role in international
affairs. Does a surface state have any sovereign control over the activity
that takes place in "outer space"? President Kennedy told the General
Assembly of the United Nations that "[t]he new horizons of outer space
must not be riven by the old bitter concepts of imperialism and sovereignty."[19] This assertion presumably implies that the development of
outer space should not proceed by states claiming exclusive control over
specified uses or regions of outer space. It looks toward the emergence
of cooperative regimes established and operated by legal institutions and
techniques. However, "sovereignty" also refers to the unilateral and
interactive capacity of states to generate legal order. But how can we
promote this capacity in view of the contradictory national policies toward territorial security espoused by the United States and the Soviet
Union? With the objective of legal order in view, let us examine the ways
in which disputes over contested uses of outer space might be handled
under circumstances of present political conflict. Here, the role of national sovereignty—not as a way to validate claims to exclusive control
but as a doctrinal basis on which to establish the legitimacy of particular
claims or to create a legal regime—is indeed complex.

[18] Both excerpts are from Leon Lipson, *Outer Space and International Law* 10 (Rand Paper P-1434, 1958). (Emphasis added.)
[19] *New York Times*, Sept. 26, 1961.

We enter a dense jurisprudential jungle at this point. The delimitation of national sovereignty, as an ordering conception, is among the most slippery subjects in international law. The relevance of sovereignty is especially problematic in a case such as this, where prior experience offers relatively little guidance. The legal order tends to resolve present controversies by referring to past practice, norms, and dispositions. When the past does not provide guidance and when the issue is important, the legal order in a centralized social system tends to generate a new solution in the form of legislation. The international legal order lacks central legislative institutions; it depends, instead, upon decentralized ordering techniques to meet the challenge of a new situation. But the outer limit of innovation in a decentralized system is reached at the point where the interests of the powerful actors within the system begin to diverge significantly. For international law, this constraint means, among other things, that an international equivalent of legislation—at least of a formal variety—can only come into being if it is able to satisfy the dominant interests of powerful national actors. It is difficult to anticipate a formal resolution of a dispute, which is not covered by the inherited legal system,[20] when the antagonistic interests of the United States and the Soviet Union arise on a subject matter bearing on relative national power and prestige.

This analysis seems suggestive for our attempt to understand the bearing of international law upon contested uses by the United States of outer space for "espionage" against the Soviet Union. Those analysts who would resolve such a controversy by negotiating an agreement on the degree of national sovereignty over outer space seem to overlook the relevance of the character of the international system to the prescription of new norms. The incapacity of the international system to provide orderly ways to test new claims is a serious cause of contemporary instability. A state is normally confronted by the choice between self-restraint and recourse to unilateral action backed by force. The danger of shifting choice back onto the national level is illustrated by Israel's initiation of the Suez campaign in 1956 and by the anticolonial revolts of oppressed peoples throughout Africa. The Samos-Midas program also illustrates the inflexibility of the system. There is no institutional-

---

20 The reference here is to the problem of adjusting the international legal system—a development of Western European culture—to a plurality of contemporary normative traditions. Josef L. Kunz, "Pluralism of Legal and Value Systems and International Law," 49 *American Journal of International Law* 370 (1955); F.S.C. Northrop, *The Taming of Nations*, New York, Macmillan, 1952; C. Wilfred Jenks, *The Common Law of Mankind*, New York, Praeger, (1958), pp. 63-172; for some strictures upon attempts to solve the problems, see Falk and Saul H. Mendlovitz, "Some Criticisms of C. Wilfred Jenks' Approach to International Law," 14 *Rutgers Law Review* 1, 4-16 (Fall 1959); and Myres S. McDougal and Harold D. Lasswell, "The Identification and Appraisal of Diverse Systems of Public Order," in *Studies in World Public Order*, Yale University Press, 1960, pp. 3-41.

ized way to determine the validity of the United States claim, and the two nuclear bloc leaders must settle the issue by give and take, since neither United States self-restraint nor Soviet forbearance is probable. Once the satellites are in orbit, a cycle of friction and retaliation is likely to begin, or at least, there is support given to the idea that a sovereign state can do whatever it can get away with, regardless of objections from other states and independent of any deference to the welfare of the international community.

Adjudication is formally possible. The issue can be formulated in a justiciable form: are observational satellites forbidden by international law? The negative considerations applicable to legislation apply *a fortiori* to adjudication. In addition, the Soviet Union has been understandably reluctant to allow legal order to emerge from supranational decisions; as a minority member of international society the Soviet Government adheres to a very conservative view of transfers of sovereign discretion from the state to an international institution. Finally, the establishment of a legal regime for outer space is a polycentric issue, and as such, probably ill-suited for adjudicative techniques and institutions.[21] The indefinite nature of the basis for any possible decision tends to undermine its acceptability to the losing litigant. States generally refuse to submit important legal controversies to adjudicative organs when they cannot, in advance, envision the general character of the legal solution. In any event, the status of the surveillance program seems to require the establishment of an entire legal regime for outer space. This breadth of determination assumes a scope of inquiry and decision that is not normally possible in the judicial process.

An alternative to a formal decision is to accept the effectiveness of the claim to orbit the satellites to operate as the determining criterion of its legitimacy. Thus, the United States is not forbidden to orbit observation satellites, but neither is the Soviet Union forbidden to shoot them down. The *Harvard Law Review* in a perceptive note phrased the issue in this way: ". . . whether the Soviet Union will choose to destroy American spy satellites when it becomes capable of doing so depends on Soviet national goals as conceived by the Soviet leaders. For the purpose of a legal analysis, however, *it is sufficient to observe that whatever the Soviet Union does in this regard will not appear to be violative of international law.*"[22] Reliance upon effective control, as a determinant of the legitimacy of "military" claims, is often an undesirable way to fill a legislative vacuum. It tends to accentuate the formative or quasi-legislative

[21] Lon L. Fuller, "Adjudication and the Rule of Law," *Proceedings of the American Society of International Law, 1960,* pp. 1-8; Clarence Morris, "Peace Through Law: The Role and Limits of Adjudication," *id.* at 15.
[22] Note, "National Sovereignty of Outer Space," 74 *Harvard Law Review* 1154, 1174 (April 1961). (Emphasis added.)

role of relative power in international affairs. Nonspace states that lack space technology are left without any protection. This stress on effective capability further promotes the bipolarization of outer space, since only the United States and the Soviet Union possess the technological base for extensive space activity in the immediate future. Effectiveness also makes coercive conflict an institutional technique for accommodation; such a resolution of conflict may often be an unavoidable last resort, but it is hardly acceptable if any alternatives can be found.

A voluntaristic theory of international obligation, as formulated by the majority decision in the *Lotus* case, provides one main line of legal analysis.[23] The basic idea of the *Lotus* decision is that the objecting state has the burden of showing that the defendant state acted in violation of an existing rule of international law. A state is entitled to do whatever it is not expressly forbidden to do by international law. In areas of international activity there is no consensus as to the nature of legal obligation —a state may do as it pleases, subject only to another state's right to act in self-defense. Specifically, the United States may launch its observational satellites and the Russians may shoot them down if they *purport* to do so in self-defense.[24] The *Lotus* approach, when coupled with the legal right of self-defense confirmed by customary international law, seems rather similar to the solution reached by the dynamics of effective control. The 1960 U-2 incident suggests that these permissive approaches can lead to serious intensifications of international tensions and may seriously impair prospects for wider patterns of accommodations.[25] In addition, we question the legality and wisdom of authorizing defensive force to test "the permissibility" of the Samos-Midas satellites. The prohibition imposed on recourse to force in Article 2(4) of the UN Charter is subject only to the qualification of Article 51 that upholds "the inherent right of individual or collective self-defense if an armed attack occurs." Certainly, the use of observational satellites in space does not constitute "an armed attack." Some Charter experts do contend that Article 51 preserves "the inherent right" of self-defense that includes the authority of a government to make a decentralized

[23] Case of the SS "Lotus," *P.C.I.J.*, Ser. A. No. 10 (1927).

[24] In other words, self-determined self-defense is a primary attribute of a decentralized legal order. International law allows a state to characterize, in the first instance, its coercive conduct as "self-defense." This is partly a consequence of the absence of a definition of aggression.

[25] Formalized expressions of public opinion—for instance, resolutions of censure in the United Nations—deserve the status of a weak sanction in the international legal system. Over-analogy, however, to the effectiveness of censure and ridicule in primitive societies is deceptive. We must not forget how much such sanctions depend upon a fairly high level of social integration among members of the community. A lack of just such integration is a major deficiency of the international order. Thus, we must be careful about the analogies between decentralized primitive societies and the decentralized international legal order.

determination of what must be done in self-defense.[26] It is contended here, however, that such a broad interpretation of the right of self-defense is less plausible and certainly less desirable than is the narrower alternative construction of the provision. Recourse to pre-Charter ideas about the exercise of the right of self-defense would also eliminate the fairly objective standard for the use of defensive force that had been written into the Charter language. The need for imposing stable limits on the use of force in a world of nuclear weapons suggests the extreme seriousness of a course of action that provides a state that deems itself a victim of injurious behavior no means of redress other than the use of defensive violence. With this thought in mind, American policy-makers should always consider carefully the advisability of presenting the Soviet Union or any other threatened state with a situation in which their vital interests can only be protected by unilateral recourse to violence.

What is the relevance of the bipolar rivalry to the quest for legitimacy in controversial areas of world affairs? The observation satellite controversy raises directly such issues of relevance, since it obviously deals with the perceived vital interests of the United States and the Soviet Union. How much should consideration of legitimacy influence dealings with the Russians or Chinese? Should the United States ignore legal restraints so as to be in a better position to meet the Communist challenge? The attitude of Admiral Ward illustrates one end of the spectrum: "Isn't it about time to free ourselves of our deception that accommodations can buy peace from the Communists, and that peace with them can be secured through law—even space law?"[27] Observance of international law, then, is a matter of unilateral self-restraint for the United States, since there is no mutuality of commitment. The Soviet Union is alleged to manipulate legal obligations to suit their political objectives and repudiate such obligations when their objectives change. The United States, in contrast, is portrayed as benignly adhering to all of its legal obligations once they have been undertaken. The result of this legalism is to sacrifice the flexibility needed for the political struggle. In Admiral Ward's view, legal restraint does not restrict Soviet freedom of action, but it does restrict options to act. The United States should henceforth eschew legal accommodations with Russians on cold-war issues as law sets a trap. Presumably, then, such reasoning would counsel the United States to move briskly forward with its surveillance program regardless of its destabilizing consequences, because the character of Soviet ideology and practice is such as to make the façade of legal accommodation self-

[26] E.g. Julius Stone, *Aggression and World Order*, Berkeley, University of California Press, 1958; Stone, *Quest for Survival*, Cambridge, Harvard University Press, 1961.

[27] "International Control of Outer Space," *Hearings Before the House Committee on Science and Astronautics*, 86th Cong., 1st Sess., p. 107 (1959), testimony of Admiral Ward.

destructive. According to this view, concerns of law and of national survival are at cross-purposes in the present world.

A more moderate attitude toward the bearing of international conflict on the role of law gives critical emphasis to strategy and experience. Legal accommodation may become desirable, but only after there has been an accumulation of enough experience to assess the bearing of a legal obligation upon the specific national interests at stake. Loftus Becker, while he was serving as Legal Adviser, wrote as follows: ". . . [A]ny sound body of law is based on a system of experience and known facts. There are a great deal of facts that we just don't know at the present time with respect to outer space and the conditions there existing."[28] To this uncertainty arising from inexperience is added deep distrust of the Soviet Union. For instance, Professor Lipson writes: "In this field [of outer space] as in other fields of international law, Soviet doctrine combines a pious attachment to the names of traditional concepts with a flexible, "instrumental" manipulation of the *content* of the concepts to serve the current needs of Soviet policy."[29] Distrust leads to an insistence on very clear lines of commitment: hence, we must be sure what we are giving up before we will agree to a bargain with the Soviet Union. In outer space, we lack sufficient experience at present to be sure whether or not a commitment we make today might not prove disadvantageous tomorrow. In this analysis, also, primacy is given to political factors, and survival is linked to freedom of choice rather than to stable limits upon choice. The processes of international law are only useful if confined to a marginal role of stabilizing areas of convergence after the facts are assessed. International law in a divided world cannot be entrusted with the more ambitious role of preparing an ordering scheme for emerging facts. In the interim, the *Lotus* style of interpreting sovereignty serves to vindicate all nonprohibited conduct. Existing law does not pertain to outer space. A state can thus do whatever it wants. Therefore, if the surveillance program is helpful to a country, then it is entitled to adopt it. Much can be said for an approach to international order that is simple and permissive; however, this kind of permissiveness fails to take account of the destabilizing effect of *novel unilateral military* claims in a decentralized social order in which the chief actors possess thermonuclear bombs. It also overlooks the horizontal and provisional ordering possibilities that arise from unilateral or cooperative patterns of self-restraint. These possibilities will not always result in a more stable system order, but restraint may at least be expected to postpone friction and might possibly even induce reciprocal self-restraint by the Soviet Union and other adversary states. The United

28 Becker, *id.* at 75.
29 See Lipson, *op.cit. supra*, note 18 at 12.

States would be faced with the choice between surrender and preventive war if it did not posit a minimum Soviet commitment to world order and to the avoidance of nuclear devastation. The United States Government often acts, however, as if few choices between these extreme positions exist. It is rational to take some risks to give order to international relations even though the conceivable beneficiary of taking such risks might be rival states.

At the other end of the juridico-political spectrum, there are a variety of scholars and concerned public officials who feel that it is essential to establish a vertical legal regime prior to the further assertion of national claims. For instance, Senator Keating stated it in these terms: "There will be no time for legal craftsmanship and judicial speculation after rival claims are made to the moon or to space itself. . . . The rule of law in the age of space is not a matter of philosophy, but a matter of survival."[30] John Cobb Cooper for years brought the weight of his learning and authority to bear in this direction. In 1960, while speaking at Leiden, Mr. Cooper noted that "international peace and the future welfare of mankind demand that the Rule of Law shall be applicable with certainty to outer space."[31] A clear agreement as to the rights and duties of nations in outer space is required:

> If the Rule of Law is to be applied in outer space, then I submit, as I have on other occasions, that the area of outer space must be determined, that its legal status be agreed upon, that the rights of States in the areas be universally acknowledged and that the legal status of flight instrumentalities to be used in outer space be also fixed.[32]

This position stressed the ordering role of law without due regard to the existing character of the international system. Without the availability of techniques for social change, states are unwilling to accept a fixed legal regime until they at least see clearly what is involved. Space and flight developments have proceeded with such rapidity that those who propose a basis for legal agreement have constantly been forced to revise their recommendations. Mr. Cooper's writings through the years provide a prominent illustration of the need to alter law in order to present an adaptive response to new technological developments.[33] Agreement on legal standards at any stage turns out to be unsatisfactory at the next technological stage; renegotiation is always difficult as a new develop-

[30] See, *op.cit supra*, note 27 at 2-3, testimony of Senator Keating.
[31] John Cobb Cooper, "Questions of Space Law," *Spaceflight*, 3 (1961), 95.
[32] *Ibid.*
[33] John Cobb Cooper, "Flight-Space, and the Satellites," 7 *International and Comparative Law Quarterly* 82-91 (Jan. 1958); Cooper, "High Altitude Flight and National Sovereignty," 4 *International Law Quarterly* 411-18 (July 1951); Cooper, "Legal Problems of Upper Space," *Proceedings American Society International Law*, 1956, pp. 85-93; Cooper, "Sovereignty in Space," *Flying*, 64 (Jan. 1959), 30.

ment has an unequal bearing upon the perceived national interests of participating states. This feature of relative nonnegotiability would apply most vividly when extralegal developments have an unequal effect on the military position of prominent and antagonist international rivals. Verticalized norms—that is, norms with the formal status of supranational obligations—could not be expected to withstand such a strain. It is probably premature, as Becker and Lipson suggest, to create vertical norms now to govern outer space. But the implementation of the potential for horizontal legal order is never premature. The alternative courses of national action are too often perceived as either comprehensive international agreement or chaos, either vertical law or lawlessness, either legal restraint or sovereign unrestraint.

The main argument of this chapter is that the effects of the surveillance program upon the stability of the use of outer space, as well as upon the use of defensive force, challenge the rationality of the unilateral assertion of claims by the United States to use outer space for the military observation of the Soviet Union. Horizontal legal order focuses inquiry upon the reasonableness of a national claim, given all relevant considerations including whatever extent the interests of other states are infringed upon. This process of inquiry, as outlined here, should have exerted some influence on the decision whether or not to orbit controversial satellites above Soviet territory. Final appraisal of this legal issue rests heavily upon access to data that remains unavailable to the public; there are several related factors—the importance of the information obtainable, the degree of Soviet objection, the probable success of Soviet attempts to shoot down or otherwise interfere with the satellites, Soviet interests in orbiting observation satellites of their own, the prospects for cooperative developments of space, and the eventual contribution to intelligence work. It is discouraging that newspaper reports and legislative hearings exhibited almost no concern for these wider implications of the space observation program. The strategic advantage to the United States of closing the intelligence gap had been accepted as a self-sufficient justification for asserting the unilateral claim. Such a foreshortening of inquiry, which seems to underrate the effect that the Samos-Midas program might have had upon international order, is unforgivable in a world where potential enemies in thermonuclear war boast of "over-kill" capacity. It may be part of the complexity of the times to acknowledge the importance of Henry Kissinger's remarks that ". . . the very intensity of our desire for peace may increase our peril."[34] But such a perception should not cause a renunciation of the rationality from which such intensity derives. We must continue to bring these energies to bear if we are ever to diminish our peril.

[34] Henry A. Kissinger, "Nuclear Testing and the Problem of Peace," 37 *Foreign* *Affairs* (Oct. 1958), 1-18.

IX. An Explanation of the Extraterritorial Extension of American Antitrust Regulation

> We do not see how the Steel Corporation can be such a beneficial instrumentality in the trade of the world, and its beneficence preserved, and yet be such an evil instrumentality in the trade of the United States that it must be destroyed.
>
> J. McKenna, *U.S. v. United States Steel Corporation et al.*, 251 US 417, 453 (1911).

IN THE late 1950's there was a great deal of attention given to the extension of American antitrust regulation to foreign business operations. The wisdom and propriety of this regulation was intensely debated. Much of the controversy emphasized jurisdictional issues, the outer limits of competence to attach American regulatory standards, and the extent to which, if at all, this competence should be modified or circumscribed because principal foreign states sought to impose quite different competitive conditions on market operations within their economies. The subject lends itself to academic commentary as the issues of substance can only be resolved by reference to fundamental conceptions about the character of the international legal order.

In essence, the debate about the legality of extraterritorial antitrust regulation raises the wider problem of national (or unilateral) regulation of interdependent (or multinational) subject matter. The Westphalia System that continues to give structure to international society is premised upon the exclusive control by a sovereign state of activity within territorial space and deference to the assertion of coordinate control by other governments within foreign territorial space. But an arrangement to restrain commerce may have multiple effects without any clear territorial base. In such circumstances, which state may prescribe its legal policies? Or more precisely, what sorts of considerations are or should be taken into account in extending extraterritorial regulation in an area wherein underlying national policies are at variance? If underlying national policies were more or less shared, then the assertion of regulatory authority would be more closely associated with a venture in cooperative law enforcement, as is the case most certainly with respect to the treatment of piracy and, increasingly, with regard to the enforcement of nonpolitical crime. The diversity of policy creates a tension between the logic of national sovereignty and the logic of reciprocity; both logics are contained in the Westphalian conception of the international legal order. The conflict of logics calls for a strategy of reconciliation. The *Restatement (Second) of Foreign Relations Law of the United States* sets out such a strategy of reconciliation, in evident response to the extraterritorial antitrust controversy, in §40. It is worth quoting in full to give a sense of the drift of American legal thinking on the enforcement of regulatory authority:

Limitations on Exercise of Enforcement Jurisdiction

Where two states have jurisdiction to prescribe and enforce rules of law and the rules they may prescribe require inconsistent conduct upon the part of a person, each state is required by international law to consider, in good faith, moderating the exercise of its enforcement jurisdiction, in the light of such factors as

(a) vital national interests of each of the states,

(b) the extent and the nature of the hardship that inconsistent enforcement actions would impose upon the person,

(c) the extent to which the required conduct is to take place in the territory of the other state,

(d) the nationality of the person, and

(e) the extent to which enforcement by action of either state can reasonably be expected to achieve compliance with the rule prescribed by that state.[1]

In approaching the subject matter of extraterritorial antitrust regulation it is worth emphasizing that the diversity of policy between economies emphasizing free competition and those emphasizing fair trade (or controlled competition) takes place within the non-Communist sector of international society. The controversial instances of regulation have mostly concerned the participation of United States capital or enterprises in conjunction with European partners. In this sense, the conflict represents a policy disagreement between countries normally identified as sharing common values, beliefs, and interests. It contrasts in this respect with a parallel set of controversies that have arisen in the same period since World War II about the legal standards governing the protection of foreign investment against expropriation.[2] In the ex-

[1] §39 sets forth the more permissive approach governing the *prescription* of policy standards. Courts are urged to mitigate prescriptive interferences with the internal policies of foreign societies in the context of application or enforcement. It is also worth considering carefully the Comments attached to §§39 and 40 to obtain a better image of authoritative legal thinking in the United States at this time. The text of §39 is as follows:

Inconsistent Requirements Do Not Affect Jurisdiction

(1) A state having jurisdiction to prescribe or to enforce a rule of law is not precluded from exercising its juris-

diction solely because such exercise requires a person to engage in conduct subjecting him to liability under the law of another state having jurisdiction with respect to that conduct.

(2) Factors to be considered in minimizing conflicts arising from the application of the rule stated in Subsection (1) with respect to enforcement jurisdiction are stated in §40.

Restatement (Second) Foreign Relations Law of the United States, St. Paul, Minn., American Law Institute, 1965, pp. 111-23.

[2] For a provocative and intelligent, if conservative, review of the relevant legal problems in the investment area since

propriation setting, the position of the United States Government has been seeking to work out compromises and accommodations with recently independent states and with societies inclining toward socialist economies: The two categories of conflict could be usefully included in any overall inventory of conflict behavior in the current international system.

It should be noted that, of course, the investor perspective is different for these two categories of economic diversity: antitrust regulation and expropriation disputes. The investor seeks to minimize antitrust regulation of foreign business operations so as to maximize the opportunities for profit of a particular firm; exemption from regulation obviously contributes to the freedom of choice open to a business enterprise, even though the exercise of that freedom may be detrimental to the economy as a whole or to the consumer of a particular product. Conduct violative of antitrust standards may take the form of cartel affiliations that may have intended or unintended political consequences of internationalizing economic relationships in defiance of political alignments. Thus the antitrust regulation contributes to political totalism in capitalist societies by assuring a minimum of national control over the patterning of international business relationships involving American participation.[3] In this sense, it is instructive to appreciate that the big surge of extraterritorial antitrust regulation occurred in the period after World War II and sought to rectify the prewar world economy in which the main political adversaries of the United States had been highly advanced capitalist countries with close economic relationships with major American companies. In the 1950's as the Soviet-American rivalry deepened and as the main level of struggle in international society was perceived in ideological terms there occurred a gradual decline of concern with anti-cartel regulatory efforts.[4] The political side effects of noncompetitive behavior in the global economy did not seem serious any longer as the entire capitalist portion of the world economy was more or less united in its opposition to socialist principles on one side and to the rising demands of the ex-colonial world for a restructuring of the international economy on the other side.

These broad considerations help to explain both the rise and fall of extraterritorial antitrust regulation in the period since World War II.

World War II see Richard B. Lillich, *The Protection of Foreign Investment*, Syracuse, Syracuse University Press, 1965.

[3] For a conservative analysis based on the desirability of a rigid separation of the political and economic sectors of a national economy see Wilhelm Röpke's defense of the international implications of nineteenth-century economic liberalism;

Wilhelm Röpke, *International Order and Economic Integration*, Dordrecht, The Netherlands, D. Reidel, 1959.

[4] For discussion of regulatory impulses throughout the world in this period see Corwin D. Edwards, *Controls of Cartels and Monopolies*, Dobbs Ferry, N. Y. Oceana, 1967, pp. 1-13.

It seems evident, albeit tacit, that the Justice Department has held back from extraterritorial antitrust regulation in recent years in response to (1) the organized pressure of the investor community, and (2) the altered character of the structure of political conflict in international society (the "enemies" of World War II are now "allies"). These same pressures have led to the opposite outcome in the expropriation area. The legislative repudiation of the Supreme Court decision in *Banco Nacional de Cuba v. Sabbatino* and the later judicial acceptance of this reversal, also represent a triumph of investor pressure and ideological anti-Communism.[5] In both settings, world order considerations have been subordinated to the superimposition of nationalistic pressures.

This chapter attempts to review the principal instances of extraterritorial antitrust regulation that have been brought before domestic courts in the United States. The focus is not upon the broader world order implications of these adjudications, but rather upon the manner with which domestic courts delimited the legal competence of regulatory authority in contexts wherein an interference with the territorial jurisdiction of a foreign state was an alleged or actual element.

I. Extraterritorial Antitrust Jurisdiction

A. THE SCOPE OF ANTITRUST JURISDICTION

American antitrust legislation has been applied to prevent even very limited restraints upon the foreign commerce of the United States.[6] "Unreasonable" restraints upon American imports or exports have been found illegal whether the acts designed to restrain trade occurred within or without the United States. The alien status of participants in the arrangement has not been effective to mitigate illegality. An act, wherever it takes place, that substantially lessens competition within the United States has been specifically declared illegal.[7] Practices normally legitimate under our foreign or domestic law, such as patent exchanges or the ownership of foreign subsidiaries, become tainted and are enjoined if their operation implements an illegal conspiracy or combination to restrain United States foreign trade. Antitrust law has not, however, been interpreted to prevent restraints that have exclusively foreign consequences.[8] In addition, American exporters are granted a limited ex-

---

[5] See further on this pattern, Chap. XIII.

[6] Some consideration of the scope of foreign trade regulation is found in Annex A. Also see Annex C, Statutory Framework.

[7] Section 7, Clayton Act, 38 Stat. 730 (1914), 15 USC §19 (1946).

[8] Foreign commerce of the United States has been construed to exclude the activities of Americans in foreign markets that

do not have domestic consequences. See Sigmund Timberg, "Antitrust and Foreign Trade," 48 *Northwestern University Law Review* 411-426 (Sept.-Oct. 1953); S. Chesterfield Oppenheim, "Foreign Commerce Under the Sherman Act," 42 *Trade Mark Reporter* 3-22 (Jan. 1952). In theory, it would be difficult to imagine a successful foreign restraint that did not have a domestic impact, at least to the extent of exemption from the Sherman Act by the operation of the Webb-Pomerene Act.[9]

B. THE RELEVANCE OF INTERNATIONAL LAW

United States prestige and policy normally reinforces patterns of adherence to the prescriptions of international law.[10] There is no clear international law pronouncement upon the permissible scope of economic regulation.[11] The modern development of international law has stressed the desirability of limiting the jurisdiction of the forum to the territory of the forum;[12] consensus, analogous holdings and dicta, and

artificially effecting potential American competition, that is, if the restraint involved only a noncompetitive price then competition would be encouraged, while if the restraint included, as it likely would, market dominance with power to exclude competitors, then competition would be discouraged. See note 14, infra, for documentation of this limitation upon jurisdiction.

[9] Cf. Annex C for treatment of this exemption.

[10] The present assertions of claims against iron-curtain violations of international law presuppose an American adherence, as well as the obligation to ad here. Membership in the United Nations carries with it an expressed willingness to obey international law. Domestic opinion still seems to favor according municipal law supremacy if it conflicts with international law. "In the absence of a clear legislative intent to the contrary, the courts of this country will apply and enforce the principle of public international law," G. W. Haight, "International Law and Extraterritorial Application of the Antitrust Laws," 63 *Yale Law Journal* 639-54 (March 1954). "An act of Congress ought never to be construed to violate the law of nations if any other possible construction remains," The Schooner "Charming Betsy," 2 *Cranch* 64, 118 (U.S. 1804).

[11] The legality under international law of the extension of a state's domestic antitrust legislation to regulate actions having an ultimate effect within but taking place outside the borders of that state is at least partially supported by the antirestrictive trade provisions applied by the Common Market under Articles 85 and 86 of the E.E.C. Treaty. On the other hand, unilateral formulation of such internationally applied economic regulations conflicts with the aims of such cooperative regional arrangements as the Common Market by considering only the economic structure and needs of the formulating

state while ignoring those characteristics of states in which activities affecting the formulating state takes place. In this respect Dr. A. J. Riedwig has contended that:

The United States has the absolute right as a sovereign state to regulate competition within the American economy as it sees fit. But by the same token other states have the same right which is inherent in their sovereignty. Application of the American antitrust concept to the economy of other nations would therefore be entirely inadmissible. As has been demonstrated, the American anti-trust laws prescribe free competition in those sectors of economic activity where such free competition is favourable to the American economy; for those sections where such free competition would not be favourable to the internal American economy, free competition is not prescribed. Application of these rules to the economy of a foreign nation would be an absolute denial of the sovereign right of that other nation to regulate its own economy as it see fit.

The remarks of the rapporteur of the Committee on Extra-Territorial Application of Restrictive Trade Legislation are found in a paper of the same title in the *Report of the Fifty-First Conference of the International Law Association*, Tokyo, 1964, pp. 357-415, at 396; for general consideration of extraterritorial application of antitrust laws in a European setting see Eric Stein and Peter Hay, eds., *Law and Institutions in the Atlantic Area*, New York, Bobbs-Merrill, 1967, pp. 517-713.

[12] Cf. J. P. Niboyet, "Territoriality and Universal Recognition of Rules of Conflicts of Laws," 65 *Harvard Law Review* 582-96 (Feb. 1952); Hessel Yntema, "The Historic Bases of Private International Law," 2 *American Journal of Comparative Law* 297-317 (Summer 1953). And see J. Story, in "The Apollon," 9 *Wheat*

statements by American treatise writers confine jurisdiction over non-nationals, at least, to events that occur within the territory of the court.[13, 14] Exceptions have been made for enumerated crimes against financial credit and national security.[15] Even the regulation of nationals for extraterritorial acts, with a primary significance in the foreign country of occurrence, is often deprecated in the literature.[16] Decisions that result in a substantial interference with the supremacy of a foreign sovereign over his territory are clearly opposed to the spirit of contemporary international law.[17] Such a decision is likely to inspire a variety of protests and reprisals.[18]

The trend of American decisions had been increasingly extraterritorial, at least until 1960 when the regulatory impulse tapered off. Until the 1960's, Sherman Act enforcement evolved steadily from the territorial

---

362, 370 (1824): "The laws of no nation can justly extend beyond its own territories except as far as regards its own citizens. They can have no force to control the sovereign or rights of any other nation, within its own jurisdiction."

[13] J. Story in "The Apollon," 9 *Wheat* 362, 370 (U.S. 1824). "A country is no more entitled to assume jurisdiction over foreignors than it would be to annex a bit of territory which happened to be very convenient for it." Lord Finlay dissenting in "The Case of the S.S. 'Lotus,'" *Permanent Court of International Justice* Ser. A, 10/9 p. 56 (1927).

[14] Herbert W. Briggs, *The Law of Nations*, New York, Appleton, 2nd edn., 1952, pp. 309-313; Charles Cheney Hyde, *International Law Chiefly as Interpreted and Applied by the United States*, Boston, Little Brown, 2nd rev. edn. 1947, I, 726-30, 904-09. Cf. the judgment in the *Lotus* case, P.C.I.J. (1927), Series A, No. 10, p. 19:

It does not, however, follow that international law prohibits a State from exercising jurisdiction in its own territory, in respect of any case which relates to acts which have taken place abroad, and in which it cannot rely on some permissive rule of international law. Such a view would only be tenable if international law contained a general prohibition to States to extend the application of their laws and the jurisdiction of their courts to persons, property and acts outside their territory, and if, as an exception to this general prohibition, it allowed States to do so in certain specific cases. But this is certainly not the case under international law as it stands at present. Far from laying down a general prohibition to the effect that States may not extend the application of

their laws and the jurisdiction of their courts to persons, property and acts outside their territory, it leaves them in this respect a wide measure of discretion which is only limited in certain cases by prohibitive rules; as regards other cases, every State remains free to adopt the principles which it regards as best and most suitable.

[15] See John Bassett Moore, *Report on Extraterritorial Crime and the Cutting Case*, Washington, Government Printing Office, 1898; Research in International Law under the Auspices of Harvard Law School, "Jurisdiction with Respect to Crime," 29 *American Journal of International Law*, Supp. (1935) (hereinafter cited as Harvard Research.) In protecting their mutual welfare and security in noneconomic areas states have used the "universality principle" to claim an international jurisdiction over crimes like piracy, slave trade, and traffic in drugs.

[16] See, e.g., Niboyet, note 6, *supra*.

[17] Modern notions of sovereignty are based upon the exclusive, or at least paramount, right of the territorial government to regulate events that occur within its borders.

[18] Judge Ryan's decree in the *ICI* case requiring the dismemberment of a Canadian Corporation having Canadian stockholders aroused vigorous protests in Canadian newspapers. Cf. Haight, 641, n8. Further disharmony caused by the *ICI* decision was manifested in British Nylon Spinners Ltd. v. Imperial Chemical Industries Ltd., [(1953)] 1 Chancery 19, where an American decision compelled a British company to violate its contractual obligations in England. The British court required *ICI* to disregard the American decree insofar as it interfered with performance legitimate under British law.

doctrine espoused in the *Banana* case.[19] American courts have sought to justify extraterritorial control by the association of jurisdiction with an act, however minor, that took place within the United States; such a spatial link has been used to justify regulation of offenses that were initiated and largely performed in foreign countries.[20] The *Alcoa* holding even ignored the absence of a United States act; an *intended impact upon domestic commerce* was the announced basis for the regulation of the activities of a foreign corporation.[21]

Few nations fully endorse the Sherman Act philosophy.[22] Somewhat comparable legislation exists in many nations, but its net effect is to subject industry to far less antitrust supervision.[23] The body of foreign judicial and legislative doctrine necessitates a finding that the restraint has actually harmed public welfare as a prerequisite to conviction.[24] While the relationship between the rise of Hitler and German cartels gave a temporary impetus to the general desire of the world community

[19] "[T]he general and almost universal rule is that the character of an act as lawful or unlawful must be determined wholly by the law of the country where the act is done." American Banana Co. v. United Fruit Co., 213 US 347, 356 (1909).

[20] U.S. v. Pacific and Arctic Ry., 228 US 87 (1912); U.S. v. Sisal Sales Corp., 274 US 268 (1927); Thomsen v. Cayser 243 US 66 (1916). These three cases most prominently illustrate the disequilibrium between the insignificance of an illegal act of the defendant within the United States and the significance accorded such an act by the court Such insignificance is emphasized by the need to assume the illegal conspiracy in order to taint the territorial act, that standing alone would have been perfectly legal. In the sardine, quinine, and potash consent decrees there was the following provision: "Nothing herein contained shall be construed to restrain or prohibit any defendant from doing any act or entering into any agreement which is entirely completed outside the United States and which does not require any act or thing to be done within the United States." U.S. v. Amsterdamsche Chininefabriek, CCH, Fed. Trade Reg. Serv. 4136 (SDNY 1928); U.S. v. Deutsches Kalisyndikat Gesellschaft, *id.* at 4188 (SDNY 1929); U.S. v. ABC Canning Co., *id.* at 4213 (SDNY 1931). See also William J. Donovan and Breck P. McAllister, "Consent Decrees in the Enforcement of Federal Anti-Trust Laws," 46 *Harvard Law Review* 885, 924-25 (April 1933).

[21] U.S. v. Aluminum Co. of America 148 F. 2d 416, 445 (2d Cir. 1945). Riedwig contends that:

Not even the U.S. cases have gone as far as is sometimes supposed. The *Alcoa* case, of course, represents the high-water mark, but Judge Hand's statement therein on the application of U.S. law to conduct wholly abroad was *dictum*. Subsequent U.S. anti-trust decisions do not go as far as the *dictum*. In no case have the U.S. anti-trust laws been applied to conduct abroad by aliens, unaffiliated with U.S. companies, where actual conduct of the aliens within the U.S. was not found. (Footnote omitted.)

In a footnote he adds: "'Limited,' the Canadian affiliate of Alcoa, engaged in the purchase and sale of aluminum products in the U.S. and maintained offices in New York City where its representatives conducted its affairs. And Judge Hand concluded: '. . . besides, only human agents can import and sell ingot.'" 148 F 2d at 444. Riedwig, *op.cit. supra*, note 11, at 378, n5a.

[22] For substantiation see Heinrich Kronstein and Gertrude Leighton, "Cartel Control: A Record of Failure," 55 *Yale Law Journal* 297-335 (Feb. 1946).

[23] See, for instance, the comparison of the application of the German and American antitrust laws outside their domestic jurisdiction in Kurt E. Markert, "The Application of German Antitrust Law to International Restraints of Trade," 7 *Virginia Journal of International Law* 47-67 (April 1967).

[24] *Ibid.*

to regulate effectively noncompetitive abuses,[25] such an impetus, even if translated into world enforcement patterns, would occur at a level far below Sherman Act standards. International joint control is expected to compel disclosure of restrictive business practices.[26] Any American effort to secure an international Sherman Act would be bound to end in failure.

C. PRELIMINARY COMPLICATIONS PECULIAR TO THE APPLICATION OF ANTITRUST LAWS TO FOREIGN COMMERCE

The unilateral regulation of multilateral activity is difficult. Regulated abuses in foreign trade are almost all multilateral.[27] Extensive regulation hostile to the values of affected nations will naturally arouse opposition. Sherman Act decisions concerned with the foreign activities of foreign corporations have created opposition.[28] The United States has an undoubted right to insist upon Sherman Act standards for domestic operations. Other countries have an equivalent right to establish different operating standards in their domestic markets. The forces and functional units that shape an economy tend more and more to operate upon a transnational level, and as such are practically immune from unilateral curtailment.[29] Therefore, without extraterritorial regulation it is impossible to eliminate the influence of nonconforming operations upon the domestic market.[30] Effective antitrust regulation, especially, requires the extirpation of the roots of restraint, or else efforts at regulation are futile, and the restraint reappears in a new or altered form.[31] Because of the particularly vigilant antitrust regulation within the United States these roots are purposefully located beyond American borders.[32] Thus antitrust authorities are up against a dilemma—*either* incur wrath and reprisal for unpopular extraterritorial jurisdiction *or*

25 Wendell Berge, *Cartels: Challenge to a Free World*, Washington, D.C., Public Affairs Press, 1944; Corwin D. Edwards, ed., *A Cartel Policy for the United States*, New York, Columbia University Press, 1945; *Restrictive Business Practices*, (Economic and Social Council, United Nations) (E/2379, E/2379/Adds. 1, 2, E/AC/37), 2, (E/AC. 37/2/Adds. 1, 2 April 29, March 13, 1953).
26 Same sources as note 25.
27 Foreign trade by definition embraces trade involving two or more countries. Agreements in restraint normally take a form that includes parties from more than one country.
28 See note 12, *supra*.
29 Cartels can endure action by a single

nation. Either they temporarily withdraw from that market or they enter in some altered form that retains the illegal power. Unilateral action can be effective if taken by a strong nation according to the analysis of Wendell Berge.
30 The only manner of securing a normal flow of aluminum imports into the United States was to exert control over the activities of Aluminum Limited.
31 Cf. Berge's discussion of the nature of cartels.
32 Berge, Edwards, *Alcoa* case. Note also the practice of the diamond cartel— it does not do business in the United States, but sells at monopoly prices to American importers who buy abroad beyond the jurisdiction of the Sherman Act.

refrain and tolerate the presence of nonconforming behavior. Naturally, a solution lies along a cautiously charted middle course.[33]

The Sherman Act seeks to promote a competitive domestic economy, but its rigorous application sometimes endangers other economic and noneconomic goals of the society.[34] There are times when effective antitrust enforcement might weaken national security. The Justice Department has explicitly advocated the toleration of noncompetitive activity in temporary deference to an overriding security consideration.[35] Some antitrust decisions have been criticized for unduly burdening the operations of American corporations in foreign markets.[36] The Sherman Act may operate to discriminate against an American participant if foreign participants are not subjected to similar regulation. Encouragement of foreign investment has always been a policy of the United States,[37] and courts have responded to this policy in their application of the Sherman Act. Particularly in the selection of a remedy, the judicial consciousness of foreign investment consequences has been evident. For example, courts have been reluctant to decree divestiture of foreign holdings from American ownership.[38] Certain other noncompetitive elements are built into the economy by statute, and generally aim to promote American industry at the expense of foreign competition.[39] These various factors to some extent obstruct the attainment of the competitive conditions envisioned by an "Adam Smith" Sherman Act, and, on occasion, may, contrariwise, make antitrust enforcement harm only the society it is designed to protect.[40]

Noncompetitive practices are sometimes incapable of regulation. Unreasonable restraints upon the American economy that are committed by foreign corporations not doing business in the United States are normally beyond our jurisdiction.[41] The *Alcoa* case seems to hold that a foreign corporation, although not doing an appreciable amount of business in the United States, is subject to Sherman Act prosecution. A conspiracy to be consummated in the United States, although conceived abroad, can be fully apprehended within the conventional definition of

[33] The Swiss Watch Cartel investigation illustrated the deficiency of Justice Department diplomacy in the enforcement of antitrust regulations, and appeared to involve a considerable interference with the authorized conduct of business in Switzerland.

[34] Cf. Annex C, pp. 318-25.

[35] During World War II there were *no* Sherman Act actions brought.

[36] Cf. dissents of Justices Jackson and Frankfurter in the *Timken* case. Timken Roller Bearing Co. v. US 341 US 593

(1951). See also Comment, 4 *Stanford Law Review* 559-574 (1952).

[37] Cf. sources, note 29.

[38] See pp. 287-98. Prominent examples are the ICI and Timken decrees.

[39] Webb-Pomerene Act, see Annex C; also tariff, duty, sudsidy, preference framework.

[40] See Annex C. There is also a need to distinguish short-run harm by enforcement from the long-run harm asserted to arise from nonenforcement.

[41] The most explicit recognition of the

the scope of territorial jurisdiction.[42] This provides courts with a doctrine able to cope with foreign elements of an action without resort to bald extraterritoriality.[43] Usually it is difficult to satisfy the formal requirements of jurisdiction when the defendant is located outside the territory of the forum.[44] Numerous devices have been developed to circumvent antitrust laws by operating domestically through independent subsidiaries or exclusive agencies. Antitrust prosecutors have countered with agency and imputation arguments. Often foreign evidence necessary for a successful prosecution cannot be obtained. For example, the Ontario Legislature passed a bill forbidding Ontario corporations from removing records from the province in order to stifle an incipient action against the Canadian newsprint monopoly.[45] Even a guilty verdict is futile if no foreign assets come within the reach of the court. Regulation of alien corporations, not doing a large amount of business in the United States and not conspiring with American corporations, tends to be sporadic, arbitrary, expensive, and inconclusive.[46]

The doctrine of sovereign immunity also interferes with the elimination of nonconforming behavior from the domestic market. An act that qualifies as a sovereign act is granted immunity from American jurisdiction. One justification for the *Banana* holding arose from the determination that the complaint dealt with abuses committed by a sovereign. American courts have come to disregard the formal appearance of sov-

---

limitation of jurisdiction to activity that affects American commerce directly was given in the consent decrees dealing with the quinine, potash, and sardine cartels. These decrees stated that there was no prohibition of foreign activities of the defendant cartels contemplated. See note 14.

[42] Limited did only a negligible amount of business within the United States. The court found that Limited was independent of Alcoa, despite the family management and common ownership. This prevents explaining the decision as an instance of the "conspiracy exception." A foreign corporation that conspires with an American corporation commits a crime against American law. Robert T. Molloy, "Application of the Anti-Trust Laws to Extra-Territorial Conspiracies," 49 *Yale Law Journal* 1312-19 (May 1940). See Harvard Research for a general enunciation of this rule that all conspirators and acts of implementation can be legitimately assimilated into the territory where the conspiracy is consummated.

[43] If Judge Hand had found Limited conspiring with Alcoa then the Alcoa decision could have avoided the problems of extraterritoriality. And the presence of

such a conspiracy is established by the provision in the Swiss agreement forbidding exports by members to the United States. Why, without a tacit reciprocal promise by Alcoa not to export, would foreign producers be willing to adopt voluntarily a self-restraint that exempted the lucrative American market? The later divesture of Limited from the ownership of Alcoa's controlling stockholders indicates Alcoa's cartel participation was achieved through the representation of Limited. 91 F. Supp. 333 (SDNY 1950).

[44] See US v. Scophony, 333 US 795 (1948); US v. Alcoa, 20 F Supp 13 (1937); US v. ICI, 100 F. Supp. 504 (SDNY 1951). These cases discuss interesting facets of the techniques and limits of formal jurisdiction over the person and subject matter of an antitrust action.

[45] *Hearings before House Committee on the Judiciary, Subcommittee on Study of Monopoly Power,* 81st Cong., 1st Sess. 82d Cong., 1st Sess. Pt 6A, Exhibit N-44 (1949-51), ("Celler Committee").

[46] See *Alcoa* case, p. 443; discussion of extraterritorial crime in Moore's Report on the *Cutting* case.

ereignty—the veil is often pierced to reclassify an act that claims immunity in a category subject to jurisdiction. Undue restraints upon commerce committed by state purchasing and selling agencies have been held normally entitled to this immunity. In this area, courts are particularly quick to rely on a technicality that will strip away sovereign prerogatives and make the commercial unit subject to American regulation.[47] It is conceivable that a pattern of zealous antitrust regulation might drive foreign industry into the shelter of sovereign immunity by inducing the transfer of ownership to the government. This prospect no longer seems plausible. Such a centralization of wealth, with its accompanying potential for monopoly and for participation in cartels, would be most inconsistent with economic policies prevailing in the United States and would certainly be an ironic consequence of antitrust regulation. The tapering of regulatory efforts in recent years makes this alleged danger of regulation no longer very relevant to an analysis of the subject.[48]

II. The Unlawful Purpose Test Applied to Antitrust Decisions

A. THE NEED FOR A COMPREHENSIVE APPROACH

The use of the same doctrines throughout the foreign trade field might aid in the formulation of needed general principles. Existing antitrust

[47] A Sherman Act prosecution of the French potash cartel was defended on the grounds of sovereign immunity. The French Ambassador testified that operation of the potash mines was a government activity; 11/15 of the capital stock was owned by the government; proceeds are used for government purposes; and the board of directors is controlled by French ministerial officials. Even so, the United States court found no immunity—relying upon a letter from the U.S. Secretary of State and the recommendation of the International Economic Conference held at Geneva in 1927, the opinion found that there was no immunity accorded to an activity essentially equivalent to private activity. The holding, narrowly construed, however, avoided the immunity question by finding the defendant to be a sham government activity that was really acting as an agent for private concerns. US v. Deutsches Kalisyndikat Gesellschaft 31 F (2d) 199 (SDNY 1929).

Deprivation of immunity is a function of the executive; the judiciary will accord immunity to state activities without contrary direction from the executive branch. J. Hough said: "If the Republic of Chile considers it a governmental function to go into the carrying trade, as would appear to be the case here, that is the business of the Republic of Chile; and it we do not approve of it, if we do not like it, if we do not wish any longer to accord that respect to the property so engaged, which has hitherto been accorded to government property, then we must say so through diplomatic channels, and not through the judiciary." The Maipo 259 F 367, 368 (SDNY 1919); approved by the United States Supreme Court in Berizzi Bros. Co. v. SS Pesaro 271 US 562, 576 (1926). For a discussion of the concepts of sovereign immunity and act of state as approached under the extraterritorial application of U.S. antitrust law see Anthony W. Graziano, Jr., "Foreign Government Compulsion as a Defense in United States Antitrust Law," 7 *Virginia Journal of International Law* 100-45 (April 2, 1967) at 118ff. See also the Second Circuit adoption of the restrictive theory of sovereign immunity as subscribed to by the U.S. Department of State in Victory Transport Inc. v. Comisaria General de Abstecimientos y Transportes 336 F 2d 354 (2d Cir. 1964), *cert. denied*, 381 US 934 (1965).

[48] See Annex C for a discussion of the statutory objectives of the Sherman Act.

cases in this area suffer from an atomistic treatment that has failed to clarify the distinction between permitted and proscribed activity.[49] The suggested approaches, briefly described immediately below, are intended to illustrate issues of method rather than exhaust matters of content. No completely satisfying comprehensive approach to the extraterritorial antitrust regulation has been developed.[50] More than one approach may be necessary, and it would probably be desirable in important judicial opinion to reinforce the main approach with supplemental approaches.

1. *Conflict of Laws.* Sherman Act jurisdiction is subject to the limitations of the conflict of laws.[51] A basic conflicts rule, known as *lex loci delicti*, is that the creation and extent of liability is governed by the place where the alleged offense was committed.[52] This is especially true in interpreting a criminal statute. Antitrust prosecution is criminal prosecution.[53] There are two alternative constructions of *lex loci delicti*: first, the physical act or subjective territorial theory; secondly, the place of harm or objective territorial theory. The *Banana* case expresses the traditional physical act theory that limits jurisdiction to the place where the illegal act physically occurred. Courts have implicitly moved toward the place of harm theory, and in *Alcoa* jurisdiction was upheld because an agreement made in Switzerland caused harm to the United States, although no significant act, albeit an omission, was committed within the United States.[54] This latter construction, permitting the regulation of any

[49] Experts have been unable to render this distinction with any precision. Significant attempts have been made by Sigmund Timberg, "Antitrust and Foreign Trade," 48 *Northwestern University Law Review* 411-26 (Sept.-Oct. 1953) and by S. Chesterfield Oppenheim, "Foreign Commerce under the Sherman Act," 42 *Trade Mark Reporter* 3-22 (Jan. 1952). But their statements are so vague as to be not helpful to those seeking to remain upon what Timberg calls "the thick part of the antitrust ice."

[50] The most satisfying overall approach to this subject matter is Kingman Brewster, Jr., *Antitrust and American Business Abroad*, New York, McGraw-Hill, 1958.

[51] "It is quite true that we are not to read general words, such as those in this Act [Sherman Act], without regard to the limitation customarily observed by nations upon the exercise of their powers; limitations which generally correspond to those fixed by the 'Conflict of Laws.'" Alcoa, 148 F. 2d 416, 443 (2d Cir. 1945). This conflicts approach was suggested by the analysis of the Steele et al. v. Bulova Watch Co. Case 344 US 280 (1952) by a

Note in 47 *Northwestern University Law Review* 677-87 (Nov.-Dec. 1952).

[52] Restatement, Conflict of Laws § 378 (1934); Herbert F. Goodrich, *Handbook of the Conflict of Laws* §92, St. Paul, Minn., West Publishing Company, 3rd edn., 1949.

[53] "The territorial principle is applicable to Sherman Act prosecutions because these proceedings are penal." G. W. Haight, "International Law and Extraterritorial Application of the Antitrust Laws," 63 *Yale Law Journal* 639, 640 (1954). See also note 6 where Haight states that offenses proscribed by the Sherman Act are "criminal offenses in the sense that they are public wrongs redressed at the instance of the State in proceedings which have as their objective the infliction of punishment or the imposition of penalties remissible only by the State." This definition of criminal law may not conform to the municipal definition, but Haight claims it applies in the antitrust context whenever foreign elements are involved.

[54] In keeping with *Alcoa*'s extension of extraterritorial application of U.S. antitrust legislation, the *Restatement (Second)*

undesirable foreign activity, provided only that the defendant can be hauled before the court, has been challenged for its flexibility.[55] However, if courts talked in terms of place of harm in their consideration of alleged violations, clear and predictable limits to jurisdiction might begin to appear as the process of meaningful comparison would be facilitated by a common doctrinal approach. Other analogies drawn from the conflict of laws might be helpful in untangling foreign antitrust cases. No decided Sherman Act case has invoked a conflicts' rule to justify its holding.

2. *Rule of Reason—Illegal Per Se.* Foreign trade cases have rarely explicitly adopted the rule of reason–per se approaches that have helped to clarify the area of illegality in the domestic Sherman Act realm.[56] Because of the comparatively greater complexity of foreign trade

---

Foreign Relations Law of the United States notes in §18 that:

A state has jurisdiction to prescribe a rule of law attaching legal consequences to conduct that occurs outside its territory and causes an effect within its territory, if either

(a) the conduct and its effect are generally recognized as constituent elements of a crime or tort under the law of states that have reasonably developed legal systems, or

(b) (i) the conduct and its effect are constituent elements of activity to which the rule applies; (ii) the effect within the territory is substantial; (iii) it occurs as a direct and foreseeable result of the conduct outside the territory; and (iv) the rule is not inconsistent with the principles of justice generally recognized by states that have reasonably developed legal systems.

[55] "[The objective territorial principle] is often said to apply where the offense 'takes effect' or 'produces its effects' in the territory. In relation to elementary cases of direct physical injury, such as homicide, this is unexceptionable, for here the 'effect' which is meant is an essential ingredient of the crime. Once we move out of the sphere of direct physical consequences, however, to employ the formula of 'effects' is to enter upon a very slippery slope; for here the effects within the territory may be no more than an element of alleged consequential damage which may be more or less remote. . . . If indeed it were permissible to found objective territorial jurisdiction upon the territoriality of more or les remote repercussions of an act wholly performed in another territory, then there were virtually no limit to a State's territorial jurisdiction." (Footnotes omitted.) R. Y. Jennings, "Extraterritorial Jurisdiction and the United States Antitrust Laws," 33 *British Yearbook of International Law* 146-75 (1957) at 159.

Riedwig, *op cit, supra,* note 11, has noted that "Nearly all European writers have been critical of the Restatement's notion of extraterritorial application of a State's law to aliens." The European Advisory Committee on the Restatement commented: "In our view, the exercise of jurisdiction based on territory is not justified in cases where all that has occurred within the territory is the effects of certain conduct and not at least part of the conduct itself." Riedwig, at 372-73. A criticism of the Restatement's reliance on decisions of European courts is found at 373-74.

For a discussion of the "objective territorial principle" see 1 Brewster, *op.cit. supra,* note 40 at 65-75; Wilber L. Fugate, *Foreign Commerce and the Antitrust Laws,* Boston, Little, Brown, 1958, 25-27; Note, "Extraterritorial Application of the Antitrust Laws," 69 *Harvard Law Review* 1452-62 (1956); Note, "Limitations on the Federal Judicial Power to Compel Acts Violating Foreign Law," 63 *Columbia Law Review* 1441-95 (1963); and John M. Raymond, "A New Look in the Jurisdiction in Alcoa," 61 *American Journal of International Law* 558-70 (1967).

[56] US v. American Tobacco Co., 211 US 106 (1911) used the rule-of-reason approach, but it did not segregate the foreign aspects of the cases sufficiently to have any imprint upon international Sherman Act law. And see Eastern States Petroleum Co., Inc. v. Asiatic Petroleum Corp. et al. 103 F. 2d 315 (2d Cir. 1939) in which complaint was dismissed on grounds that the alleged restraint was reasonable.

a rule-of-reason approach is advocated to enable courts to consider the extenuating circumstances of each case. Fairer results are predicted by experts if courts use a case-to-case method of rendering decisions.[57] The *per se* rule, with its automatic application, is less desirable in the international context where goals other than the attainment of competitive conditions may be of paramount importance. And due to the variety of inducements to limit competition in foreign trade the reasonableness of the restraint becomes a more significant factor—that is if regulation is to be functionally meaningful rather than merely mechanically consistent.[58]

3. *Underlying Unlawful Purpose.*[59] This chapter investigates the relationship between the alleged antitrust violation and the manifested underlying purpose of the defendant. The important cases will be divided into areas clustered about the major devices used by business concerns to attain illegal objectives in their foreign trade operations. "Unlawful purpose" refers to restraints upon American imports, exports, and domestic commerce whether achieved by some form of price-fixing, market division, or market exclusion. None of the litigation in the foreign trade area has concerned a situation in which the sole offense was market dominance as such. Foreign antitrust defendants have always been charged with active abuses.[60]

B. UNLAWFUL PURPOSE TEST APPLIED TO THE DECISIONS

. . . [T]he general and almost universal rule is that the character of an act as lawful or unlawful must be determined wholly by the law of the country where the act is done. . . . For again, not only were the acts of the defendant in Panama or Costa Rica not within the Sherman Act, but they were not torts by the law of the place, and therefore were not torts at all, however contrary to the ethical and economic postulates of that statute.

Holmes, J., *American Banana Co. v. United Fruit Co.,*
213 US 347 at 356, 357 (1909).

[57] See 42 *Trade Mark Reporter* 3-22 (Jan. 1952) and 4 *Stanford Law Review* 559 (1952) for persuasive arguments to this effect.

[58] Although private restraints are not permissible defenses against foreign trade barriers (*Timken*) still greater tolerance may or should be accorded where such barriers exist. See hint by J. Wyzanski, in US v. Minnesota Mining & Mfg. Co., 92 F. Supp. 947 (D. Mass., 1950). Also cf. hypotheticals in 4 *Stanford Law Review* 559, 570 (1952) where the need to permit restraint is argued to be the only alternative to freezing out American investment.

[59] This approach is used with a different organization in Oppenheim's excellent article in 42 *Trade Mark Reporter* 3 (1952).

[60] The transportation cases seem to utilize the domestic §1 standard to determine the existence of foreign trade violations. See US v. Pacific and Arctic Co., 228 US 87 (1913); US v. Hamburg-Amerikanische Packet-Fahrt-Actien-Gesellschaft et al. 200 Fed. 806 (1911); Thomsen v. Cayser 243 US 66 (1916).

1. Cartel Participation

The fundamental *object* was control of both importation and sale of sisal and complete monopoly of both internal and external trade and commerce therein. (Emphasis added.)

McReynolds, J., *U.S. v. Sisal Sales Corp.*, 274 US 268 at 276 (1927).

. . . [I]t is settled law—as "Limited" itself agrees—that any state may impose liabilities, even upon persons not within its allegiance, for conduct outside its borders that has *consequences* within its borders which the state reprehends; and these liabilities other states will ordinarily recognize. (Emphasis added.)

L. Hand, J., *U.S. v. Alcoa*, 148 F. 2d 416 at 443 (1945).

As a result of these decisions clarifying the broad statements of the *Banana* case, the law of extraterritorial conspiracies is fairly settled. As with domestic conspiracies, the essential element necessary to turn a common plan or understanding into a conspiracy subject to the Sherman Act is activity which has an effect on American commerce, foreign or interstate. If such effect is present, it is immaterial whether the common understanding was entered into in the United States or abroad. In the absence of an effect on our commerce the Sherman Act does not apply to acts committed here or abroad in furtherance of a common understanding entered into at home or in foreign countries. But once jurisdiction has attached, all activities, foreign as well as domestic, are covered by the antitrust laws.

Application of the Antitrust Laws to Extraterritorial Conspiracies, 49 *Yale Law Journal*, 1312, at 1316-17 (1940).

The majority of foreign antitrust cases include some alleged relationship in restraint with one or more foreign corporations; such a relationship constitutes cartel participation.[61] A cartel has an unlawful purpose if it seeks to restrain the domestic or foreign commerce of the United States. A restraint, exclusively limited to a foreign market and foreign competitors, does not violate the American antitrust laws.[62] Extenuating circumstances, limiting the competitive possibilities, may mitigate the illegality of cartel participation.[63] Cartels most frequently restrain international commerce by varying kinds of market allocations. An agree-

[61] See Cartels, Annex B.

[62] This can be properly drawn from the Eastern States Petroleum Co. Inc. v. Asiatic Petroleum Corp. et al. 103 F. 2d 315 (2d Cir. 1939) where the majority opinion held that no matter how reprehensible the defendant's conduct it was not subject to punishment by United States courts as it did not restrain American commerce. The case was a private treble damage action under the Sherman Act.

[63] See *Minnesota Mining* case discussion, *infra*. Also the Webb Act exemption is relevant.

ment among producers, domestic or foreign, not to export or import into the United States, clearly violates the Sherman Act. The fact that the agreement was made outside the United States does not lessen illegality.[64]

The development of the content of unlawful purpose in foreign antitrust law can be traced by reference to three major judicial landmarks—the *Banana*, *Sisal*, and *Alcoa* decisions. The *Banana* opinion relying upon a presumption of territoriality, denied that the Sherman Act had any extraterritorial application.[65] Justice Holmes ignored the plaintiff allegations of restraining *effects* upon United States commerce, and apparently limited physical acts to their area of commission.[66] The Sherman Act only apprehended unreasonable restraints that were physically performed in whole or in part in the United States. The Supreme Court also rejected a potential interpretive dichotomy between extraterritorial application to nationals and a territorial application to nonnationals. The *Banana* case defendant could have been subjected to jurisdiction by the use of the internationally approved "Nationality Principle."[67] The courts have never justified their assertion of antitrust jurisdiction by a reliance upon the nationality of the defendants. This much of the *Banana* case has been followed in subsequent cases.[68]

The *Sisal* approach relies upon a conspiracy theory.[69] The elements necessary for conspiracy to be found under federal law are consent between two or more parties, an overt act within the territorial jurisdiction, and personal jurisdiction over the defendants.[70] The breadth of this approach depends upon the requirements fixed by the judiciary to satisfy the "overt act" element.[71] If only an "effect" is necessary, the *Sisal* approach is capable of unlimited application, while the scope of applicability becomes greatly limited if an "integral physical act" is required as the *Banana* decision seems to hold. Also conceivably the *Sisal*

[64] See *Alcoa*, p. 444.
[65] American Banana Co. v. United Fruit Co., 213 US 347 (1909).
[66] See quotation of Justice Holmes at the start of this section. Also see use of *impact* construction of the Sherman Act in the District Court opinion, 160 F 184 (1908). One should, however, note the limited facts of the *Banana* case. Graziano points out that: (1) none of the acts alleged in the complaint took place in the United States, (2) the plaintiff did not claim an effect on U.S. commerce, but instead focused its allegations on the production, sale and purchase of bananas in foreign markets, and (3) the Court interpreted the plaintiff's main theory to be that although the Governor of Panama and the soldiers of Costa Rica directly caused most of the damage, the defendant

was liable because it persuaded these government representatives to act. Graziano at 103, citing 213 U.S. at 355 and 357-58 and Fugate at 49.
[67] Cf. Harvard Research, see note 9, *supra*. Also see US v. Bowman 260 US 94 (1922).
[68] For example, the *Sisal* case could more easily have been decided under the "Nationality Principle."
[69] United States v. Sisal Sales Corp. 274 US 266 (1927).
[70] 49 *Yale Law Journal* 1312, 1315 (May 1940).
[71] "The most important element in the determination of whether an extraterritorial conspiracy comes within the Sherman Act is the nature of the overt act necessary for jurisdiction." *Id.* at 1315.

doctrine could be interpreted to necessitate at least one of the conspirators to be a United States corporation.[72]

The *Sisal* complaint alleged violations of the Sherman Act and Section 73 of the Wilson Tariff Act.[73] Two American corporations conspired in the United States with a Mexican corporation to dominate the sisal hemp market in the Yucatan, a state in Mexico, that produced 90 percent of the world supply. The "unlawful purpose" of the defendants was to restrict the flow of sisal imports into the United States in order to maintain an artificially high price in the American market. All competitors of the defendants were excluded and the defendant became the sole importer. The Yucatan monopoly was facilitated by favorable legislation solicited from the Mexican government by the Mexican conspirator; the defendant became the exclusive selling agent of sisal in the Yucatan.[74] The *Banana* holding was distinguished on the ground that here, in *Sisal*, the contract of conspiracy was entered into and made effective within the United States, although the restraining acts themselves were performed in Mexico. The agreement to conspire, the higher domestic prices, and the resultant elimination of competitors were enough to constitute an overt act within the United States. The trial court dismissed the government's complaint upon the authority of the *Banana* case. The Supreme Court, in an opinion by Justice McReynolds in which Justice Holmes joined, reversed the dismissal.

This expansion of the content of "unlawful purpose" enabled the court to convict the defendant for acts that were legal where committed —the behavior in restraint was accomplished in Mexico with the sanction of Mexican law. No analytical weight should be accorded to the fact that the physical act of agreement was entered into in the United States, as this is a fortuitous and easily avoidable circumstance. Also the fact of United States participation is seemingly irrelevant, as the Court did not rely upon the nationality of the defendant to justify its claim of jurisdiction.[75] An *effect* upon United States imports—a restriction of supply and a consequent price rise—would seem sufficient by itself to taint with illegality any act of implementation wherever and by whomever committed. An extraordinary implication of this holding is that the Sherman Act has the power to control the manner in which a foreign business is to be conducted outside the United States if it expects legally to export to a United States market. Such a foreign business establishment must obey not only its own local regulations but the American

---

[72] This is rather dubious as the court lays little stress upon the nationality of the defendants. It is a fact that the principal defendants were American corporations, thus permitting a later court to escape application of *Sisal* by limiting its application to these facts.

[73] 274 US 268 (1927).
[74] *Id.* at 274.
[75] The *sole* justification claimed for jurisdiction was the right of a nation to punish any element, including foreign elements, of a conspiracy consummated within its territory.

Sherman Act as well. A further implication of the *Sisal* decision is virtually to repeal the *Banana* case by reinterpreting the Sherman Act either to have extraterritorial control over foreign acts or to redefine acts to include effects.[76] The *Sisal* holding has been cited frequently in subsequent holdings. And the consent decrees issued against the quinine, potash, and sardine cartels all rest upon the explicit authority of *Sisal*.[77] These decrees provide an important tentative footnote to the *Sisal* definition of "unlawful purpose" by applying *Sisal* to alien corporations and by explicitly disavowing any Sherman Act attempt to influence the conduct of exclusively foreign business.[78]

The "unlawful-purpose" test has received its most influential exposition in Judge Learned Hand's comprehensive opinion in the *Alcoa* case.[79] The *Alcoa* decision, endorsed subsequently by the Supreme Court, embodies more than any other single opinion the essence of contemporary international Sherman Act theory. Yet the validity of the grounds selected to justify the *Alcoa* holding appears to be quite tenuous.[80]

The court turned to the international aspects of the allegations after finding Alcoa guilty of monopolizing the manufacture and distribution of virgin aluminum ingot in violation of the Sherman Act. Limited was organized in Canada to take over Alcoa's properties that were located outside the United States.[81] The original common stock issue of Limited was all distributed to the common stockholders of Alcoa. The management of Limited was conducted by the same two families that owned Alcoa. Limited had received favorable treatment in a number of transactions with Alcoa.[82] Limited participated in foreign cartels, and seemed to be acting on behalf of Alcoa.[83] Yet the District Court and Judge Hand found that Limited was a separate corporate entity, that there was no proof of a conspiracy between Limited and Alcoa, and that Limited

[76] There is little room left for the *Banana* territorial construction of the Sherman Act if *Sisal* is followed.

[77] For the relevant facts and consequences of these consent decrees see 46 *Harvard Law Review* 885, 924-25. See note 14 for citations. See also Continental Ore Co. v. Union Carbide & Carbon Corp., 370 US 690 (1962).

[78] There were no American participants in the cartels. All the decrees contained a disclaimer as to acts "entirely completed outside the United States and which does not require any act or thing to be done within the United States."

[79] 148 F. 2d 416 (2d Cir. 1945). The international trade part of the opinion begins at 439.

[80] That is, the *impact* upon domestic prices approach in preference to the *conspiracy* approach.

[81] *Id.* at 439.

[82] *Id.* at 440. The manufacture of alumina for Limited in Alcoa's East St. Louis factory at mill cost. Also Alcoa did some cheap fabricating and financing for Limited—friendly gestures unknown in arms-length dealing among "economic men."

[83] *Id.* at 440-41. Limited participated in foreign cartels, and tacitly secured for Alcoa freedom from the competition of imports. Unless it acted as Alcoa or under payment from Alcoa there is no explanation for the division of world markets that resulted from the Alliance cartel.

was not acting as agent for Alcoa.[84] Thus Alcoa could not be convicted for cartel participation. However, Limited, which participated in a Swiss cartel, Alliance, sought to maintain the world price by limiting production of the members to a fixed quota. The United States was not explicitly mentioned in either the 1931 or 1936 agreement yet exports to and from the United States during the period of the cartel's operation were negligible despite the profitable nature of the American market.[85] The court found that the 1936 agreement by its limitation of production had the *intent* to curtail United States imports.[86] Although the *actual reduction* of imports was not established by the government, Judge Hand ruled that once intent was established then the burden of proof shifted to the defendant to disprove actual effect, and this burden Limited failed to sustain.[87] Therefore, Limited, a foreign corporation doing a negligible amount of business in the United States, was held to violate the Sherman Act because it had entered into an agreement abroad with other foreign producers not to export to the United States; these producers also did little business in the United States. Taken at face value this is an extraordinary holding—it means that foreign corporations can be guilty of violating the Sherman Act by committing acts of omission—by the failure to export to the United States. The decision on this level requires corporations in all countries to respond to a competitive allocation of resources in determining their distribution policy. It would seem likely, if frequently followed, to provoke widespread protest.[88] The application of such an "unlawful-pur-

---

[84] *Id.* at 442. "For these reasons we conclude that Alcoa was not a party to Alliance."

[85] *Id.* at 442.

[86] With regard to the operation of intent in bringing violators outside its territorial jurisdiction within the scope of U.S. antitrust legislation, Graziano notes that the *Alcoa* case "establishes a distinction between jurisdiction over acts and agreements outside of the United States involving Americans alone or acting in concert with foreigners, and those involving only foreigners. When Americans are acting alone or in concert with foreigners, no actual effect on United States commerce need be shown. Just as in purely domestic cases, the mere attempt to unreasonably restrain trade is prescribed by the Sherman Act." See e.g., United States v. United States Alkali Export Assn., 86 F. Supp. 59, 66 (SDNY 1949); cf. United States v. Socony-Vacuum Oil Co., 310 US 150, 224-26, n59 (1940). "However when foreigners alone are involved, a consideration of the 'limitations

customarily observed by nations upon the exercise of their powers,'" 148 F 2d at 443, led Judge Learned Hand to conclude that the Sherman Act applies only where there is both an intent to affect and some actual effect upon United States commerce. 148 F. 2d at 443-44. In this context, "intent" does not mean a specific intent to affect United States commerce. A foreigner is presumed to intend the normal consequences of his act. See e.g., United States v. General Electric Co., 82 F. Supp. 753, 884, 890-91 (D.N.J. 1949); N. Osborough, "The Extra-Jurisdictional Impact of Antitrust Enforcement," 16 *Northern Ireland Legal Quarterly* 239, 242 (1965), at 103-04, 15. Compare Riedwig's comments in note 15, *supra.*

[87] *Id.* at 444. "We think, however, that, after the intent to affect imports was proved, the burden of proof shifted to Limited."

[88] See Haight and Whitney articles, *op.cit.* Also see the Swiss Watch controversy and note 5, *supra.*

pose" test would result in a dangerous interference with the sovereign control of other nations over their economic affairs.[89]

The *Alcoa* holdings are more reasonable if explained by factors not explicitly relied upon by the court. Despite the express finding that Limited acted independently of Alcoa, the cartel agreements and the decision do not make sense unless the intimate relationship between Alcoa and Limited is stressed. Why else should Limited refrain from exporting to the profitable United States market? Why else did Alcoa refrain from exports after the organization of Limited? How else can the treatment by Alliance of the American market be explained? Under this explanation the "unlawful purpose" remains participation in a conspiracy to restrain domestic commerce, with at least one conspirator doing business in the United States. It seems legitimate that the United States should have the right to insist upon conformity to a Sherman Act standard by any direct or indirect participant in the domestic market. But the failure to do business in the United States, by itself, does not qualify a foreign actor who is guilty of a restraint on trade as a market participant. If a corporation situated as was Alcoa is regarded as a tacit conspirator then it is permissible to punish foreign co-conspirators although all their acts are outside the jurisdiction of the forum state provided only that the conspiracy is intended to be *consummated* within the forum state.[90]

If the explicit *Alcoa* holding had become the basis for the assertion of regulatory authority it might have been unfortunate. *Alcoa* in an undiluted form would have overexpanded the application of the Sherman Act to foreign commerce. It would have produced vague and arbitrary results—the fortuitous circumstances of the availability of personal jurisdiction would become crucial, the choice of defendants by the Justice Department would inevitably become discriminatory, and the degree of enforcement would likely be disappointing. Adequate Sherman Act protection of the American market is achieved by retaining the *Sisal* rule and limiting it to restraints of commission; punishing acts of omission—the *Alcoa* case—represents an overextension of Sherman Act jurisdiction.

These particular cases raise many problems relating to conduct outside of the United States by foreign competitors seeking entry to the domestic market. To what extent would American laws require competitive prerequisites to doing business here? The noncompetitive organization of foreign industry would seem to be no concern of American regulation provided no restraint was imported. A cartel like the Alliance might be permitted to do business in the United States if it did not re-

---

[89] *Id.*
[90] Cf. *Sisal* case discussion, *supra*, and the Harvard Research authorization under the Objective Application of the Territorial Principle.

strain United States trade, but such a cartel could not have been formed legally within the United States. Thus the place of agreement, contrary to Judge Hand's view, can be significant.[91] The *Swiss Watch Cartel* case reinforces this contention by its emphasis on the relevance of the territorial sovereign's legal compulsion to a determination of compliance with the requirement of the antitrust laws.[92]

2. *Foreign Affiliated Ownership*

In a world of tariffs, trade barriers, empire or domestic preferences, and various forms of parochialism of which we are by no means free, I think a rule that it is a restraint of trade to enter a foreign market through a separate subsidiary of limited competitors is virtually to foreclose foreign commerce of many kinds. It is one thing for competitors or a parent and its subsidiaries to divide the United States domestic market which is an economic and legal unit; it is another for an industry to recognize that foreign markets consist of many legal and economic units and to go after each through separate means. I think this decision (of the majority) will restrain more trade than it will make free.

> Jackson, J., dissenting in *Timken Roller Bearing Co. v. U.S.,*
> 34V US 593, at 607-608 (1951).

No citation of authority is any longer necessary to support the proposition that a combination of competitors which by agreement divides the world into exclusive trade areas, and suppresses all competition among the members of the combination, offends the Sherman Act.

> Rifkind, D. J., *U.S. v. National Lead Co.,*
> 63 F. Supp. 513, at 523 (SDNY 1945).

The gloss of separate corporate entities employed to insulate General Electric from the consequences of these maneuvers avails nothing in the face of the plain intent to monopolize the incandescent lamp industry in the United States and protect this dominant position from foreign competition.

> Forman, D. J., *U.S. v. General Electric,*
> 82 F. Supp. 753 at 843 (SDNY 1949).

---

[91] For example, a combination of foreign competitors entered into in a foreign country would not offend the Sherman Act. And the "combine" could even do business in the United States provided it did not engage in prohibited practices. United States antitrust laws have never been invoked to control the manner in which foreign industry is organized. However, if several foreign competitors combined within the United States the transaction might violate the Clayton Act by threatening to lessen competition substan-tially. This relevant provision of the Clayton Act applies only to domestic commerce —and thus only to mergers carried on by competitors operating in the U.S. economy.

[92] United States v. Watchmakers of Switzerland Information Center, Inc., 1963 Trade Cases para. 70600 (SDNY); for helpful interpretation see Anthony W. Graziano, Jr., "Foreign Governmental Compulsion as a Defense in United States Antitrust Law," 7 *Virginia Journal of International Law* 100-45, at 138-42 (1967 2).

Foreign subsidiaries of American corporations are not intrinsically illegal. A subsidiary is only violative of the Sherman Act if it is used by the parent as a device to accomplish some underlying "unlawful purpose"—usually a restriction of imports and exports by a market division scheme. The determination of "unlawful purpose" depends largely upon the intent of the parent. The mode of acquisition—whether by the purchase of an existing competitor or the formation of a new competitive unit—is also considered by courts. This factor suggests an important analytical inquiry—does the creation and operation of this subsidiary restrain or actually promote competition? Competition is promoted if a new competitor is enabled to enter the market. In this area of application, a rule-of-reason approach is well adapted to accomplish sensible results. The mechanical *per se* decisions tend to overlook mitigating circumstances that may make the seeming restraint quite justified on occasion.[93] For example, a policy of finding subsidiaries that are jointly owned by competitors automatically illegal glosses over the situation in which neither owner could finance the operations of the subsidiary alone. The final question in evaluating the legality of a subsidiary should be—"Is this a reasonable means of achieving a legal end?" Courts could return to the common law doctrine of the legality of ancillary restraints to uphold the formation of a subsidiary incidental to legitimate business operations. On the other hand, to strike down a subsidiary used as a subterfuge to circumvent the Sherman Act courts could support their finding by relying upon the *Yellow Cab Company* line of cases.[94] Courts also have been expected to cope with the contention that the foreign trade Sherman Act standards should be relaxed sufficiently to permit successful American competition. Standard doctrine explicitly declares that "defensive" restraints are not within the province of legitimate business operations, and so the existence of foreign uncompetitive conditions does not excuse an "unlawful-purpose" subsidiary.[95] Private industry must await government protection to counteract foreign abuses. But the conditions existing in the foreign market do affect the determination of intent, and thereby influence a finding of "unlawful purpose."[96] Cases have provoked great controversy.[97]

[93] See *Timken* majority opinion; Oppenheim, *op.cit.*

[94] US v. Yellow Cab Co., 332 US 218 (1947); Kiefer-Stewart Co. v. Seagram & Sons 340 US 211 (1951); Schine Chain Theaters, Inc. v. US 334 US 110 (1948).

[95] Otherwise the Webb Act would be either superfluous or exempting conduct beyond the express intent of Congress, see Annex C. Generally see R. D. Hale and G. E. Hale, "Monopoly Abroad: The Antitrust Laws and Commerce in Foreign Areas," 31 *Texas Law Review* 493, 495-98, 524-31 (May 1953).

[96] See especially the subsequent discussion of the *Minnesota Mining* case.

[97] Law journal reaction has been abundant and sharply differing—see particularly the commentary on the *Timken* case in 4 *Stanford Law Review* 559 (1952); 21 *George Washington Law Review* 677 (June 1953); 42 *Trade Mark Reporter* 3-22 (Jan. 1952).

Subsidiaries have been prominently used to obtain monopoly advantages. American corporations have sought to participate in cartels through the representation of a foreign subsidiary.[98] Subsidiaries are a covert technique of attaining an "unlawful purpose," as the "unlawful purpose" emerges from the final competitive pattern rather than from the character of its individual operations.[99]

In addition to activity declared illegal because of the "unlawful-purpose" test, the purchase of a foreign firm by an American corporation may be prevented by Section 7 of the Clayton Act if the "effect . . . may be substantially to lessen competition" within the United States.[100] Thus transactions with innocent business motives can be prevented if the resultant impact upon the competitive framework is regarded as unhealthy. Beyond this, the merger or purchase of competitors in foreign markets may not be permitted, if the consequence of the transaction results in dominance by a single competitor in the relevant market, on the authority of the *Columbia Steel* case ruling.[101] Both these subordinate weapons of antitrust regulation against restraints in this area seem limited in application to *American operating* firms; there is some question as to the status of an acquisition of a purely foreign concern by an American company that gives market dominance sufficient to discourage potential American competition.[102]

The geographical dispersion of a business organization may represent a response to needs rather than manifest a desire to obtain some form of monopoly power.[103] An American firm may directly invest in a foreign concern in order to attain a more economical integration of its overall business process or to jump a tariff barrier or to legitimately escape the confining effect of an export ban. United States policy favors foreign investment generally, and particularly when it coincides with our program for the development of backward countries. Thus the creation by an American corporation of a foreign operating branch is by itself legal.[104] The functional equivalent, a subsidiary formed as a foreign corporation in the area in which it expects to do business, is often regarded with more suspicion by courts.[105] In addition to the normal business advantage of decentralization, a subsidiary may have a tax advantage by

98 See especially *Alcoa* and the two *General Electric* cases.

99 Cf. 42 *Trade Mark Reporter* 3-22 (Jan. 1952).

100 38 Stat 730 (1914), as amended, 49 Stat 1526, 15 USC §13 (1964). See Brochin comment in 64 *Yale Law Journal* (Feb. 1955) for further development of the Clayton Act application.

101 U.S. v. Columbia Steel Co., 334 US 495 (1948). The Supreme Court felt that the acquisition of 14 percent of the market was not such a prohibited dominance; there was a dissent.

102 That is, does the potential exclusion of an American exporter from a foreign market come within the scope of the Clayton Act? It seems possible to regard such an event as possibly lessening competition within the United States.

103 This paragraph has relied upon a passage in Hale and Hale, *op.cit.*, note 95, at p. 523.

104 *Id.* at 525.

105 *Id.* at 526-27.

enabling some degree of income splitting, it may avoid local laws discriminating against foreign corporations—such as the imposition of unlimited liability, and it may be better able to stimulate local investment and patronage.[106]

Case law can be conveniently divided into two groups centering around the *Timken* and *Minnesota Mining* decisions. The *Timken* case raises all the problems associated with the use and abuse of the right to decentralize American foreign trade by a resort to local organization. The *Minnesota Mining* opinion is separately considered because it displays an interesting inquiry by the court into the defendant's contention of the legality of a "defensive" and "balancing" combination in restraint.

a. *The Timken Area*

. . . [A] conspiracy to divide territories which affects American commerce violates the Sherman Act.

> *U.S. v. I.C.I.*, 100 F. Supp. 504, 592 (SDNY
> 1951), citing the *Timken* case as authority.

[A] Santa Claus for British competition.

> Frankfurter, J., of *Timken* District Court opinion,
> 19 *U.S. Law Week* 3291, 3293 (1951).

. . . In some countries a foreign corporation can't own property without forming a domestic company . . . (. . . compliance with the Sherman Act would require illegal operation under foreign law) . . . if that's true the Sherman Act sets up just such a world imperialism as Russia accuses us of fostering. . . . I don't think the purpose of the Act is to compel persons in foreign countries to pay our prices which they can't possibly afford.

> Jackson, J., in course of *Timken* Argument, 19
> *U.S. Law Week* 3291, 3293 (1951).[107]

The Timken Roller Bearing Company, American Timken, was charged with conspiring to obtain an "unlawful purpose"—monopoly control and the exclusion of competition—in the world market for antifriction roller bearings. The effect of the conspiracy, justifying territorial jurisdiction, was the reduction of United States imports and exports. Since 1909 American Timken had continuously sought to obtain this illegal end. A series of agreements with its chief competitor and later co-conspirator, British Timken, sought to allocate world markets in

---

106 *Id.* at 525.

107 This is strong language and presumably refers to the higher prices that would result from requiring foreign consumers to buy in the United States; it assumes the dependence of foreign markets upon American exports. Actually this argument is specious in the *Timken* context where the territorial market, England, did its utmost to keep American competition out.

1920, 1924, and 1925. American Timken became the world's largest bearing producer and in 1927 acquired 30 percent of the stock of its only important competitor, British Timken. British and American Timken jointly organized and equally owned French Timken. Each of the three companies was dominant in its field of operation.[108] The District Court found that these three companies had allocated trade territories, fixed prices on products of one sold in the trade territory of the other, cooperated to exclude outside competition, and participated in cartels designed to restrict United States imports and exports.[109] Timken had sought to comply with the letter of the antitrust laws by seeking its illegal objectives through the medium of "joint venture" and trademark control.[110] Both the District Court and the Supreme Court disregarded the former defense as mere "corporate gloss."

The decision found that American and British Timken were separate corporate entities.[111] Therefore, in a given foreign market they were competitors. Thus these agreements to allocate territories or fix prices unreasonably restrained competition. The partial ownership relation does not confer Sherman Act immunity. The Supreme Court relied upon the *Yellow Cab Co.* holding that an illegal conspiracy may result from agreements in restraint between elements of a corporation affiliated under common or integrated ownership.[112] And agreements between affiliated elements, even if parent and subsidiary, to restrain outside competition are clearly illegal.[113] The courts made it plain that a "joint venture" was permissible provided it did not exist to cloak Sherman Act violations. Here, it seems likely that any further acquisition of British Timken by American Timken could be found to violate either Section 7 of the Clayton Act or Sections 1 and 2 of the Sherman Act.

The *Timken* decision stimulated a strong dissent and much adverse comment.[114] Much criticism concentrates upon the undue penalty inflicted upon an American concern's foreign investment, with a consequent fear that foreign development by American capital would be discouraged. Emphasis is accorded to the efforts of American Timken to enter the British market that was insulated by protective barriers, and the consequent necessity to invest in British companies to obtain a share of the British market.[115] These reactions are unresponsive to the context of the *Timken* decision—American Timken's manifest objective was the re-

---

[108] U.S. v. Timken Roller Bearing Co., 83 F. Supp. 284, 288 (N.D. Ohio 1950).
[109] *Id.* at 306.
[110] *Id.* at 314.
[111] Timken Roller Bearing Co. v. US, 341, US 593, 597 (1951).
[112] *Id.* at 597.
[113] Kiefer-Stewart Co. v. Joseph E. Seagram & Sons, 340 US 211 (1950).

[114] Justice Frankfurter and Justice Jackson each wrote a dissent; see criticism not well taken in 4 *Stanford Law Review* 559 (1952); and the cogent attack upon the *per se* approach in 42 *Trade Mark Reporter* 3-22 (Jan. 1952).
[115] Jackson dissent, 341 US 593, 606 (1951).

straint, not the expansion, of competition, and it was this "unlawful purpose," achieved by a variety of ingenious circuities, including foreign investment, that the court declared illegal. To do otherwise would have been to invite Sherman Act intervention by immunizing the restraints of affiliated concerns. Thus competing corporations would merely exchange stock and proceed to restrain trade under the protective label "joint venture." To read the *Timken* case as a doctrine of foreign investment restriction, as do the dissenters, is to lose sight of the "unlawful purpose" by an overfocusing upon the punishment of foreign investment by an American business.

There is a greater justification for Justice Jackson's argument that the majority is using a "technical conspiracy doctrine" to penalize form. Namely, that American Timken could have accomplished the same restraining result by setting up divisions in various countries under a single unified management. But could they? Antitrust laws could perhaps prevent the elimination of British Timken through the Clayton Act prohibition. Also it may be reasonable to use the existence of hostile foreign attitudes, for example the British resistance to foreign competition, to secure competitive conduct by an American concern—that is, but for British resistance American concerns could set up a "legal" system of restraining corporate subsidiaries, but since there is this British resistance, let us certainly prevent the equivalent "illegal" restraint.[116]

A most legitimate position of the dissent is to attack the *per se* approach of the majority.[117] Although the *Timken* decision is eminently reasonable, an inquiry into reasonableness in this matrix seems likely to assure a preservation of Sherman Act standards without unnecessarily restricting American business opportunities. This flexible approach recognizes the futility of regulatory claims being completely divorced from the climate of business opportunity. This treatment would promote maximum trade and competition by endorsing the tacit assumption that in certain contexts of foreign trade an expansion of competition requires participation in restraint so long as there is so much toleration of noncompetitive behavior outside of the United States. Also there are certain special cases where combinations of competitors become essential and reasonable—to jointly finance a big project, to share an exclusive agency, to make an economical integration, to serve the needs of certain markets, and so on.[118] The alternative projected by the *Timken* majority tends to develop an automatism that leaves an arbitrary trail of decisions, and

---

[116] Viz., to advocate the utilization of any factor in the relevant market, no matter how fortuitous, to achieve the antitrust objective of minimizing unlawful purpose. This kind of approach may, however, produce a capricious pattern of regulation.

[117] 341 US 593, 607. Also see Oppenheim 42 *Trade Mark Reporter* 3-22 (Jan. 1952).
[118] 4 *Stanford Law Review* 559, 568 (1952).

so a chaotic body of law arises to introduce needless uncertainty as to the legality of conduct.

Despite the widespread interest stirred by the *Timken* decision, courts have subsequently held that a foreign subsidiary cannot be used to seek an "unlawful purpose" under the Sherman Act. For example, in the *General Electric Lamp* case the district court held that the operation of foreign subsidiaries with the "dominant intent" to maintain its mastery over the United States domestic market was illegal.[119] In the *ICI* case, jointly owned subsidiaries were established by the corporate defendants to exploit common markets with monopoly power; the purpose for which a subsidiary was organized was the elimination of competition.[120] In *National Lead* and the *General Electric* titanium cases courts did not permit antitrust defendants to accomplish ends by using a subsidiary to accomplish the "unlawful purpose."[121] In the later *Holophane* opinion the court disallowed cartel participation through the representation of the parent by a foreign subsidiary.[122] All these cases indicate that part of the function of foreign subsidiaries is to represent the parent in a cartel. The parent has not avoided responsibility, and is charged, as principal, with the illegal conduct of its agent.

b. *The Minnesota Mining "Innovation"*

. . . the nub of the case is not whether defendants' political and economic exhibits are admissible but whether they, taken together with other evidence in the case, prove that defendants could not have profitably exported from the United States a substantial volume of coated abrasives to the areas supplied by their jointly owned factories located in England, Canada, and Germany. . . .

It is axiomatic that if over a sufficiently long period American enterprises, as a result of political or economic barriers, cannot export directly or indirectly from the United States to a particular foreign country at a profit, then any private action taken to secure or interfere solely with business in that area, whatever else it may do, does not restrain foreign commerce in that area in violation of the Sherman Act. For, the very hypothesis is that there is not and could not be any American foreign commerce in that area which could be restrained or monopolized.

Wyzanski, J., *U.S. v. Minnesota Mining and Manufacturing Co.*, 92 F. Supp. 947, 958, 959 (D.C. Mass. 1950).

[119] US v. General Electric Co. 82 F. Supp. 753, 842 (D.C.N.J. 1949).
[120] US v. ICI, 100 F. Supp. 504, 592 (SDNY 1951).
[121] US v. National Lead Co., 63 F. Supp. 513 (SDNY 1945), modified and affirmed, 332 US 319 (1947); US v. Holophane Co. 119 F. Supp. 114 (S.C. Ohio 1954).
[122] 119 F. Supp. 114, 119.

Courts have refused to distinguish the degree of illegality arising from "defensive" restraints of trade in the past. It is the existence of an unreasonable restraint, and not its character as "defensive" or "aggressive" that has concerned former decision-makers. Analogous reasoning is expressed by the *General Dyestuff Corp.* court:

> The second argument advanced by the defendants is that the arrangements, designed to keep foreign chemicals from entry into the United States, cannot be deemed against public policy because they serve the same policy as the tariff acts. But the intention of Congress is quite unambiguous. It subjects the imports of foreign commodities to public control and regulation and prohibits such control and regulations by private combinations.[123]

Thus in an area of similar reasoning, a private restraint, that facilitates a government policy of public restraint as embodied in the tariff acts was not regarded as a worthy defense by the court to a charge of an antitrust violation. Private industry cannot supplement government protection in any way that is not expressly sanctioned by the antitrust laws, and amendments thereto. Thus exporters could not combine to defend against cartels without the legislative authorization of the Webb-Pomerene Act. Conversely, the absence of a Webb Act would imply that the government intended no exemption from antitrust laws for other classes of participants in foreign trade, and that "balancing" restraints in the international context are just as illegal as they have always been regarded in a domestic context.[124] Any other inference would amount to a delegation of legislative authority. Private restraints cannot fulfill the needs of American business; if protection is needed it must come from the government under present law. The *Minnesota Mining* case seems to depart somewhat from this traditional position.

In *Minnesota Mining* American manufacturers of coated abrasives controlling four-fifths of the export trade formed a Webb Act association. The export association has at all times been in competition with foreign manufacturers who "have ties of nationality, local preference and sometimes governmental subsidies or low labor costs" to bolster their market position.[125] Also the association competes with nonmember domestic exporters; in fact, their share of the market increased from 18 percent to 39 percent during the life of the association (1929-1948).[126] The defendants sold their exported abrasives at a higher price than their competitors. The association also organized a holding com-

---

[123] U.S. v. General Dyestuff, 57 F. Supp. 642 (SDNY 1944).
[124] 31 *Texas Law Review* 493, 506 (1953).

[125] US v. Minnesota Mining & Mfg. Co., 92 F. Supp. 947 (D.C. Mass. 1950).
[126] *Id.*

pany, Durex Company, that held the stock of foreign subsidiaries located in England, Canada, and Germany.[127] These subsidiaries sold abrasives locally, and were organized to combat post-World War I economic nationalism. Foreign subsidiaries were claimed to be necessary to hurdle restrictionist barriers, and to take advantage of local, as compared to alien, operation. The District Court found that the subsidiaries were only used by the association when foreign discrimination made it advantageous to do so. Exports of abrasives from the United States declined—the defendant explained this decline by the political and economic barriers erected by foreign countries. The members of the association agreed not to export to the territories in which the respective foreign subsidiaries operated. It is apparent that the defendants sought to enhance prices through the medium of curtailing American exports. Why else impose a self-restraint? Profit could be maximized apparently by controlling the supply, and this implies the absence of substantial nonmember competition in these areas. This is a blatant Sherman Act violation—an agreement to curtail exports from the United States— and made the actual decision easy. The interest of the case arises from its carefully reasoned endorsement of the "rule-of-reason" approach.

The court, in an opinion by Judge Wyzanski, upheld the government's allegation of Section 1 and 2 violations. However, as was said, the importance of the case lies in the "rule-of-reason" treatment of the facts. Evidence of the reasonableness of forming the foreign subsidiaries to meet foreign competition was accepted by the court.[128] The court did find that the defendant was not so justified. After using this flexible approach it set forth a rather mechanical test that "defensive" combinations in the form of foreign subsidiaries would be tolerated, but only if the domestic exporters could not otherwise profitably export. The abrasive association only showed that it was *less* profitable to export. An initial reaction to the decision is to question the apparent discrimination against the export of capital—unless a restraint beyond the fact of combination is established, as it was not, then it seems overtechnical to permit exporters to combine to ship goods, but disallow those same exporters the right to combine to export capital to form foreign units of production.[129] This latter method may be a more economical mode of serving certain foreign markets, and the antitrust laws should not in-

[127] This activity of operating foreign subsidiaries was outside of Webb Act protection. The Webb Act deals only with export *qua* export.

[128] 92 F. Supp. 947, 959 (1950).

[129] There seems no reason to prevent this activity as there was in *Timken*, see note 105. Unless the export of capital in conspiracy is fostering an unlawful purpose—an undue restraint—then it would seem desirable to encourage such a form of foreign investment. Therefore, it does not seem sensible to punish a practice when the result is desirable and could legally, but with more economic difficulty, be achieved by an alternative practice.

terfere with the optimum use of resources, restraint absent. Once more reference to the underlying purpose of the subsidiary should become the focus of a court.

The *Minnesota Mining* case seems definitely to validate the admissibility of evidence showing foreign economic and political barriers.[130] Thus a Sherman Act defendant can defend an alleged violation on grounds of "necessary restraint"; viz., even though this was an undue restraint within the meaning of the Sherman Act, still it is not illegal if such restraint is the *sine qua non* of profitable competition in foreign markets. That is, there could be no restraint without something to restrain. This defense is foreclosed if there is a domestic *effect* arising from the foreign combination. The court says that "joint foreign factories like joint domestic price-fixing would be invalid *per se* because they eliminate or restrain competition in the American domestic market."[131] Thus applying the "no profit" test of Judge Wyzanski, and adding to it *per se* illegality if there is a domestic effect, there remains a very small range for the "necessary restraint" doctrine—a defendant must show that alternative export of goods would yield no profit and in addition that the goods produced in foreign subsidiaries do not decrease the flow of American exports. The production of the joint subsidiary must be *additional* and not *alternative* to exports. It is true that a finding of "no profit" would be a *prima facie* indication of no domestic effect, as producers will not export at a loss. But the "no profit" result may arise only after a certain volume of exports, and then the establishment of a foreign subsidiary might reduce exports by supplying the foreign market at a lower cost. Also it might appear that if there are any U.S. exports of a given product then the production of the same product in a foreign subsidiary would in a competitive market reduce the price of the product, including American exports, to the extent of the increase in supply. And if there are no U.S. exports of the product, it would be difficult to envision direct domestic impact from the tolerance of a joint foreign subsidiary. However, if a foreign transaction has no domestic repercussions it is beyond the scope of the Sherman Act.[132] Therefore, Judge Wyzanski's doctrine exhibits an apparent confusion—for either there is a domestic impact and the conduct is illegal *per se* or there is no domestic impact and consequently no regulation of foreign activities.[133] Thus a defendant does not need nor is helped by evidence of foreign trade barriers, and the introduction of such evidence serves

130 The *Holophane* case admits such evidence also.

131 *Minnesota Mining* at 960.

132 The *Alcoa* rule allows the repercussions to consist merely of an impact upon domestic prices, but there must at least be an impact.

133 If such is Judge Wyzanski's intention, then it should be so stated; if it is not, then his reasoning is unclear as it suggests this dilemma.

no justiciable purpose. Insofar as the Wyzanski ruling does have substance it would seem to formulate policy in excess of legislative intentions;[134] recent jurisprudence would justify this kind of statutory expansion-by-construction as the natural consequence of the judicial duty to freely adapt a broad statute to the changing times.[135] The wisdom of authorizing "balancing" combinations is suspect, and judicial endorsement could increase the difficulty of administering the antitrust laws.[136] The *Minnesota Mining* decision does not seem likely to provoke future alterations of the character of "unlawful purpose" unless it is misread. It will remain illegal to form subsidiaries to restrain domestic commerce or American import and exports. However, the decision may yet preclude the development of a doctrine of "necessary restraint" to permit the solution of rare emergencies with the flexibility characterized by the *Appalachian Coals* opinion in a somewhat parallel domestic context.[137]

3. *Patent and Trade-Mark Rights*

We have found that the various patents and processes agreements were made in furtherance of the conspiracy alleged. These agreements, irrespective of their *per se* legality, were instruments designed and intended to accomplish the world-wide allocation of markets; their object was to achieve an unlawful purpose—an illegal restraint of trade prohibited by Section 1 of the Sherman Act. The agreements are illegal because they provided a means for the accomplishment of this purpose and objective. We have also found that these agreements did, in operation, result in restraint of United States trade.

Ryan, J., US v. ICI, 100 F. Supp. 504 (SDNY 1951).

Courts have traditionally had a more difficult time condemning a patent scheme as an illegal instrument of an "unlawful purpose."[138] There is a basic conflict between encouraging the exchange of patent information and seeking to guard against patent infringement on one side of the fence, and maintaining a free market on the other side. Patent protection is a policy objective, as compared with the policy neutrality of the other inherently legal devices used to obtain an "unlawful pur-

[134] Judge Rifkind has said, if a private corporation claims that a cartel is necessary to do business in a cartelized world this is a subject for legislative, not judicial, revision. Courts cannot grant Sherman Act immunity. US v. National Lead Co., 63 F. Supp. 513, 526 (SDNY 1945).

[135] Jerome Frank among others has developed this point of view.

[136] Even if the burden was upon the defendant it would still raise an imposing obstacle to the prosecution if a "straw man" defense of this nature was attempted.

[137] Appalachian Coals Inc. v. US 288 US 344 (1933).

[138] Cf. Theodore J. Kreps, "Experience with Unilateral Action Towards International Cartels," in Edwards, *op.cit.*, note 18.

pose."[139] Therefore, to find against the patentee in the interests of Sherman Act enforcement requires a sacrifice of such protection. American courts have proceeded with such reticence in this area that commentary has described the patent pool as a "loophole" or "blind spot" of the antitrust laws.[140] However, in view of the *ICI, National Lead,* and *General Electric* cases, this criticism retains only an historical interest. In all these opinions the judges, with some expression of regret, declared that the rights afforded a patentee neither included nor permitted a privilege to violate the antitrust laws. The inherent legality of patent exchange plans is lost if there is dedication to an "unlawful purpose."

In the *National Lead* case, which is typical of the category, it was found that National Lead and Du Pont dominated the domestic titanium industry and choked off imports through the device of an international patent pool.[141] The exclusive operation in the area allocated by a cartel is obtained by a registration of all patents by the territorial monopolist. Competition is regulated by licenses influencing production and pricing and by refusing licenses to nonconformers or by a complete refusal to license. Competitors face the expense and danger of infringement actions by the established patentee. This technique was used by General Electric to dominate another facet of the titanium industry.[142] Courts have encountered difficulty in decreeing a remedy "that will fit the crime," but is not so severe as to completely destroy the value of the patent.[143]

Many of the patent agreements designed to reach an illegal end include very complicated licensing schemes. An attempt by American courts to disrupt the operation of illegal licensing arrangements caused a dramatic sequel to the *ICI* case.[144] A British court forbade ICI to default in its performance of a contract with a third party, and thereby required ICI to disobey the American decree.[145]

In the *General Electric Titanium* case the defendant used basic patent control as the anchor for a comprehensive body of restraints that managed to tie in future patents and unpatented products.[146] The court declared the patent scheme illegal after examining the reasonableness of the restrictions, upon the express authority of the *Standard Oil* "rule of reason." It stressed the evidence of active abuse, distinguishing the *Alcoa* emphasis upon the evidence of monopoly power, invoking the

[139] Patents are sought to be protected by legislation in order to foster invention.
[140] Edwards, note 128.
[141] US v. National Lead Co. 63 F. Supp. 513 (SDNY 1945), modified and affirmed, 332 US 319 (1947).
[142] US v. General Electric Co., 80 F. Supp. 989 (1948).
[143] See *ICI, GE* titanium, and *GE* lamp remedies.
[144] British Nylon Spinners Ltd. v. ICI Ltd., 1 Ch 19 (1952).
[145] But see Judge Ryan's dictum in *ICI* that nothing in his opinion is intended to contravene obligations under foreign law.
[146] 80 F. Supp. 989 (SDNY 1948).

theory that courts are more willing in the patent context to find a "lawful monopoly" that has been "thrust" upon a defendant.[147] But GE's record of questionable practices indicated an "unlawful purpose" that tainted with illegality the various patent control devices.

In summary, it can be said that patent exchanges between major companies are lawful so long as they are reasonably ancillary to some legitimate business purpose, such as the acceleration of technological progress. But patents used to implement conspiracies in violation of the Sherman Act are likely to be declared illegal. The most common techniques of misuse are to include in the agreement covering the exchange of patents restrictions beyond the scope of the legally protected patent right, a tie-in clause covering unpatented subject matter, and a clause assigning all future patents to the signatories.[148]

Trademarks present the same general problems, and have evoked similar judicial reactions, and therefore do not require an extended separate consideration. Section 33(b) (7) of the Trade-Mark Act specifically forbids the use of a trademark as a device to violate antitrust laws. In the *GE lamp* case a District Court found that the trademark Mazda was used as an instrument in aid of violating the Sherman Act; a similar finding was made in the *Timken* case. Thus a trademark is granted protection if it is not used to obtain an "unlawful purpose"—it is primarily a way of distinguishing products of different producers and of thus preserving goodwill. Unlike a patent, a trademark has no right to monopoly; the owner of a trademark has the *exclusive* right to use a certain brand name, and that is all.[149]

4. Export Associations. Combinations of domestic exporters are authorized by the Webb Act.[150] These combinations are called "associations" and are given a partial exemption from the Sherman Act. Their operations are subject to Federal Trade Commission regulations and to antitrust prosecution if they act to restrain domestic commerce or the exports of domestic competitors. Thus antitrust immunity is lost if the association becomes just another device to attain an "unlawful purpose," and "unlawful purpose" here is defined in a similar way as in other foreign trade contexts.[151] As with claims of sovereign immunity, the principal task of the court becomes the discovery of judicial techniques for enjoining activities that are superficially legal *per se*—the form of

[147] *Id.* at 1015.
[148] 42 *Trade Mark Reporter* 3-32 (Jan. 1952).
[149] For a trade-mark action under the Lanham Act see Steele v. Bulova Watch Co., 344 US 280 (1952). This case also expresses the contemporary Supreme Court attitude toward extraterritorial jurisdiction. It shows clearly a movement away from the *Banana* days—cf. "A Half Century of Jurisdictional Development: From Bananas to Watches," 7 *Miami Law Review* 400-08 (April 1953).
[150] See Annex C, part 4.
[151] Except that domestic competitors for export purpose may combine to control export prices and supply.

legality must be discarded or limited if the substance of activity is the effectuation of an "unlawful purpose." There is only one important case, the Alkali opinion, that deals with defining the distinctions between legal and illegal Webb Act conduct, and so the law in this area remains unsettled. A potential offense exists, however, whenever an association's actions are accompanied by a depressive impact upon the domestic economy.

The government in its *Alkali* complaint sought an equity injunction enjoining undue restraints of two Webb Act associations, thirteen member corporations, and one British conspirator.[152] Four offenses were charged—restricting American imports and exports, eliminating competition, fixing domestic prices, and curtailing production. Alkasso, a Webb Act Association acting as the exclusive foreign selling agent for the major American alkali producers, was described as the principal defendant. Foreign co-conspirators of the cartel agreement who did no business in the United States were not joined as defendants. The court decided that there were two levels of inquiry—was the alleged conduct illegal under the Sherman Act? If yes, was it exempted by the Webb Act?

Defendant Alkasso participated in a foreign cartel that sought to divide the world market. The court invoked Section 5 of the Webb Act that condemned restraints upon domestic commerce wherever committed. The intent and effect of the cartel agreement was to insulate the American market from foreign competitors.[153] The court's evaluation of the evidence led to attributing the small volume of imports to the cartel agreement and not to the economic unfeasibility of importing alkalis into the United States market.[154]

The opinion is especially significant for its statutory construction of the Webb Act. The Webb Act does not authorize an association to join a world cartel—its purpose was to enable American exporters to better compete, not to better restrain.[155] Federal Trade Commission interpretation of the Webb Act (here the Silver Letter) has no binding force in court.[156]

Alkasso also acted to eliminate domestic nonassociation exporters from competition. Members agreed to make Alkasso their exclusive agent and any production in excess of a member's allocated portion of the cartel-decreed quota for the US market was bought up by Alkasso. Purchasers who bought from a seller other than Alkasso were blacklisted from further dealings with Alkasso.[157] Alkasso did everything it

---

[152] US v. US Alkali Export Association, 86 F. Supp. 59 (SDNY 1949).
[153] *Id.* at 72-73.
[154] *Id.* at 72.

[155] See Annex C, discussion of Webb Act objectives.
[156] *Id.* at 66ff.
[157] *Id.*

could to gain the full export quota assigned to the United States market by the cartel.

Alkasso also was found guilty of facilitating the fixing of the domestic price of caustic ash. The court determined this result largely from the stable domestic prices contrasted to the volatile prices in foreign markets. The strangeness of this price behavior was accentuated by the failure of the United States price to drop after a huge increase in supply was made possible by the invention of the electrolytic process of manufacturing caustic ash. Further factors helping the court to discern a domestic intent and effect included the greater export of caustic ash compared with other alkalis, the practice by Alkasso of keeping the domestic surplus in a huge warehouse, there awaiting the discovery of profitable disposal opportunities, and the preferential treatment accorded caustic-ash supports by excessive overage allocation.

The court enjoined the enforcement of the contracts that made these restraints operative. Thus it struck a blow against the export association as an antitrust escape vehicle. And it carried into judicial pronouncement the legislative intent not to permit domestic restraints to flow from a Webb Act association. Because Alkasso so flagrantly violated the Webb Act, a finding of guilt was easy. The subtler contours of the extent of Webb Act tolerance cannot be suggested until more difficult cases come before the courts.[158]

5. *Sovereign Immunity and Acts of State.*[159] Private industry has sought to utilize the shelter of sovereign immunity to exempt itself from antitrust regulation.[160] There is doubt whether immunity is accorded to organizations engaged in commercial activity even if they are categorized as sovereign. Courts have demonstrated a decided reluctance to extend the scope of the sovereign immunity doctrine beyond its traditional applications to the activities of foreign diplomats. American judicial opinion, one imagines, would be adverse to encouraging government ownership of economic resources.[161] Foreign capital, that relies upon sovereign immunity to excuse noncompetitive behavior, can be expected to encounter strong resistance. There is very little significant case data thus far reported.

The *Banana* case did seem to suggest the availability of an "act of state" umbrella. In that prosecution, the defendant, a private corporation, had induced the governments of Costa Rica and Panama to act as its agents to oppress the property of the plaintiff corporation. Justice

---

[158] For a more recent consideration of the antitrust status of a Webb Act association, the majority opinion disallowing exemption from the Sherman Act, see United States v. Concentrated Phosphate Export Ass'n Inc. *et al.* 392 US 199 (1968).

[159] See pp. 274-75, particularly note 47.
[160] See Annex A and C.
[161] Cf. Annex A and C, for explanation of adversion felt by a capitalist economy for being a party to the encouragement of any kind of industrial socialization.

Holmes, for the Supreme Court, relied upon the inability of a plaintiff to complain about acts of a foreign sovereign within the territory of that sovereign, and the opinion made no effort to pierce the formal veil of sovereignty and attribute the acts to the defendant, as principal by resort to an agency analogy.[162] This decision, because of its alternative holding—no application of the Sherman Act to extraterritorial events —was not a strong precedent upon which to base an interposition of an acts of state defense. Its spirit did seem to regard the acts of a sovereign in an economic sphere beyond subsequent challenge. But here the acts were all performed within the territory of the sovereign and they were the kinds of acts—police power—that sovereigns are traditionally accorded the right to perform unmolested. Redress against such a sovereign would ordinarily proceed through diplomatic, rather than judicial, channels.

In the *Potash* cartel proceedings against a French government owned potash producer, the court went quite far to disregard the form and to hold the defendant liable as a private defendant.[163] The "public" corporation was owned and operated by the government. And if this kind of a defendant was found to be "private" it hardly seems possible to qualify as "public," and receive an antitrust exemption. But the court left alive the ghost, at least, of potential immunity, by explicitly basing its holding upon the nonsovereign status of the defendant. And so by negative inference, the attainment of such status, difficult as that may be, carries with it immunity or at least leaves the question open.

But the court did seem to rely heavily upon a letter from the Secretary of State advising the court that the executive branch felt that government agencies engaged in ordinary mercantile activity were not entitled to sovereign immunity. The feeling of the judge in the *Potash* case was that the scope of immunity was primarily defined by the executive branch, and that the judiciary was bound to follow expressions of executive discretion in this area. Obviously this latter avenue to a no-immunity holding has more sweeping implications, and would, if adopted by later courts, completely foreclose the sovereign immunity defense to "government" defendants engaged in economic activity that was normally performed by private concerns in our economy.

Similar considerations apply with regard to the closely related doctrine of acts of state. As with sovereign immunity, acts of state are within general limits accorded universal recognition—thus international law comity bids all states honor and recognize the validity of an act *officially performed* in any one state. Thus Justice Holmes regarded the acts, sanctioned by the sovereign, in the *Banana* case. The decision to defer to foreign sovereigns presents many international law problems

[162] 213 US 511, 513 (1909).
[163] See note 47 for facts, US v. Deutsches Kalisyndikat Gesellschaft, 31 F. 2d 199 (1929).

beyond the scope of this chapter, but if seems evident that courts should regard with a measure of "realism" foreign acts-of-state in the economic realm, or risk the creation of a new escape valve from the operation of antitrust regulation.[164]

The *Swiss Watchmakers* case dealt with the same kind of contention: namely, that the defendants were in some sense acting to fulfill, or at least to conform with, the policies of the foreign country, in this case Switzerland. The trial judge used some appropriate language of limitation: "If, of course, the defendants' activities had been required by Swiss law, this court could indeed do nothing. An American court would have under such circumstances no right to condemn the governmental activity of another sovereign nation."[165] Deference, then, is limited to situations of established legal compulsion; mere conformity with the policies or the customs of the foreign state is not sufficient to earn the defendant corporation an exemption from the normal sweep of American antitrust regulation.[166] This kind of dividing line seems to compromise sensibly between the functional interdependence of international business activity and the territorial independence of sovereign states in a decentralized legal system. At the same time, the problems of application are formidable as it is not so obvious to determine what constitutes "compulsion" in a specific instance; it is also necessary for a domestic court to assess whether the intended sphere of compulsion is within the jurisdictional competence of a foreign state.

So long as the regulatory impulse remains strong, it is likely that American courts will seek to manipulate and strictly construe international law doctrines to prevent the utilization of this means to accomplish an "unlawful purpose" within the antitrust framework. The pressure will be strong to disregard the formal appearance of government action whenever there has been established a restraint of American commerce.

6. The Potential Exclusion of American Competitors from Foreign Markets. American courts do use the nationality principle to protect American competitors from foreign restraints. A particular objective of this facet of regulation is to avoid a depressive effect upon American exports through noncompetitive behavior.

[164] There is an obvious comparison between the policy issues of deference for the expropriation and the extraterritorial antitrust subject matter. Both kinds of issues are generally within the sphere of "legitimate diversity," but the jurisdictional justification in the antitrust area seems stronger because of the interdependence of the foreign and domestic economies. For a more complete policy analysis in the expropriate setting see Falk, *The Role of Domestic Courts in the International Legal Order*, Syracuse, Syracuse University Press, 1964, pp. 21-52, 64-114. See also Chapters XIII, XIV.

[165] United States v. Watchmakers of Switzerland Information Centre, Inc., U.S. District Court, Southern District (1962), Trade Cases para. 70, 600 at 77, 456.

[166] But cf. Anthony W. Graziano, Jr., "Foreign Governmental Compulsion as a Defense in United States Antitrust Law," 7 *Virginia Journal of International Law* (#2, April 1967), 100-45, at 147.

Branch v. Federal Trade Commission[167] involved the validity of an FTC order requiring the defendant to desist from alleged misrepresentations in foreign markets. All the noxious acts occurred in Latin America where Branch maintained a correspondence school. The offense consisted of the fraudulent inducement of customers through exaggerated claims about the status of the school. The court found that the FTC has the power to prescribe competitive standards of operation, even though all acts occur outside the United States. The declared beneficiaries of such regulation were American competitors whose goodwill suffered from the defendant's evil practices; the injured Latin American customers were told to seek redress in their own courts, and preventing injury to them was specifically stated not to have been a factor in formulating the court's decision. Again the "unlawful purpose" of the defendant to restrain American commerce, and nothing else, was the touchstone of decision by a court seeking to regulate foreign trade.

Annex A—Foreign Trade

The subject matter of foreign trade concerns export and import activities, or more broadly, any events that influence the flow of goods and services across national frontiers. This definition seeks to embrace the operation of the American corporation abroad, the foreign corporation in the United States, and, in fact, any series of acts, foreign or domestic, committed with an intent to effect or having an actual effect upon the character or extent of our foreign trade.

Foreign trade regulation by the United States Government is premised upon the desirability, despite certain exceptions, of sustaining competitive conditions.[168] Antitrust control particularly seeks to prevent the operations of foreign commerce from introducing noncompetitive forces into the domestic economy.[169] Domestic standards of competition are applied to foreign corporations doing business in the United States upon the authority of the territorial principle due to the intrinsic policy of forbidding noncompetitive practices and the justice of applying the

[167] 141 F. 2d 31 (1944).

[168] Exceptions concern various artificial components of US trade policy. The most notable noncompetitive component is the export association structure fostered by the Webb-Pomerene Act, to be discussed below. Other such elements are tariffs, subsidies, duties, and such nonlegal policies as the failure to enforce existing law in certain areas or at certain times. A glamorous example was the failure to bring suit or apply remedies during World War II for Sherman Act convictions; see for instance the *Alcoa* case, 148 F. 2d 416 (1954).

[169] Of course, without a free world market it is impossible to attain a truly competitive domestic market, as the artificial prices in a foreign market exert an influence upon the allocation of factors in the free domestic market. This occurs whenever a foreign material, subject to monopoly control, is desired for production or consumption at home, equally when an American producer alters his production to take advantage of monopoly prices abroad, or whenever some element of production or its substitute is subject to monopoly control abroad.

same standard of regulation to all participants in the domestic market. The degree of actual enforcement depends upon a multitude of economic, and sometimes noneconomic factors—the extent of domestic competition in the specific area of production; the amount of foreign business conducted within the United States; the extent of violation, the need or desire for the products of the foreign producer; the condition of the nation—peace, war, depression, prosperity, Republican, Democratic; the nation of the violator—ally or enemy; and so on.[170] An American corporation that does business in the United States and also abroad tends to be more strictly regulated than the American corporation that does all its business abroad.[171] This is because it is operationally impracticable to apply two regulatory standards to the same functional unit as the foreign and domestic aspects of a business are interrelated, and cannot be mechanically separated; and thus the tolerance of noncompetitive practices outside of the United States would inevitably lead to their introduction into the United States. However these considerations do not apply to an American corporation, operating exclusively abroad, which is beyond the normal scope of American jurisdiction:[172] its operations do not as directly affect the American economy nor are they as likely to injure American competitors; and further the regulation of these events that occurred outside the United States would be expensive, inconvenient, and inconclusive;[173] the impropriety of declaring illegal acts legal acts where done; the desire to encourage foreign investment, the absence of legislative coverage of commerce of American corporations on foreign markets; these factors operate to minimize the quantity and quality of antitrust restraint in this area. Vigorous regulation is often urged whenever an American business abroad enters into embracing restrictive arrangements with foreign or other American corporations.[174] Foreign corporations, not doing

---

170 Each factor raises a series of subsidiary questions. The need for a specific product may raise the alternative policies of fostering domestic production by excluding the foreign producer, instead of making concessions to the practices of the foreign producer. The condition of the nation—peace, hot or cold war, prosperity, depression, and the economic philosophy of the dominant political party are particularly significant in determining the shape of solution adopted to meet any monopolistic encroachment upon the American market.

171 The issues raised by such an arrangement is found in the discussion of the *Timken* case, pp. 288-91.

172 Cf. p. 269 for treatment of the exceptional nature of resorting to the nationality of the individual as the basis of

jurisdiction in Anglo-American countries where the emphasis has always been upon the territorial principle. An additional problem is the classification of businesses abroad—should there be any distinction between subsidiaries and departments of American corporations? To what extent will foreign investment be discouraged by forcing corporations to be governed by the canons of competition in a noncompetitive context?

173 The difficulty of obtaining evidence and witnesses is obvious.

174 Cf., e.g., Sigmund Timberg, "Antitrust and Foreign Trade," 48 *Northwestern University Law Review* 411-26 (Sept.-Oct. 1953); or Wendell Berge, *Cartels: Challenge to a Free World*, Washington, D.C., Public Affairs Press, 1944.

business in the United States, have only been *directly* regulated when they act with an intent to restrain American commerce and there is, in fact, a restraint.[175] The effectiveness of such extraterritorial regulation depends mainly upon the ability of American courts to reach assets or to enjoin operations of the defendant, enabling enforcement. It is dangerous regulation that evokes angry protests and threatens reprisals against American commerce. Such regulation is normally termed extraterritorial, and thus contradicts the traditional insistence of America upon territorial jurisdiction in other contexts.[176]

After this preliminary examination of the areas of foreign trade subject to antitrust regulation, we proceed to a specification of the objectives of antitrust regulation in the foreign trade context. This is a necessary prerequisite to an intelligent evaluation of its application. It is convenient to cluster objectives into noneconomic and economic categories.[177] For purposes of this chapter the body of antitrust legislation will be treated as having accurately incorporated the objectives that stimulated its enactment.[178]

We look to judicial interpretation, legislative intent, and analysis of consequences to learn the basic impact of the antitrust laws upon our economy. No distinction will be attempted between *the objectives* of domestic, as opposed to foreign antitrust legislation, at this time.[179] Mr. Chief Justice Hughes told the public that the economic purposes of the Sherman Act are "to prevent undue restraints of interstate commerce, to maintain its appropriate freedom in the public interest, to afford protection from the subversive or coercive influences of monopolistic endeavor."[180] That is, the thrust of the Sherman Act is directed toward the prevention of "undue restraints" upon competition. Perfect competition is not an ideal.[181] A moderately competitive economy best

[175] Cf. the famous formula of Judge Learned Hand, 148 F. 2d 416, 445. Judge Hand also mentions the possible, though yet undecided, right of American courts to hear cases where an intent alone or an effect alone is charged to the foreign corporation.

[176] Cf. *Lotus* case, dissent of John Basset Moore; also Moore's report on *The Cutting Case*, reported in Briggs, *op.cit.*, pp. 571-80. Both discussions espouse standard American doctrine of strict territoriality.

[177] The tone and some of the material of this brief discussion of antitrust objectives is derived from Eugene V. Rostow's article "The New Sherman Act: A Positive Instrument of Progress," 14 *University of Chicago Law Review* 567-600 (June 1947).

[178] This avoids the necessity of discussing the compatibility means and ends in the existing legislation. Also cf. discussion of the statutes available for the control of foreign trade restraints.

[179] This does not mean to blur the distinction, later to be stressed, between the domestic and foreign application and administration of the Sherman Act. Also see discussion of Webb-Pomerene Act for an important distinction in prescribed behavior standards; and see Judge Frank's dissent in Adams-Mitchell Co. v. Cambridge Distribution Co., 189 F. 2d 913, 930 (2d Cir. 1951), for an expression of the unusual view that there is no manifested objective to proscribe restraints among importers.

[180] Appalachian Coals v. United States, 288 US 344, 360 (1933).

[181] Perfect competition is a textbook fantasy. But even the highly competitive

allocates resources in accord with consumer preferences and national needs, without sacrificing business cycle control, conservation programs, or freedom of investment. Further competition inspires invention and efficiency, it promotes optimum scale business organization and efficiency, it promotes optimum scale business organization, and creates a closer relationship between production and profit. More important than these positive advantages of competition is the prevention of noncompetitive abuses. Antitrust legislation seeks to prevent and punish such abuses. Monopoly power tempts the producer to limit production and raise prices to the point of most profitable utilization. Depending on the inelasticity of demand, the price may be much higher than the normal accommodation of production and cost to produce a "fair" price that occurs in a competitive market. The virtual absence of competitors discourages many technological improvements of process and product. For example, why should a tire monopolist increase the durability of his rubber? Exclusion of competitors limits investment opportunities, and thus may accentuate cyclical movements by reducing future expenditures, employment, and purchasing power. Economies of scale are encouraged in a competitive economy, but there is a tendency toward excessive, uneconomical size in noncompetitive operations. Judge Learned Hand observes that "[m]any people believe that possession of unchallenged economic power deadens initiative, discourages thrift, and depresses energy; that immunity from competition is narcotic . . . that the spur of constant stress is necessary to counteract an inevitable disposition to let well enough alone."[182] Important monopoly power tends to rigidify the economy, making it less responsive to "pump-priming," "deficit financing," and other efforts of the central government to avoid or confine business depressions and unemployment. A noncompetitive economy produces few goods of a lower quality at a higher price in a depression-vulnerable market.[183] Thus, antitrust legislation has *the economic goal* of avoiding monopoly and fostering moderate competition.

We turn now to examine the political consequences of the Sherman Act's tendency to resist concentrations and incentives to concentrate wealth.[184] There are special relationships of cartels to political issues

markets that do exist are increasingly subject to regulation. See John Maynard Keynes, *The General Theory of Employment, Interest, and Money*, New York, Harcourt, 1936, who has so influentially advocated tampering with competitive forces to maintain employment.

[182] See US v. Alcoa, 148 F. 2d 416, 427 (1945). The documentation for the propositions made in this general discussion of the economic facts underlying the antitrust laws can be found in the first eight

pages of E. V. Rostow's article cited in note 177. Also see US v. Columbia Steel 334 US 495, J. Douglas, dissent at 534.

[183] The treatment of international monopoly is saved for a summary of the claims and abuses of cartels.

[184] The incentive to concentrate wealth is usually motivated by the desire to act in restraint, and by the effective outlawing of action in restraint the incentive itself is removed.

that will be discussed more appropriately in connection with cartels. Here, we are concerned with the political objectives of the antitrust philosophy that are relevant to an appraisal of the application of such regulation to foreign trade restraints. The main antitrust effort is to prevent and discourage the accumulation of economic power, with its concomitant political influence, inconsistent with the pluralistic principles of a democratic society. The preservation of democracy is best guaranteed by a dispersal of wealth so that no single individual, group, or even government gains enough power to suppress others directly or indirectly by legislative favor. The intimate relationship between aggregations of economic and political power was expensively demonstrated in Germany and Italy, and presently reveals itself in several countries with highly centralized control over economic activity. Individual freedom has never flourished in an atmosphere in which the individual has become but an animate tool of the giant producer. His standard of living is suppressed, freedom of opportunity is curtailed, and the mass tends to be exploited, in the Marxist sense, by the few. The rationale of self-preservation has led the dominant capitalist elements in American society to accept certain restraints upon competitive excess, and the antitrust law is among the chief implements that have been used to harmonize the inevitable clustering of power inherent in modern industrial operations with the continued growth of individual freedom and opportunity.[185] These considerations apply with greater force to the foreign economic operations of American buying and selling, as in the world arena national security itself becomes another pawn in the grasp of the cartelist. The horrors of war have been often brought on by callous business aspirations that disregard human welfare to expand the market demand for a product. Correlatively the failure of the monopolist to produce to market capacity or to develop the best product leads to nonoptimum production in times of war when demand is unlimited. Finally, when people are free to become wealthy by the exercise of competitive initiative they are less tempted to revolt against political institutions. Thus democratic government requires many, rather than a few, centers of economic strength, with none so powerful as to be able to abuse the welfare of society. Vigorously enforced antitrust laws give some protection against such abuse from domestic and foreign business, and thus tend to stabilize the internal political framework and to strengthen the economy against

---

[185] Other implements, automatic or not, are the increased strength of other groups in society to balance the power of big industry; the more active role of government in the functioning of the economy by possessing the power to redistribute the balance of industrial power (e.g., use of surplus equipment from World War II to foster competition in the aluminum industry by helping Kaiser and Reynolds), but the rise of the national security state in the 1950's and 1960's casts grave doubt on the American experience.

external threats by helping create conditions for more and better production.

There may arise a danger of a tendency to foster the concentration of foreign economic and political power arising from the process of co-erced decentralization—namely, that foreign capital will be assimilated into government by any of a number of devices so as to obtain immunity from antitrust prosecution. This facilitates authoritarian political conse-quences by aggregating the control factors necessary to regiment a so-ciety. And authoritarian government, besides being opposed to American ethical and religious values, tends to be ambitious extraterritorially, thus causing antagonisms that have flared into costly wars in recent decades. War is a far-fetched consequence of even zealous antitrust reg-ulation, but this possible causal chain is sufficiently undesirable to be worth consideration even if its occurrence is seemingly remote.

Annex B—Cartels

Fulfilling the opportunities of world trade requires at least some con-trol over the activities of cartels.[186] Foreign trade, carried on in a free market, results in a greater variety and quantity of goods more cheaply available to all participants. It confers these benefits by securing more economical world production through its stimulation of an increasing division of labor, and consequent specialization.

Thus a nation that does not have to produce all the goods needed upon the domestic market may concentrate production upon those products that are most economical to produce either by reason of tech-nological advantages, availability of the particular resources, factor cost location and nature of markets, or a combination of these and other factors. And such specialization will lead to a surplus beyond domestic needs that can be exported in exchange for the goods that were more costly to produce at home. This process results in more total production being sold, because of the increased supply, at a lower unit cost; such an increase tends to promote a higher standard of living for all, provided there exists reasonable distribution among members of society of the fruits of this economic gain. This analysis applies the fundamental eco-nomic principle of a free society by allowing market preferences to allo-cate labor, capital, and resources to those uses that are most profitable in terms of total consumer demand and supply. It must be enlarged to incorporate non-economic welfare, and so production must not only be guided by economic factor allocation, but as well, by considerations of

[186] Cf. p. 272 for the economic and political justification of competition. See also Berge, *Cartels: Challenge to a Free World, op.cit. supra,* note 25, in which the author calls cartels "the greatest obsta-cle" to taking advantage of economic op-portunity in the post-World War II world.

human dignity, national security and political instability. Thus inefficient domestic production of a product more cheaply available by trade, is justified if the foreign supply is insecure. Obviously during a war or period of war tension political factor allocation is predominant. There are certain other more or less subsidiary criteria of factor allocation.

An increasingly important factor is the humanitarian considerations such as health, social service, and emergency relief which constitute an "uneconomic" influence upon allocation.

Foreign trade operations can thus be evaluated from this dual perspective of what we will call the principles of political and economic factor allocation. What I mean by these principles is indicated by a concrete illustration. An extreme instance of political factor allocation was the costly dedication of resources by the United States to develop synthetic rubber during the Second World War, a time when cheap Malayan rubber was unavailable due to Japanese occupation. The principle of economic factor allocation is more complicated to illustrate—products X and Y are both needed in countries A and B; it costs A \$1 to make X, \$5 to make Y, while B can make either X or Y for \$2; if there is no trade and each country devotes \$100 to equal production of X and Y, then A would produce 50 units of X, 10 units of Y, and B would produce 25 units of X and 25 of Y; with complete specialization A could produce 100 units of X, B, 50 units of Y; trading half their production of each good, A would have 50 units of X, 25 units of Y; while B would now have 50 units of X, retaining 25 units of Y. Therefore, trade based upon specialization benefits each country.

Cartels, restraining economic and political allocation, by artificially eliminating opportunities for factor utilization limit the benefits of world trade. Berge, for example, shows how the American desire to allocate resources to develop synthetic rubber was prevented by cartel agreements, and so with the coming of war imperiled national security.

Optimum economic allocation suffers whenever there is a restraint upon the free competitive use of men, money, or resources.[187] For instance, a territorial division of markets that restricts foreign trade in a product eliminates the possibility of taking advantage of specialization opportunities. Plainly there is no purpose in expanding production in country A when export to B cannot take place. The stimulus to divide up markets is the desire to increase profits by restricting supply and raising prices. This means, in very simplified form, that the noncartelized consumer is paying as much or more money for less goods, leaving the cartelist with a proportionately increased profit margin.

This section discusses the degree of antitrust regulation applied to the

187 See, supra, the relationship between competition and dispersal of wealth.

activities of cartels. The Sherman Act applies, apparently, only to restraints by foreign and national companies upon imports to and exports from the American market.[188] Thus a cartel that operates exclusively in foreign markets and does not exclude American exports, has not been subject to regulation even though a foreign-domiciled American corporation is a participant.[189] But a conspiracy to restrain American exports or imports can certainly be punished by the Sherman Act if the occurrence of an integral overt act is found within the United States.[190] But Judge L. Hand in the *Alcoa* case finds that a Canadian corporation, Limited, had violated the Sherman Act when it agreed with foreign producers in Switzerland to curtail its exports to the United States.[191] Limited was found to have perpetrated, with intent, an actual restraint upon American imports. Judge Hand explicitly leaves moot the power to regulate in situations where there is only an intent to restrain or where there is an unintended but actual restraint upon American imports or exports.

It is also necessary to seek the standard imposed upon foreign corporations doing business in the United States. Clearly a foreign corporation is subject to regulation if it unreasonably restrains business on the domestic market. To what extent a foreign cartel can do business in the United States is moot, and specific problems will be dealt with in relation to jurisdiction. Noneconomic considerations are peculiarly relevant in this context, where antitrust regulation by the exclusion of the cartel may cause a considerable diminution of the market supply of a rare and crucial product.[192]

---

[188] There is no reported case that I have seen that seeks to do anything more than prevent a restraint upon the export or import trade of the United States.

[189] Berge suggests regulation of the American participant on the theory that few cartels could survive without the co-operation of the American members of the market. Such jurisdiction is clearly legitimate under international law; it is treated under the doctrinal denomination, nationality principle, but it has rarely been invoked outside of a traditional area of crimes.

[190] Prior to very recent cases, the Supreme Court clung to the occurrence of some overt act within the United States upon which to base a finding that a foreign conspiracy violated the Sherman Act. And to this effect see US v. Pacific and Arctic Co., 228 US 87 (1913); Thomsen v. Cayser, 243 US 66 (1916); U.S. v. Sisal Sales Corp., 274 US 268 (1927). This reliance upon an overt act within the United States is derived from a curious interpretation of the authority of American Banana v. United Fruit Co., 213 US 347, 355 (1909); commented upon in 31 *Texas Law Review* 493, 499 (1953).

[191] The government in its brief alleged the commission of certain trifling acts within the United States—a conversation between the owner of Alcoa and Limited and a refusal of Limited to sell to Bausch. Limited was not doing any significant business in the United States in the normal sense, as even its few exports were sold FOB the loading point in Canada, legal title passing then to the American buyer. Limited did not engage in distribution activities in the United States, rather American buyers came to Canada. The court found for the government on the theory that the Swiss agreement to limit exports to the United States intended and actually affected the price on the American market, and made no attempt to justify jurisdiction upon acts done by the defendant in the United States.

[192] Of course a crisis could be averted by Government buying from excluded cartels and reselling to private consumers. But

Foreign cartels are resourceful at circumventing the antitrust laws. Cartel power and organization usually survive, perhaps in altered form, unilateral antitrust action. Some cartels have great strength, political as well as economic, and so are in a position to gain at least toleration, and sometimes protection and encouragement, from a foreign government. Many nefarious cartel activities can be insulated from the reach of antitrust jurisdiction by merely having the government render performance and claim shelter from the "sovereign acts and immunities" doctrine.[193] And to the extent that foreign governments are bent upon evading the Sherman Act, local industry could be nationalized. Thus the Sherman Act would encourage the creation of even greater centralization in foreign industry if its application were to become oppressive to other nations.

Depending upon the character of the market, the strength of the cartel, the importance of the American producer, the attitude and power of the foreign government, the accessibility of foreign assets sufficient to enforce a decree, and countless other factors, the overall consequence of a particular instance of antitrust regulation will be revealed. A very significant factor in evaluating cartel prosecution is a determination of who the real victim of the action will be and thus anticipate the effect on foreign trade. Often the only effect is to exclude the American producer from the cartel, which in turn may reduce U.S. foreign trade, or it may actually increase the volume of trade by causing the disintegration of the entire cartel. Of course, this is a complex undertaking involving a balancing of the long and short run impact on trade, the resentment of the victim, the possibility of protest and reprisal, and reference to the previously introduced noneconomic factors. As Berge says on page 18 of *Cartels: Challenge to a Free World*: "It is doubtful, indeed, whether any major international cartel can effectively control world markets without the participation and cooperation of the American segments of the industry. There is a real question whether foreign cartels can long survive in many industries if American cooperation is not extended to them."

A cartel is here defined as any business arrangement between two or more participants that has the purpose or effect of restraining competition in world trade.[194] This definition seeks to embrace any agreement,

---

this tends to centralize economic power in the government, thus frustrating the decentralization objective of the Sherman Act.

[193] In US v. Deutsches Kalsyndikat Gesellschaft, 31 F. 2d 199 (1929) the defendant raised the defense of sovereign immunity—the court found for the plaintiff on the grounds that the corporation was a separate legal entity that could not be absorbed into the French government

for the purpose of granting immunity for illegal acts committed in foreign jurisdictions.

[194] Also see definitions of cartel on page 1, Corwin D. Edwards, *Economic and Political Aspects of International Cartels*, a monograph published in 1944 for the Kilgore Committee on Military Affairs of the U.S. Senate, and see Fritz Machlup's similar definition in an essay "The Nature of the International Problem," in Corwin D.

whether formal or informal, and any participant, whether public, private, or somewhere in between. It also seeks to focus upon the actual restraint of foreign trade, rather than upon the structure, domestic or international, of the restrictive organization.[195] Excluded from this definition is the purely domestic monopoly that seeks to restrain competition only within the nation of its operation, but does not try to control imports or exports.[196] It is useful to differentiate the restrictive action of a combine in which participants, in addition to a common business purpose, also have affiliations of ownership.

Cartels use a variety of restraints to attain their objective of market control. The most frequent instrument of restraint used by cartel members operating in a common market is to resort to some form of price fixing. The level at which the price will be fixed depends on the degree of market control,[197] the elasticity of demand,[198] the ethics of the cartelists, and their anticipation of the possibility and effect of regulation.

There are many variables that influence the tenability and character of a cartel arrangement within a given area of economic activity: the number and size of firms; the homogeneity of the product; the elasticity of supply and demand; the importance of patents in the production process; the actual or potential ownership affiliation between the important firms; the attitude of the relevant governments; the geographical dispersion of markets and producers; the health or disease of the world economy—combination is more frequent and regulation less stringent in bad times. The relationship between the governments whose corporate citizens seek cartel relations; the ability to exclude potential competitors by raw material dominance; the amount of capital necessary to enable efficient production; the ability to squeeze nonmembers out —depends mainly on strength and on the proportion of fixed costs, etc.

Cartels often seek to divide the world market. Such division is usually organized by one or more of these three principles of allocation: territory, function, or technology. Territorial market division works well for the cartel with nearly complete market dominance by a small number

---

Edwards, ed., *A Cartel Policy for the United Nations*, New York, Columbia University Press, 1945, p. 3.

[195] This definition avoids a kind of semantic preference found in Justice Department writings limiting a cartel to a multi-nation arrangement, in order to avoid the necessity of classifying the Webb-Pomerene export associations as cartels. There seems to be confusion created by the resort to this euphemism; see also George W. Stocking and Myron W. Watkins, *Cartels or Competition?*, New York, Twentieth Century Fund, 1948, p. 3, definition limiting the term cartel to "producers engaged in the same line of business."

[196] This is an unrealistic exclusion as theoretically a non-socialist world economy suffers some restrictive impact from any action in restraint, even if confined to a single market, to the extent that the total world market supply and demand schedule are affected.

[197] A significant variable is the extent to which future competition could be excluded from undermining a high price.

[198] Elasticity will depend upon the desirability or necessity for a product and the relative availability and quality of substitutes.

of members. Each member is assigned a geographical area for exclusive operation. This permits the members to exercise various kinds of monopoly control in different places to accommodate the peculiar characteristics of local market.

Cartels make increasing use of trademark and patent devices as restrictive supplements to territorial allocation. The common trademark technique is for the member firms to each register a common trademark in their exclusive operating area. Then other members can legally be prevented from competing in violation of the cartel agreement. This use of the trademark law enables cartels to assure compliance with territorial allocation. It is thus a tool employed to maintain self-discipline by the cartel, and does not affect the status of nonmembers producers.

The patent device can be used both to discipline members, to achieve lower costs by the cartels, to exclude competitors, and to halt the progress of nonmembers. Patents can be territorially divided up among members, as were trademarks; members can agree to exchange new patents and to promise not to sell patents or licenses to nonmembers; a patent grantor can agree not to compete with any of his grantees. These agreements are enforceable by patent infringement actions in many nations, including the United States, who profess antitrust policies. The result is to enable cartels to pool their technological achievements and to control access into an industry by denying potential competitors licenses necessary for production.

In a technological market division each producer is allowed to supply particular kinds of products or use specific processes. Thus in a three-member cartel of industry X capable of making products $A, B,$ and C, Company X produces only A, Company X_2 produces only B, and Company X_3 produces only C. This perhaps maximizes economies of scale, and fosters lower production costs by specialization. It enables a larger number of producers to divide up the market, provided the industry is engaged in a wide range of activities. A functional market allocation restricts the members to production for particular categories of customers, and often acts to supplement a functional market allocation.[199]

Cartels sometimes express their power by restricting the selling activities of their members in various ways. Subtle modes of artificial control can be exercised through discount, rebate, and credit term manipulation. More obvious restrictions upon competition occur when production quotas or quality controls are used. Production limits, with penalties for violations, are used by cartels where the number of producers is large and/or the urge to produce is great.[200] A cartel of this type has found it

[199] See Machlup, Edwards, Berge, Stocking and Watkins for details on the allocations devices used by cartels. These authors deal in detail with all aspects of cartels here discussed.

[200] A diminishing costs industry in

difficult to divide the market and has insufficient power to fix effectively prices directly.[201] Therefore, it is essential to the successful functioning of such a cartel that it have available sanctions to punish members who violate the agreement.

Cartels, as an international institution, have generated considerable pro and con debate. It is a naive American predisposition to regard cartels as evil *per se*. Many impartial observers, including prominent economists, have at various times in different industries urged some degree of cartelization. And even the United States has had its own flirtation with cartels; although the evil connotation has been removed by the euphemism, export association. However, the close relationship between the rise of Hitler and the Farben cartel acted to swing the great weight of impartial opinion over to a position favoring some degree of control over cartel activities in the postwar world.[202] Pro-cartelists have sought to create a dichotomy between "good" and "bad" cartels, the distinction being based upon the intent and the effect of a particular cartel agreement. Kronstein and Leighton attribute continental tolerance of cartels to the early acceptance by courts of the validity of this distinction.[203]

There have been many abuses attributed to cartels: selling goods at artificially high prices; selling inferior goods as a result of the absence of quality competition; destroying incentive; reducing production and employment; undermining the stimulus to invent; suppressing the invention that does occur; promoting an inefficient allocation of factors, especially if much idle capacity exists; fostering authoritarian government; reducing consumption; increasing trade barriers; causing supply to be uncertain in stress if cartel member fails to develop domestic resource; causing wastes encouraged by cartel quotas based on productive capacity; hampering national security in time of war as cartel is either in control of an adversary government or it has no patriotic impulse of loyalty;[204] generating wars that will increase the demand for their goods;

which most profitable price requires restriction of supply that leaves some producers with high unit costs and excess capacity.

[201] Machlup, p. 8..

[202] The corpus of literature describing various facets of cartel evils is tremendous. A few representative authorities have been studied: U.S. Senate, Kilgore Committee, *Cartels and National Security* (1944); Corwin D. Edwards, ed., *A Cartel Policy for the United Nations*, New York, Columbia University Press, 1945; Wendell Berge, *Cartels: Challenge to a Free World*, Washington, Public Affairs Press, 1944; George W. Stocking and Myron W. Watkins, *Cartels or Competition*, New York, Twentieth Century Fund, 1948; Heinrich Kronstein and Gertrude Leighton, "Cartel Control: A Record of Failure," 55 *Yale Law Journal* 297 (1946).

[203] Kronstein and Leighton, note 11 *supra*, p. 300 quote an 1891 decision of Cour de Paris, "no objection to the cartel was allowed if its goal was 'the defense of the common interests' of the people engaged in the industry."

[204] Berge shows that Farben exercised some governmental control, while an American cartel member, like Esso, seems to display more loyalty to the successful perpetuation of the cartel than to the American war effort.

and generally to use the factors of production in a manner unresponsive to consumer preference or to social or national welfare—that is, to misdirect production by seeking the highest profits.

The plea for cartels is often phrased in Keynesian generalities, being a plea for the stability of the world economy through cartels that are able, as an aggregate unit, to withstand cyclical change. Cartels can eliminate destructive price wars by making price agreements; maximum economies of scale can be realized; the cartel can provide the market with an assured and steady supply; and a cartel can help to overcome industrial maladjustment by adjusting supply to demand so as to maximize industrial earnings. There are certain subsidiary benefit claims by cartelists: the elimination of competitive wastes, the technological rationalization of industry, the prevention of evils greater than cartels—combines and nationalized industry; and cartels theoretically enable a facilitation of invention by providing for free exchange of research information.

Although the bulk of impartial opinion, especially of the economists, favors the regulation of cartels by an international agency, its establishment remains highly unlikely. Unless the regulation was limited to requiring cartel agreements to be publicized, and perhaps to the power to regard certain cartel contracts as *contra bonos mores*, thus rendering them unenforceable. Clearly this would be a step forward, but it is not a standard of regulation required to attain an international market free from competitive restraints. For such an aspiration, an "International Sherman Act" is necessary.[205] However, Europe still seems willing to tolerate, at least, the well-behaved cartel. And the time lag since the conclusion of the war has enabled some of the old cartels to reorganize and reassert their tremendous influence. In Germany, Allied occupation of the Western zone consciously sought to prevent the reappearance of a united I. G. Farben, but efforts to split up this cartel of cartels have not been successful.[206]

Reliance upon the unilateral action of the United States is not enough to create free world trade, or even to keep the domestic economy free from noncompetitive characteristics. However, strict enforcement of the

[205] An "International Sherman Act" would alone enable the American market to be free from noncompetitive elements. It could regulate the interference at its source, rather than, perforce, capriciously punish its appearance. Metaphorically, limited jurisdiction to allow only the plucking of leaves, while effective enforcement necessitates the extirpation of roots that is possible only with unlimited jurisdiction.

[206] Cf. proceedings related to the projected International Trade Organization. Also for a regional attempt, stimulated by the United States, see the Havana Charter. For a discussion of the recreation-of-cartels-in-Germany problem see Lewis, "The Status of Cartels in Post-War Europe," in Edwards, ed., *A Cartel Policy for the United Nations*, 1945. Also Charles A. Welsh and Joseph Borkin, *Germany's Master Plan: The Story of Industrial Offensive*, New York, Duell, 1943.

Sherman Act, and the use of supplemental anticartel techniques by the United States, could possibly limit the operations of cartels to those products where production is concentrated in a few closely cooperating corporate giants.[207] Thus Kreps finds that "the only international cartels that can resist or defy unilateral action by the United States are those similar to the aluminum or electric lamp bulb cartel" in which this requisite concentrated control has the power to oppress the entire international market.[208] Such cartels are truly supranational economic units that have acquired monopoly control over patents, scarce deposits, and know-how, and are capable of adjusting to any degree of regulation attempted by a single nation without sacrificing monopoly advantages.

American unilateral regulation could eliminate flagrant restraint from the vast majority of foreign trade markets in which there exists an important United States concern. In fact, wherever the cartel agreement requires either actual American participation or access to the American markets it is vulnerable to unilateral regulation. The formal competence of American courts extends to a consideration of any nonconforming activity by a domestic firm, once it is found to be domestic, anywhere in the world. The actual utilization of this competence is blocked by the limitation of the Sherman Act concept of foreign trade to exports and imports and by a reluctance of the Justice Department to prosecute fully under the enabling legislation. Foreign corporations are subject to American competence if their activities restrain imports or exports. However, before an American court can hear a case the formal prerequisites of jurisdiction must be satisfied.[209] A foreign corporation doing business in the United States on the domestic market is completely subject to territorial legislation, including the antitrust laws.

America has been chided for inconsistency between its direct opposition to cartels on the one hand as expressed in the Sherman Act, regulatory commissions, and postwar disposal of property with an aim to encouraging competition, and, on the other hand, its tolerance of Webb-Pomerene export associations, its high tariffs, its patent system conducive to monopoly abuse, and its lax incorporation charters in American states, like Delaware.

Unilateral antitrust regulation is beset with certain serious difficulties in even a moderately cartelized world economy:

1. Only insufficient protection can be offered to the American con-

---

[207] This is the opinion of Kreps, "Experience with Unilateral Action Towards International Cartels," in Edwards, *supra*, note 18, who finds that "competition keeps breaking through" in the areas of foreign trade in which the Sherman Act has been applied.

[208] *Op.cit.*, p. 74.

[209] Requires a finding that the foreign corporation is doing business in the United States or that it was "found" in the United States, and found means something more than passing through, although foreign property need not be present in the United States if the action is brought *in personum*.

sumer of essential imports that sell at a cartel price. Unless the government buys at a high price and resells domestically at a lower price the importer must pay the exorbitant going rate. The cartel can be excluded from doing business in the United States, but if it monopolizes production of an essential and irreplaceable product then Americans must go abroad to purchase from the cartel. The diamond, cocoa, quinine, and tin cartels are prominent instances.

2. Unilateral action may not always be adequately able to protect American exporters, as has been dramatically indicated by the legal authorization of export associations.[210] In most instances American exports are so much in demand that they need no protection. Experts find that private boycott or the action of foreign governments only occasionally has required an American competitor to comply with a cartel quota.[211] There are a number of common contexts in which exporters may ask for protection—when a cartel uses monopoly techniques to drive the American exporter from its foreign markets;[212] when a contract enjoined by American courts is held to be legally enforceable outside the United States;[213] when the exporter is faced with state monopoly competition in foreign markets.

3. Without the cooperation of foreign governments it is almost impossible to enforce antitrust laws. For example, it is hard to get access to cartel records kept outside the United States.[214] Evidence and witnesses are often impossible to obtain. Prosecution is expensive and very slow.

4. If an American firm is prevented from joining a cartel it may be excluded from sharing the fruits of technological advances. If it attempts to compete against a cartel with patent control it may be balked by infringement actions.

5. Unilateral antitrust regulation must put up with certain cartel practices officially sanctioned or practiced by the United States Government that tend to weaken ideological insistence upon competitive world markets and to make irrational the pattern of permitted and precluded behavior in foreign trade. The Webb-Pomerene export associations and the patent law that induces monopoly abuse by its liberal receptivity to

---

[210] E.g., Kreps, *supra*, note 18, p. 81.

[211] *Op.cit.*, p. 82. see especially note 42.

[212] By thus acting to restrain American exports the cartel is violating the Sherman Act, but often its operations are beyond the jurisdictional competence of American courts if it has neither property nor officers in the United States, nor a subsidiary American corporation that could be served as an agent of the parent.

[213] For such a situation see the British Nylon Spinners Ltd. v. ICI Ltd. [1953] 1 Ch. 19, sequel to the American ICI

decision.

[214] For example the Canadian Legislature of Ontario so resented an attempt of the Attorney General to subpoena the records of an alleged Canadian newsprint monopoly that it enacted a bill making it illegal for a Canadian corporation to remove its records for any reason from the province of Ontario. See Exhibit N-44, *House Special Subcommittee on the Study of Monopoly Power of the Committees on the Judiciary*, 82nd Cong., 1st Sess., Pt. 6A.

infringement actions are prominent withdrawals from a strict insistence upon competitive conditions.[215] The foreign trade of the United States is noncompetitively affected by tariffs and export preferences. Not only do tariffs reduce the volume of international trade, but export preferences that vary the export duty by reference to the destination of the goods distort the competitive flow of goods in foreign trade. Also the effect of preferences to certain exports is to discriminate against other products. The American Trade Proposals to the ITO included a so-called safeguard clause that enables the participant countries to prevent sudden and widespread injury to domestic producers arising from excessive imports from unforeseen circumstances by restricting such imports.[216] Also in the past the United States has in a few areas resorted to quantity trade restrictions that limit absolutely the amount of permissible imports and exports. Since the war we favor the elimination of such restrictions except when there is a domestic emergency requiring limitation, there is a balance of payment problem, or there is an applicable intergovernment commodity agreement that must be honored. Previously world trade was limited by control exercised over the purchase and sale of foreign exchange, and trade with a foreign country could be prevented by the control of payments to a foreign country. Stabilization provisions in the Bretton Woods agreement limits the postwar need to exercise exchange control to assure payment. The United States has engaged in the diversion of goods into uneconomical markets for military or political purposes through the use of arbitrary methods in the assessment of duties and by the comparatively high internal charges levied upon imported goods.

America has been chided for the apparent inconsistency of stamping its feet when a foreign corporation violates the Sherman Act, while closing both eyes to its own forms of restrictionist activity. In some areas cartel behavior is tolerated for purposes of a realistic adjustment to the market. Other restraints upon trade are stimulated by pragmatic considerations of economic and political policy. The existence of these inconsistencies calls into question the ethical justification of the extraterritorial Sherman Act by at least suggesting the interpretation that America is insisting upon competition only when it benefits America. That is, we permit these noncompetitive practices whenever the United States fails to gain control of the foreign market by the superiority of its competitors. This is a manifestly unfair evaluation since American industry often suffers most from antitrust regulation. Further, to require a

---

[215] The Webb-Pomerene export associations are discussed on pp. 302-307.

[216] Robert P. Terrill, "The American Trade Proposals," U.S. Department of State Bulletin, 14 (March 24, 1946), 455. This authority is the source of the information on government restraints on trade.

Sherman Act America to compete disadvantageously in a cartelized foreign market may be likened to the caviling of those Sophists who ridicule the sincerity of a rich socialist who is unwilling to give away his wealth in a capitalistic economy. One can conform to the reality antagonistic to one's goals without losing the sincere desire or ceasing the effort to attain such goals.

This chapter does not attempt an actual evaluation of the overall consequences of unilateral action by the United States. However, a methodological approach can be suggested. Analysis should proceed to examine the results from a pragmatic and an idealistic perspective. A pragmatic investigation would seek to determine the extent of influence that permissible unilateral action has exerted upon the character and volume of foreign trade, the relative change in the American share of foreign trade that can be fairly attributed to antitrust regulation, and the reaction and impact of protest and reprisal by foreign governments angry about an attempt by America to extend its competitive standards beyond the United States. Also we must examine the extent to which antitrust regulation encourages economic readjustments, such as state trading and nationalization, that retain monopoly power behind the now unassailable facade of sovereign immunity. The danger of fostering centralization and concentration, more permanent and powerful than a private cartel, may become a serious consequence of overzealous extraterritorial antitrust regulation.

The idealist survey would seek to determine the extent to which our unilateral regulation interfered with the contrary policies of foreign governments, the location of the interference, and the harm suffered abroad by American regulation. Further it must establish the limits imposed by international law, and the flexibility and justification for these limits. And perhaps it must conduct a survey of the relationship between the application of antitrust regulation and the promotion of an impartially selected value framework.

Annex C—The Statutory Framework of Foreign Antitrust Regulation

Various laws have been enacted to supplement the sweeping coverage of the basic legislation supplied by the Sherman Act. This appendix briefly seeks to set forth a statement of the fundamental legislation in this area. It will also be possible to indicate briefly the policy objectives underlying these laws. A complete survey would have to include some sort of progress evaluation. This will not be attempted in this chapter, but there will be incidental attention paid to the relationship that exists between the legislative means and the policy ends. It is from these laws, and particularly the Sherman Act, that one should attempt to infer the content of "unlawful purpose."

1. THE SHERMAN ACT[217]

A. *General Considerations.* The broad language of the Sherman Act is explicitly made applicable to commerce "with foreign nations." The extent of application is less, however, in the foreign realm than in the domestic realm. This is due to the many technical factors than underlie a greater difficulty and a smaller incentive to foster the vigorous enforcement of the Sherman Act against foreign commerce.[218]

Because of the number of different relevant markets and the difficulty of proving monopoly, Section 2 is practically inoperative, except as a support, in the foreign context. Section 1 has contributed the bulk of international antitrust law. It deals with all contracts, combinations, or conspiracies in restraint of trade with foreign nations.[219] Both foreign and domestic corporations and individuals are subject to its mandates. However, no attempt to apply the Act to foreign acts is made unless there is an impact upon the domestic economy. And for best results, in terms of international harmony and tolerance, the impact should be, it is felt by this author, substantial, direct, and intended.[220] Unless it is substantial, direct, and intended.[220] Unless it is substantial, there is no justification for invalidating foreign acts; unless it is direct, enforcement becomes capricious and remote; and unless it is intended, there is an unjustified interference with the conduct of economic affairs outside out borders—as the alleged restraint evidently arose from an unintended and presumably incidental aspect of acts that were mainly implementing some end that was not condemned by our antitrust laws. Therefore, one regrets the *Alcoa* decision being based upon an *impact* theory. Within our economy, the plenary power of the Sherman Act can be applied to any foreign firm regularly doing business here. We have the right to prescribe competitive standards and the further prerogative to coerce, if coercion is necessary, adherence to such standards. However, here again we must not seek to interfere with the foreign activities of an

[217] 26 Stat 209 (1890), as amended 50 Stat 693 (1937), 15 USC §1 (1946). This discussion of the legislation will assume some familiarity with its content.

[218] The mechanical problems of assembling a case built upon unobtainable evidence of restraints often committed outside of American territory are considerable. In addition, the expense of such a prosecution is discouraging in view of the fact that a successful verdict can bring only a partial remedy. The interest in prosecuting American violators is diluted if their foreign co-conspirators cannot be subjected to similar apprehension. Also the economic loss from noncompetitive behavior in the foreign realm is less direct. Further, many noneconomic forces inspire toleration of certain practices in a foreign context that would be condemned in a domestic context.

[219] For a description of the scope of Section 1 in foreign trade see William Dwight Whitney, "Sources of Conflict Between International Law and the Antitrust Laws," 63 *Yale Law Journal* 655, 659 (March 1954).

[220] An overvigorous prosecution of foreign defendants for foreign acts will inspire enmity and reprisals, especially in a period in which American political power is less supreme, and in which there is less economic dependence upon U.S. aid. Also America claims to be dedicated to preserving maximum self-determination for a sovereign within its lawful territory.

alien resident corporation or its manner of organization unless there is a good justification, in terms of the domestic economy, for such interference. Also if American regulation becomes too burdensome foreign industry will retreat from our jurisdiction, thus either depressing world trade or forcing us to do business on noncompetitive terms in a foreign market. It is indeed difficult to develop a Sherman Act record that has come to cope with the functional realities of multi-nation modern business sufficiently to keep the domestic economy reasonably competitive and yet not unduly interfere with the economic conditions prevailing in foreign markets.[221] And by and large American courts are to be congratulated on their progress from the mechanical physical acts construction of the *Banana* case to the functional impact construction of the more recent cases.[222] Such progress has come to deal effectively with the increasing interdependence of modern business. Courts have also been vigilant in their detection and punishment of "unlawful purpose" in disguised forms—as in export associations, joint ventures, and patent exchange agreements. Thus the Sherman Act has been allowed to grow to meet new needs, and thus it has retained the vitality necessary to guard the domestic economy from many "evil practices." This is most remarkable in a world community that has more or less come to tolerate cartels and many noncompetitive abuses.

This is not the time to revive the exploration in the *Addyston Pipe* case of the relationship between the common law policy to punish non-ancillary restraints and the statutory condemnation contained in the Sherman Act. It is enough to recognize that the Sherman Act carries forward the common law belief that the societal weal prospers most when resources are left free to respond to the competitive bids of their different users. Adam Smith and his followers convinced our society that maximum wealth comes to a community that has a free market. This belief persists in the United States, but today we recognize the necessity of regulating abridgers of market freedom and the reciprocal futility of blithely relying upon "automatic" allocation. And so the Sherman Act has arose to insulate our economy from the evil-doers—no matter *where* they "do" or *who* they are. The Sherman Act also fosters the goals of a democratic society by resisting the concentration of wealth and by preserving the freedom of economic opportunity.[223]

Mr. Chief Justice Hughes most clearly enunciated the spirit with

---

[221] There is no doubt that foreign acts must be regulated, as often the source of the interference is extraterritorial. Such an interference must be dealt with directly, or else not at all—for example, the *Sisal* case required an interference with the domination of the Yucatan sisal market in order to terminate the domestic restraint.

[222] The *Alcoa* case is a clear exposition, though a bad application, of the impact approach. Other cases—*Bulova*, *Timken*, and *Alkali*.

[223] Annex A, p. 302. Notice the political organization is Nazi Germany, Fascist Italy, and Soviet Russia where extreme concentration of wealth was permitted.

which courts should approach the Sherman Act.[224] Calling the Act "a charter of freedom" he advocated "a generality and adaptability comparable to that found to be desirable in constitutional provisions." This is a caveat to courts that narrow legalism is to be avoided in this area— and that the criterion of legality must constantly be reintegrated in terms of the policy objectives sought by the Act. This is especially necessary in the foreign trade matrix where complex circumstances and conflicting goals make a nonmechanical focus on the function and objective of the law crucial. And this is precisely why the rule-of-reason approach is here advocated to enable the flexibility derivative from a case-to-case appraisal of the allegedly illegal conduct. The predictability and facility of *per se* analysis is not used to advantage in contexts in which the Sherman Act cannot be content with the inherent illegality of economic practices. As the *Minnesota Mining* case suggested, courts must be ready to grant some degree of tolerance to "necessary restraints," if such become the *sina qua non* of foreign commerce. Also there must be allowances made for adjustments to foreign market conditions—thus the *Timken* case could better have been decided had it evaluated the use of a foreign subsidiary in terms of the required business organization for profitable operations in the British market as opposed to the "unlawful purpose" of the particular Timken organization instead of merely condemning the *per se* illegality of market division. As Jackson suggested in his dissent, the converse to allowing formal appearance to disguise "unlawful purpose" is to infer "unlawful purpose" from the facade alone. Thus if the same results could have been perfectly legitimately attained by an alternative facade then a court should hesitate before it convicts, and becomes convinced that there is a prosecuted "unlawful purpose" present that would justify conviction regardless of the facade.

B. A Few Special Considerations

1. Criminal and/or Civil. The classification of the Sherman Act as criminal or civil is of considerable procedural importance. This is particularly true in reference to the more limited jurisdiction normally competent to deal with a crime. There exists, among authorities, considerable disagreement as to the criteria of classification.[225] The Sherman itself provides both a criminal and a civil remedy. But Haight feels that the necessity of a government prosecution or the award of exemplary damages gives all Sherman Act proceedings a criminal character. If accepted, such an interpretation suggests more self-restraint in the application of the Act to foreign acts.

---

[224] Appalachian Coals v. US 288 US 344, 360 (1933).
[225] Cf. G. W. Haight and Murry Broch-
in: Haight, 63 *Yale Law Journal* 639, 640 (March 1954); Brochin, 64 *Yale Law Journal* 581-89 (Feb. 1955).

2. Double Standard. There is in practice and in theory a need for a different Sherman Act standard for foreign and domestic commerce.[226] The objectives in foreign trade are more mixed, and the emphasis is upon avoiding restraints upon American commerce (foreign and domestic) and not so much upon attaining a competitive market. The degree of control exercisable by American regulation is very much dependent upon the nature of the particular offense—and in some foreign trade cases the unavailability of a complete remedy may require a careful consideration of the consequences of a partial remedy. In some instances a partial remedy against a nexus of restraint will merely eliminate American competition. In other words, there is more room for judicial discretion and flexibility in the foreign context than in the domestic context.

3. Adams-Mitchell Dissent.[227] Judge Jerome Frank takes the position that the Sherman Act does not apply to imports after the Wilson Tariff Act. Rather imports are freed from antitrust regulation by an implied appeal of the Sherman Act inferred from subsequent legislation.[228] This position is aberrational.[229]

2. SECTION 7 OF THE CLAYTON ACT

Section 7 applies to stock acquisitions whose effect "may be to substantially lessen competition, or to create a monopoly." The government must establish the relevant market and product. There need be no conspiracy to attain an "unlawful purpose" present. The anticipated restraint upon competition is measured by "reasonable probability." Oppenheim finds the Sherman Act test used in the *Columbia Steel* decision less strict than Section 7. There must be a domestic orientation to the restraint, that is, it must be American competition that will be lessened by the stock acquisition.

3. THE WEBB ACT[230]

The Webb-Pomerene Act (hereinafter referred to as the Webb Act) became law in 1918, two years after a report, following an extensive investigation, by the Federal Trade Commission recommended such legislation. The Webb Act intended to exempt partially American export trade from the application of the Sherman Act. It was stimulated by the desire to improve the position of the American exporter in the international market, and, specifically, to enable American exporters

[226] 37 *Cornell Law Quarterly* 821 (Summer 1952).

[227] Adams-Mitchell Co. v. Cambridge Distributing Co. 189 F. 2d 913, 921 (2d Cir. 1951).

[228] *Id.* at 921.

[229] See implication of note 4, 31 *Texas Law Review* 493, 494 (1953).

[230] On Webb Act see Brewster, *op.cit. supra*, note 50, at pp. 108-20.

to combine into bargaining units that would equalize the strength of monopolies and monopsonies that were becoming more prevalent in the world market. Incidental objectives of the Webb Act were to encourage the small domestic producer to export by providing this opportunity to share the advantages of aggregated bargaining power; to realize savings in exporting by splitting up the marketing costs, thereby eliminating duplications while simultaneously gaining the economies of large-scale operation; to encourage a greater proportion of export trade, out of total production, thus relieving the home market of depressive surpluses; and to obtain a higher price in export markets, and so raise the dollar volume of foreign trade, by virtue of the higher prices obtained by greater bargaining strength.

With debatable success, the authors of the Webb Act anticipated the dangers inherent in granting a wholesale Sherman Act exemption to all American exporters. The main dangers that were quite properly raised upon the eve of legislative endorsement of export cartels, were the creation of powerful economic units that would exploit rather than compete in the unorganized portions of foreign markets; the facilitation of international cartelization by uniting the American market into a one-producer territory; the restrictive impact upon the domestic market that would inevitably arise from this tolerance of combination together with the administrative impossibility of preventing the creation of some prohibited domestic restraints; the establishment of conditions that would tempt the member exporters to squeeze nonmember competitors out of the export market.

The Webb Act represented a serious attempt to permit certain business combinations, while still resisting the adverse consequences of combination, in the export context. The principal provisions of the Webb Act, as contained in Section 2, are:

(1) domestic producers may without violating the Sherman Act form an association solely to carry on export trade, provided actual exporting occurs;

(2) the Sherman Act shall not apply to an agreement made by the association in the course of exporting, provided that:

    (a) there is no resultant restraint upon United States trade;

    (b) there is no resultant restraint of a domestic nonmember competitor;

    (c) there is no enhancement or depression of prices and/or no substantial lessening of competition in the United States.

The statutory language sets out with care the coverage of the Act, and seeks to specify what is meant by "association" and "export trade." In Section 4, the Federal Trade Commission is given jurisdiction over the occurrence of unfair competitive practices in the course of export, whether they take place within or without the United States. This extra-territorial claim of authority has provoked debate, centering around the international implications of such a claim. In Section 6 the FTC is given the power to investigate alleged violations of the Webb Act, recommend reforms, and refer the case to the Attorney General for further action if the association fails to comply with the recommendation.

The Webb Act has apparently enjoyed little success. Exports comprise only 7 percent of the total dollar value of American annual production, and of this amount, only 7 percent has been transacted by Webb Act export associations. Up to 1940, 125 associations had been formed, but only 44 had survived. Thus the Webb Act can have a direct effect on only a small part of the economy. Expert observation has concluded that the successful associations have flourished in industries with a few large producers, that the total effect of the Act has been to oppress the domestic exporter, especially the small member and nonmember; that there is no evidence of cost savings through association operations; that cartel participation has been engendered; that the association has used permitted export combinations to cloak prohibited domestic restraints, and that enforcement of violations has been difficult and sporadic.

The situation of the association was obfuscated in 1924 by the celebrated Silver Letter written by the FTC to advise the silver producers that although foreign producers could not become members of a Webb association, there was no reason why an association could not make an agreement with a foreign producer covering operations in a foreign market. The Silver Letter was widely interpreted as endorsing the permissibility of cartel participation by an association, and this interpretation was not decisively refuted until the *Alkali* decision. The paucity of judicial pronouncement, reflecting a reluctance to prosecute rather than a high degree of compliance, has increased the difficulty of safely distinguishing prohibited and permitted conduct under the Webb Act.

Assessing the overall results of the operation of the Webb Act is not an easy task in view of the relatively little information that has been made public by the FTC. But informed opinion seems to feel that considerable amendment, if not repeal, is indicated by more than fifty years of Webb Act experience. Suggested amendments take the form of advocating the building-into-the Act of certain standards of eligibility. One suggestion is to require exporters to apply for an association license from the FTC that would be granted only if there was a foreign monoply or monopsony to balance, thereby restricting the Webb Act to "defensive" associations, and, in addition, the applicants could be required to demonstrate that the legitimate trade economies would be realized through the proposed association. This licensing arrangement would be difficult for the FTC to administer and for the judiciary to review. Another suggestion is to set out in detail certain "internal checks" intended to guarantee adherence to minimum standards of respect for the protection of nonmember competitors and small members. These standards would seek to preserve the operational independence of a maximum number of competitive economic units. Again, however, this reform, even if practicable, could not eliminate the larger deficiencies that have arisen in the course of Webb Act operations.

Another faction of opinion favors a complete repeal of the Webb Act, thus acknowledging the inability and undesirability of weakening standards of competition as a foreign trade subsidy. The argument for repeal is based upon a number of considerations—there is no evidence that export associations have cut the costs of exporting; American exporters can normally market their products without the aid of an artificial strengthening of their bargaining position; the existence of Webb associations encourages the growth of foreign organized purchasing agencies and combinations; the competitive atmosphere on the domestic market would improve; the revitalization of competitive export conditions would make American participation in world cartelization more difficult to arrange and sustain; and the American argument for free world trade would be more convincing after we had taken steps to remove our free trade barriers. The record of Webb Act experience, when added to the practical impossibility of reform by amendment, makes the case for repeal strong.

PART THREE

MAKING INTERNATIONAL LAW

EFFECTIVE IN NATIONAL

AND INTERNATIONAL ARENAS

Introduction

THERE IS an obvious intellectual and sociopolitical continuity between the emphasis of Part Two upon the nature of authority in the international legal order and the emphasis of Part Three on problems of effectiveness. Inquiries into authority concern conceptual and jurisprudential issues that involve explaining how law comes into being and passes away; there is also the complementary need to identify who exercises authority for what purposes in a decentralized system as intricate as is the international legal order. Inquiries into effectiveness presuppose that the authoritative prescription is clearly identified and then go on to consider various procedures for implementation. These procedures for implementing authority—enforcing the law—entail an explication of the sanctioning processes that exist to deter or punish noncompliance in international society; as well, the account of effective international law needs to include an account of why compliance is so often automatic in the sense of not being dependent upon sanctions in many characteristic instances. A consideration of implementing authority requires both (1) a description of the enforcement process and (2) an explanation of the extent to which enforcement is unnecessary.

The stress in domestic law upon the relationship between rule and sanction often leads observers of the world scene to question the legal quality of the international legal order because effective sanctions are often unavailable in the setting of intense, violence-laden conflict among sovereign states. Such questioning also overlooks the extent to which the implementation of authority can be induced by action within states, that is, by decentralized sanctioning procedures that are sustained by a logic of reciprocity. To make authority effective it is essential to correlate the locus of power with the locus of authority. Therefore, in the international legal order with power predominantly wielded by state actors, and predominantly by a few of the principal ones, it seems clear that the most promising bases of effectiveness involve reliance upon national enforcement capabilities. Therefore, to strengthen the international legal order appears at present to depend more on mobilizing these national capabilities than upon building up "the authority" of international institutions. The activities of domestic legal institutions with respect to the interpretation and application of international law deserve careful and systematic scrutiny. At this time, several centuries after the initiation of serious international legal studies, we continue to lack serious comparative studies of the role of domestic courts—and other domestic institutions—vis-à-vis international law in the main subject matter areas. Such lack bespeaks the persisting strength of the misleading presupposition that international law is concerned with relations *between* (and more accurately *among*) states rather than within them, and that enforcement entails supranational actors. In actuality, the only practical alternative to augmenting the role of national enforcement procedures is to work toward the centralization of power (as well as authority) in the international legal order. Such centralization implies a transformation of system changing proportions, including at the very least drastic disarmament at the national level. One reason why the subject of effectiveness is so bewildering at the present time is that there has been a premature centralization of apparent legal authority in the Charter of the United Nations without any corresponding centralization of either loyalty patterns on a level of human attachment or of power resources on a national level. It seems obvious that international law will suffer a crisis of confidence provoked by raising false expectations whenever the basis of authoritative decision is disjoined too sharply from the basis of effective implementation. Such a crisis of confidence has occurred after both World Wars I and II as a consequence of the ability of antiwar reformers to influence authority patterns combined with their inability to influence power distributions.

In considering the effectiveness of the international legal order it is important not to lose sight of the diversity of functions served by the international legal order. There is a natural tendency to emphasize those functions concerned with the restraint of behavior within permissible limits when discussing the implementation of authority claims. But, especially in situations of international conflict and crisis, the function of international law is to establish a system for continuous communication despite the hostility of adversaries to one another. The possibility for reliable communication—whether by means of hot lines or through a variety of visible and invisible diplomatic forums—allows parties in conflict to identify and act upon converging interests at the earliest possible time. It might be objected at this point that the processes of international communication have nothing much to do with international law. This is less true than it appears to be. The procedures for communication are usually sustained and sanctioned by treaty, the outcome of communicating is often expressed as a formal act, and much of the discussion often concerns the relative legal rights and duties of the parties to the dispute. International law provides common norms of reference that are available to every international actor regardless of size or ideology; in this sense legal argumentation is a universally respected international medium of rhetorical exchange. The criteria useful to assess the effectiveness of the international legal order are quite different if the center of inquiry is the communications function than if it is the restraint function. It is almost worth belaboring the point, so common is the assumption that the sole function of any legal order, and especially of international legal order, is to restrain behavior within formally established limits.

The chapters in Part Three explore some aspects of this complex set of problems. Chapter X considers the diversity of meanings that can be attached to the idea of compliance, thereby illustrating the complexity of any analysis of effectiveness adequate to the character of the international legal order. Chapter XI analyzes problems of treaty interpretation, especially focusing upon the merits and defects of the New Haven approach to treaty interpretation. The proper craft and discipline of interpretation are essential to the integrity of the agreement process in international society; problems of treaty interpretation illustrate the special task of reconciling conflicting interests of stability and adaptation in the present system of international legal order, a task intimately related to the prospect for effective law in world affairs.

Chapter XII examines certain issues of effectiveness as they appear from the perspective of the International Court of Justice when it is asked to decide a legal controversy for which the prospects of an enforceable judgment are low—The South West Africa Cases. It is a controversy in which neither side is likely to accept the outcome of an adverse judgment. Should such a controversy be adjudicated? How does one assess the role of the Court faced with such an indeterminate prospect of resistance to its legal determinations? Chapters XIII and XIV focus upon certain distinctive issues of law and policy posed whenever international law controversies are resolved by the action of national institutions. In considering the processes whereby the authority of international law is upheld it is quite illuminating to contrast the effectiveness of supranational and national action in implementation. The contrast eventually needs to be developed in detail to permit account to be taken of differences in national settings *inter se* and in the nature and subject matter of disputes.

X. Some Thoughts on Identifying and Solving the Problem of Compliance with International Law

TO CAUSE compliance by nations with international law it is necessary to influence behavior; but to assess compliance it is only necessary to judge behavior. The two subjects, however, are not mutually exclusive, since the ability to identify authoritatively an instance of noncompliance can deter a prospective violator and, in addition, may help the community to organize a sanctioning response in the event of a violation. For example, the effectiveness of the response by the United Nations to the Suez invasion of 1956 can be attributed in part to the rapid formation of an effective consensus that perceived the conduct to involve noncompliance with legal norms prohibiting aggression.

The distinctive character of a dispute about compliance with international law is rather difficult to specify. A typical dispute between two sovereign states serves as an instructive example. One state accuses the other of violating a rule of international law. The accused nation denies the allegation. What happens next? This question arises because there is no regularly available procedure in international society to resolve disputes about what international law requires in a particular instance and thereby to determine whether the alleged violation has actually taken place. Each national government posits its adversary presentation as descriptive of "the law," and inquiry is often terminated at the adversary stage. This termination of legal inquiry at the adversary stage encourages a widespread perception of international law as providing nothing more than a system of rhetoric useful in statecraft whenever rationalization of national conduct is needed to satisfy the demands of public opinion.

There are two important reasons why it is essential to obtain a more authoritative judgment about the character of a legal obligation than can be offered by either party to the dispute. First, an argument is not a determination; the requirements of law are not known until a choice can be made as to which adversary is correct in his contention about the requirements of law. Second, in international society it is sometimes difficult to distinguish between adversary and judge; there are often no judges accepted by the community as competent to act. Therefore, if international law is to develop into more than heated diplomatic conversation between adversaries, there is a critical need to develop techniques able to appraise as authoritatively as possible opposing claims about the nature of legality.

Part of the popular tendency to explain international behavior by reference to national power is a product of the failure of international lawyers to provide an adequate account of what the law really is in a social system that lacks a regularly available judiciary. If every national government has the discretion to describe the law as it sees fit and if this description is the final determination, then the more powerful of the two adversaries can normally be assured that its view of what is legal will prevail in an important controversy. But such an assurance produces an outcome of a controversy rather than clarifies the nature of legality or casts light on the comparative merits of the adversary contentions.

This chapter outlines three arguments: First, that is possible to obtain quasi-authoritative resolutions of international law disputes without necessarily having recourse to international adjudication; second, that it is desirable to accord international law experts some role as a source of authoritative guidance, provided that it is feasible to reduce the confusion caused when these experts give adversary interpretations disguised as impartial analyses; and, third, that we must become more aware of the techniques available to transcend an adversary standoff.

I. *The Limited Role of International Adjudication*

Lawyers in the West have a tendency to assume that the most worthwhile way to enhance the role of law in world affairs is to strengthen the World Court and, more broadly, to expand the role of international adjudication. Part of this support for adjudication arises because courts are frequently thought of as the only effective source of impartial decision-making in any legal system. Such a reliance upon the judicial mechanism exhibits a familiar inclination to shore up international law by a slavish imitation of law devices that have proven successful in domestic societies. The nature of the compliance problem in international law cannot be appreciated unless the tyranny of domestic models of legal order can be eliminated. To this end, it is necessary to take the distinctive features of international society into account. This perspective implies, first of all, the realization that the weakness of international (or central) judicial institutions is an almost inevitable consequence of the existing decentralization of power and loyalty within international society. Given this extralegal setting, an increase in the authority of central institutions without a corresponding acquisition of political power is likely to weaken the prospects for the growth of world law by calling attention to the conjunction between authority to declare the law and impotence to enforce it. Given the reality of decentralization, it is hardly surprising that states remain unwilling to accept as binding those judgments that are rendered by international tribunals about the content of legal obligations. Most governments and their populations continue to deem it improper to guide national conduct by deference to supranational decision-making in critical areas; therefore, states are reluctant to entrust international tribunals with any dispute the outcome of which is perceived as vital to national power, wealth, or prestige.

This reluctance, of course, does not mean that international courts are entirely irrelevant to the search for an authoritative determination as to what it means in a given case to obey the law. It does, however, indicate that the role of courts will almost necessarily remain marginal as long as the nation-state continues to be the preeminent center of power and loyalty in world politics. And this marginality will be especially characteristic, I would suppose, in those disputes about the requirements of law that develop in the course of international crises; tension and distrust will normally preclude using courts to determine whether a state has been wrongly or rightly accused of violating international law.

II. The Role of the International Law Expert

It is traditional to assume that an expert on international law can guide us toward an authoritative judgment. A skeptical attitude toward this expectation is disclosed with engaging candor in the play of Jean Giraudoux, *Tiger at the Gates*. The royal family of Troy has received word that a Greek navy is approaching their city to avenge Paris' theft of Helen; their chief desire, not an unfamiliar one, is to maintain peace while upholding the honor of their city. If the Greeks have violated their rights, then Troy must declare war; if not, not. At this point they call upon Busiris, "the greatest living expert on the rights of nations" who by "a lucky chance" is passing through Troy on his way home to Syracuse. The Trojan leaders agree to be guided by Busiris' judgment: "You can't say that he's a biased witness. He is neutral. Our Senate is willing to abide by his decision, a decision which all other nations will respect." Busiris alleges that the Greeks are guilty of various breaches of international law, of which the two most serious are to fly their flags in a hatchway salute instead of from the masthead (thus signifying the greeting appropriate for a cattleboat rather than for a great city) and to sail their ships in an aggressive-defensive frontal formation (thus violating the law that prohibits a defensive-aggressive frontal formation when foreign ships are approaching a friendly shore). On the basis of this legalistic hocus-pocus, Busiris advises Troy on the issue of war and peace. The precedents suggest that when these breaches occurred at Orphea and Magnesia, war was declared by the insulted cities and thus honor was upheld, although at some cost, since both Orphea and Magnesia were promptly destroyed and left as rubble. Despite these dismal precedents, Busiris insists that Troy must declare war upon the Greeks to defend Trojan honor. Hector, King of Troy, opponent of war, and policy-scientist supreme, refuses to accept the analysis of Busiris who, he points out, hails from rival Syracuse and would hence welcome Troy going the way of Orphea and Magnesia: "You [Busiris] are going to provide me with an argument which will allow our Senate to say that there has been no fault whatever on the part of our visitors, and with our pride untouched we [will] welcome them as our guests. . . . My dear Busiris all of us here know there's no better way of exercising the imagination than the study of law." Busiris protests that his expert counsel is not a matter of discretion, that his judgment has been formed by knowledge of the law and by a commitment to truth. However, when Hector tells Busiris that in the event of war he will be imprisoned for its duration, Busiris reconsiders his stand and produces compelling counterarguments of great cunning: e.g., a hatchway salute is not an insult if given when approaching a fertile shore; rather, it is a form of compliment by the sailors to the farmers. In this vein, he reconstrues Greek behavior to make it accord with rules of law. Busiris concludes that, since there has been no violation of international law, Troy need not greet the Greeks in hostile fashion.

Busiris' reversal illustrates the dangers that are involved in a reliance upon the impartiality of the international law expert. First, "he who pays the fiddler calls the tune"; Busiris fiddles at Hector's request. Second, that the international law expert is vulnerable to corruption, which casts doubt upon according him automatic respect as a source of impartial judgment—even the Trojan Senate was expected to follow Busiris' guidance. Third, although premised on the same set of facts, legal analysis is capable of generating contradictory legal arguments, each of which may possess logical coherence. Fourth, a failure to distinguish between an adversary presentation of law and an impartial judgment contributes to the formation of a cynical image of the role of international law.

The reason for recourse to Busiris is, perhaps, rather transparent. In an era of severe international conflict and tension, there is a tendency for international lawyers to shed the mantle of impartiality and to replace it with the adversary's cloak. I regard this sacrifice of impartial analysis and commentary to be most unfortunate, since it tends to harm the development of law as a source of independent insight, guidance, restraint, and reconciliation in world affairs. Underneath this plea for impartiality is a judgment about priorities, namely, that it has now become more important to use international law as a basis of world order than to emphasize its capacity to serve as an instrument for the realization of national interests. It also seems plain that the restraints of law may not always be consistent with a course of national action, especially when the choice of policy is made in a period of crisis and entails the use or threat of force to defend perceived national interests.

Part of the intellectual problem arises from the tendency to dichotomize inquiry by asking whether an entire course of action is legal or illegal. This level of abstraction is normally too high to make much sense of an appraisal of compliance. For one thing, it is more useful to think of compliance as a position on a compliance continuum, rather than to conceive of compliance as a two-way switch that is either on or off; if we adopt the idea of a continuum, then legality is a matter of degree varying with the circumstances of the case. Certainly the craft and influence of law and lawyers are to be praised for exerting a restraining influence during international crises by minimizing the extent of departure from fundamental legal norms applicable in the particular context. Such an effort to achieve a posture of minimum noncompliance helps to convey accurately and nonprovocatively the precise nature of a controversial national claim to adversaries. In facilitating crisis communication among adversary governments, international law discourages excessive and escalatory responses. In comparable spirit, it is desirable for the controversial claimant state to submit its cause to review by any operative regional institution, as well as to the appropriate organ of the United Nations. The willingness of a state to comply with international law can be reflected in the choice of the means used to reach an end that perhaps could not itself be fully reconciled with its legal obligations. To induce such juridical responsibility is itself a very substantial achievement. It also provides occasion for optimism about the relevance of law to the management of international conflict. This sense of juridical accomplishment is jeopardized whenever exaggerated claims of legality are made in a situation of controversy, such that only partisanship can account for the clarity of legal position.

At the 1963 Annual Meeting of the American Society of International Law, Mr. Chayes, who was then Legal Adviser to the Secretary of State, pointed out, but for somewhat different purposes, that it is not very fruitful to focus analysis and argument upon whether or not challenged national conduct is legal.[1] I would add that, given the character of international legal order, the tools of analysis and the facts available to international lawyers do not very often permit authoritative legal inferences as to whether crisis behavior is or is not legal. Legal analysis is able, however, to indicate the arguments on either side of a dispute. This inability to come always to clear legal conclusions admits the shortcoming of international law as a source of guidance, since it

[1] *Proceedings American Society of International Law 1963*, pp. 10-11.

concedes that it may often be impossible to identify which of several courses of action are legal in any final sense. Any more ambitious conception of international law encourages international lawyers to encroach upon the independent responsibilities of policy-makers in areas of legal uncertainty. Such usurpation is both widely detected and keenly resented.

The international lawyer's role in the solution of the compliance problem is potentially very substantial. If a style of detached analysis prevails, then an impartial source of judgment is available to test the extent of compliance, although this judgment must often content itself with indefinite conclusions about the central or overriding issue of legality. If, on the other hand, the analyst comes forth as a disguised advocate of the policy of his national government, then the whole enterprise of law as a regulative process is put in question, except possibly by patrioteering groups that always are ready to welcome self-serving argumentation.

III. Nine Ways of Looking at Compliance

In this final section, I would like to illustrate some techniques that can be used to overcome an adversary dispute about the requirements of international law, that is, a dispute in which one state accuses another of violating international law and the latter denies it. The unifying procedure used to assess compliance involves substituting a more authoritative perspective for an adversary perspective. In domestic societies, this substitution is performed mainly by judicial and administrative third-party decision-making according to prescribed procedures. The decentralized character of world society, however, causes the formal procedures of third-party settlement to play a much smaller role in international affairs. Furthermore, to insist that an independent judiciary is the only form of decision-making that is sufficiently authoritative is undesirable, both because present prospects for an expansion of judicial action are bleak and because available nonjudicial approximations of authoritative judgment may then be overlooked and deprecated.

Adjudication and expert testimony as an important nonjudicial approach to authoritative decision about compliance can be supplemented by others. An array of possible approaches to authoritativeness exists, the relative aptness of each should be evaluated in relation to the particular features of a given dispute. There is no single method that assures an authoritative perspective in the international legal order. Often more than one approach is both used and useful. We can classify disputes about compliance in light of how they are resolved. A first step is for statesmen to grow aware that international law already possesses a wide variety of distinctive techniques to make rather authoritative appraisals of adversary claims about what the law requires. We can now consider some of these techniques. They are not mutually exclusive; for some disputes several alternatives exist, and perhaps more than one can be used consecutively at different stages of resolving a dispute about compliance.

1. The Jurisdictional Technique. A dispute arises in a domestic court of the United States about whether or not Cuba's expropriation of American-owned sugar plantations violates rules of international law as a consequence of its treatment of alien investors. According to the *Sabbatino* decision, prior to its statutory reversal, a domestic court presupposes the validity of an expropriation for purposes of the litigation. Given the judicial validation of the statute, domestic courts will not assess whether a foreign expropriation decree is compatible with the duties imposed by international law. In a domestic judicial setting, the meaning of compliance is often determined by reference to foreign territorial law as a consequence of the act of state doctrine.

2. The Procedural Technique. A dispute about compliance may be resolved by a procedure agreed upon in advance by the parties. It is a common feature of commercial treaties to contain a provision specifying reference to the International Court of Justice or to some other mechanism of third-party settlement. The procedural technique solves the problem of the meaning of compliance, since states agree in advance to accept the assessment of a neutral decision-maker. Such a solution can also be sought on *ad hoc* basis after a dispute arises, for example, by agreeing to submit a particular issue to the World Court. The compulsory jurisdiction option is an attempt to generalize the procedural solution by making the ICJ available to resolve, in the sense of putting to legal rest, disputes about the meaning of compliance.

3. The Institutional Technique. A dispute about the meaning of compliance may be resolved upon the initiative of a political organ of an international institution. For instance, the Security Council may determine whether or not a member has violated the rules prohibiting the use of national force except in situations of self-defense. The General Assembly, as well, has the legal competence to determine by a two-thirds vote whether an accused state is violating United Nations Charter provisions governing human rights. The extent to which the institutional solution is available depends upon the status of the institution; the degree of its availability also depends upon whether a relevant consensus of states is regarded as capable of creating and implementing legal obligations, at least in the sense of construing authoritatively what it means to comply with the organic law (the Charter) of the institution.

4. The Sociological Technique. This technique is closely related to the institutional solution. The common expectations of states often provide a persuasive insight into the meaning of compliance. At the war crimes trials held in Nuremberg and Tokyo following World War II, the conclusion reached that the Axis powers had committed aggression illustrates reliance upon community expectations to assess the meaning of compliance. Resolutions of censure, or their absence, by the General Assembly or by other supranational institutions often establish a relatively authoritative link between controversial national behavior and community expectations. For instance, the resolutions of the General Assembly calling upon states to stop nuclear testing is relevant evidence, even if not decisive, in the event of a dispute as to whether or not testing is legal. The sociological solution, which is never more than supplemental to others, encompasses community activity of all kinds. It includes reference to debates in international institutions, to the reaction of experts, to public opinion, and to the press coverage given by neutral states.

5. The Clear Drafting of Rules as a Technique. A clearly understood rule exists or is brought into existence by agreement manifested in the negotiating context. Subsequent conduct of a state flagrantly contravenes the rule. The meaning of compliance is easily assessed by the widely perceived discrepancy between legal rules and challenged conduct. The overflight of territorial airspace by foreign military aircraft without permission is illustrative. If the penetration into sovereign airspace is deep enough, usually no dispute occurs about the meaning of compliance, but rather a justification is given to mitigate the violation, if not to exonerate the violator.

6. The Functional and Axiological Techniques. These solutions claim that the meaning of compliance must be determined by reference to the function served or to the values promoted by the legal rule in dispute. The norm upholding freedom of the high seas for instance, is violated by naval maneuvers only when they interfere with other characteristic uses of the oceans. Or a use of force is illegal only if it infringes by intent and effect the independence or territorial integrity of a state. The legal rule does not have a plain meaning that conforms to the perceptions of most members of the appraising community. In this event, the issue of noncompliance needs to be handled by a multifactor functional or policy analysis. If a national decision-maker is trying to decide what action the law permits his government, then this kind of appraisal may often be helpful.

7. The Technique of the Impartial Expert. A supplemental way to assess the meaning of compliance is to consult neutral experts. If we find, for instance, that three-fourths or more of the specialists in international law who made legal appraisals of national conduct in a controversial situation concluded that it was illegal, then this would be a significant element in any determination about compliance.

8. The Adversary Technique. The meaning of noncompliance may be specified by one's adversary. For instance, if an arms control measure gives a party the right to withdraw upon notice, cause, or suspicion, then the withdrawing party in this setting specifies the meaning of noncompliance. This adjustment of relations may be also worked out tacitly. For instance, North Korea's noncompliance with a provision of the Armistice Agreement governing replacements of military equipment led the United States to abrogate the provision. The meaning of compliance and noncompliance is assessed by adversary interaction. This process breaks down if it is not governed by the reasonableness of the parties, for example, if the claim to retaliate is unfounded, excessive, or misinterpreted.

9. The Equity or Legislative Technique. International society lacks a legislative organ to repeal old rules or to enact new ones. As the membership or interests of states change, the willingness to be bound by certain old rules is drawn into question. A violation of an old rule, if repeated often enough and if the violative attitude is widely and explicitly supported, may generate a new rule founded upon a new consensus; at least it may operate to nullify the binding quality of the old rule. The workings of this international legislative process can be illustrated by reference to the requirement that expropriation of foreign property be accompanied by prompt, adequate, and effective compensation. The transformed character of international society and the record of national practice in the last decade raise serious doubts about the continuing validity of classical rules that purport to specify the form and quantum of compensation. It is certainly arguable that legislative pressures have changed the measure of compensation required by international law and have, as a result, redefined the meaning of noncompliance.

These nine approaches illustrate various ways to accommodate the deficient procedures and inadequate institutions available in international society to resolve disputes among states about compliance with international law. Although these solutions overlap one another and operate at different levels of analysis, they offer both a more objective and substantial interpretation of the meaning of compliance than can be obtained by a mere reliance upon the adversary contentions of parties to the dispute. The sovereign word of a contending national government need not be accepted as the final legal word in an argument about whether or not, in what respects, and to what extent, international law has been violated.

XI. On Treaty Interpretation and the New Haven Approach: Achievements and Prospects

THIS CHAPTER will investigate treaty interpretation in the following sequence:

1. A statement of the broad relevance of interpretation to human experience without regard for the special quality of legal interpretation or the specific focus upon treaty interpretation;

2. An account of the main outlines of the New Haven approach to treaty interpretation as set forth by Myres S. McDougal, Harold D. Lasswell, and James C. Miller in a major study of the subject entitled *The Interpretation of Agreements and World Public Order*;[1]

3. A comparison of the New Haven approach with that taken by the International Law Commission in its draft proposals on treaty interpretation;

4. A critical assessment of the failure of the New Haven approach to identify the limits of treaty interpretation and a discussion of the importance of these limits to an adequate conception of the treaty interpretation process;

5. Some suggestions for next steps that might be taken to enable the New Haven approach to take more appropriate account of the limits of treaty interpretation.

I. The Wider Relevance of Interpretation to Human Experience

A point of departure is suggested by the contrast between the first and the third definitions of *interpretation* found in the *Oxford English Dictionary*: "1. The action of interpreting; explanation, exposition"; "3. The way in which a thing ought to be interpreted; proper explanation." Dictionary definitions used as a starting-point for investigation disclose, as is so often the case, an ambivalence deeply embedded in the subject matter itself. In the instance of interpretation there is disclosed the wavering between the autonomy and objectivity of the interpretative process, on the one side, and its normative, instrumental function on the other. This wavering, and the obscurity of meaning that results from it, makes interpretation at once fascinating and mysterious as an object of inquiry. In an age of propaganda, advertising, and subliminal manipulation it is essential to disentangle, as well as we can, the manipulative mode from more descriptive alternatives in our effort to comprehend the interpretative act.

[1] New Haven, Yale University Press, 1967 (hereinafter cited by page reference only).

Nietzsche conveys the radical significance of interpretation for human experience: "There are no facts, only interpretation." Our understanding of experience is totally a consequence of interpretation. The transmission of interpretations across space and through time emphasizes the relatedness of interpretation and communication.

Those who control the communication network are normally able to exert dominant influence. It is their interpretations that prevail and shape the life of the community. Self-interested interpretation presented as authoritative or objective interpretation has been an essential ingredient of all patterns of domination, veiling oppressive and exploitative relationships in the guise of that which is "natural" or "true" or "necessary." Even the most presupposed form of domination—the domination of women by men—is an expression of the male control of the processes of interpretation: ". . . men have kept the records of the race, which may explain why history is a chronicle of war, conquest, politics, hot competition and abstract reasoning. . . . Ancient writers exaggerated the biological as well as the social differences between the sexes, with the female coming off very badly indeed."[2] Two preliminary propositions are implicit: First, that the capacity to disseminate one-sided interpretations as authoritative is likely to warp the collective perception of reality in decisive respects; second, that the quest for order, justice, and truth in human affairs is very much conditioned by the interpretative process—both by the identity of interpreters and by the methods they use. An energetic commitment to the improvement of interpretation is implicit in any effort to achieve a just ordering of human affairs. "Improvement" means introducing rationality into the interpretative process by encouraging "openness" to various perspectives that bear on a subject matter—inviting women to serve as chroniclers; and "completeness"—a full exposure to the factual bases of contending interpretations. Such openness and completeness need, finally, to be supplemented by a system of communications that discloses the evidence for an interpretation as well as the content of conclusions reached and that reveals the vested interests, if any, of the interpreter.

The central place of interpretation in the legal order is obvious. The role of those entrusted with the appraisal of controversial behavior is essentially an interpreter's role, that of measuring the degrees of congruence between various contentions and the sacred text, whether the text is written or not and whether it is made sacred by individuals through private contract or by organs of the state through official acts.

---

[2] The quoted passage also points out that until relatively recently female births and deaths were not even recorded in census figures. Marshall McLuhan and F. B. Leonard, "The Future of Sex," *Look* (July 25, 1967).

The application of law involves the articulation of interpretations that are authoritative and by acquisition of this status susceptible to enforcement and deserving of respect. The mode of authoritative interpretation reflects and expresses the political values of the relevant community. In a totalitarian society the characteristic mode of interpretation is fiat implemented, as necessary, by terror; there is no premium placed upon genuine assent or explanation, although the regime may go to great lengths to induce conformity by inculcation, propaganda, and the proscription of opposing sources of evidence and belief. In a primitive society the characteristic mode of interpretation is tradition reinforced by magic; there is no effort to explain, but there may be a great deal of effort, by ritual and rite, to substantiate the credentials of the headman or divining voice to interpret the requirements of custom and tradition. In theocratically endowed societies there is normally a comparable emphasis on finding the proper way to interpret the will of God, and heresies and schisms which are usually offshoots of controversies about interpretation may merely disguise a conflict about the nature of authority, and the locus of power. Luther's insistence on "the word" unmediated by "the Church" led to the fracturing of Christendom culminating in movements historians later came to summarize as "The Reformation." The theological controversy centered upon the locus of interpretative authority to construe the will of God, and the relative role of the Bible and the Roman Church in this process of interpretation.

In democratic systems of legal order, authoritative interpreters have an eventual obligation to persuade their publics as to the reasonableness of their interpretations, reasonableness considered in light of overall value predispositions. The political myth and reality of the consent of the governed assumes and produces (or is produced by) the demand for explicit rationality as the essence of interpretation, the marshaling of evidence to convey the sense of impartiality and objectivity, the appearance of autonomy. Of course, the power-value structure animates the interpretative procedure, and the rendering of the Dred Scott decision by the Supreme Court prior to the Civil War is fully compatible with rendering Brown v. Board of Education after World War II.[3] Thus the style of persuasion is conditioned by the value expectations that dominate the community and are presumably represented in those chosen to interpret—positions of honor and substance—who are thoroughly socialized by the community that they serve and represent. A political order is fragile at those times when its class of interpreters disagrees significantly on fundamental questions; for without an underlying consensus contending interpretations are not resolved beyond the

[3] Dred Scott, 19 *Howard* 393 (1857); 483 (1954).
Brown v. Board of Education, 375 US

adversary stage of confrontation. The authoritativeness of an interpretation derives, in part, from the cohesiveness of the elite creating an aura of objectivity for its interpretative claims and, thereby, soliciting voluntary acquiescence from the general public. The cleavages in American society, for example, that have resulted from the United States involvement in the Vietnam War suggest the inevitable deterioration of all law and order that results from a failure of interpreters to sustain their burden of persuasion.

Although few of the principal governments in the world accept the postulates of liberal democracy, interpretation in international society resembles in key respects the role of interpretation in democratic society. The source of the resemblance arises from the absence of centralized procedures of interpretation and implementation in international society leading the effectiveness of a decision to depend largely on voluntary patterns of compliance. Therefore, the persuasiveness of particular interpretation is very much bound up with its authoritativeness. Persuasiveness in an international context presupposes taking account of value diversities, as well as value convergencies;[4] persuasiveness involves also weighing the perceived interests of each side in a dispute and explaining fully why a particular interpretation is selected. This set of considerations merely takes account of the international legal order as predominantly decentralized in terms of both power variables and valued ends. The consequence of decentralization is to highlight the role of communication. To appreciate the distinctive character of the international legal system is to shift emphasis from restraint functions to the communication functions of international law. This shift in

---

[4] A central issue of world order arises from the existence of value diversities and what to do about them in law settings. Some value diversities reflect fundamental disagreements in international society such that it is impossible to infer a consensus. Whereas other value diversities, such as the permissibility of colonial rule or of apartheid, reflect disagreements between the international community as a whole and individual dissident adherent states. In the former context of horizontal diversity the identification of either legal preference with the reality of an authoritative legal interpretation would be unpersuasive, whereas in the latter context of vertical diversity a legal interpretation that implements the community preference as over against the dissident state would be normally persuasive. It is necessary to say normally because legal persuasiveness is not only a matter of an authorized decision-maker passing a judgment with relevant extralegal support, but depends on other factors as well, such as deference to constitutional limits on the procedure and substance of decision-making. In fact, the dissident state is somewhat protected by the limited constitutional authority of the organized international community; the analogy to the dissenter in a democratic domestic society is, of course, obvious, as well as its limits. On the international level constitutional directives are so abstract, vague, and complementary as to make it difficult to distinguish a legally persuasive from a legally unpersuasive decision. For instance, an appeal to the prime constitutional limitation of domestic jurisdiction by a dissident state cannot be readily appraised in any specific setting. The nonoperational relevance of constitutional limits in the United Nations system tends to make political criteria of acceptability decisive; the irrelevance of constitutional restraints impairs the character of a communitywide legal system and retards its growth.

emphasis requires every effort to clarify the role of interpretation in both senses mentioned in the OED, namely that of explanation and of proper explanation.

A final introductory consideration suggests some attentiveness to the limits of interpretation. Susan Sontag has questioned interpretation in provocative form:

> The modern style of interpretation excavates, and as it excavates, destroys; it digs "behind" the text, to find a sub-text which is the true one. The most celebrated and influential modern doctrines, those of Marx and Freud, actually amount to elaborate systems of hermeneutics, aggressive and impious theories of interpretation. All observable phenomena are bracketed, in Freud's phrase, as manifest content. This manifest content must be probed and pushed aside to find the true meaning—the latent content—beneath. For Marx, social events like revolutions and wars; for Freud, the events of individual lives (like neurotic symptoms and slips of the tongue) as well as texts (like a dream or a work of art)—all are treated as occasions for interpretation. According to Freud and Marx, these events only seem to be intelligible. Actually, they have no meaning without interpretation. To understand is to interpret. And to interpret is to restate the phenomenon, in effect to find an equivalent for it.[5]

Miss Sontag is referring to the interpretation of works of art, but her comments have wider application. Underneath this modern emphasis on interpretation is Miss Sontag's contention that the interpreter is a polemicist who proposes action on the basis of suppressed goals. In such a setting it is well to be wary of interpretation and to get back into direct—or less mediated—contact with the object of study.[6] Miss Sontag states this consequence of her analysis with vivid force:

> Interpretation must itself be evaluated, within a historical view of human consciousness. In some cultural contexts, interpretation is a liberating act. It is a means of revising, of transvaluing, of escaping

[5] Susan Sontag, *Against Interpretation,* New York, Dell, 1966, pp. 6-7.

[6] In one sense, what we know is a consequence of interpretation. There is a difference, however, between an interpretation imposed by another and an interpretation evolved by oneself. An imposed interpretation is specially untrustworthy if biasing considerations have been suppressed. Of course, our contact with reality is contingent and we may ourselves be repressing biasing considerations in the process of developing an interpretation. But, especially in matters of political and legal interpretation, it is important to seek interpretations that arise from an unmediated response to "the facts." Of course, the arrangement of the facts is one way to manipulate the interpretative process; such manipulation can be resisted by insisting upon adversary presentation of both sides to the extent feasible. Especially with respect to issues of war and peace, the prospects of legal order are tied closely to the availability of less preinterpreted facts.

[346]

the dead past. In other cultural contexts, it is reactionary, imperti-
nent, cowardly, stifling.

Today is such a time, when the project of interpretation is largely
reactionary stifling . . . interpretation is the revenge of the intellect
upon art.

Even more. It is the revenge of the intellect upon the world. To
interpret is to impoverish, to deplete the world—in order to set up a
shadow world of "meanings" . . . . In most modern instances, interpretation amounts to the philistine refusal to leave the work of art
alone.[7]

To quote Susan Sontag at this length is to suggest the strength of a latent
analogy between works of art and the subject matter of international
order. We can, on occasion, achieve perspective on our subject by looking at it from the outside.[8] Those who control the process of interpretation are partisans in an intense global struggle; elaborate claims
are made about motivations, historical destiny, about who is oppressing whom, and about who is aggressor and who victim. To reach an
understanding of interpretation, thus, requires us to make our way
alone to the phenomena of struggle and turmoil throughout the world,
to find the patience and the courage to establish for ourselves a less
mediated (or, more precisely, a less interpreted) international setting.[9]
Certainly for Americans this imperative has a timely resonance in view

[7] Sontag, pp. 7-8.

[8] "An attempt to bridge the gap between political science and anthropology
has merits because such cross-disciplinary
endeavors may free one from unnecessarily
narrow assumptions which often dominate
research in a given field." Roger D. Masters, "World Politics as a Primitive Political System," *World Politics* XVI, No.
4 (July 1964), 595-619, at 596; for an
impressive comparative study of interpretation as carried on in various intellectual
settings, especially concerned with the
clarification of literary interpretation, see
E. D. Hirsch, Jr., *Validity in Interpretation*, New Haven, Yale University Press,
1967. The value of approaching legal interpretation from the relatively closed interpretative traditions of the social sciences or literary criticism or biblical
studies is to be exposed to a series of
analogous issues, procedures, and solutions
that are each formulated in a distinct
rhetoric and are each dominated by dis-
ciplinary priorities. It is not nearly so
clear in interpreting a literary text that
one should defer to the intentions of the
author as it is with respect to parties to a
legal agreement. Community morals are
much more relevant to legal interpretation than for literary interpretation because in one instance the community acts
an implementing authority and not in the
other, except in a highly authoritarian society.

[9] This advocacy, an extension of the
argument in note 6, *supra*, entails at least
a maximum effort to confront "the facts"
and a serious adoption of a planetary
orientation toward these facts. In this regard, appeals to patriotic virtues debase
the interpretative process as applicable to
the subject matter of international affairs.
Such a planetary reorientation is especially
important for international lawyers to
achieve, thereby setting up the basis for
an intellectual dialogue with those whose
task it is to implement and defend national
foreign policy on a partisan basis. The
position of impartial critic and adversary participant is a fundamental distinction in our search for authoritative interpretation of legal issues in any political
system, but especially in the international
system with its weak procedures and institutions of impartial interpretation. In
this regard, the quality of international interpretation is a function of the impartiality of the interpreter.

of the crosscurrents generated by the Vietnam War. On a simple prosaic level we witness a collision of interpretations, each reasonably connected to a preconscious selection of facts favorable to one side, adverse to the other, that sustains or repudiates the most unconstrained insistence on violence as legitimate and necessary[10] This deeper and wider role of interpretation creates the intellectual foundation for an inquiry into a narrow segment of the subject: the interpretation of international agreements. The purpose of this introductory section has been to establish both the pervasiveness of interpretation and the intimate interconnection between interpretation and the central issues of power, justice, and truth as they are presented in the world today. Dean Hardy C. Dillard has perceptively expressed the lawyer's concern with interpretation by suggesting that it is the central mission of law to serve as "a mediating device capable, when properly understood and wisely applied, of reconciling the claims of the old order under pressures from the new."[11] The interpretative context, however much it may purport to be concerned with the assessment of meanings, is more deeply understood as a battleground wherein the tension between stability and change is pulled taut. The point is that the most interesting disputes about interpretation of legal texts are superficially and secondarily disputes about language. It is rather language that provides the terrain wherein complex tasks of decisional reconciliation must occur, tasks that cannot be truly performed without some sense of the overall function of law in whatver community setting is involved in the dispute.

II. The New Haven Approach to Treaty Interpretation

The Interpretation of Agreements and World Public Order by Myres S. McDougal, Harold D. Lasswell, and James C. Miller contains the most persuasive account of treaty interpretation presently available.[12]

---

[10] An important demonstration of the biasing consequences of adversary interpretation has been made by a social psychologist concerned with developing a "scientific" understanding of issues of war and peace. Ralph K. White, "Misperception and the Vietnam War," *Journal of Social Issues*, XXII, No. 3 (1966), 1-167; a shorter version of this study has also been published: Ralph K. White, "Misperception of Aggression in Vietnam," *Journal of International Affairs*, XXI, No. 1 (1967), 123-40.

[11] Hardy C. Dillard, "Conflict and Change: The Role of Law," *Proceedings American Society of International Law, 1963*, pp. 50-67, at pp. 50-51; see also for further development of Dillard's mode of thought: "Some Aspects of Law and Diplomacy," 91 *Hague Academy Recueil des Cours* 449-552 (1967).

[12] We refer to the New Haven approach because there exist a group of scholars that have self-consciously elected to guide their studies by an application of the framework of inquiry as it has been outlined in the principal methodological efforts of Professors McDougal and Lasswell. The coordination of inquiry around a common methodology, if significant, leads to the development of "a school," an approach to the study or treatment of a subject matter that is a significant event in the history of the subject. Schools of painting and of philosophy come to mind as principal illustrations of the flowering of an approach at a given time and place. "The Vienna Circle," "The Cambridge Platonists," and "The Prague Circle" (of linguistics) are among the examples that

McDougal and Lasswell (in collaboration with Miller) have demonstrated once again the effectiveness of the New Haven approach as an intellectual strategy for restating a subject of basic importance to the international legal order.[13] By now the sweep of their several books is sufficient to regard the undertaking as the highwater mark of international legal studies in the United States and to acknowledge the total achievement to be among the impressive scholarly accomplishments of our times.

This work on interpretation embodies all the scholarly virtues that one has come to expect from The New Haven group's sensitive depiction of the problem: comprehensive survey of practice and scholarship, systematic procedures of inquiry, accurate and thorough research, openness to the relevance of innovation and dynamic technology, candid criticism of alternative conceptions, and explicit recommendations for appropriate understanding. In addition, of course, McDougal and Lasswell bring to inquiry a nonlegalistic appreciation of the ways in which law can be expected to function in an international setting that is both prone to destructive violence and organized in decentralized fashion. And finally, McDougal and Lasswell here seem to be moving rapidly away from an approach to world order that embodies the contingent time-space outlooks of mid-twentieth century United States foreign policy with its focus on the struggle to contain the spread of Communist influence.[14] Unlike earlier works in their series devoted to world public

---

come to mind. By referring to the work inspired by McDougal and Lasswell as "the New Haven approach" I am presuming both to acknowledge and to hasten the acknowledgment of this body of work as distinct and as historically significant in the development of international legal studies. By coincidence, Professor Gidon Gottlieb has written a perceptive appraisal of *The Interpretation of Agreements and World Public Order* in which he identifies the same phenomenon as "the Yale approach." "The Conceptual World of the Yale School of International Law," *World Politics*, XXI, No. 1 (1968), 108-132; see also excellent analysis in Burns Weston, "Book Review," 117 *University of Pennsylvania Law Review* 647-64 (Feb. 1969). Several other books have been published by the Yale University Press and comprise the central achievements to date of the New Haven approach: Harold D. Lasswell and Abraham Kaplan, *Power and Society*, 1950; Myres S. McDougal and Associates, *Studies in World Public Order*, 1960; Myres S. McDougal and Florentino P. Feliciano, *Law and Minimum World Public Order: The Legal Regulation of International Coercion*, 1961; Myres S. Mc-

Dougal and William T. Burke, *The Public Order of the Oceans: A Contemporary International Law of the Sea*, 1962; Myres S. McDougal, Harold D. Lasswell, and Ivan A. Vlasik, *Law and Public Order in Space*, 1963; Douglas M. Johnston, *The International Law of Fisheries: A Framework for Policy-Oriented Inquiries*, 1965; B. F. Murty, *The Ideological Instrument of Coercion and World Public Order*, 1967.

[13] I have attempted broader consideration of the work of Professor McDougal's approach to world legal order in other places: See Chap. III in *Legal Order in a Violent World*, Princeton, Princeton University Press, 1968, and Chap. II, XV, and Appendix C of the present volume.

[14] For extreme examples of McDougal's perception of problems of world legal order from the perspective of cold-war partisanship see "The Soviet-Cuban Quarantine and Self-Defense," 57 *American Journal of International Law*, 597 (1963) and the chapter on the hydrogen bomb tests in the Pacific written in collaboration with Norbert A. Schlei and printed in *Studies in World Public Order*, New Haven, Yale University Press, 1960, pp. 763-843.

order, *Interpretation* is not scarred by the distorting imprint of cold-war partisanship. The excellence of scholarly achievement makes it sensible to take this book seriously, although not by giving the impression that the treatment is so satisfying that there is nothing to criticize, nor even less, that there is nothing left to add.[15] Rarely is a scholar so generous (or deluded) as to admit that his colleague's treatment of a subject reduces him to exuberant accolades or mute acquiescence; Mc-Dougal and Lasswell would themselves proclaim that the role of a scholar is to continue inquiry in a human environment of change and ferment; the scholar does not aspire to set the process of inquiry at rest by a single cloudburst of wisdom and understanding. Accordingly, the chief value of the New Haven approach is to provide a persuasive reorientation of inquiry into the interpretative process, and not because their recommended approach is so definitive as to put to rest the need for inquiry.

The scope of the *Interpretation of International Agreements and World Public Order* is more restricted than the title suggests. The book emphasizes the task of interpreting international agreements in some international judicial forum, most characteristically the International Court of Justice. Obviously such a study contains many implications for interpreting international agreements in domestic courts, for interpreting international agreements in nonjudicial forums (such as foreign offices or international organizations), as well as for the wide process of authoritative interpretation surveyed in the first section, but the explicit efforts of McDougal, Lasswell, and Miller are organized around an inquiry into the interpretation of international agreements by international tribunals.[16]

McDougal-Lasswell-Miller evolve a comprehensive and systematic conception of how the function of interpretation is appropriately performed by a decision-maker.[17] It is a very coherent conception. In fact,

[15] The world remembers major creative enterprises long after criticisms, however well taken, are forgotten or assimilated; criticism, in this sense, is a marginal activity, constructive only to the extent that it facilitates one's own work or that of others. A critic's humility is an inevitable side-effect of the realization that his activity is a parasitical one. Such an aside seems necessary to put in some perspective the relation between the book under consideration and a critical response evoked by it.

[16] This narrowness of actual coverage of interpretative phenomena appears to contrast both with the breadth of stated purposes and the generality of Chaps. 1-3 that set forth the basic approach. See esp. the breadth of statement in the In-

troduction, pp. xi-xxi.

[17] A short statement of this conception of treaty interpretation has been made by another member of the group that adopts the New Haven approach: Peter J. Liacouros, "The International Court of Justice and Development of Useful 'Rules of Interpretation' in the Process of Treaty Interpretation," *Proceedings American Society of International Law, 1965*, pp. 161-69. Professor Liacouros' paper is a distinct contribution, especially as a consequence of its careful discussion of the choice between textualism and contextualism and of its insistence that even functionally conceived "rules" of interpretation need to be correlated with an adequate "map of social reality" (p. 167).

the approach is so persuasively presented that one is inclined to assent in the spirit of "well, of course, this is the only sensible way to interpret an international agreement." In one sense, the essence of the New Haven approach is to work out explicitly and fully the implications for a given subject matter of commonsense rationality as understood in mid-twentieth century America. Perhaps this characterization can be conveyed more definitely by a more detailed consideration of the central arguments of method and substance found in *Interpretation*.

First, it seems helpful to appreciate the extent to which the Mc-Dougal-Lasswell-Miller approach differs from that of other significant authors who have written on treaty interpretation. We find in the extensive literature devoted to the interpretation of international agreements a basic dichotomy arising from a choice between conflicting policy objectives. Many international jurists, especially those who wrote in earlier eras when the procedures of biblical exegesis provided the primary model of the interpretative process, tended to emphasize the definiteness of law as essential to authoritativeness. This emphasis produced a mechanical approach to treaty interpretation based on so-called canons of interpretation.[18] Actually, the need for interpretation was attributed to faulty drafting of an agreement; the ideal of treaty-drafting implicit in a textual view of interpretation is to employ language that is so clear and precise that no reasonable disagreement can arise with regard to the scope or meaning of the rights and duties of the parties.[19] Such an ideal was rarely attained, of course, and when disputes arose the reference to canons was supposed to resolve the interpretative issue with minimum human intervention between the text and its operational content. These canons or maxims relied upon to vindicate the interpretative act were also intended to give a decision the appearance of definiteness that was expected to nullify the inference that the interpreter was construing a document according to some arbitrary will of his own. This mechanical approach presupposes the autonomy of language and emphasizes the extent to which the task of the interpreter is to construe what has been written down and authorized by the parties to the agreement.[20] Given this orientation there is a nat-

---

[18] For a useful outline of the standard rules of interpretation with illustrative practice see Lord Arnold McNair, *The Law of Treaties*, Oxford, Oxford University Press, 1961, pp. 364-457.

[19] On the limits of language—as distinct from the context of its use—to communicate meaning it is very rewarding to consider the discussion in Ludwig Wittgenstein, *Philosophical Investigations*, New York, Macmillan, 1953.

[20] For a very suggestive account of the complexity of the interpretive task in connection with nonlegal texts see E. D. Hirsch, Jr., *op.cit. supra*, note 8 pp. 1-23. Discussions of interpretation are, of course, central to Biblical studies and to arguments about the scriptural basis of religion. For interesting accounts in a contemporary context see Paul Tillich, *Biblical Religion and the Search for Ultimate Reality*, Chicago, University of Chicago,

ural emphasis on textualism and on the acceptance of the primacy of Vattel's celebrated maxim: *"It is not allowable to interpret what has no need of interpretation."*[21] The main contention of this school of interpretation is to distrust recourse to context as importing into the interpretative process both the appearance and reality of arbitrary factors, especially since the context of negotiation, attitude, and conduct is so vague and intricate that there is created a vast opportunity for the interpreter to mold the evidence drawn from the context and interpret the obligations of the parties to defeat their intention as manifest in the agreement. There are, thus, several aspects of this approach: (1) a belief in the normal clarity of language as sufficient to dispense or minimize with the intrepretative act—the text speaks for itself; (2) a distrust of extra-textualism as encouraging the arbitrary introduction of unreliable and biased considerations in the guise of interpretation.

Since even those who advocate this approach acknowledge that the text of an agreement is not always clear, supplemental canons are enumerated to guide the decision-maker along definite channels of inquiry.[22] These supplemental canons are arranged often in hierarchical

1955; Karl Jaspers and Rudolf Bultmann, *Myth and Christianity: An Inquiry into the Possibility of Religion Without Myth*, New York, Noonday Press, 1958.

[21] Emmerich de Vattel, *The Law of Nations*, Washington. Philadelphia, T.vJ.W., Johnson (Chitty trans. 1758 edn., 1883), p. 244. (Emphasis in original.)

[22] There is an interesting contrast in approach embodied in much of the most sophisticated commentary on treaty interpretation. There are some authors, such as Liacouros, who stress the pervasive ambiguity of language as the basic orienting circumstance of the interpretative process. For instance, Professor Liacouros writes "To begin with, no agreement—and therefore, no text—is unambiguous. There are no unambiguous words, gestures, or signs. Each sign is merely a non-subjective mediator of, as yet, only hypothetically measurable subjectivities; none means anything unless related contextually by someone to somebody else (who can never be certain he received the intended subjective message)." Liacouros, *op.cit. supra*, note 17, at p. 161. There are other authors, such as Stanley Metzger, who stress the normal capacity of parties to an agreement to embody in unambiguous language the essential structure of rights and duties. Professor Metzger orients his conception of treaty interpretation upon a two-tier notion; the first tier of inquiry is based on giving effect to the clear meaning of the text; the second tier of inquiry, undertaken only if the first tier uncovers a tex-

tual ambiguity, involves reference to any contextual factors that might resolve the ambiguity in a persuasive manner. The essence of Professor Metzger's approach is expressed in the following message: "This apparent rejection [by Paul B. Larsen] of 'ordinary meaning in context', is quite unreal and impractical. Normally, legislators, and at least equally as often diplomats, know what they are saying and know the words to use to say it; they are, like lawyers who are well represented in both groups, word merchants." Stanley D. Metzger, "Treaty Interpretation and the United States—Italy Air Transport Arbitration," 61 *American Journal of International Law* 1007-11, at p. 1009-10 (1967). The controversy concerns a choice of presumptions: does one start with the presumption of normal clarity or normal ambiguity. Someone of Liacouros' persuasion initiates an inquiry with a presumption of ambiguity that requires resolution through as exhaustive inquiry into full context as the resources of the interpreter warrant (also taking account of the relative importance of the document in question). Someone of Metzger's persuasion starts an inquiry with a presumption of clarity that can be rebutted by a persuasive showing that more than one plausible reading of the disputed text can be made. There is a difference in scholarly and decisional method involved in these differing presumptions, although whether there are also differences in decisional outcomes is uncertain without serious empirical tests. It might be quite useful to construct a simulation exercise that would test the results of following each of the two presumptions.

It is not without interest to note that Metzger's approach to treaty intrepretation is very similar to that of the American Law Institute in its *Restatement (Second) of the Foreign Relations Law of the United States*. It might be appropriate to set out its central provisions on treaty interpretation, §§146, 147, 153:

Basic Function of Interpretation

The extent to which an international agreement creates, changes, or defines relationships under international law is determined in case of doubt by the interpretation of the agreement. The primary object of interpretation is to ascertain the meaning intended by the parties for the terms in which the agreement is expressed, having regard to the context in which they occur and the circumstances under which the agreement was made. This meaning is determined in the light of all relevant factors.

Criteria for Interpretation

(1) International law requires that the interpretative process ascertain and give effect to the purpose of the international agreement which, as appears from the terms used by the parties, it was intended to serve. The factors to be taken into account by way of guidance in the interpretative process include:

(a) the ordinary meaning of the words of the agreement in the context in which they are used;

(b) the title given the agreement and statements of purpose and scope included in its text;

(c) the circumstances attending the negotiation of the agreement;

(d) drafts and other documents submitted for consideration, action taken on them, and the official record of the deliberations during the course of the negotiation;

(e) unilateral statements of understanding made by a signatory before the agreement came into effect, to the extent that they were communicated to, or otherwise known to, the other signatory or signatories;

(f) the subsequent practice of the parties in the performance of the agreement, or the subsequent practice of one party, if the other party or parties knew or had reason to know of it;

(g) change of circumstances, to the extent indicated in §153;

(h) the compatibility of alternative interpretations of the agreement with (i) the obligations of the parties to other states under general international law and other international agreements of the parties, and (ii) the principles of law common to the legal systems of the parties or of all states having reasonably developed legal systems;

(i) comparison of the texts in the different languages in which the agreement was concluded, taking into account any provision in the agreement as to the authoritativeness of the different texts.

(2) The ordinary meaning of the words of an agreement, as indicated in Subsection (1) (a), must always be considered as a factor in the interpretation of the agreement. There is no established priority as between the factors indicated in Subsection (1) (b)-(i) or as between them and additional factors not listed therein.

Rule of Rebus Sic Stantibus: Substantial Change of Circumstances

(1) An international agreement is subject to the implied condition that a substantial change of a temporary or permanent nature, in a state of facts existing at the time when the agreement became effective, suspends or terminates, as the case may be, the obligations of the parties under the agreement to the extent that the continuation of the state of facts was of such importance to the achievement of the objectives of the agreement that the parties would not have intended the obligations to be applicable under the changed circumstances.

(2) A party may rely on an interpretation of the agreement as indicated in Subsection (1) as a basis for suspending or terminating performance of the obligations in question only if it did not cause the change in the state of facts by action inconsistent with the purpose of the agreement and has otherwise acted in good faith.

(3) When the conditions specified in Subsection (1) apply only to a separable portion of the agreement, suspension or termination applies only to that portion.

Cf. also the approach taken by the International Law Commission in its Draft Convention of the Law of Treaties, see pp. 363-68.

The Metzger-Restatement position accords with common sense as a practical, and yet functionally sufficient approach to interpretation, evading the cumbersomeness of presumed contextualism, and yet transcending the limits of textualism to the extent warranted by the specific sit-

form to emphasize the generality of the recommended procedure of the inquiry, reducing to the minimum the decision-maker's scope for discretion.[23] Underlying this approach is the policy of stabilizing the agreement process by means of defending and presupposing the definiteness of language as the anchor of reality, holding that what the parties have agreed to will be disclosed best in the words of their agreement and protecting the agreement from encroachment by a more freewheeling conception of interpretation.[24]

---

uation. However, the focus on the language of the text rather than upon the purposes of the parties to the agreement exhibits a certain insensitivity to the character of major disputes about interpretation. These disputes normally arise out of conflicting contentions as to purposes, perhaps complicated by opposed views as to the bearing of changed circumstances. In essence, it is the contextual character of legal argument that gives support to the insistence that an interpreter rely upon contextual modes of interpretation.

The formulation found in Article 19 of the Harvard Research Draft Convention on the Law of Treaties appears to strike the proper emphasis in this respect, an emphasis that seems more helpful than either that advocated by Professor Metzger or Section 147 of the *Restatement of Foreign Relations Law*. The text of Article 19, Interpretation of Treaties is as follows:

(a) A treaty is to be interpreted in the light of the general purpose which it is intended to serve. The historical background of the treaty, *travaux préparatoires*, the circumstances of the parties at the time the treaty was entered into, the change in these circumstances sought to be effected, the subsequent conduct of the parties in applying the provisions of the treaty, and the conditions prevailing at the time interpretation is being made, are to be considered in connection with the general purpose which the treaty is intended to serve.

(b) When the text of a treaty is embodied in versions in different languages, and when it is not stipulated that the version in one of the languages shall prevail, the treaty is to be interpreted with a view to giving to corresponding provisions in the different versions a common meaning which will effect the general purpose which the treaty is intended to serve.

Harvard Research in International Law, "Law of Treaties: Draft Convention with Comment," 29 *American Journal of In-*

ternational Law, Supp. Section III, pp. 657-1226, at p. 661 (1935); see also Comment, pp. 937-77. The Comment puts the role of the text in its proper perspective: "When interpreting a treaty, the text thereof must, of course, be respected; the interpreter must not alter it or substitute a new text. Nevertheless, the bare words of a treaty have significance only as they may be taken as expressions of the purpose or design of the parties which employed them; they have a 'meaning' only as they are considered in the light of the whole setting in which they are employed. To purport to attribute a 'clear,' or 'natural,' or a preexisting meaning to them apart from that setting is to ignore the fact that words may be given any meaning which the parties using them may agree to give them, and that few words have an exact and single meaning" (p. 947). The New Haven approach works out the systematic consequences of this point of intellectual departure, and thereby fully develops a method appropriate to a position of presumed contextualism. The Restatement approach, although to an extent far less than the International Law Commission approach, works out, although less rigorously, a method appropriate for presumed textualism. The Restatement is sophisticated about recourse to supplemental factors once the textual presumption has been overcome.

[23] For general discussion of role of principles or canons of interpretation see V. O. Degan, *L'Interprétation des Accords en Droit International*, The Hague, Nijhoff, 1963; Harvard Research, *op.cit. supra*, note 22, at pp. 939-47, for recent approaches relying on canons to guide the interpretative process see Sir Eric Beckett, "Comments on the Report of Sir Hersch Lauterpacht," 43 *Annuaire de l'Institut de Droit International* [I] 435 (1950), and Sir Gerald M. Fitzmaurice, "The Law and Procedure of the International Court of Justice," 28 *British Yearbook of International Law* 5 (1951).

[24] This restrictive approach to interpretation seeks to prevent a changed conception of self-interest to be disguised as an issue of interpretative discretion.

Courts have frequently relied upon canons of interpretation in explaining their results and have tended to accept, at least rhetorically, the injunction against the exercise of discretion. Therefore, the judicial practice of an international tribunal is replete with discussion of why the intentions of the parties must be primarily assessed by reference to the language of agreement and only if the language is not self-defining does the occasion arise for recourse to extra-textual materials.

The textualist-canonist approach to interpretation came under early attack as a dangerous deception. First, this approach was alleged to distort the description of what courts have actually done when interpretation has been involved; second, the textualist approach was regarded as providing a bad set of recommendations as to what courts should do. Language is rarely self-defining, the text is not clear unless it is "interpreted" to be so, and therefore appraisal and explanation of meaning requires recourse to evidence extrinsic to the text. Furthermore, the maxims of the canonist obscure the openness of the interpretative situation, are in internal contradiction, and suggest a simplification of the interpretative inquiry that cannot hope to assess the real intention of the parties. Effective resolution of a controversy requires more than a rule and a presumption in the case of acknowledged doubt as to the meaning of a disputed international agreement.[25]

This critique of traditional methods leads to a theory of interpretation that stresses the intelligent use of judicial discretion as a preferable substitute for its mechanical denial. Drawing principal inspiration from Charles Cheney Hyde, T. C. Yu adopts ". . . the purpose of presenting the evolution of interpretation from 'primitive formalism' to 'scientific rationalism.' "[26] He writes (in 1927) that ". . . no work has been seen in which the author has made a serious endeavor to develop the application of a new system of treaty interpretation based, not on canons, but on a scientific search for the sources of evidence."[27] Mr. Yu's orientation is developed more fully by Chang in *The Interpretation of Treaties by Judicial Tribunals*.[28] Mr. Chang argues that the emphasis on seeking evidence to assess intention with respect to disputed terms of international agreements is more descriptive of judicial behavior than any other conception of the interpretative process. "Judicial experiences in treaty interpretation on the whole reflect a general trend lead-

25 At minimum, the extratextual investigation of evidence for alternative interpretations will serve to confirm the alleged clarity of the text itself. If the context confirms the text, then it reinforces the authority of the decision, whereas if it doesn't, then the unresolved issues are more aptly resolved by considering them than by purporting a specious clarity.
26 Tsune-Chi Yu, *The Interpretation of Treaties*, New York, Columbia University Faculty of Political Science, 1927, p. 77.
27 *Id.* at 28. The exception is Charles Cheney Hyde. For Hyde's latest statement see *International Law Chiefly as Interpreted and Applied by the United States*, Boston, Little, Brown, 2nd rev. edn., 1945, Vol. 2, 1468-72.
28 Yi-Ting Chang, *The Interpretation of Treaties by Judicial Tribunals*, New York, Columbia University Faculty of Political Science, 1933.

ing to the conclusion that the function of the interpreter is simply to discover and ascertain, with the aid of various sources of evidence, the sense in which the contracting parties actually employed particular terms in a treaty. Once that significance which the parties mutually understood, consented to, and understood that they had consented to, is discovered, the function of treaty interpretation is completely fulfilled."[29] In this Yu-Chang view, the improved understanding and execution of the processes of treaty interpretation merely requires a shift of emphasis away from a rule-orientation (canons, maxims) to an evidentiary orientation. To quote Mr. Chang once more: "In short, with the function of treaty interpretation properly understood, the whole problem becomes a question of evidence, the presentation of which calls for and also permits the simplest methods of proof."[30]

Julius Stone deepens the discussion of treaty interpretation by examining the implications of the evidentiary openness that Yu and Chang affirm. He regards, also, the canonist rhetoric as essentially humbug that obscures not only the real basis of decision but also suppresses the role of judicial law-making. The use of canons has the effect of producing "the appearance of an objective decision based on compulsive legal directives, where in reality no legal compulsion does exist."[31] The purpose of this disguise (or "fiction") is "to disarm the still prevalent prejudice against judicial law-making."[32] Stone suggests that the inherent ambiguity of international agreements makes "law-making" an inevitable aspect of the interpretative act. This poses the issue as to whether it is better to present judicial law-making as such or to disguise it through the use of legal fictions purporting a false definiteness: "The important question is whether the tribunal will choose more wisely if it chooses in consciousness of its responsibility rather than in the belief that it has no choice open."[33] There is also the related question of whether the decision will be as acceptable if the role of judicial law-making is manifest; Stone is especially sensitive to the peculiar difficulty of attaining authoritativeness for the decisions of international tribunals: ". . . we still lack international tribunals which can reflect the socio-ethical convictions of the aggregate of States, in a manner cor-

---

[29] *Id.* at 182.
[30] *Id.* at 185.
[31] Julius Stone, "Fictional Elements in Treaty Interpretation—A Study in the International Judicial Process," 1 *Sydney Law Review* 334, 364 (1954); also 347: "It is notorious that . . . treaty terms may often be intended, not to express the consensus reached, but rather to conceal the failure to reach one. In multilateral instruments, especially political ones, that agreed content expressed by the terms may be far less important than the non-agreed terms concealed by them. When a case arises involving the non-agreed content of the treaty, interpretation of the terms, even if purporting to find the intention of the parties is not in fact doing so. The imputation of intention in such a case is a fiction concealing the true nature of the activity."
[32] *Id.* at 349.
[33] *Id.* at 367.

responding to that in which municipal judges reflect the convictions of a nation. And it is this relation between judges and community which, in final resort, renders judicial law-creation tolerable and consistent with liberty."[34] For Stone, then, the acknowledgment of the openness of the interpretative situation leads directly to a consideration of the limits of legal order in international society.[35] In effect, Stone's analysis suggests that if the interpretative act is properly understood, then there is no way for an international tribunal to render an authoritative judgment. Therefore, in this view the debate about interpretation is symptomatic of the wider difficulty of resolving disputes about legal obligation in a decentralized legal order that lacks shared value premises. Given this analysis there is no solution to the interpretative problem by way of method or lucidity. Thus Stone shifts the problem of interpretation from a focus on *evidence* to a search for authoritativeness in international decision-making.[36] Language is no longer of crucial significance except to illustrate the dependence of legal authority upon a collocation of socioethical consensus and police capability, which characteristics are deficiently exhibited in international society. Recalling the sweeping arguments that Susan Sontag advances against the project of interpretation, Julius Stone's approach illustrates the effort of an international lawyer to "interpret" the act of interpretation as being in essence flawed by the absence of any foundation for the assertion of legal authority in international society.[37]

This would seem to be a suitable point at which to consider the relevance of the New Haven approach to this intellectual dialogue. It would appear that their set of responses to the subject matter of treaty interpretation is shaped very largely in reaction to the Yu-Chang-Stone line of analysis.[38] To begin with, McDougal-Lasswell-Miller share and emphasize the inadequacy of various textualist approaches emanating from the classical view of interpretation found in Vattel's seventeenth chapter and sophisticated in the Harvard Research Draft Convention on the Law of Treaties published in 1935: "It is the grossest, least defensible exercise of arbitrary formalism to arrogate to one particular set of signs—the text of a document—the role of serving as the

34 *Id.* at 364.
35 Such a view of interpretation is apparent in other writings by Julius Stone. E.g., *Aggression and World Order*, Berkeley, University of California Press, 1958; "The International Court and World Crisis," *International Conciliation*, No. 536, (Jan. 1962), 3-64.
36 That is, the domestic solution is accepted whereby the authoritativeness of the interpreter is accepted as inevitably the final reference point of dispute; Julius Stone's emphasis, in part a reaction to the

false definiteness of others, tends to exaggerate the discretionary character of the interpretative process.
37 Compare the wider discussion, pp. 342-48.
38 Although these responses also represent an extension from earlier writings, especially those outlining the method of policy-oriented jurisprudence. See esp. Myres S. McDougal and Associates, *Studies in World Public Order*, New Haven, Yale University Press, 1960, pp. 43-154, 987-1033.

exclusive index of the parties' shared expectations."[39] This rejection of textual autonomy is combined with a traditional affirmation that the interpretative inquiry should be guided by a search for the genuine intention of the parties to the international agreement: "The primary aim of a process of interpretation by an authorized and controlling decision maker can be formulated in the following proposition: discover the shared expectations that the parties to the relevant communication succeeded in creating in each other."[40] McDougal-Lasswell-Miller accept the role of judicial creativity without concern.[41] Their effort is to provide a method to minimize the arbitrariness of its exercise. The essence of this method is contextualism: "the communications which constitute an international agreement, like all other communications, are functions of a larger context, and the realistic identification of the content of these communications must require a systematic, comprehensive examination of all the relevant features of that context, with conscious and deliberate appraisal of their significance."[42] The major portion of *Interpretation* is devoted to the explication of a method for carrying out this directive. The method is derived partly from a survey of judicial practice and drawn partly from an exposition of all components of context that might contain evidence relevant to the discover of "genuine shared expectations."

In effect, McDougal-Lasswell-Miller start with the directives of Yu and Chang but respond to their call for dealing with the act of interpretation as a matter of consulting the relevant evidence by supplying a procedure of inquiry which if followed will assure the decision-maker that he has been exposed to the relevant evidence. It amounts to a sophisticated "how to do it" kit prepared for interpreters of international agreements. Underneath the enterprise lies the belief—drawn into some question by Julius Stone—that maximum clarity is desirable in the search for and justification of a judicial decision.[43] The authorita-

---

[39] P. xvii; see also pp. 361-69. Note esp. the rather insistent use of visual imagery on these pages; e.g., p. 363: "The obvious fact is that the phrase-focused interpreter cannot entirely blind himself to the larger features of the dispute although his cadaver-like obedience to the textualist command may result, when his glance strays toward *travaux préparatoires*, in sensations akin to those said to be enjoyed by a peeping Tom."

[40] P. xvi.

[41] But note comment on the views of Julius Stone and Sir Hersch Lauterpacht, that suggests that an international tribunal "be modestly hesitant to impose new policies, especially in derogation of expressed apparently genuinely shared expectations. Too deliberate an assertion of control, with

doubtful authority, could have a potentially harmful effect both upon the parties and upon the development of the jurisdiction of international tribunals" (p. 265).

[42] P. 11.

[43] In general, we are dealing with the issue as to whether the authoritativeness of decision and respect for law increase or decrease as a result of disclosing the discretionary element in the decision process.

Is a decision more likely to induce respect and compliance if given a definiteness that it doesn't truly possess? The answer depends on expectations, relevant traditions, and the persuasiveness of the dispositive reasoning; it also depends on considerations of time and place.

tiveness of interpretation will flow from the effort as a persuasive and impartial application of the results of systematic inquiry into the context.

McDougal-Lasswell-Miller subordinate in the final analysis the genuine expectations of the parties to the basic norms of world legal order.[44] Therefore, the autonomy of expectations is not guaranteed—although these authors claim that it is more closely approximated than by according or pretending to accord autonomy to the text. Expectations must be reconciled with overriding community norms;[45] thus the evidence of intentions is not the whole task as Chang contends it is. McDougal-Lasswell-Miller contend that "the problem to which attention must be drawn is that of specifying precisely what international policies have been regarded, will be regarded, and ought to be regarded as so basic that they cannot be varied even by explicit agreements between states."[46] Even more important than the invalidation of expectations that conflict with community policies—probably a rare occurrence—is the use of these policies in filling up "the gaps" and the confusions that are so often embodied in complex treaty instruments, especially those of a highly abstract and multilateral character that propose regulation of a wide area of international subject matter.[47] This need for "recourse to general community policies for supplementation" is "fully recognized by most contemporary commentators—including both Lauterpacht and Stone." However, "this common recognition is often obscured by ambiguities and infelicities of expression" and "few of these formulations proceed, beyond the preliminary invocation of customary international law, to a more detailed specification of relevant community policies."[48] As with the construction of context relevant to expectations so with the determination of how world community policies enter the interpretative process, the contribution of *Interpretation* is not

[44] McDougal-Lasswell-Miller urge recourse to "the basic constitutive policies of the larger community which embraces both parties and decision-maker" whenever the search for genuine shared expectations "must falter or fail because of gaps, contradictions, or ambiguities in the parties' communication." In addition, however, they argue that to protect "overriding common interests" "decision-makers should refuse to give effect to the expectations of the parties" "when grave contradictions are found between the explicit expectations of parties to an agreement and the requirements of fundamental community policy." (All quoted phrases on p. 41.)

[45] Cf. Egon Schwelb, "Some Aspects of International *Jus Cogens* as Formulated by the International Commission of Jur-

ists," 61 *American Journal of International Law* 946 (1967) with Alfred Verdross, "Jus Dispositivum and Jus Cogens in International Law," 60 *American Journal of International Law* 55 (1967).

[46] P. 106.

[47] A good illustration of a treaty in which interpretive issues were purposely left unresolved in the text and negotiations is the Limited Test Ban Treaty of 1963. The search for a basis of underlying accord took precedence over clarifying the text with respect to whether nontest explosions for peaceful purposes (e.g., canal-building) or military nontest uses were prohibited. For convenient treaty text see *Documents on Disarmament, 1963*, Washington, Government Printing Office, pp. 291-93.

[48] Pp. 104-05.

the discovery of the need but the provision of explicit ways to satisfy it.

Therefore, the McDougal-Lasswell-Miller enterprise is one of extension and specification of the implications of the work done to overthrow the mechanical jurisprudence of the classicists. The claim being that to reject the canons of interpretation without providing a new way to order and orient the judicial task of treaty interpretation is to stop analysis at the critical stage and, therefore, to avoid the task of reconstruction. *Interpretation* rejecting the rejection of the canons of interpretation makes a persuasive argument for their use to help the decision-maker structure his inquiry into the context of an agreement.[49] The canons are converted from their Vattelian function as criteria of decision to a guidance function that calls the attention of the decision-maker to crucial aspects of context.[50] McDougal-Lasswell-Miller summarize their own position in illuminating fashion:

> The view we recommend thus rejects the excessive emphasis of recent years both upon hierarchy as in Beckett and Fitzmaurice, and upon freedom of decision as in Hyde, Stone, and others. The choice between an ordered hierarchy of rules and the rejection of all rules is one which unnecessarily restricts the available alternatives. The disciplined systematic use of such rules, not in precise application as justifications for apparent "objective" decisions, as has been suggested, but rather as specific directives to contextual factors and as procedures for guiding an examination of such factors, is, we suggest, the only reliable means of approximating, in all cases, the participants' genuine expectations of commitment.[51]

This intermediate view of the canons attempts to renew the role of traditional doctrine, not as an obstacle to policy-oriented inquiry but as an incident of it.[52] McDougal-Lasswell-Miller argue that if the rule is stripped of dogma then it will be seen to have been formulated for some

---

[49] The interpretative process is made as authoritative as possible by reliance on the canons to point toward the significant features of context without pretending that invocation of the canons can ever be dispositive of a controversy about interpretation.

[50] Rejection altogether of the role of the canons to frame inquiry leads to a fully discretionary interpretative process. This result follows from the analysis of Stone, Hyde, Yu, and Chang and is criticized by McDougal-Lasswell-Miller because it "ignores the important functions which principles can play both in specifying the detailed features of the 'sources' of expectation and in outlining systematic and disciplined procedures for their ex-

amination" (pp. 114-15). In contrast, the Yale authors contend that "the appropriate function of principles of interpretation . . . is that of calling the attention of the decision-maker, in an orderly and economic way, to the various features of the process of commitment and its context which must be taken into account in determining the parties' genuine shared expectations and identifying relevant community policies" (p. 111).

[51] P. 117.

[52] Cf. the comparable emphasis by McDougal and Florentino P. Feliciano on an intermediate approach to the interrelated conceptions of aggression and self-defense in *Law and Minimum World Public Order*, pp. 121-260.

functional reason of relevance to the overriding search of interpreters for stable agreements. Textualist emphases reflect the effort of the parties to choose the language of agreement with care; preagreement events and discussions illuminating how and why particular words were used, post-agreement events and communications illuminating how the parties understood words to be used, and the overall search for some way to over-come "gaps" and ambiguities indicating a normal subordination of specific uncertainties of obligation to general policies of establishing order.[53] Judicial practice is built around these sorts of factors approached often in what appears to be a haphazard way; *Interpretation* argues both that past practice is less haphazard than it is normally assumed to be and more haphazard than is desirable. The attempt of McDougal-Lasswell-Miller is to provide a systematic way of inquiring that minimizes the haphazard and makes the interpreter as aware as possible of what he is doing and why.

The concern of McDougal-Lasswell-Miller with treaty interpretation is part of their abiding quest to specify and encourage "the realization of a world public order of human dignity."[54] They write of being "under no illusion" about fulfilling this goal; "so comprehensive and revolutionary an achievement will require many changes in the predispositions current at any given present in the future of the world arena." At the same time these authors affirm that it would be "a crude mistake to assume" that a more adequate conception of interpretation would be "of trivial consequence for the future of law and man. On the contrary: without more adequate conceptions of interpretation the flow of decision is likely to adapt itself at unnecessary human cost to the challenges that arise in the controversies that express and in turn affect the reconstruction of world public order in an era of explosive scientific and technological growth."[55] The entire environment of accelerating change gives new prominence to the struggle to achieve stability of expectation for those who enter agreements with one another. And stability of expectation as a general goal is served by giving as clear guidance as possible to the decision-maker entrusted with construing the expectations that were written into an agreement. McDougal-Lasswell-Miller sustain the main components of their argument:

1. Interpretation of international agreements is important; the ability of governments to project mutually beneficial agreements into the future depends upon their confidence in the reasonableness of the interpretative process that will govern the obligations of the parties; this confidence can arise only if the value and policy considerations that even-

---

[53] For a very illuminating analysis of the issues posed for interpretation by gaps and ambiguities see Hersch Lauterpacht, "Restrictive Interpretation and the Principle of Effectiveness in the Interpre- tation of Treaties," 26 *British Yearbook of International Law* 46 (1949).
[54] P. 395.
[55] *Ibid.*

tuated in the language of the agreement are used to guide the process of interpretation; such confidence is not likely to arise if interpretation is mechanically performed by reference or alleged reference to rules (maxims or canons) or is perceived to be a discretionary act of the interpreter—guidelines are needed that neither sacrifice flexibility nor replace the expectations of the parties with the discretionary wisdom of the decision-maker.

2. The objective of interpretation is to construe the agreement to accord as closely as possible with the genuine shared expectations of the parties, provided only that these expectations do not violate the basic norms of world legal order; these basic norms include the prerequisites of minimum order and, possibly, some standards of human rights.[56]

3. Appropriate methods of interpretation are necessarily intricate; there is no simplification of the interpretative act that is not destructive of its main policy functions;[57]

4. The intricacy of interpretation is susceptible to systematic statement that reduces the prospect of arbitrary discretion shaping the interpretative act;

5. The appropriate method of interpretation is in the nature of drafting a map of the intellectual territory, pointing out the relevant features of the terrain and posting signposts; but not reproducing the operations with precision; the objective of such an approach is to increase the prospects of rationality of decision and justification in controversies about the meaning of international agreements.

6. The process of interpretation can be improved by taking account of the modern technology of data gathering and by advances in logical analysis of language usage; all instruments of inquiry helpful in gaining insight as to "genuine expectations" should be used by the interpreter; as well, the process of interpretation can be improved by using the classical canons of interpretation to guide inquiry to the most relevant features of context.

7. Finally, the task of interpretation can be divided between the search for relevant sources of evidence as to the meaning of the agreement (principles of content) and the agenda of operations that should guide the behavior of the inquirer (principles of procedures). Together these two sets of principles specify the recommended method of inquiry both in terms of scope and of sequence.[58]

---

[56] For examples of basic norms that override expectations see pp. 107-11. Basic community norms also are used to supplement incomplete or confused expectations by the parties.

[57] Such a stress on the intricacy of communication entails a conception of language as limited in its capacity to establish unambiguous meaning.

[58] Pp. 119-359; in addition, there is some need to relate an approach to context with an overall conception of the international environment; hence, the need for mapping and models as an adjunct to the

III. The Draft Articles on Interpretation in the International Law Commission Draft Convention on the Law of Treaties

The two most significant approaches to the interpretation of international agreements, in my judgment, are to be found in McDougal-Lasswell-Miller's volume and in the relevant provisions of the Draft Articles on the Law of Treaties of the International Law Commission (ILC).[59] The significance of McDougal-Lasswell-Miller is to develop a coherent conception of interpretation geared to the functional and policy needs of international society. The significance of the Draft Articles is of quite another sort, it derives from the stature of the ILC as the most authoritative organ in international society for the exposition of international legal doctrine.[60] The ILC is manned by international jurists of high professional status and attainment drawn from all major legal systems of the world. It is an occasion for distress, therefore, that the work of this august body on the subject of interpretation should diverge so sharply from the kind of progressive conception outlined so persuasively by McDougal-Lasswell-Miller.

The basic approach of the ILC is contained in Draft Articles 27 and 28 the full text of which is set out below:

Article 27

General rule of interpretation

1. A treaty shall be interpreted in good faith in accordance with the ordinary meaning to be given to the terms of the treaty in their context and in the light of its object and purpose.

2. The context for the purpose of the interpretation of a treaty shall comprise, in addition to the text, including its preamble and annexes:

(a) Any agreement relating to the treaty which was made be-

---

strategy of interpretation. This point is brought out well by Liacouros, *op.cit. supra*, note 17 at 167.

[59] See also the Harvard Research Draft Convention on the Law of Treaties, *op.cit. supra*, note 23 and the *American Law Institute (Second) Restatement of the Foreign Relations Law of the United States*, St. Paul, Minn., American Law Institute Publishers, 1965, §§146-54, pp. 449-75. For a very detailed comparison of the Restatement and the ILC approaches to treaty interpretation see Shabtai Rosenne, "Interpretation of Treaties in the Restatement and the International Law Commission's Draft Articles: A Comparison," 5

Columbia Journal of Transnational Law 205-30 (1966). Also see note 22, *supra*, for more discussion of these principal approaches to interpretation. Professor McDougal has written a severely critical comment on the ILC's approach to treaty interpretation: "The International Law Commission's Draft Articles Upon Interpretation: Textuality Redivivus," 61 *American Journal of International Law* 992 (1967).

[60] For an interesting assessment of the International Law Commission see Julius Stone, "On the Vocation of the International Law Commission," 57 *Columbia Law Review* 16 (1957).

tween all the parties in connexion with the conclusion of the treaty;

(b) Any instrument which was made by one or more parties in connexion with the conclusion of the treaty and accepted by the other parties as an instrument related to the treaty.

3. There shall be taken into account, together with the context:

(a) Any subsequent agreement between the parties regarding the interpretation of the treaty;

(b) Any subsequent practice in the application of the treaty which establishes the understanding of the parties regarding its interpretation;

(c) Any relevant rules of international law applicable in the relations between the parties.

4. A special meaning shall be given to a term if it is established that the parties so intended.

Article 28

Supplementary means of interpretation

Recourse may be had to supplementary means of interpretation, including the preparatory work of the treaty and the circumstances of its conclusion, in order to confirm the meaning resulting from the application of Article 27, or to determine the meaning when the interpretation according to Article 27:

(a) Leaves the meaning ambiguous or obscure; or

(b) Leads to a result which is manifestly absurd or unreasonable.[61]

The comments of the ILC attached to these Draft Articles emphasize the quasi-textual approach adopted therein.[62] Article 27 "is based on the view that the text must be presumed to be the authentic expression of the intentions of the parties; and that, in consequence, the starting point of interpretation is the elucidation of the meaning of the text, not an investigation *ab initio* into the intentions of the parties."[63] As Mc-Dougal-Lasswell-Miller note, "The position of the Commission here comes perilously close to Vattel's assumption that there are plain and natural meanings that do not admit of interpretation."[64] The idea of "context" contained in Article 27(2) is very technical and is not at all comparable to the comprehensive recourse to extrinsic evidence called for in the McDougal book. Article 28 permits a wider use of

---

[61] For a convenient text of the International Law Commission's Report on the Law of Treaties, see 61 *American Journal of International Law* 263-473 (1967) (page references to the *ILC Report* are to this text).

[62] See also McDougal, note 56, for critique along these lines; in *Interpretation* see pp. 88-90, 223-24, 275-76.

[63] ILC Comment on Article 27, note 61, at 354.

[64] P. 90.

extrinsic evidence, as does Article 27(3) (b), but only in subordination to the initial effort to obtain a clear meaning by reference to the language of the text. Article 28 as "supplementary" implies that the decision-maker should not even consider evidence of contrary intentions if the language of the text appears clear.

It is correct that Article 27(1) urges interpretation of a treaty "in good faith" and "in the light of its object and purpose." Such generality of reference permits considerable account to be taken of extrinsic evidence, although, as the Commentary makes clear, the purposes of the treaty are not at all the same thing as the intentions or expectations of the parties.[65] The clear emphasis of the Commentary is to reinforce the textualist orientation of the provisions, as well as urging that recourse to extrinsic evidence is primarily to clarify an ambiguous text, not to obtain a clearer realization of the intentions or expectations of the parties.

Maxims, canons, or principles of interpretation are omitted from the Draft Provisions, but their use as guides to interpretation in particular cases is recommended, especially when such use would clarify the search for the meaning of the text.[66] The ILC emphasizes that "recourse to many of these principles [of interpretation] is discretionary rather than obligatory and the interpretation of documents is to some extent an art, not an exact science."[67] In contrast, the New Haven approach aspires to be as "scientific" as possible and, accordingly, recommends the systematic use of the traditional principles of interpretation to survey features of the context that past practice discloses to have been important indicators of the parties' genuine expectations.

Having briefly explicated this intellectual confrontation between the ILC and McDougal-Lasswell-Miller we are led to consider two main issues:

1. What factors underlie the formulation of each of these two approaches to treaty interpretation?

2. Does it make any difference to the process of interpretation which of these conceptions of treaty interpretation is embodied in the final convention on the Law of Treaties?

As to (1), it would appear that the ILC and the final rapporteur for the Law of Treaties, Sir Humphrey Waldock, were greatly influenced by the hardness of the text as the best evidence of intention as compared to other sources of evidence drawn from the wider context of negotiations, preparations, and conduct before and after agreement. The ILC prefers evidently to risk the rigidity of the textualist orientation to inviting the wider inquiry counseled by a contextualist orientation. Why?

---

[65] ILC Comment on Article 27, note 61, at 351-52.

[66] *Id.* at 350.

[67] *Ibid.*

Presumably for the reasons emphasized by Julius Stone—the important need in international society to disguise exercises of actual or apparent judicial law-making beneath a mask of legal definiteness. Also, one suspects, the continental traditions of jurisprudence that appear to dominate the ILC are more conservative about acknowledging a role for judicial innovation and are more optimistic about the communicative clarity of the negotiated language of a treaty than is the New Haven group.[68]

Finally, and most persuasively, the ILC is setting forth its conception of interpretation in the larger framework of the law of treaties and is correctly sensitive to the importance that will be played by self-interpretation of treaty obligations by foreign offices. The text of the treaty is the common core of agreement, whereas the context is more naturally susceptible to self-serving and self-deceiving perception and manipulation. McDougal-Lasswell-Miller write sensitively about the need for a decision-maker to examine the self for evidences of partiality, but their concern with treaty interpretation is centered so clearly on the behavior of international tribunals where the problem is of much less magnitude than if decisions are made in foreign offices.[69] In an international tribunal there is normally a spatial and emotional distance from the national society, the ethos of the role emphasizes the adoption of a global orientation, the partiality of outlook is offset by other outlooks and by the dialogue between judges drawn from different national systems.[70]

McDougal-Lasswell-Miller do not deal satisfactorily with this central feature of the interpreter's orientation. It would appear, for instance, that those international agreements concerned with highly political subject matter—for instance, peace settlements—need to be drafted so as to set forth clear enough rules of action and prohibition so as to dispense with the need for extra-textual evidence of intention as nearly as possible. My own thinking on interpretation is heavily influenced by two kinds of factors that neither McDougal-Lasswell-Miller nor the ILC accord explicit attention: first, the relevance of the decision-making locus, whether national or international, whether judicial or executive, and whether governed by political officials or bureaucrats; and second, the relevance of subject matter, whether concerned with broad questions of national security in the war-peace sector or with more routine interactions.[71] Therefore, I find both the ILC Draft Articles and the New Haven approach overgeneralized in their disagreement about the relative

---

[68] I have urged such an understanding of the Judgment in the South West Africa Cases in Chapter XII.

[69] Pp. 356-59.

[70] Pp. 258-60. For very comprehensive data see Peter Liacouros, *The International Court of Justice*, 2 vols., Prelim. edn., 1962.

[71] Some of the issues relevant to the decision process that are raised by shifting the locus of decision from a domestic to an international arena are considered in Falk, *The Role of Domestic Courts in the International Legal Order*, Syracuse, Syracuse University Press, 1964.

roles of text and context in the interpretative process. We need to develop more functionally specific conceptions of interpretation that give adequate weight to these factors through the categorization of interpretative settings and through the suggestion of the appropriate mix of text and context for each category.[72] At this early stage of conceptual clarity all that can be expected is a set of presumptions about the clarity of the text that diminishes in strength as the locus of decision-making centralizes and as the focus of subject matter recedes from war-peace problems.

The second issue—does it matter which conception of interpretation becomes authoritative—is a very complex one, provoking some consideration of the entire interaction between thought and action.[73] To what extent do decision-makers do what they are told? And even if one rhetoric is used rather than another does it produce a different outcome in a dispute about interpretation? For instance, in the South West Africa Cases could one anticipate any alteration in conclusion for a judge because of a shift of allegiance from one conception of interpretation to another? Or in interpreting the Geneva Accords of 1954, the Suez Canal Convention of 1888, or the SEATO Treaty? Is not the conception of interpretation more relevant to the exposition of a conclusion about meaning than a guide to the discovery of meaning?

We do not presently possess the techniques for answering questions of this nature. There is some reason, however, to assert that it is important to choose the conception of interpretation that most closely accords with its proper functioning—even granting some skepticism about the connection between thought (or language) and action in the international legal order. The orientation of the interpreter is shaped by the conception that he adopts, and this may influence the kind of evidence that is relied upon to reach and to explain the interpretation of a disputed text. On this level the emphasis of the New Haven approach on genuine shared expectations compatible with community policies on world order conceives of law in a manner that supports persuasively its claims to regulate international affairs. The text is evidence of intention, but it is the intention, not its evidence, that is the object of inquiry. McDougal-Lasswell-Miller offer us a method to conduct this inquiry that promises, if conscientiously applied, to consider all available evidence relevant to the opposing lines of inquiry, but does not purport to settle the matter of interpretation by endowing the text with

---

[72] Professor McDougal has often acknowledged the need for such functionally specific studies in depth. See e.g., his Foreword to Douglas M. Johnston, *The International Law of Fisheries*, New Haven, Yale University Press, 1965, pp. vii-xi, esp. p. ix.

[73] For a very provocative general analysis of the interrelations between thought and action see Stuart Hampshire, *Thought and Action*, London, Chatto and Windus, 1960.

a clarity it lacks.[74] The very existence of a dispute presupposes adversary interpretations of the text, and unless one assumes bad faith or stupidity on one side, there is genuine doubt about the meaning of the text. It is misleading to suppose that a decision-maker can clearly interpret an international agreement by placing primary emphasis on textual language given controversy among the parties. Such a supposition exaggerates either the autonomy of language or the authority of interpreters, or both. Normally, openness to evidence and reasoning based on an exposure to any aspect of context deemed relevant by the parties would appear to lead to the most persuasive, and hence to the most authoritative result.

Therefore, the ILC approach, unless narrowly circumscribed to self-interpretation in the war-peace area, should be rejected in favor of the New Haven approach for two main reasons:

1. Because it establishes a more useful framework of inquiry for the interpreter; the ILC Draft Articles and Commentary give very little specific guidance except to underscore the textualist predisposition; in contrast, McDougal-Lasswell-Miller outline a method of inquiry that encourages consideration of any evidence that might lead to a better appreciation of genuine expectations;

2. Because such a wider, systematic inquiry—rejecting a false myth of textual clarity—leads to a more persuasively based interpretation and to authoritative decisions that can be more easily defended against criticism; and if textual clarity is asserted by the interpreter, then the contention of a clear text has survived the evidence produced or examined to support the basis for an alternative interpretation. The alleged self-evident clarity of textual language in isolation from its context entails a depleted understanding of language and communication; to rest interpretation on an essentially misleading view of language and communication, as does the ILC, rejects the role of reason and intelligence in the conduct of human affairs and seems to prefer implicitly the role of magic, myth, and authority.

IV. The Limits of Treaty Interpretation and Whether to Acknowledge Them

The New Haven approach is a definite improvement over the major prior efforts to explicate a method of treaty interpretation. The character of this improvement arises principally from a comprehensive specification of the contextual variables that are relevant to the interpreta-

---

[74] The clarity of the text, according to *Interpretation*, is never truly self-evident and, therefore, it is only after a look at the extra-textural evidences that it is possible to conclude that the obvious reading of the text embodies the shared expectations of the parties.

tive process.[75] The New Haven specification contrasts with the approach taken in the provisions dealing with interpretation in the draft proposals of the International Law Commission for a Convention on the Law of Treaties. The ILC, for reasons indicated in Section III, has adopted a regressive approach based upon a misleading return to textualism, supplemented by a very confusing exposition of the subordinate relevance of contextual factors. The ILC encourages a false presupposition about the clarity of international agreements and offers an interpreter very limited guidance in the event that such clarity is lacking.[76]

But beyond these matters of method and orientation, matters on which I share the outlook of the New Haven group, there lies an important issue involving the limit of *any* method of treaty interpretation. This limit is a complex consequence of the nature of the agreement process, the imperfections of language as the medium by which agreements are communicated through time and across space, the dynamic character of international public policy that shifts directives to correspond with shifts in the structure and preferences of international society, and the inability of international institutions to induce compliance with their will in relation to certain kinds of disputes about treaty obligations. In my judgment, these dimensions of treaty interpretation are not brought into sufficiently sharp focus by the McDougal-Lasswell-Miller book. In effect, I am arguing that the limits of treaty interpretation are underacknowledged and that, therefore, too little attention is given by the New Haven authors to the task of what to do about them.

In this respect, the problem of limits is obscured by the generality of method that is explicated. McDougal-Lasswell-Miller evidently regard the tasks of treaty interpretation to be homogeneous regardless of the subject matter of agreement and of the arena wherein the interpretative event is located. I feel, for instance, that McDougal-Lasswell-Miller give too little attention to whether the subject matter of agreement directly concerns problems of war and peace and whether the arena of interpretation is national or international in character. These kinds of considerations are shunted to one side by an overall call for the realization of "genuine shared expectations" of the parties as reinforced (or altered) by taking account of overriding "general community policies."[77] Such an orienting formulation, preliminary to the application of "the

[75] In this respect, the New Haven Approach is reconstructive, taking account of the critical work of Hyde, Yu, Stone, and Chang, but moving beyond criticism to offer a new orientation and a set of guidelines for any interpreter.

[76] Ambassador Rosenne does explain the process by which the ILC reached its particular outcome. He emphasizes, with the authoritativeness that only a Member of the Commission could bring to such an exposition, the extent to which decisions reflected both a responsible appreciation of the realities of practice and a necessity to reach compromises so as to bridge the gap between divergent national positions. Cf. Rosenne, *op.cit. supra*, note 59, at 212-21.

[77] P. 100.

method" for consulting context, is at once too abstract and too indefinite to give the interpreter guidance and too directive to allow the interpreter and those subject to his interpretation an awareness of "the openness" of the interpretative situation.

We are dealing here with very fundamental elements of treaty interpretation, elements for which there is no very happy reconciliation precisely because of the potentially contradictory efforts to uphold original expectations and to reflect the bearing on relative rights and duties of changed circumstances. The interpretative task is made more difficult because one side in a controversy normally wishes to underscore original expectations and the other side wishes to underscore changed circumstances.[78] The substantive arguments about the interpretation of Article 2 of the Mandate for South West Africa provide a prominent illustration of such a confrontation of interpretative perspectives and of the difficulty of finding a juridically (not to mention a sociopolitically) satisfactory resolution.[79] The New Haven approach does not totally ignore this kind of concern, but it does not contribute very much to its enhanced understanding. Nor do McDougal-Lasswell-Miller help very much with the parallel problems of what to do about an original failure of convergent expectations or about a convergence of expectation that consisted merely in evading agreement on essential terms.[80]

McDougal-Lasswell-Miller are very clear about the fundamental obligation of an interpreter to honor the original understanding of parties to an agreement:

> This primary, distinctive goal [of interpretation] stipulates that decision-makers undertake a disciplined, responsible effort to ascertain the genuine shared expectations of the particular parties to an agree-

[78] In such a situation, the core of controversy involves the degree of precedence to be given to originally shared expectations as distinct from inconsistent subsequent reinterpretations in light of shifting interests or circumstances.

[79] The dispute as to the legal consequences of the obligation to promote to the utmost the well-being of the inhabitants of South West Africa illustrates the extent to which judicial authoritativeness with regard to treaty interpretation may depend upon giving due, even decisive, weight to changed circumstances.

[80] Cf. Fred Charles Ikle, *How Nations Negotiate*, New York, Harper & Row, 1964, p. 15:

> Two consequences of ambiguity have been distinguished so far: (1) the parties have an honest misunderstanding about implications that the agreement fails to spell out; or (2) one party, while knowing what its opponent expected of the bargain, may pretend that it had a different understanding of it (i.e., the ambiguities are exploited to cover up a deliberate violation). There is a third possibility: the parties to the agreement know that the ambiguous terms mean different things to each of them. It may be more appropriate to call this *equivocality* than ambiguity. Equivocal language is used to cover up disagreement on issues which must be included for some reason in a larger settlement or which must be dealt with as if there was agreement. An equivocal agreement is similar to a partial agreement that leaves certain undecided issues for future negotiation, with the difference that the equivocal terms serve to cover up differences rather than mark them for future resolution.

ment. The link with fundamental policy is clear: to defend the dignity of man is to respect *his* choices and not, save for overriding common interest, to impose the choices of others upon him.[81]

It is on this basis that the New Haven group repudiates approaches to interpretation based on mechanical textualist and canonist notions of interpretation and, equally, on the inevitably formless discretion of the interpreter.[82]

McDougal-Lasswell-Miller criticize Julius Stone's proposal to conceive of principles of interpretation as legal fictions potentially useful to disguise the discretion of judicial interpreters.[83] Stone argues that given the weakness of international tribunals it is important to minimize the impression that courts are engaged in judicial law-making. McDougal-Lasswell-Miller write that "It is highly unlikely that international tribunals will be adequately protected against 'premature strains' by 'fictions'; neither the participants in processes of decision nor scholarly observers are likely to be tranquilized by attempts to 'conceal judicial creativeness' by such evasions, even if skillful."[84] Similarly, McDougal-Lasswell-Miller argue over and over again on behalf of the need for gaining maximum awareness of the parties' expectations by looking at all the relevant contextual evidence; they regard advocates of textualism as urging treaty interpreters "to gouge out an eye when an eye exercise would improve some limitation of vision."[85]

But what of genuine shared expectations as the informing goal of the interpretative process? Is this goal not itself often a fiction the assertion of which is not likely to tranquilize either those who observe or participate in the interpretative event? Given the vast range of agreement, given the frequent failure to crystallize expectations at the time of commitment that illuminate the meaning of controversial provisions at the time of dispute, and given the existence of complementary world order policies that are available in the event that community policies are used to supplement or override genuine shared expectation there is no very firm basis for confidence in the interpretative process. In fact, one can wonder how genuine confidence-building can take place in international society so long as it is sovereignty-centered and beset by basic conflicts among states about the proper interrelationship between considerations

---

[81] Pp. 40-41; for consideration of common interests see p. 41; see also pp. 367-68.

[82] Pp. 11-12; see also Julius Stone, *op.cit. supra*, note 31 for a discussion of the use of legal fictions to disguise the exercise of judicial discretion.

[83] Pp. 263-65; the closely related approach of Sir Hersch Lauterpacht is preferred by the authors of *Interpretation* to that of Julius Stone because of its greater emphasis on the need for judicial caution and for actual restraint (as well as for maintaining the appearance of restraint) by an interpreter situated in an international tribunal.

[84] Pp. 264-65.

[85] P. 362; see also pp. 363-64.

of order and considerations of justice.[86] There are no juridically satisfying resolutions by way of authoritative interpretation of this kind of dispute. The balancing of claims, for instance, between the imperatives of domestic jurisdiction and humanitarian intervention to secure minimum observance of human rights is not really susceptible to satisfactory resolution by means of treaty interpretation. The value input governs the interpretative output for this kind of dispute. I would argue that such an interpretative situation is characteristic for nontrivial disputes about the content of an international agreement in the present conflicted international legal system.[87]

My point here is twofold: first, McDougal-Lasswell-Miller do not illuminate this central interpretative issue in any significant way, and second, that the rhetoric of genuine community expectations and general community policies is so abstract and vague as to be properly viewed as themselves functioning "legal fictions," and therefore, subject to the criticisms directed against Julius Stone.[88] The issue is not well illuminated because McDougal-Lasswell-Miller do not correlate their recommended method for gathering evidence to the overall indeterminacy of judicial behavior. This failure of correlation then fosters an impression that genuine shared expectations and general community policies are intended to furnish decision-makers with more than vague feelings. The plain reality is that an interpreter of a broad international agreement is operating in a largely indeterminate setting. Such an interpreter may benefit from the recommended systematic search of context prescribed by McDougal-Lasswell-Miller, but it is unlikely to erode the essential indeterminism surrounding his task and restricting the authoritativeness of its discharge by any method.[89] The interpreter of an international agreement is a lonely man entrusted with an impossible

86 For instance, in determining whether force can be used, in conformity with the United Nations Charter, to end colonial and racist control of Southern Africa there is raised a basic issue of political orientation that dominates the interpretative perspective. Those who identify with African "revisionist" demands increasingly construe the Charter as authorizing force, despite the absence of "an armed attack" (Article 51) and despite the prohibition to use force against a state for purposes other than in self-defense against an armed attack (Article 2(4) read in conjunction with Article 51).
87 Stanley Hoffmann has expressed this issue in general terms very usefully by his distinction between "revolutionary" and "moderate" international systems. For a statement of his approach and his conclusions about the mixed condition of the contemporary international system see Hoffmann, *Gulliver's Troubles, or the Set-*

ting of American Foreign Policy, New York, McGraw-Hill, 1968, pp. 10-51.
88 Cf. e.g., statement on pp. 100-01. The McDougal-Lasswell-Miller reliance on the rhetoric of "genuine expectations" and community policies allows an attuned decision-maker to invoke the proper language without, in any sense, being influenced by it. In this sense, in the absence of specific operational demonstrations, the Yale authors have created a new framework of legal fictions rather than a rational framework for policy oriented inquiry.
89 The extent to which Professor McDougal believes that indeterminism of this sort is inherent in legal process has been clearly indicated in an essay. Myres S. McDougal, "The Ethics of Applying Systems of Authority" in Harold D. Lasswell and Harlan Cleveland, *The Ethic of Power*, New York, Harper & Row, 1962, pp. 221-40.

job, given the requirements of objectivity, the incompleteness of information, and presence of disagreement as to the rank-ordering and application of community policies.[90] The policy question for those, such as
McDougal-Lasswell-Miller, devising a theory *about* interpretation is
whether or not to acknowledge a high degree of loneliness and impossibility. In my view these authors *purport* to be acknowledging the interpretative situation as it really is, but that they are in actuality exag-
gerating the susceptibility of treaty interpretation to a rational methodology. It is not that the methodology proposed is not rational, nor even
less that it is not helpfully used in many situations, but rather that the
nature of the interpretative act is often (especially in highly charged
political situations) not susceptible to authoritative performance because of the dominance of contradictory expectations as to its appropriate discharge. In discussing the interpretation of the United Nations
Charter, McDougal-Lasswell-Miller suggest that given the constitutional nature of such an agreement "one could scarcely call for an interpretation which limited itself strictly to the expectations of those who
drafted the basic document."[91] Instead, they go on to suggest "the principal aim of an interpreter should be to give effect to the continuing consensus of the parties—that is, their contemporary shared expectations
concerning problems of the type being disputed."[92] The New Haven
authors allude to "the inherent difficulty of the problem," but then go to
emphasize its manageable aspects.[93] The unmanageable core of the
problem arises precisely because the interpreter is expected to interpret
in a situation where there is a contemporary divergence of expectation.[94]

V. The Limits of Treaty Interpretation and What to Do About Them

There are, at least, three main responses to the discovery of these
fundamental limits of treaty interpretation:
  1. Disguise the relevance of legal indeterminacy by fostering an illu-

[90] The quality of "loneliness" is suggested only to emphasize the fact that
there is no genuine solution to the interpretative puzzle given a conscientious
search along the lines proposed by Mc-
Dougal-Lasswell-Miller. Yet a decision
must be made and explained. The decision necessarily presupposes a genuine
solution, and its reasoning must purport
one. Otherwise there is no reason to endow a particular interpretation with authoritativeness. The dilemma must be
suppressed to uphold the prospects for a
law-ordered approach. But such suppression collides with ideals of integrity that
underlie the conception of judicial decision. Hence, often repression occurs
(i.e., unconscious suppression) to avoid
the perception of the dilemma. This psychological tension between the actualities
of the interpretative situation and the conditions of authoritative interpretation deserves careful study.

[91] P. 99.

[92] *Ibid.* Cf. McDougal and Richard N.
Gardner, "The Veto and the Charter: An
Interpretation for Survival" in McDougal
and Associates, *op.cit. supra*, note 12, pp.
718-60.

[93] P. 100; see generally, pp. 99-111.

[94] The interpreter must unify what is
inherently diverse without appearing to
identify with the policies of either contending perspective. Without such "objectivity" the basis for third-party impartiality
is undermined and the interpreter is in a
very real sense playing a disguised adversary role.

sion of false definiteness through reliance on legal fictions, high-order abstractions (human dignity, genuine shared expectations, general community policies), and a detailed methodology designed to objectify the search of context;

2. Acknowledge the central relevance of legal indeterminacy and the consequent dependence of treaty interpretation upon the value-inputs of the interpreter;[95]

3. Supplement (2) by efforts to differentiate among categories of international agreements according to subject matter, degree of generality, and demonstrated relevance to world order principles in fairly specific interpretative situations; illuminate the nature of the limits of treaty interpretation by in-depth case studies.

Response (1) does not appear to be desirable for a number of reasons. It obscures the nature of our experience and, at least from the scholarly perspective, interferes with the search for genuine understanding. The use of fictions—the illusion of definiteness—by those who exercise authority is one of the basic issues of civilization, perhaps most grandly posed by Dostoevski in the "Legend of the Grand Inquisitor." In the setting of treaty interpretation we must consider whether fostering the illusion of definiteness would enhance the authoritativeness of international procedures of interpretation, and whether, reliance on illusion is the most effective way to proceed. Can the illusion be sustained? For how long? With what effects? If scholars reject the illusion of definiteness, then will not other interpreters find it difficult to maintain?

Response (2) suggests the importance of an existentialist view of legal process. The complementary character of adversary presentation and the divergent rank-ordering of conflicting evidence and policy preferences create a situation wherein the interpreter is necessarily without decisive guidance. The interpreter can and should use a comprehensive method to appraise the genuine shared expectations and, where needed, go on to examine general community policies, but in many instances of treaty interpretation such inquiry cannot be expected to yield dispositive results. The interpreter alone is responsible for formulating an interpretation that persuasively communicates his understanding of the various plausible alternatives open to him.[96] For instance, the various

---

[95] This acknowledgment should not be confused with the Yu-Chang injunction to consider all the evidence, but is concerned with how to deal with the problems of value-diversity and of a grouping of evidence that does not resolve the interpretative issue in any decisive or even convincing way. It may be necessary to emphasize burdens of persuasion that favor one or another party in different interpretative situations. For instance, the party relying on an agreement to do something otherwise forbidden or to restrict the normal freedom of the other party might be subject to a burden of persuasion such that his contentions fail if a scrutiny of the evidence concludes indecisively.

[96] P. 265.

legal arguments about treaty interpretation in the context of the United States involvement in the Vietnam War cannot relieve the interpreter from the existential loneliness of his position. It is possible for an interpreter of the Geneva Accords or the SEATO agreement to be more or less persuasive in supporting his interpretation. And there is room for discussion of the criteria of persuasiveness in such a setting.[97] The presence of legal indeterminacy should not be taken to imply the irrelevance of legal interpretation. Quite the contrary. The interpretive act is designed to influence behavior and expectations as to permissible conduct by an appeal to facts, policy consequences, past expectations, and community consensus. The principal conclusion is merely the need to acknowledge clearly the limits of treaty interpretation, and the effect of these limits upon the use of reason.

Response to (3) involves trying to take into account various contextual variables that are not given enough attention in the New Haven approach. The nature of treaty interpretation is certainly influenced by whether the interpretative event is located within a national or an international arena. The problem of biased perception seems to be much more serious when the interpreter shares the orientation and goals of one adversary, but not the other. A foreign official in a state party to a dispute with another state may be in an excellent position to make an adversary presentation, but he is not nearly so well situated to make an impartial or authoritative interpretation. The decentralized character of the international legal order makes this factor of abiding relevance as the interpretative situation so often blends adversary and impartial perspectives to varying degrees.[98] I find that the New Haven approach has been consistently unwilling to exhibit a sensitivity to the biasing impacts of decentralized decision-making. Such an unwillingness is especially surprising in view of the intense nationalistic and ideological rivalries that have been embodied in international conflict throughout the twentieth century.

Along these lines, also, there is need to differentiate among different kinds of domestic arenas of interpretation. The degree to which the interpreter has been socialized into the acceptance of his dual role as

[97] There is, of course, a vast difference between the arena of interpretation (which may be *ex parte*) and the arena of dissemination (which may appear to be an even-handed consideration of the evidence for alternative interpretations). The gap in style results from the impulse in the first arena to mobilize a strong argument in support of a predetermined conclusion and in the second arena to be as persuasive as possible with those who do not altogether accept the predetermined conclusion. A government's legal argumentation to support its diplomacy often illustrates this tendency. Nevertheless, the final argument may be more or less convincing in comparison with other arguments made from other perspectives, including scholarly perspectives which in a free society at least are less likely to start from predetermined conclusions.

[98] I have urged in greater detail the importance of this issue for the growth of international legal order. See Chapter XV.

national official and as agent of the international legal system, the extent of judicial independence enjoyed by domestic courts in the particular society, and the extent to which the particular question of treaty interpretation has been traditionally classified as "justiciable" are among the factors that deserve enumeration in this proposed extension of the Mc-Dougal-Lasswell-Miller approach.

Case studies of interpretative problems would also be illuminating sources of insight into the problems of clarifying genuine shared expectations and of correlating these expectations (or their incompleteness) with relevant general community policies. The McDougal-Lasswell-Miller approach remains too abstract to provide an interpreter with specific guidance as to the process of correlation. The prospect of a systematic methodology for correlating expectations with other considerations does not imply the elimination of an interpreter's choice and judgment. A further elaboration of method is valuable only to the extent that it puts the interpreter in a more enlightened posture with which to choose. Case studies that I would find useful include the following illustrations:

1. "Armed attack" in Article 51 of the UN Charter; in fact, the range of interpretative situations that have arisen with respect to claims of self-defense since World War II;

2. Paragraph 7 of the Final Declaration of the Geneva Conference (July 21, 1954) in which provision was made for all-Vietnam elections by July, 1956;

3. Article 1(1) of the Limited Nuclear Weapons Test Ban of August 5, 1963 prohibiting parties from carrying out "any nuclear weapons test explosion or any other nuclear explosion" except underground;

4. Article 2 of the Mandate for South West Africa, especially the interrelation between the Mandatory's "full power of administration and legislation" and the Mandatory's undertaking to "promote to the utmost the material and moral well-being . . . of the inhabitants" in a dispute about the compatibility of apartheid with this provision.

These case studies if carried out according to a common framework of inquiry would produce some greater sense of the problems of treaty interpretation at the limits and what to do about them. In this way we would begin to consider how to make operational the rather vague directives to implement genuine shared expectations in conjunction with general community policies. Until we do these kinds of validation studies the directives for treaty interpretation offered us by the New Haven approach suffer from the same illusion of definiteness that they criticize others for disseminating. As matters now stand with treaty interpretation, for the tough cases there are rarely genuine shared expectations of dispositive significance and there is seldom a consensus about the bearing of general community policies. McDougal-Lasswell-Miller have provided a sense of direction and an exciting beginning, but there are many more steps that need to be taken to establish an adequate conception of interpretation.

XII. The South West Africa Cases: An Appraisal*

ETHIOPIA and Liberia instituted litigation in 1960 before the International Court of Justice (ICJ) to test the legality of South Africa's administration of the mandated territory of South West Africa. The ICJ received, thereby, an opportunity to deal with a major question of international concern. Hopes were raised that the role of international adjudication would be enhanced by the results of this litigation. The case was also expected to demonstrate to the new states that the procedures and institutions of traditional international law could be used to promote, as well as to retard, their distinctive goals in international life.

In 1966 hopes were dashed when the Court, by the narrowest and most adventitious of majorities, finally dismissed the complaint against South Africa on the rather formal ground of an insufficiency of legal interest on the part of the complaining states. One reaction to the decision in the *South West Africa Cases* is to consider it, at best, a painful reminder that international adjudication is suited only to the settlement of trivial questions of a highly technical character and, at worst, to regard it as an endorsement of South Africa's racial policies. These ways of understanding the case have generated widespread hostility against the ICJ and indirectly seem to have damaged the cause of international law in general. A negative attitude toward the international legal order, especially on the part of the African and Asian states, may do permanent harm to the role of law in world affairs if the first wave of dismay aroused by the decision is converted into a final assessment. Part of the purpose of the following analysis of the ICJ decision in the *South West Africa Cases* is to suggest that the results reached by the Court do not imply such a dismal future either for international adjudication as a process, or the ICJ as an institution, or even for the role of law in future phases of the ongoing dispute between South Africa and the United Nations about the status of South West Africa.

Background

The complicated background of the *South West Africa Cases* cannot be given here except in barest outline.[1] South West Africa was a German

---

* I acted as one of the counsel for Ethiopia and Liberia in the final stages of the South West Africa litigation.

[1] For a convenient survey see the Memorial submitted by Ethiopia and Liberia to the ICJ in the *I.C.J. Pleadings, South West Africa*, Vol. I, pp. 32-87 (hereinafter cited as Memorial); see also the Counter-Memorial filed by the Government of the Republic of South Africa in *ibid.*, Vol. II, pp. 1-96 (hereinafter cited as Counter-Memorial). See also Faye Carroll, *South West Africa and the United Nations*, Lexington, University of Kentucky Press, 1967, and Waldemar A. Nielson, *African Battleline*, New York, Harper & Row, 1965, pp. 110-26. The most comprehensive study now available has been written by

colony from 1892 to 1915. It was occupied by South African armies during World War I. Germany renounced its colonial interests in the territory by Articles 118 and 119 of the Treaty of Versailles in favor of the principal victorious powers. After a major diplomatic effort the views of President Woodrow Wilson prevailed and these colonies were not recolonized or annexed as spoils of war. Instead, the mandates system was evolved to establish a tutelary responsibility on the part of the organized international community for the welfare of the inhabitants of mandated territories. The essential features of the mandates system are spelled out in Article 22 of the Covenant of the League of Nations and in the text of each mandate agreement. In essence, an advanced country was selected as Mandatory to give practical effect to the intention of the League to promote the well-being of the inhabitants. The League supervised the Mandatory through its own organs, especially through a Permanent Mandates Commission that would receive annual reports and consider complaints about conditions in the various mandated territories. The League Council was the supervisory body, acting on advice from the Mandates Commission, to assure that the mandate in question was being administered so as to attain the goals set forth in Article 22 of the Covenant.

South West Africa, an enormous land area somewhat larger than Texas but sparsely populated and rather backward, was placed under mandate in 1920 and South Africa was designated as Mandatory.[2] The relatively low stage of development in the area resulted in its being classified as "C" Mandate, one that the Mandatory was expected to govern as "an integral portion of its territory."[3]

South African policies in South West Africa were mildly challenged at various points during the period of League history, especially in connection with the Bondelswarts incident, but the organs of the League were dominated by the spirit of colonial paternalism and nothing much

a Professor of Geography at the University of Witwatersrand, John H. Wellington, *South West Africa and its Human Issues*, Oxford, Clarendon Press, 1967.

[2] In 1920 when South West Africa was placed under mandate the white population was 15,000 and the black population was 81,000; in 1966 the population of the Territory is reported as 545,000, of which 72,000 are white.

[3] Article 2(1) of the Mandate reads as follows:

The Mandatory shall have full power of administration and legislation over the territory subject to the present Mandate as an integral portion of the Union of South Africa, and may apply the laws of the Union of South Africa to the territory, subject to such local modifications as circumstances may require.

South Africa aptly argued that the extension of apartheid was a fulfillment of the promise of this provision and that the Mandatory's conception of well-being was controlling provided it was carried out in good faith. It is important to appreciate that the paragraph following Article 2(1) formulates the key duty of the Mandatory to "promote to the utmost the material and moral well-being and the social progress of the inhabitants" around the meaning of which the central controversy revolved.

See also Article 22(6) of the League Covenant.

was done to interfere with the quality or quantity of South African governance of South West Africa.[4] Since the existence of the United Nations, however, the double attempt of the General Assembly to achieve rapid decolonialization and to eliminate racial discrimination has produced increasing criticism of the way in which South Africa was discharging its role as Mandatory. Three times the General Assembly turned to the International Court of Justice to obtain advisory opinions on the legal questions underlying its dispute with South Africa, and three times the Court endorsed the basic assumption of the General Assembly that the United Nations is the successor to the League of Nations in relation to the supervision of surviving mandates and that the mandated status persists and continues to govern the rights and duties of South Africa as Mandatory.[5] South Africa reacted hostilely to these judicial pronouncements, emphasized their advisory character as nonbinding and political, and continued to withhold, by and large, any acknowledgment of its obligations to the organized international community.

Efforts by the United Nations to induce South Africa to make a voluntary accommodation to international demands appeared increasingly fruitless. In 1960 Ethiopia and Liberia, therefore, with the encouragement of the overall African community of nations, instituted contentious proceedings at The Hague against South Africa.[6] The jurisdictional basis for the proceeding was provided by Article 7 of the Mandate which created an obligation to accept the jurisdiction of the ICJ in the event that a dispute between members of the League and the Mandatory that could not be settled by negotiation was submitted to the Court.[7] The applicants asked the Court in 1960, first, to reaffirm in binding form its earlier unanimous advisory finding that the Mandate had survived and that South Africa was under a consequent duty to submit to administrative supervision by the UN, and second, to order South Africa to cease forthwith the imposition of apartheid on South West

[4] The principal organs concerned with the administration of the mandates system were the Permanent Mandates Commission and the League Council as the supervisory body. For general accounts see N. Bentwich, *The Mandates System*, London, Longmans, Green, 1930; Quincy Wright, *Mandates Under the League of Nations*, Chicago, University of Chicago Press, 1930; and H. D. Hall, *Mandates, Dependencies, and Trusteeship*, London, Stevens, 1948.

[5] *International Status of South-West Africa, Advisory Opinion: I.C.J. Reports 1950*, p. 128; *South-West Africa—Voting Procedure, Advisory Opinion of June 7th, 1955: I.C.J. Reports 1955*, p. 67; and *Admissibility of Hearings of Petitioners by the Committee on South West Africa, Ad-*

visory Opinion of June 1st, 1956: I.C.J. Reports 1956, p. 23. For the interpretation of the parties in the South West Africa litigation see Memorial, pp. 51-54; and Counter-Memorial, esp. pp. 71-96.

[6] The background of this decision to institute judicial action is described in Ernest A. Gross, "The South West Africa Case: What Happened?," *Foreign Affairs*, 45, No. 1 (October 1966), 36, 39-42.

[7] Ethiopia and Liberia were the only African Members of the League aside from Egypt; the transformation of Egypt into the United Arab Republic would create a technical question about whether the latter was a "Member of the League" within the meaning of Article 7 of the Mandate.

Africa on the ground that apartheid was not compatible with the Mandatory's obligation to promote the well-being of the inhabitants.

South Africa, somewhat surprisingly, in view of the prevailing assumption that it was certain to suffer legal defeat in the ICJ, participated in the proceedings by raising a series of jurisdictional objections. As is normal, the Court decided to deal with these objections as a separate phase of the dispute and, after extended oral argument, rejected South Africa's objections to jurisdiction by the unexpectedly close vote of 8-7 in 1962. On this basis both sides submitted lengthy written briefs on substantive questions and in 1965, 99 three-hour sessions comprised the oral proceedings. This enormous litigious effort led, by a vote of 8-7 in July of 1966, to the single narrow holding that Ethiopia and Liberia lacked the legal interest to obtain a judgment with respect to their contentions that South Africa was violating the Mandate. The apparent effect of the 1966 decision is a final dismissal and an abrupt termination of the long and expensive attempt to gain support from the Court for the General Assembly claims against South African administration of South West Africa. The African countries had been reluctant to delay action for the period of years needed for the judicial proceedings, but its statesmen had been persuaded that a judicial decision subject to enforcement by the Security Council would greatly strengthen the hand of those states that wanted the organization to bring maximum pressure to bear upon South Africa. The disappointment caused by the decision in 1966 immediately produced a hostile reaction to the ICJ as an adjudicating tribunal.[8]

The Afro-Asian group at the United Nations has reacted to the decision by passing a resolution withdrawing from South Africa the right to administer the Territory and conferring this right upon the General Assembly.[9] The enforceability of this resolution appears highly unlikely for the time being, and its legal bearing on the Mandate is uncertain at this time. This action by the Assembly has led the Vorster government to move in the direction of annexing South West Africa. Annexation, although obviously a violation of the Mandate,[10] would probably make it increasingly difficult to proceed separately against South West Africa and might require any enforcement action to be directed against South Africa itself. Such a requirement may not alter, in reality, the situation prior to annexation very much, as the expectation of South African opposition to any coercive moves by the UN with respect to South West Africa would not seem to increase or decrease as a function of the for-

8 E.g., see the *New York Times*, July 19, 1966, pp. 1, 16-17.
9 See the *New York Times*, Sept. 28, 1966, p. 1.
10 The first paragraph of Article 7 reads as follows: "The consent of the Council of the League of Nations is required for any modification of the terms of the present Mandate."

mal status of the territory either as this status is defined by the UN or by South Africa. The South Africa commitment to exert what amounts to *de facto* sovereignty over the territory appears to be firm enough that its attitudes toward *de jure* status are only of symbolic value; contrariwise, the attitude of the majority of the UN toward the need to eliminate apartheid from South Africa and South West Africa is already so manifest that the revocation of the Mandate can be expected only to provide a certain emotive and symbolic relief from the political realities of struggle. In essence, the conflict over South West Africa has become increasingly defined in polar terms and its resolution appears to depend almost exclusively on the ability or inability of the United Nations majority to bring overwhelming military power to bear. Nothing short of such an eventuality appears to have any prospect of altering the quantity or quality of South African control over South West Africa.

The Judgment of 1966

The members of the League are also entitled to invoke the jurisdiction of the Permanent Court of International Justice for any dispute with the mandatory involving the interpretation or application of the mandate which diplomacy fails to settle. . . . Every member of the League can regard its rights as infringed by every violation by the mandatory of its duties under the mandate, even those primarily for the benefit of the natives, and can make representations which if not effective will precipitate a dispute referable to the Permanent Court of International Justice if negotiation fails to settle it.[11]

Until they were repudiated *sub silentio* in 1966 by the ICJ no one questioned the accuracy of these words written by Quincy Wright and contained in his influential account of the mandates system. This general understanding of the right of League members to obtain judicial remedies had been apparently reconfirmed by the 1962 decision of the International Court of Justice affirming the jurisdiction to decide on the merits whether Ethiopia and Liberia were correct to charge South Africa with violating the terms of the Mandate by which it was administering South West Africa.

The Court, however, by the narrowest possible majority—a 7-7 tie being broken in favor of South Africa by "the casting vote" of the President—stunned the world by deciding, on July 18, 1966, that, after all, Ethiopia and Liberia, although members of the League, had no sufficient legal interest in the enforcement of the Mandate for the benefit of the natives to obtain judicial satisfaction.[12] Such a decision seemed to mock

---

[11] Wright, *op.cit.*, p. 475, n4.
[12] The "majority" of seven was com-

posed of Judges Sir Percy Spender (Australia), Bohdan Winiarski (Poland), Jean

the reality of international adjudication—the parties had spent millions of dollars over a period of several years on the firmly held assumption that they possessed a legal interest in obtaining a judgment accepting or rejecting their principal contentions that the Mandate was being violated.[13] After the 1962 judgment there was no evidence of any further doubt on the part of either party to the litigation that the Court would in 1966 answer these substantive questions one way or the other. The Court itself in the course of the extensive oral proceedings held subsequent to 1962 never hinted that it remained troubled by the right of Ethiopia and Liberia to obtain a judicial pronouncement upon their charges that South Africa was violating the Mandate.[14] Several of the judges questioned both sides on many aspects of the case but always on the apparent assumption that the prior questions of competence had been fully resolved in the 1962 judgment.[15] Even South Africa itself, although its talented legal staff presented in depth every conceivable argument in support of its position, appeared to acquiesce in the assumption that the Court's decision in 1966 was going to be directed at whether or not the Mandate continued to exist and, if it existed, whether or not it was being upheld.[16]

Spiropoulos (Greece), Sir Gerald Fitzmaurice, (United Kingdom), Gaetano Morelli (Italy), André Gros (France), and J. T. Van Wyk (South Africa); the dissenting minority of seven was composed of Judges V. K. Wellington Koo (China), Vladimir M. Koretsky (Soviet Union), Luis Padilla Nervo (Mexico), Isaac Forster (Senegal), and Sir Louis Mbanefo (Nigeria). Judges van Wyk and Sir Louis Mbanefo were nominated by the litigants as judges ad hoc as provided by Article 31 of the Statute of the ICJ.

[13] Namely, that the Mandatory was acting in violation of Articles 2(2) ("well-being") and 6 (administrative accountability to the League Council) of the Mandate.

[14] It might be appropriate to quote a relevant passage written by Sir Gerald Fitzmaurice in an essay honoring Lord McNair's period of service on the ICJ:

A necessary ingredient of any sound legal system is that of the "certainty" of the law—that the parties in going to law, must be able, not indeed to predict the outcome, but to be reasonably sure as to the legal basis from which that outcome will proceed, and the principles which will be applied in reaching it;—in short the parties must be able to feel that a court of law will not go off at a tangent and decide the case on some wholly new footing thought up by itself and not discussed in the course of the argument. This objection

is justified in the sense that although the jurisprudence of the International Court firmly establishes its right to raise points, and decide on the basis of them *proprio motu*, it should at least raise them before deciding them, and this not merely in its private deliberations but at the public hearing, so that the parties may have an adequate opportunity of arguing them.

("Judicial Innovation—Its Uses and Its Perils—As exemplified in Some of the Work of the International Court of Justice during Lord McNair's Period of Service," in *Cambridge Essays in International Law,* London, Stevens, 1965, p. 26.)

[15] The only "preliminary question" that *seemed* to remain open at the stage of "merits" concerned whether the Mandate had indeed survived the dissolution of the League, a question answered unanimously in the affirmative by the Court in 1950 when it was acting in its advisory capacity.

[16] There was great stress placed in the pleadings of South Africa upon whether the alleged violation of Article 2(2) was justiciable. The issue had been discussed in great detail in the joint dissenting opinion of Judges Sir Percy Spender and Sir Gerald Fitzmaurice in 1962. They comment upon the "well-being" language of Article 2(2) [the relevant language is quoted above in note 3] as follows:

There is hardly a word in this sentence which has not now become loaded

This setting alone makes it difficult indeed to give an account of why the Court disposed of the case by throwing the plaintiff states out of Court on technical grounds although the majority took pains to argue that it was deciding on "the merits." This point is confusing. The basis of denial appears procedural in the prevailing sense that the applicant states were denied capacity to obtain a substantive determination, but the majority holds that this kind of denial of capacity involving the sufficiency of the legal interest to pursue the specific claims is a matter that pertains to the merits of the controversy. Assuming men of reasonable intelligence and integrity were involved, can we explain the 1966 judgment in the *South West Africa Cases*?

The Opinion of the Court: The Holding and Its Legal Rationale

The narrow holding of the Court was that the applicant states did not possess the legal interest needed to obtain a judgment on their contention that South Africa, as Mandatory, was violating several provisions of the Mandate. Wellington Koo, the Vice President of the Court, invoked the proverbial wisdom of China to confess his own frustration: "Why write a long and big essay on such a small subject?"[17] The opinion of the Court is written in tortured prose, dwells upon hypertechnical elaborations of its basic conclusions, and seems utterly unconvincing in its main argument. In fairness, the prevailing faction of the Court seemed determined to avoid the apparent authority of the judgment in 1962 without actually repudiating its earlier reasoning. Therefore, the majority opinion relies upon highly technical and artificial reasoning to demonstrate that the 1962 judgment does not preclude a "procedural" dismissal in 1966. This way of proceeding is in line with the judicial conservatism of the majority.

"Judicial conservatism" implies a very narrow conception of the judicial function; it also usually involves a sharp separation of law and morals and of law and politics; in an international context this conservative orientation normally accords great deference to the nation-state

---

with a variety of overtones and associations. There is hardly a term which would not require prior objective definition, or redefinition, before it could justifiably be applied to the determination of a concrete legal issue. . . . As at present advised we have serious misgivings as to the legal basis on which the necessary objective criteria can be founded.

(*South West Africa Cases* [*Ethiopia v. South Africa*; *Liberia v. South Africa*],

Preliminary Objections, Judgment of 21 December 1962: I.C.J. Reports 1962 [hereinafter cited as *South West Africa Cases, Preliminary Objections*], pp. 466-67). A considerable portion of the subsequent reasoning of the applicant states was directed at satisfying "these serious misgivings."

[17] *South West Africa Cases, Second Phase, Judgment, I.C.J. Reports 1966* (hereinafter cited as *South West Africa Cases, Second Phase*), p. 220.

and to the doctrine of national sovereignty. Such conservatism is reluctant, as a rule, to accord the will of the international community any legal effect and regards with skepticism the formal acts of the political organs of the United Nations, especially if these acts are relied upon as legal data. It is important to emphasize, however, that this kind of conservatism is not necessarily sympathetic with the values underlying South Africa's racial policy and that an individual adherent may find such policy as fully abhorrent from a moral perspective as would a judicial progressive (the reverse is also possible). The main insistence of the judicial conservatives would seem to be that the ICJ is not the appropriate forum for the settlement of the kind of controversy that Ethiopia and Liberia brought before it.

The Court chose to examine, first, the question of whether the mandates system contemplated a right of judicial protection of the sort relied upon by the applicant states of Ethiopia and Liberia,[18] Here, the opinion of the Court is quite straightforward although directly in conflict with the interpretation of the same issue that is found in the 1962 judgment. The administration of the mandates system on behalf of the organized international community was considered by the majority opinion to have been *exclusively* entrusted to the organs of the League of Nations, especially the Council and the Permanent Mandates Commission. In the last analysis the Court reasons that the Mandatory could not be subjected to legal compulsion. The voting rules of the Council gave the Mandatory a veto and the operation of the mandates system confirms this interpretation, suggesting that disagreements between the League organs and the Mandatory had to be resolved by negotiation and conciliation or not at all.[19] The League Council could obtain an advisory opinion from the Permanent Court of International Justice (PCIJ), but such judicial conclusions were, of course, not binding upon the Mandatory.[20]

Members of the League according to the opinion of the Court had no separable role in the observance of the Mandate except to the extent that their *special interests* as a state were involved. Thus, in the context of "C" Mandates, of which South West Africa was an example, the only special interest conferred upon League members in their individual capacity was the right to send missionaries and have them reside and travel in the mandated territory.[21] Such a special interest was protected

---

[18] Principally conceiving of the mandates system in terms of the provisions of Article 22 and of the practice during the League period; the provisions of the mandate agreement covering South West Africa was not, in this general inquiry, accorded special attention.

[19] *South West Africa, Second Phase*, p. 31.

[20] *Ibid.*, p. 33.

[21] Article 5 of the Mandate reads as follows:

Subject to the provision of any local law for the maintenance of public order and public morals, the Mandatory shall

by a provision in the Mandate obliging the Mandatory to accept the compulsory jurisdiction of the Permanent Court of International Justice in the event that a dispute could not be settled by negotiation. This compromissory clause had to be construed in light of the overall nature of the mandates system as exhibited by the relevant documents, intentions, and practice. For the majority of the Court in 1966 the evidence establishes beyond doubt that individual members of the League possessed no judicial remedy to secure the general observance of the Mandate as distinct from the judicial remedy restricted to special interests. As a consequence a distinction is drawn by the Court between "special interest" provisions for which there is a judicial remedy and "conduct" provisions for which there is not. The case against South Africa is concerned only with conduct provisions and hence it is a controversy for which League members have no sufficient legal interest in the observance of the Mandate to support recourse to adjudication.

Having arrived at this conclusion by reasoning that resembles in many respects the interpretation of the mandates system to be found in the joint dissenting opinion of Spender and Fitzmaurice in 1962,[22] the majority goes on to consider two apparent obstacles to their analysis: First, the judgment in 1962 had dealt with these issues and resolved them the other way—therefore, it would seem necessary to acquiesce in the interpretation of the mandates system given in 1962, or, if not, then to reverse it; second, the language of Article 7, the compromissory clause, seems to be so sweeping in its coverage as to deny the limitation upon the scope of legal interests of League members that the Court finds to have been contemplated in the mandates system.

As to alleged conflict with its 1962 judgment, the Court suggests that "the essential point is that a decision on a preliminary objection can never be preclusive of a matter appertaining to the merits."[23] Therefore, whatever was settled in 1962, even if it touched on the merits "can do [so] only in a provisional way."[24] All that was decided in 1962 was that Ethiopia and Liberia, despite the dissolution of the League, were to be deemed members for purposes of invoking Article 7 and that the dispute was encompassed by Article 7 as it related to the interpretation of a provision of the Mandate: "Hence . . . it remained for the Applicants, on the merits, to establish that they have this right or interest in the carrying out of the provisions which they invoked, such as to en-

---

ensure in the territory freedom of conscience and the free exercise of all forms of worship, and shall allow all missionaries, nationals of any State Member of the League of Nations, to enter into, travel and reside in the territory for the purpose of prosecuting their calling.

[22] See *South West Africa Cases, Preliminary Objections*, pp. 478-82.

[23] *South West Africa, Second Phase*, p. 37.

[24] *Ibid.*

title them to the pronouncements and declarations they were seeking from the Court."[25] On this basis the Court's analysis in 1962 of the legal interest possessed by the applicants is classified as pertaining to "the merits" and therefore outside the scope of the binding portion of the judgment in 1962. Hence, the Court in 1966 is free to treat as *dicta* any discussion of the existence or generality of the legal interest in the 1962 judgment, the earlier consideration being a *predetermination* of an issue that could be resolved only at the merits stage of the proceeding. This juristic reasoning seems logical enough, but it does not appear to reflect either past judicial practice or the understanding in the case that apparently had been shared by the parties and judges since 1962.[26]

The argument that the language of Article 7 is so sweeping as to preclude the distinction between "special interest" provisions and "conduct" provisions was also considered by the majority. The text of Article 7 includes the following paragraph:

> The Mandatory agrees that, if any dispute whatever should arise between the Mandatory and another Member of the League of Nations relating to the interpretation or the application of the provisions of the Mandate, such dispute, if it cannot be settled by negotiation, shall be submitted to the Permanent Court of International Justice provided for by Article 14 of the Covenant of the League of Nations.

The Court emphasized in its opinion that a jurisdictional clause does not determine by itself whether or not a party possesses a legal interest enabling the adjudication of a particular claim. Article 7 is concerned only with the right of League members to activate the Court, but it is irrelevant to whether they have the legal interest needed to establish standing before the Court in relation to a specific controversy. The latter question of standing must be established *independently* of jurisdiction, by reference to the overall intentions, as of 1920, of the creators of the mandates system. As we have seen, the Court concluded that no intention existed to give individual members any legal interest in the enforcement of the conduct provisions of the Mandate aside from their role as participants in the activities of the organs of the League.

This conclusion is reinforced by an insistence upon sharp separations between law and morals and between law and politics. The opinion of the Court rejects the implications of the applicant states and several dissenting judges that it should be sensitive to those humanitarian consid-

[25] *Ibid.*, p. 38.
[26] Judge Jessup forcefully develops this line of attack in his dissenting opinion in 1966, concluding that "The Court now in effect sweeps away this record of 16 years and, *on a theory not advanced by* the Respondent in its final submissions of 5 November 1965, decides that the claim must be rejected on the ground that the Applicants have no legal right or interest." (Emphasis added.) (*Ibid.*, p. 329; see also *ibid.*, pp. 323-30.)

erations that would make it desirable to treat the applicants *as if* they possessed the legal interests that they claimed to possess; it also rejects the implication attributed to Article 92 of the United Nations Charter that the Court as "the principal judicial organ of the United Nations" should give legal effect to political attitudes prevailing in the United Nations and decide this case as the majority in the General Assembly wanted it decided. The Court, in a spirit that is true to the character of the conservative temper of the continental jurist, implies that its sole task is to adjudicate in accordance with its understanding of the legal rights and duties in the mandates system as existent as of 1920. Nothing subsequent, whether the increasing disapproval by the organized international community of the policies pursued by the Mandatory or an increasing refusal by the Mandatory to cooperate with the United Nations, has any capacity to enlarge the original competence of the Court to entertain legal action brought against the Mandatory by members of the League.

THE 1966 JUDGMENT AS THE COVERT OVERRULING OF THE 1962 JUDGMENT

The most plausible line of explanation is to conclude that the effective majority of the Court wished in 1966 to reverse the conclusions reached in 1962 or, more precisely, the legal assumptions accompanying the earlier decision. The 1962 judgment was reached by a slim majority of 8-7. In the interim, changes in the composition of the Court kept the strength of the 1962 dissenters at seven while reducing the original majority from eight to seven. The intervening election of Sir Percy Spender as President enabled Sir Percy to cast a second vote in the face of the 1966 tie, thereby giving the dissenting group of seven a majority of eight. It is worth noting that of the ten judges participating in both decisions, all those who voted with the majority in 1962 were in the dissent in 1966 and vice versa.[27] It requires a peculiar kind of legalistic myopia to ignore the impression of reversal created by a combination of changes in the voting membership of the Court and these voting statistics.[28]

[27] The ten judges who participated in both phases are Spender, Wellington Koo, Winiarski, Spiropoulos, Fitzmaurice, Koretsky, Jessup, Morelli, Mbanefo, and van Wyk.

[28] Some of the adventitious circumstances, each of which worked against the applicants, can be mentioned:

1) The disqualification of Sir Muhammad Zafrulla Khan (Pakistan) from the proceeding because of his orginal nomination as an *ad hoc* Judge by Ethiopia and Liberia prior to his election by the General Assembly as a regular Judge of the Court.

2) The death of Judge Abdel Hamid Badawi of the United Arab Republic in the course of the oral proceedings in 1965, who in 1962 had voted with the majority of eight in favor of accepting jurisdiction.

3) The disabling heart attack of Judge José Luis Bustamante y Rivero (Peru) who had also voted with the majority in 1962 and had appended a separate

The reasoning of the 1962 majority opinion fully confirms the impression that the decision in 1966 amounts to a covert reversal. In 1962 great stress was laid upon the unambiguous scope of the compromissory clause in Article 7 of the Mandate. As the Court concluded in 1962: "The language used is broad, clear and precise: it gives rise to no ambiguity and it permits of no exception."[29] As Wellington Koo emphasizes in his dissent in 1966, if the drafters of the test of the mandate agreements had intended to impose a more restricted obligation upon the Mandatory to submit to compulsory jurisdiction, then certainly such an intention would have been expressed in the language of Article 7.

There is little doubt that in 1962 the judgment affirmed the right of League members to use the Court to test compliance with any provision of the Mandate. In explaining the workings of the mandates system the 1962 Court pointed out, for instance, that "Under the unanimity rule (Articles 4 and 5 of the Covenant), the Council could not impose its own view on the Mandatory. It could of course ask for an advisory opinion of the Permanent Court but that opinion would not have binding force, and the Mandatory could continue to turn a deaf ear to the Council's admonitions."[30] Only a decision in a contentious proceeding—that is, a proceeding initiated by a member of the League against the Mandatory—could supply the international community with some assurance that in the last analysis it could establish a legal basis for compelling due performance from an unwilling Mandatory: "The only effective recourse for protection of the sacred trust would be for a Member or members of the League invoke Article 7 and bring the dispute as also one between them and the Mandatory to the Permanent Court for adjudication. It was for this all-important purpose that the provision was couched in broad terms embracing 'any dispute whatever.' "[31] This construction of the mandates system is clearly repudiated by the Court in 1966; the requirement of unanimity of League voting is relied upon

---

opinion strongly endorsing the legal theory upon which the applicants' case rested.

4) The highly unrepresentative political and jurisprudential outlook of Judge Winiarski from Poland who is misleadingly referred to as "the second Socialist" on the Court.

5) The fact that a member of the conservative faction of seven *happened* to be President of the Court; if Vice President Wellington Koo had been President the Court would have set legal history in the other direction.

[29] *South West Africa Cases, Preliminary Objections*, p. 343; later in the same paragraph on p. 343 the Court has this to say:

For the manifest scope and purport of the provisions of this Article [7] indicate that the Members of the League were understood to have a legal right or interest in the observance by the Mandatory of its obligations both toward the inhabitants of the Mandated Territory, and toward the League of Nations and its Members.

[30] *Ibid.*, p. 337.

[31] *Ibid.* The Court concludes the passage by saying "It is thus seen what an essential part Article 7 was intended to play as one of the securities in the Mandates System for the observance of the obligations by the Mandatory." (*Ibid.*)

in the latter decision to demonstrate the intention to avoid the judicial creation of legal obligations binding on the Mandatory whereas in 1962 this same voting requirement was, as we have seen, invoked to establish the necessity for vesting judicial protection in the members of the League.

In 1962 the Court could not have been more definite in its repudiation of the distinction drawn in the 1966 decision between "conduct" provisions and "interest" provisions:

> While Article 6 of the Mandate . . . provides for administrative supervision by the League, Article 7 in effect provides, with the express agreement of the Mandatory, for judicial protection by the Permanent Court by vesting the right of invoking the compulsory jurisdiction against the Mandatory for the same purpose in each of the other Members of the League. *Protection of the material interests of the Members or their nationals is of course included within its compass, but the well-being and development of the inhabitants of the Mandated territory are not less important.*[32]

On these bases it does seem rather clear that the 8-7 vote in 1966 is, in effect, a reversal of the 8-7 vote in 1962. Why, then, did a Court composed of distinguished jurists strain to reconcile the two decisions? Why, in other words, was not the covert reversal rendered in overt form? There are several possible explanations. First, an overt reversal of an earlier phase of the same proceedings might appear to emphasize the juridical relevance of purely adventitious changes in the composition of the Court. By *distinguishing* rather than *reversing* the 1962 decision it is possible to contend that the changes in composition were of no direct significance, as the earlier phase of the proceedings was not put in formal jeopardy by the later phase. Second, and perhaps more to the point, the 1966 decision represents a victory for judicial conservatism with respect to a restrained delimitation of judicial function. To reverse an earlier phase of the same proceeding is a radical instance of judicial progressivism that is entirely at odds with the jurisprudential outlook of the 1966 majority. The 1966 decision goes out of its way to underscore its narrow conception of judicial function.[33]

Third, and most prosaically, the judges constituting the majority in 1966 undoubtedly had some difficulty in reaching a consensus as to a satisfactory legal rationale. The legal rationale given may have reflected

[32] *Ibid.*, p. 344. (Emphasis added.)
[33] See, e.g., *South West Africa, Second Phase*, esp. pp. 47-51; pp. 51-52 summarize the attitude of the majority toward the narrow scope of judicial function that controlled the decision in 1966.

the lowest common denominator among those opposing the contentions for various procedural and substantive reasons.[34]

If it is correct to interpret the judgment in 1966 as a covert reversal of the judgment reached in 1962, then criticisms of the bad effect on the morale of litigating states are highly pertinent. These criticisms are made with devastating force by Judge Jessup in 1966 in the course of his long and careful dissenting opinion. The frustration and expense, the interminable delay, and the demoralizing impact on disputants considering adjudication as a means of pacific settlement are among the criticisms made.

The 1966 Judgment as the Triumph of Judicial Conservatism

The fundamental policy issue dividing the ICJ cuts far deeper than a technical disagreement about the scope of legal interests possessed by League members in the enforcement of the Mandate or about the extent to which the findings in 1962 were *res judicata* in 1966. The basic disagreement dividing the ICJ is concerned with the character of international law and the implications of this character for international adjudication. The majority in 1966 is positivistic in its orientation and takes very seriously the role of sovereign discretion in the formation of legal obligations. As such, this conservative perspective is antagonistic to any attempt to compel a sovereign state to alter conduct performed within its national domain. The mandate concept must be, in this view, reconciled with the notions of sovereign discretion prevailing at the time of its creation. In this regard it would have been unthinkable for South Africa to be compelled to justify its basic social system before an international tribunal, a social system that it was expected to extend to South West Africa by the very terms of the Mandate and Covenant.[35]

According to this view General Assembly initiatives against South Africa's policies are expressions of moral and political disapproval that conflict with this voluntaristic conception of international society. The ICJ should not implement these initiatives as its role is to apply "the law" regardless of its moral or political effects.

In contrast, the 1962 majority deplores these attitudes. International law develops under pressure from the will of the international community. The General Assembly is a forum within which evolving normative standards can be accurately identified. Especially in the context of a trust relationship, as established by the mandate notion, the evolv-

[34] For a general analysis of the intra-judicial bargaining process see Walter F. Murphy, *Elements of Judicial Strategy*, Chicago, University of Chicago Press, 1964.

[35] See esp. Article 22(6) of the Covenant and Article 2(1) of the Mandate (text of the latter above in note 3).

ing will of the international community is legally relevant. The discretion of a sovereign state must be reconciled with, and even subordinated to, the need of the international community to find legally effective means to discharge its responsibilities to safeguard the welfare of mandated territories.[36] The ICJ, as the judicial arm of the organized international community, should facilitate the discharge of this overriding responsibility. Thus, the majority in 1966 can be associated with the precepts of legal positivism whereas the minority may be associated with functional jurisprudence, sometimes called sociological jurisprudence.[37]

To understand this distinction somewhat more concretely it may be helpful to examine the controversy about the justiciability of the contention that apartheid violates the duty to promote well-being in Article 2(2). Judges Fitzmaurice and Spender in their joint dissent in 1962 write that they are "not unmindful of, nor . . . insensible to, the various considerations of a nonjuridical character, social, humanitarian and other, which underlie this case."[38] The next phrase in their opinion exposes the underlying controversy among the factions of the ICJ about the nature of law and the function of courts: *"But these [humanitarian, social and other considerations] are matters for the political rather than the legal arena."*[39] The jurisprudential gravamen appears to be that the sort of question presented to the Court for adjudication by the contention that the policies of the Mandatory are violating the legal duty to promote the well-being of the inhabitants is essentially nonjusticiable. That is, there exist no legal criteria available for adjudication that are sufficiently objective to be applied by a court of law.[40] The 1966 majority considers that Ethiopia and Liberia came to the World Court with a *political* dispute between the United Nations and South Africa that is not convertible into a *legal* dispute susceptible to adjudication. There is no very satisfying approach to this basic question of distinguishing political disputes from legal disputes. I find the distinction a misleading way to raise the key problem of identifying a category of disputes for which a court is unable to render a judgment that will be accepted by the overall community as authoritative. In this regard I think that a court must be able to rely in its legal reasoning either upon legal rules that have been laid down by the traditional law-creating procedures set forth in Article 38 of the Statute or upon a consensus in the international community as to the values that should animate the evolution of

---

[36] It is realistic to conceive of "this dispute" as one between the organized international community and South Africa. Ethiopia and Liberia are in the role of agents of the organized international community, especially as manifest in the General Assembly. Article 34 of the Statute of the Court allows only states to initiate contentious proceedings.

[37] For a discussion of these issues of jurisprudential orientation see Chapter XV.

[38] *South West Africa Cases, Preliminary Objections*, p. 466.

[39] *Ibid.* (Emphasis added.)

[40] See *ibid.*, pp. 466-67.

legal standards. If such a consensus as to values is present, then the ICJ is in a position to evolve by its own reasoning legal criteria that govern the controversy and render a decision that will be accepted as authoritative by the overwhelming majority of states in the world community. In this respect the *South West Africa Cases* setting is one in which the issue of justiciability seems far less severe than in the setting of the advisory opinion in the *Certain Expenses of the United Nations* case.[41] In the latter controversy, especially in retrospect, it is now quite plausible to contend that the Court should have refused to pronounce upon the questions presented for legal assessment because the answers were neither provided by clearly relevant preexisting legal criteria nor was there a sufficient consensus on the underlying values at stake to anticipate the acceptability of newly evolved legal criteria. In effect, I am arguing that under these circumstances of value divergence it is predictable that the decision of the Court will be received as nonauthoritative or arbitrary by an important segment of the legal community and that this reception will diminish the prestige of the Court as well as make it difficult to mount a campaign, if such is necessary, to coerce respect with its decision.

This interpretation of the division on the Court throughout the South West Africa controversy as one of antagonistic jurisprudential outlooks becomes more persuasive if it can be shown that the judgment in 1966 was not intended as a covert decision in favor of South Africa on the real merits. One superficial reaction to the judgment has been that the artificial rationale based on a denial of legal interests was advanced to cover up a disposition to decide the substantive questions in South Africa's favor. As might be expected, South African officials hailed the judgment of the World Court as "a complete justification of South Africa's sustained denial of any right to interference by other states in the Republic's administration of South West Africa. . . . Any further attempt at interference by other means would spring from a spirit of persecution and should find no support from any respectable state or organization of states."[42] Such statements deliberately, and quite understandably, blur the distinction between a *jurisdictional dismissal* and a finding for South Africa on the *real merits*. It is important to emphasize that the Court refused to inquire whether South Africa was or was not acting in conformity with the provisions of the Mandate. The decision in 1966 determined only that it was impossible for a League member to test compliance in a judicial forum. Such a bar on inquiry does not, in any

---

41 *Certain Expenses of the United Nations (Article 17, paragraph 2, of the Charter), Advisory Opinion of July 20, 1962: I.C.J. Reports 1962*, p. 151.

42 E.g., Charles Swart, State President of South Africa, in a speech opening the new session of Parliament, Release of Information Service of South Africa, June 1966.

formal respect, impair the capacity of Ethiopia or Liberia to allege and establish noncompliance in some other forum—for instance, in General Assembly. It is possible for South Africa or other states to argue that a determination in a nonjudicial forum is nonauthoritative and is, therefore, not binding upon South Africa.

Sir Percy Spender attached a declaration criticizing those judges who in 1966 went beyond the opinion of the Court to deal with the real merits. Sir Percy wrote that "in my view there are grounds other than as stated in the Judgment upon which the Applicants' claims or certain of them could have been rejected."[43]

There is some language in the opinion of the Court in 1966 that might seem to confirm South Africa's basic contention that the governance of the Territory is a matter within the domestic jurisdiction of South Africa rather than subject to surviving obligations of international accountability. In fact, to curtail this implication the United States evidently felt compelled to issue an official statement affirming its adherence to the teaching of the three advisory opinions of the Court.[44] Despite the rhetoric of the release issued by the United States Government, the 1966 decision definitely weakened the authority of the 1950 advisory opinion that had been supported by a unanimous Court.[45]

On the basis of reading the dissents in 1962 it might have been reasonable to anticipate that some of these judges, at least, would have denied as nonjusticiable the allegations with respect to "well-being" under Article 2.

No problem of justiciability attaches to the interpretation of the Mandatory's duties of administrative accountability contained in Article 6. However, the Court in 1966 expressly points out that it neither affirms nor denies the survival of the Mandate. South Africa contended vigorously that the Mandate lapsed upon the dissolution of the League of Nations and that it exercises sovereignty over South West Africa by virtue of rights of conquest as during World War I South Africa had occupied South West Africa, then a German colony, as enemy territory. The majority in 1966 concludes that the survival of the Mandate need not be determined because of the failure of Ethiopia and Liberia to establish a legal interest. If the applicants had established their legal interest, then, and only then, would it have been necessary to deal with the issue of survival before inquiring into the merits of the alleged violations. The Court also declared that it would be improper to consider that

[43] *South West Africa, Second Phase,* p. 52.
[44] For the text of the statement see "ICJ South-West Africa Judgment: U.S. Appraises Legal Situation," *Department of* *State Bulletin,* 55, No. 1416 (Aug. 15, 1966), 231.
[45] See, e.g., *South West Africa, Second Phase,* esp. p. 19.

the decision in 1962 had already established the survival of the Mandate.

It may clarify the preceding analysis to distinguish several separate clusters of issues that are relevant to an appraisal of what was done and what was not done by the ICJ in 1966:

1. *Standing*: The requirement that a complaining party possess a sufficient legal interest to test the alleged violations of the Mandate. The Court holds that League members do not possess such a legal interest with respect to conduct provisions. Failure to establish standing is the ground of dismissal in 1966 and was treated by the Court as the first preliminary question.

2. *Survival*: The determination that the Mandate arrangement created under the auspices of the League of Nations survives the dissolution of the League. The Mandatory would not be subject to the mandate agreement, including the obligation to submit disputes to the ICJ, if the Mandate is considered to have lapsed. This issue was mentioned by the majority opinion as the second preliminary question in the case, but since the applicants were defeated on the first, it was not necessary to reach the second.

3. *Justiciability*: The requirement that legal criteria of sufficient definiteness exist to enable the identification of a violation of the asserted obligation. Disagreements about justiciability pertain only to the interpretation of the Article 2 portion of the controversy and are manifest in several of the separate and dissenting opinions of 1962 and in the dissenting opinions of Judges Jessup, Tanaka, Nervo, and Sir Louis Mbanefo in 1966. The majority opinion in 1966 never reaches the issue of justiciability.

4. *Jurisdiction*: The determination that the ICJ had the competence to adjudicate the controversy and inquire whether the parties had standing.[46] This competence was affirmed by the 8-7 decision in 1962. The most troublesome jurisdictional question in 1962 was whether there existed "a legal dispute" between the parties.[47] If there was no dispute, then there is, of course, no basis to adjudicate. These questions were set-

---

[46] The specific objections considered in the preliminary were that:

1) The Mandate was never and is no longer "a treaty or convention in force" within the meaning of Article 37 of the Statute of the Court;
2) neither Ethiopia nor Liberia is "another Member of the League" within the meaning of Article 7 of the Mandate;
3) the alleged disagreement between Ethiopia and Liberia and South Africa is not a "dispute" within the meaning

of Article 7, especially as the disagreement does not concern the material interests of these governments or their nationals; and
4) the alleged conflict is not a "dispute" that "cannot be settled by negotiation" within the meaning of Article 7.

[47] For clear analysis on this issue, favorable to South Africa's contentions, see Judge Morelli's dissenting opinion in *South West Africa Cases, Preliminary Objections*, pp. 564-74.

tled in 1962 and remain settled in 1966 except with regard to the interpretation of the scope of Article 7—"the compromissory clause."

5. *Substantive Compliance*: The determination by an authorized decision-maker that South Africa was violating or complying with specific provisions of the Mandate. The ICJ refused, of course, to make these determinations in 1966 although several dissenting judges and one concurring judge did so.[48] The General Assembly has frequently "determined" that South African policies violate the Mandate. Is the General Assembly an authoritative decision-maker? The answer is determined, in part, by settling whether the General Assembly succeeds to the role of the Council upon the dissolution of the League. One can contend that this question was settled affirmatively by the ICJ in its unanimous advisory opinion of 1950 and never subsequently contradicted. Even if this line of reasoning is accepted, South Africa can emphasize that it is not bound by ICJ determinations that are set forth in an advisory opinion.

The 1966 Judgment: A Cost Accounting

It is very hazardous to speculate about the consequences of the 1966 judgment in the *South West Africa Cases*. No legal institution deserves to be assessed on the basis of a single case. The United States Supreme Court has made great contributions to the cause of racial equality despite supporting slavery in Dred Scott and endorsing the compatibility of segregation with the Constitution in Plessy v. Ferguson.[49]

The 1966 judgment in the *South West Africa Cases* does not seem to support any general conclusions about the usefulness of the ICJ in future situations, especially in view of the fact that the outcome was so largely a consequence of fortuitous factors that allowed the 1962 minority to achieve an artificial and temporary majority in 1966. It seems safe to predict that the triumph of judicial conservatism in 1966 will be the last such triumph in the ICJ for many years to come, especially in light of the recent election of five new judges.[50]

One consequence of the decision in the *South West Africa Cases* is likely to be quite ironic. The unpopularity of the results reached by the

[48] South Africa's *ad hoc* Judge van Wyk did write a long opinion on the merits largely endorsing South Africa's contentions throughout the litigation. (*South West Africa, Second Phase*, pp. 65-215).

[49] This point is substantially borrowed from Professor Oliver J. Lissitzyn's oral statement at a forum on the South West Africa litigation held under the auspices of the African-American Institute in New York City on September 28, 1966.

[50] Fouad Ammoun (Lebanon), Charles D. Anyeama (Nigeria), Cesar Bengzon (Philippines), Manfred Lachs (Poland), and Sture Petren (Sweden) are the five new judges; three of the vacancies were created by the retirement of Judges Sir Percy Spender, Spiropoulos, and Winiarski, all of whom voted with the majority in 1966. The two other vacancies arose from the death of Judge Badawi Pasha and the disablement of Judge Bustamante, neither of whom had been able to vote in 1966 although both appeared favorable to Ethiopia and Liberia.

ICJ in 1966 has already set in motion pressures that will make such a determination far less likely in the future. But the disappointment caused by the 1966 decision has seriously undermined confidence in the ICJ to such an extent—especially in the eyes of the Afro-Asian group—that no opportunity is likely to provide the Court with an opportunity to signal a revival of jurisprudential progressivism in its operations. To overcome this ironic situation from inhibiting recourse of the ICJ and to international adjudication in general it is important for observers to appreciate the combination of improbable circumstances that allowed the judicial conservatives to muster a majority in 1966 and the probability that the judicial conservatives will exert a declining influence in future activities of the ICJ.

The dissatisfaction caused by the 1966 judgment does create pressure and hence provides an occasion for judicial reform. The present procedures of the ICJ for hearing the argument of the parties need to be streamlined to cut down on expense and delay. It is important, of course, to give a sovereign state its day in court in the fullest sense, but it is also crucial to reduce the time period between invoking the jurisdiction of the Court and receiving a final judgment. The South West Africa proceedings were shockingly wasteful; a great corpus of superfluous and redundant material is to be found in both the written pleadings and in the oral arguments. The Court should either confine the parties by fixed rules on the length of pleadings and the duration of oral argument or exercise more discretion to exclude material already substantially before the Court.

Another proposal, likely to be made in the near future, is to enlarge the number of judges on the Court to assure greater representation for the Afro-Asian group as the enlargement of the size of the Security Council has already done. The enactment of such a proposal would probably make the Court more receptive to litigation with political and moral overtones although it might also build an image of the Court as a rubber stamp of the General Assembly and thereby diminish its prestige as a judicial organ.

It has also been suggested that Article 34 of the Statute of the ICJ be amended to allow the United Nations to appear as a litigating party in certain cases.[51] To confer standing on the United Nations would not appear to improve prospects for securing a judicial remedy in the context of the dispute over the administration of South West Africa although it might be desirable in general terms. South Africa would not, in all probability, agree to participate in such a proceeding and the compromissory clause in Article 7 of the Mandate refers only to disputes between the Mandatory and members of the League. Of course, it would

[51] See Gross, *op.cit.*, note 6.

be juridically possible, although politically unlikely, to make it mandatory for a state to submit to the jurisdiction of the ICJ in any dispute in which an organ of the United Nations acted as the initiating party.

A more far-reaching reform proposal of the same sort would be to obtain an amendment of Article 96(1) of the Charter so that the General Assembly could request the ICJ to render binding judgments on legal questions referred to it for adjudication. The present form of Article 96(1) leads to advisory opinions in the event of General Assembly referrals. Such a revision of the Charter, although not entirely free from legal obstacles,[52] would allow the activation of the enforcement procedures of Article 94(1) without an adverse judgment against South Africa. The legal basis for collective action against South Africa would be much stronger if the advisory opinions—described by some as authoritative in any event—were made subject to direct implementation by the Security Council. Such a judicial proceeding would not require either South African consent or a judicial finding that the litigation was within the scope of Article 7 of the Mandate. As such, this Charter amendment would reopen the ICJ to the states aggrieved by the conditions in South West Africa and assure judicial scrutiny of the charges of substantive noncompliance with Articles 2 (well-being) and 6 (administrative supervision) of the Mandate.

It is possible to argue that the decision in 1966 saved the ICJ from choosing between rendering an irrelevant or an unenforceable decision in favor of Ethiopia and Liberia. As became evident in the aftermath of the advisory opinion given in the *Expenses* case, there is no widespread disposition to accord respect to judicial pronouncements of the ICJ if these pronouncements collide with basic policies of important states. In the event of a finding in favor of Ethiopia and Liberia, depending on the form of relief granted, South Africa might either have rejected the findings or complied with them in some *pro forma* manner. In the face of a rejection of the Court's finding it is true that an appeal to the Security Council for enforcement would have been appropriate. But would the prospects for effective enforcement have been favorable? The reluctance to take effective action to nullify the assumption of governmental control by the Smith regime in Rhodesia, up through the summer of 1969, discloses a reluctance by major states to implement the will of the international community with regard to questions affecting southern Africa. It is plausible to contend that an unenforceable or irrelevant decision would give rise to a more deep-seated, if somewhat delayed, skepticism about the contribution of the ICJ to the processes of conflict resolution. In reacting to the 1966 judgment it is possible to stress ephemeral fac-

---

52 E.g., see the problems discussed by the Permanent Court of International Justice in *Eastern Carelia Case, PCIJ Publications*, 1923 (Series B, No. 5).

tors and to anticipate their disappearance in due course. But suppose the views of Judges Jessup, Tanaka, et al. had prevailed? We do not know, of course, what sort of judicial relief a different decision would have provided to restore compliance with the Mandate. It is prudent to suppose, however, that South Africa would not have voluntarily changed its policies in South West Africa in any fundamental respect and that the organized international community would have been unable to coerce South Africa against its will for as long ahead as it is possible to see. However, if the opinion of the Court had affirmed South Africa's obligation as Mandatory under Article 6 to submit annual reports and accept the administrative supervision of the General Assembly, then a clear-cut issue of enforcement would have been presented that the Security Council could not have evaded easily. From this perspective of enforcement, at least, the issue of administrative supervision seems somewhat more important than does the more dramatic and humanitarian question of the compatibility of apartheid with the obligation to promote the well-being of the inhabitants. On the issue of apartheid the Court would probably not have rendered a decision in enforceable terms but rather used some variant of the relief granted by the United States Supreme Court in the desegregation cases—"all deliberate speed."[53] Compliance with such a judgment itself would seem to require subsequent judicial interpretation and the Security Council might well conclude that no enforcement issue was presented for its consideration.

On this basis, then, was it premature to invoke the ICJ in this sort of dispute? One would suppose that many jurists would agree that a court should not be asked to resolve controversies unless the prospects are good that its pronouncements will be respected. The counterargument, which seems persuasive to me, is that a judicial pronouncement in the setting of the *South West Africa Cases* would have been an important additional lever available to those countries seeking to mobilize political support for their objectives in South West Africa and elsewhere in southern Africa. The United States and the United Kingdom, having often proclaimed their commitment to the procedures of international adjudication and having commended the African states for their recourse to these procedures, would be subject to pressure to implement a judgment once rendered. The process of enforcement might not have been immediate if the Jessup-Tanaka views had prevailed in the ICJ, but the start on the long path leading to effective enforcement would have been made. And part of that start, so dramatic in the circumstances of Brown

[53] The applicant states requested more definite relief in their submissions—namely, an order by the ICJ that South Africa "cease forthwith" the practice of apartheid in South West Africa. But even so strong a supporter of the Ethiopia-Liberia case as Judge Jessup implied an unwillingness to grant relief in such drastic form.

v. Board of Education, is to symbolize a serious political commitment through its embodiment in the legally binding form of a court judgment.

One enduring legacy of the *South West Africa Cases* is the discussion of the legal issues found in several of the dissenting opinions, especially the opinions of Judges Jessup and Tanaka. These dissents are likely to shape consideration of the legal issues for some time to come, as well as to foreshadow the approach of the ICJ in the event that a similar legal controversy is brought before it. Judge Jessup interprets the Mandate very much in the spirit of an American constitutional lawyer, emphasizing the relevance of evolving community values to the judicial interpretation of a legal obligation to promote well-being. Apartheid is incompatible with Article 2 of the Mandate because international standards have emerged to condemn such a system of compulsory segregation on the basis of race. These standards are authoritative guides to the interpretation of the Mandate, especially in view of the Mandatory's role as the agent selected to carry out on behalf of the organized international community a sacred trust of civilization vis-à-vis the welfare of the mandated territory.

Judge Tanaka, adopting a line of reasoning that is also evident in the dissenting opinions of Judge Padillo Nervo and Sir Louis Mbanefo, goes beyond Judge Jessup's rationale to conclude that the international standards condemning apartheid had evolved to a point at which they amount to a valid rule of international law that is binding independent of the Mandate.[54] Such a finding disposes of the central South African contention that Article 2(2) of the Mandate must be read in conjunction with Article 2(1) of the Mandate:

> The Mandatory shall have full power of administration and legislation over the territory subject to the present Mandate as an integral portion of the Union of South Africa, and may apply the laws of the Union of South Africa to the territory, subject to such local modifications as circumstances may require.[55]

Judge Jessup's reliance on standards imported in the Mandate context as guides to interpretation is not convincing on this issue of balancing Article 2(2) against 2(1). No state, and *a fortiori* no state in the role of Mandatory, has the discretion to violate rules of international law. Therefore, however wide the discretion of the Mandatory is conceived to be, it must, as a minimum condition, administer the mandated territory in conformity with applicable rules of international law. Judge Tanaka's rationale has the important side effect of making illegal the

[54] *South West Africa, Second Phase*, p. 300.
[55] Cf. Judge Tanaka's sensitivity to the delicate task of relating the Mandatory's discretion in Article 2(1) to the Mandatory's duty to promote well-being in Article 2(2) (*ibid.*, pp. 283-83.)

practice of apartheid anywhere, including South Africa.[56] To find that a rule of international law has emerged from the formal acts of condemnation and declaration by the General Assembly is to endorse and augment the trend toward substituting consensus for consent as the basic law-creating energy in international society.[57] Judge Tanaka exhibits a keen awareness of the jurisprudential significance of his approach, summarized by his conclusion that "The method of the generation of customary international law is in the stage of transformation from being an individualistic process to being a collectivistic process."[58] Such a transformation is, in effect, from a sovereignty-centered international system to a community-centered international system. Judge Tanaka may well have written an historic dissenting opinion; certainly it is a document worthy of the closest study by all those concerned with the growth of international law.

The multiple legacies of the *South West Africa Cases* are difficult to balance off against one another. A careful sorting out of adventitious factors is a first step toward assessing the permanent significance of the 1966 judgment. Perhaps the greatest danger is that these adventitious factors will be treated as permanent and typical features of international adjudication. It is essential that Afro-Asian disappointment be dealt with by a careful accounting of what did *not* happen in 1966.

As far as South West Africa is concerned, judicial action in the future is not foreclosed by the decision in 1966. The advisability of relitigating some of the issues will depend upon both the prospects for a legal victory in a fairly short period of time and the outlook for translating a legal victory into an enforceable judgment of some significance soon thereafter, especially in light of what might be the new legal status of South West Africa created by the resolution of the General Assembly terminating South Africa's responsibilities as Mandatory.[59]

It is well to realize, also, that the failure of the Court to render a decision that bore some relation to community expectations as to the range of acceptable judicial outcomes produced a very strong African-led political backlash in the General Assembly. It would not have been possible to mobilize a consensus in favor of General Assembly Resolution 2145 (xxi) except in the context set by a regressive decision of the ICJ. In this sense, recourse to judicial action paid off for the complainant states because it accelerated the political procedures being invoked against South Africa. We need a much more sophisticated comprehen-

---

[56] Cf. Judge Jessup's apparent opposition to this conclusion (*ibid.*, pp. 432-33, 441).

[57] For a discussion of the problem in general terms see Chapter VI. For a discussion of the general legal issues involved see Oscar Schachter, "Towards a Theory of International Obligation," 8 *Virginia Journal of International Law*, 300-22, (1968).

[58] *South West Africa, Second Phase*, p. 294; see also the discussion on pp. 291-94.

[59] G. A. Res. 2145 (xxi); see also G. A. Res. 2248 (s-v).

sion of the interaction between judicial and political remedies on the international level. The South West Africa dispute is best understood as a processive phenomenon that unfolds over time in a variety of legally relevant arenas. The principal adversaries in such a dispute need a strategy that seeks to realize principal goals in the shortest time with the minimum expenditure of effort. Such a general strategy helps put tactical moves, such as recourse to judicial remedies at various stages of the dispute, in proper intellectual focus.

XIII. The *Sabbatino* Litigation and After: The Complexity of the Supreme Court Decision and the Simplicity of the Legislative Epilogue

THIS CHAPTER is essentially an analysis of the original decision by the United States Supreme Court in the case of *Banco Nacional de Cuba v. Sabbatino*.[1] It considers briefly in a concluding section the postdecisional developments that culminated in the so-called Second Hickenlooper Amendment and the relitigation of the controversy leading to a judicial outcome favorable to the expropriated investors.[2] The point of refocusing attention on Mr. Justice Harlan's majority opinion in the original *Sabbatino* controversy is to underscore the importance of the doctrine therein enunciated to the development of an adequate conception of the role of domestic courts in the international legal order. The critics of *Sabbatino* have temporarily prevailed, but it remains pertinent to continue the controversy to the extent that its present disposition curtails both the creative potentialities for domestic courts in international law cases and reinforces the view that national arenas of judicial application of international law are likely to be self-serving and provincial in their modes of operation. Nothing less than the whole future of the decentralized dimension of the interpretation and application of international law in a divided world is at stake.[3] To look back favorably, then, upon the principal opinion in *Sabbatino* is, in effect, to argue toward a reconsideration of the policy priorities that produced the Second Hickenlooper Amendment and the judicial action that has so far upheld the claims of the Amendment.[4]

In pondering the issues raised by the *Sabbatino* litigation it seems apposite to call attention to the cases coming before domestic courts in

---

[1] 376 US. 398 (1964) (hereinafter referred to as *Sabbatino* and cited by page reference alone; 58 *American Journal of International Law* 778-79 (July 1964).

[2] I find that the most persuasive account of the current status of the *Sabbatino* range of issues is to be found in an article by Louis Henkin, "Act of State Today: Recollections in Tranquility," 6 *Columbia Journal of Transnational Law* 175-89 (Fall 1967).

[3] For the most comprehensive critique of the kind of approach taken in this chapter see Eugene F. Mooney, *Foreign Seizures: Sabbatino and the Act of State Doctrine*, Lexington, University of Kentucky, 1968; a very perceptive, significant, and appreciative appraisal of this book has been written: Burns H. Weston, "L'Affaire Sabbatino; A Wistful Review," 55

Kentucky Law Journal, 844-62 (Summer 1967).

[4] In this connection, notice that Judge Waterman in his opinion on behalf of the Court of Appeals pointed out that for purposes of decision it was sufficient to to apply the minimum content of international law without passing upon the validity of the maximalist claims embodied in the Hickenlooper Amendment. Therefore, as yet, there has not been a full judicial endorsement of the Hickenlooper approach. For Judge Waterman's views see Banco Nacional de Cuba v. Farr, 383 F. 2d 166 (2d Cir. 1967). For further discussion of the problems posed here by the interaction of legislative and judicial views see the concluding section, pp. 423-25.

the United States as a consequence of the Vietnam War. These cases, many of which have not yet been fully adjudicated, raise in settings of draft resistance and tax refusal various arguments alleging that the United States involvement in the Vietnam War is illegal for a variety of reasons. Domestic courts have so far refused to pass on these legal issues, relying heavily on either the lack of standing of the complainant, the nonjusticiability of the issues, or merely upon the judicial abstention that results from a broad application of "the doctrine of political questions" to problems of war and peace. In the litigation arising from the Vietnam War the relevant standards of international law are drawn from legal instruments such as the United Nations Charter that enjoy virtually universal adherence. There is no question of assessing whether a consensus among sovereign states lends support to such legal standard. The main question posed is whether a domestic court will pass judgment upon the legality of action by its own government to the same extent in foreign affairs as it is accustomed to doing in domestic matters. There is the further question as to whether judicial deference to executive discretion in the area of war and peace continues to be based on sound policy in the late 1960's. The idea of nonreviewable executive discretion in foreign affairs arose and made more sense in earlier decades when international law made no consistent claim to place recourse to war within a framework of law. The Kellogg-Briand Pact of 1928, the United Nations Charter, and the Nuremberg Judgment have, however, created a new legal environment wherein national discretion is significantly bounded by legal standard.

A significant kind of doctrinal counterpoint seems to emerge from a comparison of considerations and recommendations made in the very distinct settings of *Sabbatino* and of litigation pertaining to the Vietnam War. Such a comparison may elicit a clearer overall expression of policy priorities held by international law experts arguing from distinct jurisprudential orientations. This kind of inquiry might also help to disclose different conceptions of the overall role of domestic courts in the international legal order. Such a comparison of judicial roles in distinct subject matter areas (protection of foreign investment, war/peace) needs to be supplemented by the comparative assessment of how domestic courts in various foreign countries handle, or might be expected to handle, these kinds of controversies.

I. The Context of Controversy

On March 23, 1964, the Supreme Court of the United States concluded by an 8 to 1 majority in the *Sabbatino* case that the act of state doctrine prevents a domestic court from questioning the validity of a Cuban expropriation of sugar located within Cuban territory at the time of the taking. Thereby the Supreme Court upset the rulings of two Federal courts that had decided that this expropriation was not entitled to respect in an American court.[5] As well, the Supreme Court disappointed the expectations of many lawyers and their clients who had hoped and even predicted that the highest court in the land would strike down Castro's program of expropriation with a ringing denunciation of its confiscatory and discriminatory features.

The several main lines of attack upon the *Sabbatino* decision were easy to foresee and can be briefly depicted. The Supreme Court refrained from condemning a political enemy of the United States for violating what many observers regard as clearly established rules of customary international law governing the taking of property owned by aliens. Furthermore, a domestic court refused to apply substantive rules of international law in a case coming before it. What is worse, this judicial refusal was based primarily upon a servile acceptance of executive para mountcy. The decision allegedly compromises the status of rules of customary international law protecting foreign investment and this, it can be said, undermines the effort to build a stable world economy. On a less sophisticated level, the decision is held to exhibit a solicitude toward Cuban interests at a time when the United States was using every form of coercion short of violence to make life miserable for Castro's regime. It seems especially odd to some observers that the executive branch of the United States Government should have intervened to urge the Supreme Court to decide in favor of the Cuban Government, which had initiated the litigation through the complaint of its agent, Banco Nacional de Cuba.

Especially in light of the triumph of the critics, it seems important to meet this vexed reaction with an explanation of why the Supreme Court was probably right in most respects to decide in 1964 as it did. But it is also important not to get overly sidetracked by these polemics. *Sabbatino*'s permanent significance has nothing to do with Castro and rather little to do with the legal protection of foreign investment.

Sabbatino offers an interpretation of the proper role for a domestic court to play in an international law case.[6] This interpretation is subject to just criticism as being too responsive to the federal character of the American political system and somewhat unresponsive to the decentralized (horizontal) character of international society. The balancing of this dual perspective indicates the reason why this case is of such general interest. This duality of concern controls most of the discussion of three main facets of the *Sabbatino* case in the pages that follow: first, the character of the reaffirmation of the act of state doctrine; second,

---

[5] The lower court opinions are reported in 193 F. Supp. 375 (SDNY, 1961), and 307 F. 2d 845 (2d Cir., 1962).
[6] See Chapter XIV.

the nature of federal authority exercised by courts in the field of international law; and, third, the treatment accorded by domestic courts to a foreign sovereign with whom the United States maintains no diplomatic relations.

II. Act of State Doctrine

Of course the original excitement engendered by *Sabbatino* arose from its application of the act of state doctrine to the facts of a confiscatory Cuban expropriation of American owned property. Apparently a major cause of consternation is that the Supreme Court has been understood as saying that, even if the foreign governmental act is alleged to violate international law, a domestic court is helpless, at least until it has been formally released by receipt of a *Bernstein* letter, to do anything about it. Critics resent both this helplessness and the dependence of courts upon executive authorization. In both respects, even if one accepts, as I do not, the orientation of those critics who want to enlist domestic courts in the struggle to make national views on the protection of foreign investment prevail in contemporary international law there is some reason to question whether domestic courts are suitable vehicles of such protection.[7]

A review of the pre-*Sabbatino* precedents is not necessary. Mr. Justice Harlan has done this persuasively in Section IV of his opinion.[8] The Underhill decision is appropriately emphasized, and its formulation of the act of state principle is quoted to emphasize the breadth of the doctrine that courts of one state "will not sit in judgment on the acts of the government of another within its own territory."[9] There is no hint in *Underhill* or elsewhere in the act of state cases at the Supreme Court level that this principle of deference might admit of exception. An examination of the subsequent act of state cases fails to manifest any "retreat from *Underhill*. . . . On the contrary in . . . *Oetjen* and *Ricaud*, the doctrine as announced in *Underhill* was reaffirmed in unequivocal terms."[10]

The one apparent exception "to the unqualified teachings of *Underhill, Oetjen,* and *Ricaud*" was a product of executive intervention in the

---

[7] Even if it is agreed that the requirement of a stable international economy includes the protection of private capital abroad, it is doubtful whether either domestic courts or customary international law have much to contribute at this stage of international history. Given the attitude of the new states toward their imperial past and given the ideological outlook of the socialist states, it is futile to try to impose substantive standards that predated their appearance on the international scene as independent actors. To protect contemporary foreign investment it is necessary to start over and to base protection on rules of compensation that receive active assent from the effective majority of governments that *now* constitute international society.

[8] Pp. 416-20.

[9] Underhill v. Hernandez, 168 US 250 (1887); quoted by Justice Harlan at 416.

[10] Pp. 416-417.

second *Bernstein* case.[11] At maximum, *Bernstein* stands for the proposition that the operation of the act of state doctrine can be suspended by a court if it has received an explicit executive mandate to this effect.[12] But, as Justice Harlan points out, "whatever ambiguity may be thought to exist in the two letters from State Department officials on which the Court of Appeals relied . . . is now removed by the position which the Executive has taken in this Court on the act of state claim."[13] In other words, even if it were reasonable—as it most certainly was not—for the Court of Appeals to construe executive action as equivalent to a *Bernstein* letter,[14] this construction was not at all tenable after the executive branch entered the *Sabbatino* controversy with an argument in favor of applying the act of state doctrine.[15]

In passing, *Sabbatino* mentions that "This Court has never had occasion to pass upon the so-called *Bernstein* exception, nor need it do so now."[16] It need not precisely because the executive has made no attempt to relieve a court from the normal obligation to apply the act of state doctrine. However, the Supreme Court clearly went out of its way to deprecate the teaching of *Bernstein*: "It is highly questionable whether the examination of validity by the judiciary should depend on an educated guess by the Executive. . . . We do not pass on the *Bernstein* exception, but even if it were deemed valid, its suggested extension[17] is unwarranted."[18] Certainly this undermining of the authority of *Bernstein* falls far short of a reversal, but it does disclose a judicial mood that appears favorable to a reconsideration, if not to a repudiation, of the *Bernstein* exception, given the opportunity. This gratuitous questioning of the *Bernstein* decision in a setting where it was not really relevant

---

[11] Pp. 418-419; Bernstein v. N.V. Nederlandsche-Amerikaansche Stomvaart-Maatschappij, 173 F. 2d 71 (2d Cir., 1949), digested in 44 *American Journal of International Law* 182 (1950); 210 F. 2d 375 (2d Cir., 1954), digested in 48 *American Journal of International Law* 499 (1954).

[12] It is "at maximum" because, (according to the rationale of *Sabbatino*, it was unnecessary to apply the act of state doctrine to the Bernstein facts even without an executive dispensation; a consensus condemned the racist basis of Nazi confiscations and the government whose acts were being appraised was no longer in existence. Therefore, Judge Learned Hand was not necessarily correct in deciding the first *Bernstein* case as he did, that is, as if a domestic court had no choice but to validate German acts of state so long as judicial review had not been authorized by executive mandate. See Bernstein v. Van Heyghen Frères Société Anonyme, 163 F. 2d 246 (2d Cir. 1947), digested in 42 *American Journal of International Law*

217 (1948); 332 US 772 (1947).

[13] P. 420.

[14] E.g., see persuasive argument to this effect developed by Richard B. Lillich, "A Pyrrhic Victory at Foley Square: The Second Circuit and Sabbatino," 8 *Villanova Law Review* 155-76 (Winter 1963).

[15] See brief for the United States as Amicus Curiae, filed in the Supreme Court on Sept. 10, 1963, in the case of Banco Nacional de Cuba v. Sabbatino, 376 US 398 (1963) (reprinted in 2 *International Legal Materials* 1009 [1963]).

[16] P. 420.

[17] Refers to suggestion that act of state doctrine is only applicable to violations of international law if the Executive expressly requests the courts to refrain from passing on the question of validity. See Association of the Bar of the City of New York, Committee on International Law, *A Reconsideration of the Act of State Doctrine in United States Courts* (1959).

[18] P. 436; see also note 10, *supra*.

to the outcome does function to warn the executive to ponder the consequences of writing such a letter and invite a litigant to challenge its relevance should it ever be written.[19]

Therefore, it does seem reasonable to conclude that the *Bernstein* exception to the act of state doctrine has been cast in some disrepute by *Sabbatino*. To the extent that this is correct, it is beneficial. The role of domestic courts is made more independent of executive will. The treatment of an act of a foreign government is made to rest upon judicially created principles of deference and assertion instead of upon the executive's *ad hoc* advice. The outright repudiation of the executive prerogative implicit in *Bernstein*, something that must await a direct test, would contribute to the goal of judicial independence for domestic courts in international law cases.

There are two reasons to highlight the willingness of the *Sabbatino* court to reproach the *Bernstein* precedent. First, because it runs counter to the general rationale of judicial abstention that is developed by the *Sabbatino* majority in support of the act of state doctrine. And, second, because the repudiation of *Bernstein* might be used as the opening wedge in an overdue attack upon the authority and validity of the principles enunciated in the *Pink* decision.[20] In *Pink*, the Supreme Court made some critical pronouncements about the duty of domestic courts to decide litigation before them so as to promote the foreign policy of the executive. This duty took precedence over the parallel duty to apply domestic and international law to the controversy. This duty must be eliminated if domestic courts are to regain their proper role in international law cases, and this means that the thinking in *Pink*, if not *Pink* itself, must be rejected.

But if the *Bernstein* letter cannot suspend the operation of the act of state doctrine, then it might appear that courts would never be able to inquire into the legality of a contested act of a foreign government. If an absolute act of state doctrine is affirmed, then, regardless of whether the rationale stresses accommodating diverse systems of public order in international society or internal constitutional requirements, an occasion for judicial scrutiny never arises. Therefore, it is important to investigate whether *Sabbatino* offers any new exceptions to substitute for the *Bernstein* exception, should it ever be fully eliminated. Because *Sabbatino* does offer grounds for exception, it can justly be hailed as a

---

[19] E.g., brief for the United States as Amicus Curiae, pp. 37-38: "a 'Bernstein letter' invoking the exception and waiving the act of state doctrine seems to have been issued only once, in the *Bernstein* case itself, so in practice the exception is an exceedingly narrow one. The circum-stances leading to the State Department's letter in the *Bernstein* case were of course most unusual."

[20] United States v. Pink, 315 US 203 (1942); 36 *American Journal of International Law* 309 (1942).

progressive decision from the point of view of the application of international law in domestic courts.

Sabbatino definitely does not formulate an absolute act of state doctrine. Courts are urged to pursue a flexible approach determining in each context whether the policies served by the act of state doctrine would, on balance, be served by its application to the facts of the particular controversy.

ACT OF STATE DOCTRINE: ITS SCOPE

The *Sabbatino* decision enumerates no less than four occasions on which the act of state doctrine might not apply. First of all, the doctrine would not shield from judicial scrutiny a foreign governmental act alleged to be in violation of a rule contained in an international agreement or treaty binding upon the parties to the dispute. The act of state doctrine applies only to the review of foreign governmental acts that are said to be in violation of rules of customary international law. The distinction between customary and conventional international law properly reflects the greater definiteness and mutuality of treaty obligations as compared to customary norms.[21]

However, according to *Sabbatino*, there are, aside from the *Bernstein* precedent, three kinds of facts that might justify a court's willingness to review a contested act of state by reference to rules of customary international law: first, where a consensus exists in support of the standard supplied by the rule of customary international law; second, where the case before the court has an unimportant bearing upon the conduct of foreign relations; and, third, where the foreign government whose act is being challenged is no longer in existence. These three broad grounds for exception to the doctrine's scope are offered as illustrative of the kinds of considerations that might make it inappropriate to apply the act of state doctrine, and do not purport to be the only such grounds. *Sabbatino* is in the mainstream of policy-oriented jurisprudence by virtue of Justice Harlan's pointed insistence that the scope of the act of state doctrine must be determined from case to case by reference to "the balance of relevant considerations."[22]

The scope of *Sabbatino*'s version of the act of state doctrine is partly disclosed by the narrowness of the substantive holding:

> Therefore, rather than laying down or reaffirming an inflexible and all-encompassing rule in this case, we decide only that the Judicial Branch will not examine the validity of a taking of property within

---

[21] Rules of customary norms arise in an uncertain manner, there is no way to reform or repudiate their content, and there is a tendency not to regard their validity as dependent upon changes in the character of international society, however fundamental.

[22] P. 428.

its own territory by a foreign sovereign, extant and recognized by this country at the time of suit, in the absence of treaty or other unambiguous agreement regarding controlling legal principles, even if the complaint alleges that the taking violates customary international law.[23]

Crucial Section VI of the majority opinion in *Sabbatino* begins with this key sentence:

> If the act of state doctrine is a principle of decision binding on federal and state courts alike but compelled by neither international law nor the Constitution, its continuing vitality depends on its capacity to reflect the proper distribution of functions between the judicial and political branches of the Government on matters bearing upon foreign affairs.[24]

This statement summarizes the findings in Section V of the opinion that international law does not require domestic courts to apply the act of state doctrine, nor does the Constitution make its application mandatory. Nevertheless, the act of state doctrine does have " 'Constitutional' underpinnings," which apparently means that it is an expression of the idea of separation of powers in the context of foreign affairs.[25] The executive branch has been given exclusive responsibility for the conduct of foreign affairs. The judiciary must not allow its adjudications to interfere with the proper discharge of this responsibility. Hence, the act of state doctrine is a jural device enabling the courts to refrain from reaching decisions that might in some way interfere with executive policy in matters of foreign affairs. The *Bernstein* exception conforms to this concept because it allows courts to suspend the act of state doctrine only when it becomes executive policy to encourage an adjudication on the merits of the complaint about foreign governmental action.

The most intriguing aspect of *Sabbatino*'s treatment of the act of state doctrine is its stress upon the relevance of consensus among nations to the application of the doctrine: "It should be apparent that the greater the degree of codification or consensus concerning a particular area of international law, the more appropriate it is for the judiciary to render

---

[23] *Ibid.* Cf. also the sentence on pp. 436-37 articulating the holding in narrow terms: "However offensive to the public policy of this country and its constituent states an expropriation of this kind may be, we conclude that both the national interest and progress toward the goal of establishing the rule of law among nations are best served by maintaining intact the act of state doctrine *in this realm of its application.*" (Emphasis added.)

[24] Pp. 427-28.

[25] P. 423; for an excellent interpretation of this aspect of the *Sabbatino* decision see Louis Henkin, "The Foreign Affairs Power of the Federal Courts: Sabbatino," 64 *Columbia Law Review* 805-32 (May 1964).

decisions regarding it, since the courts can then focus on the application of an agreed principle to circumstances of fact."[26]

If consensus exists with respect to customary norms, then a court is not forbidden from considering an argument that the challenged acts of the foreign government violate international law. Without such consensus the Court reasons, decisions made in the name of international law will probably be perceived as an assertion of national policy rather than as an authoritative decision of law.[27] In fact, a satisfactory explanation of the validity of rules of customary international law would seem finally to rest upon a continuing consensus in support of them.[28] *Sabbatino* glimpses, although it stops short of an explicit statement to this effect, a connection between the reality of a legal obligation and its support by an active consensus of nations. Justice White, in his dissent, seems confused about the significance of consensus, or its absence, to the existence of binding international legal obligations.[29] His is the traditional view of legal obligation—the customary rule either exists or does not exist. The existence of the rule is crucial, consensus irrelevant. How does one tell whether the rule exists? According to Justice White one looks back at practice for evidence of a sense of obligation sustained over time. Justice White never informs us how a customary rule, once established, is repudiated. How does a social system that lacks a legislature change its rules to reflect shifts in the values of its actors? Recourse to consensus as a factor relevant to the existence of customary obligations provides a method by which to accommodate pressure for change in a social system as decentralized as is international society. Such a method is essential for the maintenance of minimum international stability in a revolutionary period in international relations.[30]

Sabbatino makes it very clear that a domestic court that confronts a set of facts for which the rules are supported by a consensus is not bound to apply the act of state doctrine, nor, it should be added, is it instructed not to apply the doctrine. *Sabbatino* prescribes only that the presence or absence of a consensus (with respect to the customary norm in issue) is a factor that a domestic court should take into account in the course of achieving the end product of judicial inquiry—what Justice Harlan so aptly calls a "balance of relevant considerations." Thus the most that can be said is that a future court might mention the existence of a consensus to justify its decision not to apply the act of state doctrine. If such a decision stems from such reasoning, it could constitute a re-

26 P. 428.
27 Pp. 434-35.
28 This point has been developed in greater detail elsewhere. See Chapter V.
29 Pp. 455-56.

30 See Stanley Hoffmann, "International Systems and International Law," in *The International System*, Klaus Knorr and Sidney Verba, eds., Princeton University Press, 1961, 205-37.

fusal to apply the doctrine on the basis of an independent judicial inquiry without the receipt of any prior executive mandate in the form of a *Bernstein* letter. The act of state doctrine does not necessarily apply, then, to governmental acts performed with respect to a subject matter about which there is no significant controversy among nations as to the status and character of governing standards of international law.

In the presence of diversity, the act of state doctrine performs a valuable function in international society. It allocates jurisdictional competence on the basis of a reciprocal pattern of deference by which national actors are given mutual assurance that their activity will receive universal respect if carried on within jurisdictional limits (simplified in the *Sabbatino* discussion to refer to the control of tangible property located within territory). Such deference accords with the facts of decentralization and ideological cleavage that exist in international society today.[31]

Sabbatino also intimates that a domestic court might properly be more ready to suspend the act of state doctrine if the dispute did not bear significantly on the conduct of foreign relations: "The less important the implications of an issue are for our foreign relations the weaker the justification for exclusivity in political branches."[32] Evidently this, too, is a judicially determined rule that can be invoked and applied without awaiting prior executive intervention. This self-assertion by the courts advances the cause of judicial autonomy, although it does so at the expense of internal deference, that is, deference by the judiciary to the wishes of the executive. It is desirable to end this subordination of the law-applying function of courts to the diplomatic functions of the executive.[33] Such subordination is inconsistent with the growth of habits of respect for international law, as internal deference reinforces the idea that nothing takes precedence over sovereign discretion in the field of foreign relations. Is it not a central objective of international law to promote the acceptance of law as a source of limitation upon sovereign discretion? And are not domestic courts suitable arenas within which to give evidence of this acceptance? The rule of law in world affairs—a favorite rhetorical phrase in the speeches of our diplomats—is an idle pretense unless implemented. Just as the Connally Reservation dilutes our plea for the adjudication of disputes between nations, so uncritical deference by domestic courts to the political branches undercuts our

[31] See very good discussion in Oliver J. Lissitzyn, "International Law in a Divided World," 542 *International Conciliation* (March 1963), 1.

[32] P. 428; such a conclusion takes account of most of the considerations mentioned by Justice White in his complaint that the majority is too rigid and defer-

ential in its delimitation of the separation of powers. Pp. 461-72.

[33] For a clear statement of the opposite position see Michael H. Cardozo, "Judicial Deference to State Department Suggestions: Recognition of Prerogatives or Abdication to Usurper?" 48 *Cornell Law Quarterly* 461-98 (Spring 1963).

more general commitment to work for the growth of law in world affairs.

Sabbatino also suggests that if the foreign government no longer exists, as was the case when *Bernstein* was decided,[34] a domestic court might more reasonably refuse to apply the act of state doctrine. This seems sensible. The argument for reciprocal deference is reduced, if not reversed, by the replacement or disappearance of a government in a foreign country, especially since nonexistence often is coupled with a repudiation of the government whose act is now being challenged before a domestic court. It is quite probable that either the acting government has disappeared altogether or it has been replaced by one with a radically different political orientation. In such a situation, it might turn out to be more of an affront to the present government to apply as law the acts of its predecessor than to refuse to do so.[35] *Sabbatino* properly deems this factor relevant to the availability of act of state and hints, at least, that such a consideration might have liberated the *Bernstein* court without the permission of the executive.

These grounds for refusing deference to a foreign governmental act are not made to appear exclusive or determinative in the *Sabbatino* opinion. They are enumerated as considerations that a domestic court should properly take into account when the application of the act of state doctrine is challenged by a litigant. It is important to realize this. A domestic court shall regard the presence of one or more of these three circumstances—consensus, unimportant bearing on foreign relations, nonexistence of the acting government—as entering into "the balance of relevant considerations." Other matters could presumably also enter the balance. Therefore, there are no rigid guidelines laid down as to when a court should refrain from applying the act of state doctrine. What is plain, however, is that the Supreme Court took pains to develop a nonabsolute version of the act of state doctrine and to suggest that a decision not to apply the doctrine could be achieved by judicial inquiry unaided by executive guidance. I regard this as very crucial for an understanding of *Sabbatino*: the *rationale* of act of state, as we shall see, rests heavily on judicial deference to executive prerogatives in the area of foreign affairs, but the specific *application* of the doctrine depends upon an independent process of judicial decision-making. Such a distinction makes it possible to reconcile functional deference with the achievement of judicial independence. Justice Harlan's opinion

---

[34] And so, presumably, either *Bernstein* court might have taken this factor into account as part of a decision to refuse application of the act of state doctrine.

[35] This would be especially so if the forum state and the new government were both strongly opposed to giving effect, if at all possible, to the acts of the predecessor government.

maintains a subtle balance between judicial self-restraint and judicial self-assertion.

In view of this conception of act of state, why does the balance of relevant considerations lead the Supreme Court to insist upon application of the doctrine to the *Sabbatino* facts? Several reasons are outlined in the majority opinion.

First, no consensus exists to support the relevant rules of international law. Second, the dispute is deeply embedded in foreign relations. And, third, the government whose act is challenged remained fully in existence at the time of the suit. The opinion also considers such other possible grounds for the nonapplication of the act of state doctrine as the hostile state of Cuban-American relations and the appearance of the Cuban Government in the litigation as a plaintiff taking advantage of its own act of state. Justice Harlan's opinion concludes that neither of these latter two circumstances is an appropriate basis upon which to upset the balance of relevant considerations. Hence, the *Sabbatino* facts are within the proper scope of the act of state doctrine. Note that the first three reasons for making an exception to the act of state doctrine are regarded as good reasons, but their relevance is rejected because they do not apply to the *Sabbatino* facts. In contrast, the last two reasons are viewed as bad reasons for making an exception to the doctrine, although the *Sabbatino* facts exhibit their relevance.

Of course, the most controversial aspect of *Sabbatino* involves the determination that no consensus exists to support those rules of international law that condemn a confiscatory and discriminatory taking. The objections to this conclusion exist on three levels, each of which is mentioned in Justice White's dissent. On the first level, the facts of dissensus are disputed; evidence can be collected to show widespread support for some measure of compensation as a mandatory part of expropriation valid under international law. On the second level, the identification of relevant rules is contested. The *Sabbatino* majority is rather vague about just what are the customary rules that lack a supporting consensus. In contrast, Justice White is very specific about contending that a discriminatory and retaliatory taking of foreign-owned property is prohibited by rules that are supported by a consensus of nations reflected both in their practice and doctrinal pronouncements. It makes a great deal of difference whether one is denying a consensus for the rule that "prompt, adequate, and effective compensation" must accompany a valid expropriation rather than for the rules that prohibit discrimination against the nationals of one country or forbid a confiscatory expropriation in which no compensation at all is offered. The *Sabbatino* majority does not seem sensitive to the importance of identifying rather specifically the customary norms that are at issue. Judge Waterman, in the Circuit Court of Appeals, was very careful to state his holding in terms far narrower than those used by Judge Dimock to void Castro's expropriation in the District Court.[36] It might be argued that *Sabbatino* should have affirmed the decision of the Circuit Court, substituting its rationale for exceptions to act of state deference for Judge Waterman's strained and misguided conclusion that the executive had written, in effect, a *Bernstein* letter.

Finally, on the third level, the argument is made that even if there is no consensus to support the rules, nevertheless such a taking should be struck down because it violates customary international law as established by authoritative and unrepudiated precedents. The pros and cons of this dispute are difficult to assess. The *Sabbatino* majority is persuasive in its view that the protection of foreign investment is a subject about which there is such salient conflict and that it is an area in which domestic courts are not presently capable of positing authoritative standards. The explicit holding in the Supreme Court makes reference to the capacity of domestic courts and not to the status of the customary norms. All that *Sabbatino* says is that a domestic court is not an appropriate forum wherein to apply a rule of customary international law unless that rule is supported by a consensus at least wide enough to embrace the parties to the dispute. Such judicial self-restraint may not be appropriate if the forum is an international tribunal entrusted with competence by both sides, but the situation is different for a domestic court. The appearance of impartiality is as important to the formulation of authoritative law as is the actuality of impartiality. The consequences is that a domestic court, however manfully it struggles to achieve impartiality, will not be able to render an authoritative judgment when the adjudication requires it to decide whether the forum state or the foreign state is correct about its contentions as to the content of customary international law. The act of state doctrine, in the absence of a firm agreement on the rules of decision, acknowledges this incapacity of domestic courts.

If a domestic court were to pass upon the overall validity of the Cuban expropriation, it could reach one of two unsatisfactory results. Either it could hold the expropriation illegal and render a decision that would be perceived as nothing more than an expression of national interest, or it could find the expropriation legal and gravely compromise the diplomatic posture of the United States. *Sabbatino*'s dual concern for judicial independence and for executive-judicial harmony made this an unacceptable dilemma.

Justice White's dissent rejects this entire line of analysis. He argues that a consensus exists to support relevant norms of customary interna-

[36] Banco Nacional de Cuba v. Sabbatino, 307 F. 2d 845, 864 (1962); 56 *American*   *Journal of International Law* 1085 (1962).

tional law, but that even if it does not, a domestic court is always capable of applying and obliged to apply international law. The unacceptability of a decision by one's ideological adversaries is not, the dissent contends, a relevant reason for restraint.[37] If the rule exists, then international law is promoted by applying it to settle a legal controversy. On the issue of judicial interference with executive policy, Justice White has this to say:

> I would not disregard a declaration by the Secretary of State or the President that an adjudication in the courts of the validity of a foreign expropriation would impede relations between the United States and the foreign government or the settlement of the controversy through diplomatic channels. But I reject the presumption that these undesirable consequences would follow from adjudication in every case, regardless of circumstances. Certainly the presumption is inappropriate here.[38]

This excerpt discloses much about Justice White's view of *Sabbatino*. In the first sentence, one wonders whether Justice White wants to distinguish a declaration by the Solicitor General, the Deputy Attorney General, and an Assistant Legal Adviser from that of the President or Secretary of State. Why? Surely these high officials speak for the executive branch with sufficient authority. In *Sabbatino* they did speak, although the dissent could maintain that since their declaration was based on a general doctrine of separation of powers, and as it proceeded "regardless of circumstance," its directive should not have received judicial acquiescence.

The second sentence in the excerpt from Justice White's dissent is either an echo of the majority opinion or a misunderstanding of it. Justice Harlan's opinion expresses as much dissatisfaction with an abstract and mechanical notion of act of state as does Justice White. In fact, the majority, as we have discussed, details an approach based on the "balance of relevant considerations." It emphasizes the absence of a consensus in support of customary norms of international law applicable to foreign investment in reaching its conclusion that internal deference (judiciary to executive)[39] is appropriate here, especially so in view of the executive intervention to urge upon the Supreme Court the application of the act of state doctrine. In contrast, Justice White regards internal deference as inappropriate here. First of all, the exec-

---

[37] This argument is most persuasive if the holding is fashioned in the narrow form adopted by Judge Waterman in the Circuit Court of Appeals. Cf. Justice White's emphasis on the fact that the Cuban decree "is alleged not only to be confiscatory but also retaliatory and discriminatory" (p. 459).

[38] P. 462.

[39] External deference: forum state to foreign state.

utive has already contended in formal diplomatic notes that Castro's expropriations violate international law. And furthermore, a decision on the merits by a domestic court, even in the unlikely event that it comes to the conclusion that the expropriation carried out by Cuban Law No. 851 is legal, is not going to cause the executive "greater embarrassment" than does the *Sabbatino* rationale that there exist no "widely accepted principles to which to subject the act."[40] Except on the issue of embarrassment to the executive, however, the alternative of deference or substantive judgment is not equivalent. For Justice White considers a judgment on the merits, while not endangering legitimate executive interests, to possess the great advantage of giving a litigant his day in court. Justice White puts the choice this way: "As to potential embarrassment, the difference is semantic, but as to determining the issue on its merits and as to upholding a regime of law, the difference is vast."[41]

The dissent analyzes the situation without revealing any awareness of the distinctive character of international law as a legal order. Most specifically, Mr. Justice White does not appear sensitive to the constraints placed upon domestic courts by their dependence upon the horizontal mechanisms of international law. Without adequate central legal institutions of interpretation and enforcement, the area of consensus and common interests sharply restricts the domain of effective international law. The majority opinion in *Sabbatino* is partly significant because it seems to appreciate this limiting condition, although it undermines this appreciation to some extent by relying so heavily upon an argument favoring judicial deference to executive action, instead of trying to rest its judgment principally upon United States deference to Cuban action.

Sabbatino's RATIONALE

Prior discussion has indicated that the *Sabbatino* decision, despite its many virtues, rests upon two unfortunate characteristics. First, it overgeneralizes the customary norms at stake to be apparently coterminous with the entire law of foreign investment and, thereby, forfeits the opportunity to suspend the operation of the act of state doctrine by narrowing the norms at issue to those prohibiting discriminatory and confiscatory taking. Second, it rests the argument for the act of state doctrine principally upon separation of powers (internal deference) rather than upon conflict of laws (external deference). Although these criticisms have been made in passing already, it is important now to examine the case for and against separation of powers as the principal basis of decision.

40 P. 465.   41 Pp. 465-66.

Justice White rejects the relevance of the separation of powers analysis to the *Sabbatino* situation. Instead, he emphasizes that the act of state doctrine is best understood and used as a doctrine in the conflict of laws that has developed as an expression of the territorial sovereignty of national actors.[42] His opinion argues that the act of state doctrine is an American equivalent to the rule "adopted in virtually all countries, that the *lex loci* is the law governing title to property."[43] The dissent associates the deference implicit in the act of state doctrine with the need for comity and reciprocity in the international legal system: "Where a clear violation of international law is not demonstrated, I would agree that principles of comity underlying the act of state doctrine warrant recognition and enforcement of the foreign act."[44] Such a statement is tantamount to saying that where authoritative standards are not available, then the logic of a horizontal legal system requires validating the separate legal claims of each unit within its spatial sphere of competence. This does seem to be the most persuasive rationale for the act of state doctrine.

Unfortunately, the majority opinion rests its case for the act of state doctrine almost entirely upon its internal aspect, that is, as an appropriate technique for the allocation of competence between the executive and the judiciary when the subject matter of litigation touches upon foreign affairs. But, as the dissent demonstrates, this is a rather shaky justification for deference when adopted in the form of a general principle rather than as a possible outcome of a case-by-case analysis. Justice White points out that quite often a judicial appraisal of foreign governmental acts would not be inconsistent with the proper discharge of executive function in the field of foreign affairs.[45] It is not very convincing to contend, Justice White suggests, that an appraisal of legality is, *in general*, likely to be embarrassing for the executive. If international law is to be an important source of law, then its application should not be subordinated by domestic courts to hypothetical political considerations. For this reason, the emphasis upon the internal aspect of deference seems to be unnecessarily deprecatory of the role of domestic courts in the field of international law.

Justice White is arguing somewhat against an imaginary adversary. The majority concedes most of what he is purporting to argue against. As we have said, Justice Harlan does not regard deference as automatic or as dependent upon executive mandate. Justice White's complaint would be more apposite if it were restricted to the case at hand: why

42 Pp. 444-50.
43 P. 445.
44 P. 458.

45 Of course, the majority opinion leaves room for such an exception where a court deems it apt.

defer in *Sabbatino*? The majority, despite its language about a balance of relevant considerations, does not investigate very carefully the reasons why a court should defer to the executive in the *Sabbatino* setting. A clearer, stronger case for deference could be made by reference to the dependence of international society upon patterns of mutual respect for territorial law. Such an argument is persuasive with regard to the *Sabbatino* facts unless the dispositive issue is narrowed beyond expropriation in general to the discriminatory and confiscatory quality of this particular expropriation.

III. Federal Authority

Less celebrated, but not less significant, is the attempt of *Sabbatino* to clarify the basis and extent of federal authority in the field of international law. The decision strongly affirms the unified control of the central government, as expressed through the Supreme Court, over the interpretation and application of international law by domestic courts, whether they be state or federal. Such an affirmation is very important to make in a federal system such as our own. Without it, there is an element of uncertainty and nonuniformity introduced into the process of giving domestic effect to international obligations that hampers the capacity of a state to participate effectively in international society.

Professor Henkin has written so definitively on this aspect of *Sabbatino* that it is only necessary here to state the conclusions reached by the decision in their bare outline.[46] *Sabbatino* confirms federal authority to establish uniform standards binding on lower courts, whether state or federal, with respect to the application of international law. This conclusion eliminates the suspicion that *Erie v. Tompkins* might to some extent require federal courts to follow state law in international law cases.[47] *Sabbatino* also makes it plain that the application of international law by state courts is a federal matter to which the supremacy principle applies. This is obviously a sensible result. The United States can best participate in the international legal system as a single political unit, not as an assemblage of fifty subunits, each having its own sphere of competence. However, every rosebush has its thorns. The centralization of federal control facilitates the use of domestic courts as vehicles for the pursuit of national policy objectives. In that sense, courts are made more vulnerable to pressures for conformity to the national will than if each were subservient to the more local policies operative at the state level.

[46] Henkin, note 20, *supra*.
[47] Pp. 425-27; Erie R. Co. v. Tomkins, 304 US 64 (1938); see Philip C. Jessup, "The Doctrine of Erie Railroad v. Tomp- kins Applied to International Law," 33 *American Journal of International Law* 740-43 (Oct. 1939).

IV. Access to Domestic Courts

Sabbatino holds that the severance of diplomatic relations does not affect the access of a foreign sovereign to a domestic court in the role of a plaintiff.[48] Thus the Supreme Court refuses to adopt the *Cibrario* precedent as guidance for the treatment of a government with which the United States has broken diplomatic relations. It will be remembered that *Cibrario* dealt with a claim of access to a New York state court put forward by the unrecognized Soviet government;[49] in a companion case, *Wulfoshn v. Russian Socialist Federated Soviet Republic*, the same court held that the Soviet government, although unrecognized, could nevertheless bar prosecution against itself by an appeal to the doctrine of sovereign immunity.[50]

This conclusion seems sensible. A foreign government should be able to have recourse to a domestic court so as to obtain an adjudication of its legal rights. Maximum recourse is consistent with the wider international effort to encourage reliance upon third-party procedures to obtain the peaceful settlement of international disputes. It is also expressive of a policy of making the work of domestic courts in the international law field as independent as possible of the vagaries of foreign relations. An American court should adjudicate a legal controversy between litigants without reference to the state of Cuban-American relations or to the locus of the forum within the territory of the United States. Such an adjudication emphasizes the supranational quality of the rules of international law and indicates that national courts are institutions within the international legal system rather than servants of the national political will.[51]

Sabbatino, perhaps to avoid questioning old precedents, rests its conclusions too heavily upon the distinction between severance of diplomatic relations and nonrecognition of a foreign government. Mr. Justice Harlan writes for the majority that "the refusal to recognize has a unique legal aspect. It signifies this country's unwillingness to acknowledge that the government in question speaks as the sovereign authority for the territory it purports to control." Furthermore: "Political recognition is exclusively a function of the Executive."[52] Such language makes the out-

48 Pp. 408-12, 437-38.
49 Russian Socialist Federated Soviet Republic v. Cibrario, 235 N.Y. 255 (1923).
50 Wulfsohn v. Russian Socialist Federated Soviet Republic, 234 N.Y. 372 (1923).
51 This orientation also tends to reduce the relevance of the national locus of the forum to the outcome in a domestic court. Uniformity of judicial outcome is, of course, an ideal nowhere attained at present. Its closer approximation is an important aspect of the overall commitment to the development of a universal system

of legal order. And its explicit denial in the name of national values is a regressive acceptance of sovereign precedence in world affairs.
52 P. 410; and see p. 411, n12 which calls attention to the literature that has criticized the preclusion of even unrecognized governments from access to our domestic courts; as with *Bernstein*, here, too, there is evident, at least, a judicial willingness to reconsider. The indication of this willingness is a signal worth noting.

come depend upon a *doctrinal* rather than a *functional* allocation of competence between executive and judiciary. The executive is just as much in charge of severance as of nonrecognition, and the two modes of response to disfavored foreign governments may be pursued for identical reasons. There is no reason to treat Mao's China differently from Castro's Cuba in United States domestic courts merely because one government is unrecognized whereas diplomatic relations with the other have been severed.

It would seem preferable to stress the executive competence to resolve judicial doubts about the facts of foreign governmental control. Thus, if a civil war is going on in a foreign country, the court might obtain guidance from the executive as to which government is in control of what. If the factual existence of a foreign government is not in doubt, then there is no more justification to deny access to an unrecognized government than to a government with which we have broken diplomatic relations. The *Cibrario* rule implies that it is a favor to gain access, suggesting that the availability of an international law solution should depend on a prior record of friendship and good behavior between the forum state and the plaintiff state. It is important to persuade all states, whether friend or foe, to develop good law habits in foreign relations. One way to dramatize this point is to make clear that access to our tribunals is quite compatible with otherwise hostile political relations.

Sabbatino decided that a judicial determination of reciprocity was an unwise condition precedent to access. It refused to extend the approach developed in *Hilton v. Guyot* to deal with the conclusiveness of foreign judgments to a situation in which the foreign government sought access as a plaintiff.[53] *Sabbatino* correctly pointed out that "Re-examination of judgments, in principle, reduces rather than enhances the possibility of injustice being done in a particular case; refusal to allow suit makes it impossible for a court to see that a particular dispute is fairly resolved."[54] However, this assessment does not argue the complex case of how to balance the particular against the general claims of access to domestic courts. The opinion is quite correct to suggest how difficult it would be for a court to resolve the issue of reciprocity. The merits and difficulty of executive scrutiny are not considered. Perhaps they should be, as this might be an appropriate occasion for the reliance of the judiciary upon an executive conclusion in an international law case.

Sabbatino mentions that "The freezing of Cuban assets exemplifies the capacity of the political branches to assure, through a variety of techniques . . . that the national interest is protected against a country which is thought to be improperly denying the rights of United States

[53] Hilton v. Guyot, 159 US 113 (1895).   [54] P. 412.

citizens."[55] Thus, even if the plaintiff government is permitted access and wins the controversy, the executive is still in a position to deny the fruits of the litigation to the victorious party. This executive capacity indicates the difference between adjudication and diplomacy, and it is a risk that even the most inexperienced foreign government must realize when it goes to the trouble and expense of initiating litigation. Even if no money is collected, however, the favorable outcome is a valuable asset. It provides the foreign government with an impartial determination that its contention, which often extends beyond the adjudicated controversy, is correct. Such support may have immediate psychological value and it is almost certain to be taken into account if a general political settlement is reached in the future.

The prerogative of the executive to freeze foreign assets illustrates the continuing dependence of international society upon the primitive sanction-remedy of self-help. The remedy is primitive because its application is self-determined by a party to the disputes, making its appropriateness hinge upon the overall validity of the claim. It also is primitive because its coercive nature suggests the extent to which international society tolerates the use of coercion other than outright military violence in the course of settling an international dispute. Such an imperfect system of legal order is an almost inevitable consequence of the absence of compulsory procedures of peaceful settlement in international society. This absence, in turn, expresses the fact that national actors retain predominant control over the outcome of international disputes, and have yielded only marginal competencies to international institutions. As long as this is the case, there are bound to be sharp limits imposed upon the opportunities for developing universal procedures and standards to deal with disputes among nations. In recognition of these limits, ideas of reciprocity and mutuality emphasize the dependence of international society upon horizontal forms of international legal order.

V. The End Result

Sabbatino has certainly become a landmark decision in the field of international law. It has been both hailed and condemned. Of course, time must intervene before its overall impact upon the development of international law can be accurately discerned and appraised. It is not too early, however, to praise the craftsmanship of *Sabbatino* for achieving the qualities of distinction that Dylan Thomas commended for a poet: "The best craftsmanship always leaves holes and gaps in the works of the poem so that something that is not in the poem can creep, crawl, flash or thunder in."[56]

---

[55] P. 412.
[56] George J. Firmage, ed., "A Garland for Dylan Thomas," New York, Clarke and Way, 1963, p. 152.

VI. The Critics Triumph: A Postscript

The Supreme Court in its decision of 1964 remanded the case to the District Court for the Southern District of New York for action consistent with its determination. While the case was pending the Congress enacted the Second Hickenlooper Amendment.[57] This statute, embodied in foreign and domestic legislation, obliged domestic courts to disregard the act of state doctrine for any expropriation of property by a foreign state that took place subsequent to January 1, 1959. Courts were instructed to adjudicate in accordance with the requirements of international law as these requirements were set forth in the First Hickenlooper Amendment.[58] These requirements were established to impose on the President an obligation to suspend foreign aid to a violating recipient country, and obliged the expropriating country, in the language of the statute, to comply with international law "including speedy compensation for such property in convertible foreign exchange, equivalent to the full value thereof."

In the Second Hickenlooper Amendment the President is given authority to secure application of the state doctrine by an explicit suggestion to the domestic court. This suggestion is supposed to rest upon a prior determination "that application of the act of state doctrine is required in that particular case by the foreign policy interests of the United States."

[57] The Second Hickenlooper Amendment was originally a rider to the Foreign Assistance Act of 1964, effective only for cases commenced before January 1, 1966. 78 Stat. 1009, 1013 (1964). It was modified slightly and made permanent legislation in the Foreign Assistance Act of 1965, 79 Stat. 653, 22 U.S.C. §2370(a)(2) (Supp. I, 1965). In its present form, the section provides:

(2) Notwithstanding any other provision of law, no court in the United States shall decline on the ground of the federal act of state doctrine to make a determination on the merits giving effect to the principles of international law in a case in which a claim of title or other right to property is asserted by any party including a foreign state (or a party claiming through such state) based upon (or traced through) a confiscation or other taking after January 1, 1959, by an act of that state in violation of the principles of international law, including the principles of compensation and the other standards set out in this subsection: *Provided*, That this subparagraph shall not be applicable (1) in any case in which an act of a foreign state is not contrary to international law or with respect to a claim of title or other right to property acquired pursuant to an irrevocable letter of credit of not more than 180 days duration issued in good faith prior to the time of the confiscation or other taking, or (2) in any case with respect to which the President determines that application of the act of state doctrine is required in that particular case by the foreign policy interests of the United States and a suggestion to this effect is filed on his behalf in that case with the court.

79 Stat. 653, 659 (1965).

[58] The First Hickenlooper Amendment required that the President suspend foreign aid to any country that expropriated properties (50 percent or more of which was American owned), unless that country complies with international law "including speedy compensation for such property in convertible foreign exchange, equivalent to the full value thereof, as required by international law." Foreign Assistance Act of 1962, as amended, 78 Stat. 1013, 22 U.S.C. §2370(e)(1) 1964).

As a consequence of this intervening legislation the District Court found for the American property owners.[59] The Second Hickenlooper Amendment was given precedence over the earlier mandate contained in the Supreme Court decision, and the argument directed at the retroactivity of the legislation was rejected. The Court of Appeals upheld the District Court and the Supreme Court denied petition for *certiorari,* bringing the extended judicial proceedings to a close on March 4, 1968.[60]

Such an outcome seems discouraging for a number of reasons.[61] First, the Congress repudiated a Supreme Court decision by acting in response to pressures generated by special interest groups. Secondly, the Second Hickenlooper Amendment exhibits an insensitivity to the problems facing a domestic court that seeks to apply international law to a subject-matter for which the rules are in doubt. Thirdly, this insensitivity is aggravated by the Hickenlooper Amendment's insistence that domestic courts apply a rule of international law that exceeds the customary rule of international law and is partial to the interests of the foreign investor. Fourthly, the creation of a right of executive intervention in judicial proceedings that is accorded the President seriously compromises the judicial independence of domestic courts by making explicit the subordination of normal adjudicative procedures to foreign policy considerations. The effect of such legislation is undoubtedly to undermine any emerging confidence in domestic court as agents of an emerging international legal order. The Second Hickenlooper Amendment rejects the effort by the Supreme Court in the *Sabbatino* decision to emphasize the judicial independence of domestic courts in international law cases and to take account of the need to rest adjudication of substantive issues upon widely endorsed legal standards if decisions were to enjoy respect. The post-statute outcome is consistent with the most cynical perceptions of the coincidence between national interest and the outcome of international law cases in domestic cases. The whole point of the act of state doctrine in the *Sabbatino* sort of setting is to encourage domestic courts to exercise judicial self-restraint in those circumstances when the prospects of authoritative judgment are low.[62] It is a matter of conserving the

---

[59] After remand, as a consequence of the substitution of the sugar brokers, Farr, Whitlock & Co., for the temporary receiver appointed to hold the proceeds of the sugar pending disposition, Peter Sabbatino, the case was renamed. Therefore, the District Court decision is known by the following citation: Banco Nacional de Cuba v. Farr, 243 F. Supp. 957 (SDNY 1965). A supplemental opinion dealt with the failure of the executive branch to exercise its option under the statute to file a suggestion that the court apply the act of state doctrine. See 272 F. Supp. 836 (SDNY)

1965.

[60] 383 F. 2d. 166 (2d. Cir. 1967); cert. denied, *United States Law Week* 3341 36 No. 968 (March 4, 1968).

[61] The outcome of the *Sabbatino-Farr* litigation is brilliantly assessed in Louis Henkin, see *op.cit. supra,* note 2.

[62] This point has been persuasively made by Wolfgang Friedmann in a symposium entitled "Act of State: *Sabbatino* in the Courts and Congress," 3 *Columbia Journal of Transnational Law* 103-07, at 104 (1965).

real potentialities of domestic courts for those occasions when their activism might be a constructive contribution to a genuine system of world legal order.[63]

Conduct by the United States, just because it is the principal state with a continuing concern for world order issues, has a particular importance as a precedent and as a learning experience. Other governments and specialists emphasize, and others emulate, American patterns of practice. Therefore, it seems particularly regrettable in the *Sabbatino* controversy where the choice was clearly posed between a nationalistic and an internationalist direction that the United States should have come down so firmly on the regressive side. Even today the approach embodied in the Second Hickenlooper Amendment need not be accepted as desirable or permanent. It is essential that the defects and short-sightedness of its approach be exposed, that efforts at repeal be organized, and that the original orientation of the Supreme Court in *Sabbatino* be encouraged to reemerge. The world order constituencies and pressures groups are diffused in their concerns and command small resources when compared to various vested and special interest groups. Nevertheless, perhaps it is not sentimental to believe that there is coming into being a wider sense of the need to redefine the national interest so that it reinforces, rather than erodes, the growth of a genuine world community of distinct states committed to diverse belief systems and operating at different stages of social and economic development.

[63] My own views on this world order dimension are presented in greater detail   in the next chapter.

XIV. Domestic Courts, International Law, and Foreign Acts of States: Executive Prerogatives and Judicial Imperatives

THERE ARE two categories of cases involving the application of international law in domestic courts that need to be distinguished:

1. There are those cases, exemplified by the *Sabbatino* controversy, in which a litigant invokes international law to challenge the validity of the official acts of a foreign government;[1]

2. There are those cases, exemplified by the *Spock* and *Mora* litigation, in which a litigant invokes international law to challenge the validity of official acts of a *domestic* government.[2]

In category 1 the main issues concern the role of domestic courts in an international legal order of sovereign states.[3] In category 2 the main issues concern the availability to individual litigants of judicial remedies in situations in which executive action is alleged to transgress limits on governmental action set by rules of international law. Categories 1 and 2 share a concern about the proper distribution of legal competence between the executive and judicial branches, although the resolution of this concern brings into play essentially distinct considerations. This chapter devotes itself solely to category 1 problems.

I. Some Issues Stated

The controversial nature of the role of domestic courts in various categories of international law cases centers primarily upon a disagreement about the extent to which courts should be independent of executive supervision in cases impinging upon the conduct of foreign relations. A somewhat less important area of disagreement concerns the stability of substantive rules of international law in the broad area of state responsibility for injury to alien interests. This chapter argues on behalf of maximum judicial independence. It also takes the position, although

---

[1] Cf. Chapter XIII; see also Frank G. Dawson and Burns H. Weston, "Banco Nacional de Cuba v. Sabbatino: New Wine in Old Bottles," 31 *University of Chicago Law Review* 63-102 (Autumn 1963); Martin Domke and Hans W. Baade, "Nationalization of Foreign Owned Property and the Act of State Doctrine—Two Speeches," *Duke Law Journal* 296 (Spring 1963); Richard B. Lillich, "A Pyrrhic Victory at Foley Square; The Second Circuit and Sabbatino," 8 *Villanova Law Review* 155-76 (Winter 1963); Stanley D. Metzger, "The Act of State Doctrine and Foreign Relations," 23 *University of Pittsburgh*

Law Review 881 (June 1962); John R. Stevenson, "The Sabbatino Case—Three Steps Forward and Two Steps Back," 57 *American Journal of International Law* 97-99 (Jan. 1963).

[2] There is an unfulfilled need for comparable scholarly attention being devoted to category 2 problems.

[3] A more complete attempt to develop a framework for thought about these problems is to be found in Falk, *The Role of Domestic Courts in the International Legal Order,* Syracuse: Syracuse University Press, 1964.

it does not document its evidentiary value, that many of the traditional rules governing state responsibility are now obsolete.[4]

Analysis of these issues is confined to the perspective of the United States. This narrowing of perspective deprives the analysis of generality for several distinct reasons. The character of American political institutions and traditions undoubtedly influences the interpretation. The federal nature of the United States has led to the idea of dual sovereignty for domestic governance; this creates special difficulties for the United States (and for other federal states with nonauthoritarian political structures) insofar as the maintenance of unified policies is considered desirable and necessary for a state that participates in international affairs as a sovereign actor. In addition, the doctrine of separation of powers causes Americans to have a set of expectations about the character of judicial independence that, if disappointed, undermines their respect for court proceedings and for the sanctity of law in general. Executive interference in the activities of domestic courts because a legal dispute involves the application of rules of international law is an evident discrimination against this category of law—a discrimination that might be expected to weaken public confidence in the viability of international law as a legal order. It is true, of course, that the executive branch is responsible for the conduct of foreign relations, and that foreign relations may be affected by domestic litigation. But should the dictates of foreign relations dominate a private dispute between litigants seeking a vindication of their legal rights by an appeal to rules of private and public international law?

A refusal to allow the pursuit of a civil remedy by interposing diplomatic considerations infringes the basic dignity of individual rights by assuring that domestic judicial authority is exercised in such a way as to subordinate private rights to some hypothetical public interest. Especially in a democratic society, it is important to preserve the private sector and to resist encroachments of government. Access to courts is symbolic of the right of a free individual. The paternalistic claim that the government can protect its citizens better if they are denied a judicial remedy in an international law case is not only unnecessary, but undermines the effort to transform the law of nations into a law of mankind.[5]

Eventually, it is essential to disentangle what is American from what is universal about the role of domestic courts in the international legal system. Such disentanglement must await, however, detailed comparative studies of constitutional tradition, political reality, and public expecta-

[4] For an excellent analysis of the question of substantive obsolescence in the *Sabbatino* context, see Dawson and Weston, note 1, *supra*.

[5] Such a transformation has been suggested, discerned, and commended with admirable clarity in C. Wilfred Jenks, *The Common Law of Mankind*, London, Stevens, 1958, pp. 1-22.

tion in the major domestic societies of the world.[6] In the interim an assessment of the role of domestic courts within the international legal order will have to remain incomplete and tentative. Nevertheless, an argument in favor of judicial autonomy can be developed from an American perspective on two principal bases: first, to uphold domestic values and traditions and second, to advance the cause of world legal order. This line of argument is not intended as an endorsement of a provincial outlook. On the contrary, domestic courts should be encouraged by international lawyers to construe the character of international law from as nonnational a perspective as possible.

There are two forms of autonomy: the autonomy of the judicial institutions within the framework of the domestic political system, and the autonomy of the rules of international law within the law-applying context. The first form of autonomy without the second may be less satisfactory than the elimination of both. A failure to achieve the second form, the impartial application of existing rules of international law, causes the judiciary to be politicized and transforms adjudicative proceedings into *ex parte* argument. This failure is probably more damaging to the development of international law than the exercise of discretionary control by the executive over the courts in a frankly political fashion.[7] If a domestic court construes controversial rules of international law to accord with national values, courts become politicized by their own independent action. The adoption of a provincial orientation causes the content of international law to be shaped by national interests, leads foreign parties with antagonistic values to expect and receive unfair treatment in a domestic court, and makes a judicial outcome depend more upon the values and outlook of the forum than upon the uniform impact of rules of international law on the controversy. Such a pattern neither produces domestic justice nor promotes international law. It seems clear, then, that both institutional and normative autonomy are

---

[6] A multinational inquiry of this sort would allow us to appraise the prospects for integrating domestic courts into a global set of institutions administering a common legal system according to common principles. National societies that have completely centralized political power and have subordinated all law to the demands of politics would not be very likely to permit their domestic courts to develop an autonomous tradition in cases involving international law.

[7] Throughout this chapter a contrast is made between law and politics that can be easily misunderstood. The plea for judicial independence and the arguments against political decision-making are intended to emphasize the difference between executive and judicial behavior. However, it is certainly not suggested at this late day that judges can or should decide difficult cases without recourse to policy considerations, or that judges are immune to political pressures generated by national passions. Certainly not! It is a matter of degree. Courts are normally foreclosed, especially if they are so instructed, and refrain from giving expression to temporary policies, whereas the executive, especially in foreign policy as developed in the American tradition, is frankly pragmatic and *ad hoc*, making the best of the combination of immediate interests.

inextricably bound up with one another in an assessment of the activities of domestic courts.

The issues governing autonomy combine problems of allocating legal competence with problems of construing substantive rules. The initial question is not what is the governing rule, but rather who shall supply it; the executive has a primary interest in reaching settlements of a category of disputes involving a conflict of interests among states, whereas the judiciary has a primary commitment to the solution of a specific dispute. To reach an executive settlement, the application of legal rules is only one of several elements that enter into intergovernmental negotiations. Few international law specialists would deny either that the executive branch should use diplomatic techniques to resolve international disputes or that diplomacy that must search for a settlement according to law is often likely to be futile and dogmatic in international relations. Yet recognition of a proper sphere of diplomatic action need not imply that the judicial outcome of specific controversies should be suppressed to avoid interference with the parallel pursuit of diplomatic remedies. The executive branch overgeneralized the issues in its brief in the *Sabbatino* case and argued that a diplomatic settlement is *more effective* than a judicial settlement—as if one prohibited the other.[8]

In what way is executive disposition more effective? There are two sets of interests, each of which is valid within its proper sphere: (1) the public interest in reaching a settlement on a state-to-state basis, the effect of which settlement might also be of indirect benefit to a class of private claimants, and (2) a private interest in having courts available to determine alleged infringements of individual rights. An assumption that the public interest in a general settlement outweighs the private interest is unwarranted unless one is prepared to dismiss as irrelevant, or at least as trivial, the legal protection that is given to individuals by the rules of international law. The material satisfaction of a maximum number of claimants may not be the broadest interest to be served. The judicial opportunity to reinforce the expectations of private parties that disputes will be settled according to international legal standards serves a general interest that may outweigh the special interests of a class of claimants disadvantaged by the default by a foreign government in a particular instance. Moreover, a judicial settlement exhibits the role of law,

---

8 "The primary and most satisfactory way to deal with foreign acts of state which violate international law is the exercise of diplomacy. In the absence of an international tribunal with power to settle controversies arising from sovereign acts, it seems evident that the effective and important means for dealing with acts of sovereign states which violate international law is not through sporadic American judicial decisions but through the exercise of diplomatic power by the Executive."

Brief for United States as amicus curiae, p. 28, "Banco Nacional de Cuba v. Sabbatino," 376 US 398 (1964), reprinted in 2 *International Legal Materials* 1009, 1018 (1963).

as distinct from politics, in the struggle to create a stable system of international remedies, the process of which is itself a valuable learning experience.

In a domestic law context, it would not occur to anyone to foreclose a normal judicial remedy available to individuals so as to improve the prospects for a general settlement. The effort of the federal government to improve the status of blacks in the Southern states might benefit from federal-state diplomacy, but hardly anyone would want to contend that encouragement of diplomatic negotiations might come to justify foreclosing the pursuit of a remedy by an individual black. The President's responsibility for supervising federal-state relations does not generate an incidental power to interfere with the ordinary functioning of federal courts. Thus, why does the President's responsibility for foreign affairs generate an incidental power to prevent normal adjudication? No discernible functional need is served by the assumption of such an incidental power.

II. The Scope of Executive Discretion in Foreign Affairs: The Precedents

Properly construed, the earlier Supreme Court decisions affirming executive prerogatives in the area of foreign relations are not inconsistent with the advocacy of judicial independence.[9] *United States v. Curtiss-Wright Export Corp.*[10] concerns the extent of discretion that Congress may vest in the President to control shipments of private arms from the United States to parties engaged in a foreign war. As the Supreme Court correctly affirmed, "in this vast external realm, with its important, delicate, and manifold problems, the President alone has the power to speak or listen as the representative of the nation."[11] This general observation was related to the functional needs of the executive for discretion in this kind of factual situation:

It is quite apparent that if, in the maintenance of our international relations, embarrassment—perhaps serious embarrassment—is to be avoided and success for our aims achieved, congressional legislation which is to be made effective through negotiation and inquiry within the international field must often accord the President a degree of

---

[9] The responsibility of the executive for the conduct of foreign affairs has been frequently affirmed by the courts as a guiding principle. See, e.g., Carter v. Carter Coal Co., 298 US 238, 295 (1935) (and cases there cited); Mackenzie v. Howe, 239 US 299, 311 (1915). However, the existence of the principle does not deter-

mine the *scope* of the executive competence. The two principal cases considered in this section support a limitation of scope by reference to the functional requirements of the executive undertaking.

[10] 229 US 304 (1936).

[11] *Id.* at 319.

discretion and freedom from statutory restriction which would not be admissible were domestic affairs alone involved.[12]

The opinion by Mr. Justice Sutherland went on to stress the President's need to rely on "confidential sources of information" to assess the foreign situation, the disclosure of which might be harmful. Since the issue in *Curtiss-Wright* was the governmental regulation of American business to prevent an unintended involvement of the country in foreign wars, either by establishing an American "presence" on one side by the introduction of United States' arms or by interfering with a national aim to restore peace to the area. As a precedent the case stands for the conclusion that the Constitution allows the legislature to confer wide discretion on the executive when the subject matter, by its very nature, involves foreign relations. But it should be understood that the *Curtiss-Wright* case presents the extreme instance—the relationship between the United States and a foreign war to which it is not a party. Such litigation does not suggest the extent to which, if at all, the executive power over foreign relations impinges upon the normal scope of judicial function in civil litigation in international law cases.

The other important Supreme Court case, *Chicago & S. Air Lines v. Waterman S. S. Corp.*,[13] likewise confirms the authority of the executive to carry out specific foreign relations duties entrusted to it. In *Waterman* the issue involved presidential authority to approve certificates of convenience and necessity issues by the Civil Aeronautics Board (CAB) to foreign carriers or for foreign routes. As in *Curtiss-Wright*, the Supreme Court emphasized the reliance of the President upon intelligence reports to exercise his responsibility of assuring that the action of the CAB is compatible with national security interests. The combination of administrative and executive action is declared unreviewable by the courts, for "it would be intolerable that courts, without the relevant information, should review and perhaps nullify actions of the Executive taken on information properly held secret."[14] Furthermore, these are "decisions of a kind for which the Judiciary has neither aptitude, facilities nor responsibility and which [have] long been held to belong in the domain of political power not subject to judicial intrusion or inquiry."[15] An appropriate claim of executive preemption is raised by this case, since the nature of the disputed question—the propriety of the grant or the denial of the certificate—cannot be decided by judicial techniques without appraising the President's judgment about national security. But does the *Waterman* holding militate against an affirmation of judicial independence for civil litigation arising in the area of international law?

---

[12] *Id.* at 320. This conclusion is, perhaps, stated in rhetoric that is unnecessarily sweeping, given the character of the case.

[13] 333 US. 103 (1948).
[14] *Id.* at 111.
[15] *Ibid.*

The disputed issue in international law cases is quite susceptible to a judicial resolution since it rests upon an appraisal of the legality or legal effect of a foreign government's conduct. There is only an indirect and most uncertain connection between the civil case and the conduct of foreign relations. From a technical viewpoint, the domestic court is competent; no political ingredient is necessarily embedded in that kind of case.

Of course, in a particular judicial setting, trends in world politics may make a judicial act relevant to foreign policy. It may be desirable in one situation to avoid a rebuff to France, whereas in another it may be desirable to rebuff Cuba; therefore, an assurance of judicial support may facilitate the achievement of executive objectives. But this kind of executive interest is based on *ad hoc* considerations of foreign policy, and if such considerations are allowed to control judicial behavior, then courts are nationalized without serving any general executive function and without taking account of limits upon judicial competence. There is no regulative principle, as distinct from *ad hoc* pressure, to justify the particular executive claim or to explain judicial abdication. In this sense, the executive claim is unlike *Curtiss-Wright* or *Waterman*.

The tradition of judicial deference to *ad hoc* executive policy can be traced to the influence of *United States v. Pink*,[16] a principal case standing for the subordination of judicial outcome to the foreign policy of the moment. While it is often proper for judicial deference to arise solely as a consequence of the structural characteristics and functional requirements of the executive's responsibility for foreign relations, it is generally improper for judicial deference to be a consequence of the vagaries of shifting patterns of foreign policy. In the latter instance, the court can and would decide the issues in dispute, permitting the execu-

---

[16] 315 US 203 (1942). The *Pink* case involved a determination of the effect of diplomatic recognition upon the disposition of some Russian assets located in New York, which the Soviet government had attempted to confiscate by extraterritorial decree. To reestablish good relations, the Soviet Union agreed in the Litvinov Assignment to assign its claims to American-located assets to the United States Government. The latter was then expected to use them to satisfy American claims against the Soviet government. By normal rules of conflict of laws, a state court in New York had decided that the Soviet decree, because of its confiscatory nature, was unable to affect ownership of assets physically present in the United States; there being nothing to assign, the assignee acquired nothing more than the assignor possessed. The Supreme Court reversed on broad grounds, stressing executive supremacy in the area of foreign affairs and a consequent judicial duty to carry out the executive will. In *Pink* this conception of executive-judicial relations was used to hold that, in view of the objectives of U.S. recognition policy, the Litvinov Assignment must be held to transfer the New York assets to the federal government. This gave the Soviet confiscatory decree retroactive validity; such validity, ironically, could *only* be accorded because the Soviet government was unrecognized at the time that it acted. This holding illustrates the extent of judicial subservience to executive authority. See also Michael H. Cardozo, "The Authority in Internal Law of International Treaties: The Pink Case," 13 *Syracuse Law Review* 544 (Summer 1962).

tive disposition to manipulate judicial behavior to serve a temporary national interest. To hallow the *Pink* tradition is to erode the prestige and role of domestic courts in the international legal system. The whole problem of executive-judicial relations in international law cases cannot be satisfactorily resolved without a reexamination, and an eventual repudiation, of the judicial thinking that prevailed in *Pink*.

III. Conflicts of Interest: National and International

Domestic courts necessarily function as national institutions and as agents of international legal order. This much is noncontroversial; the controversy arises when, as in *Sabbatino*, it becomes necessary to attribute significance to the reality of this dual membership in a specific instance, especially one in which contradictory lines of action emanate from national and international sources of legal authority. In such an instance, it becomes necessary to choose and by choosing to identify which of the two affiliations is paramount. There is no way to compromise or otherwise avoid the thorny issue of paramountcy.

The nature of the contradiction can be illustrated by the conflict between the conduct of foreign policy and the application of a rule of international law. From the perspective of a national government, domestic courts are subordinate instruments of policy in the area of foreign relations; the executive branch has the chief responsibility and possesses the necessary authority to act on behalf of the state. From the perspective of the international system, a court should apply rules of international law as independently and as consistently as it applies rules arising from any other source of law. Domestic courts are in a position to develop international law, to manifest respect for international law, and to demonstrate that normal standards of judicial independence are just as operative in an international law case as in a domestic case. The usefulness of domestic courts as international institutions, that is, as institutions responsible for upholding international law and for displaying it as a common system of law peculiar to no single state, depends on the capacity of these courts to withstand internal political influence when confronted with an issue of international law. To the extent that domestic courts set aside the normal application of international law to serve the foreign relations of the national government, they confirm cynical perceptions of international law as a body of law that is subordinate to or a rationalization of national policy. In addition, if domestic courts act as a branch of national government, their capacity to declare and develop international law is impaired. The law-giver, to be authoritative, must not appear partisan.

Yet, can the executive afford to have a domestic court impose its provincial views of the character of international law and relations upon legal controversies having important consequences for foreign policy? The action of a domestic court is often perceived as the action of the state as a whole, especially by officials serving in those foreign states domestically unaccustomed to an independent judiciary. If the court in state X renders a decision hostile to the interests of Y, then Y is likely to regard the judicial conduct in X as tantamount to a hostile foreign policy decision, a decision perhaps calling for a reprisal by Y, and certainly productive of tension. It is reasonable to maintain that, given the delicacy of the political balance in contemporary international politics, the executive needs the authority to control the behavior of courts.

An incident reported in February 1967 involving the seizure of Cuban fishing vessels on the ground that they were improperly present in the territorial waters of the United States illustrates a genuine problem. The seizure itself raised tensions at the time and led Cuba to retaliate by interfering with the normal water supply available to the United States' naval base at Guantanamo. In turn, this hostile Cuban act led the United States to discharge some of its Cuban employees at Guantanamo. Domestic voices in the United States were heard advocating more drastic responses, some ardent patrioteers even urged a complete blockade of Cuba until Fidel Castro turned on the water again, others demanded a military intervention to restore the water supply at Guantanamo. The Cuban Government indicated that the normal supply would not be restored until the fishermen and their vessels were set free. Convinced after investigation that these vessels were being operated for fishing purposes only and were not engaged in a mission hostile to the United States, the Department of State apparently favored prompt release of the vessels and crews.

That action might have terminated the crisis. Florida authorities, however, wanted to prosecute these fishermen under a state statute making it a crime to fish without a license in Florida's territorial waters. A citizen of a Communist state was statutorily ineligible to obtain a Florida license. The federal government turned the Cubans over to Florida authorities, enabling prosecution and conviction of the four boat captains. The action of the Florida courts might well have inflamed Cuban-American relations in a manner contrary to the will and wisdom of the State Department, although the federal decision, in this instance, to make possible the Florida prosecution by turning over the defendants suggests no real conflict between federal and state policy. Does not the federal government need to retain the competence to withdraw such litigation from Florida courts?

In this instance the executive possessed the original competence to deny court action because it had obtained custody over the prospective defendants. The federal government could certainly have effectively refused Florida's request since, in a criminal case where federal custody exists, initial executive control over the prosecution is assured. If instead the incident had grown out of a state enforcement action, that is, if the jurisdiction over the defendants and their vessels had resulted from a Florida seizure and prosecution, one can visualize that the problems posed by the conflict between the United States' form of federalism and its foreign relations could be potentially very serious.

This kind of problem is created by the political context within which any executive decision to prosecute is made. Since a criminal prosecution is a matter of executive discretion, it is, therefore, properly construed as an aspect of foreign relations. Whether a state with a federal system that involves the decentralization of executive authority should develop a competence to assure federal control is a special, although important, question. It is probably not reasonable to expect a foreign government to accede to the degree of autonomy enjoyed by federal subunits as an excuse for action to which they object. On the other hand, the authority of the fifty states to apply their own law to events within their jurisdiction is an essential attribute of the federal system, as it has evolved in the United States.

The incident involving Cuban fishing boats is interesting partly because it powerfully demonstrates why the executive branch might want and need to exercise control over domestic litigation so as to execute properly fundamental national policy in foreign affairs. There are special elements in the case, however, that require greater emphasis. First, the illustration concerned a criminal prosecution, i.e., a public act of the prosecuting government, that is by its discretionary nature inevitably political and thus reasonably construed as political by foreign governments. This point becomes more evident when one recalls the reaction in the United States to foreign criminal prosecutions of American servicemen, even when those prosecutions occurred in friendly states. States are habitually sensitive whenever their nationals are made defendants in a criminal prosecution, and this sensitivity is accentuated if the prosecution seems motivated by hostility toward the nation to which the defendant owes allegiance. If there is a political background to the prosecution, it then often appears that the foreign state is the real defendant with the private litigant being victimized as, in effect, a representative of the foreign state. It is hard to imagine in the current international setting a seizure by the Coast Guard of Mexican fishing vessels operating under circumstances similar to those of the Cuban vessels, and it is almost inconceivable to suppose a Florida prosecution of such Mexican fishermen after a federal willingness to release.

Second, by discrimination against certain foreign states on the basis of their political system, the underlying Florida licensing law incorporates a viewpoint toward international relations tantamount to the adoption of a foreign policy for Florida. Here again, the federalist structure of the United States complicates legal analysis. The doubtful utility of Florida's statutory policy does not support restrictions upon the role of domestic courts. Rather the issue provoked concerns the extent to which unified federal control is, can, and should be maintained over the legislative capacity of the fifty states so as to exclude these federal subunits from participating too actively in the foreign policy-making function.

Lastly, the prosecution itself, when and if it takes place, does not necessarily involve an issue of international law. It is certainly quite possible for the defense to contend that ships traversing territorial waters are not bound to obey the subnational laws of Florida and that, in any event, the Florida licensing statute is illegal under an international rule of nondiscrimination and therefore unenforceable. To the extent that a Florida prosecution involves arguments about the application of rules of international law to a dispute, the case is correctly treated as one that concerns the proper function of domestic courts.

IV. Arguments Favoring Executive Preemption

An international law case is one in which the judicial outcome depends at least in part upon a dispute over the application or character of international law rules. If the suit has been genuinely initiated by a private party, the controversy presumably does not reflect a governmental decision to prosecute. Nevertheless, it may not resemble ordinary private litigation; "complications" may arise. For example, an inconsistency may arise between the diplomatic representations of the United States and the determination of its domestic courts. If an American court finds that an expropriating state need not always pay prompt, adequate, and effective compensation, it is more difficult for the State Department to maintain the contrary position in the course of international negotiations. It seems clear that in certain circumstances judicial action might prejudice diplomacy covering the same subject matter. Also it could be urged that a court is less competent than the executive to interpret rules of international law. Furthermore, since the executive must necessarily take a position when disputes about international law arise, it may be both confusing and embarrassing to risk an inconsistent judicial position. It can be contended with some force, therefore, that either courts should be kept silent when a controversial rule of international law is at stake, or they should interpret international law in accord with executive will to the end that the judiciary and executive branches speak with a single national voice in international law disputes. And finally, in certain situations, the *Rich* case, for example, the executive might want to bargain a judicial release for a foreign favor; that is, the American executive branch in the United States may wish to give up its jurisdiction over a foreign ship in exchange for the return of United States' hijacked planes in foreign possession.[17] A recognition of executive paramountcy provides a bargaining counter in international negotiations that can be valuable on occasion.

These considerations demonstrate that disadvantages may arise if domestic courts achieve real independence in international law cases, and that the executive may sometimes have good reason for seeking to restrain or manipulate domestic courts. Clearly, the conduct of foreign relations might be adversely affected by the treatment accorded an international law case by a domestic court, but likewise foreign relations can be adversely affected by the investment policies of United States' corporations conducting business abroad. This potential for adverse effects should be balanced against the potential for beneficial effects. In weighing the balance, it is evident that one is faced with a problem of scheduling utilities and arranging priorities. Is it more important to encourage the independent operation of a domestic court or to assure the executive control over activity that might influence the conduct of foreign relations? In the final analysis, this question can be resolved only through a value judgment. An objective comparison of the net effect of judicial autonomy versus executive control does not appear possible.

V. Arguments Favoring Judicial Independence

Despite the acknowledgment that values govern one's judgment about the proper role of domestic courts in the international legal order, it is possible to outline a supporting rationale for a judiciary that is independent in noncriminal and nonpunitive international law cases.[18]

1. Purely international tribunals are not conveniently available for the litigation of disputes about international law.

2. Respect for the claims of international law as a legal system is lost if adjudication is made subservient to diplomacy.

3. Domestic courts, especially in principal sovereign states, have an excellent opportunity to develop international law if allowed to operate as reasonably independent tribunals.

4. The domestic location of the forum should normally not be treated as an essential aspect of the controversy. The *Sabbatino* litigation could just as easily have taken place in a foreign forum; some of the cases testing the validity of the Iranian and Indonesian nationalization pro-

---

[17] Rich v. Naviera Vacuba, S.A., 295 F. 2d 24 (4th Cir. 1961).

[18] Only a listing of the reasons can be given here.

grams took place in domestic courts of countries that did not have an interest in the expropriated property.[19]

5. The independence of the judiciary in international law cases is one way to shatter the illusion that sovereignty allows a state to reconcile its obligation to uphold international law with the promotion of its national interests. In fact, the depoliticalization of courts in international law cases might help to overcome the regressive notion that states are the only significant actors in international relations.

6. An awareness by the general community of states of the independence of the judiciary would probably itself mitigate many of the burdens that such independence is alleged to impose on the executive. Part of the need for executive control arises from the illusion abroad—especially in states that lack independent political institutions and a system of intragovernmental checks and balances—that executive control actually exists and that judicial behavior is properly comprehended as nothing but a product of executive will.

7. An independent judiciary preserves a private sector of international transactions that is not vulnerable to government control, and thereby resists the trend toward totalization of the exercise of control over human activity by the modern state. It is desirable to allow the state to speak with several voices in foreign affairs if the effect is to resist the tendency of the public sector to take over all private, nonnational activities. Application of international law by domestic courts should satisfy expectations created by law, rather than be made responsive to the needs of world politics or foreign policy.

8. Domestic courts are in a better position, in part because of their visibility and disciplined mode of operation, to resist domestic pressures to apply international law in a partisan manner. Public opinion, legislative pressures, and interest groups have more opportunity to influence executive and legislative than judicial processes of decision-making.

9. Domestic courts can educate the public about the character and importance of international law by writing opinions in this area, particularly if these opinions manifest a nonpolitical approach to interpretation and application of rules of international law. Such forms of

[19] Anglo-Iranian Oil Co. v. S.U.P.O.R. Co., Civil Tribunal of Venice, *International Law Report* (1955); Anglo-Iranian Oil Co. v. Idemitou Kosan Kabuskiki Karsha, *International Law Report* 312 (High Court of Tokyo), (1953); Martin Domke, "Indonesian Nationalization Measures Before Foreign Courts," 54 *American Journal of International Law* 305-23 (April 1960) (discussion of and excerpts from the opinions of the District Court in Bremen and the Hanseatic Court of Appeals in N.V. Verenigde Deli-Maatschapijen v. Deutsch-Indonesische Tabak-Handelsgesellschaft M. b. H.). See also Hans W. Baade, "Indonesian Nationalization Measures Before Foreign Courts—A Reply," 54 *American Journal of International Law* 801-35 (Oct. 1960).

communication may also persuade the states of Asia and Africa to consider international law as a serious source of mutual constraint.

10. The dangers of the nuclear age make it desirable to take risks, even to make sacrifices, to promote the growth of world legal order. The constructive use of domestic courts encourages a fuller and more responsible participation by states in the international legal system.

VI. After Judicial Independence, Then What?

Suppose that domestic courts do liberate themselves from executive constraints in private litigation involving the potential application of rules of international law to the contested action of foreign governments. That is, suppose a complete repudiation of the *Pink* tradition occurs and is replaced by an affirmation of the need for judicial independence in international law cases. Then what?

At first glance the effects of judicial independence appear trivial. Adherence to the act of state doctrine requires a domestic court in the United States to refrain from reviewing the validity of official action taken by a foreign government.[20] For the purposes of the litigation, the foreign act of state must be treated as valid by a domestic court. Thus, even though the executive branch does not instruct the court on what it must do, the court by its own rules of deference is foreclosed from doing anything.

Judicial independence does, however, make an important difference in at least one respect. The executive loses the competence to suspend the operation of the act of state doctrine by writing a *"Bernstein* Letter."[21] The loss of this kind of executive competence, unrelated as it is to functional considerations of the *Curtiss-Wright* or *Waterman* variety, would end the practice of allowing *ad hoc* foreign policy motives to influence judicial outcomes. It is submitted that the requirements of judicial independence necessitate a repudiation of the *Bernstein* doc-

20 For a more complete discussion of the nature and scope of the act of state doctrine, see Falk, note 3.

21 The idea of a *Bernstein* letter arises from a series of cases dealing with German acts of state during the Hitler period. These acts of state took property without compensation from Jewish owners. In Bernstein v. Van Heyghen Frères Société Anonyme, S.A., 163 F. 2d. 246 (2d Cir. 1947), Judge Learned Hand held that the act of state doctrine prevented a domestic court from questioning the validity of the German confiscatory acts. A second case involving similar facts, Bernstein v. N.V. Nederlandsche-Amerikaansche Stoomvaart-Maatschappij, 173 F. 2d 71 (2d Cir. 1949), also refused inquiry into the validity of the challenged German acts of state until

such inquiry was authorized by a letter sent to the court by the Acting Legal Adviser to the State Department. 210 F. 2d 375 (2d Cir. 1954). The letter stated that it is "the policy of the Executive, with respect to claims asserted in the United States for the restitution of identifiable property (or compensation in lieu thereof) lost through force, coercion, or duress as a result of Nazi persecution in Germany . . . to relieve American courts from any exercise of their jurisdiction to pass on the validity of the acts of Nazi officials." *State Department Bulletin* 20 (May 8, 1949), 592. On the basis of this letter, the court in the second Bernstein Case invalidated the German acts of state and awarded the property to the complainant.

trine,[22] which is, in effect, a corollary application of the *Pink* view of the duty of domestic courts to implement foreign policy as it was being pursued at the time by the executive.

This shift in executive-judicial relations does not necessarily mean that there can be no exceptions to the deference accorded by the act of state doctrine. It only means that exceptions must be judicially created and, hence, judicially justified by reference to functional considerations. It has been advocated that the basis for an exception should be the existence of universal consensus.[23] This position entails an interpretation of the external aspects of the act of state doctrine as a means of affirming the legitimate diversity of national conduct in relation to all activity for which a common standard was not supported by a consensus. Such a view implies that the basis of obligation in international law is primarily a reflection of community will and only secondarily a reflection of national will. That is, if nations are in agreement, a foreign state's conduct should be appraised by reference to common standards; if there is a significant degree of dissensus, a domestic court should treat the disputed official action of the foreign government as valid.

What establishes a consensus is a difficult, but not impossible, determination. Evidence in support of or in opposition to normative standards can be ascertained by national practice and claims, as well as by the actions of states in international organizations, by the votes and proceedings of scientific legal organizations, and by an examination of the technical literature. The discernment of consensus is most apparent with respect to many of the problems of human rights law; the discernment of dissensus is most salient with respect to the duty to compensate aliens for expropriated property and, generally, with respect to the law of state responsibility.

An insistence upon consensus as a basis of obligation in international law takes account of the structure of international society. There are no developed central legal organs able to change old patterns of law that are in conflict with new patterns of values. International law has to be administered in accord with the national governmental structure that continues to dominate international life. The dispersion of governmental institutions on the national level and the patterns of effective control both affirm the territorial nature of law. In the absence of an overwhelming consensus to the contrary, domestic courts should accept the validity of the territorial acts of a foreign government. The act of state doctrine could be easily reformulated to incorporate this set of recommendations, but such a reformulation is not necessary and it may perhaps even be deceptive.

[22] Bernstein v. Van Heyghen Frères Société Anonyme, S.A., 163 F. 2d Cir. (1947).   [23] See Chap. I.

More useful judicial decisions might result if courts come to justify deference or its exceptions by offering a functional account of their action by reference to the criteria of legitimate diversity and universal standards. One could dispense entirely with the act of state doctrine, although it would be necessary to substitute for it a presumption of validity that would be automatically attached to the actions of a foreign government so as to restrain domestic courts from giving provincial interpretations of the character of support available for the relevant rule or rules of international law. This presumption would alert courts and litigants to the need to find persuasive support for rules of international law that transcend the national outlook. In fact, it would be desirable to demonstrate the absence of any support for the claim of right implicit in the challenged action of the foreign government. This kind of demonstration would help to bring the dependence of international legal obligations upon a supporting consensus of national actors into sharper focus. If such a consensus is absent, then the presence of diversity is tantamount to a validation of territorial law. Because international society lacks central institutions, it is important not to manipulate the idea of territoriality so as to make the foreign act "extraterritorial" and hence not subject to a normal level respect by a domestic court. Effectuation of the viewpoint recommended here requires a search for neutral jurisdictional formulas that associate the activity of a foreign government with national territory in a fashion as mechanical and uniform as possible.

VII. Conclusion

There is no easy reconciliation of the national and international character of domestic courts. A functional approach based upon spheres of competence seems sensible, however, and leads to advocacy of judicial independence for domestic courts in civil litigation involving the application of rules of international law. Whatever contact such a case may happen to have with the conduct of foreign relations reflects the special character of the particular situation. The contact is not a reflection of any functional overlap, as it is when courts are asked to decide upon substantive matters that are *necessarily* within the sphere of foreign relations.[24] Where the connection between judicial outcomes is contingent and situational rather than necessary and functional, courts should serve the cause of developing the international legal system by claiming autonomy for themselves and by repudiating executive guidance.

The pursuit of judicial independence within the domestic system is

24 Examples of issues bearing on the substance of foreign relations are the grant of a certificate of convenience and necessity to a foreign airline or the prohibition of arms shipment to one faction in a foreign civil war.

not an invitation to domestic courts to assume an overly activist role when it becomes their duty to judge official acts of foreign sovereigns by reference to substantive rules of international law. Instead, a restrictive view of judicial function acknowledges the weakness of substantive international law in a world divided along ideological, cultural, and economic lines. Accordingly, the official action of a foreign government should normally be treated as valid by a domestic court unless that action violates a substantive rule supported actively by a global consensus of states. The absence of consensus with respect to many of the rules and standards in the area of state responsibility compels a domestic court to abstain from challenging the legality of the foreign government's official action. In this way can domestic courts operate constructively, deferring in areas of dissensus to the primacy of territorial supremacy, and implementing in other areas an existing consensus established by reference to world community standards.

PART FOUR

A PLEA FOR SYSTEMATIC

PROCEDURES OF INQUIRY

Introduction

TO DEAL adequately with the international legal order it is necessary to gather together the vast corpus of relevant data as meaningfully as possible. Too often international legal scholarship has been based upon an impressionistic survey of some of the relevant data, especially that available in the language(s) of the particular scholar or that which is reflective of national preferences. It is important to expand the scholarly base and to present the relevant material as to state practice in a form that is at once comprehensive and manageable. The relevant material needs to be organized in a systematic fashion to encourage the formulation of increasingly better evidenced generalization as to (1) patterns of behavior relevant to specific legal requirements, (2) patterns of attitude as to the character and content of legal requirements, and (3) patterns of expectation as to the reinforcement, revision, or creation of specific legal requirements. In effect, we need a survey of behavior and attitudes toward past, present, and future behavior that takes account of both the perceptions and expectations of the main participants in international life (especially those of officials in states and international institutions) as to the requirements of international law. "Requirements" needs to be broadly conceived to encompass the rules of behavior that set standards by which to distinguish compliance from violation, the procedures properly available to interpret the merits of a dispute about compliance, and the procedures properly available to enforce a judgment of noncompliance.

The development of adequate methods of inquiry with respect to the international legal order includes four main elements. These can be briefly identified:

1. The idea of systematic inquiry into the subject to coordinate its various parts and to assure a comprehensive coverage of the field;

2. The idea of comparison to assure the representation of diverse viewpoints and to highlight the present situation by comparing it with an actual past and a hypothetical set of plausible futures; that is, comparison is understood very metaphorically to include differences in outlook and situation over time and across space;

3. The idea of "the case" to assure depth, as well as breadth of inquiry, by emphasizing the degree to which the structure of the whole international legal order is caught up in any single strategic embodiment of it in an international dispute (although not, of course, one that is necessarily dealt with by a judicial forum); in this sense, the Cuban missile crisis is as much "a case" as is the judicially processed dispute over the status and administration of South West Africa;

4. The idea of a cosmopolitan orientation to enable the inquirer to

disengage himself from either advocacy or opposition to the policies and values of the national society to which he is affiliated, at least for the purpose of analyzing the overall character of the international legal order; a national orientation, if explicitly adopted, might also be beneficial in clarifying the optimal participation of a particular state in the international legal order, optimal being understood primarily in a selfish sense of the fulfillment of national goals (see Chapter XIX).

The Chapters in Part Four are all written to reflect the paramount importance that I attribute to finding an explicit and pervasive intellectual means by which to correlate international law with its conditioning international context. In a sense, then, Part Four is more an argument for using a contextual framework of inquiry than it is a mere explication. Chapter XV surveys the range of contextually oriented strategies of inquiry, pointing both to the number of fruitful alternatives that exist and the contribution made to our total understanding of the international legal order by supplementing one form of inquiry by others rather than by feeling compelled to choose among them to find "the right one." Chapters XVI-XVIII examine in some critical detail the work of several of the leading practitioners of contextual inquiry in the United States. Additional distinguished practitioners of the contextual style of inquiry such as Julius Stone, C. Wilfred Jenks, and F.S.C. Northrop are not dealt with here, although the special contributions that stem from their distinct approaches would well vindicate separate treatment. Chapter XIX outlines a strategy of inquiry that can be useful to identify the specific perspectives of any given actor or group of actors toward the past, present, and future of the international legal order. The framework is developed to fit the circumstances of the Afro-Asian world, a circumstance wherein the need for a rational assessment of the compatibility between national values and goals and those embodied in the international legal order is an obvious necessity. Such an assessment would be better performed by rational procedures of inquiry and observation than by intuitive patterns of predisposition and supposition. The framework could be adapted to analyze and determine an optimum strategy of participation for any actor in the international system.

XV. Some New Approaches to the Study of International Law

I. New Trends in Observation and Assessment in International Legal Studies

International law is both a contemplative academic subject and an active ingredient of diplomatic process in world affairs.[1] The failure to maintain the clarity of this distinction accounts for considerable confusion about the nature and function of international law in the world today. An international lawyer is also a citizen of a nation-state who often holds strong views as to preferred courses of foreign policy. One way for him to vindicate these views is to demonstrate their compatibility or incompatibility with governing rules of international law. Confusion arises in scholarly settings whenever the adversary presentation of views is not distinguished from the scholarly assessment of opposing lines of adversary presentation.

The use of military force by the United States in Vietnam offers an example of this sort of problem. The United States Department of State issued a memorandum defending American use of force as legal on the principal ground that it amounts to legitimate collective self-defense against aggression by North Vietnam.[2] This memorandum is obviously an adversary document stating "our side" in the legal controversy and making very little effort to assess impartially the facts or the law in support of the other side. North Vietnam could issue its own memorandum that could construe the facts and present the law in a manner favorable to its actions. In domestic society we have no problem distinguishing the argument of counsel from the judgment of the court; the former is understood as adversary, the latter as impartial. In international society the absence of generally competent adjudicating institutions makes it very difficult to move beyond the adversary level of discourse.

The academic international lawyer has a potential contribution to make to the extent that he is capable of substituting an adjudicatory for an adversary orientation. If the academic international lawyer succeeds in establishing for his legal analysis a reputation of impartiality, then the perception of the relationship between challenged national conduct and rules of international law can be elevated to a higher level of discourse. To revert to the legal controversy in the United States regarding the

[1] Myres S. McDougal has made the useful distinction between "theories *of*" and "theories *about*" international law to call attention to this dual role. McDougal, "Some Basic Theoretical Concepts About International Law: A Policy-Oriented Framework of Inquiry," *Journal of Con-* *flict Resolution* 4 (Sept. 1960), 337-54.

[2] "The Legality of U.S. Participation in the Defense of Vietnam," Department of State, Office of Legal Adviser, March 4, 1966; for a convenient text see *Congressional Record*, March 10, 1966, 5274-79.

PLEA FOR SYSTEMATIC PROCEDURES OF INQUIRY

use of force in Vietnam, it seems unfortunate that five of the most distinguished American international lawyers should have chosen to write an open letter to President Johnson in which they confirm the legality of the United States position as "defensible" under international law.[3] Of course, the position is defensible in legal terms, but would an impartial tribunal of experts find it more defensible than the counterarguments—and, if so, with respect to which issues?[4]

The international lawyers of the period after World War I, dominated by approaches associated with legal positivism or natural law, achieved a different sort of policy irrelevance from the policy justifications of recent years. These earlier international lawyers detached law from the political context of world affairs and made very rigid analyses of the regulation of state conduct by invoking supposedly fixed and unambiguous rules of restraint. They relied for a new system of world order upon agreed legal rules but they failed to develop an adequate appreciation of the social and political difficulties of making these rules into effective behavioral norms.[5] The Covenant of the League, the Kellogg-Briand Pact, and the general seriousness with which prohibitions upon the use of aggressive force were taken by international lawyers are indicative of this general failure to understand the limited effect of rules of restraint upon the central activities of the nation-state in a social system as decentralized in its distribution of power and as horizontal in its institutional structure as is international society.

In the 1940's and 1950's, new critiques of international law as legalistic and moralistic were salutory efforts to persuade well-intentioned governments away from any general reliance upon such rules in the pursuit of their interests and the defense of their values.[6] A modicum of realism suggests that rules governing recourse to violence can be manipu-

---

[3] The letter to President Johnson, dated February 14, 1966, was signed by Professors William W. Bishop, Jr., Richard R. Baxter, Myres S. McDougal, Louis B. Sohn, and Neill H. Alford, Jr.; it may be found in the *Congressional Record*, February 23, 1966, 3694-95. An earlier letter supporting the legality of U.S. action was sent to the President after it had been circulated by Professor E. Ernest Goldstein and signed by thirty-one professors of international law; see *Congressional Record: Appendix*, January 27, 1966.

[4] These counterarguments concern the charges of breaking faith with the Geneva Agreements of 1954, the degree and nature of North Vietnamese infiltration, the relationship between the National Liberation Front and Hanoi, the claims of American intervention in South Vietnam, and so on; legal issues include allegations of violations

of the laws of war, disproportionate use of force in self-defense, and armed attack against North Vietnam.

[5] Cf. Walter C. Schiffer, *The Legal Community of Mankind*, New York, Columbia University Press, 1954; Julius Stone, *Legal Controls of International Conflict*, New York, Rinehart, 1954; Charles De Visscher, *Theory and Reality in Public International Law*, Princeton, Princeton University Press, 3rd rev. edn., 1968.

[6] Among the most influential critics of a legalistic-moralistic approach to foreign policy have been George F. Kennan and Hans J. Morgenthau. See Kennan, *American Diplomacy 1900-1950*, Chicago, University of Chicago Press, 1951, pp. 95-96; Morgenthau, *In Defense of the National Interest*, New York, Knopf, 1951, pp. 101, 102, 144.

lated; the complementarity of a system of legal rules assures that a legal pretext, at least, will always be available to a government.[7]

And given the absence of impartial procedures to review contradictory legal claims put forward by nation-states in a dispute, there is no very persuasive means to appraise the relative merits of the legal argument. The understanding of a legal order, then, must be expanded to include an awareness of the prospects for upholding a fairly stable set of expectations about what is permissible and what is impermissible conduct, an awareness that shifts inquiry from the rules to the social and institutional means available for their effective implementation. The leading international lawyers in the period following World War II have been increasingly sensitive to this need to examine the role of law in light of the overall setting of international politics. Some of the most impressive work along these lines has been done by Myres McDougal, C. Wilfred Jenks, Rosalyn Higgins, Oscar Schachter, Eric Stein, Julius Stone, and Wolfgang Friedmann. These scholars give great attention to the definition of realistic goals for international law in light of the decentralized character of international society. There is almost a consensus present among contemporary international lawyers that such an intellectual orientation is essential to the fruitful study of international law. The result of this orientation is to bring the study of international law into ever closer association with the outlook, method, and concerns of the social scientist.

An international lawyer cannot afford to hold constant the context within which law is created and applied or within which legal controversy takes place. For the student of domestic law the institutional social context is fairly clearly established and can more easily be taken for granted, although the bearing of changing pressures and values upon the development of all phases of law is now widely accepted. For international lawyers the first task, in a sense, is to find functional equivalents for the legislature, court, and executive and then to measure the degree to which these equivalents produce law-conditioned behavior in international affairs. So long as international lawyers conceived of the search for functional equivalence in terms of mechanical identity the results of their labors produced either artificial enthusiasm or premature despair. Such a mechanical approach tends to give exaggerated prominence to the central institutions that do exist in international society—especially to the International Court of Justice—and produces either an attitude that such institutions as do exist constitute the international legal sys-

---

[7] For an extreme articulation of the notion that legal order is constituted by complementary norms, see Myres S. McDougal, "The Ethics of Applying Systems of Authority: The Balanced Opposites of a Legal System," in Harold D. Lasswell and Harlan Cleveland, eds., *The Ethic of Power*, New York, Harper & Brothers, 1962, pp. 221-40.

tem or the conclusion that despite the formal existence of equivalent institutions their impact on international behavior is so marginal and sporadic as to deprive of legal quality the ordering of relations among states.

The development of a more sophisticated approach to the notion of functional equivalence makes it possible to achieve a richer sense of the character of international law. In particular, increasing stress is now being put upon the distinctive ordering characteristics of an international society conceived of in predominantly horizontal and decentralized terms.[8] The most pronounced consequence of this stress is to shift the focus of inquiry from the activities of primitive international institutions to the activities of national legal institutions in generating, enforcing, and repudiating the rules and expectations associated with international law. It is a commonplace hypothesis that it is necessary to correlate patterns of authority with patterns of power in an effective social order. One can thus infer, in a manner relevant to the study of international law, that the effective locus of international authority will be on the national level. Systematic attention is now being given for the first time to the role of national institutions and decision-makers in upholding and developing international law, but it has yet to proceed very far on a comparative basis.[9]

Roger Fisher has done notable work that points out very forcefully the extent to which international law attains a certain effectiveness merely because it is woven into the complex bureaucratic structure of the modern state.[10] Bureaucratic decision-making is by its nature rule-governed. A bureaucrat called upon to act on behalf of the state would not normally even consider that the commission of a violation to promote national policy was an option open to him. Of course, there exist both a wide area of discretion within which to interpret rules and many subject matters for which rules (which are, after all, only crystallized expectations about permissible behavior) are not established, but the whole impulse of a bureaucratized response is to find a consistent formula that can deal with recurrent situations and that will be acceptable to as many of the relevant actors as possible. Accommodation and reciprocity operate to structure a legal response and thereby tend to minimize

[8] See e.g., Myres S. McDougal, "International Law, Power, and Policy: A Contemporary Conception," 82 *Recueil des Cours* 139-258 (1953); also Falk, *The Role of Domestic Courts in the International Legal Order*, Syracuse, Syracuse University Press, 1964, pp. 21-52.
[9] Some interesting material on the role of national decision-makers is to be found in H.C.L. Merillat, ed., *Legal Advisers and Foreign Affairs*, Dobbs Ferry, N.Y., Oceana, 1964; cf. also Richard B. Bilder, "The Office of the Legal Adviser: The State Department Lawyer and Foreign Affairs," 56 *American Journal of International Law*, 633-84 (July 1962).
[10] Roger Fisher, "Bringing Law to Bear on Governments," 74 *Harvard Law Review* 1130-40 (April 1961).

friction arising from conduct and to maximize the prospects for regularizing the conduct in question. One form of "technical assistance" that may promote the effective implementation of international law among the new states consists of helping these states to build into their developing bureaucracies a place for legal advice in foreign affairs, through the provision of a trained cadre of bureaucratic specialists in international law whose dignity and influence depend on the acceptance of this advice. Similarly, in the developed countries a way to enhance greatly the role of law in world affairs would be to raise to cabinet level the status of the legal adviser and to appoint to the post a prominent man of influence, ambition, and competence.

There is a need to complement the work on bureaucratic decision-making with more searching forms of inquiry into the relevance of law to political decision-making. In certain international situations of conflict and crisis the overriding goals of national policy are chosen almost independently of what the law, impartially assessed, might be supposed to require. Consequently there exists a rather misleading and destructive tendency to conclude that international law has nothing whatever to do with the behavior of states or with the maintenance of international stability in this sort of political setting. Government lawyers are called in, if at all, to provide legal arguments for a decision taken on other grounds, so that official action will seem legally defensible, especially in the eyes of domestic public opinion. This rationalizing function of international law has seemed to determine the lawyer's role with respect to the military participation of the United States in Vietnam or to the armed intervention of 1965 by the United States in the Dominican Republic.[11] And in Soviet international practice there is almost no indication that international lawyers in their role as experts on international law advise on policy or are permitted to comment objectively on the relationship between Soviet practice and relevant rules of international law. The role of international law has in these situations been restricted to one of rationalization, and there is little indication that the existence of international law has had much bearing on the execution of the various phases of foreign policy. An exclusion of law from the procedures of political decision-making suggests a willingness to conceive of national interest as exclusively defined by national will and by the relative capabilities of interested parties to assert control over the event in question.

Political decision-making does not require the exclusion of interna-

---

[11] For a general analysis see Wolfgang Friedmann, "United States Policy and the Crisis of International Law," 59 *American Journal of International Law* 857-71 (Oct. 1965). It is generally true that Communist states have not even bothered to put forth serious legal arguments to support their positions in international disputes.

tional law. The formulation of a political position in terms of distinct legal claims may clarify the stakes of an international controversy and make rival actors somewhat less likely to overreact. International law can operate as an assured medium of diplomatic communication, allowing for interactions of claim and counterclaim to delimit the area of dispute and clarify the stakes of a particular conflict. The degree to which international law facilitates international communication is a developing subject of scholarly investigation.[12] An informed awareness of legal expectations in a situation of crisis may also strengthen inclinations to exercise maximum self-restraint in achieving the political end in view. One way to command support for or to minimize opposition to political claims, especially those involving the use of force, is to exhibit deference to relevant rules of international law.

A characteristic of a decentralized social system is that the political claims of the powerful nation-states serve as legal precedents for other, less powerful, members of international society. Nuclear testing by the United States and the Soviet Union created permissive precedents that are very difficult to repudiate. Relative power plays a much greater role in creating precedents than in repudiating them. There is a kind of reciprocity and symmetry operative in international society, as in all social systems, that makes the assertion by one state of a legal claim to act in a specified way available to other states similarly situated. Such symmetry owes much to the external aspects of the ideology associated with national sovereignty, an ideology that has contributed so centrally to the constitutive structure of traditional international law through ideas of the equality of states, the absoluteness of territorial jurisdiction, and the doctrine in nonintervention.[13, 14]

An implication of such symmetry is to underscore that the capacity of a powerful state to assert unilaterally a claim on behalf of its own immediate interests may have a rather detrimental system-wide impact upon the satisfaction of its intermediate-term interests. That is, the characteristic processes of political action in world affairs are shaped in part by rationales designed to legitimize the claims issued by powerful states pursuing unilateral and partisan aims. The Soviet Union's endorsement of support for wars of national liberation—a departure

[12] See Stone, op.cit. supra, note 5 at p. xiv. A perceptive stress on communication as a function of international law is found in the recent work of William D. Coplin. See his "International Law and Assumptions About the State System," World Politics 17 (July 1956), 617-34, and his book, The Functions of International Law: An Introduction to the Role of International Law in the Contemporary World, Chicago, Rand McNally, 1966.

[13] Cf. Leo Gross, "The Peace of West- phalia, 1648-1948," 42 American Journal of International Law 20-41 (Jan. 1948). See also Richard N. Rosecrance, Action and Reaction in World Politics, Boston, Little, Brown, 1963, pp. 17-191.

[14] It is, of course, important to distinguish legal doctrine from political behavior. Despite a doctrinal insistence upon territorial sovereignty, frequent examples exist of intervention by the powerful in the affairs of the weak.

from the Charter conception of permissible use of force—provides a complex example of unintended consequences flowing from an original departure in doctrine and practice from legal expectations. Among the consequences of such a departure is that it weakens the impact of Soviet objections to the more militant posture of the Chinese and to the interventionary anti-Communist policies and practices of the United States. Likewise the unilateral nature and the scale of the United States role in support of the Saigon government in Vietnam is generating precedents (especially with regard to outside participation in civil wars) that seem to impair existing precedents of neutrality and limited intervention that might have been strengthened had the United States chosen alternative courses of action.

Part of the inquiry directed at the role of international law on the domestic level is to take note of the increasing use of international law by private citizens, at least in democratic societies, as a way to restrain, or dramatize opposition to, the undertakings of their own national governments. This development is attributable, in part, to a withering of nationalist sentiment in the developed countries, reflecting both a universal humanistic ethic popular among intellectuals of all countries and a widespread fear that even the most powerful nations must act with caution in the nuclear age.[15] The existence of this trend is some indication that international lawyers are adopting an outlook based on an extranationalistic view of international law, which can serve as a transnational source of judgment on issues of disputed legality. Dramatic evidence of this outlook is the effort to present cases in domestic courts to test the willingness of these courts to question the legality under international law of government conduct. Notions of sovereign immunity are giving way as barriers to such challenges on behalf of international law. The idea that international law is of concern only in state-to-state relations is also giving way, undermined, in part, by the imposition after World War II of criminal responsibility on the leaders of Germany and Japan because of their alleged violation of international law. The precedent of the Nuremberg Judgment is now being invoked against those who helped to create it, the argument being that if individuals have a duty to avoid violating rules of international law, then this duty of the individual must be protected by the domestic system, and thus that a domestic court must not decline to determine whether or not its own government is violating international law (just as it determines whether or not its own government is violating domestic law).[16]

[15] See Chap. XXIII.
[16] For a relevant argument on this issue see the Steel Seizure Case: Youngstown Sheet and Tube Company v. Sawyer 343 US 579 (1953).

By and large these attempts to make use of domestic courts in this fashion have failed, the court refusing to regard the plaintiff as competent to raise the issue or itself as competent to decide it. Typical reasoning of this sort was used in the Pauling cases, instituted to prevent further contamination of the atmosphere by continued nuclear testing.[17] Another example is the *Eminente* proceeding brought by a French national in 1965 against President Johnson, Robert McNamara, and Dean Rusk to collect $1,000,000 in damages to plaintiff's property allegedly sustained in United States bombing of North Vietnam in violation of international law.[18] The most celebrated litigation arising out of the Vietnam War to date has been the criminal prosecution, conviction, and sentencing of Dr. Benjamin Spock, Rev. William Sloan Coffin, Michael Ferber, and Mitchell Goodman for an alleged conspiracy to counsel draft resistance;[19] in their defense presentation, Spock and Ferber relied heavily upon arguments that the United States' role in the Vietnam War violated rules of international law. The trial judge excluded any testimony on or other consideration of the international law issues, and this exclusion at the trial level was not touched upon in the appellate judgment. However, the mere presence of these cases on court dockets is significant to the extent that it can dramatize a shift in the locus of loyalty from the national scene to the common law of mankind. To the extent that domestic courts dismiss such claims because the conduct of foreign policy is a nonreviewable exercise of executive discretion, these cases serve to highlight prerogatives claimed by a state in its foreign affairs that it would not dare claim for domestic affairs. Further, these cases call attention to the discrepancy between the appeals of statesmen for the rule of law in world affairs and their insistence upon the nonreviewability of their own conduct within their own domestic courts. If the conduct of foreign policy is not subject to review in a forum as sympathetic and conversant with national perspectives as a domestic court is normally inclined to be, then the outlook for entrusting vital legal disputes to international tribunals is indeed dim.

The relevant point here is that the study of international law can benefit greatly by more systematic and comparative attention to the extent to and manner by which domestic institutions apply international law. The *Sabbatino* controversy is an excellent example of the use and abuse of international law by the main branches of government in the

[17] Linus C. Pauling and others v. Mc-Namara, 331 F. 2d 796 (1964); Pauling v. McElroy, 278 F. 2d 252 (1960).

[18] Emilio Eminente v. Lyndon Baines Johnson, McNamara, Rusk, No. 19, 802, U.S. Court of Appeals for the District of Columbia (1966).

[19] United States v. Coffin *et al.*, Criminal Docket No. 68-1-F, U.S. District Court, Massachusetts, 1968; the international law arguments are set forth in the Memoranda in support of Michael Ferber's and Benjamin Spock's Motions to Dismiss the Indictment.

domestic system; it has led to a legislative formulation of a rule binding upon domestic courts because it is posited as the "authoritative" domestic interpretation of international law.[20]

A Japanese domestic court in the *Shimoda* case provides the only example of an attempt by a legal tribunal to assess the legality of the atomic attacks upon Hiroshima and Nagasaki.[21] The court's decision is particularly significant, first, because it involves a review under international law of belligerent action carried out in the course of a major war by the victorious powers and, second, because the review was undertaken at the insistence of individuals, five survivors of the attacks. The conclusion reached by the Tokyo court that the atomic raids violated international law has an impact, the ultimate strength of which is as yet unmeasurable, upon the status of nuclear weapons as legitimate military weapons. To the extent that such an impact exists it illustrates how the growth of international legal standards may be the result of determinations of law reached at the domestic level. The case illustrates as well that individuals may be beginning to make a legislative input to the international system, thereby complicating further the notion that rules of international law can be formed only by the consent of sovereign states.

Contemporary approaches to international law are searching for ways to encompass the role of actors other than nation-states, ways that are descriptive of the relevance of law to international behavior.[22] Wolfgang Friedmann has called attention to the relevance of regional actors to the growth of effective international law in a world divided on such fundamental matters as human rights and the ownership of private property.[23] As yet no adequate work has been done on the degree to which regional actors are bound either by the rules governing nation-states in their relations with other regional actors or by some nascent interregional law of a distinctive sort. In addition, only very primitive speculation has taken place on the relations between the United Nations, regional organizations, and nation-states. There are important issues involving the danger of regional aggression against a state that opposes the regional consensus in some fundamental way, as Israel opposes the

---

[20] For full documentation see Lyman M. Tondel, Jr., ed., *The Aftermath of Sabbatino*, Dobbs Ferry, N.Y., Oceana, 1965, which includes texts of the first three judicial opinions.
[21] See Falk, *Legal Order in a Violent World*, Princeton, Princeton University Press, 1968, pp. 374-413; for the complete text of the court's decision see Falk and Saul H. Mendlovitz, eds., *The Strategy of World Order: Toward a Theory of War Prevention*, New York, The World Law

Fund, 1966, Vol. I, 314-53.
[22] For one attempt to redefine the scope of law in world affairs to include actors other than nation-states see Quincy Wright, "Toward a Universal Law of Mankind," 63 *Columbia Law Review* 440-60 (March 1963).
[23] Wolfgang Friedmann, *The Changing Structure of International Law*, New York, Columbia University Press, 1964, pp. 60-71.

Arab League, Cuba, the Organization of American States, and South Africa the Organization of African Unity.[24] International lawyers are growing sensitive to the need to adapt their framework of inquiry to take account of the contemporary structure of international society, especially the relevance of regional actors and international institutions to the regulation of all sorts of behavior with transnational implications.

A different source of regulatory authority arises from the efforts of bloc actors to moderate the limits of conflict by establishing rules of the game in their relations *inter se*.[25] The significance of these rules depends upon the degrees to which certain relations are perceived in bipolar terms and upon the acceptance of and reliance upon processes of communication to establish commonly perceived limits of conflict. The Soviet Union and the United States are both competing for political influence in the new states of Asia and Africa. One consequence of this competition is the manipulation of civil strife so as to produce desired outcomes; another, in special cases, is intervention with overt military power. At the same time, these two preeminent world powers seek to avoid an escalation of small wars above certain thresholds. Therefore, rules of the game that limit the extent and nature of participation in civil wars would seem to serve the common interest of both powers without unduly interfering with their freedom of political action. Among the most significant of these rules is a prohibition upon the use of nuclear weapons to support one's proxy faction. Another rule calls for the confinement of the geographical scope of violence to the territorial limits of the state that is the scene of the violence. The decision in February of 1965 to extend the war in Vietnam by bombing north of the seventeenth parallel is a very significant challenge to this rule unless the civil war is viewed as a struggle between North Vietnam and the Saigon elite in South Vietnam.[26] Given the inability of the United Nations to interpose itself effectively in situations of cold-war violence, these informal rules of the game are an important ingredient of contemporary world order, and their importance is to some extent dependent upon their character as norms being perceived and understood

[24] For some relevant observation see Falk, *op.cit. supra*, note 21, at pp. 324-35. See also Inis L. Claude, Jr., "The OAS, the UN, and the United States," *International Conciliation*, No. 547 (March 1964).

[25] See Edward McWhinney, "Soviet and Western International Law and the Cold War in the Era of Bipolarity," 1 *Canadian Yearbook of International Law* 40-81 (1963).

[26] The official U.S. justification claims collective self-defense against an armed at-tack by North Vietnam. One difficulty with this argument is that the pattern and character of this conflict more closely resembles a civil war. If the conflict is treated as a civil war, then there is no legal basis for bombing North Vietnam, even if the factual basis is prior intervention on behalf of the National Liberation Front. Counterintervention may be permissible, but not when it takes place outside the territorial limits of the political entity enduring the civil war.

by relevant decision-makers.[27] If law is identified with community expectations and a violation of law consists of the disappointment of these expectations, then there is no real problem presented by assimilating this kind of "rule" into the analysis used to deal with rules created by the more traditional procedures associated with treaty-making and customary international law.[28]

In fact, one of the major issues challenging time-honored approaches to international law is the development of a more adequate theory of the basis of legal obligation in international society.[29] C. Wilfred Jenks has been particularly articulate in suggesting the need to supplant a sovereignty-oriented notion of consent with a community-oriented notion of consensus.[30] Considerable recent attention has been given to the law-creating potential of various sorts of resolutions passed by the General Assembly.[31] Considerable work needs to be done to formulate the conditions under which and the extent to which various categories of resolutions do have a law creating impact. It is also necessary to investigate the interaction between resolutions and attitudes toward permissible and impermissible behavior and thereby to achieve some understanding of when and how the General Assembly can exert an effective influence, as well as to identify some of the occasions upon which its actions are likely to be futile.

Some authoritative insight into the juridical status of these issues has been given in several of the dissenting opinions in *The South West Africa* cases decided by the International Court of Justice in June of 1966. In the course of this complex litigation the argument was made that the practice of apartheid is "illegal" because of the law-creating effect of formal acts of the General Assembly supported by an overwhelming majority of the membership.[32] It is also relevant to take note of the use by the *Shimoda* decision of "declaratory" rules of air warfare to draw and support inferences about obligatory standards of behavior. The main point is that the traditional dichotomy between what is obligatory and what is permissive is crumbling and that therefore international lawyers need a more adequate and comprehensive theory of legal

---

[27] Relevant patterns of strategic thinking can be adapted to the analysis of the operation of international law in crisis situations; see especially Thomas C. Schelling, *The Strategy of Conflict*, Cambridge, Harvard University Press, 1960.

[28] For a clear account of traditional processes of law creation, with some attention to recent developments, see Clive Parry, *The Sources and Evidences of International Law*, Dobbs Ferry, N.Y., Oceana, 1965.

[29] For the background of traditional thinking see the title essay in James L.

Brierly, *The Basis of Obligation in International Law and Other Papers*, Oxford University Press, 1958, pp. 1-67.

[30] E.g., Clarence W. Jenks, *Law, Freedom and Welfare*, Dobbs Ferry, N.Y., Oceana, 1963, pp. 83-100.

[31] E.g., Oscar Schachter, "The Relation of Law, Politics and Action in the United Nations," 109 *Recueil des Cours* 171-249 (1963); Rosalyn Higgins, *The Development of International Law Through the Political Organs of the United Nations*, London, Oxford University Press, 1963, pp. 1-10.

[32] See Chaps. V and XII.

obligation than that developed to serve an international society consisting only of states, in which the existence of law subserves the ideology of national sovereignty.

II. *From Impressionism to Scientific Inquiry:*
A *Focus on Developing Methodologies*

The new methodologies available for the study of international law are seeking, above all, to move beyond the impressionism of earlier approaches. In each area of international law there are a body of practice and a set of attitudes associated with the interesting legal questions. These data need to be collected and organized in a systematic fashion to permit the formulation of well-evidenced generalizations. In turn, these generalizations can then be formulated as propositions about the relation of law and behavior which are subject to validation and refutation. Only in this manner can international legal studies begin to acquire a scientific character, a character that assures that the expansion of knowledge is cumulative and not just accumulative.

The term "impressionism" is used to characterize approaches, still accepted by some, in which legal analysis is based upon a partial selection of relevant material and in which the criteria for selection are arbitrary reflections of the researcher's values, national locus, and imperfect factual knowledge. To move legal research techniques beyond impressionism there is a need for a fuller investigation of the extent to which the advances in the technology of knowledge can be put to work by international lawyers. However, although admirable efforts have been made in the field, there is considerable reason to suppose that the data of international legal studies are not generally susceptible to quantification in any form that will not trivialize or even distort inquiry. International practice is not sufficiently iterative to permit the aggregation of instances of recurrence. What seem primarily needed to advance inquiry, at present, are (1) a systematic framework of inquiry adapted to various relatively specialized subject matters and (2) coordinated efforts by scholars willing to conduct inquiry within a suitable framework. In a later chapter a method is outlined for assessing the participation of the recently independent states of Asia and Africa in the international legal system.[33] If implemented, even by a less-than-global program of study, it would produce a body of knowledge, organized on a comparative basis, which is considerably "harder" than the speculative interpretations upon which international lawyers have, by necessity, previously relied. On the basis of this knowledge, generalizations could be advanced with more confidence and their validity could be confirmed

[33] See Chap. XIX.

or challenged by direct observation of behavior. Such a reorientation of international legal studies is more likely to come about in a social science setting than in the law schools, whose principal educational function remains one of vocational training, a function best served by teaching students to think about legal problems in ways sensitive to their resolution through counseling, diplomacy, and adjudication.

The study of international law has been heretofore dominated by lawyers mainly concerned with developing these particular skills. Research has concentrated on the analysis of legal issues in problem areas or on the presentation of more or less exhaustive informational surveys that collect the experience of the past. This is a beneficial tradition of continuing validity. It merely needs to be complemented by the approaches to knowledge that are developing within the social sciences for the observation and assessment of human behavior.

In the United States today there seem to be present four main methodological orientations used in the study of international law: policy science, functionalism, quantitative empiricism, and systems theory; a fifth methodological orientation, less well established than the other four, can be identified under the label of "phenomenological perspectives." These approaches are not mutually exclusive; each accords attention to the social and political setting of law and each takes seriously the bearing of the interests, goals, and values of the participants in international society upon the character and nature of international law and its prospects for effective growth. This evidence of agreement on a common point of methodological departure is a remarkable achievement, reversing as it does a long tradition of legal studies devoted only to a detached observation of "legal data" (that is, treaties, judicial decisions, formal diplomatic correspondence, and the like). Attentiveness to the international context of international law has also produced a far livelier awareness of the relations between law and power in world affairs, thereby introducing realism and avoiding the inclination toward wishful thinking, legalism, and moralism evident in earlier generations of international lawyers. Among the evils inflicted by strict adherence to the precepts of legal positivism, and now being overcome by the newer approaches, is a tendency to create an artificial distance between the "is" of international politics and the "ought" of international law.

As Myres McDougal has so ably demonstrated, one role of law is to help a social system move toward the attainment of its goals.[34] An acceptance of this role leads international lawyers to adopt prescriptive as well as descriptive postures and makes necessary a sharp discrimina-

[34] Myres S. McDougal, "Jurisprudence for a Free Society," 1 *Georgia Law Re-* *view* 1-12 (1966).

tion among the different legal tasks undertaken by the scholar. But this emphasis upon prescription is not legalism or moralism; it is an articulation of the contribution that can be made in legal contexts to the goals of those actors possessing power and professing adherence to certain values.

In matters of approach, some disagreement arises about the extent to which policy alternatives can be prescribed in "scientific" terms in concrete instances.[35] Some jurists contend that an analysis of international law can only clarify the nature of choice, whereas others allege that it can indicate the proper decision as well. In the former instance, the legal authority supporting and opposing various policy options is presented without any claim that lawful action can be identified; in the latter instance, not only are the legal implications of the choice set forth but the legal argument is accorded priority according to its relative capacity to promote the policies at stake in the decision-making situation.

Further disagreement centers upon the way in which the political context is to be made relevant to legal appraisal. The discussion of the problem of distinguishing the national from the cosmopolitan perspective is important here. Does one analyze the policy content of legal choice in terms of national policy, of worldwide policy, or of some combination of policy outlooks? International lawyers have not yet taken clear or successful account of what J. David Singer has so usefully identified as the "level-of-analysis" problem.[36]

Policy Science. This approach is associated with the work of Myres S. McDougal, supported by the influence and collaboration of Harold D. Lasswell and emanating from the atmosphere in American legal thought established by the legal realist movement.[37] Inquiry is organized in terms both of factual events in community process and of the decision-

---

[35] E.g., Leo Gross, "Problems of International Adjudication and Compliance with International Law: Some Simple Solutions," 59 *American Journal of International Law* 48-59 (Jan. 1965).

[36] J. David Singer, "The Level-of-Analysis Problem in International Relations" in Klaus Knorr and Sidney Verba, eds., *The International System*, Princeton, Princeton University Press, 1961, pp. 77-92; see also McDougal's analysis in "The Impact of International Law upon National Law; A Policy-Oriented Perspective," in Myres S. McDougal and Associates, *Studies in World Order*, New Haven, Yale University Press, 1960, pp. 157-236.

[37] See further comment on the work of McDougal in Chaps. I, II, XI, and in Appendix C. McDougal's principal writings to date, mostly in collaboration, have been (in addition to the collection of essays cited in the previous note and the Hague Lectures cited in Note 10) *Law and Minimum World Public Order* (with Florentino P. Feliciano) New Haven, Yale University Press, 1961; *The Public Order of the Oceans* (with William Burke 1962), New Haven, Yale University Press; *Law and Public Order in Space* (with Harold D. Lasswell and Ivan Vlasic), New Haven, Yale University Press, 1963; *The Interpretation of Agreements and World Public Order* (with Harold D. Lasswell and James Miller), New Haven, Yale University Press, 1967.

maker authorized to make legal decisions. McDougal, with the help of a series of distinguished collaborators, has tried to take systematic account of all the variables that a fully rational decision-maker would want to take account of. These variables include all the factors bearing upon common interest and arising from what has happened in the past, what is expected in the present, and what is desired in the future. Thus the decision "required" by law is not determined exclusively by applying the past legal rules and precedents governing the situation.

The control asserted by the legal past is further diminished by McDougal's emphasis on the complementary norms relevant to any legal controversy. Viewed from the perspective of the decision-maker, then, there is available a plausible legal argument for almost any line of decision that seems to maximize the desired policy outcome. Assuming a national decision-maker, the content of desired policy should be an accommodation of the global (inclusive) interests of the world community and of the more exclusive interests of the nation-state on whose behalf he acts. McDougal relies heavily on Scelle's notion of *dédoublement fonctionnel* to conclude that the national decision-maker, since he is alternatively claimant and judge, can serve simultaneously both national and world policies.

The stress on the national decision-maker follows from McDougal's emphasis on the international legal order as relatively decentralized. Therefore, the most important authority functions are performed by the decision-makers attached to the actors with the predominance of effective control over behavior. As a result national decision-making is the basic focus for legal inquiry, and rather subordinate attention is accorded the central institutions of international affairs.[38]

McDougal has given a generalized description of the decision-making process, one that is free from conventional predispositions about the location and nature of the decision-maker. Thus it is not biased, as legal inquiry so often is, in favor of judicial decision-makers. Given McDougal's stress on the conjunction of power and authority, the focus of inquiry is upon the political official called upon to assert claims on behalf of the national system to act in world affairs or to react to foreign claims that affect its interests. It is participation in this claiming process that gives rise to the most typical situation in which international law is applied and shaped to conform to preferred policy. Such a dynamic orientation contrasts with the static conception of the relation between rules of law and behavior that normally dominates the legal imagina-

[38] See Myres S. McDougal, Harold D. Lasswell, and W. Michael Reismann, "The World Constitutive Process of Authoritative Decision," which will appear as a chapter in *The Future of the International Legal Order*, C. E. Black and Falk, eds., Princeton, Princeton University Press, Vol. I, 1969.

tion.[39] The notion of a legal decision as a claim, with promise of reciprocity, to act in a specified way authorized or challenged by a given decision-maker is very well adapted to the patterns of interaction in a decentralized political system. Such an approach also makes it possible to encompass different sorts of decision-makers with varying roles in national or international systems.

The test of legality (or of whether an action is in accordance with law) is the degree of an action's conformity to relevant community expectations as determined by authoritative decision-makers. This test of legality upsets traditional notions because, as contrasted with rule-orientation, it appears indefinite and subject to manipulation, and results in conclusions that will often be expressed as degrees of illegality. Its great advantage is that it reflects realistically both the decisiveness and the limits of decision-making in construing the requirements of law. In the first instance the content of law is determined by examining conclusions reached by those entrusted with the authority to make decisions.

The ultimate vindication of law for McDougal and his associates is its secularly based capacity to promote the fulfillment of social values specified in terms of human dignity, together with the realism with which it reflects the genuine shared demands and expectations of people. The content given to human dignity is rather clearly derived from the individualistic ethics of a progressive democratic society in the West. Each decision-maker, according to McDougal, is supposed to use the authority at his disposal to promote human dignity. Decision-makers are not encouraged to exercise a free-wheeling discretion, as the content of human dignity is to be objectively specified in terms of community preferences as understood through techniques of the social sciences and of other contemporary modes of acquiring knowledge. McDougal takes into account that one important community preference is that authority be used in a predictable fashion and that this use requires the decision-maker to accord considerable weight to precedent.

This comprehensive framework of inquiry has served McDougal and his associates well in their efforts to restate major portions of the substance of international law. A series of significant volumes has given a new insight into the traditional materials of international law in such areas as the law of outer space, the law of the oceans, and the law governing the use of violence. The quality of this scholarly achievement certainly places it among the great milestones in the history of international legal thought and assures it a permanent place in the study of the subject matter of international law.

Functionalism. There is a widespread acceptance by a group of influ-

---

[39] For an extreme example see Hans Kelsen, *The Principles of International Law*, New York, Rinehart, 1952.

ential international lawyers of the belief that the way to improve upon a positivist, rule-oriented approach is to correlate the development and study of international law with the satisfaction of certain social functions in the international system. The functionalist approach is represented, to varying degrees, by Percy Corbett, C. Wilfred Jenks, Wolfgang Friedmann, and Julius Stone. The functionalist point of departure is the sharp separation between interests *perceived* by nation-states as vital or as nonvital. So far as interests perceived as vital are concerned, it is realistic to conclude that states are not yet disposed to entrust their realization to the rules and procedures of international law. So far as interests perceived as nonvital are concerned, states are willing to entrust their realization to "the rule of law" and to support specialized international institutions dedicated to upholding them. These nonvital interests include such matters as postal service, telecommunications, health, conservation, safety, and cultural exchange. In such areas important policies are at stake, and international institutions can work effectively to bring satisfaction without in any way appearing to challenge the prerogatives of the sovereign state. Such an image of international legal order is especially appealing to those jurists who are rather skeptical about the capacity of international law to regulate the use of force by nation-states.

Recent functionalist work has thrown into useful focus the inventive capacity of legal technique to fashion solutions for social problems. Wolfgang Friedmann has demonstrated, for instance, the manner in which the idea of the international corporation and the joint venture has arisen to meet the needs of the developing countries for investment capital without at the same time arousing their suspicion of and hostility to the foreign investor.

Functionalism is really not a coherent framework of inquiry in the manner of McDougal. It is instead only a jurisprudential orientation that generates a certain style of inquiry and concentrates upon certain sorts of legal developments. Its basic outlook emphasizes only those activities not regarded by national governments as politically significant. Therefore, functionalists concentrate on the role of law at the margins of international conflict. Friedmann sums up the functionalist claim rather well: "The functionalist approach is thus no miracle solution, but it affords an important means of bypassing the propagandist atmosphere of political international assemblies, and of bringing the nations together in practical tasks of mutual interest and benefit."[40]

The approach closely parallels the efforts of David Mitrany to gain attention for the functionalist dynamic operative in international specialized agencies. He views these agencies as the most promising arenas with-

[40] Wolfgang Friedmann, *An Introduction to World Politics*, 5th edn., New York, St. Martin's Press, 1965, p. 57.

in which to promote political integration at the international level and to erode through time the preeminence of the sovereign state. It was Mitrany's central presupposition that if nations would cooperate in the satisfaction of the common needs, then an internationalist ethos would emerge among the civil servants working in these international institutions. These activities could begin modestly with such uncontroversial subject matter as the provision of an international postal service and the development of techniques to halt the international spread of disease. Gradually more sensitive subjects could be dealt with, such as labor standards or capital loans. As states gained confidence in the capacity of international institutions to perform services, and as the institutions gained confidence and independence, there would take place, according to the Mitrany view, a gradual expansion of activities and a slow withering away of state power. However, as Stanley Hoffmann, among others, has shown, the dynamics of functionalist growth do not assure a spillover into areas in which the vital interests of states are engaged.

Ernst Haas has recently reformulated Mitrany's conception of functionalism in a stimulating manner; he takes particular interest in the degree to which political conflict can contribute to rather than hamper (as Mitrany supposed) the growth of international institutions.[41] Using the experience of the International Labour Office as a principal example, Haas shows that the use of the I.L.O. by Western states to embarrass the Soviet Union for failures to allow trade unions requisite freedom created institutional precedents that were subsequently invoked by Afro-Asian states to bring pressure on Portugal and South Africa. Haas argues that the original precedent was a product of "politics" and that without this precedent it would have been impossible to organize the later action. A principal conclusion of Haas's study is that the avoidance of "politics" is not necessarily conducive to the growth of international institutions. This line of analysis can also lead to a parallel reformulation of the functionalist approach to international law, and especially it can lead to examinations of the law-creating potential of international crisis and conflict. Such a reexamination of the prospects for the growth of law could combat the literalism usually found in the functionalist literature, a literalism that assumes that the growth of law is dependent upon convergent interests and values and upon the voluntary acceptance of the benefits of international law in areas where cooperation seems possible without political friendship. The Haas variation on traditional functionalism suggests that out of a political clash there may arise a precedent that can be used for unintended future purposes.

[41] Ernst Haas, *Beyond the Nation-State*, Stanford, Stanford University Press, 1964.

Quantitative Empiricism. In recent years there has been a surge of interest and effort on the part of international lawyers seeking to apply the quantitative methods and canons of behaviorialism to the subject matter of international law and organization. Much of this work is at a relatively too early stage to assess in any very definitive fashion. What seems clear, however, is that the data of international legal studies are susceptible to manipulation by the newer techniques associated with modern statistical methods and with computer analysis. It seems clear that future work on international legal materials, especially the work of nonlegally trained social scientists, will give increasing prominence to these "harder" techniques of data collection and analysis. A behavioral methodology assures the elimination of rampant intuitionalism and of covert moralism, features that have been most responsible for downgrading international law as a concern of the political science discipline.

Some of the most interesting work currently being done involves the interrelated use of computers for data-coding and factor-analysis for data-interpreting. Studies of the voting patterns in international organizations and multilateral conferences illustrate this approach. The studies by Haywood Alker and Bruce Russet of United Nations voting behavior and by Robert Friedheim of the voting patterns of the Geneva Conferences (1958, 1960) on the Law of the Sea are, perhaps, the best examples.[42] Large-scale use of computers is also being made to analyze the contents of documentary materials, such as international agreements or parliamentary debates in international organizations. An outstanding illustration of work along these lines is the exceedingly ambitious United Nations Treaty Series Project being conducted at the University of Washington under the direction of Peter Rohn. In a series of articles Rohn has reported his interim findings that bear directly on very central questions about the volume, shape, and character of formal interactions between states and groups of states.[43] Rohn appears to be building up a rigorous empirical base upon which to erect a new, more persuasive account of international legal order as a functioning reality.[44]

[42] Haywood R. Alker, Jr., and Bruce M. Russett, *World Politics in the General Assembly*, New Haven, Yale University Press, 1965; Robert L. Friedheim, "Factor Analysis as a Tool in Studying the Law of the Sea," in Lewis M. Alexander, ed., *The Law of the Sea*, Columbus, Ohio State University Press, 1967, pp. 47-70.

[43] See e.g., Peter H. Rohn, "Canada in the United Nations Treaty Series: A Global Perspective," *Canadian Yearbook of International Law, 1966*, pp. 102-30;

id., "Institutionalism in the Law of Treaties: A Case of Combining Teaching and Research," *Proceedings American Society of International Law, 1965*, pp. 93-98; for general assessment see Richard W. Edwards, Jr., "Electronic Data Processing and International Law Documentation," 61 *American Journal of International Law* 87-92 (1967).

[44] E.g., Rohn, "A Legal Theory of International Organization," *Turkish Yearbook of International Relations, 1964*, pp.

Other related work has been done by social scientists that deserves attention. Efforts have been made to study problems of arms control and disarmament through reliance on the interrelated techniques of gaming and simulation.

In general, the present period is a time of experimentation and innovation. The critics of quantitative empiricism are often overly impatient, complaining about the truistic character of the findings or about the research being focused upon what is quantifiable rather than upon what is significant. It seems too early to pass judgment; we are still only dealing with first-generational efforts at quantitative empiricism. Methodological receptivity seems appropriate, especially as the proliferation of actors and data makes the task of systematic research and analysis increasingly difficult to conduct along traditional lines.

Other approaches to international legal studies would appear, at minimum, to benefit greatly from the selective application of quantitative methods to work within their domain of concern.

Systems Theory. A fourth major approach evident in international legal studies arises from a reliance upon "the international system" as a basic concept by which to organize the contextual data relevant to the role of law. System theorists tend to specify historical or analytical models on the way in which power is distributed and conflict conducted as a basis upon which to assess the role of law. The rationale for this approach is that (1) context is relevant and (2) the relevance of context can be established through the specification of a small number of strategic variables. The distribution of power among the units in a system and the stakes of conflict are especially significant variables in identifying the system and distinguishing it from another.

Morton Kaplan has done the most fundamental work to vindicate the use of systems theory as the basis for the study of international law.[45] Kaplan's analytic models of plausible international systems suggest rather clearly the usefulness of investigating the extent to which the character and role of international law are conditioned by the character of the international system. In collaboration with Nicholas deB. Katzenbach, Kaplan has taken a further step in this direction in *The Political Foundations of International Law*.[46] The Kaplan-Katzenbach book demonstrates the value of the systems approach by its very incisive analysis of norms of nonintervention in the balance-of-power and loose bipolar international systems. Kaplan and Katzenbach effectively dis-

19-53; *id.*, "Turkish Treaties in Global Perspective," *Turkish Yearbook of International Relations, 1965*, pp. 119-60.
  [45] Morton A. Kaplan, *System and Process in International Politics*, New York, Wiley, 1957. See also Oran R. Young, "A Systemic Approach to International Politics," Research Monograph No. 33, Princeton University, Center of International Studies, June 30, 1968.
  [46] New York, Wiley, 1961.

close the relevance of political factors to the operation of law in world affairs. Their approach interestingly appraises the strengths and weaknesses of international law by reference to the kind of international system that is posited.

Stanley Hoffmann has tried to orient the systems approach to international law in the tradition of historical sociology.[47] Thus Hoffmann endeavors to construct a system by observing the patterns of conflict in a past period of international relations and by correlating these patterns with prevailing social structures operative in international society. This effort is in contrast, one would suppose in view of Hoffmann's earlier critique of Kaplan's approach,[48] to the more analytic models of the international system. The difference appears to be mainly one of intellectual style, Kaplan preferring an analytical mode of rhetoric and Hoffmann a more historico-sociological mode. Further, Kaplan derives many of his models from the history of the main currents of international politics, whereas Hoffmann seems responsive to the conceptualization of the main systemic alternatives that have been derived by Kaplan. The analytic mode does permit somewhat greater freedom of inquiry, as it encourages projection of trends in world affairs and allows an inquirer to posit possible future international systems.[49] This orientation toward the future is compatible with those features of McDougal's approach that call upon the international lawyer to engineer a new international order that more clearly fulfills the values of human dignity.[50]

The work of Kaplan has stimulated a more programmatic use of models of the future of the international legal order by Saul Mendlovitz and the author.[51] We posit a future international system in the form of the Clark-Sohn plan for a vastly strengthened United Nations operating in a totally disarmed world.[52] The Clark-Sohn model gives more specific content to an international system than does the analytic style of Kaplan. Our efforts might be regarded as using the rather utopian proposals of Clark and Sohn to write one possible history of the future and thereby to achieve the same kind of empirical grounding in the actuality of social structure and political conflict that Hoffmann derives from his scanning of the history of the past.

47 "International Systems and International Law," in Knorr-Verba, note 36, pp. 205-37.

48 See Hoffmann's excerpt from his own essay in Stanley Hoffmann, ed., *Contemporary Theory in International Relations*, Englewood Cliffs, N.J., Prentice-Hall, 1960, pp. 40-50.

49 See Chap. XXI.

50 I have undertaken with Cyril E. Black of Princeton a multivolume study along these lines under the general title *The Fu-*

ture of the International Legal Order* (cited in note 38).

51 *The Strategy of World Order*: Vol. I, *Toward a Theory of War Prevention*; Vol. II, *International Law*; Vol. III, *The United Nations*; Vol. IV, *Disarmament and Economic Development*, New York, World Law Fund, 1966, 1967.

52 Grenville Clark and Louis B. Sohn, *World Peace Through World Law*, Cambridge, Harvard University Press, 3rd edn., 1966.

We use the distance between the present international system and the Clark-Sohn model posited as a preferred future international system as the real center of inquiry. We argue and organize the data of international law to emphasize the prospects for and obstacles to transition from one international system to another. This brings analysis to grips with the hard problems of assessing the limits of political attainability, whereas at the same time the approach accepts the commandment issued by McDougal and Lasswell that the international lawyer employ his professional training to invent, appraise, and create a better international legal order.

Phenomenological Perspectives. There is, finally, an approach to the study of the international legal order that emphasizes depth analyses of single "cases." The objective of these analyses is both to clarify the particular set of issues involved in a dispute and to illuminate the general structure of the legal order. Brainerd Currie has used this approach to cast great light upon fundamental problems in the field of the conflict of laws.[53] In my judgment, cases such as *Sabbatino, Shimoda,* or *The South West Africa Cases* all offer the international lawyer excellent material for the development of general theory from a phenomenological perspective, that is, from a perspective that emphasizes the concrete phenomena of legal experience and finds support in the philosophical tradition associated with phenomenology.[54, 55]

The extension of phenomenology to international legal studies should be made in explicit terms. There is a need for a jurisprudential rationale. It is important to distinguish between the penetration of a particular case to discover the general attributes of the legal system and the traditional analysis of a line of cases to discern the evolution of legal doctrine. The phenomenologist is interested in the case as a useful example only when it both typifies and enacts fundamental legal controversies of the sort that go on in a variety of distinct substantive settings.

"The case" as the unit of analysis requires some explanation. A judicial decision is a convenient example of a case, but is only one example. A particular civil war might serve as a case for the study of the inter-

[53] Brainerd Currie, *Selected Essays on the Conflict of Laws,* Durham, N.C., Duke University Press, 1963.

[54] For attempts to carry out this procedure see Falk, *The Role of Domestic Courts in the International Legal Order,* Syracuse, Syracuse University Press, 1964; id., *Legal Order in a Violent World,* Princeton, Princeton University Press, 1968, pp. 374-413. See also Chaps. V and XII.

[55] For the character of phenomenology see Joseph Quentin Lauer, *Triumph and Subjectivity: An Introduction to Transcendental Phenomenology,* Fordham University Press, 1958; A. T. Tymiemiecka, *Phenomenology and Science in Contemporary European Thought,* New York, Farrar, Straus, 1962. For backgrounds see E. Husserl, *Ideen zu einer reinen Phänomenologie und phänomenologischen Philosophie,* Halle, M. Niemeyer, 1913; English translation published under the title, *Ideas: General Introduction to Pure Phenomenology,* New York, Collier Books, 1962.

national law of civil wars,[56] or a debate in the Security Council might serve to provide a phenomenological basis for the analysis of the international protection of human rights, the scope of domestic jurisdiction, or the legal character of peacekeeping operations.[57]

In conclusion, then, the phenomenological approach is a technique useful for combining concrete analysis of legal problems that are intrinsically interesting with the formulation of more general ideas about the relationship between international law and international behavior.

[56] In 1966 the Carnegie Corporation awarded the American Society of International Law a grant to enable the study of a series of specific civil wars as "cases" to create empirical support for generalizing about the international law of civil war in the contemporary world.

[57] This type of analysis is used in the fourth lecture of the series cited in note 31. The cases used are the Security Council debates concerning Goa (1961), the U.N.'s Stanleyville Operation (1964), and Indonesia's guerrilla activity in Malaysia (1964). See Chapter IV.

XVI. Wolfgang Friedmann

The Changing Structure of International Law incorporates and organizes most of the important thinking that Wolfgang Friedmann has devoted to problems of international law throughout his distinguished career. As such, it offers a convenient focus for an appraisal of Friedmann's work.[1]

Changing Structure provides an extraordinary *tour d'horizon* of happenings significant for understanding the character and development of modern international law. It is extraordinary, in part, simply because Friedmann knows so much and possesses a talent for combining generalization and concrete example. This talent is notable for at least two reasons. First, the use of examples allows us to follow closely the argument of the book at each of its numerous stages. There is no ambiguity and no excuse for being in doubt about Friedmann's meaning. Second, the willingness to generalize enables a reader to come away with a nontrivial and coherent view of the substantive issues treated. Friedmann is evolving a general view of the structure of international law that can be adopted by an inquirer as a continuing frame of reference that may help organize further study of specific subject matters.

In addition, Friedmann combines an impressive awareness of the political constraints that hamper the growth of law in world affairs with the sort of pragmatic idealism that is constantly searching for feasible ways to foster the extension of the rule of law. Friedmann is always on the lookout for particular solutions to particular problems. The intellectual enterprise is carried on in a nonpartisan spirit that admirably succeeds in excluding from analysis *ex parte* perspectives of nationality and ideology. *The Changing Structure of International Law* can be read with benefit and without irritant by students of the subject situated in any social system or culture in the world.

I am particularly grateful for Friedmann's nonpartisanship. Let us be clear. Nonpartisanship does not imply neutrality in relation to the outcome of major international conflicts. It implies only a posture that emphasizes the nonpolitical character of legal analysis. Rules are not manipulated to rationalize those we like or castigate those we abhor; the jurist does not volunteer for the role of national advocate. Part of the reason that I wish to call special attention to this virtue of Friedmann's book is that it is not a very fashionable virtue. For instance, the extraordinary achievements of Myres S. McDougal and the fine

---

[1] New York, Columbia University Press, 1964 (hereafter page references are indi- cated by insertion in parentheses in the text).

effort of Kenneth S. Carlston[2] are seriously flawed by their inability to suppress either the rhetoric or the attitudes of Western statesmen in their discussion of the role of law in the control of international conflict. Their inability to purge their analyses of the accident of nationality undermines the confidence of noncommitted readers and blurs the distinction between legal analysis and national propaganda. It is one thing for a great international lawyer either to take on a client (whether it be corporate or governmental) or to write broadsides as an impassioned citizen; to analyze and appraise the developing character of international law as an impartial expert with a point of view transcending the national angle of vision entails an objective orientation, or at least the quest for objectivity. Friedmann sustains the outlook of an impartial expert, appraising developments from the perspective of world legal order, describing law and behavior without taking pains to avoid national self-criticism or making special exertions to vindicate national policy of dubious legality.

In a sense, the ability to achieve political distance from the events under analysis expresses Friedmann's more fundamental intellectual style. This style emphasizes command over the specifics in the relevant subject matter and shows most concern with problem-solving in limited situations. Friedmann distrusts grand strategy, the systemic overview, and even the rigorous methodological canons of modern social science. He prefers, instead, the sober, informed, and conscientious analysis of an intelligent observer who approaches problems without a heavy freight of dogma or passion. Values are relevant, but as a constituent of the facts and as conditioned by the various constraints of a particular setting. In his Foreword to his influential text, *An Introduction to World Politics*, Friedmann makes explicit his conviction that it is essential to grasp the facts in all their complexity to achieve a responsible outlook relevant for world order issues. Friedmann is keenly aware of the dangers that arise when a government explains away recalcitrant problems by blaming "an enemy": "Distortion by oversimplification is one of the most dismal features of present-day international propaganda. . . . And one of the greatest threats to democracy is the increasing temptation to imitate the totalitarian example, by singling out an arch-enemy, as a substitute for sober thinking."[3] I refer to Friedmann's general outlook here because it discloses clearly what underlies and informs his approach to international law. In putting the approach to work Friedmann honors his own code. The work is problem-centered; ideals are conditioned by practicalities; the complexities have been mastered and great restraint is displayed in offering solu-

2 See Chap. XVIII.
3 Wolfgang G. Friedmann, *An Intro-* *duction to World Politics*, New York, St. Martin's Press, 1965, 5th edn., p. XII.

tions. Hopes are neither falsely dashed, nor falsely raised. Friedmann achieves the responsible prudence he commends.

Such prudence does not imply that Friedmann reaches trivial conclusions. Quite the contrary. A mastery of the facts discloses the vast changes in international law that have taken place and must be understood. It is not enough to modify and extend traditional conceptions about the nature of international law, for "it is submitted that the extent of the structural changes in international relations in our time requires a far more basic reorientation of our thinking in international law" (p. 3). Friedmann seeks to achieve this reorientation by dividing contemporary international law into three main divisions: (1) the international law of coexistence; (2) the international law of cooperation: universal concerns; and (3) the international law of cooperation: regional groupings (pp. 60-71). The first of these three categories is roughly identified with the traditional effort of international law to delimit respective spheres of sovereign authority and to set up standards and procedures for the resolution of disputes between nations. These ordering tasks remain valid and crucial and should continue in the midst of intense and dangerous ideological and political antagonisms. In the nuclear age the search for minimum world public order can never be suspended. As the importance of avoiding large-scale warfare has increased, the need has grown gradually more urgent to adjust or contain differences, however severe, by nonviolent means.

But alongside this essential type of ordering activity, there has grown up a series of positive demands for cooperation in an ever more interdependent and complicated world. Friedmann highlights this new emphasis in international affairs by stressing the developmental and cooperative features and potentialities of this evolving international legal order. He adapts this functional emphasis on cooperative relations to the realities of political conflict by separating those subject matters where world conflicts do not matter (universal concerns) from those where they do (regional or subsystemic concerns). Friedmann's interpretation of the growth of international law is creative and important because international conflict is presented neither as a decisive obstacle nor is it presumed irrelevant to the growth of the international law of cooperation. The prospects for cooperation depend in each instance upon a careful scrutiny of the particular subject matter. Where the subject matter is not yet perceived as important to the resolution of political conflict, as with weather control, international communications, or conservation, then the international law of cooperation can develop rapidly on a global basis. However, when, as with human rights or business regulation, there are strong basic disagreements about what should be the governing policy, then it will be impossible to build universal legal standards, and this should be frankly acknowledged. In this regard, Friedmann criticizes Jenks for his tendency "to gloss over the divisive factors in his enthusiasm to promote a universal legal order" (297-98 n.1).[4] Friedmann submits that in the event of a value consensus insufficient to support global standards and institutions, it is appropriate to examine the situation on a regional level. Friedmann summarizes trends toward regional law, giving special attention to the emerging law of European legal communities. Here, shared values and interests, similar stages of economic development, and common problems may support a degree of legal integration impossible on the universal level. "The general approach to the changing structure of international society . . . leads to the conception of international law as a stratified structure, moving on three different levels." (p. 58).[5] Friedmann informs us that "the substantiation" of this approach is the main substance of *The Changing Structure*.

This substantiation takes various forms. Friedmann first undertakes to specify the nature of cooperative international law. "Unlike the traditional law of nations, which is predicated upon the assumption of conflicts of national interests, which it seeks to stabilize and regulate, cooperative international law requires a *community* of interests" (p. 57). A requirement of some sense of community does not presuppose "the abolition of self-interest," but it does "radically affect the dimensions and objectives of self-interest" (p. 57). Throughout his analysis, Friedmann accepts the continuing primacy of national interests in shaping the behavior of states involved in building a new international law. In fact, he views ideological, cultural, and economic differences among states as subordinate to the tendency of all states, regardless of their particular orientation, to promote the maximization of their relative power, prestige, and privilege within the overall international system. For this reason he is suspicious of reliance upon national decision-makers to develop common standards of international law in areas where there exists a conflict of interest among principal national actors, e.g., foreign investment.[6] Accordingly, Friedmann is critical of "too easy an acceptance of George Scelle's conception of the *dédoublement fonctionnel*, the dual function of state authorities as organs

---

[4] Cf. C. Wilfred Jenks, *The Common Law of Mankind*, New York, Praeger, 1958, pp. 63-172.

[5] Cf. Stanley Hoffmann has proposed a quite different division of the international law found "in stable systems" into "the law of the political framework," "the law of reciprocity," and "the law of the community." Hoffmann, "International Systems and International Law," in Klaus Knorr and Sidney Verba, eds., *The International System*, Princeton, Princeton University Press, 1961, pp. 205-37, see esp. pp. 212-13.

[6] E.g., at 371: "The contributions of the national courts have to be viewed with caution since the interpretation of international law through national courts is subject to national prejudices and passions, as has been clearly evident in recent years in the various national judicial reactions to nationalisations of foreign property."

of the respective national communities and of the international community." (p. 148). It is too easy because it "conceals the tension" between the dispositions of national policy and the desiderata of world order. This issue is, in part, at the center of the controversy about the usefulness of the act of state doctrine in the *Sabbatino* context: Can a national court be trusted to develop useful rules of customary international law to govern compensation for the expropriation of alien property located abroad?[7] The answer depends somewhat on the extent to which one has confidence in the present capability of a national court to detach itself from national values when deciding a dispute in which one of the parties is challenging those values. Friedmann adduces evidence to support his distrust of domestic courts. In practice, national judges rarely find that international law thwarts national policy. The nationality of the forum, more than the logic of the legal authority or the persuasiveness of policy considerations, is the best indicator of the probable outcome when a case presenting a challenge to national preference comes before a domestic court. I would add to Friedmann's appraisal the point that the authoritativeness of international law in general is reduced by entrusting its interpretation in prominent instances—such as expropriation cases—to decision-makers who cannot be regarded as impartial.

Friedmann also regards the gradual emergence of a more globally interdependent content for national interest as the world's best single hope to avert nuclear catastrophe. Friedmann does not put much faith in the gradual triumph of altruism in international politics. He does, however, take seriously the capacity of men to reorganize the world to avoid their own destruction: "Peace on earth may either be the implementation of the love of man for all fellowmen, as preached by all the great religions of the world, or it may be seen as an indispensable condition of human and national survival, and it is this aspect which is more likely than love to guide the policies of nations" (p. 53). Friedmann avocates the pursuit of enlightened self-interest, to promote the growth of a tolerable system of world order.

Friedmann is dubious about "the constitutional approach," which proposes control over world politics by greatly augmented international institutions. This kind of approach, of which the Clark-Sohn plan is taken as the prototype, represents an instance of grand strategy, the value of which Friedmann doubts.[8] Friedmann writes of the Clark-Sohn plan that it ignores "the basic social factors of international society," and most of all, it fails to appreciate the fact that international

---

[7] Cf. Chaps. XIII and XIV.
[8] Grenville Clark and Louis B. Sohn, *World Peace Through World Law*, Cambridge, Harvard University Press, 1966, 3rd rev. edn.

conflict cannot be overcome by devising organs and procedures, however appropriate (p. 276).

"By contrast, a functional approach to international organization correlates the development of international law and organization with political and social realities and tendencies of international life" (p. 276). The functional approach will give importance to the distinction between regional and universal concerns at the present stage of international society and correlate a strategy for world order with the specific needs of various subject matters. Functional growth produces a patchwork development of institutions and legal order, arising from the spirit of flexibility that encourages regimes of legal order to be tailored to particular configurations of needs and interests. Friedmann concludes that "[t]here is, of course, no doubt that it is the functional approach which has triumphed in post-war international organization, resulting in a complex pattern of organizations with different objectives, constitutions and powers. What is asserted here is not only that this is the actual pattern of international organization but that it is the only possible one at this time, reflecting the actual structure of international relations" (p. 277). This assessment may unnecessarily claim too much. Is there any necessity to choose between the constitutional and the functional approaches? Friedmann has not been very successful in demonstrating that functional and constitutional approaches to world order are incompatible, nor does he try. The piecemeal bias, common to lawyers of gradualist persuasion, expresses a distaste for metaphysics, utopias, and grand conceptions. But where is the evidence against radical system changes? The frequency of domestic revolutions attests to the occurrence of such changes in domestic society. Why can there not be comparable changes in international society? The rapidity of the process of decolonization offers an example of rapid, drastic change in the character of the international legal order. And after major international wars, serious institutional changes have been introduced by agreement of dominant national governments. Rather than proposing a choice between the functional and constitutional approaches, it would be more convincing to analyze the prospects for both, regarding functional development not only for its own sake but to set the stage for the constitutional revision, and looking upon constitutional revision as an eventual necessity, whether the necessity is borne of catastrophe or enlightenment.

Friedmann's attempt to substantiate the changes in the structure of international law leads him down many avenues of inquiry. There are useful discussions of regional developments in Europe, of such new participants in international life as the public international corporation, the private corporation, and the individual, of the extension of international law to cover the activities of non-Western states and of their distinct cultural perspectives, of such new subfields as international constitutional, administrative, labor, criminal, commercial, economic development, corporation, antitrust, and tax law, of the problems of regulating the use of force and of facilitating welfare activities, and of the impact of communist ideology and of underdevelopment upon the effectiveness and shape of international law.

Changing Structure is impressive, in part, because Friedmann displays a masterly command over the specifics in these many disparate areas, and yet manages to demarcate the general developmental trends. General assessments emerge naturally from an exposure to evidence and trends, rather than by the authority and appeal of the noted author. As well, Friedmann demarcates the province of law by focusing upon legal technique and instrumentality without confining analysis to a stultifying emphasis upon legal doctrine. Friedmann's analytical focus is always upon what law is doing to solve live social problems, given the constraints on legal action properly attributable to the political environment.

Despite this sophistication about the political setting of international law, Friedmann writes as if modern social science did not exist. There is no attempt to take account of the relevance of the literature dealing with the structure and resolution of conflict, economic development, the new states, civil strife, modern war, and so on that has been written by nonlawyers. Friedmann is also unconcerned with the development of better methods by which to analyze the phenomena of international law. Friedmann calls in vague and general terms for greater collaboration between international lawyers, comparative lawyers, and substantive specialists (pp. 186-87). No attention is given as to the forms of thought that should guide such a collaboration. McDougal's contribution to the understanding of the international legal order is so great, in part, because he has developed a systematic style of thought. Friedmann is a traditionalist when it comes to methodology. He relies upon intelligence, erudition, and a few pervading themes (e.g., the precedence of interests and the threefold division of international law) to organize the material. For this reason *Changing Structure* is more to be read than studied. Its principal pay-off is informational. Once one is familiar with the information and the point of view, there is little left to learn. In this respect it is like most books, but not nearly so seminal in Anglo-American traditions of legal thought as is Carlston's *Laws and Organization in World Society*, the major writings by McDougal and his associates, or Kaplan and Katzenbach's *The Political Foundations of International Law* (1961). Innovative methodology, radical reinterpretations, and definitive reference works create the milestones in legal research. It might be possible to consider Friedmann's book to be a radical interpretation. Such a conclusion would certainly be in order if the main themes had been introduced more systematically into the substance of each chapter. In many of the chapters, however, one feels that the contention about the simultaneous development of an international law of coexistence, of regional and of global cooperation, is brought in, if at all, as something of an afterthought in the spirit of a theoretical embellishment or flourish. There is no integral organizing conception that pervades the substantive discussions.

Having characterized *The Changing Structure* in general terms, it may be useful to consider briefly Friedmann's treatment of a few representative topics. The value of the book arises in part because it contains nonsuperficial discussions of many central questions in international law. My selection gives no more than a glimpse of Friedmann's remarkable control over the subject matter of the discipline; the subject matter of international law is more and more intimidating as a result of its growing complexity and magnitude. The following topics have been selected to illustrate Friedmann's approach and outlook: force, foreign investment, the new states, and human rights.

Force. Friedmann's discussion of the role of law in regulating force in international society is both excellent and disappointing. It is an excellent discussion because it takes imaginative account of the relevance of nuclear weapons to the problem of waiting until attacked to assert the right of self-defense and it gives appropriate emphasis to the significance of indirect aggression as the major impermissible use of violence in world affairs today. There is an informed account of the main forms of indirect aggression and of the limited role that international law can expect to play in view of the conflict of interests that continue to block efforts at fact-finding and regulation by third-party procedures.

The discussion of international force is disappointing because it is misleading in some respects. For instance, Friedmann gives credence to the notion that "game theorists" are responsible for the main outlines of nuclear strategy (p. 259). The logic of deterrence has become complicated, but it has not, except for some very special and limited cases, been worked out in light of the postulates and methods of game theory. There is also the suggestion made, although somewhat qualifiedly, that the existence of nuclear weapons eliminates traditional incentives to have recourse to war (p. 253). This overlooks the continuing temptation of secondary powers to commit aggression to attain national objectives and resolve international disputes of subsystemic dimension. Indonesia, China, the United Arab Republic, even India have not pursued policies that suggest an acceptance of the conclusion that war is obsolete. Friedmann gives no sustained attention to varieties of conventional and subconventional war between states that are unrelated to the occurrence of indirect aggression or intervention. As a result, the problem of force and security is understood almost exclusively from the viewpoint of the nuclear superpowers. From their viewpoint the problems of anticipatory self-defense and indirect aggression are so central that Friedmann's conclusion about "the tacit abandonment of war, at least major wars" does not seem too unreasonable (p. 254). But what makes a war "major"? Friedmann provides no indicator; as a result it becomes impossible to construe either the accuracy or the significance of his statement.

Friedmann makes the point that "[t]he organization of peace differs from that of any other human interest in that it can only be universal" (p. 258). What underlies this view is that "the amalgamation of states in larger non-universal groups . . . only reduces the number of potential belligerents" (p. 258). Thus, regionalism is no final solution to the problem of war. So long as there exist two or more centers of power, the danger of global warfare remains. It is clearly if vacuously correct to point out that international war remains a theoretical possibility so long as there exists more than one pole of military power in the world. But the stress on this theoretical possibility distracts attention from assessing the risks and dangers of an international system with strong regional actors relative to present risks and dangers. The emergence of regional units would result in a transfer of authority and capability away from the national level without any likely corresponding transfer of political allegiance. As a consequence, ordering capabilities may become less closely tied to the emotive energies of nationalism.

Regional institutions may also play valuable implementing roles in disarming or disarmed worlds. It is not necessary to claim that regional institutions will or can be made to play a positive role in a peace system, but in more modest vein, that we do not yet know enough to reject their relevance out of hand, as Friedmann does.

I would like to suggest some reasons for supposing that regional institutions might be in a position to make a constructive contribution to the creation and maintenance of an effective peace system. The relevance of regional security arrangements at this stage in the development of international society would seem to depend upon the character of intraregional conflict, and upon whether there exists any serious expectation of the development of globally organized security and welfare systems. The appraisal will probably vary from region to region.[9]

[9] For an analysis that develops this, idea of the variable character of regional politics and the variable interactions between regions and global political patterns see Oran R. Young, "Political Discontinuities in the International System," *World Politics*, xx, 3 (April 1968), 369-92.

The prospect of interregional conflict is also dependent on the extent to which dominant modes of international conflict are between rather than within regions; as well, this prospect depends on global control capabilities. It may be that if regional organizations were to become effective security organs for intraregional conflict, then disarmament could be more easily negotiated to eliminate the capability for inter- regional warfare. A regionally based system of global security might evolve that was reinforced by a universal system of disarmament. Thus regional arrangements might both set the stage for drastic disarmament and assume a major share of responsibility for peacekeeping in a dis- arming world. The anticipation of a disarmed world, to the extent that it takes place seriously at all, is usually envisaged as involving a choice between international and supranational systems.[10] The supranational system is assumed to be centralized in global institutions, including a world police force more powerful than any state or combination of states. One might, however, think about a supranational system organ- ized around regional and/or superpower poles of power and authority as an approach intermediate between international and global supra- national conceptions. Such an intermediate image has the apparently attractive feature of appearing to compromise the United States and Soviet view of a disarmed world. This regional variant of existing schemes for world order is attractive because it may allow the disarma- ment process to proceed to drastic levels despite the persistence of rather intense modes of intraregional conflict. It is also attractive as a model because it does not completely centralize power in a disarming world, thereby preserving values of autonomy and making the world less vulnerable to whatever praetorian inclinations on the part of the world police appeared. It might also be easier to agree on peacekeeping and verification machinery if regional actors were allowed to manage intraregional conflict and to have a share in the administration of dis- armament. Whatever the merit of these speculations, they underscore how little is now known about the conditions of a stable world peace system. Because so little is genuinely known there is neither reason nor occasion to accept Friedmann's flat statement that the prospects for world peace are directly dependent on the evolution of a universal and nonfragmented system of world security.

Foreign Investment. Friedmann is at his very best on the subject of foreign investment, although his treatment of the subject is dispersed

[10] Cf. Klaus Knorr, "Supranational ver- sus International Models for General and Complete Disarmament," in Falk and Richard J. Barnet, eds., *Security in Dis- armament*, Princeton, Princeton University Press, 1965, pp. 384-410; see also "The Russian Idea of a World Without Arms," Appendix to Arthur Larson, ed., *A War- less World*, New York, McGraw-Hill, 1963, pp. 175-209.

throughout the book.[11] His very considerable assets include knowledge, a sympathetic appreciation of the contending perspectives, and an imaginative sense of the relevance of technique to the solution of issues of principle and policy. Friedmann is aware of traditional patterns of investment, of the attacks upon it, and of the new forms of investor protection. As such he discusses with wisdom and ingenuity issues such as the balance between sovereign control over economic development and the protection of the foreign investor.[12] He proposes, for instance, adapting the principle of unjust enrichment to controversies about how much compensation international law requires an expropriating state to pay.[13] This suggestion cuts through the rather banal debate about whether the standard of "prompt, adequate, and effective" persists, or, in fact, ever existed. Reliance upon the logic of unjust enrichment permits, indeed requires, a decision-maker to take specific equities into account in fixing the level of appropriate compensation. The proper measure of compensation may be reduced if a foreign investor's concession "has been granted under conditions of political and military domination and under financial conditions starkly different from those prevailing in an open market." As Friedmann says, "it would be neither realistic nor equitable not to take into account the 'unjust' enrichment that has accrued to the foreign interests as a result of their privileged position" (pp. 208-09). The proper level of compensation is achieved by "a balance of relevant considerations."

Friedmann's approach encourages a fresh, nondogmatic start on the need to rest international law upon the *perceived* common or convergent interests of the capital-exporting and capital-importing states. The formerly colonial states, in particular, are understandably hostile to legitimizing economic relationships established decades ago as a by-product of their colonial or subordinated status. The overall attitude of this large group of states toward international law may be poisoned simply by the insistence that what is widely conceived of as a legacy of imperialism remains valid as a consequence of its embodiment in customary international law. It is essential to discover ways to distinguish between meritorious and illicit investment claims. Friedmann has sketched out the basis for one reasonable approach. His approach is able to distinguish between the squealing exploiter and the defrauded investor, that is, between business interests that have taken long advantage of unequal bargaining conditions and political corruption, and those that

---

[11] See esp. pp. 176-84, 200-01, 356-61.

[12] Friedmann's approach follows rather closely the line developed so well by Garcia Amador in his work on state responsibility for the International Law Commission. See esp. "Fourth Report on International Responsibility," U.N. Doc. A/CN. 4/119 (1959).

[13] This use of unjust enrichment illustrates Friedmann's sensitivity to the relevance of general principles of law for the solution of various problems of ordering relations among states.

have entered on reasonable conditions with reasonable expectations that correspond to normal business arrangements in developed countries.

Friedmann also considers recent developments affecting the making and protection of foreign investment. He discusses, for instance, the relevance of investment guaranty programs, the new law of economic development, the importance of "joint ventures" that merge foreign and local capital, and the increasing role of international lending institutions in providing equity and stability in a situation of capital acquisition. Among his many valuable discussions, I would single out for special commendation his subtle discussion of the interpenetration of public and private elements in the typical international transaction between the developed and developing countries.

Human Rights. Friedmann does not discuss human rights in any great detail, but he is skeptical about the attainment of universal standards in a divided world: "The sphere of human rights is the field in which the divisions of values and ideologies are the deepest, and most inimical to a universal order" (pp. 297-98 n1). This kind of perception leads Friedmann to observe that "[i]t is not, therefore, surprising that the only effective implementation, on a limited scale, of an international protection of the individual against violation of certain human rights has been achieved within a limited and more closely knit community of states, the Council of Europe" (p. 243). Therefore, human rights are approached as the subject par excellence to illustrate the thesis that what world conflict obstructs on a universal level can often be attained on a regional level.

Friedmann's analysis appears far too concerned with the ability or nonability of sovereign states to agree upon enforcement machinery for human rights conventions. I regard the European promotion of human rights as an interesting experiment in international organization, but rather unconnected with the actualities of protection. In the European setting the participating national governments are subject to alterations of policy arising from changes in governments committed to upholding minimum standards for the human rights subject to regulation. No evidence has emerged to suggest that the European system has any influence whatsoever over a determined violator. The repressive regime that came to power in Greece during 1967 has shown no responsiveness to adhere to European standards of human rights.

Actually the development of a universal concern with the attainment of racial equality is one of the few areas in which common values have joined political rivals in a genuine common cause. The cause of racial equality is undoubtedly the great transnational movement of the modern period, one in which both organs of the United Nations and private pressure groups are likely to play an increasing role. Already the existence of a dramatic consensus in the United Nations against racial oppression seems to have influenced the whole climate of national opinion on these issues. The success and pace of the civil rights movement in the United States during the 1950's and early 1960's seems to have been decisively conditioned by sentiments of the Afro-Asian states, reinforced by the belief that the overall success of United States foreign policy depended upon the national image on this issue that formed in "the third world." It is precisely because this attitude toward human rights is so universally shared that it achieves a degree of political effectiveness even without any formal sanctioning activity. Objection to the racial policies of the Republic of South Africa present a major international dispute in which almost all states agree as to its proper outcome and as to the dependence on supranational coercion to reach it. There is little doubt that external pressure will grow and that either the government of South Africa will succumb to the will of the international community or face the prospects of internal war and external attack. Already the disposition exists to use the authority of the United Nations to impose sanctions short of war. I stress the South Africa question at length because it shows that the main area of concern about human rights, is not an arena of divisiveness in the modern world, but rather gives basis for the most solid hope of legal ecumenicism in the contemporary world.[14] In this regard, the ability of the General Assembly to endorse the Principles of Nuremberg and the Declaration of Human Rights is a signal progressive step, and not without influence on the development of national ideals and practices.[15]

New States. Friedmann has an original and powerful interpretation of the entry into international society of the states of Asia and Africa after World War II, and of the significance of this entry for international law. Friedmann does not consider the differing cultural outlooks of the new states very relevant to the nature of their participation in international society.[16] He definitely disagrees with Northrop who contends that an adequate contemporary international legal order depends upon first embodying in international law a cultural synthesis. Friedmann also disagrees with Jenks who contends that if the main independent cultural traditions are examined carefully enough a consensus supportive of the

[14] I have made this argument at some length in Falk, *The Role of Domestic Courts in the International Legal Order*, Syracuse, Syracuse University Press, 1964, pp. 71-77, 64-114.

[15] See Egon Schwelb, *Human Rights and the International Community*, Chicago, Quadrangle Books, 1964.

[16] Stanley D. Metzger agrees with Friedmann that interests are the main force shaping the attitudes of the new states of Asia and Africa toward international law. See Metzger, " 'Nations' and the Rules of International Law—a Commentary," 8 *Howard Law Journal* 122 (Spring 1962).

main lines of the modern system of international law as it has historically grown out of Western European life is disclosed.[17] Friedmann thinks that the behavior and interests of national governments do not express cultural predisposition to any important degree: "Since even an historical perspective reveals such remarkable similarities in the behavior of nations with differing cultures, it is even more surprising than it would otherwise be to find that the modern states representing these different cultures do not appear to differ to any significant extent, in the practical conduct of their international relations and in their attitude to international law, from that of the Western nations, which have constructed the main structure of contemporary international law" (pp. 313-14). Friedmann regards "[t]he continuing supremacy of the 'national interest' as the dominant value of international life" (p. 298). It is attention to interests, not to cultural predisposition, that gives the deepest insight into the role of international law in the foreign policy of these new states. "India," Friedmann writes, "in the practical conduct of international relations and in her attitude to international law, behaved very like other states. It has preached peace and the observance of international law while being guided in critical moments by the supremacy of national policy and national power aspirations" (p. 314). Unlike some other commentators of late, Friedmann does not make invidious comparisons that suggest how irresponsible the new states are compared to the Western states.[18] In fact, Friedmann goes so far as to admit that Western statesmen regard "any action inconsistent with obligations under the United Nations Charter as justified by the overriding interest of national policy" (pp. 302 03).

Friedmann does assert that the stage of economic development may give a group of states a similar outlook, but this similarity is not evidence suggesting the importance of culture or ideology: "To confuse policies born of changing postures of interest with religious, cultural, or other values inherent in the national character or the cultural pattern of a people, can only lead to a grave distortion of the real problems of contemporary international politics and law" (pp. 322). Friedmann adds that "[t]he so-called African-Asian bloc is an illusion, in any sense other than that of a temporary and shifting coalescence of interest positions, dictated by political and economic circumstances" (p. 323). Certainly this is too clean a position unless "interests" are defined broadly enough to encompass cultural variables, but in the event that "interest" is conceived broadly then the dismissal of culture as an illusion is unwar-

[17] F.S.C. Northrop, *The Meeting of East and West*, New York, Macmillan, 1946; Northrop, *The Taming of Nations*, New York, Macmillan, 1952; Jenks, *op.cit. supra*, note 4.

[18] E.g., Alwyn Freeman, "Professor McDougal's Law and Minimum World Public Order," 58 *American Journal of International Law* 711, 712 (July 1964); see Appendix C for criticism of Freeman's views.

ranted. It may be reasonable to conclude that in most respects the new states, like the old, act to maximize national power, national wealth, and national prestige. Such an emphasis on interests corrects the tendencies to criticize the new states for their refusal to abide by the traditional legal system, or to exonerate them for whatever they do because the tides of history are running in their favor. However, once this much is admitted, then it can also be admitted that various cultural attitudes toward authority, law, violence, and dispute settlement are relevant to the formation of the attitudes displayed by a national polity in the international system.[19]

Similarly, when Friedmann examines Soviet theory and practice he emphasizes conflicts of interests and discounts ideological differences. This encourages an objective account of Soviet behavior, but as with the states of Africa and Asia, it tends to underestimate the extent to which ideological preferences continue to shape goals and influence the choice of action taken to reach them (p. 338). To regard ideological considerations as a separate variable is not at all meant to imply that peace and prosperity may not take precedence in Soviet policy-making over the promotion of revolutionary objectives. The narrower point being made is simply that ideology is one of the forces guiding Soviet policy-making having influence on the selection and rejection of opportunities for international action.

Friedmann's reliance upon an undifferentiated cluster of "interests" leads to unfortunate consequences. One consequence is to produce rather vapid overgeneralizations, which even if interpreted, as Friedmann does (pp. 47-48), to embrace enlightened national interests, elide significant differences among states in outlook and behavior. For instance, to assert the precedence of national interests over world community interests gives no indication as to when a given state will use violence to reach its objectives. We could learn much more by specifying what risks various states will take and what methods they will employ under varying conditions, than by affirming that all states pursue national interests.[20] Certainly Germany in 1939 and Germany in 1969 are both, in some sense, devoted to maximizing their perceived national interests, but this similarity is far less interesting than are the differences separating Germany then from Germany now.

Despite these criticisms, Friedmann's work is a valuable contribution to the literature of international law. It combines a sensible recon-

[19] For a fuller statement of my views on these matters see Falk, "The New States and International Legal Order," 118 *Recueil des Cours* (1966—II), 1-103.

[20] "All systems of law tend to break down in crisis situations. In such situations, there is a major provocation to act politically with little deference to pre-existing rules." Kaplan and Katzenbach, *The Political Foundations of International Law*, p. 6.

ciliation of fact and fantasy and exhibits the author's success in reconciling his humanistic hopes for world order with his sense of realistic possibility. Friedmann's erudition and common sense enable a student of his approach to obtain a very reliable awareness of the major developmental trends in international legal order.

XVII. Morton A. Kaplan and Nicholas deB. Katzenbach

MACHIAVELLI begins his *Discourses* by observing that "the curious nature of men, so prompt to blame and so slow to praise, makes the discovery and introduction of any new principles and systems as dangerous almost as the exploration of unknown seas and continents." *The Political Foundations of International Law* runs this hazard, as it is both a splendid pioneering venture and vulnerable to serious criticism.[1] Although it most suggestively studies the theoretical interaction of law and politics, it provides scant doctrinal support. Although it brilliantly applies systems analysis and prudently uses decision-making theory, structural functional approaches, institutional studies, and a subtle form of historicism, it hints provocatively at the relevance of game theory to the role of law in international affairs. Although it advances its views of international jurisdiction with unprecedented sophistication, it resorts to amateurish simplification when discussing the United Nations Charter or the significance of European regionalism. In sum, *Political Foundations* is at once profoundly stimulating and frustratingly unrealized. However, the achievements are so far greater than the defects that it warrants high praise and mild rebuke.[2]

Political Foundations has deep affinities with the excellent work of Myres McDougal, Charles De Visscher, and John Herz; as well, it builds significantly upon Kaplan's *System and Process in International Politics* and Katzenbach's long article, "Conflicts on an Unruly Horse: Reciprocal Claims and Tolerances in Interstate and International Law."[3] As collaborators Kaplan and Katzenbach examine international legal phenomena in sociopolitical contexts, and employ analytical techniques of social science far more than traditional juridical modes of logical analysis and doctrinal interpretation. As such, *Politcal Foundations* can be regarded as the methodological antithesis of the Kelsenite approach to international law.

Kaplan and Katzenbach make two special contributions that I should like to identify at once. First, *Political Foundations* demonstrates the value of systems analysis for the study of international law. Although the authors do not purport to make a rigorous application of systems analysis, they do enough to convince one of its usefulness as a methodological innovation, especially with respect to evaluating the effectiveness of legal norms. Second, without sacrificing the sophistication of

---

[1] New York, Wiley, 1961.
[2] For an articulate analysis that finds the balance of virtues and defects to be negative see Robert W. Tucker, Book Review, *Journal of Conflict Resolution*, VII (1963), 69-75.
[3] New York, Wiley, 1957; 65 *Yale Law Journal* 1087-1157 (July 1956).

the legal realists, Kaplan and Katzenbach manage to generate some confidence in the capacity of legal norms to establish stable limits in international affairs. Decision-making theory is used, but in moderate form, and as only one of several ways to study normative phenomena. This diluted focus on the decision-maker's process of decision avoids the tendency of unrestricted "rule skepticism" to dissolve the objective quality of legal obligation. A clear sense of normative guidance in the international legal system underlies the development of law habits, especially as principal actors often possess contradictory policy objectives. It seems desirable to encourage the perception of common legal norms and procedures by national actors with different instrumental and ideological orientations in the system. Advocates of a decision-making approach to international law—principally McDougal and Lasswell—appear to underestimate this important implication of their analysis.

There is an additional special reason to single out Kaplan and Katzenbach for high praise: they have written profoundly about the effects of current patterns of bipolarity upon international law without embracing the Manichean heresy. Part of this success may be attributed to the depersonalized tendency of systems analysis. Inquiry into characteristic behavior patterns makes one less susceptible, perhaps, to the self-manipulating effects of national and political ideology. If this is true, it would be an important beneficial side-effect of systems analysis, since international legal scholarship so frequently disguises national advocacy; advocacy disguised as scholarship happens especially under political conditions of challenge and crisis such as have existed in recent decades. It is, however, not a new phenomenon. The Grotius-Selden debate in the seventeenth century on the freedom of the high seas is but one of numerous historical examples. One prominent instance among numerous contemporary examples was the elaborate defense by McDougal and Schlei of the "legality" of nuclear testing by the United States on the high seas.[4] The Communist counterparts are far less subtle; the legal attacks made by Korovin and Zhukov in *International Affairs* (Moscow) upon the right of the United States to orbit observational satellites over Soviet territory provide typical illustrations. Such a provincial tendency in the serious literature of international law has the special effect of obscuring the dimly perceived and bewilderingly relevant novelty of the present situation.

For one thing, politics in a nuclear age challenge deeply the traditional delimitation of national interests. A national concern with survival now gives new incentive for the attainment of a higher quality of international order. It appears more dangerous for national governments to

---

[4] See McDougal and Associates, *Studies in World Public Order*, New Haven, Yale University Press, 1960, 763-843.

impair the ordering techniques provided by international law through their manipulative use. The advantages of international stability seem to outweigh, with certain rare exceptions, any national gains that might be won by a selfish shaping of legal claims to suit immediate national convenience. It seems essential that the nuclear powers, at least, *perceive* the link between world order and national interest, and *act* accordingly in specific instances. As principal states set the tone for behavior throughout international society it is especially significant to appraise their behavior as constructive or not.

The United States, as the dominant nonrevolutionary nation with a deep cultural commitment to legal order, has a self-proclaimed responsibility for exercising leadership in this regard. It must, in the first instance, seek to convey to Soviet leadership a perception of the connection between national interest and international legal order. Such a perception follows from a universal will to avoid nuclear catastrophe. This common ground remains the bedrock of minimum order in the world. For this reason it is disturbing to observe the tendency of the United States to depart from a law-oriented approach to world affairs under the pressure of its struggle to prevent the expansion of Communist influence. The most damaging and sustained departure from a low-oriented foreign policy has been an outgrowth of United States participation in the Vietnam War.[5] The U-2 incident, American sponsorship of the Cuban invasion of April 1961, and the Dominican intervention of 1965 are other examples. It is unrealistic to expect revolutionary nations to *perceive* the benefits of legal order when *status quo* nations *act* in violation of applicable legal standards. Such an assertion rests upon several propositions: first, that the national interest of the principal nuclear powers urgently requires stable limits upon permissible conduct; second, that national elites perceive and act upon this awareness; third, that the initiative of older law-oriented states is a necessary condition for increasing the prospect that revolutionary nations will perceive that their national interest also depends upon adherence to legal norms; and, fourth, that the significance of a law-oriented approach to foreign affairs has evidently not been appreciated by United States policy-makers entrusted with making critical decisions affecting the use of military power.

Kaplan and Katzenbach provide a lucid account of the international legal system that encourages one to see clearly why it is mutually advantageous for the nuclear powers to work toward international stability by reciprocal adherence to applicable legal norms. With great skill, *Political Foundations* depicts the distinctive quality of international law as a predominantly *horizontal* legal order in a highly *decentralized* social

[5] For full argument to this effect see Falk, *Legal Order in a Violent World*, Princeton University Press, 1968, 224-323.

system.[6] Norms govern the behavior of formally equal units. Insufficient central enforcement exists to achieve satisfactory standards of implementation in certain areas of international legal regulation. However, a level of order is reached by horizontal ordering techniques. Reciprocity and self-interest play a dominant role in this process. A national unit tends to refrain from claiming more than it is willing to permit other units in the system. U-2 flights by the United States over Soviet territory would discourage, if not altogether preclude, the United States from objecting to corresponding overflights of American territory. It is important that nations perceive and act upon a calculation of self-interest that includes this factor of reciprocity.[7] A norm of international behavior is entitled to the status of law even though there is no central enforcement. To understand international law we must learn to see its distinctive attributes, and not to appraise its reality by the degree to which it conforms to our images of domestic legal order.

The effectiveness of international law arises, as well, from the habits of compliance that government officials develop. The observance of international law is routinized in the standard bureaucratic operations of most states. Suspension of a rule (or its deliberate violation) requires an extraordinary decision at high echelons of government and, for this reason alone, tends to be infrequent. Such a view of international law does not overlook the weakness of a decentralized system that seeks to keep order between hostile units, but it does point to important areas of structural support given the norms of international law.

Kaplan and Katzenbach add to this description a strong sense of the relationship of function, interest, and effectiveness. For instance, the law of neutrality was developed to limit the scope of belligerency, thereby serving the interests of all states so long as the outcome of a war did not endanger nonparticipating states. As the politics, tactics, and technology of major war began increasingly to endanger neutral states, their governments grew unwilling to abide by the rules of neutrality. Norms lose effectiveness when they no longer promote the reciprocal interests of most nations under most conditions. This loss of effectiveness applies particularly to norms bearing upon national security interests. The rules governing and limiting belligerent rights—blockade and visit

---

[6] A legal order is vertical if it possesses a hierarchial arrangement of norms backed by an institutional hierarchy that assures effective implementation. Modern nonfederal states possess vertical legal orders. A legal order is horizontal if implementation of norms usually depends upon self-help and self-restraint on the part of formally equal participants in the legal order. That is, there is no compulsory procedure for resolution by appeal to a higher level in the legal system. This is generally the case in international law. Of course, the distinction between horizontal and vertical is a gross first approximation of the quality of international order. It is useful, however, to highlight a contrast between international law and developed systems of domestic law.

[7] A fuller consideration of these issues is to be found in Chap. VIII.

and search—could not be expected to retain effectiveness after the advent of economic warfare and the development of submarine and aerial combat.

Finally, the absence of legislative institutions and the difficulties of reaching explicit agreement among governments place a heavy responsibility upon major nations to moderate their unilateral claims to act by self-limiting appraisals of reasonableness. The "legitimacy" of a national claim arises partly from a unilateral display to the rest of the world that the claim is reasonable in view of an objective balance of benefits and burdens. At minimum, a sovereign government should seek to restrict injury to other nations when it acts. This refers especially to claims with military implications. Such a stress upon self-limitation is a necessary restriction upon sovereign discretion. It supplements the generally acknowledged burden of obeying normative restraints that have the status of "law" with the more subtle general burden of refraining from the assertion of "unreasonable" claims. An understanding of the self-ordering role of reasonableness is fundamental to a proper appreciation of the international legal system. Such a perception involves a minimum commitment by members of the system to some degree of stability, at least with regard to resort to force. The prospect of mutual destruction arising from excessive instability should provide the nuclear nations with adequate incentive to moderate their unilateral claims.

Kaplan and Katzenbach show how the pattern of power distribution in the world influences the effectiveness of particular legal norms and shapes the role of supranational legal institutions. Building upon Kaplan's provocative earlier work in systems analysis, *Political Foundations* relies upon the balance of power and the loose bipolar models as its basic interpretative images. The book argues that international law grew up to meet the political needs of the balance of power system that lasted until World War I. After a period of transition to bipolarity—tested by the struggle of Germany and Japan for bipolar world domination—the end of World War II produced a genuine condition of loose bipolarity. The looseness of the bipolarity derives from the existence of blocs of nations (rather than single national empires), from uncommitted nations, and from the presence of a universal mediating organization like the United Nations. Many norms inherited from the balance of power system—for instance, the doctrine of nonintervention or the law of neutrality—are not effective in a loose bipolar world in which national actors seek to expand their bloc by the absorption of new members and in which no nation can be indifferent to the destabilizing effect of changes in the relative strengths of the blocs. Underlying *Political Foundations* is the belief that international restraints upon national behavior will be effective only so long as they correspond roughly to the survival interests of the major national actors in the world. This belief, in turn, rests upon the assumption that national survival and strength depend upon certain characteristic behavior that results from the nature of the international system, and especially from the distribution of power within it. The attractiveness of this approach includes provision of a way to distinguish between effective and ineffective norms in the prevailing legal order, and hence suggests the kind of doctrinal reform that is necessary to promote increasing adherence to law.

An illustration helps to suggest the value of using system models: the Kaplan-Katzenbach treatment of the Congo crisis especially as it bears upon the role of the United Nations in a loose bipolar world. A characteristic of the loose bipolar model is the development of a universal organization to mediate between the blocs and to control peace-endangering situations that arise independently of the main lines of strategic conflict in world affairs. The United Nations, then, is much more likely to be effective for violent nonbloc disputes than for interbloc disputes. Korea was an exception resulting from the domination of the United Nations by the Western bloc, accentuated by the adventitious circumstances of the temporary Soviet boycott. The original decision by the United Nations in 1960 to enter the Congo was made when the situation appeared not to involve very directly Soviet-American rivalries; in fact both the Soviet Union and the United States appeared to favor using United Nations capabilities to protect the recent independence of the Congo from Belgian reencroachment. However, the displacement of Lumumba meant that the Congo would no longer have radical internal leadership. The Soviet Union was not eager for a restoration of internal order in the Congo except in Lumumba's favor. When the Secretary-General chose a contending faction that seemed inclined toward the Western bloc, the Congo controversy became an interbloc dispute of first magnitude, involving the future political orientation of the whole continent of Africa. As such, the Soviet perception of the Secretary-General as an agent of the Western bloc was quite predictable, as were the resulting Soviet efforts to undercut his effectiveness. The high stakes in the Congo made the Soviet Union particularly sensitive to the antagonism between its policies and those of the Secretary-General.[8] Kaplan and Katzenbach emphasize the normal Soviet preference, at least outside the socialist group of states, for instability as

[8] For a very persuasive presentation of the Secretary-General's role in the Congo and Congo-type situation see Leon Gordenker, *The UN Secretary-General and the Maintenance of Peace*, New York, Columbia University Press, 1967, 137-319; for studies focused on the Congo situation see Arthur Lee Burns and Nina Heathcote, *Peace-Keeping by U.N. Forces: From Suez to the Congo*, New York, Praeger, 1963, 23-160; Paul-Henry Gendebein, *L'intervention des Nations Unies au Congo 1960-1964*, Paris, Mouton, 1967.

the political setting most generally favorable to the spread of Communism. Since the United Nations seeks stability as its primary objective, the activities of the Organization are bound to collide frequently with Soviet interests and preferences. By such reasoning Kaplan and Katzenbach provide a simplistic view of the limits of effective United Nations efforts in behalf of world stability, a view that overlooks the partisan control of the UN in its early years by a Western coalition and is insensitive to trends toward a UN role in promoting selective instability as a consequence of the growing influence of the Afro-Asian group within the organization.

The analysis of Kaplan-Katzenbach facilitates an appraisal of the Troika proposals for restructuring the United Nations.[9] The basic Kaplan-Katzenbach hypothesis suggests that the revolutionary impetus of the Sino-Soviet bloc puts it in continuing opposition to the United Nations, whereas the commitment of the Western bloc to stability gives it a continuing incentive to strengthen the Organization. This world political split makes the United Nations vulnerable to serious disruption. Suppose that control should pass to the revolutionary nations? Kaplan and Katzenbach argue that such an event would be likely to "increase intervention in the internal affairs of other nations and to decrease normative constraints on that kind of activity" (p. 313).

The loose bipolar model suggests an interpretation (not made by Kaplan and Katzenbach) of the intense historical forces pressing toward radical social change in many parts of the world. Is it not also important to consider the stabilizing value of encouraging United Nations intervention on the side of the internal faction with a radical program of social change? Can these pressures for change be accommodated except by civil strife and intervention? These questions point to the absence of supranational legislative institutions. Might it not be better to centralize, and hence moderate, the interventionary process in the United Nations?[10] Thus, a potential contribution to international stability might result from giving the revolutionary nations greater influence in the administration of the United Nations. The Kaplan-Katzenbach analysis of systemic behavior fails to comprehend the impact of these pressures upon the possibilities for international stability in the world today. Their focus upon the international distribution of power gives crucial insight, but if it is not supplemented by reference to other behavioral variables it becomes a rather monolithic interpretative per-

9 See, in general, Sydney D. Bailey, "The Troika and the Future of the United Nations," in Falk and Saul H. Mendlovitz, *The Strategy of World Order—The United Nations*, New York, World Law Fund,

1966, III, 326-51.
10 For further discussion along these lines see Falk, *op.cit. supra*, note 5, 336-53.

spective unable to provide concrete insight for policy-makers or students of the subject.

This is part of a more general criticism. The simplicity of the loose bipolar model entails some sacrifice in understanding. Kaplan and Katzenbach, for instance, suggest that the shift from the flexible alignments of the balance of power world to the rigid alignments of the loose bipolar world undercuts the political (or systemic) support for the doctrine of nonintervention. There is virtually no attention given to the influence of nuclear weaponry upon the interventionary pattern of contemporary world politics. Coercive strategies depending on covert and low-scale violence become a *feasible* way to advance external political objectives without taking substantial risks of nuclear war. Such a selective use of violence tends to limit the scope of conflict without giving up the politics of expansion or of counterrevolution.

There is a further consideration in this regard. The focus upon the loose bipolar model leads to a natural emphasis upon external relations among the political units that make up the system. Scant attention is given to the relevance of the internal distribution and orientation of power within participating national units. One finds, it is true, a perceptive discussion of the tendency for domestic courts to become "apologists for national policies determined by the political aims of government" (p. 268) instead of acting as independent agencies of a developing world legal order. However, once depicted, this phenomenon is ignored. The instance of domestic courts suggests the heuristic quality of the entire Kaplan-Katzenbach endeavor. There is abundant occasion for further probing of this subject. The process of politicalizing the national judiciary detracts greatly from the stability of normative standards under present conditions. It has found its way into the treatment of the act of state doctrine in the Restatement of the Foreign Relations Law of the United States and is expressed in the Hickenlooper Amendment overruling the effort of the Supreme Court majority in *Sabbatino* to establish a more independent judiciary for international matters.[11] This trend acts to disrupt the territorial distribution of policy-making authority. It interferes with the basic jurisdictional allocation of authority among national units in the decentralized world system.[12] This seems undesirably destabilizing for those problems, such as the status of alien-owned property, that arise from a legitimate diversity of policy on the part of various social systems. In settings of legitimate diversity the tradition of deference to official foreign governmental policy continues to serve the cause of world order.[13]

[11] For fuller account see Chap. XIII.
[12] For a more complete discussion in the context of extraterritorial antitrust regulation see Chap. IX.

[13] Argument developed in Falk, *The Role of Domestic Courts in the International Legal Order*, Syracuse University Press, 1964, 21-52.

The growth of law depends partly upon a combination of the development of mutual respect for diversity and joint action in areas of genuine agreement. Thus the universality of formal sentiments supporting basic human rights, especially on matters of racial discrimination, does provide national courts with a foundation of universal sentiments that encourages the application and development of universal norms. The institutional deficiencies of international law make it imperative that we try to restrict executive and legislative interferences with the autonomy of domestic courts. Only by establishing a tradition of autonomy can domestic courts function as part of the international structure. However, this objective makes some degree of political decentralization in the sense of separation of powers a precondition for the effective creation of international norms in national institutions.[14] This forms part of the effort to make national decision-makers aware of the current connection between the national interest and world order. I suggest that the distinction between legitimate diversity and universal consensus provides some guidance for a domestic judiciary ready to contribute to international stability.

Systems analysis appeals to us because it is an advance over *ad hoc* empirical observation.[15, 16] It tends to show the wider implications of

---

[14] More development of this theme is to be found in Chap. XIV.

[15] I find Robert Tucker's assessment overly harsh, especially such a comment as the following: "A substantial number of the conclusions reached after labored analysis are not only truisms but very banal truisms at that." Tucker, *op.cit. supra*, note 2, at 70. Professor Tucker does make a convincing point of the failure of Kaplan and Katzenbach to clarify the explanatory value of isolating power as a variable in the international environment as they do in classifying international systems solely by reference to the distribution of power within international society. Unless this procedure can be demonstrated as valuable for purposes of explanation or prediction the failure to emphasize other variables produces a simplistic and essentially distorted conception of international legal order and its distinctive politico-historical properties. For example, Tucker appropriately emphasizes the presence in international society of a major revolutionary actor as a very critical variable that conditions the varying significance of norms at different stages of international history. Stanley Hoffmann puts principal stress upon the revolutionary-moderate character of the relations among principal sovereign states as the crucial variable in his adaptation of sys-

temic thinking to problems of international law. See Stanley Hoffmann, *The State of War*, New York, Praeger, 1965, 88-122. Hoffmann's conception of an international system is multifactorial, the differentiating criteria being expanded considerably beyond Kaplan-Katzenbach's stress upon the distribution of power among international actors or units. This difference in conception is clearly evident in Hoffmann's definition of an international system: "An international system is a pattern of relations among the basic units of world politics, characterized by the scope of the objectives pursued by those units and of the tasks performed among them, as well as by the means used to achieve those goals and perform those tasks. This pattern is largely determined by the structure of the world, the nature of the forces that operate across or within the major units, and the capabilities, patterns of power, and political cultures of those units" (*id.* at 90).

[16] For a very useful critical survey of the principal attempts to apply systems analysis to the study of international politics see Oran R. Young, "A Systematic Approach to International Politics," Research Monograph No. 33, Center of International Studies, Princeton University, June 30, 1968. Professor Young's mono-

particular behavior for the stability of the entire social order. Thus it widens the horizon of relevance, enabling a more rational grasp of the risks of normative ineffectiveness. It also closes the gap between structure and process by providing an overall image of the society in motion. Kaplan and Katzenbach make a very beneficial use of systems analysis. Among other things, its employment builds a persuasive case for the existence of international law. This is done by showing the systemic bearing of normative phenomena upon international relations. The models of international behavior, however, remain primitive, as they do not reflect a variety of other factors that influence the pattern and effectiveness of international law in any given international setting: nuclear weapons; socoeconomic, ideological, moral, and cultural convergence and divergence; distributions of power *within* the basic participating unit of world affairs; the historical pressures favoring radical social change. Kaplan and Katzenbach give us a superb heuristic introduction, but it is a starting place rather than a terminal point. *Political Foundations* has exerted a helpful influence upon serious thinking about international law in the years since its publication. One hopes that the approach initiated in this book will inspire a new generation of studies that are more rigorous in procedure, more specific in scope, and more sustained in research and analysis.

---

graph contains very complete bibliographical references to the more interesting developments in the systemic approach (including his own). Very little of this work done since the publication of *Political Foundations* in 1961 has been concerned directly with the international legal order, although there are many suggestive discussions in this growing literature of the relevance of norms to behavior under various systemic conditions.

XVIII. Kenneth S. Carlston

IT IS intriguing to speculate about what it will take to mobilize the political energy to organize international society anew, really anew—on some basis, that is, that eliminates the preeminence of the nation-state as the center of political life and military capability. Obviously, neither recent wars nor the prospect of future wars are sufficient agents of transformation. No matter how much gloomy evidence is amassed, all the instruments of reckoning agree that only modest changes in the structure of international society are likely to occur in the foreseeable future. If we accept this diagnosis as accurate, then one consequence is to place severe constraints upon a sense of what it is possible to do about reducing the risks of large-scale violence. One remains free, of course, to think more grandiosely about world government and general and complete disarmament, but, as the prospects for realization are almost nil, these schemes must continue to be discounted as outside the realm of practical politics.

It seems safe to conclude that this conservative judgment about what can be done to eliminate the prospect of war is shared by most people who have thought about the problem. There is, in fact, a further tendency to suppose that since nothing radical can be done, there is nothing worthwhile to do. This kind of thinking illustrates a habit of the human mind to convert partial knowledge into total ignorance. In this case it is a false inference, because much can be done to reduce the prospects and curtail the magnitude of international violence short of achieving some spectacular reordering of power and values in international society. Increasingly, those with a concern for securing world peace are exhibiting an awareness that patience and hard thinking are essential preconditions to real contributions. It is from this perspective that a realistic appreciation of the relevance of international law to the patterns of international behavior becomes both possible and necessary. Few international lawyers have combined a concern for the maximization of world order with a realistic sense of the international environment within which the law must operate and develop.[1] Kenneth Carlston exhibits this kind of sophistication in his major book, *Law and Organization in World Society*.[2]

Before considering Carlston's specific contribution to international

---

[1] There are, of course, notable exceptions: for example, Charles de Visscher, *Theory and Reality in Public International Law*, Princeton, Princeton University Press, 3rd rev. edn., 1968; P. E. Corbett, *Law and Society in the Relations of States*, New York, Harcourt, Brace, 1951; Louis Henkin, *How Nations Behave*, New York, Praeger, 1968; William Coplin, *The Functions of International Law*, Chicago, Rand McNally, 1966.

[2] Urbana, University of Illinois Press, 1962 [hereinafter page references are indicated by parentheses in the text].

legal studies, it seems useful to consider briefly the case for and against taking international law seriously. To argue about the value of international legal studies is necessary on account of the continuing skepticism of many acute observers of international politics about the significance of law to an understanding of the behavior of states. It seems possible to challenge successfully this skepticism. However, first it seems essential to understand its rationale.

This understanding is, in part, vital because much of the present generation of skepticism about international law has arisen as a healthy reaction against the exaggerated claims on behalf of their discipline put forward by an earlier international lawyer. Few would now dispute the Kennan-Morgenthau critique of a foreign policy-making process comprehended as subservient to legal rules.[3] The idea that rules of law could or should by themselves govern state behavior, regardless of the absence of reliable means to assure their enforcement, was unsound, as it was evident that national governments could not put themselves in a position to uphold various national interests merely by conforming to a regime of rules.

This prudent conclusion arose from an interpretation of the character of international society. It can be shown that international society has at various times, if not always, contained one or more principal actors intent upon using force to improve their relative position in the international system. Such revisionist actors tend to be far less responsive to the restraining claims asserted in behalf of law than do their conservative rivals. Given this situation, it becomes important for all states to be equally unrestrained. Otherwise the more virtuous and defensive states encourage and abet the ambitions of the more expansionist and aggressive states. If a revisionist state could rely upon the restraint of others, then it could proceed slowly to satisfy its ambitions and benefit from a competitive advantage in a struggle for regional or even global dominance. The outcome of this analysis is to counsel states to play the game of international politics according to the rules set by the players rather than according to the unrealistic rules posited by international law. Copious illustrations exist to bring home the need to retain discretion to uphold national security interests. No illustration is more persuasive or apropos than the evident encouragement given Hitler by the law-abiding behavior of liberal democracies during the middle

[3] For representative statements of the Kennan-Morgenthau position see George F. Kennan, *American Diplomacy, 1900-1950*, Chicago, University of Chicago Press, 1952; Kennan, *Realities of American Foreign Policy*, Princeton, Princeton University Press, 1954; Hans J. Morgenthau, *Dilemmas of Politics, Chicago*, Chicago, University of Chicago Press, 1958; Morgenthau, *In Defense of the National Interest*, New York, Knopf, 1951. See also Dean Acheson, "The Lawyer's Path to Peace," 42 *Virginia Quarterly Review* 337 (1966); Acheson, "The Cuban Quarantine —Remarks," *Proceedings American Society of International Law, 1963*, pp. 13-15.

1930's. The lesson is often symbolized by contrasting the noninterventionary policies of the liberal democracies during the Spanish Civil War with the policies of Germany, Italy, and the Soviet Union, states that intervened even though they had formally pledged adherence to a nonintervention pact. The alleged lesson to be learned is that whenever the basic arrangement of powers and actors in international society is being challenged by a formidable revisionist state or coalition, adherence to international law by other states promotes negative results. The formulation of the issue may appear dogmatic depending on whether coercive approaches to revision are regarded as necessarily undesirable or only as selectively undesirable.

It is obviously important to grasp the merit of this critique of international law. However, the attack is usually stated in such an unqualified form as to be overstated. There is much more to international law than rules about the use of force, and, besides, international lawyers have been educated along with others by their critics. Today greater account is taken of the relevance of political, social, and procedural factors to the possibility of effective international law. Furthermore, there is now widespread among international lawyers an acknowledgment that if one state persistently violates a particular rule, then the duty of others to obey that rule is likewise suspended. It is now time, accordingly, for nonlawyers to reexamine the status of international law as a stimulus to thought about world order and as a framework for restraining governmental behavior within normative limits and procedures. This call for reexamination reflects a conviction that international law, realistically conceived, can make significant contributions to war prevention that are not yet generally appreciated by social scientists concerned with this range of subject-matter areas and issues. Although diplomats manipulate legal rules to reinforce preferred national positions, the habit of legal argument sharpens the issues in dispute and helps to keep minor disputes minor. Especially between rivals not eager for war, international law provides a process by which claims to act are asserted and counterasserted, thereby valuably encouraging communication even in the midst of the worst crises. This maintenance of communications curtails the tendency of disputes to get out of hand. An argument about the legal merits of opposing claims provides a way to keep a conflict within perceptible boundaries, and more readily permits concessions that are not resisted on the ground that they sacrifice national honor. International law has played this regulative role in many recent crises, helping to shape the conflict so as to maintain thresholds resistant to escalation; recourse to "the hot line" during the Middle East War of 1967 is a very explicit instance whereby Soviet-American rivalry did not inhibit conflict-restraining recourse to communication facilites provided and sustained by the techniques and rhetoric of international law.[4]

Part of the failure to acknowledge the positive uses of international law arises from a tendency to evaluate the success or failure of a legal system by the extent to which actors abide by its restraints. Such a criterion for evaluation has been borrowed from domestic settings wherein it has somewhat more validity, given the more hierarchical social and political structure. To assess international law on the basis of a record of compliance is especially misleading because it tends to withhold from view the multiplicity of functions served by international law. One crucial function, relevant in situations of international crisis, is to allow rivals to cooperate, or more accurately, to restrict their noncooperation in such a way that mutually destructive results are curtailed, if not altogether avoided. Diplomatic controversy carried on in the rhetoric of law is one way to achieve the kind of tacit bargain in international relations that Thomas Schelling and others have written so instructively about.[5]

It is important that specialists appreciate these tangible achievements of international law. Otherwise the debilitating connection between attitudes toward world order and its actual character promotes the most pessimistic outcomes. A lack of confidence in law as an existing and potential source of common restraint gives statesmen no alternative to national self-reliance. A skeptical consensus among critical decision-makers and social scientists tends to be self-vindicating, the belief system creating the data that are being assessed, thereby maintaining the cycle.

How does one dislodge the skeptical predisposition by persuasive means? This task is made especially difficult because habits of thought about violence and security have deep roots in human consciousness. A rational appeal, however convincing its supporting evidence, is unlikely to affect a reorientation of basic patterns of human thought and action. Hence it is often assumed that the only way out of the dangers of the present system is to prepare for the trauma induced by the next catastrophe. It may be plausible to suppose that a traumatic event —such as a nuclear war—might decisively undermine confidence in the existing order, as well as create the openness needed for drastic modification in the existing distribution of power and authority in world affairs. Historical evidence gives some support to this kind of expecta-

[4] Arab-Israeli negotiations of a cease-fire in the Middle East War of 1967 seemed facilitated by the continuous operation of Security Council as a forum for authoritative communication. Such a forum encourages more reasonable formulations of adversary positions so as to secure maximum support for their contentions and makes it more possible to identify any convergence of adversary position that might be converted into an agreement.
[5] See Thomas C. Schelling, *Arms and Influence*, New Haven, Yale University Press, 1966.

tion. All major attempts to reorganize international society for purposes of war prevention have been undertaken during the aftermath of a war widely perceived as the cause of intolerable damage: Westphalia after the Thirty Years' War, the Congress of Vienna after the Napoleonic wars, the League of Nations after World War I, and the United Nations after World War II. Only after such a total breakdown has the international situation been sufficiently fluid to induce leaders and supporting publics of dominant nations to join seriously in the task of reorganizing international society to avoid a repetition of the terrible events just experienced.

There has been a consistent growth of organizational control over various dimensions of international life.[6] However, if this growth is considered in connection with the problems of preventing warfare, the achievements of the past must be regarded as disappointing. It becomes evident that the traumas of the past have not induced a sufficient transformation of international society to serve the cause of war prevention. After the catastrophe the will to do something fundamental to avoid its repetition is more apparent than real.[7] As a consequence the old order has survived intact, perpetuated and sustained by those whose status and ideals remained tied to the past. Soon after the rubble is cleared and the corpses buried, national egoism reasserts itself to prevent any serious diminution of sovereign authority. The memory of the preceding trauma quickly fades amid the renewed pursuit of the traditional goals of foreign policy—national prestige, power, and wealth. New patterns of international conflict emerge. Once more world society grows vulnerable and its elites exhibit increasing insensitivity to its vulnerability to ruinous war. The cycle has been maintained throughout human history; the termination of the next general war can be expected to provide yet another occasion for a collective effort to prevent subsequent occurrences of major warfare.

Such reasoning supports a pessimistic set of conclusions about the future of international society. First, apparently only a trauma sets in motion political forces of sufficient magnitude to reform international society in fundamental respects. Second, past traumas, however grave their impact seemed at the time, failed to reorient the thinking of elites sufficiently to produce genuine reform; that is, the old pattern of inter-

---

[6] Some of the more interesting trends in these regards are to be found in C. W. Jenks, *The Common Law of Mankind*, London, Stevens, 1958; Wolfgang Friedmann, *The Changing Structure of International Law*, New York, Columbia University Press, 1964.

[7] Postwar reconstructions of international society have normally led to a compromise between appearance and reality: the appearance of significant change and the reality of nominal change. For supporting analyses see especially Walter Schiffer, *The Legal Community of Mankind*, New York, Columbia University Press, 1954; F. H. Hinsley, *Power and the Pursuit of Peace*, Cambridge, Eng., Cambridge University Press, 1963.

state rivalry resumed dominance and the new cooperative endeavor did little more than create a new superstructure in international life. Third, each effort at reform was in fact unable to prevent an eventual breakdown in the form of an international war.

These conclusions imply a judgment about the prospects for a system change in international society.[8] They are not meant to cast doubt upon the stabilizing role of ordering devices in international society as it now operates. Two parallel endeavors exist: first, the effort to stabilize the existing system; second, the effort to initiate a peaceful process of transition to an improved international system. The two endeavors are connected. Improvements in the existing system may, if perceived as supporting further changes, also constitute transition steps generating the confidence to proceed in the direction of a new system.

It seems inadvisable to rely too heavily upon a pessimistic assessment.[9] We know too little about social reality to accept positively the result of a pessimistic analysis, however persuasive on the basis of available evidence. If those with a progressive view of world order abandon the cause, an intellectual vacuum is left to be filled by those with regressive positions. There are many reasons to explore the possibilities for transformation. Despite the failures of the past, there is a faint movement in the direction of greater world order discernible, and some finite possibility of realization if the appropriate steps are taken. A continuing effort to prescribe the constituents of world order may help to create an intellectual climate that can, at minimum, take more constructive advantage of whatever fluidity is created by the next catastrophe.

Kenneth Carlston's view that "the failure of the scholar of international law, and, to a lesser extent, the scholar of international relations, to develop for the purposes of their disciplines a model of international relations which will couple comprehensiveness and fidelity to the elements of international order with simplicity, precision, and elegance of structure, is increasingly becoming a cultural catastrophe" (p. 139) is a particularly strong form of appeal. It is part of a wider

[8] The preceding discussion has emphasized the elimination of war through the consciously instituted structural change of international society. Such a direction of change presupposes that it is the nature of the state system and the character of interstate rivalry by means of military competition that is primarily responsible for the pervasiveness of war in human experience. Important alternate approaches emphasize the need to overcome the aggressive component in human nature and the need to eliminate coercively organized national societies. These three main approaches are not mutually exclusive, but varying emphases on one or another factor as primary does produce very different strategies of world order. For a very lucid survey of the theoretical literature on these matters see Kenneth W. Waltz, *Man, The State, and War*, New York, Columbia University Press, 1959; see also Falk, *Legal Order in a Violent World*, Princeton, Princeton University Press, 1968, pp. 8-38.

[9] An unusually clear statement of rationale is found in a section of a recent book entitled "Why Speculate Far Ahead?": Herman Kahn and Anthony J. Wiener, *The Year 2000—A Framework for Speculation*, New York, Macmillan, 1967, pp. 1-5.

need to adapt our understanding of international society to new urgencies. As Carlston puts it: "As the character of our lives is being changed by massive forces in the international arena, the need to provide a rational order for these forces and for the international system becomes increasingly desperate" (p. 141). Kenneth Carlston has contributed significantly to this end.

Law and Organization in World Society is a particularly important book because it gives such firm support to an interpretation of international law that lies in the middle quadrants of thought separating utopians from skeptics. As such, it manages to affirm the importance of international law, while at the same time calling attention to the very considerable deficiencies of international law as an existing or prospective basis for world order. Carlston favors the active managerial use of law to realize human and societal values.[10] If Carlston's viewpoint is grasped and disseminated it might eventually influence the orientation of intellectuals and policy-makers. In any event, there are several reasons to urge nonlawyers who are expert in international affairs to give attention to Carlston's conception of an evolving international legal order.

In part, reading Carlston might convince social scientists that the perspective of law is not alien to their interests and techniques. The rehabilitation of law in social scientific thought is not a problem peculiar to, although it is perhaps most severe in, the international field. It is more severe here because international law appears to be an extreme example of a tendency, throughout all juristic thought, to explicate detailed formal structures without assessing the extent of correlation with actual patterns of human behavior. In contrast, the social sciences have been increasingly successful in their insistence that the actualities of human behavior constitute the prime object of their study. In the course of establishing themselves as disciplines, the social sciences have emphasized their rebellion against the stultifying narrowness of a juridical approach to man in society. One consequence of this intellectual rebellion has been the distortion and depreciation of legal studies by implying that legal analysis necessarily exhibits the excesses of the most formal and legalistic juridical practitioners.

Now that the social sciences have largely earned their right to exist as autonomous and respected disciplines, it seems important that social scientists reassess the relevance of law to their work. For law *need* not be conceived as a corpus of rules or as a collection of static structures. It can be conceived, as it is by Carlston and others, as a mode of social

[10] In this regard compare Amitai Etzioni, *The Active Society: A Theory of Societal* and *Political Process*, New York, The Free Press, 1968, esp. pp. 550-613.

process (as well as formal structure) by which men living in groups organize their lives to realize common values and goals. That is, law is a dynamic instrument of social fulfillment, constantly adapting itself to the changing conditions of its particular societal milieu.

Legal scholarship has benefited from the revolt of the social sciences. A continuing process of self-criticism and reform led to the emergence of a new jurisprudence in the 1930's, associated mainly with the work of Oliver Wendell Holmes, Jr., Roscoe Pound, Louis Brandeis, Jerome Frank, and Thurman Arnold. This new jurisprudence stressed the importance of the methods and findings of social science research for legal analysis. The social sciences provide the best-evidenced insight into the quality of social existence and, thereby, assist experts studying and operating within the legal system to adapt law in each context to the social values at stake. The study of law can no longer be regarded as a discipline in which the primary objective is to gain mastery over an esoteric and complex body of interrelated doctrine. The new jurisprudence conceived of law primarily as a set of analytical techniques available to decision-makers who are responsible for maximizing the values of the particular community. The jurist thus becomes a principal consumer of social scientific knowledge.

The social sciences amount to a series of specialized interpretations of social life; the various constituent disciplines do not themselves play a role in society. Law, however, is both a specialized interpretation and a central ingredient of societal life. Through legal institutions the findings of the social sciences can assume a policy relevance and avoid for themselves the fate that, in part, led to their emergence—that of being a barren and futile reflection of the life of the community rather than a vital part of it.

The extension of the new jurisprudence to international society has been accomplished with great brilliance and influence by the work of Myres S. McDougal and his associates.[11] McDougal's intimate collaboration with Harold Lasswell has emphasized the extent to which the methods and insights of the social sciences can be fruitfully introduced into legal science. In fact, Don Quixotes of legal positivism continue to attack McDougal's work precisely because it refuses to confine the concept of law to formal structure and doctrine. Legalism, it is contended by these jurisprudential romantics, is essential to preserve a clear sense of what law is.[12]

But as Carlston shows, the nature of law is inseparable from its particular setting and from the functions it is expected to serve in a given

---

[11] Cf. Chapter XI and Appendix C.
[12] For a creative adaptation of neo-positivistic thinking to an analysis of the character of international law see H.L.A. Hart, *The Concept of Law*, Oxford, Clarendon Press, 1961, pp. 208-31.

social system. Carlston helpfully points out that law has always been most creatively perceived as the central ordering process at work in society. He quotes Plato's statement that law is "the leading string, golden and holy" of a society (p. xi). Plato seems to mean by his statement that law contributes form and order, the enduring elements, to community life. Carlston observes that, "As it is the scientist's faith that there is an ultimate symmetry, order, and truth in nature, so it is the lawyer's faith that the body of law will express the full image of the society which it unites" (p. xi). It is this architectonic idea of law that makes *Law and Organization in World Society* a bold intellectual venture.

It is also a necessary venture. Too little is known about the modes of thought that might be useful to those engaged in working toward a just and reliable order in international affairs. There are, as yet, no very authoritative models available by which to specify the *distinctive* nature of legal order in international society. This deficiency is not trivial. It encourages the retention of sloppy habits of thought. Familiar domestic models of law, order, and justice developed over centuries to fit the circumstances of centrally organized territorial states are made to serve as explanatory tools in a social system dominated by national actors and lacking effective governmental institutions of its own.

In his preface Carlston writes: "To find the place and function of law in the provision of order in the world society is the ultimate concern of this study" (p. xii). Carlston seeks to develop a theory of great generality, and at the same time, to demonstrate its applicability to the solution of concrete problems emerging in international life. In the latter vein, Carlston investigates practices of nationalization by host governments of concession agreements (e.g., the right to explore for and extract mineral resources) with foreign investors, to illustrate the impact and usefulness of his general theory, as well as to assist in its derivation. Carlston's strategy of inquiry is to combine inductive and deductive modes of thoughts in a single interactive process, each acting upon and reacting to the other.

A consequence of this form of inquiry is to produce two quite separate studies that one is never quite sure should have been brought together in a single volume. Chapters I, II, III, IV, and VII are devoted to the nationalization of concession agreements, whereas Chapters V, VI, and VIII develop a general framework for the analysis of law in world society. The experiment, although innovative, is not entirely successful. For one thing, the two levels of approach are not very explicitly integrated. Each stands rather too much on its own and does not appear to depend sufficiently on the existence of the other. The persuasiveness of the general approach is not increased by reading the chapters dealing with nationalization, nor is Carlston's treatment of nationalization any more convincing if read after studying his general theory.

There are certain obvious reasons why nationalization was a problem area with appeal for Carlston. First, states currently disagree as to the status of legal norms pertaining to nationalization. Second, the differing interests of capital-investing and capital-importing states disclose a contemporary need to develop legal rules and procedures offering mutually beneficial arrangements for the reciprocal sets of interests. This latent reciprocity reinforces the argument of a functionalist like Carlston that the basic law task is to construct a system permitting actors with diverse interests to participate in such a way that values of each are optimalized; each type of actor needs to understand that it will benefit from a compromise. Third, nationalization of concession agreements is a subject matter that illustrates the need for lawyers to grasp the economic and other extralegal consequences of alternative legal standards. The economics of modernization and investment are pertinent to the construction of a system of law that reconciles reciprocal interests. Furthermore, an explanation of the advantages of private investment for the achievement of domestic goals of rapid development makes the *real* interests of the new states, as contrasted with their more apparent ideological interests of opposing the investment legacies of colonialism, quite compatible with the protection of foreign investment. The functionalist approach to law and order in world affairs strives to cut through the layer of apparent interests—the dogmatic insistence on sovereign control over national wealth-producing procedures, or the equally dogmatic insistence upon the inalienable nature of investor rights—and encourages the development of legal standards based upon a classification and reconciliation of the real interests at stake for each party. Carlston impressively argues that a functionalist approach to nationalization discloses a basic compatibility between the investor and the new state that is easily overlooked in current debates, even in debates dealing with legal doctrine pertaining to foreign investment that continues to be applicable.

Carlston's choice of nationalization as the problem by which to test his general theory does have certain serious disadvantages. The subject of nationalization is so beset by controversy that it becomes difficult to distinguish advocacy from analysis. It might be felt by some readers, for instance, that Carlston is employing the supposedly impartial tools of functionalist analysis to disguise, so as to make more authoritative, an argument in favor of a substantive position that expresses his special values and outlook. Carlston's approach arouses suspicion because it appears to embody the typical values held by a Westerner of mildly liberal persuasion. Thus, although attempting to deal fairly with alien viewpoints, Carlston seems more comfortable and convincing when advancing an argument in support of investment claims. This assessment is reinforced by Carlston's championship (without giving consideration to its drawbacks) of the private corporation as an optimal mode for the economic development of the new states and by his unsuppressed hostility toward patterns of state-trading engaged in by the socialist states. Carlston's appreciation of world affairs is shaped by a rather orthodox anti-Soviet perspective typical of American intellectuals in the late 1950's. Unfortunately, then, a functionalist analysis does not necessarily achieve, as it promises, a liberation from the national value-system of the analyst. The rhetoric of the analysis may be global, but the animating spirit can remain provincial and ideological.

Carlston would serve the cause of functionalism better if he would remove his judgments about the Soviet-American rivalry from his statement of a general theory of law and organization; at best, such judgments are ephemeral and distract a reader from the enduring merits of the approach and its underlying analysis. Disguised partisanship will be resisted as more insidious than partisanship openly avowed. In the former case the supposedly impartial analysis becomes manipulative if it claims to govern the outlook of those who disagree with its particular values. Carlston might be more convincing to skeptical readers by choosing for investigation problems that are less deeply embedded in the ideological rivalry between East and West than is the legal status of foreign investment.

Carlston's general theory often rises above contemporary patterns of rivalry in world politics. He offers a coherent set of carefully delineated concepts useful for the analysis and appraisal of legal rules in world society. It is, in fact, precisely because the general framework is so carefully and usefully worked out that Carlston's special pleading becomes so objectionable. Carlston could enhance the importance of his work if in a subsequent edition he removed from the text conventional criticisms of the Soviet Union.

Carlston's theoretical orientation is both imaginative and rigorous. In the long theoretical chapters (V and VI) his presentation takes the form of a series of principal propositions, augmented by subpropositions, and explicated by discursive commentary. This form of presentation facilitates systematic explanation and study. It also exhibits Carlston's self-discipline. He takes great pains to define carefully and to correlate his ideas into patterns of analysis, patterns that will be useful for the consideration of any specific problem in international life. In fact, the care is so evident that stylistic felicity is sacrificed upon an altar of definitional diligence. This subordination of style to the rigors of precision makes *Law and Organization* neither easy nor pleasant to read; nevertheless, this book is very nearly required reading for anyone concerned with the study of world order. There is a grandeur about the whole conception, the way the parts fit smoothly into a coherent whole and illuminate one another, that is suggestive of the intellectual excitement produced by systematic theology at its very best. This sense of coherence as it emerges makes one forget the drabness of style, a drabness that is an almost unavoidable outcome of Carlston's quest for conceptual precision.

Both the drabness and the precision can be illustrated by examining Carlston's conception of law. "Law comprises those norms for conduct which embody valued expectations in the functioning of a social system, deviation from which leads to measures of control, which may or may not be institutionalized in a judicial organ but which are designed to prevent the further occurrence of such deviance and to repair the resultant injuries" (p. 131). This kind of formulation is not much fun to read, nor, I suppose, to write, but it is difficult to propose a more felicitous alternative that does not sacrifice some of Carlston's meaning. Carlston puts a great deal into the definition, including an awareness of the need to insist upon a measure of freedom from either the traditions of legal positivism or natural law. Law is identified with social expectations; it is not tied to any specific sources, institutions, or metaphysical foundations. Instead law is conceived as a process used by a social system to realize values, discourage deviance, and obtain behavior that accords with societal role expectations. Such a view of law is indispensable for assessing the normative element in international life. For international society remains decentralized. The formation, interpretation, and application of law is carried on mainly by officials acting for the nations that comprise the system or for the international system itself. As such, it is useful to compare expectations and responses to deviance as a measure of the way in which law regulates interstate activity in the absence of a police force or even of a compulsory system of courts capable of settling disputes about what is legally expected in a given situation.[18]

Carlston makes explicit the dependence of law upon the character of the social system. "The regulatory process in primitive society is institutionalized in a variety of behavioral patterns, applying sanctions of differing degrees of constraint, ending, of course, in the application of force. In the state, it is institutionalized in the judicial organ" (p. 131). This statement has several significant aspects. First, the function of the judicial organ is relative to the degree to which the social system is de-

---

[18] For an exploratory generalized study of the functioning of law under these circumstances see Michael Barkun, *Law Without Sanctions: Order in Primitive Societies and the World Community*, New Haven, Yale University Press, 1968.

veloped; therefore, given the primitive condition of international society, it is a mistake to emphasize the role of the judiciary. Second, coercive self-help plays an important role in international society. If force is exercised in accord with community expectations, then it is a fulfillment not a denial of the effectiveness of international law. Third, the pressures used to obtain a high degree of compliance with international law need to be specified to accord with the operation of the system, rather than with some set of abstract criteria.

Carlston creatively emphasizes the particularities of the organizational setting within which political action takes place. The specific character of the organization exercises a very formative influence upon the way in which individuals perform their roles. This emphasis leads Carlston to affirm that "[o]rganizations and not individuals may justifiably be characterized as the principal actors in the international system" (p. 70). States are regarded as the principal organizational actors, but regional and universal actors are also considered to be international actors.

He argues "that interaction among states and other actors in the world society has not as yet assumed the pattern of a single system" (p. 66). He reaches this conclusion because "the peoples of the world . . . do not interact with one another with a sense of realization of unity, belonging together, and sharing a common culture and institutional framework." (p. 66). Carlston considers this failure to qualify as a system to be a depressing conclusion about the condition of international society as he regards the state mechanism to be no longer able to bring a tolerable degree of order to international relations or to promote human values in satisfactory fashion.[14] Carlston discusses the dangers of nuclear war and the need for coordinated economic behavior as being among the principal reasons for lamenting the inability of international society to evolve the mechanisms and beliefs that would enable it to operate as a single system.

Carlston carefully shows the interplay of power, authority, and values in international society. His efforts yield an unusually high degree of conceptual clarity. Authority is established "when commands or directions of an actor are regularly followed by action of others in conformity with such commands without reasoned explanation or persuasion of the rationality of their content" (p. 79). One simply obeys the commands of the police. Power, as an adjunct to authority, is defined as the ability to employ resources "in such a manner as to render disadvantageous a decision not to accept . . . commands" (p. 22).

[14] For a provocative discussion of the nation-state in the present international system see Stanley Hoffmann, "Obstinate or Obsolete? The Fate of the Nation-State and the Case of Western Europe," *Daedalus* (Summer 1966), 862-915.

That is, power assures compliance with commands and thereby fulfills claims to control behavior posited by law. Carlston regards extensive reliance upon power to fulfill the commands of authority as a precarious basis for social organization. It reveals the extent to which societal values are being frustrated, rather than implemented, by the authority structure. In a well-functioning society, authority is a principal mode of value realization for the members and compliance is generally voluntary, power being used to deter and apprehend the marginal violator. "As the available energy of the social system is diverted from a widespread realization of values of its members to those of a restricted élite and the resultant resistance is held in check only by an increasing use of power to support authority, the social system will eventually lose rationality to such a degree that integration will cease and the system will disintegrate" (pp. 85-86).[15]

This conceptual framework is used to analyse the deficiencies and prospects for world legal order. It leads Carlston to adopt a view of law and social process that is, at once, sophisticated and manageable. Carlston does not confuse the growth of legal order with net increases in the corpus of rules governing international behavior nor even with the expansion of institutional facilities. At the same time, Carlston is able to avoid the complexity of the McDougal-Lasswell framework of analysis with its numerous categories. Carlston believes that the "problem of creating a viable world organization" entails "the most careful exploration of those ways in which ordered progress to a different kind of a world society can be achieved" (p. 98). He is one of the first legal scholars to call scholarly attention to the development of a system of world order adequate to the needs of the day. The essential element in such a system will be its affirmation "by all participants." Only then will it be plausible to reduce the use of force "to its proper role, that is, the preservation of the system as a means for the realization of the important values of all actors therein, instead of the particularistic values of actors possessing a preponderance of power" (p. 98).

Carlston places stress upon the development of a sense of community on the part of the major participants in world affairs. This requires, among other changes, that national actors increasingly perceive the optimal functioning of regional and universal organizations as necessary for the attainment of overriding national goals. Without the development of such perceptions, states will refuse to allow supranational authority structures to engage in significant undertakings. To build

---

[15] The stability of many repressive regimes of both left and right make empirically questionable this kind of conclusion. There is no convincing evidence that democratic values, if put into operation, necessarily produce a more stable society. There are, however, many reasons aside from stability to prefer democratic modes of governance.

confidence Carlston recommends that international organizations narrow their activities to those that promote the shared values of their members. Somewhat paradoxically Carlston seems to be urging growth by a strategy of curtailment. He is, perhaps, unduly skeptical about the capacity of an international organization to deal with political conflict.[16] Given Carlston's orthodox stance on the Soviet-American rivalry, the skepticism may merely reflect his insistence that an agreement upon values is a prerequisite for effective political coordination. It is at this point that functionalists often desert their own cause, by forgetting that a common function (e.g., peacekeeping) may take precedence over value antagonisms (e.g., Congo), and may generate a mutual interest in reconciliation sufficient to override temporarily, at least, the facts of antagonism.

Carlston's persistent contention is that decisions involving the application of international law take account of the needs of international life. Such a contention tries to liberate law from any mechanical bondage to the past. Legal precedents are to be constantly appraised and reappraised in light of their current contribution to the successful functioning of an international system. Carlston asks the judge in an international tribunal or an official in a foreign office to look beyond state practice and come to decisions that are sensitive "to their suitability for promoting the viability of the international order and the opportunity of its actors to realize their important values by participation in that order" (p. 215). This complements Carlston's view that "[a]ction in the international system is not to be viewed solely from the confines and perspectives of separate states. International law as a science must find a world perspective outside and above the state" (p. 219). This demand, of course, states a widely held view, although there is considerable disagreement about the extent to which it is feasible to supersede the state at this stage and about the selection of the best available supranationalizing strategies.[17]

Among those who share Carlston's dissatisfaction with the state system in the nuclear age, the most conventional supranationalizing strategies seek to achieve world government and disarmament.[18] Carlston is skeptical about such goals, and seems surprisingly unconcerned about either world government or disarmament. He regards the development

[16] For a view that the introduction of political conflict into the work of international organizations, including especially the functional agencies, facilitates, rather than impedes, the growth of supranationalism see Ernst Haas, *Beyond the Nation-State: Functionalism and International Organization*, Stanford, Stanford University Press, 1964, pp. 429-97.

[17] Many of these issues are considered in Raymond Aron, *Peace and War: A Theory of International Relations*, Garden City, Doubleday, 1966.

[18] The range of supranationalizing strategies is surveyed in Chap. XXI.

of "at least a surface mass culture and system of shared values" as an essential precondition to the growth of a strong world organization. In the interim, national control over power and wealth assures the predominance of the nation and its officials in world affairs. Therefore, Carlston puts his stress upon the need to orient the national official toward world community values rather than upon institution building on a supranational level. In his view, ". . . not until states as actors are faced with situations of disfunction preventing the realization of highly prized values, which can be resolved only by the exercise and acceptance of centralized authority, will they be ready to become members of a world organization" (p. 121). The threat of nuclear war is not enough of a situation of disfunction to foster the requisite realization. Therefore, the prospects for supranational growth are bleak. This bleakness is reinforced by Carlston's insistence that the confrontation between East and West represents a clash of fundamental values. If the growth of a world organization depends upon the prior realization of shared values and if the major actors have contradictory values, then there is no basis for political and legal integration.

Such a conclusion leads Carlston to enter a plea for wisdom on the part of nations. Nations are urged to act for the common good because their interests are inevitably bound up with each other's welfare. Carlston's emphasis upon concession agreements and expropriation leads him to illustrate this wholeness of international life by reference to the reciprocal interests of capital-importer and capital-exporter. The importer needs capital and markets; the exporter requires an attractive investment opportunity. A successful investment relationship needs the host country to perceive a net benefit from the investment. If it is too one-sided in favor of the investor, then the domestic pressures mount to dislodge the investment and to reassert sovereign control over national resources. But if the host succumbs too easily to this pressure, other investors will be scared away and this is self-defeating for the new state, as the desired level of economic development depends upon its continuing ability to attract foreign capital. Thus, Carlston reasons, if both sides would exercise restraint their mutual advantage would be well served. Carlston chastises the new states because their short-sighted claims to expropriate without compensation defeat their own more major interests in modernization. He criticizes, for instance, Egypt for its refusal to nationalize the Suez Canal in accord with those rules and procedures of international law that have been developing to reach a compromise between the interests of investor and expropriator (p. 152). Carlston calls upon the new states to perceive and give expression to the interest they have in common with the developed states—namely, the stability and promotion of international trade and investment.[19]

Throughout Carlston's book there is this plea for wisdom and the assumption that wisdom requires the transcendence of a national outlook and the adoption of a global perspective. There is something curiously naive about this position. For if national decision-makers can acquire the disinterested wisdom to substitute global for national values, then the perception of common values required for world organization exists. Yet Carlston despairs about the growth of supranational institutions.

This combination of injunction and despair may not be quite as irreconcilable as it may sound. Carlston contends that a functional analysis of national self-interest indicates that what is good for the world is good for the nation. This analysis should guide national policy-making in the international system. However, the acceptance of the analysis does not necessarily give birth to the will to reorganize the world by transferring power and authority to global institutions. It is far easier to preach enlightenment to a national political elite than to convince it that it ought to divest itself of status and power. If one keeps this distinction in mind, it seems reasonable to conclude that Carlston draws a realistic boundary line between feasible and utopian projects for the enhancement of world order. As in other respects, Carlston's image of what is desirable and feasible in international affairs well warrants serious study by those social scientists concerned with the study of war-peace issues.

[19] For a comparable argument see Muhamed A. Mughraby, *Permanent Sovereignty Over Oil Resources*, Beirut, The Middle East Research and Publishing Center, 1966.

XIX. The Recently Independent States: A Framework for Systematic Inquiry

1. *International Law as a Strategy of Participation.* One of the most notable developments in international society since World War II has been the attainment of sovereign independence by former colonies. These recently independent states, located throughout Asia and Africa, are very different from one another in terms of scale, wealth, ideological orientation, internal stability, and external foreign policy. As a consequence these differences establish a range of national governments encompassing the most conservative and the most militantly radical regimes. At the same time these states, together to some extent with Latin American countries, create a distinct "presence" in international society by virtue of their shared outlook and priorities. All of these states are to some extent committed to developing their domestic system into a modern state and all look toward the richer, already modern states to facilitate this process.[1] It is this common feature of outlook that has led some observers of the international scene to speak of a north-south split.[2]

From the perspective of international law it is essential to gain a more sophisticated sense of what the participation of these recently independent, modernizing states signifies for the future of the international legal order.[3] One aspect of the overall subject is the extent to which the governments that fit within this loosely delimited categorization of "recently independent" states react to the received doctrines, procedures, and institutions of international law.[4] The leaders of these states are often ill-disposed toward international law because they regard it as uniquely the product of Western civilization, especially in its role of providing legitimation for colonial title to political rulership. At the same time, as weaker and poorer members of international society these ex-colonial states stand most to gain by strengthening the international legal order, especially with respect to those sectors wherein their goals are most intense. The limited capabilities of the states of Africa and Asia

[1] On modernization see C. E. Black, *The Dynamics of Modernization*, New York, Harper & Row, 1966; David E. Apter, *The Politics of Modernization*, Chicago, University of Chicago Press, 1965.

[2] For some sense of these issues see Branislav Gosovic, "UNCTAD: North-South Encounter," *International Conciliation*, No. 568 (May 1968), 1-80.

[3] Cf. Oliver J. Lissitzyn, *International Law: Today and Tomorrow*, Dobbs Ferry, Oceana, 1965; R. P. Anand, "Attitudes of the Asian-African States Toward Certain Problems of International Law," 15 *International and Comparative Law Quarterly* 782-91 (1966); R. P. Anand, "Role of the 'New' Asian-African Countries in the Present International Legal Order," 56 *American Journal of International Law* 383-406 (1962); J.J.G. Syatauw, *Some Newly Established Asian States and the Development of International Law*, The Hague, Nijhoff, 1961.

[4] A fuller development in Falk, "The New States and International Legal Order," 118 *Recueil des Cours* (1966-II) 1-103.

make them uniquely dependent on mobilizing external support. One strategy of mobilization has to do with influencing the shape and character of international law so as to shift its value bias from its historical center in Europe to something more reflective of globally relevant perspectives.[5] Such a strategy presupposes a clearer sense than now exists of what are appropriate goals for these recently independent states. To improve the tools of analysis at the disposal of international lawyers is to improve the prospects for international law itself. The presentation of the international legal order by international lawyers has consistently influenced the status and role of international law in world affairs. Given crucial changes in the international environment today there is a need, as yet unsatisfied, for a major reformulation and reorientation of the basis and character of international legal order. An important ingredient of such a reformulation would involve taking account of the effects that active participation of the recently independent states have had on the international legal order and are likely to have in the years ahead.

To assure the basis for appropriate reformulation and reorientation, however, there is a need for the adoption of a common framework of inquiry within which to collect and organize relevant data about the recently independent states and international law. A task of first priority is to organize inquiry on a comparative basis. The suitable scope of inquiry would probably be subregional (that is, smaller than the formal regional groupings but larger than a nation-state) for such areas as East Africa or Southeast Asia and national for the more important states among the recently independent states such as are India, Indonesia, and the United Arab Republic.[6] Inquiry along comparative lines would provide a solid empirical foundation upon which to construct a more comprehensive descriptive theory about the participation of the new states in the international legal system. To reach this objective, however, requires the acceptance of a reasonably common framework of inquiry and the collaboration of a large team of scholars. To provoke a consideration of the merits and feasibility of such a proposal, this chapter offers some guidelines for a common framework of inquiry.

If international law is to be a developing field of knowledge that keeps abreast of other perspectives of inquiry, it should modernize its

---

[5] A very significant case along these lines has been made by F.S.C. Northrop in a series of books. See, especially, *The Meeting of East and West*, New York, Macmillan, 1946; *The Taming of the Nations*, New York, Macmillan, 1952.

[6] For considerations bearing on the unit of analysis see Bruce Russett, *International Regions and the International System*, Chicago, Rand McNally, 1967, pp. 1-12.

A creative discussion of the interrelations between regional and global systems is found in Oran R. Young, "Political Discontinuities in the International System," *World Politics* 20 (April 1968), 369-92; see also Roger Masters, "A Multi-Bloc Model of the International System," *American Political Science Review*, 55 (Dec. 1961), 780-98.

methodology. International legal studies continue to be dominated by their double derivation from moral philosophy and diplomatic practice.[7] These two traditions can be crudely correlated with the jurisprudential traditions of natural law and legal positivism.

Natural law as the principal basis of international law produced rules so vague and sentiments so lofty that it was almost impossible to identify a violation with any persuasiveness. With the disappearance of any centralized authority in Christendom as a result of the Reformation, sovereign states asserted the authority to interpret rules of international law in a self-interested fashion and to deny external actors legal capacity to challenge such interpretations. By emphasizing self-interpretation, Vattel generalized these facts of international life and offered a reconciliation of natural law and state sovereignty in clear form that produced a conception of the international legal order that continues to be both descriptive and persuasive. From such a conception no very satisfactory account of why states are bound to obey international law can emerge; hence, the continuing debate as to whether international law is really "law."

Vattel's approach to international law also reflected the impulse to find rules of action of more specific content than could be derived by deductive forms of reasoning popular among natural lawyers. Such an impulse was reinforced by the rise of natural science based on an empirical tradition of close observation. In international legal studies this intellectual attitude was expressed by elaborate collections of diplomatic practice, illustrative of what states actually did in various instances of statecraft. The basis of international obligation was traced to evidence that sovereign consent had been given to the rule in question, the consent being established either in the form of binding agreement with one or more other sovereigns (treaty law) or in the form of patterns of practice undertaken in the spirit of obligation (customary law). This description of international law was supposed to provide a realistic sense of the limited role of law in the relations among states, as well as to associate the rule of law with "facts" rather than with "preferences." International law aspired to be a descriptive science—assembling and systematizing operative norms into a coherent order—and the international lawyer was expected to refrain from approval or disapproval of these norms and from advancing norms that might be argued to be binding because they were essential to uphold Christian morality or to satisfy the requirements of world order.

Especially in a period of rapid change in international society such a positivistic conception of international law seems insufficient. During changing conditions there exists the need to emphasize the instrumental

7 But see Chap. XV for some different trends in research and approach.

or engineering role of law and explain how law might help realize the values of various categories of participants in world affairs. Given the revisionist perspectives of many ex-colonial states toward international legal order, it becomes desirable to examine the role of law in world affairs in less static terms so as to grasp better dynamic interactions among the participants. One task of examination created by the emergence of the recently independent states is to assess which portions of international law conform to or oppose the joint and several interests of these states. This legislative style of interest analysis shifts the attention of the observer to the means available to achieve particular ends, including the extent that the international legal order is capable of experiencing reform from within.

We hope, then, to achieve an interest-oriented perspective on the participation for *each* of the new states or, at least, for each group of similarly situated new states in the international legal system. International law is conceived of as a strategy among strategies for national governments planning their action in world arenas. The value or disvalue of a specific rule, procedure, or institution of international law depends on its perceived relationship to such goals as nation-building and anti-colonialism. These perceived relationships might be expected to vary from state to state as a result of variations in background, problems, controversies, leadership, and ideology. Most frequently in the late 1960's nation-building refers to economic development and the creation of a centralized governmental apparatus—especially institutions of stable government and a trained, reliable bureaucracy.

There is also need for greater sophistication about the concept of "interest." To act on the basis of self-interest is to be a rational participant in a social and political process, but to assess self-interest in a narrow-minded form is to engage in self-destructive behavior, however self-assertive it might appear. In particular, the dominant concern of various states with facilitating the internal processes of nation-building cannot be safely divorced from the broader problems of regional and world order in the area of war and peace. Modernizing states can use their numerical strength and solidarity in international institutions to bargain on war-peace issues, offering their ideological support in exchange for the economic and military capabilities of the great powers. The virtual silence of most new states on the war in Vietnam illustrates a shortsighted unawareness of the linkage between warfare in Southeast Asia and effective pressure on southern Africa, as well as a deficient awareness of their bargaining leverage. The rather lackadaisical attitude of revisionist states toward the selection of judges for the International Court of Justice is part of what made possible the anachronistic outcome in *The South West Africa Cases*. To react to such an occurrence by condemning international legal order as regressive is to neglect both the potentiality for reforming the Court through a more rational pattern of participation and the responsibility for having in the past failed to organize opposition to candidates for judgeships known to be hostile to the main goals of the new states in international society.

The broad guidelines for a framework of inquiry presented here are designed to orient legal analysis toward discovering and assessing the operative strategy of participation of the particular state under investigation and to establish, by aggregating case studies, a corpus of comparable data that will support generalizations about the relevance of the new states to international legal order. Such an empirical methodology could, if adopted, have broad applicability and be used to guide inquiry into any major problem of international law.

2. *Guidelines for a Framework of Inquiry into the New States.*

(1) *A relevant national profile.* To assess the background of participation it is essential to have a grasp of the socioeconomic situation of a particular state, including the special shape of the domestic social order.

(a) *Historical and cultural sketch.* This outline should include a consideration of the record of relations with the international community, an account of the degree of internal stability, and a description of the main cultural traditions. The period covered should extend back to precolonial times.

(b) *Ethnolinguistic considerations.* Many of the new states operate within artificial boundaries established during the colonial period. The mapping of ethnolinguistic groupings may point up problems associated with internal security and with the acquisition of legitimacy by the central government. Often the colonial administrator allowed considerable tribal autonomy, but such autonomy is not consistent with building a centralized modern state devoted to national economic growth. The creation of a nation is vastly complicated if the society includes antagonistic ethnolinguistic units of significant size, especially if these units spill over into contiguous, unfriendly states. The problems of national stability encountered in the Congo and Nigeria during the 1960's illustrate the issue.

Furthermore, transnational ethnolinguistic groupings may make it very much more difficult for a government to establish a satisfactory level of internal security, especially where the political boundaries are uncertain and porous, as in Southeast Asia. One of the underappreciated obstacles to nation-building in Southeast Asia arises from the severe discontinuities throughout the area between ethnolinguistic boundaries and political-territorial boundaries.[8] Understanding these discontinuities helps explain the degree and quality of conflict—often shrouded in ideological terms—within a new state and with the state's neighbors. The importance of ethnolinguistic factors may be diminished or enhanced by geopolitical factors, especially by the topographical naturalness of the boundary and the political orientation of contiguous states. If a state is separated by water from its neighbors or has strong fraternal and ideological ties with them, then the artificial ethnolinguistic separations may prove less divisive.

The quality of national independence may be crucially affected by the degree to which foreign states can render effective military support to a government. The relative ease or difficulty of logistic access will often have a considerable bearing on the political alignment and diplomatic flexibility of the incumbent regime, influencing the willingness of outside states to come to its rescue in the time of crisis.

(c) *Vital statistics.* It is important to gather statistical information, including trends and projections where applicable, on such matters as size, population, rate of population growth, per capita income, cost of living, gross national product, resource inventory, agricultural productivity, exports and imports, literacy rate, degree of education, hospital facilities, hydroelectric power, and military capabilities. The idea here is to present the scale of the nation-state and to gain specific insight into its problems, potentialities, and rates of progress. Most of this information can be readily found in statistical yearbooks in tabular form and should perhaps be presented in three- to five-year intervals with projections into the future if possible. The proper focus for this statistical information should be upon the approach taken to the tasks of nation-building and modernization. Where possible, it would be extremely useful to seek quantitative indicators that might be illuminated by comparative experience. Domestic and international mail flows are among the indicators of modernization that have been proposed by social scientists. The underlying assumption of this focus is that the external role of a new state will be shaped very largely by the form of its experience with nation-building and modernization.

(d) *Patterns of investment.* The forms of investment, as well as its rate and quality, bear vitally on the modernization process and reveal clearly the extent and variety of social mobilization. As well, the treatment of investment is indicative of the character of a state's participation in the international system. Recourse to expropriation of alien property, with or without compensation, is a symbolic, as well as a highly practical, policy choice, with possibly far-reaching implica-

---

[8] See John T. McAlister, Jr., "The Possibilities for Diplomacy in Southeast Asia," *World Politics*, xix, No. 2 (Jan. 1967), 258-305.

tions for the future. Many of the new states profess to adhere to a form of socialism as a development strategy that most naturally combines ideals of social justice with the achievement of various nation-building goals, including the centralized management of economic growth. It is important to discover the behavioral attributes of the varieties of socialism throughout the new states, as well as to chart the international consequences of socialism, especially the consequences for the attraction and protection of private sources of foreign investment.

A further useful study would include a doctrinal account of the attitudes of various governing elites in each state toward foreign invest-ment, especially their views on the compatibility of private investment and foreign investment with the goals and values of the polity. In addi-tion, it would be useful to obtain statistics on the quantity of private investment and the distribution between foreign and domestic owner-ship; also it would be useful to discover the percentage of foreign in-vestment held by the former colonial power or its nationals and the per-centage of the domestic investment held by colons, as distinct from natives.

(e) *Capital assistance and foreign aid.* The amount and source of capital assistance and other forms of foreign aid from abroad should be taken into account. It would also be useful to gather information about the receipt of loans and grants from foreign countries and from international lending agencies, the record of use and repayment, and the sorts of projects involved.

(f) *The colonial period and decolonization.* The character of a new state is vitally affected by the length and form of colonial rule and the process by which national independence was achieved. The patterns of colonial administration varied considerably, from a loose and limited control to a very complete displacement of the native culture and mores by those of the colonial power. Britain, for instance, was gen-erally able to give up its colonies more easily than was France because the British colonialist ethic was separatist rather than assimilationist.

The process of decolonization is also crucial to understanding the particular character of a given new state. If decolonization came grad-ually, after a violent struggle on a large scale, the process usually pro-duced a strong military elite that supplied much of the political leader-ship after independence. The politics of struggle may have developed capacities for self-rule and created a national ethos that would not exist in a situation where independence was granted suddenly, with neither a unifying struggle nor a guided transition. The anarchy and violence of the period following the independence of the Belgian Congo in 1960 is a spectacular illustration of the dangers and tragedies that can ensue if minimum prerequisites for nationhood, such as central authority, bureaucratic structure, and intertribal arrangements, have not been brought into being in the course of decolonization. Perhaps it would be useful to approach this particular inquiry by examining the policies of the colonial power toward the indigenous independence movement. Postcolonial economic and political relations between the newly independent state and the colonial power must also be examined.

(g) *The political system.* The structural characteristics of domestic government should be included in the background profile. The pattern of leadership, the tolerance of an organized political opposition, the creation and identity of political parties, the use, frequency, and freedom of elections, the degree to which individual rights and duties are respected in accordance with legal rules and procedures, and the freedom of judicial institutions from political interference are some of the points of obvious inquiry.

Some new states are federalist or quasi-federalist in character. An important source of insight into their participation in international legal order may arise from examining their approach to interunit legal relations within their natural boundaries. In particular, it would be useful to search for indigenous practice and thought associated with conflict-of-laws problems—in both their intranational and international dimensions. In general, the practice and thought associated with the behavior of domestic legal institutions, especially courts, are neglected in constructing a theory of national participation in the international legal order. Such neglect is politically naive, in view of the concentration of power and influence on the national level in the international system.

It is also very important to examine the role of violence in the domestic life of the state. Have changes in leadership taken place by constitutional or extraconstitutional means? What use has been made of terror and suppression to eliminate or curtail political opposition, or, in contrast, to seize control of the apparatus of the state? Has the revolutionary elite, if it exists, linked itself avowedly or secretly to foreign states or to an international political movement? Is there evidence of foreign participation in the political life of the state through subversion, infiltration, propaganda, education, financing, and military means?

Such questions point to an inquiry into the degree of national autonomy that has obtained at various stages since independence. Certainly a basic world order issue for many of the new states is the preservation of their independence in the face of foreign intervention. But to control the consequences of foreign intervention presupposes a capacity for internal self-government and some success in the pursuit of viability. Otherwise, given the ease of penetration of the new state and the antagonistic goals of the principal developed states, the politics of competitive intervention are almost certain to overshadow domestic initiative. The intervention variable is among the most important, and whatever information on economic, political, military, or ideological intervention is available should be presented. It may be difficult to distinguish intervention (in the sense of interference) from participation as a consequence of interdependence and the natural linkages between the weak, poor, and inexperienced states and the strong, rich, and experienced states. The ascription of "intervention" to these relationships between a new state and other states should be justified in behavioral terms.

We need, also, some analytical distinctions. First of all, intervention in favor of the incumbent should be distinguished from intervention in favor of counterelites. Second, intervention by the former colonial power, by cold-war rivals, by imperialist neighbors, and by international institutions should be distinguished. Third, the objective of intervention should be identified to the extent possible—for instance, to neutralize intervention by another state, to influence government policy, to change the structure and authority pattern of the government in a decisive way, to prevent, foment, or influence the outcome of civil strife. And fourth, the means of intervention should be classified in a systematic fashion, as being of an ideological, military, economic, or diplomatic character.

(h) *The indigenous legal tradition.* As one of the basic themes in international legal inquiry has been a comparison of the native legal background with the structure and content of international law, it is desirable to assemble some relevant data.

It might be useful to search for indigenous attitudes toward law, authority, sovereignty, justice, legal obligation, private property, inheritance, dispute settlement, and the liberty of the individual. Certainly the belief supposedly widespread in China that just as there is only one sun in the sky so there can be only one empire in the world is an important conditioning variable affecting China's entry into a political order such as the international legal order, based as it is on notions of coordination rather than subordination and superordination. It would be useful in examining a state's attitudes toward law to obtain as much information as possible about its relations with countries in the region. The overall objective is to identify in what respects, if any, national attitudes toward domestic law and order affect attitudes toward international law. Of especial concern is any evidence that particular portions of international law will be rejected in the event of a conflict with domestic law. Also it would be useful to find out whether there are any specific incompatibilities between the indigenous legal traditions and specific rules and procedures of international law. Such an inquiry might cast light on the Jenks-Northrop debate on whether comparative law research will mostly disclose national experience supportive of international law or mostly reveal vital points of incompatibility.

Legal attitudes toward the role of force to settle domestic and foreign disputes are also important to discern, as is the degree to which national practice confirms or contradicts these attitudes.

(2) *Participation in the international legal order.* In section (1) the objective of the guidelines is to obtain a descriptive background that locates a particular new state in the spectrum of new states active in the international legal system. Section (2) proposes a descriptive survey of the facts of participation in the international legal order. Here the attempt is mainly to gain basic insights, not to produce a detailed accounting.

(a) *The facts of participation.* It would be useful to have an idea about the degree of diplomatic contact maintained by a new state with foreign countries and with international institutions. An inventory of membership and figures on the relative size and importance of delegations and missions would be useful. Information on relative budgets would also be suggestive of the distinctive patterns of participation. One might expect to confirm the hypothesis that, compared with the older countries, most new states devote a greater proportional diplomatic effort to international institutions than to traditional internation diplomacy. It would be useful to know the extent to which dues owed global and regional international organizations were paid and to appraise the national contributions to the operations of the organizations through providing their leadership and civil service.

The facts of nonparticipation or nominal participation might be just as interesting as the data on high-priority participation. The overall pattern of diplomatic activity might give some sense of the implicit and explicit thinking of the governing elite in a new state about the ways it might best serve its interests through participating in the international system with the limited economic means and diplomatic talent at its disposal. Certainly skepticism about the role of international law in the behavior of the relatively modernized countries is supported by comparing their enormously greater expenditure of resources and talents on alliances than on the activities of international institutions.

The attitude of the state toward the International Court of Justice might be especially important to assess. Article 93 of the United Nations Charter makes all members of the Organization *ipso facto* parties to the Statute of the International Court of Justice. Given the lack of any obligation to submit disputes to the Court, this minimum formal affiliation is not very significant. More revealing indicators of the state's attitude include an examination of the actual participation in Court proceedings, the state's attitude toward reference of its disputes to the

Court, the practice of the state with respect to the insertion of compromissory clauses in treaties, its acceptance of compulsory jurisdiction with or without reservations, its promoting or opposing use of the advisory jurisdiction of the Court, and its views and practice bearing on compliance with the Court's determinations.[9]

It is also revealing to detail the participation of the state in large international conferences of a law-making character. The conferences dealing with draft conventions on the law of the sea and consular immunities are obvious examples.[10]

Likewise, the debates in the Sixth Committee of the General Assembly could reveal shifts in national positions that bear on attitudes toward international legal order.

(b) *An inventory of international disputes and claims.* It would be helpful to have on hand an enumeration of claims and disputes, prospects for their settlement, and expressions of willingness to use the rules and procedures of traditional international law as the basis for settlement. It might be useful to classify these disputes and claims by economic and territorial subject matter.

It is especially important to gain evidence of official and expert thinking, as well as national practice, on jurisdictional issues, especially on the extent and bases of national jurisdiction over various categories of subject matter. International legal order depends largely on patterns of claims and deference; therefore, the presentation of jurisdiction attitudes of a new state would be quite suggestive of its overall attitudes toward international legal order. It is especially important to determine whether the new state protects its self-interest by overclaiming, as when states enlarge the whole breadth of territorial waters to vindicate a particular claim to exclusive offshore fishing rights. The avoidance of overclaiming (and underclaiming) is indicative of the extent to which a state has assimilated the logic of reciprocity in its rational definition of national self-interest vis-à-vis potential adversary states. The self-limitation of claims in the interests of achieving a reconciliation of interests with some potential counterclaimants may be an important aspect of a rational strategy of participation in the international legal system.

It is also important to assess attitudes toward the vertical aspect of jurisdiction—the relationship between the competence of international institutions and the sanctity of the domestic jurisdiction. In what settings, by what criteria, with what rationale has the new state sought to specify the scope of and exceptions to domestic jurisdiction?

---

[9] Cf. Ibrahim F. I. Shihata, "The Attitudes of New States Toward the International Court of Justice," *International Organization*, XIX (Spring 1965), 203-22, at 205-16.

[10] See R. L. Friedheim, "The 'Satisfied' and the 'Dissatisfied' States Negotiate International Law: A Case Study," *World Politics*, XVIII, No. 1 (Oct. 1965), 20-41.

Some of the claims may have to do with the process of repudiating old law and creating new law. The new states incline toward favoring a limited legislative role for the General Assembly and appear to accord greater significance to its actions than do the advanced countries that are concerned with keeping the United Nations within its constitutional limits. To endow the will of the international community with a quasi-legislative role to be exercised by the formal expressions of consensus in the General Assembly is to alter traditional conceptions of law-creation in international society, especially by reducing the role of the sovereign state in the process. Traditional notions of obligation in international law have accorded a virtual veto to the sovereign state by making its expression of consent to be bound an indispensable precondition of a legal obligation. This veto has also kept in being a rule that had lost the support of much of the international community. It would be useful to gather any evidence of thought and action by the new states in relation to these issues.

One exceedingly hopeful sign is the approach taken by the African countries toward boundary disputes. There exists an almost limitless number of overlapping boundary claims that are of the sort that have in the past led revisionist movements to war. Despite their total repugnance for the colonial period the African states have resolved "to respect the frontiers existing on their achievement of national independence" (i.e., colonial frontiers).[11] The Council of Ministers of the Organization of African Unity has played a very constructive role in making mediation available under its auspices in the two main disputes that have so far erupted—Algeria-Morocco and Ethiopia-Somalia.[12]

(c) *Attitude toward state succession.* One of the more revealing areas for assessing the attitude of a new state toward the international legal order involves problems of state succession, namely, whether the state regards itself as bound by some or all of the international legal obligations incurred by predecessor regimes. Does the new state have the right to pick and choose among inherited legal obligations? The attitude taken on this question goes to the essence of whether the new state feels that it has been created by and born into a preexisting and objective world of law or whether as a latecomer to the international scene the new state feels it can determine for itself the extent to which it is bound by rules devised by others. Part of the issue is whether international law is regarded as Eurocentric in certain respects and whether these perceptions are allowed to support a selective process of acceptance and rejection. A more important part of the issue is whether the leaders

[11] See the text reprinted in Colin Legum. *Pan-Africanism*, New York, Praeger, 1962, p. 303.
[12] *Id.* at 139-40.

of the new states consider traditional rules as satisfactory bases for present conditions.[13]

A further problem is posed in the event that in the period since the recovery of national independence, governments have obtained political control by unconstitutional methods and have repudiated the legal obligations assumed by postindependence predecessor regimes. In a certain sense we have one set of problems relevant to succession that can be associated with the transition from colonial status to national independence and another, quite distinct, set of problems that can be associated with instabilities and revolutionary politics in the new state. Both of these processes foster attitudes that may direct challenges at portions of the international legal system, but the causal explanations and policy consequences are quite different.

A refusal to be bound by obligations descending from the colonial period may very well accord with notions of unjust enrichment and with the general repudiation of the exploitation and injustice associated with colonialism. If this repudiation is sharply distinguished from postcolonial and voluntary acceptances of new obligations, then there is no reason to suppose a permanent impairment of the credibility of international legal obligations. But if the successive governments in new states undergoing modernization insist upon discretion to repudiate postcolonial international undertakings of predecessor regimes, then a serious loss of confidence in international commitments is bound to result. Because some postcolonial legal commitments may be "neocolonialist" (i.e., a continuation of unfair colonial prerogatives reflecting the values and interests of the governing elite in the "independent" state), it is impossible to insist upon a rigid distinction between colonial and postcolonial classifications. A constructive compromise might be achieved by requiring an external or impartial decision-maker to uphold a specific claim of unjust enrichment justifying the repudiation of a legal obligation (on a succession-of-government rationale) incurred after national independence was achieved, whereas an internal decision-maker would suffice for the repudiation of obligations dating from the colonial period.

(d) *The domestic reception of international law.* Closely connected with the inquiries into problems of state succession is the attitude taken toward the application of international law in disputes that are handled within the domestic legal system. Given the decentralization of international legal order, it is very important to strengthen international law by the action of national institutions. This is especially important for the new states, as relatively weak members of international society. For

[13] In general, see A. A. Fatouros, "International Law and the Third World," 50 *Virginia Law Review* 783-823 (June 1964).

this reason, it would be useful to discover whether by constitutional provision or by statute international law is the supreme law of the land and to find out under what circumstances a specific rule of international law must be received by an act of the national legislature as a precondition of its internal validity. As well, judicial experience or opinions of a state's legal adviser on foreign affairs would be very revealing.

A focal point of inquiry, although one for which evidence may not be available, is whether the courts of the new state are subject to political influences in international law cases. Even in advanced countries with long-cherished traditions of judicial independence, it is unclear whether a domestic court is generally free to apply international law in an impartial fashion. Foreign policy and ideological considerations often dominate the domestic legal scene. The *Sabbatino* controversy that has had such a long and colorful history in the United States is an illustration.[14] In gathering data on the new states it is most important to gain whatever material and practice is relevant to the role of domestic courts in international law cases, as well as to obtain some understanding of the distribution of authority between the executive, judicial, and legislative branches in the domestic application of international law. One would expect that the weak traditions of constitutionalism in many of the new states would lead to a centralization of authority in the executive on these matters and that the domestic application of international law would be on a rather *ad hoc* basis.

It would be useful to inquire into the conditions under which an individual can appeal to international law in a domestic court. Issues of standing and justiciability are present and are now the subject of dramatic litigation challenging the legality under international law of military participation by the United States in the war in Vietnam. The most interesting of these cases involves objections to military service by individuals subject to selective service obligations. In addition, approaches to sovereign immunity and the act of state doctrine are important indicators of the extent to which domestic courts will be permitted to examine the validity of governmental action—foreign as well as domestic—in response to a legal complaint by an individual.

Domestic courts can operate to generate quasi-legislative data by their international law decisions, introducing new standards and questioning old ones. Recalling that international legal order is characterized as a value-realizing process, one sees that national arenas are ideal contexts within which to register value claims posited by the new states.

(e) *State responsibility for injury to aliens.* Traditional international law devoted considerable attention to the establishment of rules protect-

---

[14] For a description see Falk and others, *The Aftermath of Sabbatino*, Dobbs Ferry, N. Y., Oceana, 1965.

ing aliens resident in non-Western countries, protecting their persons and their property. Sometimes this protection operated as incidental to imperialism. Notions of extraterritoriality or capitulary regimes expressed an unwillingness by the colonial powers to submit this alien interest to domestic legal institutions in the non-Western world. Such an unwillingness flowed from the wider idea that international law had been developed by and for the benefit of the colonial powers. The new states have legitimized their claim to subject foreign interests to domestic control by a supportive resolution of the General Assembly.[15] But that same resolution requires respect for property interests in accordance with international law and includes an acceptance of a duty to pay out appropriate compensation in the event of expropriation. It establishes a framework within which new legal norms might emerge to govern relationships between capital-exporting countries and capital-importing countries on the basis of equality and mutual advantage.[16] There is a need for a legal atmosphere that is not dominated by the colonial and imperialist past when the law of state responsibility was evolved on the basis of inequality and one-sided advantage, often amounting to exploitation.

In gathering data it would be useful to collect any information on the regulation of foreign investment, including laws, court decisions, and administrative rulings.[17] It is especially important to narrate any investment disputes, not only outright expropriation but also complaints relating to concession agreements, currency regulation, repatriation of profit, tax rates, domestic ownership requirements, and so on. In the event of an expropriation, it is important to examine the offer of compensation, the response of the investor, and the entire sociopolitical context and merits of the dispute. In the absence of expropriation it would be useful to analyze the factors that have enabled foreign investment to remain or increase in the postcolonial period and to identify the sectors of the economy where foreign investment has been either encouraged or discouraged.

Subsidiary attention should also be given to noneconomic aspects of state responsibility, especially to the use of international law as a way to promote fairness in the treatment of aliens accused or prosecuted for crimes under local law. There are potential issues of human rights involved here which have received scant attention in the contemporary period.

[15] G. A. Res. 1803 (XVII).
[16] Cf. e.g., E. I. Nwogugu, *The Legal Problems of Foreign Investment in Developing Countries*, University of Manchester Press, 1965; Muhamad A. Mughraby, *Permanent Sovereignty over Oil Resources*, Beirut, The Middle East Research and Publishing Center, 1966.
[17] This section on legal data should be correlated with the corresponding section, pp. 518-19 on factual data associated with foreign investment.

It would also be desirable to examine the treatment given to a claim made by an alien that his rights under international law were being infringed by the territorial government. If such a claim is made by an alien in protesting action to government officials, is it taken seriously or brushed aside as mere propaganda? Such an inquiry might also include a determination of whether there are local remedies available for violations of international law and whether it is difficult to exhaust these remedies in order to render a claim "ripe" for diplomatic negotiation prior to a last-ditch resort to an international tribunal.

(f) *Supranationalism.* Many of the recently independent states are not yet viable political entities, as determined by the successful discharge of either economic or military functions associated with the exercise of national sovereignty. It has, therefore, been necessary for these countries to find external support to survive. Such a necessity compromises the pride of these countries, especially to the extent that it reveals new forms of dependency in fact if not in formal status. In such circumstances the possibilities of supranational integration have been seriously considered. The idea, of course, is to achieve certain national objectives by enlarging the unit of political organization sufficiently to achieve higher levels of viability—and thereby to solve problems associated with independence without inviting the intervention of the great powers. Supranationalism also is ideologically appealing to many societies in Africa and Asia, partly because it is a way of taking advantage of the feelings of solidarity and unity arising from transnational religious, racial, or tribal identifications. These supranational symbols of coherence often have greater mass appeal than do symbols of national solidarity and unity that are artificially imposed by the governing elites. It is a fact that several African countries have made constitutional provisions for this shift of sovereign powers to a unit broader than the nation-state.

The important feature relevant to the international legal order is that the new states, despite a very emotional attachment to nationalism in certain respects, have acknowledged from the outset the possibility of organizing international life on the basis of units other than the nation-state. And especially with respect to specialized tasks associated with economic development, the new states have not questioned the compatibility of sovereignty and supranationalism. In fact, often the only alternatives to supranationalism are a frustrated nationalism unable to project or meet reasonable domestic goals or a nominal nationalism subject to great-power intervention, if not covert hegemony.

There is now such a bewildering variety of international institutions operative in international life that it is important to develop a taxonomy by which to present the extent of supranationalism. In particular, it would be useful to assess exactly what kind of sovereign prerogative has been supranationalized and for what purpose. Statistical indicators related to budget, delegations, and so on, might reveal the scale and pattern of commitment to some extent, as might a summary of the formal obligations and procedures entailed by active membership in various institutions, together with the record of participation.

(g) *General role on strategic war-peace issues.* The Afro-Asian states have been generally naive about working out a rational strategy of participation in the war-peace area. Their influence in the General Assembly as a voting majority gives them some bargaining potential vis-à-vis the West. If the United States and Britain are reluctant to support Afro-Asian demands for a rapid rectification of the situation in southern Africa, then the Afro-Asians might consider mobilizing action to refer uses of force by the great powers to the International Court of Justice for an Advisory Opinion. Such a reference of a conflict to adjudication—for instance, the conflict in Vietnam—might have an intrinsically beneficial effect, but beyond this direct effect there is created an opportunity for world order "trade-offs": American support on policy toward southern Africa might be solicited in exchange for Afro-Asian forbearance on the Vietnam issues. If the emphasis of a new state entering the structured environment of international society is upon devising a strategy of participation that maximizes its interests, then it is essential to take note of unused potentialities, as well as to inventory manifested attitudes and actions.

It might also be illuminating to examine the positions taken in various settings on war-peace issues. Such an inquiry might help to reveal the degree to which a particular state has played a constructive role in international society when its own immediate interests were not involved. Several African countries, for an apparent variety of motives, supplied the United Nations with much of the manpower used to carry out the Congo operation. Afro-Asian conferences have been increasingly sensitive to the connection between the economic savings associated with drastic disarmament and the imposition of a duty on the rich nations to transfer some of their wealth to the poor countries.

As nuclear proliferation proceeds, the more important new states are themselves confronted with the need to make critical choices. The acquisition of a nuclear capability by China has put great pressure upon India to do the same or to receive some effective equivalent addition to its security, perhaps in the form of a system of guarantees by the nuclear superpowers. At least India has acted to keep the option available, and Indian security interests are likely to provoke crucial debate as to whether India should, in the event of a signature at Geneva, ratify a nonproliferation treaty. If India decides to acquire nuclear weapons

—it already possesses an incipient capability that is roughly equal to China's present capability—its decision will probably provoke Pakistan, possibly Japan, Indonesia, and Australia to do the same. South Africa, too, has an industrial base that might encourage it to acquire a nuclear capability to deter its African neighbors. Israel and the United Arab Republic have maintained a rather ambiguous posture in their respective nuclear development programs.

The new states, then, are now entering an early phase of the nuclearization of their international relations.[18] In the period between 1945 and 1964 the new states were largely spectators in the strategic military arms race conducted between the Soviet Union and the United States and were to some extent potential victims as a consequence of contamination of the atmosphere by fallout from testing or from a war or conceivably as a consequence of providing the first nuclear battlefield (some American leaders proposed using nuclear weapons in the Korean War).

Certainly the leaders of the new states are in some sense aware that a nuclear form of World War III would produce such economic and political disarray as to imperil their own nation-building enterprise. But as frightened and somewhat self-righteous spectators, these states have largely confined their role to moralizing and formulating abstract pleas for drastic disarmament. The strategic arms race, which the outstanding Afro-Asian leaders have associated with great-power politics, has had a rather abstract remoteness for them. But with China, Indonesia, Ghana, and the United Arab Republic all emerging as regional military powers with ambitions to dominate or intimidate foreign countries, the attitude of the new states toward war-peace issues has become increasingly serious.

In studying a particular new state's participation it might be useful to break down inquiry into four subcategories: (i) disarmament, (ii) collective security, (iii) rules of world order, (iv) just-war doctrine.

(i) *Disarmament.* Participation in disarmament conferences, ratification of the limited test ban, attitudes toward the draft treaties on nonproliferation and general and complete disarmament, and policy on domestic acquisition of nuclear weapons are relevant here. Some attention might be paid to the state's voting record on disarmament issues in the United Nations and the contributions to debates on the subject. Finally, it would be useful to determine whether a state considers disarmament only as disarming of others or whether its consideration in-

18 For a general analysis see essays by Richard A. Falk, Robert C. Tucker, and Oran R. Young published under the title *On Minimizing the Use of Nuclear Weap-* *ons*, Research Monograph No. 23, Center of International Studies, Princeton University, March 1, 1966.

cludes a serious willingness to engage in self-limiting arrangements. It should be noted that the new states have taken some initiative in trying to establish nuclear-free zones in the main geographical divisions of the southern hemisphere.

(ii) *Collective security.* The extent and nature of support given the United Nations in undertaking its various efforts at peacekeeping and peaceful settlement should be described. Some attention might also be given to the position taken on the financing dispute, which indicates to some extent a state's attitude toward endowing the United Nations with a certain degree of financial independence in situations affecting international peace and security. Attention should also be given to the issue of whether the response of a state in the United Nations seems motivated mostly by the world-order criteria embodied in the Charter or reflects very short-term ideological calculations relative to a particular use of force. Is the state opportunistic about limiting collective security to measures on behalf of national interests? As an example, was there an unconcern about Soviet uses of its military power to suppress the East European uprising in 1956 or was the relative inactivity of the Afro-Asian states a consequence of a feeling that nothing could be done by the United Nations against one of the superpowers as an adversary?

(iii) *Rules of order.* The new states have joined the Soviet bloc in espousing the adoption of rather abstract rules of world order as part of the effort to maintain a peaceful world. The nonintervention resolution adopted by unanimous vote in the General Assembly is a recent example of a carefully drafted document that is unlikely to have the slightest impact upon the interaction among states.[19] In an interdependent world the proscription of intervention in general terms seems to be a naive or misleading act, one that tends to take attention away from support for *procedural* techniques. For instance, a fact-finding agency or a border-control capability would appear to contribute something, whereas rules defining nonintervention or peaceful coexistence are unlikely to make any contribution and may often degenerate into mere tools for the conduct of hostile propaganda.

With regard to defining aggression, self-defense, and armed attack, the same limitations are apparent, although to a lesser degree. A set of *procedural* requirements for compliance with the obligation to specify the facts justifying a claim of self-defense to the Security Council might discourage the sort of pro forma compliance with the Charter that the United States has purported to achieve during the war in Vietnam.

In some areas legislative claims in the form of General Assembly

19 G. A. Res. 2131 (XX) [adopted by a roll-call vote of 109 in favor to none against, with one abstention (United Kingdom)].

resolutions may have a constructive, though unspectacular, effect. The new states have, for instance, without the blessings of the great powers (and over the real opposition of the United States) passed a series of resolutions questioning the legality of nuclear weapons. G. A. Res. 1653 (XVI) went so far as to declare that the use of a nuclear weapon would constitute *ipso facto* a war crime. Such a resolution is certainly helpful to those seeking to establish a tradition of nonuse for nuclear weapons equivalent to that applicable to poison gas. The new states can play a role in this process by creating an overall climate of opinion that brings some pressure on the great powers and strengthens peace-minded domestic factions in those countries.

(iv) *The just-war doctrine.* Each state by deed and doctrine has taken certain positions on the use of force to achieve preferred policy objectives. The new states have been particularly active in calling for the use of force to terminate colonialism and to establish majority rule in southern Africa. Some new states, most notably the more expansionist, have also advocated the use of force to combat neocolonialism. Indonesia's claims against Malaysia are, perhaps, the most flagrant example, but by no means an isolated one. In this area we should obtain as much insight as possible into the degree to which various priorities in the foreign policy of a state are accorded precedence over the total renunciation of nondefensive force expressed in Article 2(4) of the Charter. It should be emphasized that the promotion of just-war objectives in the guise of collective security operations appears to be compatible with international law. It is the insistence on using force without authorization by the United Nations that sets up a conflict between the just-war doctrine of the state in question and the Charter.

(h) *The revision of the international legal system.* It is important to discover what the spokesmen of the new states assert as desirable and feasible in the way of reforming the international legal system. To begin with, it would be helpful to distinguish between changes demanded in specific rules (width of territorial seas, compensation of foreign investment, trade preferences) and changes sought in the structure of international society (redistributions of the power, wealth, and prestige, especially transfers to international institutions and to the new states by the rich and dominant states). Then, too, it would be helpful to examine what has been done to promote these various reforms, to what extent these demands are symbol-wielding and rhetorical and to what extent they represent real action goals posited as part of national policy.

Inquiry into these matters should clarify the extent to which a particular new state can be considered as revolutionary, reformist, or conservative in its impact upon international legal order.

3. *Conclusion.* The collection of information in accord with this outline for a framework of inquiry should permit a better-evidenced discussion of the new states and international legal order. Such an endeavor might also illustrate the importance of introducing more rigorous techniques of observation and analysis into the study of international law.

PART FIVE

STRENGTHENING THE INTERNATIONAL

LEGAL ORDER

Introduction

THERE IS a long tradition of confusing facts and values in the presentation of the international legal order. In particular, there has been a tendency for international lawyers to present personal preferences or national outlooks as if they were analyses of international law as it is. The mixing of analytical and normative modes of inquiry has been one of the reasons why the pronouncements of international lawyers are so often greeted with suspicion.

To overcome this suspicion more recent generations of international lawyers have tended to either reject the normative dimensions altogether and concentrate their energies upon explicative analysis or to ignore the descriptive dimension and concentrate their energies on the advocacy of a better system of world order. The analysts tend toward trivializing the subject matter of international law, whereas those who fully indulge their normative inclinations are likely to become so detached from the political realities of the times as to make their prescriptive commentary virtually irrelevant.

A group of outstanding international lawyers of our time including Myres S. McDougal, Julius Stone, Wolfgang Friedmann, Charles de Visscher, and C. Wilfred Jenks have struggled to achieve a reunion of analytical and normative modes of inquiry that is neither foolishly idealistic nor cynically manipulative. Two central ideas permit this reunion to be fruitful: the idea of "process" which is suggestive of the inevitable movement toward the future implicit in the environment of any legal order, and the idea of "function" which is suggestive of a criterion of choice that measures what is desirable by what carries out certain tasks set by the broader social and political system. These newer intellectual styles of inquiry generate candid proposals to strengthen the international legal order that are rooted in an awareness of the restraints created by present realities. More significant, perhaps, than the proposals themselves is a new way of thinking about the future of the international legal order that is characterized by combining the virtues of pragmatism with those of idealism, by seeking improvement in terms of what is feasible. There is, of course, considerable disagreement as to what makes what feasible, as well as about what constitutes an improvement.

In the United States with its legal heritage shaped by the common law tradition there is a strong tendency to assume that what is feasible is gradual and incremental rather than sudden and drastic. This tendency of thought is not supported by any testable theory of change nor is it confirmed by recent international history. Certainly the process of decolonialization as it unfolded between 1945 and 1965 is illustrative of a fundamental change in the character of international society that came about suddenly and proceeded at a rate that seems predictable, if at all, only when considered in retrospect. The skeptical attitude taken toward drastic changes in the international legal order through the transfer of sovereign prerogatives to international institutions at a regional or global level may not be feasible at all, or it may be feasible either gradually or suddenly depending on the relevant conditioning variables. Not enough is yet known about how change takes place in complex political units to support any dogmatic form of affirmation or rejection of any specific strategy of change. It is certainly desirable that a conception of how to strengthen international law builds its case from the available evidence and that it connects the present with a preferred future through some explanation of the transition process.

The chapters in Part Five are experimental studies carried on in this spirit. Chapter XX examines how the trend of "law reform" has fared in a classical area of international concern—the regulation of ocean fisheries. The problems posed by substituting a community-oriented pattern of regulation for a state-oriented pattern raises many of the problems of compromising sovereign discretion through voluntary agreement. The logic of decentralization is challenged by newer conceptions of community management and social engineering. The result has been a kind of disorderly compromise that seeks to uphold the basic claims of each principal category of sovereign states. These claims are not mutually consistent and so the incentives for law reform are unequally present in international society. Chapter XXI attempts to depict four plausible models of the shape of future international systems and to assess the law-consequences of each. In this exercise the objective is to confront the present international legal order critically by comparing it with some significant alternative ordering patterns, but to refrain from judging which pattern is better or from predicting which pattern is likely to emerge. The only part of the analysis that is mildly predictive is the assertion that present international legal order is likely to persist approximately as we know it throughout the foreseeable future unless there occurs some cataclysmic event of the proportion of a third world war.

In Chapter XXII the special difficulties of law and policy created by the continuation of the Vietnam War are considered, with special concern being devoted to the normative basis for military intervention in the internal affairs of sovereign states. Does the invitation of a constituted elite—an incumbent regime—*always* make legal an intervention, regardless of magnitude, duration, impact, and wider community attitudes? Under what circumstances of humanitarian concern or community disposition is it proper to give assistance to a counterelite, whether it be a secessionist counterelite (Biafra, Katanga) or an insurgent elite (the National Liberation Front in South Vietnam, some future anti-apartheid uprising in South Africa or South West Africa)? These questions underlie a critical examination of the central lines of policy inference drawn by the advocates and the critics of the United States role in the Vietnam War. Chapter XXII tries to discover and promote a middle ground between the neo-Wilson rationalization of a world role for the United States and the neo-Kennanist critique that has been set forward as a response.

And, finally, Chapter XXIII, analyzes the shaken foundations of political loyalty in the United States that have resulted from the adoption of "military approaches" in Vietnam and in the cities of America to essentially nonmilitary problems. The chapter examines the case for a reorientation of loyalty in postindustrial society toward a more cosmopolitan, less nationalistic, value base, and associates the success of this reorientation in principal sovereign states with the prospects for a strengthened international legal order in the decades ahead.

XX. Settling Ocean Fishing Conflicts:
The Limits of "Law Reform" in a
Horizontal Legal Order

The Westphalia System and the Pressures Upon It

Despite certain very critical centralizing tendencies, the international legal order remains, as it has for several centuries, largely horizontal or decentralized. Decentralization in international society implies that principal decisions are typically made and implemented by officials acting on behalf of national governments. A decentralized legal order tends to be voluntaristic, especially with respect to normative change; that is, changes in the structure of international law require widespread assent from the state units that are the subjects of regulation. A further consequence of this voluntarism is that it is very difficult to adapt the legal order to changed circumstances whenever states perceive their interests as significantly diverse. Such difficulty is especially pronounced when some national governments perceive their interests to be best preserved by adherence to the earlier scheme of legal order, however obsolescent such a scheme may appear to the majority of states or to the collective perceptions of world community welfare.

The issue, in its most general terms, is to understand the problem of "legal reform" on an international level. Once the issue is clearly stated there is the further possibility of examining alternative strategies of accommodation. The purpose of this chapter is to depict the issue and to consider some accommodating strategies in the specific substantive setting of the international law of ocean fisheries.

It is my view that the underlying problem of achieving a functional reordering of the international law of ocean fisheries is an excellent, if bedeviling, illustration of the general phenomenon of legal reform in international society. More specifically, the basic legal arrangement created in earlier centuries was designed to stabilize the scope of state jurisdiction; it was designed to clarify the realm within which a particular government was allowed to exert its sovereign control. Once the oceans were determined to be "free" (and not subject to sovereign appropriation) and certain coastal fringes of ocean made subject to qualified sovereign authority, largely to uphold security interests, then the pattern of legal authority as well as its supporting rationale were easily developed. The international law of fisheries is a special instance of the distribution of legal competence over the oceans for all purposes, and this distribution is itself derived from the more general conception of a decentralized international order constituted by sovereign states and first laid down in concrete and authoritative form at the Peace of Westphalia (1648).

The animating functional logic of the Westphalia system expressed a drive to solve the jurisdictional problems that dominate a social and political order lacking any prospect of a governmental center.[1] This jurisdictional solution seemed compatible with the requirements of ocean fishing. The nature of fishing technology automatically confined most fishing efforts to areas of ocean near the coastal state. Overlapping fishing interests of any significance were comparatively rare. Of more importance, the scale of exploitation did not appear to infringe upon supply —the fishery resources of the sea were supposed to be virtually inexhaustible and it was desirable, hence, to allow nationals of any state to fish freely on the high seas. Such presuppositions supported a decentralized ordering of legal competence that did not generate any significant evidence of dissatisfaction; the Westphalia system as applied to ocean fisheries appeared generally adequate until after World War II. To be sure, there were indications that certain species of fish might be depleted, even extinguished, by the permissive standards of exploitation associated with decentralization, but there was no general awareness that such exceptional issues could not be dealt with by *ad hoc* conservation effort.[2] There was, in other words, no systemic dissatisfaction with the basic scheme of the Westphalia system—permissiveness for all on the high seas and exclusiveness for the coastal state with regard to a narrow band of territorial waters. And, in fact, there was little evidence of extended coastal claims to reserve exclusive rights to fisheries beyond the three-mile limit.

Beginning late in the nineteenth century, however, certain developments created some dissatisfaction that has grown to express a widespread sense of international concern about the adequacy of a jurisdictional conception of legal order with respect to fisheries disputes.[3]

---

[1] A jurisdictional approach to world order emphasizes the task of allocating legal competence to apply national law. The primary role of international law becomes one of providing clear-enough allocational rules so that contradictory national claims to possess legal competence are kept at a minimum. Such a concern with the allocation of legal competence should be sharply distinguished from a concern with the substantive content of law.

[2] For a discussion of the international regulatory efforts to conserve certain endangered species of whales see Douglas M. Johnston, *The International Law of Fisheries—A Framework for Policy-Oriented Inquiries*, New Haven, Yale University Press, 1965, pp. 396-411 [hereinafter cited as Johnston].

[3] The concern that has developed encompasses fishery problems in a wider frame of reference applicable to all those subject matters for which the realities of growing interdependence suggest the need for common substantive standards and agreed compulsory procedures of dispute-settlement. Decentralized legal order is functionally sufficient only when the degree of interdependence of use is marginal and when the decentralized actors share reasonably common interests. The exploitation of ocean fisheries, of course, has experienced trends of accelerating interdependence and of diverging interests. There is also some potentiality for functional arrangements that result from bargaining trade-offs that involve an exchange

First of all, technological innovation progressively encouraged the exploitation of evermore distant fisheries. Secondly, new fishing techniques seemed, in some instances, to be so effective that the maintenance, and in some cases even the survival of significant species of fish seemed endangered, especially under conditions of unrestricted interstate competition. Thirdly, ocean fishing was often done in a wasteful manner, resulting in unnecessary depletion of stocks. Fourth, an increasing awareness emerged that ocean fishing was an important basis of support and earnings for certain otherwise underprivileged states and a potential source of food supply for many of the hungry and crowded countries of the world. Fifth, the uneven modernization of fishing technology enabled certain states, most notably Japan, but more recently the Soviet Union, Peru, and even South Korea, to fish very heavily and profitably in a considerable zone of waters contiguous to the narrow belt of territorial waters.[4] Sixth, the United States by claiming national competence to regulate the continental shelf underlying ocean waters established a kind of precedent for other spectacular claims to exclusive control over vast sectors of ocean at the expense of the inclusive or community sector of "freedom."[5] Seventh, smaller, less developed states eager to safeguard potential fisheries against exploitation adopted preemptive strategies and extended greatly, and in various forms, claims to establish exclusive fishing zones.[6]

The cumulative impact of these developments helps to explain the numerous arguments against retaining the jurisdictional focus of the Westphalia system, with its resulting permissiveness, or putting the issue more polemically, with its resulting anarchic patterns of exploitation.

---

of assertions and/or concessions in different subject-matter areas. For instance, perhaps foreign aid designed to modernize fishing fleets can be bargained for a more managerially satisfying regime for the regulation of a contested off-shore fishery resource. International lawyers have been reluctant to analyze the bargaining opportunities that may provide a basis for consensual legal order. This reluctance is deeply rooted in a static jurisprudential tradition that directs inquiry at legal doctrine rather than at the processes and procedures that have yielded or might yield doctrine.

[4] The remarkably rapid growth of the Peruvian fishing industry over the last decade offers the less modernized states of the world a very suggestive model of what it is possible to do in a short period. Ocean fishing appears to be a sector wherein rapid development can take place and wherein a contribution to food supply, and often foreign exchange, constitutes a valuable and immediate reward. For statistics on the total catch of the leading fishing countries in 1938, 1948, 1958, and 1962 see tabular presentation in Johnston, p. 19.

[5] Johnston has effectively expressed the point in the following language: "The main criticism is that framers of this regime [of the continental shelf] were apparently careless of the effects it would have on claimants to extensive unshared authority over floating fisheries who lack a shelf and therefore fail to benefit from this act of bounty. It is certainly true that there is more in common between floating and sedentary fisheries than between sedentary fisheries and oil" (p. 458).

[6] For sympathetic consideration of these new claims to enlarged legal competence by coastal states see F. V. Garcia-Amador, *The Exploitation and Conservation of the Resources of the Sea*, Leyden, Nijhoff, 1959, pp. 13-85, 134-212.

A reform consensus seemed to be pursuing several objectives. First of all, there emerged a majority disposition to place limits on the breadth of coastal waters that could be claimed as an exclusive fishing zone. Second, there was a virtually universal acknowledgment that "freedom" to fish on the high seas needed to be selectively subordinated to conservation considerations (at least, that is, where fishing patterns were leading to reduced total yields); there was some further evidence of a demand that the traditional freedom to fish needed to be harmonized by regulation with community goals to increase the world food supply.

Third, there was a tacit agreement by governments on the need to eliminate the voluntarism implicit in the Westphalia system. A consensual approach to legal obligation allows any state to refuse to participate in a conservation scheme governing high seas activities; such a refusal by any significant fishing state undermines all prospects for effective regulation through *ad hoc* agreement. To restrain some exploiters while leaving one or more user states unregulated creates an unacceptable situation. The noncooperative state is the beneficiary of the conservation scheme; its refusal to restrict its own operations diminishes, if it does not altogether preclude, any prospect of successful conservation. The permissiveness of Westphalia then creates a functional basis for increasing the scope of sovereign authority of the coastal state. That is, the only feasible way to establish unified conservation authority over "the high seas" is for the coastal state to claim exclusive rights.[7] Such an extension of exclusive authority is not as likely to reflect the common interests of the other fishing states as is a negotiated agreement. An exclusive claim even if justified by an appeal to conservationist goals may be partially a pretext to discriminate against non-coastal fishing states.

Fourth, the awareness among interested governments that spatial regimes are not very well correlated with conservation needs, since fish do not normally confine their movements within easily delimited zones; as well, different kinds of fish have vastly different movement patterns. For extreme instances, an anadromous species—such as salmon—can only be effectively regulated by controlling internal waters as well as by regulating fishing activities over vast stretches of high seas.[8]

---

[7] A very perceptive consideration of the relationship between the development of conservation policy and the extension of coastal state legal authority can be found in Myres S. McDougal and William T. Burke, *The Public Order of the Oceans— A Contemporary International Law of the Sea*, New Haven, Yale University Press, 1962, pp. 964-1007 [hereinafter cited as McDougal and Burke].

[8] For example, the discovery was made that an obstruction at Hell's Gate Canyon on the Fraser River was seriously depleting the stock of sockeye salmon. The removal of such a cause of depletion depended, of course, on action taken totally within the realm of territorial sovereignty, but without such action the efforts to conserve and manage ocean salmon fishing would be seriously hampered. For discussion see Johnston, pp. 384-86; a detailed consideration of more recent problems of de-

Fifth, the diverse interests and claims of states, accentuated by modern technology and by the more active participation of many more states in international life (especially, in the case of fishing, of the Latin American states) exhibited the vulnerability of international legal order to minimal patterns of prohibition and to voluntary procedures of settlement. The state that is enlarging its competence at the expense of others is not normally even obligated to respond to the objections of other states by accepting a demand for recourse to third-party procedures.

Sixth, it may also be noted, perhaps with a faint sense of irony, that the problems created by the Westphalian system have been deepened by the growth of restraints on police uses of force by principal states (the main beneficiaries of maximum freedom on the high seas) to coerce adherence to norms by lesser states;[9] the United States, for instance, is now inhibited from using force even in its sphere of greatest geopolitical influence, Latin America, for purposes other than its overriding global mission to curb extensions of actual or expected Communist influence. The competition between East and West for influence reinforces this inhibition. This competition has even induced the United States to reimburse its fishermen who pay fines imposed by Latin American countries upon fishing operations conducted beyond the twelve-mile limit, that is, on waters we regard as beyond the territorial jurisdiction of the coastal state, and, therefore as legally fishable by nationals of all states.[10]

Two conclusions can be drawn from this presentation of the pressure mounted against the Westphalia system—first, a jurisdictional solution is no longer functionally sufficient to deal with fisheries problems; second, different categories of states—those with distant-waters fleets and those without, those with long coasts and those with no coasts or short ones, those with an extensive continental shelf and those with a small shelf, those with major off-shore fisheries and those with none, those who have real socioeconomic dependence on fishing and those who don't—have sharply divergent interests in modifying traditional legal

limiting the geographical scope appropriate for regulating salmon fishing in the Northeast Pacific is found in Ralph W. Johnson, "The Japan-United States Salmon Conflict," 43 *Washington Law Review* 1-43 (1967) [hereinafter cited as Johnson].

[9] On the diminishing utility of force in general terms see Klaus Knorr, *On the Uses of Military Power in the Nuclear Age*, Princeton, Princeton University Press, 1966; in a legal context some of the adverse effects of inhibiting recourse to force upon the enforcement of rights are considered by Julius Stone, *Aggression and World Order*, Berkeley, University of California Press, 1958, and upon the maintenance of international stability in Peter Calvocoressi, *World Order and New States*, New York, Praeger, 1962.

[10] See "Foreign Seizures of U.S. Fishing Vessels," *Hearing before Subcommittee on Fisheries and Wildlife Conservation of the Committee on Merchant Marine and Fisheries*, House of Representatives, 90th Cong., 1st Sess., June 22, 1967 [hereinafter cited as Foreign Seizures].

conceptions governing the use of the oceans by sovereign states. It appears accurate to say that coastal states with large zonal claims and states with technologically advanced fishing fleets normally benefit from the high degree of permissiveness and decentralization built into laissez-faire doctrines of allocation and dispute-settlement, whereas states more concerned with conserving, developing, and sharing limited resources are generally inclined to favor a more managerial and conservationist approach to fishing rights and dispute-settlement.[11]

The Geneva Compromise

This split between states was very evident at the Geneva Conferences of 1958 and 1960[12] and resulted in an inability to establish authoritative limitations on coastal state prerogatives; the 1958 Convention on Fishing and Conservation of the Living Resources of the High Seas, a document that embodies many of the demands for a functional reorientation of Westphalia, especially by its elaborate provision of compulsory third-party settlement procedures, has predictably not achieved an impressive record of ratification, especially on the part of states with important distant-fishing fleets.[13] Therefore, both at the negotiating stage, and emphatically at the ratifying stage, the difficulties of promoting a functional reorientation of the international law of fisheries are evident. These difficulties really illustrate and confirm the general observations about "law reform" in international society set forth in the introductory paragraphs. Given the uneven interest of states in a functional reorientation of one segment of international law—such as fisheries—there is no very effective way for the reform-oriented majority to bargain with those states whose privileged position appears to depend on the retention of what governments of the majority of states regard as a dysfunctional legal system. In essence, consensus has not replaced consent in many traditional settings of international behavior, and

[11] A Japanese specialist on the law of ocean fisheries has written: "it is too premature to generalize any principle supporting the artificial allocation of fish resources for the benefit of some historically or geographically privileged States, or to discard the principle of free competition endorsed by modern history in many fields as one of the basic values. *Few will doubt that, until the time comes, when, as in municipal society, some super-authority can guarantee equitable sharing of different resources among the nations, the states will continue to argue for adoption of principles most favorable to their own interests in the field of high seas fishing.*" Shigeru Oda, "Japan and International Conventions Relating to North Pacific Fisheries," 43 *Washington Law Review* 63-73, at 73 (1967). (Emphasis added.) [Hereinafter cited as Oda].

[12] See Robert L. Friedheim, "The 'Satisfied' and 'Dissatisfied' States Negotiate International Law: A Case Study," *World Politics* xviii (Oct. 1965), 20-41.

[13] Of the 1958 Geneva Convention on Fishing and Conservation of the Living Resources of the High Seas, Johnston notes that it was the last of the four Geneva conventions to come into force and notes that "it was scarcely a child of love" (p. 463). In general, on the limits of a global approach to the regulation of ocean fishing see Johnston, pp. 445-65.

the granting or withholding of consent remains especially critical whenever "law reform" proceeds by the treaty method.[14]

The Geneva Conventions, despite their shortcomings by way of internal ambivalences and external vaguenesses, attempt to reform the Westphalian jurisdictional system to the extent that was politically feasible. This impressive attempt rested upon two sets of conclusions: first, a complete reorientation in light of a functional ideal was not feasible because a few important states benefited more from the Westphalia system than from any other conceivable system of legal order and these states would be able to veto any proposed changes adverse to their interests;[15] second, there were certain general shifts in emphasis from a jurisdictional (permissive) to a conservationist (managerial) perspective that could attract widespread rhetorical support in the context of a world conference; these general shifts were commingled with a reaffirmation of the spatial-jurisdiction ordering scheme—freedom on the high seas and a loosely delimited preferential status for the coastal state with regard to coastal waters—*despite* the prevailing awareness of its basic obsolescence.

Contradiction and compromise are the strategies of system-wide law reform in a decentralized (sovereignty-oriented) social order in any substantive setting where there are insufficiently shared and perceived common interests. The characteristic contradictoriness, perhaps more accurately regarded as internal inconsistency, results from the unwillingness to repudiate the old ordering scheme (The Westphalia system) in the very process of reordering the relevant behavioral sector. Spatial regimes—despite their ecological irrelevance to conservation and management objectives—and the freedom to fish on the high seas were retained at Geneva.[16] But the Geneva Convention on Fishing and Conservation of the Living Resources of the High Seas was couched almost completely in the rhetoric of management and conservation. In particular, the conventions signified a trend toward the subordination of zonal thinking to conservation considerations.

Patterns of regulation are authorized in terms of Article 2's criterion of "rendering possible the optimum sustainable yield from those resources so as to secure a maximum of food and other marine resources." The realities of decentralized legal order are fully appreciated by rely-

[14] Such an observation appears true wherever the treaty method is used to legislate or develop new legal standards and procedure rather than to clarify or declare existing law. This observation is relevant as the primary effort of the Geneva Fisheries Convention was to develop new law, and not merely to achieve an authoritative declaration of existing law.

[15] Norm-creation by treaty-making procedures illustrates the operation of what Morton A. Kaplan calls "the unit-veto system" in which each actor has a veto over the behavior of the entire community. See Morton A. Kaplan, *System and Process in International Politics*, New York, Wiley, 1957, pp. 50-52.

[16] See Johnston, p. 464.

ing upon unilateral assertion of conservation authority over high seas fishing when the nationals of only one country are engaged in fishing (Article 3) and by the preferential status given to a coastal state with regard to fisheries adjacent to its territorial sea (Articles 6 and 7).[17] If there is a situation of multinational fishing, then the Geneva Convention seeks, first, to bring a conservation-management scheme into being through voluntary agreement, and second, in the event that no agreement can be reached any state engaged in exploiting the fishery is entitled to invoke the compulsory arbitration machinery of Article 9. The points of interest are, of course, the primary competence of the states themselves to identify a conservation issue and to work out its solution by agreed sharing and restrictionist schemes. Such a competence presupposes that states have the relevant knowledge and policy commitment, as well as that conservation encroachments upon normally unregulated fishing activity can be effectively made. If the Geneva solution received universal application, then its effect would be to introduce major modifications in the spirit, if not the actuality, of the international law of fisheries. But the record of adherence is not yet notable, especially on the part of those states whose fishing patterns pose most of the conservation difficulty because of their distant fleet technology or because their exclusive claims encroach upon community interests in wider patterns of shared use. The failure of adherence by a state such as Japan should not be construed simply as a rejection of management in favor of anarchy; Japan's stand may only indicate a bargaining strategy natural for a state that has been very successful—as compared with other states—in exploiting ocean fisheries under the Westphalia system. By not formally endorsing a universal or global reorientation, Japan retains the possibility of proposing specific settlements of fishery disputes without jeopardizing its legally advantageous position;[18] it may be that solutions based on compulsory arbitration always tend toward equalizing and leveling results that work to the advantage of the less powerful and the less efficient and to the disadvantage of the more powerful and the more efficient. There are, then, two quite distinct issues here: (1) the rationale for nonadherence to the Geneva framework; and (2) the effects of nonadherence upon the effort to bring about functional reorientation.

We have considered (1) and now comment upon (2). The authoritative endorsement of a global framework of principles is likely to achieve

17 There are several levels of legal restraint: (1) unified international (a cooperative or voluntary model of community law); (2) unified sovereign control (an imperial model of community law); (3) decentralized sovereign control by means of self-assertion and self-restraint (an anarchic model of community law).

18 See Oda, pp. 63-72 for a sympathetic discussion of recent Japanese diplomatic practice with regard to settlement of fishing conflicts.

a law-ordering significance that exceeds the network of formally binding legal obligations that results. A consensus document of the sort represented by the Geneva Convention on Fishing helps to establish a new pattern of legal expectation as to what constitutes reasonable behavior. This new pattern induces pressures toward voluntary compliance and it influences the course of international negotiations outside the Geneva framework. Nonadhering states such as Japan acknowledge conservationist objections to their exercise of freedom and enter negotiations to restrict free competition that are really quite at variance with the logic of Westphalia.[19] The real point is that the pattern of treaty adherence and formal implementation is only one indicator of the extent of impact upon national behavior that might properly be attributed to a globally conceived regulatory pattern. A further indicator concerns the effect of that pattern in creating a broad framework of legal expectation that guides the behavior of normal national governments almost all the time. It is rare, especially outside the area of war and peace, for a state to pursue its interests without due regard for what is globally deemed reasonable in the context. The importance, then, of the Geneva Convention may be more to promote a redefinition of reasonableness that shifts the functional orientation of international order from one of jurisdiction toward one of conservation and resource management.[20]

Within the somewhat confused general normative framework created by the fusion of the diverse logics of spatial jurisdiction and conservation management, a series of specific solutions to fishing disputes by way of negotiated compromise have been worked out in recent years. These solutions seek to protect the diverse interests of negotiating states with regard to their historic share of the fishery and to promote the common interest of states in developing further the fishery resource, or at least in guarding against its depletion. These negotiated compromises tend to be functionally specific in the sense of taking account of the species that is of principal concern. Such functional specificity tends to produce patterns of regulation that move far away from such classical organizing principles as "sovereignty" and "freedom." The several negotiated arrangements in the North Pacific and North Atlantic reflect a subtle blending of vested interests (that is, upholding past

---

[19] E.g., consider this quotation by Professor Soji Yamamoto: "Traditionally, Japan has subscribed to the doctrine of free exploitation of ocean resources, but today she recognizes the need for certain controls in the interests of conservation." Yamamoto, "The Abstention Principle and its Relation to the Evolving International Law of the Seas," 43 *Washington Law Review* 45-61, at 46 (1967).

[20] The Geneva Conventions posit a rather authoritative pattern of norms and procedures. The result is spontaneous authoritativeness that creates a status for these conventions additional to and independent of their formal character as international treaties binding upon ratifying states. At minimum, such conventions represent the conclusion of statesmen and experts as to the most desirable pattern of mutually beneficial regulation that can be agreed upon at the time.

fishing rights in relative proportion),[21] of preferential criteria (that is, subordinating historically based preferential positions to either contiguity or socioeconomic dependence),[22] and of long-term disposition to maintain or expand the fishery. Dissatisfaction with these arrangements arises when ecological conditions shift—for example, salmon go out beyond the regulatory zone or when there is an exempt area that allows one party to exploit at the expense of other parties[23]—in such a way that the negotiated settlement appears to restrict one side more than it does the other. In general, however, given the continuing decentralization of international society and given the sharply divergent national interests of different groups of states with respect to fishery regulation, the most effective regulatory patterns are evolved by *ad hoc* agreement among the states engaged in exploiting a given fishery. To reiterate, however, it is clear that bargaining for specific solutions is influenced by shifts in community attitudes concerning both proper goals of regulation and the relative priority of different categories of claims and claimants.

Where a negotiated compromise is not reached, then the international legal order relies upon the interaction of claims and counterclaims by sovereign states to generate change and produce stability.[24] The Geneva

[21] The argument put forward by the United States in favor of "the abstention principle" is the most explicit and systematic effort to accord preference to established patterns of exploitation. For discussions of the abstention principle see McDougal and Burke, pp. 956-60, Johnson, pp. 27-34.

[22] E.g., the phased extinction of British claims to fish off Norway and Iceland illustrates this trend. See Johnston, pp. 185-87.

[23] Professor Oda writes of the Northwest Pacific Fisheries Convention of 1956 as follows: "Theoretically, the reduction in quotas affects both nations [Japan and the Soviet Union], but in fact only Japan is regulated because the convention extends to territorial waters only. Because salmon are an anadromous fish, the Soviet Union is able to take significant quantities of salmon by operating within territorial waters. The Soviet Union is theoretically free to take as many salmon as it wishes inside its own territorial waters.

"The quota system, like the abstention formula, is ostensibly designed to conserve particular stocks of fish. In fact, these principles seem to provide a scheme whereby the coastal state is able to regulate the high seas activities of Japan, thereby reducing the Japanese take, while maximizing its own fishery production." Oda, p. 69.

[24] See Article 6 of the Fisheries Convention the text of which is as follows:

Article 6

1. A coastal state has a special interest in the maintenance of the productivity of the living resources in any area of the high seas adjacent to its territorial sea.

2. A coastal state is entitled to take part on an equal footing in any system of research and regulation for purposes of conservation of the living resources of the high seas in that area, even though its nationals do not carry on fishing there.

3. A state whose nationals are engaged in fishing in any areas of the high seas adjacent to the territorial sea of a coastal state shall, at the request of that coastal state, enter into negotiations with a view to prescribing by agreement the measures necessary for the conservation of the living resources of the high seas in that area.

4. A state whose nationals are engaged in fishing in any area of the high seas adjacent to the territorial sea of a coastal state shall not enforce conservation measures in that area which are opposed to those which have been adopted by the coastal state, but may enter into negotiations with the coastal state with a view to prescribing by agreement the measures necessary for the conservation of the living resources of the high seas in that area.

5. If the states concerned do not

Convention partly acknowledges this feature of the new ordering pattern by conferring special status upon the coastal state with regard to ocean waters contiguous to its territorial sea. In addition, the legally indeterminate breadth of the territorial sea, and many national claims of expanding scope, have resulted in unilateral transfers of waters from "high seas" to "territorial waters." In regulatory terms this shift entails a shift from the domain of "freedom" to that of "sovereign control." In a decentralized legal order there is often no prospect for a-community-based system of regulation. The expansion of national responsibilities and competencies, in these circumstances, may actually, if unexpectedly, offer the optimal way to establish regulatory authority in the *common interest*. Of course, as the lateral expansion of exclusive fishing zones suggests, this process of nationalization control may also promote inefficient monopolistic control over fishery resources and avoid the effects of competitive exploitation.[25] However, as has been argued in many comparable contexts, national officials may sometimes be induced to act in a double capacity—both as agents of the international legal order and as public officials of the national government that they serve; the regulatory capabilities at the disposal of sovereign states enable a possibility of constructive resource management that global machinery, because of its rudimentary quality, is unlikely ever to achieve.

The related, more ambiguous point, is that in a decentralized legal system the unilateral claiming process of *principal* sovereign states tends to evolve patterns of normative expectation as to what is reasonable for the community of states. Therefore, the extension of sovereign authority by the United States and the Soviet Union over vast areas of the high seas to test nuclear weapons established a clear precedent for other lesser states to make *identical* claims, and acted as a persuasive precedent for the assertion of *equivalent* claims. The United States claim to exercise sovereign authority over the continental shelf cannot be completely disjoined, especially for coastal states without a large shelf, from extensive claims over floating fishing resources. Just as the Geneva framework, even if not widely ratified or implemented, shapes normative expectations, so do unilateral claiming patterns of principal sovereign states. These patterns build up a common law of international fisheries that automatically adapts, although not necessarily in a beneficial manner, what is legally permissible to ever-changing circumstances. Therefore, the degree of functional perceptivity and responsibility that at-

reach agreement with respect to conservation measures within twelve months, any of the parties may initiate the procedures contemplated by Article 9.
[25] This argument is often directed in various forms against the Latin American claimants who purport to be acting in a conservationist role in justifying their assertion of extensive authority over fisheries far from the coastline.

taches to these unilateral claiming patterns is vitally connected with the capacity of the international legal order to bring functionally adequate "law reform" into being.

The issue is gravely complicated by the radiating effects of interrelated claims and interests. For instance, the United States and the Soviet Union as claimant states tend to subordinate economic considerations to security and other political considerations, and what is functional for one set of considerations may be dysfunctional for another.[26] Principal states, in addition to their ordering role as precedent-setters, can play a significant role through the effective assertion of counterclaims so as to induce compliance with legal standards. The rationale for the Hickenlooper Amendment—cutting off foreign aid to a country that expropriates United States owned property without adequate compensation—is to deter violations of international law by prospective expropriators. The same sort of idea has been proposed by Congressmen to deter foreign states from excluding United States fishing operations in ocean areas that we insist belong in the "high seas" category.[27] But such a proposal has been rejected as imprudent in the area of fisheries because such punitive action may produce bad side-effects on the conduct of United States foreign policy.

The Post-Geneva Outlook for Ocean Fisheries Disputes

On the global level there exists some pull toward acknowledging conservation considerations and some sense of obligation to seek a third-party resolution of a dispute that cannot be resolved by intergovernmental negotiations. But the overwhelming thrust appears to be one of seeking negotiated settlements along functionally specific lines—a series of subregional and bilateral, trilateral, and multilateral *ad hoc* settlements. As yet there is no very significant record of third-party settlement, partly because the criteria for settlement may not be firmly enough established and partly because the data needed for a managerially satisfactory solution are not available. The Geneva machinery in Articles 9 to 12 and the other procedures for compulsory settlement express a commitment to discourage resolution of disputes about fisheries questions by legalistic criteria or even by any very strict application of adjudicative techniques of assessing the adversary merits of a complaint. Traditional legal norms are too ambiguously related to both behavioral

---

26 It is generally assumed that Soviet support for a twelve-mile fishery zone arises from a governmental decision to give priority to off-shore security. Such a decision entails a subordination of the competing Soviet interest in narrow fishing zones, an interest presumed to exist in the light of the large-scale Soviet distant-fishing fleet operations.

27 Interesting discussions of these issues are to be found throughout House hearings, cited as Foreign Seizures, see note 10.

patterns and to functional goals to encourage states with diverse fishing positions to look at this time toward lawyers, judges, and courts for authoritative guidance and decision.

Conclusion

The problems of rationalizing the international law of fisheries are a microcosm for the general problem of recreating the conditions of tolerable order in contemporary international society. Divergent national interests are sufficiently strong to preclude the emergence of a functional reorientation of fishing rights that would serve the overall welfare of the world. At the same time a consensus favoring the shift from jurisdictional to managerial legal conceptions has been embodied in the Geneva framework and has helped shape a new normative climate.[28] This normative climate has also been influenced by the claiming, counterclaiming, and settlement patterns of principal sovereign states. In such a context there is not much immediate prospect of achieving a formal and complete repudiation of the Westphalia system as it applies to ocean fisheries. Instead for the indefinite future there is likely to be a transitional or amalgamated international system that combines in a messy totality the logic of Westphalia with the logic of central planning.

During this period of transition it is important to emphasize the prospects for accommodation through *ad hoc* compromise. Such prospects can be improved by the clarification of converging and contending interests with respect to regional, subregional, and species exploitation. Reliable ecological data, especially with respect to practices and yield levels that would increase, as well as maintain, relevant fishing resources, are especially needed. The Japanese-Korean commitment in their normalization treaty to establish joint survey zones offers a good example of constructive bilateral action designed to create a basis to avoid future conflict as well as settle present disputes. Research may provide ideas about how to exploit a given fishery in such a way that preserves or increases the return on effort and the future prospects of all interested states.

There remain some difficult issues for the present period: (1) An adequate response to the Latin American claims of large zones of quasi-exclusive control; (2) The extent to which newcomers to an ocean fishery are bound to defer to claims of earlier exploiters in situations calling for allocation; (3) The degree to which the proliferation of distant-fleet fishing states will so overload present allocation patterns as to

---

[28] The exact impact of this normative climate on specific disputes is, of course, difficult to assess. Some sense of impact may be achieved by comparing regulatory agreements with the rhetoric, rules, and procedures of the Geneva Convention on Fishing. For some speculations on this issue in quite another context see Falk, *Legal Order in a Violent World*, Princeton University Press, 1968, pp. 414-35.

induce a genuine crisis of control; (4) The absence of any very widely accepted preference schedule for rank-ordering and satisfaction of claims based on humanitarian (food supply), socioeconomic (poor states; fish-dependent states), historical (past exploitation record), competitive (cost-efficiency of operations), vested interest (past investment) and contiguity criteria.

These issues specify some of the divergent interests of claimant states and reinforce the conclusion that accommodations are most likely to proceed by the legal techniques associated with a decentralized political order in the years ahead. No prospect for a general solution commanding global or near-global respect is likely to be forthcoming under such circumstances of acute and multiple based diversity of interest among sovereign states. In a situation of conflict among actors, the main alternatives are either compromise or coercion. If population growth puts severe pressure on food supply, then the danger of violence cannot be ruled out. The problems of devising a rational strategy for law reform given the constraints of a decentralized international legal order is one of the great challenges of our time. Perhaps the relative obscurity of fishery disputes may provide a social laboratory wherein to work on the fundamental international problem of adapting international life as smoothly as possible to the cumulative impacts of continuing technological innovation and of accelerating demand for scarce resources. In one sense the problem for international lawyers is to work out the policy consequences and choices that result from growing social, economic, and political interdependence along every dimension of human experience. The deepest cause of the obsolescence of the Westphalia system arises because it has become so unrealistic to treat states as autonomous units within sovereign space and as capable of anarchic coexistence in extrasovereign realms such as the high seas and outer space. In effect, the functional reorientation that appears called for by the urgencies of contemporary life is some variant of limited world government. It is, perhaps, a useful exercise to grasp the argument for world government (*as distinct from the prospects for its realization*) in a substantive setting as uncataclysmic as a discussion of the international law of ocean fisheries.

XXI. The Prospects for World Order: Models of the Future

THERE ARE many reasons to be deeply troubled about the present condition of international society. Two of the most prominent causes of distress arise from the existence and spread of weapons of mass destruction and from the growing shortage of food in the world. These disturbing developments provoke questions about whether the present system of world order is adequate and whether, if it is not, there are better systems that can be brought into being. This chapter considers some alternative systems of world order that might be preferable to what now exists and gives some attention to whether system-change at the international level is desirable and attainable.

In undertaking such an exercise of speculation there is some danger of being provincial, of seeing issues and potentialities from the confines of one's own cultural situation. For this reason, especially, we need to generate a global dialogue approaching the subject of world order from every significant cultural, moral religious, ideological, and socioeconomic perspective. Each principal world civilization possesses a long and distinguished tradition of thought about order and justice in international affairs that needs to be brought to bear on contemporary problems of world order.[1] Some consensus must be reached as to what is both possible and desirable with respect to the future of world order. We need first to become aware of what is possible and then we can begin to become architects of our own future.

This orientation toward the subject matter of world order has received a specific inspiration from Pope John XXIII, especially from ideas powerfully presented in his encyclical *Pacem in Terris*. In this history-making document Pope John emphasized that "At the present day no political community is able to pursue its own interests and develop itself in isolation, because the degree of its prosperity and development is a reflection and a component part of the degree of prosperity and development of all other political communities." (Paragraph 131) The early exploits of the space age further demonstrate the extent to which it makes increasing sense to think of the earth as one organic unit rather than as an assemblage of sovereign entities. Nevertheless, nation-states retain predominant control over the instrumentalities of military power and do control the shape and outcome of international conflicts. It is this imbalance between the objective requirements of human welfare and the stark actualities of national power that accounts for the

[1] For an excellent survey of much of the most salient of this literature see W. Warren Wagar, *The City of Man*, Baltimore, Penguin, 1967.

dramatic culmination of *Pacem in Terris*: "It can be said, therefore, that at this historical moment the present system of organization and the way its principle of authority operates on a world basis no longer corresponds to the objective requirements of the universal common good." (Paragraph 135) Such an orientation gives a special urgency to inquiry into the conditions and prospects for world order.

There is a great danger that someone in the United States thinking about the future of world order will introduce, however unwillingly, United States biases and value priorities into his analysis. It may even be the case that the United States preoccupation with organizing the world to prevent World War III is a concern that is overweighted out of proportion to other concerns by thinkers who are situated in relatively modernized societies that are gravely endangered only by the specter of nuclear disaster. It may be, as a consequence, that from a characteristic perspective of the poorer countries, the effort to reorganize international society in such a way as to diminish the prospects of large-scale violence must be accompanied or even preceded by comparable revisions in the structure of international trade and investment, revisions that assure above all greater growth potential for the states of Latin America, Asia, and Africa. It may be that a global fiscal procedure introducing "progressive taxation" to the same extent on the international level as it is now established on the domestic level of the richer, more developed societies is the first order of priority. It may even be that from the perspective of an African or Asian international lawyer first priority should be given to the creation of strengthened procedures to eliminate the remnants of colonialism and to abolish racial discrimination of the sort that continues to prevail in South Africa and in South West Africa.

Thought on world order problems in Asian and African countries is increasingly likely to work through the use of process models for the study of the future, that is, models setting forth a series of preconditions arranged according to a priority schedule and phased in corresponding sequence. The effort here is, in contrast, to posit structural models to contrast the world order consequences of four main, plausible systems for organizing international life. Regardless of ideological or intellectual perspective, however, it seems fruitful to direct some energies toward the emerging future of international society, if only to grasp present trends and to improve prospects for shaping these trends, to the extent possible, to better reflect value preferences. The values of freedom and national independence call for the development of aspirational models conceived of in personal, national, regional, and global terms. A comparison of the law consequences of four models of the future of international society aspires, above all else, to encourage communication among thinkers differently situated in the international system whose concern it is. Perhaps by generating patterns of intellectual interaction a new constructive vision of the common good in international affairs will emerge that cuts across barriers of national, cultural, and ideological separation.

Contemporary movements to promote "world peace through world law" often seem to possess an innocence not encountered in the world they seek to reform. Such innocence assures the irrelevance of their efforts. It is only by acknowledging that neither individuals nor governments act in accordance with the dictates of reasonableness that we begin to grasp the problem of war and the enormous difficulties that confront all enterprises that would eliminate or diminish the danger of future wars. Only by facing these difficulties, overwhelming as they are, can we ever hope to overcome them.

There are many reasons to explore whether better ways to organize international society exist and can be put into practice. We live at a time when the danger of nuclear war threatens to inflict senseless and awesome destruction upon societies built up over centuries of effort. We live at a time when communications and transportation have created the possibility for a unified society on earth with no part remote from any other, and at a time when the early explorations of space emphasize the smallness and identity of the earth in a larger cosmic setting. At such a point of shifting consciousness there seems to be present an unprecedented concern about planning and understanding the future. The climate of opinion now seems suitable for clarifying main alternative future systems of development on the international level. Emphasis will be given to those world order systems that are most likely to accompany different shifts in the structure of power. This effort of analysis assumes that the single crucial variable concerns the distribution of power and the identification of how decisions involving the exercise of power are made in different international situations. National government officials exert major control over the exercise of power in the world as we know it today, and this single fact shapes the structure of conflict and authority in world affairs.

A concern with future systems of world order different from the present system implies a concern with change and how it comes about. In international society there has been a tendency for the main lines of reformist thought to be either naive or cynical about the prospects for consciously directed change. One result has been a utopian literature that projects a future world order that fulfills the values of reasonable men but is insensitive to the corpus of political history that bears extensive witness to the failure of reason to regulate the behavior of political groups toward each other. A further result is a cynical literature that refuses to contemplate an altered future because its creators believe man to be a sinful creature incapable of building a good society at any level of his existence; restraint of human aggressiveness in this tough-minded view can only be achieved by fear and deterrence. Such a cynical outlook seems to overlook the good societies that have been brought into being and the extent to which men and groups are motivated by beneficent, as well as hostile, energies. As well, it overlooks those sectors of international society in which states live in security and peace without any dependence on defensive military capabilities. Somewhere between the utopian and cynical outlooks lies the constructive area for thought about the future of the world.

Of course, one of the more plausible alternatives for the future is a continuation of the present basic international system. That is, a system of sovereign states controlling territory and commanding the overriding loyalty of the bulk of their populations, a system in which military power is wielded by a few of the strongest of these states. Military power is a relational as well as an intrinsic reality. As of 1968 only the United States approaches being a fully global power, that is, capable of exercising effective military power in relation to any country in the world. The Soviet Union has the capacity to destroy any foreign society, but it lacks the nonnuclear capabilities to bring its power significantly and directly to bear in many parts of the world. India and China are regional powers, whereas the United Arab Republic is a subregional power. Security in this international system is largely sustained by deterrent threats to inflict unacceptable damage on the nation-state that is responsible for breaking the peace. The present international system is a largely decentralized one in which formal order and diversity arise from the activities of governments carried on largely within territorial boundaries, although foreign intervention is a significant element of domestic government for many countries in the world. The possession of weapons of mass destruction by adversary states inhibits a projection of this world indefinitely into the future, especially if it is acknowledged that interstate rivalry has in the past always led sooner or later to warfare of an intensity that relied on the most effective military capability available. Poison gas and biological weapons were not used during World War II, although their use was urged to facilitate the United States efforts in the Pacific theater of combat. The explanation of the refusal to use these weapons is controversial, some believing that use was inhibited by a fear of retaliation, others believing that the prohibited status of these weapons was the key consideration, and still others believing that poisons would have been used had their use been regarded as decisive at any point by any belligerent. It can be argued that the radioactive fallout of the atomic bombs dropped on Hiroshima and

Nagasaki amounted to the use of poison; it can also be argued that had atomic weapons been subject to the same prohibitions as were lethal gas and biological agents, these weapons would not have been used against inhabited areas. The main conclusion is, however, that so long as national governments possess the capability to wage war there is no very reliable assurance that the most destructive weapons will not be used, even if in retrospect such use appeared to be self-destructive. History includes many Carthages. What is peculiarly awesome about the future is the extent and consequence of nuclear disaster.

To feel insecure about the prospects for international order in the world as it is presently constituted is not necessarily to feel optimistic about alternative security systems. It is not clear that any given alternative is either desirable (we prefer it to what we have got), or attainable (we can imagine the circumstances whereby what is desirable can be brought into being at tolerable costs). We will consider first, the question as to whether desirable alternatives exist and how they are to be identified in advance, and second, whether and under what conditions that which is desirable could become attainable.

Because of widespread anxiety about the recurrence of warfare and the danger of a nuclear war, there is some tendency to neglect the virtues of an international society constituted by semi-autonomous and quite diverse units called sovereign states. Winston Churchill once made the observation that democracy is "the worst possible system except for all the others that have been tried." Does this observation have relevance to international society in the last half of the twentieth century? Might not an international system that bases the security of its members upon threats and counterthreats, intermittently reinforced by violent struggle at subnuclear levels seem preferable to some unipolar, disarmed world in which a single set of governing values and institutions —whether bland or tyrannical—is imposed on the whole world? Let us not, in other words, underrate the virtues of the existing system or the hazards of alternatives, in our haste to avoid a specific danger— that of nuclear warfare.

As to feasibility, it is chastening to recognize that significant modifications of the structure of international society have taken place only as part of a peace settlement after a major war. The international system seems exceedingly rigid during the "peaceful" periods between wars, the inertia and vested interests of the constituted order effectively precluding any real shifts in the structure of power and society. Therefore, to consider an alternative to the present international system may appear tantamount to postcatastrophe planning, by its tendency to focus upon what might become possible after whatever major wars occur in the future.[2] Even if we regard it plausible for a new system of world order to arise in postcatastrophe settings, still further grounds exist for skepticism when thought is directed at what can be done in the future through a consideration of what has been done in the past. World Wars I and II produced a negative reaction to major warfare. The commitment "to save succeeding generations from the scourge of war" was written into the Preamble of the United Nations Charter. This verbal commitment to modify international society to prevent major warfare in the future was, however, more apparent than real. National control over the use of military power has been left undisturbed, despite the growth of verbal prohibitions upon its employment. The main locus of human loyalty continues to coincide with the main locus of military capability—namely, the sovereign state.[3] It is this capacity of those who control military capability to command human allegiance that underscores the dangers of violent conflict in a world of intense political antagonism and extraordinary technological proficiency.

Some attention has been given to issues of desirability and attainability, as well as to the general question of the prospects for changing the structure of international society in any fundamental respect, and to the need to be convinced that the particular changes sought will produce a world that is more desirable than what we now have. Of course, one difficulty is that different states, sectors, and strata of the same states, and distinct individuals have different perspectives, interests, and goals, some of which are mutually inconsistent and many of

[2] Analytical skepticism, although needed as an antidote to wishful thinking, does not tell the whole story. The complexity of the world environment is such that our evidence of the past cannot be extrapolated to enable any very reliable explanation of the present or prediction of the future. This general insufficiency of the intellectual apparatus available for the study of world order problems is accentuated by several novel contemporary factors such as weaponry of mass destruction, the active involvement in world affairs of non-Western societies, and the accelerating formation of elites with a transnational consciousness. Given these circumstances, engineering for a future that we prefer is the height of rational sophistication. It is another kind of naiveté to overweight certain indications of how difficult it is to alter the structure of international society by consciously directed action. In view of the difficulty, given the importance of the task, there is a special need to educate into being values and understandings supportive of a safer and juster system of world order, to organize a movement that seeks to propagate a political myth arising out of such values, and to forge an ideology of world order. One optimistic note is that in the latter decades of the twentieth century efforts along these lines appear to be on the increase.

[3] But there are hopeful signs emerging: intellectuals, professional workers, common citizens, students, minorities who identify increasingly with transnational symbols of identification. Functional tasks of international institutions are proliferating rapidly, making it possible for more and more people to feel that governmental institutions of an international character are performing tasks relevant to human convenience, security, and welfare. National governments are losing their monopoly over welfare and service functions. There are, thus, various tendencies eroding the claims of nation-states to serve as the main organizing center of human experience. For a useful analysis emphasizing the continuing predominance of the nation-state see Stanley Hoffmann, "Obstinate or Obsolete? The Fate of the Nation-State and the Case of Western Europe," *Daedalus* (Summer 1966), 862-915.

which are in different priority schedules. The rich, developed countries would benefit from a world society within which their existence was not threatened by nuclear war, whereas the poor societies would benefit from a world society that taxed the rich countries for the benefit of the poor ones. It is possible to satisfy both aspirations up to a point, but are rich societies prepared to give up their privileged position reinforced by their superior military capability at present in response to demands for economic equalization on a global scale? Or are poor societies prepared to eliminate the role of violence as a main energy of reform unless they receive enough aid to permit economic growth at desired rates? Or are political expectations ever reducible to such formulation of the needed rate of satisfying basic interests?

It seems appropriate to consider at this point the role of international law both as a source of stability and as an instrument of change. Two preliminary comments seem relevant. First, law is a relatively passive reflection of whatever social and political environment it operates within. This passivity is as characteristic of national as it is of international society. Law is an instrument by which governing values are put into operation in accordance with expectation patterns. World law groups often commit the legalistic fallacy of treating international law as an independent force capable of realizing the common good for mankind. Rules cannot by themselves alter basic patterns of group behavior, nor can blueprints of ideal legal systems be brought into being unless supportive attitudes toward security, welfare, and loyalty are held by those who control the power of decision. The attitudes that presently prevail continue to emphasize the national character of security, welfare, and loyalty. Peace groups of short-run and long-run perspective, whether castigating the refusal of the United States to abide by rules of international law in Vietnam or advocating world federalism, encourage the dismissal of their positions if they do not make the hard effort to relate law to the concrete particularities of the overall international environment.

The second comment emphasizes the extent to which the means of transition to some alternative system of world order will itself influence its character and hasten its attainment. There is no difficulty perceiving the strategic role of transition procedures in other contexts. For instance, no one would doubt that ex-colonial societies have been influenced by the manner in which their national independence was attained, especially the extent to which sustained violence played a role in that process. Even a primitive appraisal of the future of world order should distinguish between a future international system that comes about as a consequence of the trauma and violence of world war, and one that comes into being peacefully and gradually through consensual means.

Such a distinction suggests the utility of comparing the role of international law in four alternative future international systems. Each system is set forth in rudimentary form to suggest the main properties:

(1) *Coercive Decentralization.* Basic international order maintained as today by deterrence, reciprocity, and alliances;

(2) *Coercive Centralization.* Basic international order maintained by the global organization of international life, including some kinds of central regulatory mechanism to coerce compliance everywhere;

(3) *Volitional Decentralization.* Basic international order maintained by consensual harmony among the sovereign states that constitute the international system, but without major reliance being placed on military power for security against external danger;

(4) *Volitional Centralization.* Basic international order maintained by a centralized set of procedures and institutions brought into being and sustained thereafter by the agreement of sovereign states.

These four arrangements of international security emphasize the importance of the way power is distributed between sovereign states and international institutions. Emphasis is also given to the role of coercion in attaining and maintaining whatever power distribution prevails. The role of international law is treated only in relation to the use of force to resolve disputes among states. No particular preference is accorded one model rather than another from the viewpoint of avoiding war, although each has very distinct implications for the role of law and for the relative importance of the sovereign state as the organizing center of human loyalty and political activity. It is now appropriate to give somewhat more detailed attention to each of the four basic models or ideal types.

Coercive decentralization is essentially a continuation of the present international system—with some marginal adjustments, of course. In fact, the continuation of the present security arrangement appears highly likely unless a third (or fourth) world war takes place, subject only to the caveat about the limits of analytical understanding.[4] The basic structure of this international system arises from state control over military force. Sovereign states have accepted formal legal commitments to use this military power only in individual or collective self-defense against an armed attack or under the authorization of the United Nations. The significance of these commitments is restricted by the inability to define clearly or uniformly what constitutes an armed attack or self-

[4] See note 1. Postcatastrophe transition is the simplest case, but it is not the only international setting in which drastic change in the structure of international society may come about.

defense, and furthermore, by the inability of the organs of the United Nations to identify, in a particular situation, which state is the wrongful or illegal user of force. A more fundamental defect, perhaps, is the insistence by the more powerful sovereign states on self-determining the occasions on which it is permissible for them to use force without accepting community review procedures. Formal legal efforts to restrict the use of international violence are also bound to be hampered by the absence of peaceful procedures of change and reform. The domestic legal order, if nonoppressive, depends on a delicate balance between stability and adaptation to changed circumstances. International society has no legislative institutions. States with real or imagined grievances about the character of international society rarely have any legislative alternative to violence at their disposal. In this regard, the attempts by the United Nations Charter to outlaw war without assuring a procedure for peaceful revision of international relationships were bound to produce tension and lead to failure. Widespread support for certain wars of national liberation, Afro-Asian support for uses of force to overthrow the remnants of colonialism and racism, especially in southern Africa, and Western support for anti-Communist wars of national defense[5]—all are indications of the extent to which Charter conceptions of legitimate force have been expanded by state practice and policy. There is some tendency to move from an awareness of these imperfections of the international legal order to a total denial of its relevance. It is well to remember that even in domestic societies with strong democratic traditions that it is difficult to induce basic social reforms without the threat or experience of political violence.[6] The demonstrations, riots, and warnings of more to come certainly acted as an impetus for the progress in civil rights that has taken place over the past decade or so in the United States.

It is obvious that national security in such an international system depends primarily on deterring potential enemies by building up national military capabilities and augmenting these capabilities by entering into alliances. National efforts to attain security for a nation

[5] It may be a misleading euphemism to write of "anti-Communist wars of national defense." In the shadow of the Vietnam War, it appears essential to take seriously allegations of a new version of colonialism, so-called neocolonialism, involving the use of military power belonging to a powerful external elite to sustain in governmental control an internal elite lacking a popular social or political base in the country involved. The United States role in Laos, Thailand, Formosa, South Korea, the Philippines, and, of course, South Vietnam offer the clearest domain within which to examine the phenomenon of neocolonialism in action. The use of force of varying degree to constitute and sustain the neocolonial internal elite is a separate phenomenon. For a short critique of American foreign policy along these lines see David Horowitz, *The Free World Colossus*, New York, Hill & Wang, 1965.

[6] Cf. Harold L. Nieburg, "Uses of Violence," *Journal of Conflict Resolution*, VII (March 1963), 43-54.

take clear precedence over international efforts. The amount of time and money spent by the United States to achieve its own military prowess or to find a satisfactory basis for cooperation with its European allies far overshadows its commitment of resources or thought to the United Nations. When the chips are down, states are dependent upon their own capabilities to sustain their existence against determined adversaries. Switzerland and Israel have in different ways dramatized the fact that even a small nation can, if sufficiently determined, protect its independence against a series of more powerful neighboring states. An appeal to the United Nations and to the principles upon which it rests is only likely to be effective when the great powers are willing to back up the Organization as the United States has done at the time of Korea or during the Suez crisis. The United Nations plays a minor and symbolic role in the present world security system, a role that is very much dependent on the degree to which its principal members agree or disagree in a particular setting. If disagreement is sharp, as with regard to the war in Vietnam, the potential role of the United Nations is marginal, but if agreement is present, as with respect to restoring peace to the strife-torn Congo of 1960, then the role for the United Nations is considerable. But as the tragic course in the Congo disclosed, the strain on the United Nations grows when the basis for united action among the superpowers—the United States and the Soviet Union—is lost.

Despite the predominant control exercised by sovereign states over the use of military force, international trends are evident that disclose the recent emergence of important restrictions upon sovereign discretion in the area of war and peace. The mass suffering caused by World Wars I and II, together with the fear of nuclear warfare, have at least withdrawn the halo of glory that used to surround exploits of war and conquest. War is now looked upon by leaders and their populations as a desperate necessity.[7] As a result of this emerging attitude toward war there is a new prudence evident in even the most intense international rivalries carried on by the superpowers. Part of this prudence is expressed by a general willingness to abide by basic legal expectations about the use of force. Especially, recourse to military force to expand the domain of national territory appears to be very infrequent in present international society, except to clarify disputed borders in the period following national independence. The major dangers to world order (aside from the danger of nuclear war itself) arise from *covert*

---

[7] Of course, it is hardly necessary to emphasize, the statement in the text is an overgeneralization that is misleading if applied uncritically. Specific leaders, specific national, and even regional orientations and specific conflict situations exhibit a much more positive reliance upon war as an instrument of change and dispute-settlement.

uses of force to extend influence to foreign areas by helping a sympathetic governing elite to take or maintain control, and from *overt* uses of force to influence the outcome of domestically based struggles for political control that mix the pressures of revolutionary nationalism with the incitements of foreign intervention. Vigorous great power competition for influence in the recently independent Afro-Asian world has produced a series of interventionary uses of military power in external arenas. In these postcolonial and neocolonial contexts, international law offers certain tacit rules of mutual constraint by emphasizing the role of national boundaries as a limit upon the arena of violence, and by reinforcing such reciprocal forbearances as the nonuse of nuclear weapons in such a setting. International law also offers certain procedures and devices that can be used by adverse parties interested in formalizing and maintaining a settlement. In other words, states locked in conflict may govern their conduct in accordance with the substantive rules of international law, thereby restricting the scope and magnitude of violence and avoiding the extremes of bitterness where compromise and conciliation are presently impossible. International law also offers states a framework with which to transform a condition of war into one of peace or quasi-peace whenever their converging sense of self-interest so permits.

In this international system the basic role of law is to clarify common standards of self-restraint applicable at the national level. If the foreign policy of principal states can be made more responsive to these standards of self-restraint, then the safeguarding of world order interests can be strengthened greatly without altering the structure of international society. One problem with this system is that national governments tend to perceive external conflict in such a way as to reinforce their own particular biases and preconceptions. When perceptions result in contradictory understanding by principal states, the stage is set for a conflict in which each side views the other as responsible for "aggression."[8] Civil war situations illustrate this danger very dramatically because of the tendency to select self-vindicating facts, one side emphasizing the revolutionary situation within and the other side emphasizing the interventionary pressures from without. The savage and tragic conflict in Vietnam from the end of World War II to the present epitomizes this awful vulnerability of international society to the disruptive impacts of incompatible interpretations of who is responsible for what, each interpretation being reasonable given the national level of outlook, and neither being reasonable given the global interest.

International order may also be upset by the illusion or reality of

[8] See a very important book that develops this position persuasively: Ralph White, *The War Nobody Wanted*, Garden City, New York, Doubleday, 1968.

military superiority arising from some perceived advantage or disadvantage in the arms race, especially at the nuclear level. The balance of terror is delicate, and however irrational a conscious assumption of the risk of war may be for any state, there are possibilities for major war arising from miscalculation, accident, and escalation. Lesser warfare, subnuclear and confined to a single state or subregion, is likely to remain a zone wherein adversary governments employ and threaten limited violence against one another to achieve political gains.[9]

Coercive centralization essentially relies upon a shift of military power to a single center of political authority, maintained by a single military center of power. The most likely form of such centralization is a type of world empire. This result is unlikely to come about except through the prior subjugation of present contenders for world power, either by outright conquest or by intimidation. Dante's *De Monarchia,* written early in the fourteen century (1310-1317), argues in favor of a world government established by means of a globally organized Roman Empire. In effect, a single state expands its writ to reach the entire world and withholds any substantial military capability from the subordinate units in the system. This kind of enforced disarmament at the national level seems to imply the disappearance of the sovereign state as we know it and its replacement by a single superstate, but without the development of a parallel structure of government on the supranational level. The expansion of an established state to the exercise of global functions of control thereby contrasts with the creation of a world government outside the structure of the existing state system.[10]

In such a world empire system, considerable autonomy could be accorded the units in the system or not, depending upon the ideology of the imperial elite and the process by which coercive centralization was attained. International law in such a system would resemble more closely the role of law in any hierarchical domestic state; military power would be monopolized by the imperial structures of power and authority. Depending on the political ethos of the system, force could be used in an arbitrary repressive manner or its use might be confined by legal procedures to authorized police functions. Central institutions of interpretation and enforcement would exist. The ambiguity that arises from each national government interpreting its own obligations under international law would, of course, disappear. A possibility of insurgency, secession, and civil strife would maintain a threat of large-scale and prolonged

---

[9] Fuller discussion of these issues can be found in Falk, *Legal Order in a Violent World*, Princeton, Princeton University Press, 1968, pp. 8-79.

[10] A very perceptive discussion of these issues, including the consideration of "empire" as constituting an illustration of "premature expansion" is to be found in Amitai Etzioni, *The Active Society*, New York, The Free Press, 1968, pp. 579-613.

interunit violence. Centralization is not always an assurance of peace, especially when imposed upon population groups lacking any loyalty or identification with the central structures of authority. The American Civil War was the most costly and violent encounter of the latter half of the nineteenth century, far bloodier than any international violence among the leading sovereign states of Europe during the period between 1815 and 1914.

Volitional decentralization would characterize an international system in which political authority was distributed among a large number of relatively sovereign units, but in which there was no significant reliance upon military power to uphold security interests arising out of external relations of states. The relations of Canada and the United States are not dependent on any form of deterrent threat, direct or indirect, but are largely a consequence of the reciprocal acceptance of each other's basic identity and the confidence that this acceptance will be virtuallly permanent. Generalizing this relationship on any global basis would seem to require very important prior transformations of either human nature or of the relationship among sovereign units. Pierre Teilhard de Chardin's vision of the future contemplates a human order in which men would have a much greater altruistic regard for each other.[11]

Another image of the underlying transformation involves the successful human emulation of animal species that have eliminated aggressive behavior within a single species—for example, the dolphin. Such a reconstituted human nature might lead to the disappearance of aggressive behavior from intergroup relations. The recent interest in the work of animal ethologists alive to the implications of their work for the control of human conflict represents a new line of approach to world order problems.

Norman O. Brown writes: "The problem of war is the problem of idolatry, or literalism."[12] For Brown, the cure involves a symbolic substitution of the bloodless for the bloody sacrifice, a psychoanalytic recreation of the primal and violent conflicts that is enacted by each father and each son; the only satisfactory resolution of these conflicts is through its symbolic external embodiment in the form of a poem. Such a conception leads to a radical reinterpretation of the task of world order: "The next generation needs to be told that the real fight is not the political fight, but to put an end to politics. From politics to metapolitics."[13] Brown's reinterpretation of human conflict falls within the wider ambit of "voluntary decentralization" by its argument that the

[11] Pierre Teilhard de Chardin, *The Phenomenon of Man*, New York, Harper, & Brothers, 1959.
[12] Norman O. Brown, *Love's Body*, New York, Random House, 1966, p. 173.
[13] Brown, "A Reply to Herbert Marcuse," *Commentary* (March 1967), 83.

one and only way to eliminate war is to develop a new human consciousness.

Immanuel Kant and Lenin, each quite distinct from the other, consider the transformation of national political life to be the key to permanent world peace and to obviate the necessity for structural changes in international society by way of world government. Kant regards the universal emergence of republican forms of government on the national level assuring human liberty to be the essential and sole precondition for the elimination of warfare, whereas Lenin regards the universal triumph of Communism as achieving the same result. Each thinker denies the need for centralization of political authority to any significant degree, but each regards the attainment of certain basic values in every national society as the sole precondition to international solidarity and to the removal, thereby, of the kinds of antagonism that results in conflict and leads to violence among nations.

International law in such a system would probably no longer be administered by the governments of sovereign states. If the sovereign state no longer confronted external enemies and no longer provided the basis for national security, then it would be unlikely to retain its pivotal role in the political consciousness of man. Other actors of a functional or regional kind might play increased roles, and there might be a greater stress on the individual human being as the main subject and object of a new emergent legal order. C. Wilfred Jenks has developed this conception of the future as the culmination of present trends in his pioneering book, *The Common Law of Mankind*.[14] Jenks argues, although not altogether convincingly, that we already possess much of the Kantian moral and political basis on the national level needed for a universal legal order centered on the rights and duties of the individual person, instead of merely reflecting the interaction of sovereign states. Myres McDougal and Harold Lasswell offer somewhat the same moral vision but interpret the political and moral realities in a manner contradictory to Jenks, concluding that contending systems of public order exist on the national level, with each doing its best to eliminate the other and each holding very different views as to the character of social fulfillment.[15] McDougal and Lasswell regard the competition for influence between the Communist states and the liberal democracies as the main illustration of the contending public order system that is not taken account of by the universalism of Jenks.

Volitional centralization would involve some kind of voluntary agreement by existing governments to centralize political authority in

---

[14] London, Stevens, 1958.

[15] See Myres S. McDougal and Harold D. Lasswell, "The Identification and Appraisal of Diverse Systems of Public Order," in McDougal and Associates, *Studies in World Public Order*, New Haven, Yale University Press, 1960, pp. 3-41.

a limited world government. The governmental center would be responsible for police functions, as well as, perhaps, for other matters relating to welfare and human rights. Disarmament would have to take place on the national level and much greater compulsion would have to be available to assure the peaceful settlement of disputes among states. The widely circulated plan of Grenville Clark and Louis B. Sohn for limited world government (published in the form of a drastically amended United Nations Charter) is the most carefully articulated conception of volitional centralization in recent times.[16]

International law in the Clark-Sohn world would be administered to a much greater degree than at present, especially in the war-peace area, by international institutions. The sovereign state, however, would be likely to remain a more dominant focus for human loyalties than in the conception of world order based on coercive centralization. Essentially, the system would be created and maintained by the voluntary action of sovereign states acting in concert, and would not entail the coercive destruction or the withering away of the state system. The voluntary relinquishment of sovereign prerogatives appears to contradict the egoistic bias of state sovereignty and does not appear analytically plausible except in the wake of catastrophe or after the gradual evolution of global consciousness. The only precondition for volitional centralization is adherence by states to a formal agreement; as such, there is in this conception the belief that the permanent arrangement of security can be instituted at any point that governments are persuaded to act reasonably and, thereby, to promote the common good. The expectation that reason will be applied to solve such intractable human problems as war is reminiscent of problem-solving during the era of the Enlightenment in the eighteenth century.

The abrupt adoption of a plan for world government is unlikely, but it may be possible to work out a strategy by which to satisfy certain social and political preconditions of world federalism. The functionalist approach is one example of a gradualist technique that looks toward the eventual emergence of global political institutions. Regional institutions may rapidly develop the ability to satisfy human needs to such an extent that they capture some of the loyalties now monopolized by the state. A partial regionalization of international life might make feasible the further consolidation of political control at the global level. Therefore, volitional centralization can be achieved in stages, and not, as is naively supposed, only now or never.

---

[16] *World Peace Through World Law,*   rev. edn., 1966.
Cambridge, Harvard University Press, 3rd

A Concluding Note

Only the grossest implications for law reasonably to be associated with the four different kinds of international systems have been sketched. Aristophanes has written that "Ideas . . . become fascinating when they move men, especially when they are misunderstood and move men to foolishness." Theorists of international order have yet to move men to foolishness. Perhaps, when proponents of a new international order begin to be treated as dangerous to the welfare of the sovereign states and locked up in prisons, as were the pre-World War II nationalist opponents of colonialism, then, and only then, will it be possible to be optimistic about voluntary modifications of the structure of international society. As things stand now, the only way that we can envision a future that is radically distinct from the present is to envision it emerging out of the smouldering ruins of nuclear devastation.

To contemplate a new world order is to be engaged in the creation of social science fiction. In this spirit it may be less than fatuous to contend that the creation of a future international system that is less prone to prolonged international violence (including nuclear war) may depend on the widespread dissemination of a credible myth of extraterrestrial aggression. If we believed the earth was endangered by an enemy in outer space, then a new seriousness about global organization might suddenly develop that would support the creation of a new system of world order, one that would make sense even if the provoking cause is false and there is no threat from space.[17]

[17] In fact, *only* if there were no real threat from space. In this connection see André Maurois, *The Next Chapter—The War Against the Moon*, New York, E. P. Dutton, 1928. In M. Maurois' fictive account the "era of Inter-Planetary War" is initiated by an attack by the earth on the moon, the attack having been motivated by the belief that a credible extraterrestrial aggression myth alone could eliminate war on earth. The belief backfired because the earth did not realize that a populated moon of comparable technology could and would retaliate if attacked.

XXII. The Quest for World Order, and the Vietnam War: A Second American Dilemma

THE POSITION of this chapter arises from the following sequence of intellectual steps:

(1) An explanation of why the Vietnam War has crystallized "a second American dilemma" in the form of a contradiction for the United States Government between its espousal of world order ideals and its patterns of diplomatic practice;

(2) A comparison of the dominant ideological perspectives that have emerged in the course of the debate produced by the Vietnam War, these perspectives being roughly identified as neo-Wilsonianism (pro-administration) and neo-Kennanism (anti-administration);

(3) A consideration of the Vietnam War as a phenomenon that is, in fact, radically inconsistent with its rationalization as the fulfillment of a neo-Wilsonian foreign policy;

(4) Some illustrations of the reliance by supporters of United States policy in Vietnam upon unconvincing neo-Wilsonian patterns of justification;

(5) A rejection of the neo-Kennanist response to the second American dilemma, and a consideration of the specific tensions between practice and norms that are exhibited in a Vietnam-type war;

(6) An outline of reorientation of foreign policy with respect to Vietnam-type political violence that rests upon the logic of a functionally conceived system of world order—conceived, that is, to combine the inevitability of competitive diplomacy with the feasibility of establishing a relevant framework of minimum world order;

(7) A conclusion suggesting that the United States, as a consequence of the Vietnam War, is at a critical crossroads and, finally, that the world order proposals outlined in (6) can help to resolve the second American dilemma provided they can be authoritatively incorporated into a new American world order creed.

A Second American Dilemma

The conflict between ideals of American foreign policy and its patterns of actual practice prompted including the enigmatic phrase "a second American dilemma" in the chapter title. There are interesting substantive and methodological similarities between Gunnar Myrdal's depiction of race relations as "the American dilemma" and the contradiction between norms and practices exposed by American involvement in the Vietnam War. Myrdal defined the American dilemma as follows:

The ever-raging conflict between, on the one hand, the valuations preserved on the general plane we shall call the "American Creed," where the American thinks, talks, and acts under the influence of high national and Christian precepts and, on the other hand, the valuations on specific planes of individual and group living where personal and local interests; economic, social, and sexual jealousies; considerations of community prestige and conformity; group prejudice against particular persons or types of people; and all sorts of miscellaneous wants, impulses and habits dominate his outlook.[1] (Emphasis removed from original.)

There appears to be such a gap between the norms and the practices at the present time which is characteristic of the present world order position of the United States. Myrdal contended that social science research could demonstrate the identity and breadth of this gap between conduct and creed. This demonstration encourages an awareness of the gap that is itself regarded by Myrdal as a valuable achievement. It is valuable because it tends to produce a gradual political mobilization of the political system in favor of the creed. This mobilization process is significantly aided, according to Myrdal's view, if the legal system can be induced to enforce the creed, as it will tend to do if it is convincingly confronted by proof of the gap. Since 1944, the year that *An American Dilemma* was originally published, it has become clear that the American creed, based on an equal right of participation in the dominant white society, does not provide a solution for race relations in the United States. The creed itself needs to be reformulated so as to be more responsive to group patterns of black perceptions of the social and political determinants of their own dignity.[2] The nonresponsiveness of this American creed as conceived in traditional terms of constitutional democracy and Christian ethics accounts for some of the appeal and success of the black power movement.

Today we are faced with a second American dilemma in the form of

[1] Gunnar Myrdal, *An American Dilemma*, New York, McGraw-Hill, 1962 edn., p. lxxi (1st edn., 1944). A somewhat parallel, although totally distinct, analysis of American foreign policy relying on Myrdal's framework has been made. See Charles A. Barker, "Another American Dilemma: Multilateral Authority versus Unilateral Power," *The Virginia Quarterly Review*, 45 (Spring 1969), 230-52.

[2] For a striking illustration of the impact on black consciousness of this gap between creed and practice see Eldridge Cleaver, *Soul on Ice*, New York, McGraw-Hill, 1968. See especially the opening paragraphs of the first essay on pp. 3-4 describing the importance of the Supreme Court decision of 1954 in shaping Cleaver's militant outlook. One short passage is expressive on the overall importance of an authoritative statement of creed: "The Supreme Court decision was only one month old when I entered prison, and I do not believe that I had even the vaguest idea of its importance or historical significance. But later, the acrimonious controversy ignited by the end of the separate-but-equal doctrine was to have a profound effect on me. This controversy awakened me to my position in America and I began to form a concept of what it meant to be black in white America" (p. 3).

a gap between our foreign policy and the American creed. This gap has been dramatized by the role of the United States in the Vietnam War, but its existence and extent are quite evident apart from Vietnam. Myrdal's argument with respect to race relations appears applicable in its structure, not its substance, to foreign policy: The demonstration of a gap between conduct and creed will tend to produce a movement to reconcile the differences in favor of the creed. In the international context the argument is made more urgent at present by a group of influential critics of American foreign policy who are urging that we abandon any normative framework as a basis for action in international society. Arguing for an abandonment of creed is quite different than urging, as seems persuasive, that, as with race relations, the traditionally conceived American creed underlying foreign policy be reformulated since it is not functionally adequate to satisfy either the selfish pursuits or the altruistic needs of international order toward which it is directed. The foreign policy evolved and explained by President Johnson, Dean Rusk, and Walt Rostow is unconvincing on its own terms as applied to the Vietnam War; as well, the terms themselves seem misguided. The purpose of this chapter is principally to establish that the terms that constitute the American creed are misguided in the setting of the Vietnam War and only incidentally (partly because by now it seems so clear) to demonstrate that even within the traditional framework of analysis there is an American dilemma vis-à-vis foreign policy parallel to the dilemma Myrdal depicted in the domestic context.[3]

The two levels of analysis (demonstrating the gap and reformulating the creed) are interconnected because it is first necessary to show the gap between the Rostow-Rusk position and the phenomena. It is especially relevant to illustrate the gap as it emerges in the legal analysis of, for instance, John Norton Moore and Myres S. McDougal.[4] Nevertheless, if the gap between norms and behavior can be established, we should avoid concluding that world order considerations either are irrelevant to our foreign policy or, worse, operate only as ideological disguises for imprudent and evil policies. There is serious danger that the

---

[3] Myrdal's depiction, however, presupposed the adequacy of the creed relevant to race relations. On closer scrutiny, however, it seems clear that American ideals were built around individual realization through equality of treatment. The Negro as an oppressed group increasingly appears to be calling for a new creed based on group dignity achieved through community responsibility. This direction of sentiment has been crystallized by "the black power movement." Herein, the analogue to foreign policy; in both settings there exists one gap between creed and practice and a second gap between a traditional creed and a reformulated creed responsive to new conditions and new perceptions.

[4] For John Norton Moore's views see Falk, ed., *The Vietnam War and International Law*, Princeton University Press, 1968, pp. 237-70, 303-17, 401-44. For Myres S. McDougal see Remarks, *Preceedings American Society of International Law, 1965*, pp. 77-78; Foreword to Roger H. Hull and John C. Novogrod, *Law and Vietnam*, Dobbs Ferry, N. Y., Oceana, 1968, pp. vii-ix.

ideological trappings currently surrounding the official explanation of the American position in Vietnam will serve to discredit law further as a source of relevant guidance for foreign policy. It would be desirable, then, if at all possible, to rehabilitate the role of international law in shaping foreign policy by demonstrating that American actions in the Vietnam War are a *repudiation* rather than an *enactment* of normative influences. Furthermore, we need to move beyond criticism to postulate a constructive role for world order considerations in future foreign policymaking operations of the United States Government. To exercise this constructive role requires a substantial revision of the world order creed of the United States, at least as far as this creed exerts an influence upon responses to revolutionary violence throughout the world.

Neo-Wilsonianism Versus Neo-Kennanism

Before examining the ideological underpinning of American foreign policy in the setting of the Vietnam War, it is essential to put this inquiry in perspective. There are two main purposes in continuing to subject the American involvement in the Vietnam War to critical scrutiny: to help end the war and to learn from our mistakes.

THE RESOLUTION TO END THE WAR IN RESPONSIBLE FASHION

By exposing the gap between norms and behavior in Vietnam, we may help to mobilize the kind of resolve needed to end the Vietnam War in a responsible fashion. Such a position requires a clearly discernible deescalation by the United States including a unilateral termination of bombing North Vietnam, according status to the National Liberation Front, and inducing the Saigon regime to release non-Communist political prisoners such as Quat and Dzu. This initiative must also involve negotiations seeking a cease-fire, a coalition government, a deferred procedure on reunification, neutralization of South Vietnam and if possible other contiguous states, guarantees against reprisals, provisions for receiving exiles, massive economic aid for the entire war zone, and possibly a policing responsibility for the United States under Asian auspices.[5]

[5] President Lyndon Baines Johnson's speech of March 31, 1968 (see *New York Times*, April 1, 1968) restricted bombing of North Vietnam to the territory below the 20th parallel and announced his intention to withdraw from the presidency. These steps appeared for a time to indicate a peace initiative on the part of the United States; North Vietnam responded positively and talks started in Paris on an unconditional cessation of all bombing and other war acts against North Vietnam. However, in the months subsequent to March 31st the United States has flown more missions and delivered a greater tonnage of bombs against North Vietnam than ever before. The geographical concentration of the bombing sharply increased the human costs. The principal targets appear to have been heavily inhabited village communities. In early April 1968 the United States military command organized a sweeping attack labeled Operation Certain Victory, hardly a designa-

The Lessons of the Vietnam War

It is important to shape the future along constructive lines, especially with respect to the character of world order. There is a great deal to learn from the massive and tragic failure of United States policy in Vietnam. The most important lesson of the Vietnam War is the need to reorient the relevant sector of United States foreign policy to make it more constructively responsive to those types of political violence throughout the world that are linked to revolutionary movements. We must achieve an understanding of the Vietnam War that will not yield to the regrettable habit of statesmen of preparing for the future by overreacting to the past.

The reorientation of policy that I propose is an alternative to the two main approaches to Afro-Asian violence that presently dominate the debate on the world order dimensions of the Vietnam War. The first approach is labeled "neo-Wilsonianism" and can be fairly associated with the official arguments of the Johnson administration, especially as articulated by Dean Rusk and Walt Rostow, supporting the American role in Vietnam. Neo-Wilsonianism, as it will be here designated, entails reliance on a series of world order arguments to sustain the legitimacy of employing force in the course of carrying on an interventionary foreign policy. These neo-Wilsonian arguments seem incapable of explaining the American role in the Vietnam War. In addition, a reliance on this kind of argumentation to explain and justify what is now widely believed to have been an imprudent Vietnam involvement tends to discredit altogether the relevance of a world order perspective to the conduct of foreign policies.

The second approach, which has risen to prominence in reaction to the first, will be designated "neo-Kennanism." The neo-Kennanist critique of the Administration position contends that United States policy has been overly guided by a series of sincerely held but misguided convictions of leading policymakers about an American mission to build world order. This missionary energy is held responsibile by neo-

tion supportive of the search for peace. And, finally, the Second Honolulu Conference was the occasion in July of 1968 of another endorsement by President Johnson of United States support of the Thieu regime in South Vietnam. Therefore, the pattern since March 31st in this light appears to be aimed at immobilizing the Peace Movement and at appeasing public opinion on the issue of peace. For a general critique of the approach of the United States Government to peace in Vietnam see David Kraslow and Stuart H. Loory, *The Secret Search for Peace in Vietnam,* New York, Knopf, 1968. The diplomatic posture in the months since President Nixon's election has also exhibited a contradiction between the search for peace and the intensification of battlefield pressure in the most cruel and destructive fashion. See Gabriel Kolko, "Vietnam: The War and Diplomacy Since January 1968—An Analysis of United States Policy," Stockholm Conference on Vietnam, May 16-18, 1969, pp. 1-41.

Kennanists for some of the rigidity of American policies toward Vietnam. Further, the neo-Kennanists assert that if the United States would abandon the world order rhetoric and candidly act to realize the national interests of the United States, then "commitments" like the one to Vietnam would be readily perceived as absurd and irrational. In essence, the best way for the United States Government to reform its foreign policy orientation is to give up its pretensions about creating world order; instead, policymakers should carefully specify national interests and guide foreign policy toward a protection of these interests in the relatively egocentric manner of a principal sovereign state of the nineteenth century.

It seems preferable to avoid both of these approaches to the conduct of foreign policy. It is desirable for United States foreign policy to seek world order objectives but only after they have been reformulated in a functionally specific manner. If we are to avoid future Vietnams, if we are to avoid regional warfare and very destructive civil strife, if we are to cope with a series of security problems associated with nuclear proliferation, and if we are to assist with legislative efforts to promote social and political justice throughout the world, then we need a foreign policy that acknowledges a world order dimension as relevant. The international system is extremely unstable, and it is a cynical form of political romanticism to revive, under these world circumstances, a balance-of-power approach as the viable foreign policy alternative to *Pax Americana*.

The United States in Vietnam: A Betrayal of Neo-Wilsonian Ideals

The Vietnam War exhibits an extraordinary disproportion between the magnitude of the United States military effort on the one side and the small-power military capabilities of its North Vietnamese adversary on the other. This disproportion is accentuated by the ability of the NLF and North Vietnam to frustrate the pursuit by the United States of a military solution for the Vietnamese conflict. It has been estimated that the United States has spent in Vietnam, by the beginning of 1968, an equivalent of $3,000 per Vietnamese square acre and had dropped an average of 100 tons of bombs per square acre. The results of the American military intervention have been to combine political futility with incredible societal devastation and human suffering.

John McAlister, an academic specialist on Southeast Asia, testified before the Senate Committee on Foreign Relations on March 7, 1968, that on the basis of past guerrilla-warfare force ratios the United States could require as many as 15 million men to succeed militarily in Vietnam.[6] This estimate makes General Westmoreland's post-Tet request for an additional 206,000 American fighting men (above the 525,000 then committed) appear as a small ascent on an escalation ladder that must be climbed to much higher levels if genuine military requirements for United States military success are to be satisfied.[7] As of March 1968, in the wake of the Tet offensive, the NLF-DRV had regained considerable control over the countryside and commands the allegiance of a significant portion of the population, whereas the incumbent regime continues to be ineffectual and compromised by its own dissension and incompetence, its political inability to secure support from non-Communist nationalist elements, and its utter dependence for survival upon a non-Asian power that appears to be fighting the war without any concern for the well-being of the Vietnamese or of their society. The United States has used its influence to keep shaky Saigon regimes in power since 1954. Despite the nationalist outlook of Premier Ngo Dinh Diem, the Vietnamese we have supported in power are basically Vietnamese successors to the colonial regime of France and express the interests of those Vietnamese who fought on behalf of the French. In this situation the United States has been playing a role in Vietnam since 1954 that resembles that of a colonial power.[8] The reality of this role is expressed in many ways, including the degree of United States command and control exercised over the war policy in Vietnam and the degree to which the conditions for negotiations, a cease-fire, and a political settlement are determined in Washington rather than Saigon. For the United States to charge that South Vietnam is the victim of aggression and armed attack under these circumstances is to go against the moral and material drift of modern history, a drift that we ourselves have supported when it was not intertwined with cold-war issues, a drift of history and conscience that we still support to the uncertain extent that we endorse the demands of black Africans rather than side with the colonial and racist claims of the ruling groups in the white redoubt of southern Africa. Legitimacy may attach to certain revolutionary efforts and is partly established by the overwhelming support given to the revolutionary position by the international community. A revolutionary effort may gather impressive political strength if it is well organized and if the constituted regime is vulnerable to fundamental chal-

---

[6] Cf. Statement of John T. McAlister at Hearings before the Senate Foreign Relations Committee, "The Nature of Revolution," February 19, 21, 26, and March 7, 1968, p. 161.

[7] Even such a projected military victory presupposes no offsetting escalation of effort on the other side. Should North Vietnam solicit and receive volunteers from China, the parameters of conflict might alter sufficiently so that the prospects for military success would have to be reevaluated.

[8] Vice President Nguyen Cao Ky offered a startlingly candid characterization of the United States role in these terms: "The foreign colonialists cannot use their material aid at this critical juncture to put a yoke around our necks," *New York Times*, April 29, 1968, p. 3.

lenge. A revolutionary situation may generate political movements that can be crushed, if at all, only through inordinate military efforts. The costs of such military efforts are likely to be especially high whenever the counterguerrilla elite is a client, or semi-puppet regime, as is the case in South Vietnam. This aggravation is true even if the particular puppet is one of those which the United States seems fond of building, a puppet with special aptitudes for manipulating the puppeteer. The politico-military dynamics of modern revolutionary nationalism produce a special kind of warfare which is not susceptible to legal analysis either as a civil war purely internal to a single society or as an attack or aggression by one state against another.

The war in Vietnam is *not* usefully analogous to the Korean War, and no amount of rhetorical insistence by our leaders can make it so. The key element in South Vietnam since the war for Vietnamese independence resumed in 1960 was not North Vietnamese support for the insurgency in the South but the combined failure of the Saigon regime either to govern adequately or to motivate and organize its own fighting forces. The reality of the revolutionary situation was created by the continuing control of this southern portion of Vietnam by a reactionary, oppressive government that owed its continuing existence to non-Asian power and wealth. The United States does not openly question support given by Algeria, Tanzania, and others to the liberation movements directed against the five governing regimes of southern Africa. Hardly anyone, least of all South African Nationalists, questions the potential revolutionary situations created by oppressive and reactionary white rule in this part of the world. It is worth noticing, however, that the governments in control in these countries have the capacity to govern; consequently, there is as yet no genuine revolutionary prospect. The point relevant to Vietnam is that external support is *not* the critical factor. We abundantly trained, guided, and supported Cuban exiles to mount the Bay of Pigs operation in 1961, but there was neither an anti-Castro revolutionary situation in Cuba nor an inability of the Castro regime to govern or to respond to security threats. It is the combination of inadequate domestic government and a revolutionary situation that produces a war of the Vietnam type. Entering this kind of war on behalf of the beleaguered government has little in common with genuine collective self-defense and collective security, whether this collective procedure is of the type dependent on United Nations action or an outgrowth of an alliance of the SEATO type. It is most important to distinguish decisively between genuine applications of the collective security effort of the Korea type and the spurious collective security claims of the Vietnam type.

Professor McDougal at the 1965 Annual Meeting of the American

Society of International Law made a series of comments that appear to ignore the considerations of the preceding paragraphs. I quote this somewhat dated statement by Professor McDougal only because he has been willing to reiterate subsequently[9] his attachment to the same legal sentiments: "We do not need new law nor to be so pessimistic" about the existing law when it is considered in relation to the conflict raging in Vietnam. Professor McDougal went on to explain that

> it should not be so difficult to apply the Charter and customary international law to the events in Viet-Nam. The people in South Viet-Nam were being subjected to the most obvious aggression in all its forms. The established government of that country had sought our assistance in self-defense. The South Viet-Namese and ourselves were the objects of continuous armed attack, and the response we were making with the military instrument was certainly no more than proportional to the attacks. . . . If the question were seriously asked whether the continued assistance or withdrawal by the United States would promote the genuine freedom of choice of the people of South Viet-Nam, there could be but one answer. Our moral—and legal—position in South Viet-Nam is sound.[10]

This remarkable statement was made by one of the most creative and sensitive jurists of our time. Is it any wonder that opportunistic statesmen seize upon such an analysis that purports to be a legal assessment? Is it any wonder that statesmen turn from international law with dismay? The main legal arguments that have been put forward to support the administration are variations on this theme, variations aptly focused by the government itself through the words of its Legal Adviser to the Secretary of State, Leonard C. Meeker: "The crucial consideration is that North Vietnam has marshalled the resources of the state and has used instrumentalities of the state including units of its regular armed forces sent into South Vietnam to achieve state objectives by force—in this case to subject the South to its rule."[11] Leaving aside the one-sidedness of these interpretations of the factual situation—the failure to take into account what the United States was doing with its resources to sustain the Saigon regime in power—Mr. Meeker's statement accepts the underlying notion that the same legal tests and images can be used to appraise the legality of an antiregime challenge in Vietnam as were suitable to assess the uses of force in 1950 against South Korea and in 1956 against the United Arab Republic in the Suez.

Professor McDougal's view is that the United States is acting in

9 Foreword, see note 4.
10 Remarks, see note 4, pp. 77-78.
11 Leonard C. Meeker, "Viet-Nam and the International Law of Self-defense," in Falk, *op.cit.*, note 4, pp. 318-32, at 326-27.

defense of the Vietnamese people by supporting the Saigon regime. This claim seems macabre and absurd in light of several million refugees and the untold devastation and destruction inflicted on Vietnam without even the prospect of successful military and political action. Jonathan Schell's account of the Vietnam War is a very compelling portrait of the battlefield impact of the American military presence; as such, Schell provides a foundation on which to rest a legal and moral appraisal of these issues. For Schell, these features of the United States role are most salient:

> The immense disparity in size and power between the two adversaries, the fact that Americans are fighting ten thousand miles from home, the fact that the Vietnamese are an Asian and non-industrialized people, the fact that we are bombing North Vietnam but the North Vietnamese are incapable of bombing the United States, the fact that our bombing in South Vietnam can be met only by small-arms fire, the fact that it is often impossible for our men to distinguish between the enemy and friendly or neutral civilians, the anomalousness and the corruption of the Saigon government, the secondary role played by the South Vietnamese army we are supposedly assisting, the fact that that enemy is fighting a guerrilla war while we are fighting a mechanized war, and, finally, the overriding, fantastic fact that we are destroying, seemingly by inadvertence, the very country we are supposedly protecting.[12]

This "overriding, fantastic fact" is a central aspect of the present setting. The United States Government has found no way to conduct the war in Vietnam except to turn the country into a land of scorched earth, mistreated refugees, and corpses. Let there be no mistake or shyness about labels. The cumulative effect of the tactics of the United States must be minimally construed as tending toward being genocidal in character in the sense of entailing the systematic destruction of an innocent alien population of distinct ethnic identity.[13] And let me also be clear that this awful reality is not the fault of our soldiers or even primarily of their immediate commanders, who were given hopeless military assignments by their political leaders. It seems necessary to place central blame upon those American leaders and policy-makers who insisted upon a quasi-idealistic interpretation of the Vietnam War as the defense at all costs of a quasi-society against aggression. Consequently, some of the fault lies with a theory lodged in the minds of statesmen,

[12] Jonathan Schell, "A Reporter at Large, Quang Ngai and Quang Tin-I," *The New Yorker* (March 9, 1968), 39-128, at 39.
[13] For a rather full presentation of the genocidal indictment of United States war policies in Vietnam see Jean-Paul Sartre, "On Genocide," *Ramparts* (Feb. 1968), 37-42.

such as Dean Rusk and Walt Rostow, and made more pernicious by the sincerity and conviction of its espousal by these two proponents.

The Neo-Wilsonian Interpretation

Nowhere has this false idealism about world order been better exhibited than in Walt Rostow's address to an English university audience at Leeds in the winter of 1967. There Mr. Rostow argued that "we are confident that what we are seeking in Viet Nam is right and essential if we are to move successfully through the great transition; that is, toward an orderly world of peacefully coexisting states." Mr. Rostow insisted that

> . . . we are honoring a treaty which committed us to "act to meet the common danger" in the face of "aggression by means of armed attack" in the treaty area. And we are answering, as we had to answer on other occasions, the question: Are the word and commitment of the United States reliable? For the United States cannot be faithful to its alliances in the Atlantic and unfaithful to its alliances in the Pacific.[14]

Mr. Rusk echoed these sentiments when he said before the Fulbright Committee in March of 1968, "I don't know what would happen to the peace of the world if it should be discovered that our treaties do not mean anything."[15]

This kind of rationale based on the existence and interrelation of collective defense commitments is then buttressed by an acceptance of the Mao-Giap thesis that the Vietnam War is a test case for wars of national liberation. This assessment assumes an array of revolutionary leaders around the world awaiting the outcome of the Vietnam War to set their own course of action. Does Mr. Rostow really believe that African liberation groups or Latin American insurgent leaders would alter their plans or tactics depending on the outcome of the Vietnam War?

It is perhaps true that frustration, despair, and exhaustion will influence future United States policy and may lead the United States to withdraw altogether from the Afro-Asian arena or to remain only under some revived doctrine of massive retaliation. An Indian journalist, M. S. Prabhakar, has suggested a scenario for ending the Vietnam War that reveals the policy impasse confronting the United States in a form that is not nearly as implausible as we might want it to be.[16] Prabhakar

[14] W. W. Rostow, "The Great Transition: Tasks of the First and Second Postwar Generations," *State Department Bulletin*, 56 (March 27, 1967), 491-504, at 503.

[15] Excerpts from Rusk testimony on Vietnam, *New York Times*, March 12, 1968, p. 16, col. 3.

[16] M. S. Prabhakar, "The Vietnam War Ends," *Atlas* (March 1968), 50-51.

begins his picture account with President Johnson appearing on national television to explain why he suddenly ordered a unilateral withdrawal of United States troops from Vietnam followed by nuclear attack on all of Vietnam. The projected date of the hypothetical occasion is October 2, 1968. Prabhakar writes of "the hard step" President Johnson "was compelled to take to protect the freedom and integrity of South Vietnam from the North." He attributes to President Johnson the following explanation:

> A series of forty bombs, each of half-a-megaton potency, were dropped at different points of the country, thus affecting maximum range and destructive power and totally neutralizing enemy action. . . . I am glad to announce that all the aircraft have returned safely after their mission. . . . We could hardly use our nuclear capability without subjecting our own men to certain death. It was with this objective that I announced an unconditional withdrawal of all American troops. The enemy, I am glad to say, fell into the trap, and came out into the open to demonstrate his happiness at the so-called "victory." Little did he realize how firm and complete our commitment to defend the freedom and integrity of South Vietnam was.[17]

Prabhakar's piece is disturbing, in part because it carries to a grotesque conclusion the logic of the combat that Schell has written about. Prabhakar's satire is only an extreme form of Schell's "overriding, fantastic fact" that we are destroying the very country that we are supposedly protecting. It is then with awesome incredulity that we consider a further excerpt from Dean Rusk's testimony before the Senate Foreign Relations Committee: "We have undertaken not the task of the world policeman, but we have undertaken certain aspects of it." Secretary Rusk urged that the American effort in Vietnam be understood as the search for organized peace! "Now the central problem, Mr. Chairman, before the human race is how to organize peace in the world."[18] Like Secretary Rusk, Mr. Rostow professed no concern for anything so provincial and self-serving as the national interest of the United States, not even in terms of upholding Asian and Pacific stability. Mr. Rostow concluded his Leeds lecture by saying that "if the argument I have laid before you is correct—and if we have the common will to hold together and get on with the job—the struggle in Viet-Nam might be the last great struggle of the postwar era."[19]

[17] *Ibid.*, President Johnson's withdrawal from the campaign for the presidency on March 31, 1968 and offer of negotiations does not invalidate the satirical reality of Mr. Prabhakar's fantasy.
[18] Rusk, *op.cit.*, note 15, p. 16, col. 2.
[19] Rostow, *op.cit.*, note 14, p. 504.

The Neo-Kennanist Reaction

It is little wonder that idealistic explanations of this ugly, costly, and disastrous war lead prudent men of affairs to seek an ideological surgeon. These neo-Wilsonian ideals blind their adherents to the perception of contradictory facts. The invocation of these ideals recalls the self-righteous tone of Woodrow Wilson, who failed in his own effort to have the United States single-handedly reform the world. Woodrow Wilson also believed that if the American creed could be universalized, it would bring order and justice everywhere.[20] Not only did Wilson fail to persuade others, but he persuaded the United States at the time that it needed to choose the obverse of globalism—isolationism—with ruinous results as a consequence. We are again in danger of a reactive choice in opposition to the resurgence of Wilsonian foreign policy in our own era. Opponents of the Vietnam War castigate properly the self-delusive idealism that keeps us from a realistic appreciation of the facts. These critics propose instead more attentiveness to national interests in regions that have been traditionally the main concern of the United States; namely, Latin America and Europe.[21] This quest for a redefinition of our foreign policy seems to repeat, in reverse, the error of our unilateral intervention in the Vietnam War. The idea of grounding foreign policy on national interests realistically conceived rests on an obsolete nineteenth century image of statecraft and political consciousness. The facts of interdependence today do create what Albert Wohlstetter has recently called "illusions of distance."[22] It is no longer economically, militarily, or emotionally feasible to retreat from participating in what goes on elsewhere in the world, nor does spatial remoteness give much indication of significance or effect. We need a foreign policy that seeks autonomy rather than affinity for the states of Africa and Asia, a foreign policy that supports community procedures to protect states that may become victims of Korea-style aggression but does not unilaterally commit the United States to the preservation of a Saigon-type victim of an NLF-type insurgency.

[20] In recent historical reevaluations, Wilson has been charged increasingly with disguising beneath a world order design a carefully conceived defense of very particular economic and ideological interests of the United States. See e.g., N. Gordon Levin, Jr., *Woodrow Wilson and World Politics—America's Response to War and Revolution*, New York, Oxford University Press, 1968; Arno J. Mayer, *Wilson vs. Lenin—Political Origins of the New Diplomacy 1917-1918*, Cleveland, Meridian edn. World Publishing, 1963.

[21] E.g., J. William Fulbright, *The Arrogance of Power*, New York, Vintage, 1967; see also George W. Ball, *The Discipline of Power*, Boston, Little, Brown, 1968; Roger D. Masters, *The Nation is Burdened: American Foreign Policy in a Changing World*, New York, Knopf, 1967.

[22] Albert Wohlstetter, "Illusions of Distance," *Foreign Affairs* (Jan. 1968), 242-55.

Normative Options: Bridging the Gap Between
Reality and International Law

This factual assessment of the Vietnam situation uncovers three areas of normative tension relevant to legal analysis. First, United Nations Charter conceptions of aggression, armed attack, and self-defense are *not*, as properly interpreted and applied, relevant to an NLF-type challenge and response, even if there is substantial evidence of foreign instigation and support. The Charter conceptions of aggression, armed attack, and self-defense are relevant, however, when characterizing certain kinds of counterguerrilla strategies, such as the extensions by the United States of the zone of violence to include North Vietnam after February 1965. Under this line of reasoning, the United States was guilty of aggression amounting to an armed attack against North Vietnam, and North Vietnam and her allies were states legally entitled to act in self-defense. The failure of North Vietnam to respond to this American attack by calling more strongly upon its allies can be interpreted as partial appeasement of the United States; considerations of relative power and the danger of provoking a general war perhaps made this a prudent move. At a minimum, North Vietnam would seem to be legally entitled to attack United States Air Force sanctuaries in Thailand.

A second conclusion is that the Westphalian logic of independent sovereign states exercising mutual respect for one another presupposes that external coercion is not used to manipulate and establish the character of the governing elite.[23] This is especially true in circumstances such as those in Vietnam where one side, the Viet Minh, won a war of national independence fought to control the entire country and where both sides[24] confirmed at Geneva in 1954 that Vietnam was one and only one country, a view that continues to be proclaimed officially by both halves of Vietnam. In other words, legal ideas about indirect aggression and nonintervention are not simplistically applicable in situations where the target state is nonviable, where the internal faction contending for control has an equivalent basis of legitimacy, and where the external state, North Vietnam, has strong legal and political reasons to support its opposition to any effort to partition the country. The second war in Vietnam has certain similarities to a war of secession to the extent that North Vietnam has been seeking to prevent permanent

[23] For an attempt in a quite different context to specify the characteristics of an international legal order conceived on the basis of Westphalian logic see Chap. XX.

[24] "The other side" in the war of independence was the colonial war, France. Of course, such a view overlooks the claims of the Saigon regime to participate in determining the political future of Vietnam. For a careful analysis of these issues see John S. Hannon, Jr., "A Political Settlement for Vietnam, the 1954 Geneva Conference and its Current Implications," 8 *Virginia Journal of International Law*, 4-93 (1967).

partition:[25] at Geneva in 1954, only the Viet Minh and the French were accorded autonomous diplomatic status to settle the future of Vietnam, and neither of these two actors appeared to expect Vietnam to evolve into two separate sovereign states.

It would seem that the existence of a distinct state of South Vietnam came about as a result of the factual assertion of statehood by the Saigon regime combined with the acceptance of that assertion by a large portion of the international community, principally evidenced by the grant of diplomatic recognition to the Saigon government.[26] Diplomatic recognition is conferred through a subjective and decentralized procedure that can be invoked by any state, with the result that external support can be partially self-legitimized. It may or may not fulfill the values of self-determination to support one side or to remain impartial. There is no necessary correlation—as Soviet intervention in Hungary in 1956 suggests—between responding to a call for help by an elite characterized as "legitimate" and lending support to the principle of self-determination. In the Vietnam kind of situation the degree of autonomy and viability possessed by the constituted regime is a crucial factor in determining the status of claims to intervene on opposing sides. It may be more destructive of world order to rely on the CIA to manipulate the character of constituted elites in foreign countries than to infiltrate support to the insurgent elite. An insurgent elite may offer a better prospect of political stability and human welfare for a particular country. The legal tradition favoring outside discrimination in support of the incumbent government does not contribute very much to our understanding of the relative merits of specific claims to assist either the insurgent or incumbent faction. The specific context should be appraised, including the compatibility between the policy orientation of the incumbent and world community policies.

My third conclusion, which is significant for legal analysis, is that the adoption of a counterguerrilla strategy which seeks "a military solution" in a revolutionary situation, especially when adopted on behalf of a nonviable and unpopular regime, can succeed only if it is based on an extraordinary ratio of military superiority, resulting in a degree of destruction and disruption disproportionate to the value of normal political objectives. If the counterguerrilla forces cannot achieve a decisive early military advantage while the conflict is still at a small scale, the

[25] Even South Vietnam in its Constitution of 1967 in Article 1 proclaims that "Vietnam is a territorially indivisible, unified, and independent republic." Article 107, to emphasize the claim, says that Article 1 "may not be amended or deleted."

[26] The arguments in favor of considering South Vietnam as a sovereign state are well presented in an extensive legal memorandum by John Norton Moore and James L. Underwood in collaboration with Myres S. McDougal, *The Lawfulness of United States Assistance to the Republic of Viet Nam*, May 1966, pp. 5-29.

war will tend to intensify in scale and scope, moving gradually in the direction of genocidal war—necessarily a war indiscriminately waged by armed soldiers using advanced weaponry against large sectors of the domestic population. In effect, once a certain escalation threshold has been crossed, it is virtually impossible to constrain altogether a counter-guerrilla combat strategy within the Hague-Geneva conceptions of the law of war. If the escalation continues in time and magnitude, then the cumulative effect of specific violations of rules is to wage war against the entire social and political base of insurgent support; that is, against the people themselves. Such a major counterguerrilla war effort is almost necessarily conducted in modes of combat that are incompatible with the basic premises of postfeudal international regulation of warfare. These premises were, first, that the belligerent confrontation should be confined to adversary military establishments with as little civilian spill-over of destruction and suffering as possible, and, second, that opposing belligerent forces should fight within a framework agreed upon to avoid needless suffering for combatants. The military logic of a Vietnam-type war undermines these premises since the military operations in-volve indiscriminate death and destruction for all human beings situ-ated in certain zones suspected of being "enemy" strongholds with only incidental military damage.[27] As a result, these tactics induce an atmos-phere of lawlessness and provoke a sense of moral outrage. For these reasons, it becomes imperative to rethink the relevance of law to the conduct of large-scale guerrilla warfare and either revise the legal framework, abandon the legal framework, or alter the conception of what constitutes an effective and permissible counterguerrilla strategy.

Normative tension exists, then, on three levels in a revolutionary situation of the Vietnam type. First, Charter ideas of aggression and armed attack are virtually inapplicable; second, the relevance of the doctrine of nonintervention is dependent on the viability of the consti-tuted regime and on the degree of external acceptance of the group op-posing the regime's political legitimacy; and third, legal restraints are difficult, if not impossible, to sustain in a situation of prolonged large-scale guerrilla warfare given current conceptions of counterguerrilla warfare. Three sorts of responses appear plausible in this situation.

One response is to maintain the Rostow-Rusk position by continuing to describe efforts on behalf of an insurgent in such situations as in-stances of conventional aggression no different from those occasions when one army crosses a boundary to fight another army or when com-bat occurs between conventionally based military forces belonging to

---

[27] For collection of material describing violations by the United States of the laws of war in South Vietnam see study com-missioned by Clergy and Laymen Con-cerned About Vietnam, published under the title, *In the Name of America*, Turnpike Press, 1968.

adversary states. Such an argument is functionally unrelated to the character of revolutionary conflict. Even on grounds of prudence it represents a self-destructive world order position since it gives rise to gross miscalculations, such as the predictions of military success repeatedly made by American leaders throughout early stages of the Vietnam War. These predictions were made partly because the war was perceived, analyzed, and fought in terms of a set of categories applicable to the Korea-type war but not to the Vietnam-type war. The Rostow-Rusk interpretation by its failure to make clearly this distinction greatly impairs the ability of foreign policy-makers to distinguish between occasions of genuine and spurious collective security.

The second principal form of response to revolutionary situations in Asia, Africa, and Latin America is to suggest that law and notions of restraint have no real relevance to this form of conflict, that these forms of violence cannot be grasped within the traditional limiting notions of international law, and that therefore foreign policy responses should be viewed as exercises of undisguised power restricted only by prudential considerations of whether it is a worthwhile deployment of national capabilities. At least such a position relieves its adherents from the distorting impact of an ideological level of interpretation. A government adopting such a position does not have to say that treaties throughout the world are at stake, declare that it must establish that aggression does not pay, or show that wars for national liberation cannot work. This kind of neo-Kennanism guards a state against regarding every occasion of civil strife as a potential Munich in the struggle to stem the tide of Communist encroachment. Such grandiose considerations are eliminated by eliminating the relevance of norms altogether.

A Preferred Approach: Intermediate Norms

A third approach to law and revolutionary violence is to evolve a series of intermediate norms that are both functionally related to this kind of violence and operationally related to the conduct of foreign policy in the world as presently constituted. This approach presupposes the validity of distinguishing between three zones of conflict within the international system.[28] The proposal for intermediate norms is a quasi-legislative proposal for regulating revolutionary violence in the tertiary zone.[29] The primary zone consists of actors capable of main-

[28] This geopolitical conception of the management of power relationships in world affairs will be set forth more fully in other writing not yet published.

[29] "Quasi-legislative" in this setting is a way of emphasizing the prospect of emerging community law despite the absence of any formally designated legislative procedure. Such quasi-legislativeness is an incident of political decentralization in international society. For a parallel consideration see Falk, Chap. VI.

taining their own security under normal conditions and of maintaining autonomy with regard to domestic and foreign policy.[30]

The secondary zone refers to those portions of the international system where one or the other of the great powers effectively exercises a principal security role (or imperial role virtually uncontested). Eastern Europe is in the secondary zone of the Soviet Union, the imperial upholder of security for the area; Latin America also is mostly in a secondary zone where the United States is the imperial upholder of security for the area.[31]

The tertiary zone consists primarily of the ex-colonial world of Africa and Asia, the principal settings for the practice of competitive diplomacy and competitive interference. The units that constitute the tertiary zone possess a rather fragile capability to maintain their own security. At the same time, since the collapse of colonialism, no great power has been consistently willing and able to sustain either internal or external security in the tertiary zone.

In the Vietnam context, part of the difficulty arises from the apparent fact that each side may well have conceived of South Vietnam as within that portion of the secondary zone for which it was responsible. The miscalculations may have occurred because the Geneva settlement lent itself easily to self-interested but contradictory interpretations.[32] The leadership of the United States Government apparently regarded, or chose to regard, Vietnam as a divided-country situation that allowed South Vietnam to be treated similarly to South Korea and West Germany. North Vietnam, France, China, and the Soviet Union evidently regarded the first Indochina War as a war of independence that had been successfully concluded; therefore, the Geneva Settlement, just as the Evian Accords of 1962 after the Algerian War of Independence, would appropriately have been construed as a transition devised to allow for a graceful French withdrawal from Vietnam preparatory to North Vietnamese governance of the entire country.

In dealing with problems of revolutionary violence, an initial normative effort would be to clarify the contours of secondary zones as well as to allocate security roles among primary zone actors in the sec-

[30] Primary zone actors include the United States, the Soviet Union, China, and several of the principal states of Western Europe. It may as an operative fact include smaller states that have established a strong tradition of autonomy, such as Sweden or Switzerland.

[31] Cuba since the ascent to power of the Castro regime in 1959 is not any longer within the secondary zone of the United States. However, the imposition of boycotts and sanctions directed at Cuba is expressive of secondary zone prerogatives. The United States may also not be in a position to provide for the security of Brazil or the Argentine, large, remote states with strong traditions of national autonomy.

[32] Cf. Hannon, *op.cit. supra*, note 24; see also Ngo Ton Dat, *The Geneva Partition of Vietnam and the Question of Reunification*, unpublished Ph.D. dissertation, Cornell University, 1963.

ondary zone. This is necessary because China, as part of its effort to become a great power, is seeking to assert its security-maintaining prerogatives over countries contiguous to itself, thereby transforming these states from tertiary zone status to secondary zone status. The Soviet Union and the United States appear determined, albeit for rather divergent reasons and by recourse to most divergent techniques, to oppose this assertion of Chinese power beyond its boundaries.

These geopolitical considerations underlie the prospect of building norms relevant to revolutionary violence in the tertiary zone, norms seeking to decouple revolutionary violence from global politics by assuming the advantages of autonomy as against affinity. In other words, the security interests of primary zone superpowers would be redefined to presuppose the benefits of autonomous and viable national units throughout the tertiary zone. The ideological orientation of tertiary zone units would not be treated as significant for security purposes. Yet, the commitment to Korea-type deterrence would be fully endorsed. There is, then, a double proposal: first, to decouple revolutionary violence from global politics through the encouragement of relatively more viable and autonomous states, and, second, to maintain and develop collective procedures of an institutional and alliance nature that represent commitments to deter such overt forms of aggression as took place in the Suez in 1956 and in Korea in 1950.

Competitive diplomacy in the tertiary zone needs to find new modes of expression. In particular, it is essential for the great powers to avoid overt military responses to alleged covert coercion or indirect aggression. United States foreign policy, in this spirit, should seek preventive strategies of influence in the tertiary zone to substitute for reactive strategies. Such preventive strategies of influence might include diplomatic and financial support for border surveillance and boundary delimitation in situations wherein a state is vulnerable to covert coercion projected across state lines.

A further element of this proposed reorientation of United States foreign policy would entail an effort to regionalize responsibilities for stability in the tertiary zone. Such regionalization would involve promoting Asian and African supranational actors capable of insulating their region or a section of it from extraregional interferences. A growth of regional actors in the tertiary zone is an important part of any effort to decouple revolutionary violence from strategic conflict at the global level.

It would also be desirable to adhere to what might aptly be called the Farer norm; namely, a prohibition on tactical support, either openly or through military advisers and volunteers, for either side engaged in an ongoing struggle for control of a national society.[33] The Farer norm acknowledges a threshold below which external support would be tolerable as part of the rules of the game governing competitive diplomacy in the tertiary zone. Given the character of international society, it is impossible and unrealistic to try to prohibit competitive diplomacy altogether. But it is both possible and necessary to establish functional thresholds that discourage violence from rising beyond certain levels of destructivity. Limited rights to accord external support to factions contending for control of a society would also provide reasonably reliable assurance that the processes of self-determination would operate by eventually vesting control of the society in that elite which combines an effective capacity to govern with a popular base of support.

It also seems essential to rehabilitate the secondary norm that the United States has persistently violated in Vietnam since 1965; namely, reinforcing the territorial ceiling on counterinterventionary claims. If the United States or any actor is counterintervening to neutralize allegedly prior intervention on the other side, then the fixed upper limit of counterintervention should be confined to the boundaries of the country experiencing the violence.[34] Such an artificial limitation on counterinterventionary claims, however, does not assure satisfactory results in all situations of revolutionary violence. The normative objective is to establish and maintain a series of thresholds to inhibit the recurrence of the large-scale counterguerrilla warfare that unfolded in Vietnam during the late 1960's. Every counterinterventionary act, regardless of its political or military rationale, that involves extraterritorial violence would constitute a violation of provisions of the United Nations Charter concerned with the prohibition of nondefensive force. In the unlikely event that the political organs of the United Nations identified interventionary facts as constituting "an armed attack" then the customary extraterritorial prerogatives of self-defense would be operative. Action in self-defense, authorized by an international institution, enjoys a different legal status than does a self-determined claim by the counterintervening state, especially given the practices of adversary fact-finding and of competitive diplomacy typical in the tertiary zone.

A Comment in Conclusion

This recommended reorientation of the norms of involvement governing outside participation in revolutionary violence in the tertiary zone has important implications for the foreign policy debate provoked

[33] See Tom Farer, "Intervention in Civil Wars: A Modest Proposal," in Falk, *op.cit. supra*, note 4, pp. 509-22.
[34] For legal controversy on this issue of the territorial constraints on counterintervention see Falk and John Norton Moore in Falk, *op.cit. supra*, note 4, at pp. 375-86, 417-30, 490-94.

within the United States since 1965 by the Vietnam War. Such a reorientation is directed toward the future, toward a period of world history that seems destined to be fraught with revolutionary violence within states and global discord between groups of states.

In this spirit, it is possible to heed a portion of Myrdal's argument; namely, that the persuasive documentation of the gap between ideals and practices helps to close the gap in the direction of the ideals. Myrdal also argued that the methods of the social sciences—by providing evidence or data to support the inference—are able to make persuasive the underlying contention that a gap between ideals and practices exists.

In the present context, the gap is between the norms of world order relevant to revolutionary violence and the actual patterns of state practice. One shortcoming of Myrdal's argument with regard to race relations was his failure to recast the relevant norms in functionally suitable terms. In this essay I have tentatively recast the norms relevant to the regulation of revolutionary violence. Incidentally, an argument has been developed to the effect that patterns of United States practice, as disclosed in the Vietnam War, are disjoined either from traditional norms of the Rostow-Rusk variety or from the functionally specific variety outlined in the last section of this chapter. Further, an argument has been offered against reacting to the gap disclosed by the American policies in Vietnam along neo-Kennanist lines.

This is a time when it is imperative for Americans, especially those concerned with world order issues, to reexamine the relationship between the phenomenon of revolutionary violence and the normative interpretation of this phenomenon. We need to find modes of reconciliation that accord some deference to the world image we would like to see evolve in coming decades.

This essay is a preliminary attempt to suggest the form that such modes of reconciliation might take. Myrdal suggested in 1944 that the United States was at a crossroads with respect to race relations; in 1969 the United States is once again at a dangerous crossroads, this time with respect to revolutionary violence in the tertiary zone.[35]

[35] The present situation appears more serious than does the earlier one. Added to the unresolved problems of racial strife are the unresolved problems of military intervention by the United States in foreign societies. In both settings military solutions have been promoted by the government, leaving untouched the roots of tension and conflict. For many politically conscious Americans this double gap between norms and practices creates a severe crisis of conscience. The severity of the crisis is deepened by an advancing technology of destruction that threatens to convert political imprudence by national leaders into a tragedy of possibly irreversible character, bringing death and deprivation not only to one's own society, but to all peoples and to all forms of life.

XXIII. Observations on Political Loyalty at a Time of World Crisis

THIS chapter examines some of the issues of political loyalty as they are emerging in the United States during the late 1960's. The form of these issues is deeply influenced by the participation of the United States in the Vietnam War and by the interrelated phenomena of racial violence in American cities and student violence in American universities. These particularities of the contemporary scene are further agitated by more fundamental questionings directed at the functional and emotive obsolescence of the sovereign state in the nuclear age.

The observations of this chapter on the conditions of political loyalty are intended as a tentative assessment and one that pertains to the particular national situation of the United States. These observations need to be supplemented by comparable assessments of political loyalty pertaining to national circumstances different from those prevailing in the United States. It would be desirable to compare the loyalty situation in highly centralized socialist states, especially the Soviet Union and China, where the institution of censorship and government controlled education takes precedence over the values of intellectual autonomy. Such a political system subordinates the contribution of individuals to such an extent as to question the very premises of political loyalty conceived of as a volitional act of attachment and affirmation. It may be that for highly centralized political systems of both left and right there is no meaningful distinction between the orientation of the government and the outlook of the entrapped individual. The evolving domestic experience in the Soviet Union and the countries of Eastern Europe, however, suggest that even rigid state control cannot permanently stifle dissident voices or trends of thought. Some encouraging evidence now exists that these states, once in stable control of their national societies, are gradually becoming indulgent of individualist orientations toward political values. There is also some evidence that leaders of such countries will themselves be socialized so as to acquire more cosmopolitan perspectives that will be, to some extent, disseminated to the population as a whole.

The contemporary shape of political loyalty is also distinctive for those national societies engaged in the early stages of the process of nation-building. Many African and Asian societies are discovering that the widening of loyalty now from tribal or ethnic units of identification to embrace national or regional units is itself an expansion of outlook that is quite responsive to their particular circumstances. For societies engaged primarily in building a modern state the symbols and creeds of egocentric nationalism may be functionally appropriate, whereas for citizens of advanced states experiencing the shift to postindustrial society these symbols and creeds may be highly inappropriate. It is obvious that a more comprehensive account of the bearing of political loyalty on the present character and future prospects of world order would have to comprehend very great differences in national circumstances that characterize international society as a whole.

I. The Loyalty Setting

In less harassed times, the basic constituents of loyalty are taken for granted by a particular community. During periods of rapid social and political change, the proper hierarchy of loyalties to which an individual may find himself subject in a complex situation of choice and action is likely to be controversial, even though the validity of each distinct set of loyalties has not been very generally drawn into question. At present, however, we find more and more people puzzled not only by the familiar and unavoidable need to choose among loyalties so as to act in one rather than another direction, but troubled, as well, by more profound doubts as to whether traditional objects of loyalty continue to deserve affirmation. Such a loyalty crisis reflects a more total questioning of inherited belief systems and governmental institutions entrusted with the actualization of these belief systems. We live at a time of uncertainty and disruption that influences attitudes at every level of existence, including attitudes toward such fundamental institutions of our social being as family, church, and state; this experience of malaise is accentuated by the tension between the expansion of the horizons of awareness to include the possibility of contact with extraterrestrial sensate cultures and the contraction of global separateness through a technology that makes the metaphor of the world as a single human family increasingly pertinent to everyday perceptions, fears, and hopes.

Such a crisis of orientation makes it exceedingly difficult to specify what the conflict of loyalties is about and why it is important to grasp. One general observation does appear warranted: many articulate and sensitive members of advanced industrial societies have been experiencing drastic and rapid shifts in their understanding of the requirements of political loyalty and have been led, as a consequence, toward increasingly radical responses to the personal, social, and political problems of our age. A conflict of loyalties is manifest in recent surges of political energy toward radical solutions. Some changes in loyalty patterns have also come about as a consequence of changes in the relative weightings given to traditional loyalties. Thus part of the apparent dilemma of loyalty results from the elimination of confusion as to value preferences, and the adoption of new conceptions of loyalty and the repudiation of old conceptions. Commitment to a new value pattern in direct conflict with orthodox patterns of loyalty is becoming increasingly salient throughout Western civilization.

Three general levels of this loyalty crisis pertain to the regulation of violence and international conflict. The specific sociohistoric shape of this loyalty crisis has been vividly crystallized in the United States by the intensely interrelated realities of the Vietnam War and urban distress. The employment of violence by the American government in Vietnam and in its own cities produces a national dilemma of loyalty for many Americans. At the same time, the dilemma is itself connected with the deepest levels of human experience, with the whole process of organizing and vindicating the authority of the state and with the various modes of identifying and separating ourselves from groups perceived as alien because their pigmentation is different.

II. The Three Levels of the Crisis of Loyalty in Our Times

The first and most general level of loyalty crisis is a questioning of the capacity of the nation-state to satisfy fundamental human needs for group security and welfare, especially in areas of war and peace. Nuclear technology dramatizes the limitations imposed upon the capacities of even the most powerful state to provide its own population with any sense of security against a determined adversary possessing weapons of mass destruction. This loyalty crisis on the general level has also been prompted by witnessing more or less directly the great destructiveness of World Wars I and II. Aghast at the prospect of a nuclear war, observers often tend to overlook the awful destruction of life and civilization that took place in these prenuclear wars; even before nuclear weapons were developed and used, there was a widespread prenuclear revulsion with war and with the tendency of the state system to produce wars of great magnitude in the struggle of leading states to exert greater relative influence within international society. On this most general level of confidence in the sovereign state, then, the technology of destruction, combined with the growing and deepening sense of how irrational recourse to general warfare has become, tends to arouse a widespread, if largely latent, questioning of the traditional capacities of the nation-state to provide for the security of its population. This loss of confidence in the ability of the state to deliver security undermines the logic of loyalty in one objective sense. Certainly the loyalty of the citizen is not susceptible of expression in the form of a tacit bargain to give loyal adherence in exchange for group security, but the rational underpinnings for the sentiments of patriotism provided a solid foundation of largely unquestioning adherence that, once removed, engenders a more skeptical attitude toward the policies and demands of national governments. This skepticism erodes the earlier ethos of supporting one's country "right or wrong." If national security is no longer assured, in any event, the classical rationale of responsibility of an individual to his government is considerably undermined. Such an altered attitude is reflected, of course, in an individual's response to a demand by a national government that his life be subjected to greater risk by serving in the armed forces on a conscription basis; the issue is further aggravated if an individual is being asked to risk his own life and be prepared to kill others in a conflict for which he thinks the national purpose is unjust in means or ends, or both.

On a second, somewhat more specific level, is the special role that the United States has played in international society since the end of World War II, a role that appears to many at variance with the traditions of American foreign policy, at variance with American ideals concerning nonintervention in the affairs of a foreign society, at variance with endorsing the general right of revolution for a people suffering from domination or oppression, and generally, at variance with an American belief in the self-determination of peoples.[1] All of these older elements of the self-conception of the American role in world affairs have been, though not consistently and coherently, brought into question by the kind of international situation that resulted after 1945 from the simultaneous collapse of the colonial system and the expansion of the Communist system. The interaction of these two sets of phenomena has produced the peculiar crisis of ideals for American foreign policy-making, a crisis that has yet to be resolved successfully; it has not even been perceived very clearly, except at the fringes of political awareness. The policy contradiction is created by simultaneous commitments to contain the expansion of the Sino-Soviet group of states and, at the same time, to continue an espousal of fidelity to the traditional ideals of national self-determination for foreign societies. This contradic-

[1] The pattern of United States foreign policy since World War II, and the confused rationalization of it as a defensive response to Soviet expansionism and to world Communism, has been narrated in detail by several "revisionist" historians of "the cold war." See, e.g., D. F. Fleming, *The Cold War and Its Origins, 1917-1950*, Garden City, Doubleday, 2 vols., 1961; William A. Williams, *The Tragedy of American Diplomacy*, Cleveland, World Publishing, 1959; Gar Alperovitz, *Atomic Diplomacy: Hiroshima and Potsdam*, New York, Simon and Schuster, 1965; David Horowitz, *The Free World Colossus*, New York, Hill & Wang, 1965; David Horowitz, ed., *Containment and Revolution*, Boston, Beacon Press, 1967; and note the contribution of Arthur Schlesinger, Jr., to the symposium in *Foreign Affairs* on "The Russian Revolution—Fifty Years After: The Origins of the Cold War," 46 *Foreign Affairs* (Oct. 1967), 22-52; for a convincing indictment of United States foreign policy as applied to Greece see Andreas Papandreou, "The 'Greek Problem' is Really An American Problem," *New York Times Magazine Section*, July 21, 1968, pp. 8, 27, 29, 31, 34, 36.

tion has caused even conservative and moderate analysts of foreign policy to experience a sense of confusion as to what the United States is in fact seeking in the world.[2] This sense of confusion is all-pervasive and can, perhaps, be illustrated by reference to the governing policy of the United States Government toward the situation in South Africa which apparently embitters all sides in the controversy. A manifest inconsistency of words and deeds arises from championing goals of self-determination in the most militant, ideological language while withholding the capabilities to attain these goals. The reality of this gulf between word and deed is accentuated by the awareness of a national willingness and ability to make sacrifices, even sacrifices of self-determination itself, in the interests of preventing expansions of the "Communist" domain of influence. It is not necessary to refer to Saigon regimes in South Vietnam since 1954 to establish an American willingness to endorse regimes that suppress their own populations. The United States' unwavering support, through periods of massacre and discrimination, of the Chiang regime on Formosa is a grim example of long standing;[3] unfortunately, these examples could be multiplied many times by reference to Asian and Latin American regimes that the United States has sustained in repressive and reactionary control. The United States has found that its geopolitical ambitions have placed it in a position of pursuing a foreign policy that often contradicts the ideals of world order that it professes to be supporting and implementing.[4] This split between the ideals and realities of United States foreign policy tends to intensify the crisis of loyalty that many Americans have experienced in recent years. It becomes ever clearer through a growing awareness of national patterns of behavior that the Government is violating those very ideals that it most ardently urges upon American society. This circumstance opens up a wide credibility gap—namely, that the United States Government is doing one set of things and saying another. This dissonance has now become sufficiently apparent to a sufficient number of people so that the leadership of the country is called into question by a significant segment of the population; the moral pretensions of the present leadership group are increasingly resented.

[2] E.g., George W. Ball, *The Discipline of Power*, Boston, Little, Brown, 1968; Roger D. Masters, *The Nation is Burdened*, New York, Knopf, 1967; Stanley Hoffmann, *Gulliver's Troubles, or The Setting of American Foreign Policy*, New York, McGraw-Hill, 1968; Edmund Stillman and William Pfaff, *Power and Impotence—The Failure of America's Foreign Policy*, New York, Random House, 1966; Theodore Draper, *Abuse of Power*, New York, Viking, 1966.

[3] For ample documentation in the Formosa context see George H. Kerr, *Formosa Betrayed*, Boston, Houghton Mifflin, 1965; and a chapter in the excellent book: Lung-Chu Chen and Harold D. Lasswell, *Formosa, China, and the United Nations*, New York, St. Martin's Press, 1967, pp. 82-140.

[4] This theme is the main burden of the argument developed in Chap. XXII.

In the first instance this contradiction between ideals and acts was brought about by conditions that the United States had nothing much to do with—namely, the power vacuum created in an adversary international environment by the abrupt disintegration of colonialism. One result has been to lead the United States toward playing an imperial role throughout large sectors of the international system. Increasingly, an American military presence is potentially or actually felt in all non-Communist sectors of the world.[5] Despite some continuing mention of "bipolarity" as a by-product of the nuclear stalemate, it is the United States and only the United States that is exercising and discharging the role of a global power; there is a considerable reason to report a shift in diplomatic activity from a predominantly bipolar world to a unipolar world, a world in which the United States alone projects its military power overtly throughout the world, and makes the sacrifices that this projection entails.[6] The Soviet Union, despite its nuclear weapons, has been reduced to a regional power, and China appears eager to make the transition from being a national power of continental proportions to being a regional power with extranational spheres of special control.

The third, and most concrete, level of explication, the one that brings the other two levels of the loyalty crisis to full culmination, is the war in Vietnam. The American involvement in Vietnam is an extrapolation of the sorts of commitments that were made in Western Europe first and in the Middle East later—commitments that, at the time they were made, seemed to represent quite plausible directions, for United States policy—plausible because of the coercive nature of domestic Stalinism in the Soviet Union and because Soviet foreign policy appeared to be entering upon an expansionist phase. An American effort to check Soviet expansion was especially needed because governmental control in postwar Europe and the Middle East appeared vulnerable to even rather delicate amounts of Soviet-sponsored intervention. The forward and lateral extrapolation of these Europe-based policies of the late 1940's and 1950's to Southeast Asia of the 1960's is quite another matter. Some of the ex-colonial states in Asia have little immediate prospect of stability; in many Asian settings the United States is using its military might to oppose the only groups capable of providing political

[5] For some divergent interpretations of this phenomenon see sources cited in notes 1 and 2; see also George Liska, *Imperial America—The International Politics of Primacy*, Baltimore, Johns Hopkins, 1967; Ronald Steel, *Pax Americana*, New York, Viking, 1967; J. William Fulbright, *The Arrogance of Power*, New York, Vintage, 1966.

[6] The United States is the *only* state that has, aside from special circumstances arising out of World War II in Europe, stationed troops and established military bases throughout the world. The visible symbols of an American military presence in foreign countries is a major attribute of the present international system.

stability and willing to provide social and economic progress for their populations.

The war in Vietnam makes the character of the United States role in the international system more apparent. The United States Government is willing to pay enormous costs in lives and destruction, inflicted not only on its own population, but on foreign populations, to preserve what it conceives to be a favorable political situation in a very remote part of international society, remote if measured by reference to the right of a nation to defend its own security against potential enemies or by reference to some humanitarian mission to preserve "freedom." It is a dangerously circular and vague argument to contend that the outcome of a political struggle in Vietnam is associated with the security of the United States.[7] In fact, one could more persuasively argue that the United States has its security at stake in these remote regions of the world to a lesser extent than does any other country. Not only is the security argument abstract and remote to many of us, but its application to Vietnam appears to be a very unfortunate demonstration of where these containment policies lead. The state of South Vietnam is itself largely an embodied fiction of American creation. The French lost a long and bloody war of independence fought between 1946 and 1954 against the Viet Minh for the control of the entire country of Vietnam.[8] The French lost an anticolonial war, as they were later to lose in Algeria and as the Dutch lost in Indonesia. Up until 1954 there was no South Vietnam. South Vietnam was a temporary zone created in the south of the country to soften the blow of defeat for the French nation and to avoid a possible backlash in domestic French politics. The Geneva Accords were an accommodation designed to avoid further bloodshed; the French by and large accepted the Geneva settlement as an acknowledgment of defeat comparable to that reached at the end of the Algerian war with the FLN; one notices that the Evian Accords established no

[7] Of course, if the chain of sequence is sufficiently extended, any political change anywhere bears significantly on United States security (and on the security of all other states). A more sophisticated argument concerns the American role in procedures of collective defense in sectors of the international system unable to organize their own security. The test of this argument is whether these procedures of self-defense are operating in a manner that is compatible with principles of national self-determination. The case against the American role in Vietnam rests upon the assertion that the appeal to collective self-defense against aggression is largely a smoke-screen to obscure the imposition of a Western-oriented elite upon South Vietnamese society in defiance of the domestic balance of forces. In addition, it is doubtful whether the United States has any special claims, aside from its predominant capabilities, to police the ex-colonial world. The record of accomplishment, even aside from Vietnam, is not a proud one if measured by the criteria of stability, justice, or modernization.

[8] George McT. Kahin and John W. Lewis, *The United States in Vietnam*, New York, Delta, 1967; Jean Lacouture and Philippe Devillers, *Le Fin d'une guerre, Indochine, 1954*, Paris, Editions du Seuil, 1960.

separation of East and West Algeria. The policy determination of the United States to contain Communism in Vietnam became seriously intertwined with opposition to certain indigenous, revolutionary pressures that existed almost totally independent of the ideological leadership that these pressures happened to produce in Vietnam. The Vietnam conflict has exhibited the same nationalistic pressures that are making their impact felt throughout the world; these same pressures produced a movement against the French throughout Indochina. These same nationalistic forces rose up in protest against the Dutch in Indonesia, against the British in Malaya, and have been evident to varying degrees throughout Asia. The only difference, and it is an important difference, is that the leadership of the nationalistic movement in Vietnam was Communist in training and orientation, but it was a leadership that had effectively captured control over the nationalistic movement. To oppose a Communist-led movement in the ex-colonial world that has established effective and credible solidarity with the forces of nationalism in a society fighting for its independence is to take on a formidable adversary, and to work in opposition to the historical consciousness of the present era.[9]

III. Two Intensifying Factors

It is a distinctive crisis that is given a special quality by two further considerations. One consideration arises from the recollection that the United States Government prominently supported steps taken to hold the leaders of Germany and Japan criminally responsible for their role in planning and waging the Second World War; the United States participated in the proceedings at Nuremberg and Tokyo that convicted surviving leaders as war criminals; in addition, a great many other individuals who acted in a more subordinate capacity were also convicted as war criminals for engaging in specific acts that violated laws governing the conduct of war. The tribunals prosecuted individuals for their participation in an aggressive war. It was no defense to establish that their conduct conformed to superior orders given them by their government.[10] The Nuremberg Judgment held that superior orders were no

---

[9] The degree of popular support for a guerrilla war is, of course, related to its prospects for success; to fight an anti-guerrilla war on behalf of a reactionary elite, especially if it has been allied with the colonial regime, is to oppose the whole modern movement to achieve genuine national independence. The relations between a dependent domestic elite that controls the apparatus of government and its military ally from the Western world has many resemblances to the colonial relationship. The phenomenon of neocolonialism, new forms of foreign domination, is deserving of conceptual clarification and careful empirical study.

[10] For convenient texts see Louis B. Sohn, ed., *Cases on United Nations Law*, Brooklyn, N.Y., The Foundation Press, 1956, pp. 858-968.

defense against participation in an illegal war, that the legal obligations, in other words, of the individual to refrain from participating in such a war took precedence over his obligations to obey the enacted law and the commands of his own national government. This legal conclusion represented a radical departure from prior notions of individual responsibility in periods of wartime, but the departure was supported at the highest levels by the United States Government. The resulting extension of individual responsibility was endorsed unanimously by the General Assembly of the United Nations; the results of the war crimes trials have often been reaffirmed by American leaders. It seems to me that one of the implications of the Nuremberg tradition is that Americans who oppose the war in Vietnam should be entitled to test their legal qualms about the war within our own domestic court system; Americans should be able to discover from a judicial body whether the United States is engaged in a war that violates the kind of legal prohibition that served as the basis for holding responsible those in Germany and Japan who participated at high levels of policy-making throughout World War II.[11] An individual, in other words, should no longer be obliged to commit what he feels, in conscience, to be a war crime within the meaning of Nuremberg. It is true to note that giving individuals such judicial recourse would be a revolutionary breakthrough in the relations between the individual and the sovereign state. For the first time it would become possible for an individual to invoke international law to restrict the discretion of his own government in international society to an extent comparable to an individual's capacity to invoke law to restrict the discretion of the government to act in domestic society.[12]

The second special consideration worth noting—admittedly now with a certain kind of wry embarrassment—is that the United States, more than any other country in the world, has assumed leadership in the

[11] My own thinking on this matter is briefly stated in a commentary entitled "International Law and the Conduct of the Vietnam War" published as a preface to *In the Name of America*, Annandale, Virginia, Turnpike Press, 1966, pp. 22-27; see also The Nuremberg Principles, formulated by the International Law Commission of the United Nations in 1950 to summarize "The principles of international law recognized in the Charter of the Nuremberg Tribunal and in the Judgment of the Tribunal," at 43-44.

[12] At the time of the earliest thinking about the role of the executive in foreign affairs there existed almost no framework of legal restraint applicable to issues of war and peace. Increasingly since World War I, however, there has evolved a set of legal standards that govern the use of violence in world affairs. For a careful narration of these developments see Quincy Wright, *The Role of International Law in the Elimination of War*, Manchester University Press, 1961. As a consequence, the legal status of a contested use of national force is now susceptible to judicial appreciation. A domestic court seems no longer to possess an adequate basis for characterizing an issue of war and peace as "nonjusticiable" or not subject to judicial determination because of "the doctrine of political questions."

so-called rule of law movement. President Johnson has found it possible to issue a proclamation each year on Law Day declaring the intensity with which the United States respects the commitment to settle international conflicts by peaceful means and is at work to develop international institutions capable of handling conflicts that might otherwise culminate in violence. A special irony attaches to efforts by the United States to champion the rule of law in world affairs at this time; it requires only a little objectivity to perceive that the United States has become the most obvious flagrant violator of legal rules and procedures governing the use of violence.

IV. Some Countervailing Tendencies

If one goes along to some degree with this characterization of the crisis of loyalty, citizens in the United States are now confronted with a basic question as to what the implications for action are—what should be done if this general perception of the international situation and of one's relation to one's own government is accurate? Before facing the question of action, it seems important to take account of certain countervailing considerations that have not been touched upon as yet. One of the few positive things about the behavior of the United States Government during the Vietnam War has been its basic deference to democratic values, including the right of dissent.[13] There has been maintained in the United States up through March 1968 the right to oppose and to persuade; upholding even this degree of freedom of dissent during a period of war is a very remarkable achievement in the history of nations. The United States effort to shape the outcome of the Vietnam War has been supported by a majority of citizens in American society. Those of us who adopt a position of radical opposition to American involvement in the Vietnam War are confronted by very special problems of ethics and tactics concerning the limits of minority dissent in a democratic society. At the same time that we acknowledge the law-creating role of the will of the majority, it is important to appreciate the extent to which public opinion, especially on matters of war and peace, are subject to manipulation by the government, especially by the president. The character of popular support for the Vietnam War needs to be carefully examined. Some account should be taken of the fact that the mass media are predominantly controlled by ultraconservative elements in the United States. Presidents Johnson and

[13] There are some notable exceptions to this toleration of dissent. Perhaps the most prominent, and certainly the most lamentable, exception has been the prosecution, conviction, and sentencing of Benjamin Spock, William Sloan Coffin, Jr., Mitchell Goodman, and Michael Ferber, in 1968 for a conspiracy to resist compliance with the selective service laws.

Nixon have, at many stages of the war (and, it must be added, so had President Kennedy earlier), had great opportunities to change the nature of the American involvement, as well as to change the American attitude toward that war. The United States involvement in the Vietnam War has never led the policy alternatives to be as narrowly circumscribed as the course or the official defenses and criticisms of American foreign policy in Vietnam seem to imply.[14]

A second countervailing consideration that counsels caution in expressing a revised view of the nature of loyalty is that there always exists some danger that disruptive dissent may generate a repressive counterreaction by the government and its supporters. This patriotic backlash may alter the democratic framework within which we presently exist, a framework that has been beneficial in many respects. In other words, one risk of the effort to generate an effective opposition to government policy in Vietnam is to stimulate impulses toward repression. If these impulses are acted upon the result may damage the whole domestic system with respect to the longer-run realization of democratic values. Such a risk underscores the importance of civic responsibility for opponents of the war; it is especially necessary to think through the implications of dissent, both as to prospects for effective influence and as to prospects of unleashing a repressive backlash. A plea for reflective political action should not be converted into a plea for political quietism; the risks of inaction during a time of crisis are also very high.[15]

A third countervailing consideration is that the general public, including even those citizens who take a great interest in these questions, has very imperfect access to much of the relevant information. It is very difficult to argue persuasively with policy-making officials who read the daily cables about what has been happening on the battlefields of the war, about what the negotiating opportunities for settlement have been and when they occurred, as well as what could have been achieved had negotiations been more seriously sought. An ordinary citizen may experience a sense of helplessness when it comes to assessing the degree of credibility that it is reasonable to accord official explanations of the government's motivations and goals.[16] Secondly, it is very difficult to determine the true nature of United States belligerent objectives in Vietnam. It is possible for a powerful state to contend that its belligerent objec-

[14] Such is the position of Arthur M. Schlesinger, Jr., *The Bitter Heritage*, Boston, Houghton Mifflin, 1967.

[15] It is important to appreciate the limits of rational analysis in relation to concrete action. The presence of unweighted conflicting evidence, risks, and goals makes choice an essentially non-rational act even if it is vindicated in rationalistic rhetoric. Some discussion of these issues is to be found in Falk, *Legal Order in a Violent World*, Princeton, Princeton University Press, 1968, pp. 8-38.

[16] On these issues see David Kraslow and Stuart H. Loory, *The Secret Search for Peace in Vietnam*, New York, Vintage, 1968; Franz Schurmann, Peter Dale Scott, Reginald Zelnik, *The Politics of Escalation in Vietnam*, Boston, Beacon Press, 1966.

tives are modest, even altruistic, while at the same time pursuing even without using its full capabilities a set of belligerent policies that virtually destroys the weaker state's society.[17] There is no fully convincing way to correlate these verbal claims of restraint with the patterns of action undertaken. The inability to clarify what the governing policies are underscores the whole difficulty of citizen participation in the war and peace area; the membership of a modern society is subject to extreme manipulation by a government intent on mobilizing support for a war effort, even by a well-intentioned government, much less a government lacking any benign motivation.

A fourth countervailing consideration to a repudiation of traditional forms of loyalty is the absence at the present time of any viable alternative to the state as a value-realizing instrumentality with regard to maintaining the security of social groups. International institutions exist—most prominently, the United Nations—but these institutions continue to lack the capability or the consensus to undertake critical action in the war-peace area whenever principal sovereign states are among the actors directly involved in a conflict. At present it is generally accepted that no alternative exists to bestowing loyalty upon the state other than the creation of a loyalty vacuum.[18] Such a vacuum is not desirable for individual personality structure, as studies of disaffection show. Perhaps the most constructive action involves more concerted efforts to reform and reorient the actors controlling the main instrumentalities of power. The capability to influence human behavior through international violence continues to belong predominantly to the apparatus of the sovereign state. It can be argued that until there exists a reasonable prospect that other actors in the international system will implement a more cosmopolitan set of values, it is important to resist the temptation to support supranational forms of solution. Despite the fragility of the state mechanism in the nuclear age, some reformist energy should be devoted to the management of military power. It is not constructive to

[17] The rhetoric of restraint in the sense of not destroying all that might be destroyed should not be confused with "moderation." The pattern of destruction, its sensitivity to the human dimension of war, and the magnitude and duration of destructive modalities are the elements to be assessed. The existence of residual capabilities does not necessarily prove very much, especially if the risks of "a wider war" are the main inhibiting forces.

[18] That is, political communities, institutions, and creeds that command widespread acceptance do not exist. The inchoate development on a regional and global basis of a more inclusive political system has not yet engaged the loyalties of significant segments of the population. Thus, the disintegration of loyalty with respect to the national government tends not to be replaced by some alternative target of loyalty—hence, the idea of a loyalty vacuum. Increasing numbers of citizens, however, are shifting their loyalty from the state as an object of allegiance to the norms of international law as the basic standard of permissible behavior. There is evidence of an emerging loyalty to norms of world order, even in the absence of any governmental superstructure.

engender expectations that military power will be eliminated or transferred to some more enlightened actor or group of actors.[19]

These considerations suggest that we are living in a period of confusion and transition, that we can neither affirm traditional values in the form of the relevant pattern of loyalties, nor discover meaningful substitutes. It is within this context of confusion that the individual is challenged to act. There are neither clear solutions nor answers. There are only more or less clear and un-self-deceiving questions. Inquiry is valuable to explicate the connections between the overall structure of moral consciousness and individual concrete action. We need bridges between creeds and commitments. It is time to stimulate inquiry into whether the social or moral sciences have anything distinctive to contribute to this bridge-building process.[20] We do not yet know whether anything organic emerges from the interplay between theological and secular humanistic or social scientific modes of inquiry. Because of the inability to offer prescriptions with any degree of confidence or to posit solutions for the loyalty dilemma that command general assent, the most that people can do is to bear witness to the way in which they themselves build bridges. This kind of personal emphasis may disclose the way in which individuals might discover links between moral consciousness and concrete action in settings where the traditional claims of loyalty are no longer providing acceptable bases of belief or action.

V. Urban Violence in the United States and the War in Vietnam

There have been many references to the interconnection, or lack of it, between violence in the cities of the United States and the war in Vietnam. No one doubts that these two realities presently dominate and torment the political imagination of the nation, but considerable controversy attaches to whether and to what extent these two realities spring from a single challenge. It is rather significant that the Johnson administration, in its responses to the urban riots during the summer of 1967, took pains to separate absolutely the domestic situation from the international situation. President Johnson opened his speech after the large

---

[19] For a very balanced survey of the main literature of hope in the area of world order see W. Warren Wagar, *The City of Man*, Baltimore, Penguin, 1967; a positive prescription for the future deserving serious study has been written by a Soviet physicist—Andrei D. Sakharov, "Thoughts in Progress, Peaceful Coexistence and Intellectual Freedom," published in full, *New York Times*, July 22, 1968, pp. 14-16.

[20] There are various social science projects that are working out a conception of the future of world order. E.g., see the essays in "Toward the Year 2000: Work in Progress," *Daedalus* (Summer 1967), 639-934, summarizing the early efforts of the Commission for the year 2000, under the Chairmanship of Daniel Bell, and set up by the American Academy of Arts and Sciences; see also Herman Kahn and Anthony J. Wiener, *The Year 2000—A Framework for Speculation on the Next Thirty-Three Years*, New York, Macmillan, 1967.

riot in Detroit by saying, "we have endured a week such as no nation should live through, a time of violence and prejudice," obviously a week different from others, in his sense. Orthodox thinking producing the basic model of action has coupled the strategic uses of violence in foreign affairs with pleas for "law and order" in the cities. Those who are the most passionate advocates of "victory" in Vietnam are often also those who identify with the mission of the riot police in America. The basis of order in both settings turns out to be the violence of the constituted elite, police units tending toward becoming military contingents as the scale of urban violence mounts.

In opposition, those who would settle the Vietnam War by a negotiated compromise that opens the way to an eventual assertion of the domestic balance of forces are expressing a basic skepticism about "military solutions" that pertains equally to urban convulsions. It is not so much a matter of rejecting "law and order" for the cities, as it is an insistence that a military solution of such domestic problems rests on repression rather than on the consensual values of participatory democracy. The recourse to the tactics of violence, whether by blacks in the ghettoes or students on campuses, is a social signal expressive of profound distress, a call for reconstitutive response so that groups on the threshold of insurgency can be brought back into positive interrelation with the rest of society.

In contrast with the government's emphasis on separating violence in Vietnam from violence at home, militant spokesmen among student and black groups have seen the war in Vietnam as an external continuation of the policy that the United States has been pursuing within its own society. Stokely Carmichael, speaking in Havana during August 1967, is reported as saying: "We must internationalize our struggle, and if we are going to turn into reality the words of Che Guevara to create two, three, and more Vietnams, we must recognize that Detroit and New York are also Vietnams." The drama of the imagination with respect to violence and conflict is played out in its fullest and clearest form in extreme cases; the extremes illuminate what is latent in a much larger segment of the oppressed population, but is suppressed precisely because it seems unreasonable.[21] Nevertheless, the same patterns of perceiving are present in less militant persons; to understand the concrete action involving violence it becomes essential to identify the inflamed contents of the imagination.

Youth, minorities, artists, intellectuals all tend to associate urban violence with the Vietnam War. These groups do not seem strategic

[21] Literature often illuminates human character by selecting extreme situations or by relying on extreme personality types. The "Theater of the Absurd" illuminates the normal by a careful focus on the extreme; the absurd at its deepest level is only normalcy clarified to the point of comprehension.

from the perspective of power, but they are very strategic indicators of value trends. These are vanguard groups whose views are often eventually accepted by society as a whole. In all four of these strategic groups polarized attitudes are currently prominent. On the one side is a mood of apathy and hopelessness tending, in its extreme form, toward the hippie ethos, withdrawal from the system, a feeling that dominant values are at odds with the right way to live, a sense of hopelessness about reform, and therefore a move to establish little subsystems that evolve their own value and belief structure in radical rejection of the larger social framework. On the other side is the mood of militancy, tending toward a revolutionary orientation; in effect, a sense that the constituted procedures of peaceful change are insufficiently promising with regard to satisfying justice demands. Those who feel themselves dissatisfied (and their allies) are inclined toward ever more extreme action in opposition to the prevailing policies of the national government. These prerevolutionary sentiments are exhibited in the wave of urban riots, and also by recourse to more extreme tactics of dissent by those involved in opposition to the Vietnam War, such as refusals to pay taxes, advocacy of resistance to government, proposals to initiate the impeachment of President Johnson, and efforts to enjoin the continued prosecution of the war through recourse to domestic courts. The main inference that can be drawn from the evidence of apathy or withdrawal on the one hand and militancy on the other is a loss of hope, a sense of hopelessness on the part of those strategic groups that care most about the shape and direction of society; these are the groups that normally articulate new values and goals.

One of the prime features of loyalty—loyalty to something—is a premise of active minimum hope. Loyalty only makes sense when there is, in addition to the tradition of being loyal, of fostering habits of obedience and of honoring one's heritage, also an active hope that the object of loyalty is worthy, at least potentially, of affirmation. We can sustain loyalty only if we have the feeling that the overall political system is either working beneficially or that at least it is moving in a beneficial direction and at a satisfactory rate, or that organized political, social, and moral action has the capacity to transform and reconstitute the system at a satisfactory rate. Procedures for social change are also an attribute of political loyalty implying a confidence in the self-rectifying power of society, and encouraging the maintenance of loyalty during periods of failure. To lose confidence in the self-rectifying powers of the political system, as well as to lose confidence in many substantive policies embodied in it, leads inevitably to a deteriorating social and political situation. In such event, there is not only a failure of belief in the present but also a loss of hope in the future; it is possible to abide the loss of hope in either the present or future, the absence of either or the collapse of one or the other time dimension, but not both. Hope is not so important if a basic acceptance of what is going on exists, but it is demoralizing to lack both belief and hope.

The United States suffers from a double wound: the internal wound created most prominently by the condition of blacks (I would mention that other minority groups deserve attention—not only the Indians but many whites who should be seeking "white power") and the external wound opened up by the Vietnam War. As a nation we are expending the reservoir of hope and confidence built up through decades of earlier achievements. There is an urgency in relation to both sets of issues. There is need for quick and drastic action to reengage the loyalty of the individuals who feel dissatisfied by the dominant trends of American society. It is crucial to obtain an affirmation animated by a sense of individual dignity. The problem within the United States is not merely to secure a more just distribution of goods and services, but to affirm the dignity of each individual by making him feel a participant—in the sense of having a stake in making the system work. It is only with a positive stake in making the system work, and wanting it to work, that one is reintegrated. So long as the black man is the object of charity and gratuity and the beneficiary of a paternalistic dispensation of goods and services by the central government, there is only a deepening resentment. To receive welfare places individuals and groups in the position of being supposed to be grateful toward the objects of one's hostility. To express gratitude is very demeaning. We have started to appreciate that foreign countries often react this way to the receipt of economic aid.

The situation of hopelessness, or of minimum hope, itself creates the need to choose. It creates, among other things, the opportunity to choose a course of action that leads to the restoration of hope and to the eventual restoration of belief. The symbolic individual sacrifices being made by individuals who, out of conscience, refuse to enter the armed forces or to pay taxes in support of the Vietnam war should be understood as efforts to restore the basis of hope.

VI. A Concluding Comment on Political Violence

Whenever private groups have recourse to unauthorized violence to pursue their ends a wider risk to the security of the domestic community is created. Violence breeds counterviolence, and endangers values associated with the protection of life and property and with the pursuit of happiness. At the same time, a society that fails to provide for the conditions of self-realization of its citizens, especially of its main component groups, invites recourse to violence. Social change of a fundamental variety is usually a product of threatened or actual violence, rather than a belated expression of compassion. The situation of black men in our postslave society is one that fails to establish the basis for minimum dignity; the basic experience of black men is one of humiliation and misery, and it is up to the dominant social groups to take the steps, including sacrificial steps, to alter this condition by drastic action. Anything less than drastic action will sustain the present intolerable conditions, fully vindicating a radical political consciousness, including the repudiation of the framework of legal restraint on violence.

Similarly, in foreign affairs. If the United States Government ignores the rules of restraint that are supposed to constrain the use of international violence, and if reasonable recourse has been had to strategies of persuasion, then recourse to coercive strategies seems ethically justified, even demanded by the imperatives of a cosmopolitan consciousness. Although those who employ violence or its threat need to be counseled toward prudence, this counsel should even more emphatically be given those who create and sustain the conditions at home and abroad that give rise to a radical political consciousness. In this sense, it is the governing elite's failure to bring dignity to the black communities of America despite unprecedented prosperity, and the insistence of this elite on the promiscuous use of violence in foreign societies that must be held mainly responsible for emerging patterns of violence in the United States.

This chapter has considered some of the problems of loyalty in our time. The relationship between hope and belief are the main components in this approach. The role of violence in relation to the restoration of hope and the reorientation of loyalty is a critical issue. The position that we take implies neither a renunciation of violence as a social strategy nor its embrace. The human condition is interpenetrated by violence that is employed as a political instrument capable of working toward either justice or injustice; violence can defend the good against assault by the evil, and violence can be used to change and overcome conditions that are perceived as evil, but violence should be thought of as an instrumentality of last resort, as the final defense against an acceptance of hopelessness. Some violence is an inevitable incident of a just social order because the agencies of legitimate authority depend on force. Recourse to violence refuses minimum solidarity with opponents, and shatters the solidarity of the human race as a whole. Violence should always be demonstrated as necessary.

Furthermore, recourse to violence must be shown to be effective. Those who advocate violent solutions have the burden of moral responsibility to show the relationship between the violent means advocated and the social and political end in view. We must act to avoid wasteful violence; the effects of violence should be calculated to improve the situation of those dominated; this calculation applies directly to the proposals involving violence that are designed to liberate black majorities in southern Africa.[22] An irresponsible commitment to the ideals of self-determination may produce action subjecting those who are already dominated to an even more gruesome fate. A responsible conception of political violence should normally envision the proportionality between the means chosen and the end-in-view.

And finally, there is need for parsimony—no greater amount of violence should be used than is needed to attain the just reordering of the social situation. This orientation toward political violence is relevant to domestic situations in which a part of society feels itself hopelessly oppressed, and concludes that there is no choice but acquiescence or recourse to violence. Such an orientation also applies to the conduct of foreign policy. A government has a minimum obligation to justify international violence by reference to legal and moral standards of principled action.[23] The principles of necessity, of effectiveness, and of parsimony applied to the Vietnam War appear to illustrate unprincipled use of political violence on a large scale and over a long time-span. Such a use of violence by the principal sovereign state in the world gives rise to the worst kind of learning experience for other participants in the international political system. Citizen loyalty to the national community seems better exercised in such a setting by resistance to governmental authority than by mere habitual acquiescence. The defendants in the Spock-Coffin litigation gave symbolic expression to this reorientation of loyalty. We live at a time when to be a loyal citizen may require a courageous course of opposition to the directives of national policy.

If this line of argument is persuasive, then it is time for basic revisions in the constitutional conception of the discretionary power of the President to use violence in international affairs. It is a time when there is a critical need for a revitalization of the doctrine of separation of powers in the area of war and peace. Congress needs to have a more substantial role in restraining executive discretion, and the courts should be encouraged to play a more activist role in assessing citizen complaints about the legality of national uses of violence against a foreign society. The renewal of loyalty, and with it the revival of citizenship, seems to depend on the adoption of more cosmopolitan perspectives

[22] Such a rational view of violence as a political instrumentality is contrary to some very persuasive contemporary perspectives on the subject. See e.g., Frantz Fanon, *The Wretched of the Earth*, New York, Grove, 1968.

[23] Such a minimum obligation is only the first element in establishing sufficient grounds for political violence. The justification must be assessed in relation to facts, values, and consequences. On this basis it becomes possible to endorse or condemn the claim of justification.

that emphasize how the national unit can most creatively and constructively participate in the global whole. Both the dangers and the awarenesses of the nuclear age tend to make obsolete egocentric forms of nationalism and national loyalty, especially for individuals who are trying to come to terms in advanced societies with what Kenneth Boulding has designated as "the transition to post-civilization."[24] For the more recently independent state that is struggling to move toward a domestic condition of modernity, the ethical setting may be quite different, and loyalty patterns may remain usefully nationalistic in older, more egoistic terms of political reference. The excitement of the nation-building process may be so predominant for citizens in Asian and African countries that virtually the entire field of political energy is occupied by this surge forward from conditions of subjugation and primitiveness.

Trends in loyalty patterns are one of the important determinants of the future quality of world legal order. As such, it is essential that educational and other energies be applied to the task of adapting traditional forms of loyalty to a new kind of international setting. Both the prospect and quality of human survival are heavily at stake. We now are challenged by objective circumstances to establish the human preconditions of a genuine world community. To meet the challenge it is necessary, perhaps beyond all else, to resist adversary national presentations of the facts of international conflict by those entrenched through bias or status in positions of vested outlook. The cause of a world legal order can best be served by moving toward the reality of a cosmopolitan consciousness on matters bearing upon war and peace.

[24] Kenneth Boulding, *The Meaning of the 20th Century*, New York, Harper, 1965, see esp. pp. 180-99.

APPENDICES AND INDEX

Appendix A
Documents on Dispute between Malaysia and Indonesia

AGREEMENT ON EXTERNAL DEFENCE AND MUTUAL ASSISTANCE
BETWEEN THE GOVERNMENTS OF THE UNITED KINGDOM AND OF
THE FEDERATION OF MALAYA.
OCTOBER 1957. (HMSCO CMND. 263)

Whereas the Federation of Malaya is fully self-governing and independent within the Commonwealth;

And whereas the Government of the Federation of Malaya and the Government of the United Kingdom and Northern Ireland recognise that it is in their common interest to preserve peace and to provide for their mutual defence;

And whereas the Government of the Federation of Malaya has now assumed responsibility for the external defence of its territory;

Now therefore the Government of the Federation of Malaya and the Government of the United Kingdom and Northern Ireland have agreed as follows:

Article 1

The Government of the United Kingdom undertakes to afford to the Government of the Federation of Malaya such assistance as the Government of the Federation of Malaya may require for the external defence of its territory.

Article 2

The Government of the United Kingdom will furnish the Government of the Federation of Malaya with assistance of the kind referred to in Annex I of this Agreement, as may from time to time be agreed between the two Governments for the training and development of the armed forces of the Federation.

Article 3

The Government of the Federation of Malaya will afford to the Government of the United Kingdom the right to maintain in the Federation such naval, land and air forces including a Commonwealth Strategic Reserve as are agreed between the two Governments to be necessary for the purposes of Article 1 of this Agreement and for the fulfilment of Commonwealth and international obligations. It is agreed that the forces referred to in this Article may be accompanied by authorised service organisations, and civilian components (of such size as may be agreed between the two Government to be necessary) and dependants.

Article 4

The Government of the Federation of Malaya agrees that the Government of the United Kingdom may for the purposes of this Agreement have, maintain and use bases and facilities in the Federation in accordance with the provisions of Annexes 2 and 4 of this Agreement and may establish, maintain and use additional bases and facilities as may from time to time be agreed between the two Governments. The Government of the United Kingdom shall at the request of the Government of the Federation of Malaya vacate any base or part thereof; and in such event the Government of the Federation of Malaya shall provide at its expense agreed alternative accommodation and facilities.

Article 5

The conditions contained in Annex 3 of this Agreement shall apply to the forces, the authorised service organisations, the civilian components and the dependants referred to in Article 3 while in the territory of the Federation of Malaya in pursuance of this Agreement.

Article 6

In the event of a threat of armed attack against any of the territories or forces of the Federation of Malaya or any of the territories or protectorates of the United Kingdom in the Far East or any of the forces of the United Kingdom within those territories or protectorates or within the Federation of Malaya, or other threat to the preservation of peace in the Far East, the Governments of the Federation of Malaya and of the United Kingdom will consult together on the measures to be taken jointly or separately to ensure the fullest co-operation between them for the purpose of meeting the situation effectively.

Article 7

In the event of armed attack against any of the territories or forces of the Federation of Malaya or any of the territories or protectorates of the United Kingdom in the Far East or any of the forces of the United Kingdom within any of those territories or protectorates or within the Federation of Malaya, the Governments of the Federation of Malaya and of the United Kingdom undertake to co-operate with each other and will take such action as each considers necessary for the purpose of meeting the situation effectively.

Article 8

In the event of a threat to the preservation of peace or the outbreak of hostilities elsewhere than in the area covered by Articles 6 and 7 the Government of the United Kingdom shall obtain the prior agreement of the Government of the Federation of Malaya before committing United Kingdom forces to active operations involving the use of bases in the Federation of Malaya; but this shall not affect the right of the Government of the United Kingdom to withdraw forces from the Federation of Malaya.

Article 9

The Government of the United Kingdom will consult the Government of the Federation of Malaya when major changes in the character or deployment of the forces maintained in the Federation of Malaya as provided for in Article 3 are contemplated.

Article 10

The Government of the Federation of Malaya and the Government of the United Kingdom will afford each other an adequate opportunity for comment upon any major administrative or legislative proposals which may affect the operation of this Agreement.

Article 11

[Definitions—not reproduced here]

Article 12

This Agreement shall come into force on the date of signature.

Annex I
Assistance by the United Kingdom to the Armed Forces
of the Federation

The Government of the United Kingdom having already undertaken to finance certain capital costs of expansion of the armed forces of the Federation further agrees to foster the closest co-operation between the armed forces of the two countries, including joint training of unit formations; and to provide, if so requested by the Government of the Federation of Malaya:

(a) personnel to assist in the staffing, administration and training of the armed forces of the Federation;

(b) facilities, including instructional courses abroad, for training members of the armed forces of the Federation;

(c) expert advice and assistance in operational and technical matters;

(d) use of facilities within the United Kingdom for the maintenance and logistic support of the armed forces of the Federation;

(e) assistance in the supply of equipment for the armed forces of the Federation.

THE MANILA ACCORD. JUNE 1963. REPORT AND RECOMMENDATIONS OF THE CONFERENCE OF FOREIGN MINISTERS OF THE FEDERATION OF MALAYA, THE REPUBLIC OF INDONESIA AND REPUBLIC OF THE PHILIPPINES TO THEIR RESPECTIVE HEADS OF GOVERNMENT.

1. The Governments of the Federation of Malaya, the Republic of Indonesia and the Republic of the Philippines, prompted by their keen and common desire to have a general exchange of views on current problems concerning stability, security, economic development and social progress of the three countries and of the region and upon the initiative of President Diosdado Macapagal, agreed that a Conference of Ministers of the three countries be held in Manila on 7th June 1963, for the purpose of achieving common understanding and close fraternal co-operation among themselves. Accordingly, Tun Abdul Razak, Deputy Prime Minister of the Federation of Malaya; Dr. Subandrio, Deputy First Minister/Minister for Foreign Affairs of the Republic of Indonesia; and Honourable Emmanuel Pelaez, Vice-President of the Philippines and concurrently Secretary of Foreign Affairs, met in Manila from 7 to 11 June, 1963.

2. The deliberations were held in a frank manner and in a most cordial atmosphere in keeping with the spirit of friendship prevailing in the various meetings held between President Soekarno of the Republic of Indonesia, and Prime Minister Tunku Abdul Rahman Putra of the Federation of Malaya, and President Diosdado Macapagal. This Ministerial Conference was a manifestation of the determination of the nations in this region to achieve closer co-operation in the endeavour to chart their common future.

3. The Ministers were of one mind that the three countries share a primary responsibility for the maintenance of the stability and security of the area from subversion in any form or manifestation in order to preserve their respective national identities, and to ensure the peaceful development of their respective countries and of their region, in accordance with the ideals and aspirations of their peoples.

4. In the same spirit of common and constructive endeavour, they exchanged views on the proposed Confederation of nations of Malay origin, the proposed Federation of Malaysia, the Philippine claim to North Borneo and related problems.

The Macapagal Plan

5. Recognising that it is in the common interest of their countries to

maintain fraternal relations and to strengthen co-operation among their peoples who are bound together by ties of race and culture, the three Ministers agreed to intensify the joint and individual efforts of their countries to secure lasting peace, progress and prosperity for themselves and for their neighbours.

6. In this context, the three Ministers supported President Macapagal's plan envisaging the grouping of the three nations of Malay origin working together in closest harmony but without surrendering any portion of their sovereignty. This calls for the establishment of the necessary common organs.

7. The three Ministers agreed to take the initial steps towards this ultimate aim by establishing machinery for frequent and regular consultations. The details of such machinery will be further defined. This machinery will enable the three governments to hold regular consultations at all levels to deal with matters of mutual interest and concern consistent with the national, regional and international responsibilities or obligations of each country without prejudice to its sovereignty and independence. The Ministers agreed that their countries will endeavour to achieve close understanding and co-operation in dealing with common problems relating to security, stability, economic, social and cultural development.

8. In order to accelerate the process of growth towards the ultimate establishment of President Macapagal's plan, the Ministers agreed that each country shall set up its own National Secretariat. Pending the establishment of a Central Secretariat for the consultative machinery, the National Secretaries should co-ordinate and co-operate with each other in the fulfilment of their tasks.

9. The Ministers further agreed to recommend that Heads of Government and Foreign Ministers meet at least once a year for the purpose of consultations on matters of importance and common concern.

Malaysia and North Borneo

10. The Ministers reaffirmed their countries' adherence to the principle of self-determination of the peoples of non-self-governing territories. In this context, Indonesia and the Philippines stated that they would welcome the formation of Malaysia provided the support of the people of the Borneo territories is ascertained by an independent and impartial authority, the Secretary-General of the United Nations or his representative.

11. The Federation of Malaya expressed appreciation for this attitude of Indonesia and the Philippines and undertook to consult the British Government and the Governments of the Borneo territories with a view to inviting the Secretary-General of the United Nations or

his representative to take the necessary steps in order to ascertain the wishes of the peoples of those territories.

12. The Philippines made it clear that its position on the inclusion of North Borneo in the Federation of Malaysia is subject to the final outcome of the Philippine claim to North Borneo. The Ministers took note of the Philippine claim and the right of the Philippines to continue to pursue it in accordance with international law and the principle of the pacific settlement of disputes. They agreed that the inclusion of North Borneo in the Federation of Malaysia would not prejudice either the claim or any right thereunder. Moreover in the context of their close association, the three countries agreed to exert their best endeavours to bring the claim to a just and expeditious solution by peaceful means, such as negotiation, conciliation, arbitration, or judicial settlement as well as other peaceful means of the parties' own choice, in conformity with the Charter of the United Nations and the Bandung Declaration.

13. In particular, considering the close historical ties between the peoples of the Philippines and North Borneo as well as their geographical propinquity, the Ministers agreed that in the event of North Borneo joining the proposed Federation of Malaysia the Government of the latter and the Government of the Philippines should maintain and promote the harmony and the friendly relations subsisting in their region to ensure the security and stability of the area.

Meetings of Heads of Government

14. The Ministers agreed to recommend that a Meeting of their respective Heads of Government be held in Manila not later than the end of July 1963.

15. The Ministers expressed satisfaction over the atmosphere of brotherliness and cordiality which pervaded their meeting and considered it as a confirmation of their close fraternal ties and as a happy augury for the success of future consultations among their leaders.

16. The Ministers agreed to place on record their profound appreciation of and gratitude for the statesmanlike efforts of President Macapagal whose courage, vision and inspiration not only facilitated the holding of this historic meeting but also contributed towards the achievement for the first time of a unity of purpose and a sense of common dedication among the peoples of Malaya, Indonesia and the Philippines.

THE MANILA DECLARATION. AUGUST 1963

The President of the Republic of Indonesia, the President of the Philippines and the Prime Minister of the Federation of Malaya, assembled in a Summit Conference in Manila from 30 July to August 5,

[618]

1963, following the Meeting of their Foreign Ministers held in Manila from June 7 to 11, 1963:

Conscious of the historic significance of their coming together for the first time as leaders of sovereign States that have emerged after long struggles from colonial status to independence:

Desiring to achieve better understanding and closer co-operation in their endeavour to chart their common future:

Inspired also by the spirit of Asian-African solidarity forged in the Bandung Conference of 1955:

Convinced that their countries, which are bound together by close historical ties of race and culture, share a primary responsibility for the maintenance of the stability and security of the area from subversion in any form or manifestation in order to preserve their respective national identities and to ensure the peaceful development of their respective countries and their region in accordance with the ideals and aspirations of their peoples: and

Determined to intensify the joint and individual efforts of their countries to secure lasting peace, progress and prosperity for themselves and their neighbours in a world dedicated to freedom and justice:

DO HEREBY DECLARE:

First, that they reaffirm their adherence to the principle of equal rights and self-determination of peoples as enunciated in the United Nations Charter and the Bandung Declaration:

Second, that they are determined, in the common interest of their countries, to maintain fraternal relations, to strengthen co-operation among their peoples in the economic, social and cultural fields in order to promote economic progress and social well-being in the region, and to put an end to the exploitation of man by man and of one nation by another:

Third, that the three nations shall combine their efforts in the common struggle against colonialism and imperialism in all their forms and manifestations and for the eradication of the vestiges thereof in the region in particular and the world in general:

Fourth, that the three nations, as new emerging forces in the region, shall co-operate in building a new and better world based on national freedom, social justice and lasting peace: and

Fifth, that in the context of the joint endeavours of the three nations to achieve the foregoing objectives, they have agreed to take initial steps towards the establishment of Maphilindo by holding frequent and regular consultations at all levels to be known as Mushawarah Maphilindo.

MANILA
August 5, 1963

Soekarno,
President of the Republic of Indonesia

Diosdado Macapagal,
President of the Philippines

Tunku Abdul Rahman Putra Al-Haj
Prime Minister of the Federation of Malaya

SUMMARY OF FINDINGS *(PARAGRAPHS 232-246)* OF THE
REPORT OF THE UNITED NATIONS MALAYSIA MISSION
TO THE SECRETARY-GENERAL

232. In view of the terms of reference[1] established in the request to the Secretary-General, it was understood that the "fresh approach" proposed did not contemplate a referendum, or plebiscite. It was considered that it would be meaningful to make a "fresh approach" by arranging consultations with the population through elected representatives, leaders and representatives of political parties as well as non-political groups, and with any other persons showing interest in setting forth their views to the Mission.

233. In the course of visits to various localities in the two territories, it was possible to consult with almost all the "grass roots" elected representatives. In the case of Sarawak, the Mission met with about 400 of the 429 persons who had been elected in the several wards of the 24 districts into which the territory is divided. Each of these persons, or councillors, is directly elected and represents an electorate averaging about 700 registered voters. In Sabah (North Borneo) over 100 elected and nominated members of District Councils and Town Boards met with the Mission. In addition to these representatives consultations were held in both territories with national and local representatives of each of the major political groups, and with national and local representatives of ethnic, religious, social and other groups, as well as local organisations of businessmen, employers, workers, and various community and social groups. Information and expressions of opinion were provided orally and by the submission of written memoranda.

234. These consultations, coupled with examination of relevant documentary material, provided the Mission with information on the

---

[1] The terms of reference were paragraphs 4, 5, and 6 of the Manila Joint Statement.

specific questions which the Secretary-General was asked to take into consideration, and also provided a basis for analysing and evaluating the results of the recent elections and for appraising the views of the people regarding the establishment of the Federation of Malaysia both at the time of the elections, and at present.

235. With regard to the specific question which the Secretary-General was asked to take into consideration, the members of the Mission concluded, after evaluating all of the evidence available to them, that:

Elections

236. (a) In the recent elections Malaysia was a major issue throughout both territories, and was the major issue in most of the electoral wards. The members of the Mission were satisfied that the vast majority of the electorate understood the significance of the proposal that the territories become parts of the Federation of Malaysia.

(b) Electoral registers were properly compiled, as judged not only by criteria which might be considered adequate in a country with a limited experience in elections, but even by standards of countries with larger experience with the procedures and technical problems of voters' registration.

(c) The elections were freely and impartially conducted with active and vigorous campaigning by groups advocating divergent courses of action. In Sabah, almost no complaints were heard. In Sarawak, complaints of each group of advocates that the opposing group at times used unfair means of persuasion did not appear to differ significantly in kind or number from similar complaints in many elections of democratic societies with much longer electoral organizing and administering the elections, in so far as they were directly related to the Malaysia issue were not in the opinion of the Mission, adequately supported. Allegations were made in Sarawak that measures taken by the authorities in the maintenance of the security of the State, especially in connexion with and following the Brunei revolt, had the effect of limiting the effort of the group opposing Malaysia (the Sarawak United People's Party), and that the security measures had the result of depriving them of some of their officers and members, who would have assisted in the campaign, of making unavailable certain newspapers and printing presses that might otherwise have been utilised, and of deterring persons who might otherwise have affiliated with it, or have voted for its candidates, from doing so. The Mission carefully considered these allegations, and the issue which they seemed to pose, whether measures regarded as essential to safeguard the security of the State in the presence of what the authorities considered to be a clear and present danger, could, because of their effect on one group be properly considered as coercion with regard to that group. The Mission was satisfied, from the whole body of evidence available to it, that even if these events had not occurred, the final outcome of the election in Sarawak would not have been reversed.

(d) The votes were properly polled and counted, on the basis of the evidence obtained by the Mission. Recourse was available under the election laws and procedures to those who considered that there had been irregularities. In the relatively few cases where irregularities were alleged, recourse had not been sought, and in any event, the number of instances seemed within the normal expectancy of well-ordered elections.

Wishes of Persons Detained, Imprisoned or Absent

237. The Secretary-General was also asked to take into consideration "the wishes of those who, being qualified to vote, would have exercised their right of self-determination in the recent election had it not been for their detention for political activities, imprisonment for political offences, or absence" from the territory. The number of persons detained in Sarawak under the Preservation of Public Security Detention Regulations was 62 at the end of May and 103 at the end of June 1963. The Mission was informed that 75 to 80 per cent of the group are voting age (at and above) and that all members of the group oppose the Malaysia Plan. The number was in any case not sufficient to have affected the total result. Nor, in the opinion of the Mission, does the fact that the detainees included some 31 officials of the anti-Malaysia party, appear to have resulted in a substantial limitation of the campaigning potential of that party during the elections so as seriously and significantly to have affected the result. Indeed, the party had scored convincing electoral victories in many of the areas from which those officials had come.

238. Despite repeated questioning, the Mission was able to secure very little information from the persons with whom it met about persons absent from the territories. One witness provided four names of persons who were no longer at their normal place of residence, and believed to have crossed the border to another country. Of these four, the Mission found that two were registered voters, and two were not. The two wards in which they previously resided both returned anti-Malaysia candidates. From Government sources, the Mission learned that about 50 persons have been reported as missing from their normal residence, under a regulation requiring such reports. The Government believes that a large number have departed across the Indonesian border and estimates the total at about 800. However, of 81 persons

who were apprehended over the last four months while attempting to cross the border, 85 per cent were less than 21 years of age. It is therefore believed that most of the estimated 800 would also not have been eligible to vote. In any event, the total number, assuming all to be opposed to Malaysia, is not large enough to have had a significant effect on the election results.

Wishes of the People

239. The Mission considers that it is possible to approach the assessment of the wishes of the people of Sarawak and of Sabah (North Borneo) in three ways:

(1) As expressed through the established electoral and legislative processes under the present constitutional arrangements. This expression is voiced through the Council Negri, the highest legislative body in Sarawak, and the Legislative Council in North Borneo. The Council Negri is selected through a double "electoral college" system—the elected councillors in each district select from their number the members of the five Divisional Councils, and each of the Divisional Councils selects from its number the members to serve on the Council Negri. The Council Negri debated on and approved, on 8 March 1953, a motion that the Council:

(a) adopts the recommendations contained in the Report of the Inter-Governmental Committee on Malaysia which was today laid on the Table as Sessional Paper No. 1 of 1963;

(b) welcomes the creation of the proposed Federation of Malaysia by the 31st August, 1963; and

(c) authorises the Governor to select such members of the Inter-Governmental Committee as he may think fit to initial, on behalf of Sarawak, the draft of the Agreement for the establishment of the Federation of Malaysia to be entered into by the Government of the United Kingdom and the Federation of Malaya.

On 4 September 1963, the Council Negri as reconstituted with 36 elected members chosen after the 1963 elections, debated and approved, by vote of 31 to 5 of the elected members, the following motion:

WHEREAS a motion was passed without dissentient voice at the last session of this Council adopting the recommendations of the Inter-Governmental Committee on Malaysia, welcoming the creation of the proposed Federation of Malaysia by the 31st August 1963, and authorising the Governor to appoint representatives to initial on behalf of the Government of Sarawak the draft Agreement for the establishment of the Federation.

BE IT RESOLVED THAT this Council reaffirms its support for Malaysia, endorses the formal Agreement which was signed in London on the 9th July and, while regretting that the Federation of Malaysia could not be brought into being on the 31st August welcomes the decision to establish it on the 16th September 1963.

The two actions of the Council Negri and the similar actions of the Legislative Council in North Borneo constitute the formal, constitutional approval of the Federation of Malaysia, and may be regarded as the expression of the people through the established legislative institutions.

Because of the double "election college" or "three-tier" system of election of the Council Negri, the criticism has been advanced that expression through that Council may differ from the initial views of the electorate. It is true that the proportions of the several groups do vary, as measured by the popular vote, and by the seats held at the District, Division and Council Negri Level. Under the recent elections in Sarawak, the variation is as shown below, in percentage terms:

	Popular Vote[a]	District Councils	Divisional Councils	Council Negri
Sarawak United Peoples' Party (SUPP)	21.3	27.0	20.4	13.9
Party Negara Sarawak (PANAS)	14.3	13.8	11.1	8.3
Alliance	34.0	32.2	37.0	50.0
Independents[b]	30.4	27.0	31.5	27.8
	100.0	100.0	100.0	100.0

(a) Including a portion of the electorate in uncontested wards.
(b) On the basis of original party designations; some independents subsequently affiliated with one of the parties.

(2) Another means of assessing the wishes of the people regarding the Federation of Malaysia is through the representatives directly chosen by the people. In Sarawak, each represents an electorate of about 700 persons. These councillors reported to the Mission in almost every case that Malaysia had been discussed in their wards before the election, and that their stand, either for or against Malaysia, was the major factor in their election. This was corroborated by other testimony. They considered that they knew the wishes of their electorates on this issue both at the time of the election and at present. A careful analysis of the views expressed by these representatives indicates a majority in Sarawak in favour of the Federation of Malaysia of about 284 to 123, or about 66.2 per cent to 28.7 per cent. The remainder, 22 representatives or 5.1 per cent, could not be classified in either group. The

Mission also attempted to assess the division in the electorate in Sarawak on the Malaysia issue. Careful questioning of councillors, especially those elected as independents, as well as defeated candidates and others, enabled an analysis of the votes cast, plus an approximation of the comparable number of voters in the uncontested wards. The analysis, as shown in Chapter 9, indicates a probable division in the electorate of 61.0 per cent in favour of Malaysia, 22.2 per cent opposed, with the remainder, 16.8 per cent neutral or unattributable from the evidence available. The division among those whose opinions are attributable with some assurance is 73.3 per cent in favour, and 26.7 per cent opposed.

(3) In addition to hearing the views of political parties, the Mission made use of every opportunity to find out the opinions and reaction of non-political groups and organisations which submitted written memoranda and also appeared before the Mission at its hearings. The Mission concluded that the question of Malaysia was widely discussed among the people and that the majority of the population understood and were in favour of the proposed Federation of Malaysia.

240. The Mission found that the great majority of the people of North Borneo have strongly supported the proposed Federation of Malaysia from the time of the elections down to the present. The Mission noted the high degree of unity reflected by national leaders of political parties, members of political parties, chiefs and headmen, representatives of civic, religious, commercial, labour and ethnic groups and other persons who appeared before it. Security considerations and economic considerations were presented as important motives for support of the proposed Federation, which was identified with independence in the minds of the people. There exists an expectation that Federation will be conducive to harmony among ethnic groups and economic advancement in rural areas. The Mission found little evidence of articulate and organised opposition to Federation, and it seems clear that doubts and uncertainties existing among some groups and political parties prior to the electoral campaign were largely dispelled by the agreement among political party leaders which led to the formation of the Sabah Alliance. The Mission found evidence for continuing doubts among some individual members of the Pasok Momogun party but other members of the party, and particularly its national leadership, expressed strong support for the establishment of the Federation of Malaysia. The evidence would indicate a diminishing trend of opposition to Federation at this time. Doubts and reservations appear to be limited largely to some groups, mainly in the interior, and may be attributed to satisfaction with the status quo, lack of information or a lack of clear understanding of the proposal to establish the Federation of Malaysia or suspicion of unfamiliar ideas.

241. While local issues, traditional relationships, and ethnic considerations played their part in the elections, nevertheless at the time of the elections most people were familiar with the proposals for the creation of the Federation of Malaysia and the stand of the Sabah Alliance on Federation. The large number of votes received by Alliance candidates was, in most cases, indicative that support for the proposed Federation has increased since the elections.

General Assembly Resolution 1541 (XV)

242. The Mission has given careful thought to the reference, in the request to the Secretary-General, that "he ascertain, prior to the establishment of the Federation of Malaysia, the wishes of the people of Sabah (North Borneo) and Sarawak *within the context of General Assembly Resolution 1541 (XV), principle IX of the Annex*, by a fresh approach, which in the opinion of the Secretary-General is necessary to ensure complete compliance with the principle of self-determination within the requirements embodied in principle IX."

243. Resolution 1541 (XV) is concerned with "Principles which should guide Members in determining whether or not an obligation exists to transmit the information called for under Article 73(e) of the Charter." Reference to it in the Manila Joint Statement, however, clearly does not allude to the question of the transmission of information under Article 73(e) of the Charter, but must be understood as posing the issue whether the requirements for integration laid down in principle IX have been met in the case of the proposed inclusion of Sarawak and Sabah (North Borneo) in the Federation of Malaysia.

Principle IX of the Annex provides:

Integration should have come out about in the following circumstances:

(a) The integrating territory should have attained an advanced stage of self-government with free political institutions, so that its peoples would have the capacity to make a responsible choice through informed and democratic processes;

(b) The integration should be the result of the freely expressed wishes of the territory's peoples acting with full knowledge of the change in their status, their wishes having been expressed through informed and democratic processes, impartially conducted and based on universal adult suffrage. The United Nations could, when it deems it necessary, supervise these processes.

244. The Mission, having considered the constitutional, electoral and legislative arrangements in Sarawak and Sabah (North Borneo), is of the opinion that the territories have "attained an advanced stage of self-government with free political institutions, so that its peoples would have the capacity to make a responsible choice through informed and

democratic processes." Self-government has been further advanced in both territories by the declaration of the respective Governors that as from 31 August 1963 they would accept unreservedly and automatically the advice of the respective Chief Ministers on all matters within the competence of the State and for which portfolios had been allocated to Ministers.

245. The Mission is further of the opinion that the participation of the two territories in the proposed Federation, having been approved by their legislative bodies, as well as by a large majority of the people through free and impartially conducted elections in which the question of Malaysia was a major issue, the significance of which was appreciated by the electorate, may be regarded as the "result of the freely expressed wishes of the territory's peoples acting with full knowledge of the change of their status, their wishes having been expressed through informed and democratic processes, impartially conducted and based on universal adult suffrage."

246. The Mission is satisfied that through its hearings it was able to reach a cross-section of the population in all walks of life and that the expressions of opinion that it heard represent the views of a sizeable majority of the population. The Mission is convinced that the time devoted to hearings and the number of localities visited were adequate and enabled it to carry out its terms of reference.[1]

EXTRACT FROM FINAL CONCLUSIONS OF THE
SECRETARY-GENERAL, UNITED NATIONS ORGANISATION
(UNITED NATIONS SPECIAL RELEASE SPL/84
DATED 16 SEPTEMBER 1963)

The basic assessment which I was asked to make has broader implications than the specific questions enumerated in the request addressed to me by the three governments. As previously mentioned, I was asked to ascertain, prior to the establishment of the Federation of Malaysia, the wishes of the people of Sabah (North Borneo) and Sarawak within the context of the General Assembly Resolution 1541 (XV), Principle IX of the Annex, by a fresh approach, which in the opinion of the Secretary-General, is necessary to ensure complete compliance with the principle of self-determination within the requirements embodied in Principle IX. . . .

I have given consideration to the circumstances in which the proposals for the Federation of Malaysia have been developed and discussed, and the possibility that people progressing through stages of self-government may be less able to consider in an entirely free context

[1] The terms of reference were para-   Statement (Document 20).
graphs 4, 5, and 6 of the Manila Joint

the implications of such changes in their status, than a society which has already experienced full self-government and determination of its own affairs. I have also been aware that the peoples of these territories are still striving for a more adequate level of educational development.

Having reflected fully on these considerations, and taking into account the framework within which the Mission's work has performed, I have come to the conclusion that the majority of the peoples of Sabah (North Borneo) and of Sarawak have given serious and thoughtful consideration to their future and to the implications for them of participation in a Federation of Malaysia. I believe that the majority of them have concluded that they wish to bring their dependent status to an end and to realise their independence through freely-chosen association with other peoples in their region with whom they feel the ties of ethnic association, heritage, language, religion, culture, economic relationship, and ideals and objectives. Not all these considerations are present in equal weight in all minds, but it is my conclusion that the majority of the peoples of these two territories have taken them into account and wish to engage with the peoples of the Federation of Malaya and Singapore, in an enlarged Federation of Malaysia through which they can strive together to realise the fulfilment of their destiny. . . .

Bearing in mind the fundamental agreement of the three participating governments in the Manila meetings, and the statement by the Republic of Indonesia and the Republic of the Philippines that they would welcome the formation of Malaysia provided that the support of the people of the territories was ascertained by me and that, in my opinion, complete compliance with the principle of self-determination within the requirements of the General Assembly Resolution 1541 (XV), Principle IX of the Annex, was ensured, my conclusions based on the findings of the Mission are that on both of these counts there is no doubt about the wishes of a sizeable majority of the peoples of these territories to join in the Federation of Malaysia.

In reaching my conclusions I have taken account of the concern expressed with regard to political factors resulting from the constitutional status of the territories and about influences from the outside area on promotion of the proposed Federation. Giving these considerations their due weight, in relation to the responsibilities and obligations established in Article 73 and General Assembly Resolution 1541 (XV) in respect of these territories, I am satisfied that the conclusions set forth above take cognisance of, and are in accordance with, requirements set forth in the request addressed to me on 5 August 1963 by the Foreign Ministers of the Republic of Indonesia, the Federation of Malaya and the Republic of the Philippines. . . .

From the beginning of this year, I have been observing the rising tension in South-East Asia on account of differences of opinion among the countries most directly interested in the Malaysia issue. It was in the hope that some form of United Nations involvement might help to reduce tension that I agreed to respond positively to the request made by the three Manila powers. I would hope that the exercise in which my colleagues and I have been involved in this regard will have this effect, and that the coming into being of Malaysia will not prove to be a continuing source of friction and tension in the area.

The emergence of dependent territories by a process of self-determination to the status of self-government, either as independent sovereign states or as autonomous components of larger units, has always been one of the purposes of the Charter and the objectives of the United Nations. Whatever the origins of the proposal of Malaysia may have been, it seems to me in the light of actual events, including the present exercise, that we have witnessed in Sarawak and North Borneo the same process leading to self-government. I fervently hope that the people of these territories will achieve progress and prosperity, and find their fulfilment as component states of Malaysia.

AIDE-MÉMOIRE FROM THE INDONESIAN TO THE
UN MALAYSIA MISSION IN SARAWAK AND SABAH. CYCLO-STYLED
TEXT ISSUED BY THE INDONESIAN EMBASSY IN LONDON,
DATED OCTOBER 1963 AND HEADED "CONDENSED VERSION."

1. The observers arrived in Kuching on September 1, and four of them travelled on to Jesselton later that day. However, the latter group did not start observing the hearings until the next day. Consequently, the observers could not associate themselves with the hearings in Sarawak before the afternoon of September 1, and in Sabah before the morning of September 2.

2. They found that the element of "fresh approach" (mentioned in article 4 of the Manila Joint Statement and which should have assured complete compliance with the principle of self-determination embodied in UN Resolution 1541 (XV)—principle IX) was nowhere apparent in the whole operation.

3. The observers found that the hearings merely took the form of "samplings"—not even on the Gallup-poll level—and were conducted along the lines of the last elections, which could not possibly meet the requirements of UN Resolution 1541—principle IX.

4. According to this principle, an inquiry should be made whether the integrating territory has reached a state of self-government with

free political institutions. The observers had the strong impression that no such inquiry had been made—self-government was taken for granted.

They found the governmental set-up in Sarawak and N. Borneo still colonial in nature, power being in the hands of British civil servants and armed forces. The hearings clearly revealed that this colonial element must have been even stronger during the elections.

5. Principle IX provides that integration should be the result of the freely-expressed wishes of the territories' people, but the observers found that these wishes had not been expressed either in the elections or hearings. Coercion was applied to inhibit freedom of expression. The colonial administration detained anti-Malaysia political leaders, banned 3 anti-Malaysia newspapers, and restricted right of domicile of some people to certain areas. All this interfered in the forming of a balanced public opinion and greatly affected the result of the elections.

6. Principle IX requires that in expressing their wishes through informed and democratic processes, the people should act with full knowledge of the change in their status. The observers found that this had not happened. To the question, for example, whether Malaysia was the main issue in the elections, many interviewed persons gave only perfunctory replies, obviously not having a clear idea of the establishment of the Federation and the consequences of integration.

7. Principle IX requires that the people's wishes should be expressed through democratic processes and based on universal adult suffrage. The observers were not aware of a sufficiently thorough investigation regarding this; if, for instance, the voters' registers had been carefully scrutinised. Detainees testified during the hearings that a large percentage of the eligible voters were not registered, and these testimonies were amply substantiated by the figures drawn from the census, voters' registers and cast votes. Reference was also made to the absence of refugees, detainees, etc., and to irregularities in the operation of voting machinery.

8. To the question:

a. "whether Malaysia is a major, if not the main, issue," the hearings brought forward that local issues and personal loyalties dominated the elections. Granted the claim of some interviewed persons that Malaysia was a major issue, their perfunctory answers could not convince the observers that they realised the consequences of integration. It was obvious that Malaysia could never have been a major issue, let alone a main one.

b. "whether electoral registers were properly compiled." The observers did not witness a careful scrutiny of registers, but they heard allegations that many eligible voters were left out because of detention, absence from their domiciles, etc. It is doubtful whether registers were properly compiled and whether this point was carefully examined by the Mission.

c. "whether elections were free and whether there was no coercion." Coercion and intimidation against anti-Malaysia groups before and during elections were alleged. The observers found that even during the hearings the atmosphere was not free from coercion created by strong security measures, as evidenced by the presence of many troops and riot police in Kuching, Bau, and Serian. The observers were surprised to find United Kingdom observers present at the hearings, since the Manila Agreement only provided for the presence of observers from Indonesia, the Philippines and Malaya. Also, one of the interpreters in Sarawak was a presiding officer of a local court. The presence of UK observers and liaison officers no doubt influenced the way interviewed persons expressed their views.

Taking all this into account, the observers could only conclude that the elections were not free.

d. "whether votes were properly polled and counted." The observers did not witness the Mission's investigation into this matter, but in the hearings, allegations were made of irregularities, with ballot-boxes manipulated by governmental officers.

9. Pursuant to paragraph 4 of the Manila Joint Statement, the UN Secretary-General in ascertaining the wishes of the people, should consider the wishes of those qualified to vote who would have opted for self-determination had they not been detained or imprisoned for political activities.

The observers witnessed hearings of only four detainees representing 110 detainees at Kuching, and were unaware of the wishes of those in other areas, while in Sabah they had no chance to witness a single hearing. As to political refugees and other absentees, the Mission did not try to make contact with them.

DJAKARTA, *September 7, 1963*

TEXT OF A RESOLUTION OF THE SECURITY COUNCIL OF THE
UNITED NATIONS ON THE MALAYSIAN-INDONESIAN DISPUTE
VOTED UPON ON 17 SEPTEMBER 1964.

The Security Council
Taking note of the complaint of Malaysia contained in document S/5930,
Taking into consideration the statements of the parties and of the members of the Council expressed during the discussion,

[631]

Deeply concerned by the fact that the armed incidents which have occurred in that region have seriously aggravated the situation and are likely to endanger peace and security in that region,

Noting with satisfaction the desire of the parties to seek a peaceful solution of the differences between them,

Recalling the relevant provisions of the United Nations Charter,

1. *Regrets* all the incidents which have occurred in the whole region;
2. *Deplores* the incident of 2 September 1964 which forms the basis of the complaint contained in document S/5930;
3. *Requests* the parties concerned to make every effort to avoid the recurrence of such incidents;
4. *Calls upon* the parties to refrain from all threat or use of force and to respect the territorial integrity and political independence of each other, and thus to create a conducive atmosphere for the continuation of their talks;
5. *Recommends* to the Governments concerned thereupon to resume their talks on the basis of the joint communiqué issued by the Heads of Government following the meeting which took place in Tokyo on 20 June 1964. The conciliation commission provided for by that joint communiqué, once established, should keep the Security Council informed concerning the development of the situation.

Appendix B
Significant General Assembly Resolutions Since 1966 on the Status of South West Africa

1. GENERAL ASSEMBLY RESOLUTION 2145 (XXI) (114-23) 27 OCTOBER 1966

2145 (XXI). *Question of South West Africa*

The General Assembly

Reaffirming the inalienable right of the people of South West Africa to freedom and independence in accordance with the Charter of the United Nations, General Assembly resolution 1514 (XV) of 14 December 1960 and earlier Assembly resolutions concerning the Mandated Territory of South West Africa,

Recalling the advisory opinion of the International Court of Justice of 11 July 1950,[1] which was accepted by the General Assembly in its resolution 449 A (V) of 13 December 1950, and the advisory opinions of 7 June 1955[2] and 1 June 1956[3] as well as the judgement of 21 December 1962,[4] which have established the fact that South Africa continues to have obligations under the Mandate which was entrusted to it on 17 December 1920 and that the United Nations as the successor to the League of Nations has supervisory powers in respect of South West Africa,

Gravely concerned at the situation in the Mandated Territory, which has seriously deteriorated following the judgement of the International Court of Justice of 18 July 1966,[5]

Having studied the reports of the various committees which had been established to exercise the supervisory functions of the United Nations over the administration of the Mandated Territory of South West Africa,

Convinced that the administration of the Mandated Territory by South Africa has been conducted in a manner contrary to the Mandate, the Charter of the United Nations and the Universal Declaration of Human Rights,

Reaffirming its resolution 2074 (XX) of 17 December 1965, in particular paragraph 4 thereof which condemned the policies of apartheid

---

[1] *International status of South West Africa, Advisory Opinion: I.C.J. Reports 1950*, p. 128.

[2] *South West Africa—Voting Procedure, Advisory Opinion of June 7th, 1955: I.C.J. Reports 1955*, p. 67.

[3] *Admissibility of Hearings of Petitioners by the Committee on South West Africa, Advisory Opinion of June 1st, 1956: I.C.J. Reports 1956*, p. 23.

[4] *South West Africa Cases (Ethiopia v. South Africa; Liberia v. South Africa), Preliminary Objections, Judgment of 21 December 1962: I.C.J. Reports 1962*, p. 319.

[5] *South West Africa, Second Phase, Judgment, I.C.J. Reports 1966*, p. 6.

and racial discrimination practised by the Government of South Africa in South West Africa as constituting a crime against humanity,

Emphasizing that the problem of South West Africa is an issue falling within the terms of resolution 1514 (XV),

Considering that all the efforts of the United Nations to induce the Government of South Africa to fulfil its obligations in respect of the administration of the Mandated Territory and to ensure the well-being and security of the indigenous inhabitants have been of no avail,

Mindful of the obligations of the United Nations towards the people of South West Africa,

Noting with deep concern the explosive situation which exists in the southern region of Africa,

Affirming its right to take appropriate action in the matter, including the right to revert to itself the administration of the Mandated Territory,

1. *Reaffirms* that the provisions of General Assembly resolution 1514 (XV) are fully applicable to the people of the Mandated Territory of South West Africa and that, therefore, the people of South West Africa have the inalienable right to self-determination, freedom and independence in accordance with the Charter of the United Nations;

2. *Reaffirms* further that South West Africa is a territory having international status and that it shall maintain this status until it achieves independence;

3. *Declares* that South Africa has failed to fulfil its obligations in respect of the administration of the Mandated Territory and to ensure the moral and material well-being and security of the indigenous inhabitants of South West Africa, and has, in fact, disavowed the Mandate;

4. *Decides* that the Mandate conferred upon His Britannic Majesty to be exercised on his behalf by the Government of the Union of South Africa is therefore terminated, that South Africa has no other right to administer the Territory and that henceforth South West Africa comes under the direct responsibility of the United Nations;

5. *Resolves* that in these circumstances the United Nations must discharge those responsibilities with respect to South West Africa;

6. *Establishes* an *Ad Hoc* Committee for South West Africa—composed of fourteen Member States to be designated by the President of the General Assembly—to recommend practical means by which South West Africa should be administered, so as to enable the people of the Territory to exercise the right of self-determination and to achieve independence, and to report to the General Assembly at a special session as soon as possible and in any event not later than April 1967;

7. *Calls upon* the Government of South Africa forthwith to refrain and desist from any action, constitutional, administrative, political or

otherwise, which will in any manner whatsoever alter or tend to alter the present international status of South West Africa;

8. *Calls the attention* of the Security Council to the present resolution;

9. *Requests* all States to extend their whole-hearted co-operation and to render assistance in the implementation of the present resolution;

10. *Requests* the Secretary-General to provide all assistance necessary to implement the present resolution and to enable the *Ad Hoc* Committee for South West Africa to perform its duties.

> *1454th plenary meeting,*
> *27 October 1966*

2. GENERAL ASSEMBLY RESOLUTION 2248 (S-V) (85-2-30) 19 MAY 1967

The General Assembly

Having considered the report of the *Ad Hoc* Committee for South West Africa,[1]

Reaffirming its resolution 1514 (XV) of 14 December 1960 containing the Declaration on the Granting of Independence to Colonial Countries and Peoples,

Reaffirming its resolution 2145 (XXI) of 27 October 1966 by which it terminated the Mandate conferred upon His Britannic Majesty to be exercised on his behalf by the Government of the Union of South Africa and decided that South Africa had no other right to administer the Territory of South West Africa,

Having assumed direct responsibility for the Territory of South West Africa in accordance with resolution 2145 (XXI),

Recognizing that it has thereupon become incumbent upon the United Nations to give effect to its obligations by taking practical steps to transfer power to the people of South West Africa,

I

Reaffirms the territorial integrity of South West Africa and the inalienable right of its people to freedom and independence, in accordance with the Charter of the United Nations, General Assembly resolution 1514 (XV) and all other resolutions concerning South West Africa;

II

1. *Decides* to establish a United Nations Council for South West Africa (hereinafter referred to as the Council) comprising eleven Member States to be elected during the present session and to entrust to it the following powers and functions, to be discharged in the Territory:

[1] A/6640.

(*a*) To administer South West Africa until independence with the maximum possible participation of the people of the Territory;

(*b*) To promulgate such laws, decrees and administrative regulations as are necessary for the administration of the Territory until a legislative assembly is established following elections conducted on the basis of universal adult suffrage;

(*c*) To take as an immediate task all the necessary measures, in consultation with the people of the Territory, for the establishment of a constituent assembly to draw up a constitution on the basis of which elections will be held for the establishment of a legislative assembly and a responsible government;

(*d*) To take all the necessary measures for the maintenance of law and order in the Territory;

(*e*) To transfer all powers to the people of the Territory upon the declaration of independence;

2. *Decides* that in the exercise of its powers and in the discharge of its functions the Council shall be responsible to the General Assembly;

3. *Decides* that the Council shall entrust such executive and administrative tasks as it deems necessary to a United Nations Commissioner for South West Africa (hereinafter referred to as the Commissioner), who shall be appointed during the present session by the General Assembly on the nomination of the Secretary-General;

4. *Decides* that in the performance of his tasks the Commissioner shall be responsible to the Council;

III

1. *Decides* that:

(*a*) The administration of South West Africa under the United Nations shall be financed from the revenues collected in the Territory;

(*b*) Expenses directly related to the operation of the Council and the Office of the Commissioner—the travel and subsistence expenses of members of the Council, the remuneration of the Commissioner and his staff and the cost of ancillary facilities—shall be met from the regular budget of the United Nations;

2. *Requests* the specialized agencies and the appropriate organs of the United Nations to render to South West Africa technical and financial assistance through a co-ordinated emergency programme to meet the exigencies of the situation;

IV

1. *Decides* that the Council shall be based in South West Africa;

2. *Requests* the Council to enter immediately into contact with the authorities of South Africa in order to lay down procedures, in accord-

ance with General Assembly resolution 2145 (XXI) and the present resolution, for the transfer of the administration of the Territory with the least possible upheaval;

3. *Further requests* the Council to proceed to South West Africa with a view to:

(*a*) Taking over the administration of the Territory;

(*b*) Ensuring the withdrawal of South African police and military forces;

(*c*) Ensuring the withdrawal of South African personnel and their replacement by personnel operating under the authority of the Council;

(*d*) Ensuring that in the utilization and recruitment of personnel preference be given to the indigenous people;

4. *Calls upon* the Government of South Africa to comply without delay with the terms of resolution 2145 (XIX) and the present resolution and to facilitate the transfer of the administration of the Territory of South West Africa to the Council;

5. *Requests* the Security Council to take all appropriate measures to enable the United Nations Council for South West Africa to discharge the functions and responsibilities entrusted to it by the General Assembly;

6. *Requests* all States to extend their whole-hearted co-operation and to render assistance to the Council in the implementation of its task;

V

Requests the Council to report to the General Assembly at intervals not exceeding three months on its administration of the Territory, and to submit a special report to the Assembly at its twenty-second session concerning the implementation of the present resolution;

VI

Decides that South West Africa shall become independent on a date to be fixed in accordance with the wishes of the people and that the Council shall do all in its power to enable independence to be attained by June 1968.

ROLL CALL: *In favour*: Afghanistan, Algeria, Argentina, Barbados, Bolivia, Brazil, Burma, Burundi, Cambodia, Cameroon, Central African Republic, Ceylon, Chad, Chile, China, Colombia, Congo (Brazzaville), Congo (Democratic Republic of), Costa Rica, Cyprus, Dahomey, Ecuador, El Salvador, Ethiopia, Gabon, Ghana, Greece, Guatemala, Guinea, Guyana, Haiti, Honduras, India, Indonesia, Iran, Iraq, Israel, Ivory Coast, Jamaica, Japan, Jordan, Kenya, Kuwait,

Laos, Lebanon, Liberia, Libya, Madagascar, Malaysia, Mali, Mauritania, Mexico, Morocco, Nepal, Nicaragua, Niger, Nigeria, Pakistan, Panama, Paraguay, Peru, Philippines, Rwanda, Saudi Arabia, Senegal, Sierra Leone, Singapore, Somalia, Spain, Sudan, Syria, Thailand, Togo, Trinidad and Tobago, Tunisia, Turkey, Uganda, United Arab Republic, United Republic of Tanzania, Upper Volta, Uruguay, Venezuela, Yemen, Yugoslavia, Zambia.

Against: Portugal, South Africa.

Abstaining: Australia, Austria, Belgium, Botswana, Bulgaria, Byelorussia, Canada, Cuba, Czechoslovakia, Denmark, Finland, France, Hungary, Iceland, Ireland, Italy, Luxembourg, Malawi, Malta, Mongolia, Netherlands, New Zealand, Norway, Poland, Romania, Sweden, Ukraine, Union of Soviet Socialist Republics, United Kingdom, United States.

Absent: Albania, Dominican Republic, Gambia, Lesotho, Maldive Islands.

[On 13 June 1967, in pursuance of paragraph 1 of section II of the above resolution, the General Assembly elected Chile, Colombia, Guyana, India, Indonesia, Nigeria, Pakistan, Turkey, United Arab Republic, Yugoslavia and Zambia as the members of the United Nations Council for South West Africa.

[On the same date, in pursuance of paragraph 3 of section II of the above resolution, the General Assembly, on the nomination of the Secretary-General (A/6656), appointed Constantin A. Stavropoulos, the Legal Counsel of the United Nations, as Acting United Nations Commissioner for South West Africa.]

3. GENERAL ASSEMBLY RESOLUTION 2372 (XXII)
(96-2-18) 12 JUNE 1968

The General Assembly

Having considered the report of the United Nations Council for South West Africa,

Recalling its resolutions 1514 (XV) of 14 December 1960, 2145 (XXI) of 27 October 1966, 2248 (S-V) of 19 May 1967 and 2324 (XXII) and 2325 (XXII) of 16 December 1967,

Noting with grave concern that the refusal of the Government of South Africa to withdraw its administration from the Territory of South West Africa has obstructed the attainment of independence by the Territory in accordance with the relevant United Nations resolutions,

Mindful of the serious consequences of the continued foreign occupation by South Africa of the Territory of South West Africa, which constitutes a grave threat to international peace and security,

Concerned that the continued refusal of the Government of South Africa to comply with its obligations to the United Nations and to the international community as a whole, making it impossible for the United Nations Council for South West Africa to perform effectively the functions that were entrusted to it by the General Assembly, constitutes a flagrant defiance of the authority of the United Nations,

Deploring the defiance by the Government of South Africa of General Assembly resolution 2324 (XXII) and Security Council resolutions 245 (1968) of 25 January 1968 and 246 (1968) of 14 March 1968 concerning the illegal arrest, deportation, trial and conviction of South West African patriots engaged in the struggle for independence,

Conscious of the special and direct responsibility of the United Nations towards the people and the Territory of South West Africa, in accordance with the provisions of General Assembly resolutions 2145 (XXI) and 2248 (S-V),

Recalling Security Council resolution 246 (1968), in particular its last preambular paragraph, in which the Security Council took cognizance of its special responsibility towards the people and the Territory of South West Africa,

Taking into account the views expressed by representatives of the people of South West Africa in their consultations with the United Nations Council for South West Africa,

1. *Proclaims* that, in accordance with the desires of its people, South West Africa shall henceforth be known as "Namibia";

2. *Takes note* of the report of the United Nations Council for South West Africa and expresses its appreciation for the Council's efforts to discharge the responsibilities and functions entrusted to it;

3. *Decides* that the United Nations Council for South West Africa shall be called "United Nations Council for Namibia" and that the United Nations Commissioner for South West Africa shall be called "United Nations Commissioner for Namibia";

4. *Decides* that, taking into account the provisions of General Assembly resolution 2248 (S-V), the United Nations Council for Namibia shall perform, as a matter of priority, the following functions:

(*a*) In consultation and co-operation with the specialized agencies and other appropriate organs of the United Nations, which under section III, paragraph 2, of resolution 2248 (S-V) were requested to render technical and financial assistance to Namibia, the Council shall assume responsibility for establishing a co-ordinated emergency programme for rendering such assistance, in order to meet the exigencies of the present situation;

[639]

(*b*) The Council shall organize a training programme for Namibians, in consultation with those Governments which indicate their interest and concern, so that a cadre of civil servants and of technical and professional personnel may be developed who would be in a position to undertake the public administration and the social, political and economic development of the State;

(*c*) The Council shall continue with a sense of urgency its consultations on the question of issuing to Namibians travel documents enabling them to travel abroad;

5. *Reaffirms* the inalienable right of the Namibian people to freedom and independence and the legitimacy of their struggle against foreign occupation;

6. *Condemns* the Government of South Africa for its persistent refusal to comply with the resolutions of the General Assembly and the Security Council, its refusal to withdraw from Namibia and its obstruction of the efforts of the United Nations Council for Namibia to proceed to Namibia;

7. *Condemns* the actions of the Government of South Africa designed to consolidate its illegal control over Namibia and to destroy the unity of the people and the territorial integrity of Namibia;

8. *Condemns* the actions of those States which by their continued political, military and economic collaboration with the Government of South Africa have encouraged that Government to defy the authority of the United Nations and to obstruct the attainment of independence by Namibia;

9. *Calls upon* all States to desist from those dealings with the Government of South Africa which would have the effect of perpetuating South Africa's illegal occupation of Namibia and to take effective economic and other measures with a view to securing the immediate withdrawal of the South African administration from Namibia;

10. *Further calls upon* all States to provide the necessary moral and material assistance to the Namibian people in their legitimate struggle for independence and to assist the United Nations Council for Namibia in the discharge of its mandate;

11. *Considers* that the continued foreign occupation of Namibia by South Africa in defiance of the relevant United Nations resolutions and of the Territory's established international status constitutes a grave threat to international peace and security;

12. *Reiterates* its demand that the Government of South Africa withdraw from Namibia, immediately and unconditionally, all its military and police forces and its administration;

13. *Recommends* the Security Council urgently to take all appropriate steps to secure the implementation of the present resolution and to take

effective measures in accordance with the provisions of the Charter of the United Nations to ensure the immediate removal of the South African presence from Namibia and to secure for Namibia its independence in accordance with General Assembly resolution 2145 (XXI);

14. *Requests* the Secretary-General to continue to provide all possible assistance to enable the United Nations Council for Namibia to perform its duties;

15. *Requests* the Secretary-General to report to the General Assembly and to the Security Council on the implementation of the present resolution.

Appendix C
Some Thoughts on the Jurisprudence of Myres S. McDougal

EVEN so mild an affirmation of human freedom as embodied in Henri Bergson's remark that "men do not sufficiently realize that their future is in their own hands,"[1] is generally read as remote from the concrete, everyday tasks entrusted to the legal order. The legal mind seems typically inclined toward an antimetaphysical determinism in which the role of destiny is played by the heritage of society. Law tends to sustain the prevailing order—preferring old injustices to new solutions; the legal process may make marginal concessions to pacify discontented groups in society, but the law generally mobilizes its capabilities on behalf of the maintenance of an atmosphere favorable to elite groups. This conservative role of law appears endemic to legal endeavor, exhibited as forcefully today by the tendency of Soviet law to protect the managerial class as earlier in the United States by the use of law and its police adjunct to protect the interests of property owners.

Legal scholars are, accordingly, especially vulnerable to the despairing insight of Ortega y Gasset: "Men prefer service, without real allegiance, under outworn banners, to the compliance with the painful effort of revising inherited principles and setting them in accord with their own deepest feelings."[2] The intellectual achievement of Myres S. McDougal and of the scholars associated with him stands forth at this point as a brilliant exception. McDougal's own career has been devoted to a monumental project to establish a new understanding of the nature of law, conceived to help men achieve greater control over their social existence.

McDougal writes in the great rationalistic tradition of secular humanism. One discovers intellectual roots as far back as Pico della Mirandola; the earliest expression in the tradition of Anglo-American thought should probably be attributed to the work of John Stuart Mill and Jeremy Bentham. The humanistic orientation centers upon a faith in the sufficiency of human reason to fulfill (or at least to promote) the human condition. Neither God nor the past governs the destiny of man. Man is free to use his reason to build the future in accord with his deeds, values, and goals. The McDougal jurisprudence seeks to demonstrate the relevance of law to meeting this dominant challenge created by the situation of men everywhere.

McDougal pursues this high aspiration with imagination and erudition.

[1] Henri Bergson, *Two Sources of Morality and Religion*, New York, Anchor edn., 1954, p. 317.

[2] José Ortega y Gasset, *The Modern Theme*, New York, Harper & Brothers, 1961, p. 21.

Studies in World Public Order is a book of major significance. The twelve studies included in this collection appeared in scholarly journals between 1942 and 1959. However, the act of joining these separate essays into a single volume achieves more than compilation for the convenience of regular readers. The volume as a whole conveys a synoptic sense of McDougal's range of inquiry. The collective presentation vastly increases the power of the separate formulation. One is impressed by the unity of method and style, an exceptional tribute to the strength of McDougal's approach, considering that nine of the twelve essays were written in active collaboration with scholars of such independent achievement as Harold Lasswell, Gertrude Leighton, Leon Lipson, and Richard Gardner.

The special effort made by the McDougal approach to liberate law from conventional modes of perception involves the substitution of a complicated and still largely unfamiliar set of new categories. These new categories are selected to guide inquiry through the abstractions of legal doctrine to facts, problems, and policies. There is also in McDougal's work an insistence that the conception of law is broad enough to encompass law as a dynamic process as well as a static system. McDougal tries to do this in a reconstructive manner. That is, he substitutes a new systematic jurisprudence for the impressionism and legalism that have dominated legal analysis for centuries. In an appendix there is "a particularly clear and economic summary of the general mode of analysis" by Florentino Feliciano.[3] The Feliciano statement is sophisticated and lucid, but it is far too abstract to help the uninitiated across the inhibiting threshold that results from the elaborate McDougal framework of inquiry.

A reader should be prepared, if not already familiar with McDougal's writing, for an austere pilgrimage, unalleviated by witty asides or enhancing quotations. I wish to underscore strongly that the commitment of time and energy and even the occasional flush of exasperation are well rewarded in the end by a greatly sharpened awareness of the character of world legal order. Infelicity of expression is an insignificant failing in the pursuit of knowledge. Mankind cannot expect enlightenment to come only from those rare geniuses like Plato and Jeremiah who possess exceptional gifts of style with which to impart their revolutionary wisdom. There is a particular need to grasp and respond to McDougal's presentation of contemporary international legal and political conditions. McDougal provides comprehensive tools of analysis and appraisal which are developed in specific response to such challenges as ideological conflict, nuclear weapons, and the explosive energies of the newly developing nations.

[3] P. xi.

Experts in international law have often been antagonized by Mc-Dougal's obscure terminology. McDougal invites this reaction by a failure to state the purpose of the basic enterprise in simple language or to explain his reasons for evolving a specialized nomenclature. The introduction to *Studies* anticipates the content and strategy of the volume, and immediately greets the uninoculated reader with a formidable dose of prose: "The unity which is sought in these Essays . . . is that of a contextual policy-oriented jurisprudence, postulating as its overriding goal the dignity of man in an increasingly universal public order."[4] Such a sentence is not an effective lure. It encourages a facile rejection of McDougal's ideas by tempting a reader to regard the terminological armor as impenetrable by normal intellectual processes.

Risking oversimplication, it seems useful to describe the jurispruden-tial strategy that animates McDougal's approach, to point toward the significance of the approach. McDougal's basic orientation in the social sciences has been borrowed from the conceptual outlook of Harold Lasswell. This outlook has worked to develop a method that will enable a systematic use of legal techniques for the promotion of a particular conception of human welfare.

Many legal philosophers share with McDougal and Lasswell an in-strumental theory of law that transforms jurisprudence into a branch of social engineering. In fact, various forms of instrumentalism dominate American legal philosophy so far in the century.[5] The earliest articulate advocates of an instrumental approach to legal order have become known as the Legal Realists.[6] Instrumentalists of all forms join to attack those who exclude social policy from a determination of the content of legal norms no matter whether the exclusion comes, as with natural lawyers, from deference to transcendental criteria or whether the exclusion comes, as with legal positivists like Kelsen, from a sharp separation of law and morals.[7] As has been indicated, McDougal's adoption of a jurisprudence of social engineering is not at all novel. What then warrants attention? It is that, with the exception of Roscoe Pound, no other American legal thinker of consequence had advanced instru-mentalism and legal realism much beyond its polemical role as a critique of other legal theories like Austinian positivism or Thomistic natural law. McDougal's achievement is to carry the instrumental orien-

---

4 P. ix.
5 See, e.g., Grant Gilmore, "Legal Realism: Its Cause and Cure," 70 *Yale Law Journal* 1037-48 (June 1961).
6 See also Hermann Kantorowicz in A. H. Campbell, ed., *The Definition of Law,* Cambridge, Eng., Cambridge University Press, 1958; Kantorowicz, "Some Rationalism About Realism," 43 *Yale Law Journal*

1240-53 (June 1934).
7 See discussion, Lon L. Fuller, "Human Purpose and Natural Law," 3 *Natural Law Forum* 68-76 (1958); Ernest Nagel, "On the Fusion of Fact and Value: A Reply to Professor Fuller," 3 *Natural Law Forum* 77-82 (1958); Fuller, "A Rejoinder to Professor Nagel," 3 *Natural Law Forum* 83-104 (1958).

tation beyond its critical function and to develop a method that promises to make the insights of legal realism *operational in a systematic way.* It is often said that law was made for man and not man for law. But just how does a judge confronted by controversy go about fulfilling this injunction? McDougal's central effort is to provide a comprehensive answer to this question, not just for the judge, but for any actors in the political system entrusted with the task of legal decision. In *Studies* the response is restricted to the subject-matter of international law, but the method developed has general application to all situations in which law in the sense of authoritative decision is brought to bear upon human behavior.[8]

The first task of such a method is to find some reliable way to specify the content of social welfare. This task depends on building a model of human nature that is especially attentive to the social pattern of human needs and desires. McDougal and Lasswell have sought to specify human aspiration by identifying the principal values that underlie the pursuit of individual human dignity. How can we find out about the prevailing content of human values? Speculation based on intuition and impression would introduce bias, gross error, and unfertile abstraction Is it possible to be more exact? Yes, by working out a way to receive guidance from specialists in social science who have been studying aspects of human nature in varying societal circumstances. The work of McDougal's group demonstrates why legal science should encourage interdisciplinary study. If law is to achieve instrumental ends, it needs to make use of all available means to specify these ends, and this awareness can only be reliably advanced through a convincing integration of law and the social sciences.

Knowing the general direction in which human fulfillment lies is not enough. It is also necessary to work out techniques that put this knowledge in a form that has practical relevance. It is more difficult than it sounds to be creatively practical. It requires the capacity to perceive a legal problem as a conflict between competing values. The relation of fact to value is itself an enormously complex matter that continues to evade quantification. There is no ground to abandon rationality of decision because the data cannot be put in quantitative terms. McDougal

---

[8] Professor McDougal himself used this method in relation to the law of property. See McDougal and David Haber, *Property, Wealth, Land: Allocation, Planning and Development,* Charlottesville, Va., Michie Casebook Corp., 1948; McDougal and Maurice E. H. Rotival, *The Case for Regional Planning with Special Reference to New England,* New Haven, Yale University Press, 1947; see also George Dession, "The Technique of Public Order: Evolving Concepts of Criminal Law," 5 *Buffalo Law Review* 22 (Fall 1955); Harold D. Lasswell and Richard C. Donnelly, "The Continuing Debate Over Responsibility: An Introduction to Isolating the Condemnation Sanction," 68 *Yale Law Journal* 869-99 (April 1959); Nicholas deB. Katzenbach, "Conflicts on an Unruly Horse, Reciprocal Claims and Tolerances in Interstate and International Law," 65 *Yale Law Journal* 1087-1157(July 1956).

has well understood the nature of rational decision. His entire study of legal phenomena has proceeded from the perspective of the decisional situation. The jurisprudential orientation is responsive to the insights of decision-making theory. The main aim is to put the decision-maker in contact with the full factual and policy context that pertains to a potential decision, including the process of its implementation. McDougal also argues that the decision-maker should perceive the law task to be one of maximizing human dignity, rather than, as has been traditionally supposed, to use logic and history to find the legal solution that most accords with the development of self-consistent legal doctrine.

McDougal maintains, in the manner of Cardozo and Jerome Frank, that legal doctrine contains complementary sets of norms. Doctrinal support is thus available for contradictory decisions. McDougal submits, for instance, that the distinction between permissible and illegal coercion in international affairs depends upon whether the decision-maker chooses to treat the occasion of violence as an "act of aggression" or as "self-defense."[9] A legal decision, in this view, is not governed by the proper discovery of an applicable norm; there exist opposed norms of a complementary character within the system of norms that can be invoked to reach whatever decisional outcomes are preferred. How does the decision-maker in this event avoid an arbitrary role if doctrine supports any decisional outcome with equal force? As might be supposed, McDougal believes that a nonarbitrary decision depends upon the capacity to decide in systematic response to alternative value considerations, including deference to expectations about the proper legal result.

The systematic search for policy consequences makes the decision-maker aware of the values at stake. The decision itself should be framed by reference to a standard of "reasonableness." This standard is flexible and yet it embodies reference to relevant contextual variables. McDougal urges that "reasonableness will be determined, as in the interpretation of agreements, by a disciplined systematic canvas of all relevant features of the particular value change and its conditioning context."[10] The appraisal of context is guided by the commitment, postulated by McDougal as dominant, to "enhance the overriding values of a world public order of freedom, security, and abundance."[11]

This commitment to the values of human dignity prompts McDougal to urge a new emphasis in legal education upon training students to discharge decision-making roles, or to advise decision-makers. Legal education, at present, is overly concerned with teaching students how to parse doctrine. Students should also, in McDougal's view, be trained

9 P. 292.   10 P. 1016.   11 Pp. 1015-16.

to analyze and weigh policy considerations. Such an educational re-orientation would encourage decision-makers to take full account of the policy consequences of alternative decisions. The implementation of policy in actual legal decisions alone allows an instrumental view of law to become not an approach to analysis, but an influence on the shape and shaping of the human environment. Such a practical jurisprudence is, in summary, a systematic attempt to reconstruct a rational basis for making legal decisions; this reconstruction is possible because the critical insights of legal realism had earlier undercut the tendency to rely upon doctrinal extension based on logic and precedent as an adequate account of the judicial decision process.

The flexibility of international law, as a result of its primitive and decentralized quality, gives an added value to McDougal's systematic method of inquiry and appraisal. There is more obvious occasion for choice on the part of the decision-maker, and hence a greater need to ground choice upon some rational foundation that will promote the ends of men and reach a result that is regarded as authoritative. Insecurity among international lawyers has often led them to stress the technical dimension of their craft, thereby disguising the primitive social character of international law. The most popular form of irrationalism in contemporary legal thinking is to obscure policy flexibility by confining discussion of legal problems to technical issues. McDougal and his associates rigorously avoid this pitfall, not just by rhetoric but by their entire method of analysis. The New Haven Group carries forward the pioneering direction of inquiry initiated by such continental jurists as Huber, Schindler, and de Visscher.[12] McDougal supplements their emphasis upon the social context of international law by working out a systematic method to bring extralegal considerations to bear upon the legal process. This method is applied by McDougal in a variety of specific studies of substantive areas of international law.

It is the unity of McDougal's jurisprudential outlook that bind together the twelve essays that make up *Studies in World Public Order*. The subject matter is quite diverse, extending to concerns marginal to the use of law to improve the quality of world order. There is, for instance, the celebrated collaborative study with Harold D. Lasswell, "Legal Education and Public Policy: Professional Training in the Public Interest," that is devoted primarily to an outline of what should be done to make legal education serve the needs of the lawyer. This study develops a defense of the jurisprudential orientation that is used as the

[12] Central formulations are Max Huber, Peter Klein and Herbert Kraus, eds., *International rechtliche Abhandlungen*, Berlin, Rothschild, 1928; Dietrich Schindler, "Contribution à l'Etude des Facteurs Sociologiques et Psychologiques du Droit International," 46 *Hague Recueil* 233-322 (1933); Charles de Visscher, *Theory and Reality in Public International Law*, Princeton, Princeton University Press, Corbett trans., 1957.

foundation of all the subsequent inquiries into special problems of international law. "The Comparative Study of Law for Policy Purposes: Value Clarification as an Instrument of Democratic World Order," proposes the study of comparative law to promote the goal of a universal world order based on the aspiration to build a liberal democratic society characterized by an overriding concern with the human dignity of its individual members. Comparative law becomes a tool for the promotion of policy preferences central to the underlying jurisprudence. More concretely, comparative law can be related to McDougal's basic humanizing objective if the research discloses equivalent commitments to human dignity on the part of nontotalitarian national societies that otherwise might remain hidden beneath disparate doctrinal labels. The jurisprudential method proposed by McDougal is designed to allow the comparist to contribute to the growth of world order. If the research in comparative law reveals unities on the level of basic values then it is assumed that national leaders will hasten the trend toward supranational integration of legal, political, and economic functions; such information would also encourage the development of greater trust between nations on the basis of a loyalty and sense of community that transcends national boundaries.

Support for world integration needs to be balanced against the Manichean interpretation of contemporary international affairs that is put forward by McDougal and Lasswell in the chapter "The Identification and Appraisal of Diverse Systems of Public Order." The basic hypothesis of this essay is that the stakes of conflict between the Sino-Soviet bloc and the Western bloc are nothing less than the fundamental values of political organization. This conflict precludes the emergence of a universal public order since the values of the competitors are decisively incompatible. The essay warns against a spurious or premature universalism that ignores the chasm between the contenders for dominance in international society. The universalist builds on insubstantial hopes and would place democratic societies in fearful jeopardy by joining into false concert with rival ideologies. Once this obstacle to global supranationalism is understood, an international lawyer can concentrate upon promoting realistic limited forms of supranational growth between nations committed to democratic values. McDougal and Lasswell do not rule out a transition to a more democratic political base in the Communist countries, but until this takes place, genuine cooperation on world order issues, except for limited functional purposes, is impossible.

There is also a long study by McDougal entitled "The Impact of International Law upon National Law: A Policy-Oriented Perspective" which explores the constitutional and institutional structure within the

United States that operates when international legal norms and standards are received by the domestic legal process. The focus on specific problems and policies that arise for American courts in international law cases produces many valuable insights into the ways in which international law is treated at the national level. Illuminating discussions of the Connally Reservation and the Bricker Amendment are coupled with a broader inquiry into the balance between the maintenance of national identity and the constructive participation of a nation-state in the world community. McDougal urges strongly that there is no necessary or pervasive inconsistency, with respect to basic values, between the national aspirations of a democratic society and an increased trust and reliance upon a world community perspective that similarly incorporates these values. This presentation needs to be understood in relation to McDougal's skepticism about universalizing the rule of law so long as principal national societies are based on contradictory value premises.

There are seven other long chapters devoted to substantive studies of major areas of current concern in international law: the law of war (with Florentino Feliciano), human rights (with Gertrude Leighton), international agreements (with Asher Lans), the United Nations Charter veto power (with Richard Gardner), the hydrogen bomb tests (with Norbert Schlei), the law of the sea (with William T. Burke), and the law of outer space (with Leon Lipson). One notes that the framework of analysis has been worked out through the collaboration of McDougal with Lasswell, while the specific applications in each case study are the product of work done by McDougal and an associate. McDougal's recommended method of approach prevails, overcoming whatever differences separate his talented associates; the diversity of authorship is nowhere significantly apparent. High scholarly standards are maintained throughout these studies; primary and secondary legal sources document the textual material with useful precision, and imaginative references to extralegal writings illuminate the intellectual horizon. The presentation of the legal discussion is always placed in a factual context that indicates how the legal problems have emerged. Legal problems are not discussed only in doctrinal terms. In fact, the main effort is to clarify the policy alternatives of complementary legal norms. Complementarity of norms underscores the freedom of the decision-maker to choose the appropriate norm to promote the dominant policy. The McDougal group is critical of doctrinal rigidity and the type of legal scholarship that limits analysis to technical considerations. Several essays are organized around a polemical theme. For instance, the study of the veto power written with Richard N. Gardner was designed to refute an earlier article by Leo Gross which had argued that Security

Council action taken during the Soviet boycott was void, as it was not based on the "concurring vote" of the permanent members. And the long chapter with Norbert Schlei, supporting the legality of United States hydrogen bomb tests, was written to oppose an article by Emanuel Margolis that had condemned these atmospheric tests as illegal. In both instances the argument of the opposition is stated at the outset. Somewhat surprisingly, the polemical objectives do not seriously interfere with the value of the article as an authoritative depiction of the subject in issue, although the partisanship may distract adversaries from the manifest merits of the scholarship.

Each of the seven studies makes a major contribution to the specialized literature of international law. McDougal's method highlights the key problems that confront the actor entrusted with the power of decision. Two of these studies are particularly able: the law of war with Feliciano and the law of the sea with Burke. Both constitute the foretaste of a comprehensive study of a major subject-matter area. In contrast, the extended study of international agreements is too long for what it says and the hydrogen bomb test article, although impressive as advocacy, is somewhat superficial in its response to the serious policy and legal objections that could have been advanced, and should have been considered, to the tests. McDougal and Schlei appear to have used their erudition and skill to serve the immediate cause of national interest. The result of such an exercise is to ignore the deeper anxieties provoked by the use of high seas in a manner that seriously impaired the rectitude prevailing within Japan, an objecting national community; the typical Japanese family could not have approached their staple fish meal with much relish the winter after the Bikini tests. There is a rather striking discrepancy in spirit between the McDougal-Burke article on the law of the sea that builds such a strong case for favoring inclusive, community-oriented uses of the high seas and the McDougal-Schlei argument in behalf of the most peremptory, exclusive use of the high seas since the days when *mare liberum* triumphed over *mare clausum*.

McDougal seeks, as has been said, to make the legal scholar practical by concentrating inquiry upon the factors relevant to decisions—at all points in the legal system—that will further favored policies. McDougal emphasizes concern with "the making of authoritative and controlling decisions."[13] We need to identify those with authority so as to ascribe legitimacy to their acts. Likewise we should satisfy ourselves that those with authority control behavior; this criterion of effectiveness is needed to keep law in contact with social reality. It remains possible to say that Chiang retains authority to act for "China," but one would still

[13] P. 13.

be well advised to know what Mao decrees: "The conjunction of common expectations concerning authority with a high degree of corroboration in actual operation is what we understand by law."[14] Neither aspiration nor terror can serve as the basis of law. It is crucial to exclude such extremes from international legal studies where opinion has so often tended to veer toward either utopian formalism or cynical realism. McDougal mounts the narrow ridge between these positions upon which a genuine opportunity for legal development exists.

Behind this definitional focus is a flexibility that permits an understanding of international law as a *distinctive* legal order. Traditional misconception has arisen by the use of the domestic legal order of a progressive nation as the model for every legal order. McDougal emphasizes the decentralized character of the world community as a distinctive feature that controls the ordering behavior within the system. But he does not proceed from the absence of adequate central institutions and processes of enforcement to a denial of the effectiveness of international law. Instead McDougal directs us to the distinctive decentralized forms of order that are based on the logic of reciprocity. Self-restraint, adherence to norms, reasonable accommodation emerge because nations find this to be increasingly mutually beneficial in an interdependent world. The unreasonable national claim prompts imitation and retaliation. If the Soviet Union restricts the travel of American diplomats then the United States will restrict the travel of Soviet diplomats. If the United States claims sovereignty over its continental shelf then Argentina follows with a parallel claim. If the United States uses the Pacific Ocean to test hydrogen bombs then it cannot object convincingly when Communist China seeks to do the same thing. The strength of reciprocity is increased in a world in which there is a diminishing prospect of advantage from the exertion of superior force. As war grows more patently obsolescent there is every reason to transform structures of domination into structures of accommodation. With the relatively minor exceptions of Cyprus and Suez, the British perceived this, whereas until recently the French have not. This is one reason, among many, for the comparative ease with which Great Britain made the transition to decolonialism.

Especially in the study of the law of the sea (written with Burke) the idea of reciprocity is extended to give content to an idea of world community interest that unites the nations of the world in a common enterprise. In the area of international concern where resources are, to use McDougal's word, "sharable," nations have a joint interest in weighting "decision in favor of inclusive rather than exclusive claims." Nations, as well, are here counseled, in spite of relative power, to make

14 P. 14.

"an offer of reciprocity," and to exercise "severe restraint in the application of naked power." There is, in relation to the high seas, outer space, and the polar regions the prospect for overlapping cooperative use in many areas. There is no need for states to make many claims that assert an exclusive sovereign right to act. Exceptions may arise in relation to certain uses for national defense or fundamental economic livelihood. McDougal emphasizes here "the tremendous net gain in community and particular values" that would come if a shift from the exclusivity of sovereign claim to the inclusivity of community claim could be made in these areas of "sharable resources."[15] A principle of reasonableness is urged upon decision-makers to mediate between their concern for national interest and the growth of a world community. This is necessarily vague, but it does suggest a direction of thought that would be most beneficial if adopted by leading participants in the world. McDougal and Burke, writing at a time when nations are making greatly expanded claims of exclusive right to use the sea, remind us that "the choice before the states of the world in the present crisis of the law of the sea is whether, for the illusory mess of pottage obtainable in an uneconomic extension of exclusive right, they will forego their heritage of inclusive rights and its promise of even greater future achievement in community and particular values."[16] Such a choice seems to point vividly to the crisis in all phases of the struggle to build a world order before it is too late.

This formal plea for the extension of the world order is animated by a faith in the values proclaimed by the liberal democracies. McDougal seeks to achieve a world in which the dignity of the individual is the focal point of all social order. More specifically values are to be achieved by noncoercive, persuasive means within national societies. The democratic ideal of equal opportunity and respect must be promoted everywhere by peaceful process of social change. Totalitarian societies cannot participate significantly in the development of such a world order on a universal basis. Thus real global integration must await a fundamental internal shift within the national societies now members of the Sino-Soviet bloc. McDougal revives Kant's claim in *Perpetual Peace* that the reign of peace is decisively linked to the establishment of liberal democracy throughout the world.

There is a keen temptation to question McDougal and his associates about particular matters. Would it not be useful for a discerning reader, in the spirit of exegesis, to write a detailed commentary on these twelve studies? If it were well done it could support a central dialogue on the problems of contemporary international law that might deepen the gen-

[15] Quotations in this paragraph are from p. 909.   [16] P. 911.

eral climate of understanding and give professional international lawyers firmer ground to stand upon. Anyone concerned about international law should make serious contact with *Studies in World Public Order* and with McDougal's other major writings.

THERE IS a current tendency to discuss which approach to international legal studies is the correct one. This fashion produces rather sterile arguments by advocates of one approach against those of another. Such polemics overlook the important fact that the main established approaches each serve a useful function, and that this usefulness normally accounts for their existence and survival. In this respect the polemics for and against Kelsen, McDougal, or Tunkin are mainly unnecessary and misleading. They create the impression that one contemplating the use or study of international law is confronted by the need to make a mutually exclusive choice; that there exists an either/or situation in which it is desirable, if not essential, to make a clear commitment to one approach and reject its competitors; and that if one, for instance, admires Kelsen, then one must look askance at McDougal and vice versa.

It is possible to avoid this necessity for choice by understanding that each particular approach has its own set of intellectual objectives. After attaining such comprehension, the next task becomes to classify the major approaches according to their objectives. This will put us in a better position to select for a particular purpose the approach with the intellectual objectives that most clearly coincide with our own. It seems clear that an international lawyer may be interested in any one of several things. It is one thing to seek guidance as to the content of relevant rules and standards when advising a client about the extent to which international law presently offers protection against the risk of expropriation of property held abroad. It is quite another to ascertain the effectiveness of the existing rules and procedures for their enforcement. It is still different to emphasize those rules and procedures that should be brought into existence to sustain the international economy at optimum levels. And it is quite something else again to discern what rules of international law should apply to the protection of foreign investment, given a certain set of national attitudes toward the status of private property; this last is one of the central challenges confronting international lawyers writing from a socialist perspective. It is also different if one adopts a systemic outlook and tries to consider expropriation norms in light of a need for international law to achieve a proper balance between national prerogative and world community welfare. And, finally, the problems of expropriation may be studied primarily to gain insight into how international law works, rather than to receive guidance as to its doctrinal content.

Each of these inquiries fulfills a genuine intellectual need. Each inquiry expresses a predominance of certain interests over others. And each tends to reflect one jurisprudential outlook more than others. But it is an otiose exercise to excoriate some as guilty of the debasement of true international law, and to exalt others for giving it true expression. This is not to deny that the philosopher of international law can make useful criticisms of the theoretical foundations of each approach and thereby increase its potential validity and usefulness. In fact, an accurate understanding of the objectives of a particular approach is a necessary preliminary to useful criticism. For only then can we accept the approach on its own terms.

Having once satisfied this initial requirement of empathy, a critical examination of the thought of leading international lawyers can make two useful contributions. First, it can create an awareness of the particular objectives emphasized in their work to engender greater sophistication about why and when to consult whom. At the same time we will be rescued from the barrenness of trivial debates such as whether the Harvard or Yale approach, assuming either exists, provides a superior method for the study of international law. Perhaps the debate can be clarified by pointing out that no overall choice need be made. This suspension of judgment encourages a more constructive discussion among international lawyers and liberates the more passionate sectarians from the temptation to organize crusades against the heretical.

If this first contribution can be made, then a second becomes possible —namely, constructive criticism of a specific approach to international law having explicated its major objectives and having discerned its animating outlook. In this respect, one can point out that a given thinker on his own terms is inconsistent, unconvincing, or incomplete. I have felt, for instance, that Myres McDougal has never made a convincing reconciliation of his support for the legality of the use of force by Western states in cold war contexts with his more general plea for a system of minimum world order premised upon the acceptance of *all* states of certain *common* restraints.

Alwyn Freeman has written in criticism[17] of McDougal and Feliciano's *Law and Minimum World Public Order*.[18] The criticisms offered are coupled with many comments praising the authors for their achieve-

---

[17] Alwyn Freeman, "Professor McDougal's 'Law and Minimum World Public Order,'" 58 *American Journal of International Law* 711 (1964).

[18] Myres S. McDougal and Florentino P. Feliciano, *Law and Minimum World Public Order*, New Haven, Yale University Press, 1961. My views on this book are set forth in Falk, *Legal Order in a Violent World*, Princeton, Princeton University Press, 1968, pp. 80-96.

ment. Mr. Freeman's principal criticisms of McDougal-Feliciano are unwarranted, and require response, as they deal with important issues of form and content. Mr. Freeman's criticism seems to stem from certain attitudes toward contemporary international society that appear dangerous and regressive. One feels a certain reticence about bringing differences in political valuation out into the open in a scholarly forum. But this reticence is probably unwise, especially when the discussion involves the validity of McDougal's approach, an approach that devotes itself so centrally to the use of law as an instrument for the realization of the values of human dignity. Freeman's editorial is initially important because it makes clear that even among Western international lawyers as sympathetic with one another as Freeman and McDougal are, there is, nevertheless, considerable room for controversy as to the specific content of the values of human dignity.

So much by way of introduction. It is now in order to offer a response to three principal criticisms made by Mr. Freeman of the McDougal-Feliciano study: First, that the authors are not sufficiently alert to the damage that has been inflicted upon the international legal order by allowing the newly independent states of Asia and Africa to participate as full-fledged members; second, that McDougal's mode of analyzing international law could be made more effective if the language were simpler and the categories fewer; and, third, that McDougal-Feliciano-Lasswell lend their good names to an image of world community that appears to reflect socialist rather than Western values, given the present stage of international relations.

1. *The New States.* After praising McDougal and Feliciano for the overall realism of their outlook, Freeman criticizes the book for giving "too little weight to the devastating inroads which the myth of universality has chiseled into the very foundations of traditional law" (p. 712). Freeman goes on with gathering passion to claim that

> some, it is true, appear to regard this as a good thing; but a complete evaluation *must* impeach the practice of admitting into the Society of Nations *primeval entities* which have no *real* claim to international status or the *capacity* to meet international obligations, and whose *primary congeries* of contributions consist in *replacing* norms serving the common interest of mankind by others *releasing* them from inhibitions upon irresponsible conduct. [P. 712. Emphasis added.]

No examples are given. Freeman says that these new states have been "aided and abetted by the so-called socialist states," and concludes with the assurance that "an undignified compulsion to admit these new entities as full-blown members of the international society upon achieving 'independence' has impeded, not advanced, the emergence of a mature code of conduct" (p. 712). Freeman's breath-taking rhetoric is an attack, it must be recalled, upon the failure of McDougal and Feliciano to give attention to the problem.

But consider what attention, in Mr. Freeman's vein, would entail. These new states are, one presumes, those nations in Asia and Africa that have achieved independence since the end of World War II. Prior to independence these states were largely governed as colonies of the great imperial powers of Europe. What is it that is wrong with these states? Why are they primeval entities? In most cases internal order has been achieved in a society that is busy modernizing itself and is, at the same time, rediscovering its earlier indigenous cultural traditions that had been suppressed during its term as a colonial dependency. Often these countries are poor and must rely upon an elite that has had relatively little education. The economy has been generally distorted to serve the interests of the former colonial master, and often much of the wealth and wealth-producing activity remains in the hands of nationals of the colonial power or their friends among the native population.

These nations are generally resentful about their long period of foreign oppression, and there is an understandable, if unfortunate, tendency for them to be dubious about a system of international law that legitimated the colonial relationship and gave legal protection, in the form of exterritoriality and capitulatory regimes, to the privileges extorted by their foreign overlords.

The aggregate leadership of the new states represents a combined population that is almost half of the world's total. Why should not international law be revised to take account of their particular interests? Why should the traditional "code" be satisfactory for an international society that is so altered in composition? Why are not even the "so-called socialist states" (Freeman's phrase) entitled to influence the content of modern international law? Can we be so proud of such Western and "civilized" states as Hitler's Germany, Mussolini's Italy, Franco's Spain, or Duvalier's Haiti to permit ourselves to make in good faith the invidious repudiation of the new states or the socialist states? Is Indonesia's aggressiveness or India's coercive settlement of the Goa dispute out of line with the behavior of aggressor states in the West? Does not the continued reliance upon force by the great powers which find their vital interests challenged suggest that the Afro-Asians are not alone in their unwillingness to have vital interests foreclosed by the rules of international law developed to prohibit recourse to force?

What, then, would Mr. Freeman have McDougal-Feliciano say about the emergence of new states? One supposes that he longs for more rigorous standards governing recognition practice and admission to the United

Nations, as well as for an insistence upon adherence to traditional rules of state responsibility and duties of protection toward foreign investment; in other words, he seems to counsel greater fidelity to the old order. One way to achieve this greater fidelity is to deny states legal status in international society unless they give evidence of their intention to abide by the old order. If access were so restricted, then the myth of universality about which Freeman complains would no longer hold sway. Evidently the main attribute of the myth, a not very mythic attribute, is that political entities with the factual characteristics of a state qualify for membership in international society regardless of their domestic political orientation or their foreign alignments. The continuing ostracism of mainland China from the United Nations illustrates an inroad on the myth of universality, an inroad achieved at the expense of the most populous state and the seat of the oldest and one of the most glorious of all civilizations.

It seems unfair to criticize McDougal and Feliciano on this account. In fact, the opposite case can be made even more persuasively; namely, their failure to consider what changes in international law are appropriate to take account of the values and interests of these new members of international society. In any event, one of Freeman's persuasions has the duty to come forward with a more specific set of allegations and rectifying proposals. In the absence of such specificity it seems irresponsible and unfair to use such hostile language to describe the impact of the new states of Asia and Africa upon the conduct of world affairs. It should be kept in mind that these new states have consistently supported the peacekeeping operations of the United Nations, and have been a source of moderating influence on those occasions when disputes among the great powers threatened to produce large-scale violence.

2. *Simplification.* It is often said that McDougal presents his ideas in an obscure jargon that impedes comprehension and adds nothing of substance. Critics call for clear and simple formulations, and complain about his murky sentences and numerous categories. Freeman echoes this standard line of criticism when he writes that "one can still admire the intellectual resources brought to McDougal's scholarly conceptualism of law as an instrument of social and humanitarian will, without approving unqualifiedly the abstruse formulation of principles enunciated" (p. 715). Freeman observes that "the structural idiom occasionally overpowers the living thought of which it is the skin," and reminds us that "the unwary may not grasp readily the prolix esotericism enveloping the legal submissions" (p. 715). Freeman's own prolix esotericism envelops his submission in such an accusation as this: "Simple ideas are sometimes expressed in a framework which so cloaks the substance

that the dialectic casing, the vehicle, blurs the focal points of concentration."

Freeman does express a criticism of McDougal's writing that is frequently made, especially by those who privately conceded that they have not really had the time or the patience to read very much of his work. One supposes that it is much more reassuring to reject a difficult author's books *ab initio* than to do so after a careful reading.

This stylistic criticism seems unfounded. McDougal tries to achieve clear and precise expression. His sentences are almost always impossible to improve upon. Their complexity stems from an insistence upon nuance and accuracy, not from an infatuation with German metaphysics, or some inborn quality of verbal ineptitude. McDougal, with the substantial help of Harold D. Lasswell, is engaged in the formidable task of developing and applying a jurisprudence that takes *systemic account* of all aspects of social reality relevant to the processes and structures of making *rational* decisions about legal policy alternatives. This is a complicated endeavor and requires an elaborate intellectual apparatus. It would not occur to anyone to complain about Einsteinian theories of physical reality on the ground that they were abstruse and not readily susceptible to lay understanding. Well, it is time that we appreciate that theories about social reality are also likely to be comparably complicated if they are to render service. Our expectations seem quite wrong. Why should a reader be entitled to grasp McDougal's ideas on international law without special effort and training? It is an insidious form of anti-intellectualism to insist that legal analysis can always be carried on in a fashion that allows its meaning to be evident to the uninitiated or hurried reader. All that it is proper to demand is that legal analysis bring added knowledge and understanding to the adept. McDougal and Feliciano overfulfill this demand.

3. *World Image.* Finally, Freeman questions Lasswell's advocacy, in an introductory chapter, of a nonprovincial world view, one that is released from what he aptly terms "the syndrome of parochialism." Parochialism in world affairs leads nations to pursue egoistic ends at the expense of other actors. This has always been the case, but today it creates prospects of mutual destructivity on an unprecedented scale. Thus, McDougal and Lasswell contend that rational self-assertion requires men to identify increasingly their fulfillment with the welfare of political units larger than the state. Such a prescription tends to deprecate the role of the state in the global value-realizing process. It also supports, by implication, the growth of supranationalism. This so offends Freeman that he is led to ask "Would it be legitimate to inquire whether the achievement of a 'self-system larger than the primary ego, larger than the ego components of family, friends, profession or nation' (Lass-

well's introduction, p. xxxiv) is, at this writing something more akin to a socialist philosophy than that of the Western world?" (p. 716). It is ironic that two such staunch defenders of the Western conception of human dignity against the socialist attacks from the East, as are McDougal and Lasswell, should stand accused of embracing a socialist world image.

Does Mr. Freeman really concede that socialists are more advanced than others in their conception of world order? Or that the effort to supplant the nation as the primary organizing unit in world affairs is somehow "socialistic?" It would appear that Mr. Freeman's bias, as with respect to the new states, is to favor retention of traditional ideas about the actual and desirable preeminence of the sovereign state in the international legal system. One wonders what conditions would lead Mr. Freeman to perceive the need for drastic revisions in international society. Mr. Freeman's argument on this point is very strange, indeed, for it is the Soviet Union, among principal sovereign states, that most insists upon maintaining the full panoply of traditional prerogatives of national sovereignty; this insistence is maintained even in their projected version of a totally disarmed world.

Index

Aaland Islands dispute, 224
Abel, Col. Rudolf, 253
abstention principle, in fishing conflicts, 549n
accommodation, legal response in, 450-51
Acheson, Dean, 497n
act of state, antitrust regulation and, 299-301; foreign, 428-29
Act of State doctrine, 32, 406-19
actor, international, 35-36
Adams-Mitchell dissent, in Sherman Act case, 322
Addyston Pipe case, 320
Africa, new states in, 513. *See also* South Africa
Afro-Asian bloc, as "illusion," 483
Afro-Asian Conciliation Commission, 112, 114, 117
Afro-Asian states, international order and, 182; and Vietnam War, 580. *See also* South West Africa
agencies, specialized, 463-64
aggression, extraterrestrial, 569; of Indonesia against Malaysia, 91, 110-11; Korea-style, 582; by secondary powers, 477; in Vietnam, 582
aggressive behavior, elimination of, 566
Ago, Roberto, 140, 152
Air Defense Identification Zones, 251
air space, information-gathering in, 249
air warfare, "declaratory" rules of, 457
Alafraz, Arturo A., 99n
Alcoa case, 273-76, 280, 284, 309; "unlawful purpose" test in, 282-83
Alcoa Limited, 284, 309
Alexander I (Russia), 191
Alexander, Lewis M., 465n
Alfaro, Ricardo J., 231-32
Alford, Neill H., Jr., 448n
Algerian War of Independence, 587
alien-owned property, status of, 493. *See also* expropriation
Alkali case, 298, 324
Alkasso case, 298-99
Alker, Haywood, 465
Alperovitz, Gar, 594n
aluminum imports, control of, 272n
Alvarez, Judge, 163, 169, 213-14
Amador, Garcia, 480n
American antitrust regulation, extraterritorial extension of, 265-325. *See also* Sherman Antitrust Act
American Banana Co. v. United Fruit Co., see Banana case
American corporation, foreign trade regulations for, 302-07
American dilemma, Vietnam War as, 570-72
American Dilemma, An (Myrdal), 571
American Law Institute, 353n
American Revolution, 73

American Society of International Law, 336, 469n, 577-78
American Trade Proposals, 317
Ammoun, Fouad, 396n
Anand, R. P., 513n
Anderson, Stanley V., 14n
Anglo-American temperament, theory of, 38
Antarctic Treaty, 255
anthropology, political science and, 347n
anticolonialism, 33
anticolonial wars of independence, 73-74
antirevolutionary coalitions, 74
antitrust decisions, unlawful-purpose test for, 275-325
antitrust jurisdiction, scope of, 268-69
antitrust laws, foreign commerce and, 272-75; goal of, 305
antitrust regulation, cartels and, 307-18; foreign trade and, 302-07; geographical dispersion and, 287; individual freedom and, 306; international law and, 269-72; monopoly power and, 305; statutory framework of, 318-25
anti-Zionism, 33
Anyeama, Charles D., 396n
Anzilotti, Dionisio, 199n
apartheid, ix; as "delinquency," 169; illegality of, 457; international law and, 155; *South West Africa Cases* and, 380-99; and United Nations, 135, 149, 152, 183; world community and, 142
Apter, David E., 13n, 513n
Arab League, aggression by, 455-56. *See also* United Arab Republic
Argentina, coastal sovereignty of, 651
Aristophanes, 569
Arnold, Thurman, 503
Aron, Raymond, 510n
Arreglado, Juan M., 99n
Article 2(6), UN Charter, 188-90; analysis of, 200-28; constitutionality of, 218; judicial status of, 200-28; legality of, 228; legal obligation created by, 225; moral obligation under, 226; specific problems of, 214-16; theoretical interpretations of, 210-28; UN practice and, 228-41
Asamoah, Obed y, 128n, 184n
Asia and Africa, new states in, 513. *See also* Africa; Afro-Asian states
Association of South East Asia, 94n
asylum, common interests and, 159
Asylum Case, 158
atomic bombing cases, Japan, 136, 557-58. *See also* nuclear weapons
Austin, John, 41
authority, diagonal allocation of, 88-89; and international law, 19; lateral allocation of, 89; legal analysis and, 87-90; power and, 461; spiritual, 19; two forms of, 428

Suez Canal Convention of 1888, 367
Suez crisis, 46, 186, 258, 563, 578, 588
Suharto, Gen., 120
Sukarno, Achmed, 89, 91, 98, 103-07, 109-
12, 114, 117-18, 120-21, 616, 620
Sumulong, Lorenzo, 99n
superpowers, rivalries among, 563
supranational system, growth of, 658; international legal order as, 49-50
Supreme Court, U.S., 136; Act of State
doctrine and, 413-14; antitrust regulation and, 268; black militancy and,
571n; and *Sabbatino* case, 177, 404-
05, 413-14, 423
surveillance satellites, *see* observation satellites
Sutherland, George, 431
Swart, Charles, 393n
Swiss Watch Cartel case, 273n, 283, 285,
301
Switzerland, self-defense in, 563
Syatauw, J.J.G., 513n
synthetic rubber, foreign trade in, 308
*System and Process in International Poli-
tics* (Kaplan), 486
system-oriented judgment, in international
law, 49
systems analysis, social order and, 494-95
systems theory, international law and, 466-
68

Tammes, A.J.P., 141
Tanaka, Kotaro, 88-89, 126n, 127n, 129,
395, 399-401
Taubenfeld, Howard J., 256n
Tchitcherin, Soviet Minister of Foreign
Affairs, 196-97
technology, cold war and, 130
Tengku, *see* Putra Al-Haj
Terrill, Robert P., 317n
territorial waters, espionage and, 254-55
Tet offensive, Vietnam War, 576
Thant, U, 98n, 104-05
Theater of the Absurd, 604n
theory, in U.S. legal studies, 37-40. *See
also* international legal theory
third-party judgment, 25
third world, confrontation in, 93
Thirty Years' War, 500
Thomas, Dylan, 422
Thomsen v. Cayser, 271n, 278n, 309n
three-mile limit, fishing and, 541
Tiger at the Gates (Giraudoux), 334-35
Tillich, Paul, 351n
Timberg, Sigmund, 268n, 276n, 303n
Timken Roller Bearing Co. case, 273n,
286n, 288-91, 293n, 303n, 321
Tito Broz, 28
Tondel, Lyman M., Jr., 455n
totalitarianism, vs. international law, 49
total war, revolution and, 71
Touscoz, Jean, 46n
trademarks, cartels and, 312
Trampler v. High Court of Zurich, 220n

Trautman, Donald T., 250n
treaties, "authentic" interpretation of, 148;
international law and, 31; law of, 199,
357. *See also* Harvard Research Draft
on Law of Treaties
treaty interpretation, limits of, 368-77;
New Haven approach to, 342-77; world
public order and, 361
treaty law, defined, 515. *See also* treaties
Treaty of Dorpat, 196
Treaty of Utrecht, 190
troika proposals, 492
Truman Doctrine, 75
Tsune-Chi Yu, 355-58, 360n, 369n, 374n
Tucker, Robert W., 18n, 486n, 494n, 530n
Tunkin, G. I., 44n, 653
Tymiemiecka, A. T., 468n

underdeveloped nations, *see* new states
Underhill v. Hernandez, 406
Underwood, James L., 406n, 584n
Union of South Africa, apartheid in,
155. *See also* South Africa; South West
Africa
United Arab Republic, as subregional
power, 557; and Suez crisis, 578; war
outlook of, 477. *See also* Arab League;
Suez crisis
United Kingdom, Malaysia mutual assistance pact document, 98, 613-18
United Nations, action in relation to Art.
2(6), 228-41; Afro-Asian group in, 381;
authority of, 119, 185-241; bipolar world
and, 491; coercive strategies of, 81;
"compulsory" membership in, 206-07;
Congo operations of, 77; as form of
communication, 185; Franco and, 230-
32; in India-Pakistan dispute, 46; international law and, 3, 455; international
order and, 72; international society and,
21; intervention by, 81; law-creating
capacity of, 135, 144; League of Nations and, 134-35; legitimacy of, 119;
Malaysia and, 115; 620-27; membership
in, 185; nonmembers and, 185-241; ordering role of, 134; outer space and,
244-45; peacekeeping by, 21n; prior
claims over nonmembers by, 189-200;
racial oppression and, 482; restructuring of, 492; and South West Africa
Mandates, 131-45; Stanleyville Operation of, 469n; and Vietnam War, 185;
withdrawal from, 216-17; world peace
and, 224; zones of conflict and, 589.
See also United Nations Charter;
United Nations General Assembly;
United Nations Security Council
United Nations Charter, 35, 91, 101, 119;
Art. 2(5), 202, 205; Art. 2(6), 187-90,
200-41; Art. 2(7), 207-08, 233; Art. 38,
141-43, 161-62, 165, 173-74, 385-86;
Art. 96(1), 398; Art. 103, 218; confrontation and, 108; as constitution,
217; controverted issue and, 209; deci-

[675]

BOOKS WRITTEN
UNDER THE AUSPICES OF THE
CENTER OF INTERNATIONAL STUDIES
PRINCETON UNIVERSITY

Gabriel A. Almond, *The Appeals of Communism* (Princeton University Press 1954)
William W. Kaufmann, ed., *Military Policy and National Security* (Princeton University Press 1956)
Klaus Knorr, *The War Potential of Nations* (Princeton University Press 1956)
Lucian W. Pye, *Guerrilla Communism in Malaya* (Princeton University Press 1956)
Charles De Visscher, *Theory and Reality in Public International Law*, trans. by P. E. Corbett (Princeton University Press 1957; rev. ed. 1968)
Bernard C. Cohen, *The Political Process and Foreign Policy: The Making of the Japanese Peace Settlement* (Princeton University Press 1959)
Myron Weiner, *Party Politics in India: The Development of a Multi-Party System* (Princeton University Press 1957)
Percy E. Corbett, *Law in Diplomacy* (Princeton University Press 1959)
Rolf Sannwald and Jacques Stohler, *Economic Integration: Theoretical Assumptions and Consequences of European Unification*, trans. by Herman Karreman (Princeton University Press 1959)
Klaus Knorr, ed., *NATO and American Security* (Princeton University Press 1959)
Gabriel A. Almond and James S. Coleman, eds., *The Politics of the Developing Areas* (Princeton University Press 1960)
Herman Kahn, *On Thermonuclear War* (Princeton University Press 1960)
Sidney Verba, *Small Groups and Political Behavior: A Study of Leadership* (Princeton University Press 1961)
Robert J. C. Butow, *Tojo and the Coming of the War* (Princeton University Press 1961)
Glenn H. Snyder, *Deterrence and Defense: Toward a Theory of National Security* (Princeton University Press 1961)
Klaus Knorr and Sidney Verba, eds., *The International System: Theoretical Essays* (Princeton University Press 1961)
Peter Paret and John W. Shy, *Guerrillas in the 1960's* (Praeger 1962)
George Modelski, *A Theory of Foreign Policy* (Praeger 1962)
Klaus Knorr and Thornton Read, eds., *Limited Strategic War* (Praeger 1963)
Frederick S. Dunn, *Peace-Making and the Settlement with Japan* (Princeton University Press 1963)
Arthur L. Burns and Nina Heathcote, *Peace-Keeping by United Nations Forces* (Praeger 1963)
Richard A. Falk, *Law, Morality, and War in the Contemporary World* (Praeger 1963)
James N. Rosenau, *National Leadership and Foreign Policy: A Case Study in the Mobilization of Public Support* (Princeton University Press 1963)
Gabriel A. Almond and Sidney Verba, *The Civic Culture: Political Attitudes and Democracy in Five Nations* (Princeton University Press 1963)
Bernard C. Cohen, *The Press and Foreign Policy* (Princeton University Press 1963)

Richard L. Sklar, *Nigerian Political Parties: Power in an Emergent African Nation* (Princeton University Press 1963)

Peter Paret, *French Revolutionary Warfare from Indochina to Algeria: The Analysis of a Political and Military Doctrine* (Praeger 1964)

Harry Eckstein, ed., *Internal War: Problems and Approaches* (Free Press 1964)

Cyril E. Black and Thomas P. Thornton, eds., *Communism and Revolution: The Strategic Uses of Political Violence* (Princeton University Press 1964)

Miriam Camps, *Britain and the European Community 1955-1963* (Princeton University Press 1964)

Thomas P. Thornton, ed., *The Third World in Soviet Perspective: Studies by Soviet Writers on the Developing Areas* (Princeton University Press 1964)

James N. Rosenau, ed., *International Aspects of Civil Strife* (Princeton University Press 1964)

Sidney I. Ploss, *Conflict and Decision-Making in Soviet Russia: A Case Study of Agricultural Policy, 1953-1963* (Princeton University Press 1965)

Richard A. Falk and Richard J. Barnet, eds., *Security in Disarmament* (Princeton University Press 1965)

Karl von Vorys, *Political Development in Pakistan* (Princeton University Press 1965)

Harold and Margaret Sprout, *The Ecological Perspective on Human Affairs, With Special Reference to International Politics* (Princeton University Press 1965)

Klaus Knorr, *On the Uses of Military Power in the Nuclear Age* (Princeton University Press 1966)

Harry Eckstein, *Division and Cohesion in Democracy: A Study of Norway* (Princeton University Press 1966)

Cyril E. Black, *The Dynamics of Modernization: A Study in Comparative History* (Harper and Row 1966)

Peter Kunstadter, ed., *Southeast Asian Tribes, Minorities, and Nations* (Princeton University Press 1967)

E. Victor Wolfenstein, *The Revolutionary Personality: Lenin, Trotsky, Gandhi* (Princeton University Press 1967)

Leon Gordenker, *The UN Secretary-General and the Maintenance of Peace* (Columbia University Press 1967)

Oran R. Young, *The Intermediaries: Third Parties in International Crises* (Princeton University Press 1967)

James N. Rosenau, ed., *Domestic Sources of Foreign Policy* (Free Press 1967)

Richard F. Hamilton, *Affluence and the French Worker in the Fourth Republic* (Princeton University Press 1967)

Linda B. Miller, *World Order and Local Disorder: The United Nations and Internal Conflicts* (Princeton University Press 1967)

Henry Bienen, *Tanzania: Party Transformation and Economic Development* (Princeton University Press 1967)

Wolfram F. Hanrieder, *West German Foreign Policy, 1949-1963: International Pressures and Domestic Response* (Stanford University Press 1967)

Richard H. Ullman, *Britain and the Russian Civil War: November 1918-February 1920* (Princeton University Press 1968)

Robert Gilpin, *France in the Age of the Scientific State* (Princeton University Press 1968)

William B. Bader, *The United States and the Spread of Nuclear Weapons* (Pegasus 1968)

Richard A. Falk, *Legal Order in a Violent World* (Princeton University Press 1968)

Cyril E. Black, Richard A. Falk, Klaus Knorr, and Oran R. Young, *Neutralization and World Politics* (Princeton University Press 1968)

Oran R. Young, *The Politics of Force: Bargaining During International Crises* (Princeton University Press 1969)

Klaus Knorr and James N. Rosenau, eds., *Contending Approaches to International Politics* (Princeton University Press 1969)

James N. Rosenau, ed., *Linkage Politics: Essays on the Convergence of National and International Systems* (Free Press 1969)

John T. McAlister, Jr., *Viet Nam: The Origins of Revolution* (Knopf 1969)

Jean Edward Smith, *Germany Beyond the Wall: People, Politics and Prosperity* (Little, Brown 1969)

James Barros, *Betrayal from Within: Joseph Avenol Secretary-General of the League of Nations, 1933-1940* (Yale University Press 1969)

Charles Hermann, *Crises in Foreign Policy: A Simulation Analysis* (Bobbs-Merrill 1969)

Robert C. Tucker, *The Marxian Revolutionary Idea: Essays on Marxist Thought and Its Impact on Radical Movements* (W. W. Norton 1969)

Harvey Waterman, *Political Change in Contemporary France: The Politics of an Industrial Democracy* (Charles E. Merrill 1969)